The Two Narratives of
Political Economy

The Two Narratives of Political Economy

Original Material Selected and Edited by

Nicholas Capaldi and Gordon Lloyd

Scrivener

For general information on our other products and services or for technical support, please contact our Customer Care Department within the United States at (800) 762-2974, outside the United States at (317) 572-3993 or fax (317) 572-4002.

Wiley also publishes its books in a variety of electronic formats. Some content that appears in print may not be available in electronic formats. For more information about Wiley products, visit our web site at www.wiley.com.

For more information about Scrivener products please visit www.scrivenerpublishing.com.

Cover design by Russell Richardson.
Front cover illustrations. Left: Adam Smith and the pin factory taken from the current British £20 bank note. Right: "The Paving-Stone" taken from *Les Misérables* by Victor Hugo, Project Gutenberg.

Library of Congress Cataloging-in-Publication Data:

ISBN 978-0-470-94829-3

Printed in the United States of America

10 9 8 7 6 5 4 3 2 1

Contents

**Part Three: The Maturation of the Two Narratives:
The Challenge of Social Economy**

Editors' Note

A complete account of the intellectual origins and development of political economy would encompass the multiple works of many writers over several centuries. Instead, we have (1) edited the original material that captures the conversation over three centuries between what we have called the liberty narrative and the equality narrative and (2) made that conversation available in an accessible, and affordable, one volume reader. Since our objective is to let the original participants speak for themselves, we have kept editorial intrusions to a minimum.

To repeat, we are interested in a conversation about the origin and development—including its anticipated fall and rise again—of political economy. We collect under one roof, the seventeenth, eighteenth, and nineteenth century essential contributions of leading writers on behalf of the liberty narrative and the equality narrative which we identify as the two paths of political economy. Even though the liberty narrative has its roots in the Anglo-American tradition, we have excluded writers such as David Ricardo who turned political economy in a more technical direction. Similarly, we have selected authors who focus on the issue of the inter relationship between the questions of property, fairness, and religion over three centuries in our coverage of the equality tradition. And while this tradition is mainly Continental European, we have included Robert Owen as an important part of the conversation. We also assume that the reader will have ready and affordable access to the twentieth century and twenty-first century versions of the two narratives.

In short, the readings included here are intended to be instructive with respect to the origin and development of the two narratives rather than an exhaustive account of how thinkers and writers on economics advance the project of economics as a social science.

We divide the conversation into three parts roughly coinciding with the three centuries. And in each part, we focus on one or more critical thinkers and use one or more decisive events as bookends. Prior to modernity, economic activity was confined to the household and/or regulated by the religious sphere. Thus we call Part One, **The Emergence of Political Economy: Economic Activity Leaves the Household**. With the works of Locke and Rousseau, on the one hand, and the Glorious Revolution and suspicion of the Enlightenment on the other hand, the economic question enters the public sphere and we have the birth of the two narratives. We entitle Part Two, **The Arrival of Political Economy: Liberty, Property, and Equality**. The central thinkers are Adam Smith on behalf of the liberty narrative and Robert Owen and P. J. Proudhon for the equality narrative. The pivotal question is the status of property and its relationship to liberty and equality. The vital events are (a) the two revolutions that take place on opposite sides of the Atlantic in the late eighteenth century and (b) the unsettling, yet reflective, times of the 1840s. The final section of the book, Part Three, we refer to as **The Maturation of the Two Narratives: The Challenge of Social Economy**. The two critical thinkers are John Stuart Mill and Karl Marx, who "correct" the intellectual foundations of the two narratives inherited from the previous centuries. The defining opening event is the specter of yet further revolutionary activity and thought haunting Europe in 1848. We have deliberately not put a bookend to Part Three for it leads naturally into the next century.

All of the selected material is edited from original sources available at The Huntington Library or one or more of the University of California Libraries. The material is in the public domain and we have used editions that stay as close to the version approved by the author as possible. We have retained the original style, grammar, and punctuation wherever possible and sensible. We have, however, made an effort to modernize, even Americanize, the spelling. An important editorial intrusion is the addition of subheadings to the original texts where appropriate to help the reader breakdown material which at times is dense. For example, we, not Locke, divide his *Second Treatise* into 17 sections, *Toleration* into 13 sections, and *Money* into 12 sections. We have taken particular liberties with John Stuart Mill's paragraphs: often Mill will include a page or more within one paragraph and, thus, we have chopped several of them into shorter and more manageable ones. But we have also given other writers a helping hand.

The standard *The Works of John Locke* (1823) is our point of departure for the three Locke entries. *The Second Treatise, Toleration,* and *Money* written by Locke (1632-1704), and each published for the first time in 1689, are also available in affordable paperback versions and on a number of electronic sites; see for example Liberty Fund's Online Library of Liberty. G. D. H. Cole's 1913 translations of the four J. J. Rousseau (1712–1778) entries are the basis for our own versions of Rousseau's works. *The First Discourse, The Second Discourse, Political Economy,* and *The Social Contract* were published in 1750, 1754, 1755, and 1762 respectively. See also the Constitution Society website for helpful links to commentaries on Rousseau.

We rely on Edwin Cannon's 1904 edition of Adam Smith's *Wealth of Nations* as our text for the Smith entry. Also see Liberty Fund's publication and their

Library of Economics and Liberty website at www.econlib.org for the complete works of Smith (1723–1790). *The Federalist* is available in numerous forms; we use the 1788 "McLean Edition." These essays are also available in many print and electronic versions. See, for example the "Rossiter edition," updated by Charles Kesler, or George Carey's edition for Liberty Fund. See also www.teachingamericanhistory.org/ratification. There are many efforts to produce *the authentic* version of the two volumes of *Democracy in America* by Alexis de Tocqueville (1805–1859). Nevertheless, we rely on the original English translation for our selections from the second volume (1840) by Henry Reeve (1813–1895) because 1) it is in the public domain and 2) we are more interested in Tocqueville's contribution to the conversation of the two narratives than reproducing *the* definitive version of Tocqueville's *Democracy*.

For our coverage of The French Revolution, we rely on Francis Lieber's *On Civil Liberty*, edited by Theodore D. Woolsey and published by J. B. Lippincott in 1883. We rely on, but adapt, the 1794 Philadelphia publication of an English translation of Robespierre's *On the Principles of Morality*. The full title of the original was *Sur les principes de morale politique qui doivent guider la Convention nationale dans l'administration intérieure de la République Prononcé à la Convention le 5 février 1794 - 17 pluviôse An II*. See http://www.marxists.org/history/france/revolution/robespierre/index.htm for online coverage of Maximilien Robespierre (1758-1794). There are a number of reliable editions of Robert Owen's work. See, for example, *Complete Works of Owen* (1771–1790) published in 1931 by Dent. We rely on the original 1816 second edition version of *A New View of Society* also published by Dent with an introduction by John Butt. Unfortunately, there is not a full set of English translations of *Comte de Saint-Simon* (1760–1825) in the public domain. So we have provided our own translation of the essential paragraphs of his *Nouveau Christianisme* (1825). A complete collection of Saint-Simon's works is available in forty-three volumes; they were first published in Paris between 1865–1872. We include an excerpt from Sampson S. Lloyd's English translation in 1881 of Friedrich List's *National System* originally published in 1841. List (1789–1846) is not a direct advocate of the equality narrative but he is recognized as the father of the "German Historical School," and perhaps even the great grandfather of the European Economic Union within which the ups and downs of the equality narrative are in full display in the twenty-first century. Moreover his critique of Smith's individualism is central to the equality narrative and anticipates the growing importance of intellectuals in the conversation. We rely on the late nineteenth century English translations of P. J. Proudhon's works by Benjamin R. Tucker (1854–1939). Here we include extracts from *The Philosophy of Poverty* (1840) and *What is Property?* (1846) by Proudhon (1809–1865). See also http://anarchism.pageabode.com.

For the entries from J. S. Mill's *Principles of Political Economy* (1848) we rely on the 7th edition by William J. Ashley in 1909. And for *On Liberty* and *The Subjection of Women*, we rely, respectively, on the Longman, Roberts and Green version of 1869 and the Henry Holt edition of 1879. They originally appeared in 1859 and 1869. Thirty-three volumes of *The Collected Works of John Stuart Mill* (1806–1843) are available from The Online Library of Liberty. The edited versions of the three major writings of Karl Marx (1818-1883) and Frederick Engels (1820–1895)—*The Communist Manifesto, Das Kapital,* and *Socialism: Utopian and Scientific*—were translated into English by Samuel Moore and Edward Aveling in 1888, 1886, and 1892 respectively. They made their first appearance in 1848, 1867, and 1880 respectively. We rely on the English translations approved by Engels. Near the end of the Introduction to the 1888 English edition of *The Communist Manifesto,* Engels reveals his reliance on Moore: "The present translation is by Mr. Samuel Moore, the translator of the greater portion of Marx's *Capital.* We have revised it in common, and I have added a few notes explanatory of historical allusions."

We thank the following people for their insight and encouragement: Steve Ealy, Bobbi Herzberg, Kevin Honeycutt, and Martin Scrivener. We also thank Marie Ann Thaler and Christynn Vierra for their editorial assistance. Finally, we wish to thank Liberty Fund for bringing us together in the first place and for providing the opportunity to introduce earlier versions of The Two Narratives at a variety of conferences.

August 2010

General Introduction

Political Economy

Political Science and Economics are, within the present intellectual world and the university, usually presented as two separate disciplines. This was not always the case. As can be seen from the titles of the selections in this anthology, the expression "political economy" reflected the view that political and economic institutions were related in some way. Specifically, political economy was originally concerned with the relationship between production and distribution. As such, it carried normative implications for public policy or the practice of politics.

It was only in the late 19th century that economics came to be viewed (e.g., in Alfred Marshall) as an independent empirical subject employing mathematical models to study economic behavior. By the twentieth century, political science became an independent empirical subject employing mathematical models to study political behavior. As allegedly scientific disciplines, neither political science nor economics has any normative implications.

Of course, economists who make public policy judgments and recommendations both presuppose certain political beliefs and expect certain political consequences. Likewise, political scientists who make public policy judgments and recommendations both presuppose certain economic beliefs and expect certain economic consequences. Political theory as a subset of political science attempts to retain the historical and normative dimensions of political thought, usually with economics being in a subordinate role. Recent academic programs in political economy have focused on the normative dimension also with economics being seen as a reflection of political presuppositions and arrangements. Politicians are expected to make normative public policy decisions and therefore presuppose certain views about economics and politics.

But what is the relationship between politics and economics? We suggest that in the modern or post-Renaissance world there have been and continue to be two competing views or narratives about that relationship. We call them narratives. The most fundamental way in which human beings understand themselves is by telling a story, hence a narrative. Narratives are not strictly speaking arguments although they may contain arguments within them. Such narratives cannot be refuted because they reflect decisions on the part of individuals both to view themselves and the world in a certain way and to act according to that vision.

Objective of the Book

The objective of this book, which we have called *The Two Narratives of Political Economy*, is to go back in order to come back. We don't want to get stuck in the past, rather we want to learn from previous insights in order to come back and participate in the present and future. But what do we bring back from this journey of retrieval and how do we apply our rediscoveries to the contemporary situation? Our objective is not to presume that we know more about politics and economics today than previous generations. In fact, our project assumes just the opposite: we wish to retrieve the connection between politics and economics, a connection that lasted for two hundred years but which has been severely tested, if not severed, over the last hundred years by those who wish that economics would become more scientific, with efficiency as the central objective, and those who wish that politics would become more ideological, with inevitability as the driving force, along with planning by experts replacing "the anarchy of the market."

At the heart of our project of retrieval is the claim that there are two narratives at work both in the normative and empirical sense: the liberty narrative and the equality narrative. And both these narratives are informed by two versions of the enlightenment. Both of these narratives undergo internal intellectual challenges as the enlightenment understanding of physical and human nature are subjected to criticism, first in the nineteenth century, and then in the twentieth century.

We place the origin of the study of political economy with Locke and Rousseau rather than in the world of Greece and Rome. Both Locke and Rousseau took economics out of the private household where it was placed in the thought of the ancients, and placed economics in the public or political realm. This is the origin of political economy. There is something modern and even new about the issues generated by political economy that are different from the quarrels of the ancient or old world. That world argued about virtue and vice, courage and cowardice, excellence and ignorance, innocence and sin. The modern world has as its argument something new, what we have called the liberty narrative and the equality narrative.

In classical and medieval political thought, economics was not a major focus. Economics, as we have indicated, was confined to the household. The economy was largely agricultural and even trade was largely confined to agricultural products. Populations as well as economies were static. Reflection on such issues revolved around an Aristotelian perspective within which the world was seen as finite, cyclical and teleological and therefore non-evolutionary, and self-contained. In such a finite and no-growth universe, theoretical economics focused on questions of the just price and the charging of interest.

In the modern period, the world came to be viewed much differently. In physics, Galileo and Newton replaced the Aristotelian notions that rest was natural (wherein motion was problematic) and that motion was circular with the views that motion was natural (hence rest was problematic) and that motion was linear (and therefore evolution and progress were possible). Astronomers from Copernicus onto Galileo changed our perspective from that of a closed world to an infinite universe. Descartes and Bacon promoted the idea that wisdom consisted not in conforming to nature, but in manipulating it. Thus was born the Technological Project. The voyages of discovery (Columbus, da Gama, Magellan) also contributed to the notions of growth and expansion. Suddenly, nations were engaged in economic growth, expansion and competition. It is at this point that economies are viewed not as operating within a household or estate but nationally. We now see the concept of economies of states or nations (Wealth of Nations). To be sure, some early modern political economists poured the new wine into old bottles by adopting *mercantilism*, the view that while wealth was far greater than hitherto imagined, it still was finite so that one nation's gain was another's loss.

The Logic of Modernity

The most important historical development in the last four hundred years has been the rise of the **Technological Project (TP)**.[1] The TP, not the market, is the starting point for our narrative, because, although there have always been markets, it is only since the 16th century that markets have come to play such a dominant role in our lives. It is the presence of the TP that explains the centrality of markets.

The TP is the control of nature for human benefit. The TP (a) radically changed the way people in the West viewed the world and their relationship to the world, (b) led to fundamental changes in the major institutions of the West (economic, political, legal, and social), (c) led to the expansion of the West and its domination of the non-Western world, and (d) finally to Globalization—the internationalization of Western institutions.

---

1. The so-called industrial revolution is but an expression of the Technological Project. The more fundamental idea is the notion of transforming the world. See Rene Descartes, *Discourse on Method*; Francis Bacon, *Essays* nos. 13, 16–17, and *The Great Instauration and New Atlantis*.

In the ancient and medieval world (and in much of the world today) people thought in terms of conformity to nature, not transforming nature for human benefit. In large part this reflected the fact that the earliest civilizations were agrarian, that agriculture requires in its early stages a calendar, and that the earliest calendars were based upon astronomy. This understandably fostered the mind set of believing that the physical world had a structure and meaning independent of human beings, that truth consisted in the apprehension of a structure independent of human beings, and that wisdom and success depended upon human beings conforming to the external structure of the world.

By the Renaissance all of that was to change. Starting with Copernicus, Western thinkers became aware of how much of what we understand reflects the human perspective (and so did the artists of the Renaissance). Copernicus, for example, maintained that despite appearances the sun does not rise and set, rather the earth turns on its axis. Starting with Copernicus and reinforced by the work of Galileo, Descartes, and Newton, Western thinkers came to recognize how much of science depended not on naïve observation of surface phenomena but on the construction of hypothetical *mathematical* models about hidden structure. Newton and Leibniz would both go on to invent the calculus. Meaning and structure (and in a word, truth) were not to be found externally but in the internal models of the human mind. Wisdom and success were transformed from conformity to an external structure to bending or conforming the external physical world to human reason and imagination. The belief that human beings could understand and control the hidden structure of nature and that the hidden structure was conducive to human benefit was inspired by Christianity's conception of God!

The medieval Aristotelian synthesis in which all of nature and humanity were linked in an inter-locking series of organic associations arranged in hierarchical order was rejected. Nature was no longer to be viewed as an organism but as a mechanism created by God. We as individuals inspired by an internally apprehended divine vision replicated God's creativity by transforming the world through good works including commerce and industry (not just charity). There was no collective good to be authoritatively apprehended in nature, only a collection of individually apprehended goods whose continuity and coherence were vouchsafed by God.

Among the first to proclaim the TP as a self-conscious undertaking were Francis Bacon when he proclaimed that "knowledge is power" and Rene Descartes, French philosopher, mathematician, and physicist, who advocated that human beings make themselves "the masters and possessors of nature." It is worth noting that Descartes specifically singled out the importance of advances in medical science for an age in which the normal human life span was 36 years! It was also Descartes who in his *Discourse on Method* advocated the development of inner-directed individuals (autonomy) cooperating to produce innovative ideas (scientific and technical thinking) for understanding and controlling natural processes. Finally, Descartes also recognized how commercial republics like Holland in the 17th century were peculiarly hospitable to these new developments.

The TP is fostered by an environment in which human beings are given as much free reign as possible to use their imagination (a) to think scientifically in the mathematical-modeling sense and (b) to develop new ways and products for humanity to control the physical environment, to protect and heal the human body, and to make life more comfortable and enjoyable. The economic institution most conducive to the TP was the **free market economy (FME):** a system for the exchange of goods and services wherein there is no central allocation of such goods and services. The goods and services are privately owned (i.e., private property). The FME fosters competition.

In order for a free market economy to function it requires a **limited government (LG)**. The government provides the legal context for maintaining law and order and for enforcing contracts. It requires as well that the government which performs this service understands that it should not interfere with the competitive and innovative process of the market. The government exists to protect the *rights of individuals* who pursue their own individual interests from interference either by others or the government itself. It does not exist to further a preconceived collective good or to serve the bureaucracy or to serve a particular faction (James Madison in *Federalist #10, 1787*).

Part of the meaning of political equality was equality before the law, and equality before the law meant appeal to the rule of law and not the whim of political leaders. One of the institutional ways in which government is limited is through the **rule of law (RL).** *Behind the notion of the rule of law lies the historical notion that not all law is just law—that there is a higher law in terms of which ordinary law could be challenged.* Going back to the classical Greeks, a distinction was made between positive or man-made law and the law of nature—the latter being understood as normative. Aristotle explained natural law in terms of a purely naturalistic and teleological conception of the universe—everything has a purpose and the entire set of all purposes forms a natural hierarchy. Throughout the medieval and early modern period Christianity had adopted and advocated the tradition of natural law. Christians identified natural law ultimately with the will of God. Aquinas sought to harmonize Christianity with Aristotle. Aquinas posited a hierarchy of Divine law, Biblical law, natural law, and positive law. Positive or man-made law was to be judged in terms of its conformity to the natural law. Even the meaning of positive law was clarified by appeal to natural law. The latter was accessible through reason supplemented by Biblical law. Crucial to the development of the rule of law in England was the theologian Richard Hooker who adapted Thomistic notions of natural law to the Church of England and influenced John Locke who quotes him extensively in the *Second Treatise*.

The demand for equality before the law was an expression of the notion of Christian liberty. In rejecting a hierarchical conception of the world, Protestants could accept that the political realm was no longer subordinate to the religious realm. But, at the same time, the political realm had to respect the traditional spiritual realm of Christianity. That realm as understood in Protestant terms meant the opportunity to do God's work by transforming the world economically. Equality before the law came to mean that there should be no legal barriers to economic activity that did not apply equally to everyone. Placing legal barriers in the economic realm was tantamount to thwarting God's plan!

All of the above institutions both reflect a certain kind of culture and promote that kind of culture. "Purpose refers to a person's belief that life has meaning. Autonomy refers to a person's belief that it is in his power to fulfill that meaning through his own acts....creativity ultimately comes down to small, solitary acts in which an individual conceives of something new and gives it a try, without knowing for sure how it will turn out. Streams of accomplishment are more common and more extensive in cultures where doing new things and acting autonomously are encouraged than in cultures that disapprove."[2]

In order for a government to remain limited and not become either authoritarian or totalitarian or subject to mob-rule (i.e., pure democracy), it is necessary that the citizens of that government be special kinds of people. They must be autonomous people. **Autonomous people:** are those who rule themselves (i.e., they impose order on their lives through self-discipline in order to achieve goals that they have set for themselves). Kant, Hegel, Mill, and Oakeshott are the philosophers of autonomy par excellence.

Again it is important to avoid misinterpretations and misrepresentations of a culture of personal autonomy. A **culture of personal autonomy (CPA)** is not a culture of self-indulgence. Merely to acquiesce in bodily and emotional impulses is not autonomy but a form of slavery—becoming a slave to one's passions. In order to fulfill God's plan, human beings need to know how to control themselves. Moreover, autonomous beings do not impose their will on others. To define oneself in such a way as merely to defy others or to require that others be your victim is to define oneself in terms of others—the opposite of autonomy. Hence, to act autonomously is to presume that the ultimate ends of each individual are consistent with the ultimate ends of all other individuals. The will of God no longer has its locus in nature outside of human effort. Rather the will of God is discerned inwardly through self-discipline. We imitate God by freeing our will of all influences except the recognition of its freedom, by freely choosing to create a world or to help in creating a world in which the ultimate interests of all coalesce, in which the ultimate interest of each individual is to express its freedom so understood.

It is the combination of the TP, the FME, and autonomy that account for the appearance of a new persona, the entrepreneur. In the 16th century we find the

---

2. Charles Murray, *Human Accomplishment: The Pursuit of Excellence in the Arts and Sciences, 800 B.C. to 1950* (New York: Harper, 2004) pp. 394–99.

first use of the term entrepreneur, from the French verb *entreprendre*—to under-take something. The entrepreneur discovers (Israel Kirzner view) or imagines (Joseph Schumpeter view) new ways of combining resources to create new products or new methods of production. The entrepreneur engages in what Schumpeter was to call creative-destruction.

Autonomous people are inner-directed and therefore capable of participat-ing in the TP in a creative and constructive way. In fact, *the ultimate purpose of the TP is not simply to create wealth but to allow autonomous people to express their freedom and how such freedom reflects God's Will.* Wealth is a means to achieve-ment and freedom, not an end in itself. It is in this sense that **the TP is now to be understood as the spiritual quest of modernity.** The ultimate rationale for the technological project is not consumer satisfaction, or productive efficiency, but the production of the means of accomplishment. *Our greatest fulfillment comes from freely imposing order on ourselves in order to impose a creative order on the world.*

Many of the features we have described as the logic of modernity can be found in 17th century writers such as Hobbes, Descartes, and Mandeville.[3] John Locke, however, is the first to express the entire spectrum of such views and in a coherent manner. Many later 18th and early 19th century writers (Montesquieu, Hume, Constant, and Kant) will replicate Locke's narrative despite differences of philosophy or even substantive disagreements on some specific issues.

The First Enlightenment Model: Locke's Liberty Narrative

The first version of the enlightenment model takes its bearing from the natural rights and social contract teaching of Locke, and its common sense Scottish companion, and focuses on individual liberty and equality of opportunity in the economic, political, and religious dimensions. It is, on the whole, more at home with competition and consent rather than what it saw as the monopoly and coercion forces operating in economic, political, and religious life. Conse-quently, we think that it is no accident that in its seventeenth and eighteenth century versions, there was in this competitive-consensus model, an interre-lated opposition to the monopoly inclinations of "inherited" property accumu-lation under feudalism, the "divine" concentration of political power in a monarch, and the dominance of the papacy, or any other conforming tenden-cies in Christianity. The Protestant work ethic promoted the notion of the inner-directed individual, an emphasis on work, equality before the law, differentiation based on achievement, and the right of individual conscience. The insistence upon equality before the law was an expression of the notion of Christian lib-erty. Adam Smith, James Madison, J. S. Mill, and later Herbert Hoover, Milton

3. See Henry C. Clark (ed.), *Commerce, Culture, and Liberty: Readings on Capitalism Before Adam Smith* (Indianapolis: Liberty Fund, 2003).

Friedman, and F. A. Hayek all rely on the link between liberty and competition on the one hand, and choice and consent on the other in making the case for the three aspects of freedom, although the intellectual foundation has moved away from natural right via utilitarianism and into positivism.

There is, to be sure, an equality component to the liberty narrative, namely, equality of opportunity and equality before the law, that is thoroughly compatible with liberty as expressed in the following truth: all men are created, or born equal, and thus have the individual right to life, liberty, property, and the pursuit of happiness. Equality before the law came to mean that there should be no legal barriers to economic activity that did not apply equally to everyone. Nor should there be legal barriers to political and religious activity. In other words, the liberty narrative assumes the equal autonomy of human beings as a normative point of departure and the human challenge is to secure individual liberty as an empirical reality. And this task will, for a variety of legitimate reasons, produce unequal outcomes.

The early defenders of the liberty narrative placed their emphasis not simply on the superior efficiency of a free market over against government regulation and ownership. Rather the sustainability of the narrative is grounded in a moral claim that compulsion is unfair and wrong. In one form or another, the moral core of the liberty narrative was stated as truths in the United States *Declaration of Independence* by way of Locke: "all men are created equal, that they are endowed by their Creator with certain unalienable Rights, that among these are Life, Liberty and the pursuit of Happiness." Life is the necessary condition for liberty and liberty is the means by which individuals pursue happiness.

The Second Enlightenment Model: Rousseau's Equality Narrative

The second version of the enlightenment model takes its bearing from the natural rights and social contract teaching of Rousseau, and its utopian companion in the French Revolution, and focuses on community, solidarity and equality of outcome in the economic, political, and religious dimensions. It is far less at home with the virtues of competition, emphasizing instead what is seen as the vices of competition such as selfishness, greed, fraud, luxury, and anarchy. What pulls this second narrative in the direction of equality of outcome is the human sense of compassion, or deep-seated natural sympathy for others, and the duty toward the well being of other humans. And there is a compatible development in the world of politics and religion: there is an emphasis on the rule of the general will rather than the rule of law and the substitution of a civil religion, or secular humanism, for the rule of individual conscience.

This second version as it developed from Rousseau, through Marx, to the Progressives and FDR, to the New Left, to the Great Society and beyond has a very hard time accepting, even living with, the unequal distribution of income and wealth that comes and goes with the presence of competition. This suspicion that there is something fraudulent and hypocritical about the distribution of property by means of competitive markets carries over into the political and religious realms. There is a critique of, and impatience with, the competitive system of separation of governmental powers between three branches, the deliberative dimensions of representative democracy, the federal division of powers that encourage deliberation and discourage action, and even the presence of religion as "an opiate of the people." And so there is, in this second narrative, a different conception of the role government, especially what government should do and which level of government should do it. What sustains the attractiveness of the equality narrative are not the scientific claims of the inevitable decline of capitalism, or the ideological attack on bourgeoisie institutions, or the "fetishism" of religion. Rather the sustainability of the narrative is grounded in a moral claim that inequality is unfair and wrong. In one form or another Saint-Simon, by way of Rousseau, stated the moral core of the equality narrative: "from each according to his ability, to each according to his need." Or in the language of the Declaration of Rights of the French Revolution: "Liberty, Equality, Fraternity." Liberty is the necessary condition for equality and equality is the means to secure fraternity.

The Liberty Narrative Expanded

The claim of the lovers of liberty is that a free market economy is the most effective means of carrying out the Technological Project, the conquest of nature in the service of human needs. The dynamic of the Technological Project requires constant innovation, and the free market economy maximizes such innovation through competition and specialization. At least that is the claim of "classical economics."

In Locke's version of the modern "experiment," we learn the following: "God, who has given the world to men in common, has also given them reason to make use of it to the best advantage of life, and convenience...it cannot be supposed. He meant it should always remain common and uncultivated. He gave it to the use of the Industrious and Rational...not to the Fancy or Covetousness of the Quarrelsome and Contentious...for it is labor indeed that puts the difference of value on every thing... of the products of the earth useful to the life of man nine tenths are the effects of labor...."

The crucial theoretical argument for the centrality of a free market was made by Adam Smith in the *Wealth of Nations* (1776). Smith emphasized private property, competition, and the division of labor—all of which contribute to technological innovation.

Smith was also the author of *The Theory of Moral Sentiments*, suggesting that some sense of individual responsibility and common good is connected to the increase in the production of the necessities and conveniences of life. Smith replaced Locke's natural law/natural right framework for liberty with a natural history approach. Like other Scottish enlightenment thinkers he explained the emergence of liberty as part of the stages of economic growth. Smith, like his friend Hume, replaced the centrality of reason (understood as the mirror of nature) with imagination—a reflection of the inner-directed individual. It was through imagination that we could adopt a social perspective both to restrain our partiality and to sympathize with the interests of others. Rather than proclaiming pure enlightened self-interest and rather than dismissing Rousseauean protests of inequality, Smith attempted to deal with the distribution issue through sympathy and the "hidden hand." The same God (understood Deistically) who created an ordered universe hospitable to human interest, (TP) created individuals who could be sensitive to the interests of others and whose pursuit of their own interest coincidentally fostered the interest of others (FME). God's order was discovered not in physical nature but within the social world and the individual sensorium.

The market economy was not itself new. In fact, it could be maintained that private property had always existed in historical memory. The Church, moreover, had officially defended the importance of private property. What was new was the recognition of how crucial private property and a free market economy were to the TP. Why is that? Innovation cannot, by definition, be planned. To the extent that property is privately owned and not centrally controlled, and to the extent that a free market economy is *competitive*, there is a greater possibility for innovation. In his canonical work which marked the beginning of modern economic theory, Adam Smith argued in the *Wealth of Nations (1776)* that a free market economy encouraged innovation. It was innovative because the division of labor led to specialization and specialization led to innovation (labor saving devices, etc.) as well as greater productivity. Smith's example of the manufacturing of pins explains how an assembly line of narrowly focused specialists is far more productive. Once we focus on one part of a process we are apt to invent labor-saving devices. Because it is the best vehicle for innovation, the free market economy is the best form of economic system for engaging in the TP. Finally, the historical-empirical argument for the advantages of a free market economy is the post 1989 implosion of the Soviet Union and the growth of China's economy. Almost everywhere it is now admitted that a free market economy is the most efficient method for engaging in the technological project.

While private property had always existed, governments from time immemorial had regulated and controlled it in varying degrees to advance their own purposes and not for the TP. To get the maximum advantage out of a market economy it needs to be as free as possible to foster innovation. Government or the State can play a useful but limited function by providing a legal system for protecting the rights of individuals, especially private property, for enforcing contracts, and for dispute resolution. In order for a free market economy to function it requires a limited government known as a commercial republic. The government provides the legal context for maintaining law and order and for enforcing contracts. It requires as well that the government which performs this service understands that it should not interfere with the competitive and innovative process of the market. The government exists to protect the rights of individuals who pursue their own individual interests (*civil association*). It does not exist to further a collective good (*enterprise association*) or to serve the bureaucracy or to serve a particular interest group. This is the sense in which the government is limited or subordinate to the requirements of commerce. Instead of employing slogans like the 'night watchman state' or the 'minimal' state, it is more insightful to recognize that state action is best when restricted to serving the interests of a market economy within the technological project. Needless to add, Christianity had provided a tradition for limiting the government and the Church had steadfastly maintained the inviolability of private property—including and especially its own!

This form of government is called a *Republic*. It is a government of laws and not of men. A republic is designed to protect the rights of individuals not the privileges of a majority or a minority. It has a Constitution which specifies those rights. Since there is no collective good, there is a common good. The common good consists of the conditions (e.g., rule of law, toleration) within which individuals pursue their self-interest.

A Republic is not a direct democracy, for a direct democracy involves unfiltered and unchecked majority rule and not constitutional rule. From Plato and Aristotle right through the 18th century Founding, direct democracy was rejected as mob rule. Democracy technically means majority-rule, and in practice becomes a system of political economy in which the bottom 51 percent progressively loot the wealth and productivity of the top 49 percent.

Indirect Democracy was understood by the Founders as part of a system of checks and balances[4] that restrains one interest from imposing its will upon others. Indirect or Representative Democracy, as Madison made clear in *Federalist # 10*, is a negative device for blocking one powerful interest group from imposing its will on others. Representative Democracy, or democratic republicanism, was never intended as a positive device for articulating a suspect collective common good. It was during the nineteenth-century in Europe that democracy as majority rule was posited as the will of the people or even the general will as originally suggested[5] by Rousseau: the voice of the people is

---

4. Sen's paradox (1970) presents a more precise formulation of why democracy is a negative device rather than a positive one. Marxists have always been rightly contemptuous of democratic socialism because shifting majorities literally makes even the façade of economic planning impossible. Sen, Amartya, "The Impossibility of a Paretian Liberal," *Journal of Political Economy*, 78, pp. 152–157.

5. There is reason to believe that Rousseau distinguished among the General Will, the will of all, and the majority will. Later thinkers ignored such distinctions.

the voice of God. That is when Tocqueville and Mill came to view democracy as a threat, as the tyranny of the majority.[6] It evolves into the formal notion that what is right is what the majority decides or that the common good is what the majority decides it is on a given occasion.

In the post-Renaissance and Reformation period, Protestants especially saw an important connection between politics and economics. The desire for political equality was not the desire to exercise power for power's sake or to remake society. On the contrary, Protestants were largely focused on protecting the private sphere and the spiritual dimension from political corruption. The connection between politics and economics derived from the fact that government controlled large parts of the economy (granting of privileges such as monopolies, sinecures, land grants, etc.). Political equality implied economic equality in the sense that all possessed the liberty to pursue God's work in this world, not an equal distribution of the spoils.

This is the sense in which the government is limited or subordinate to the requirements of commerce. And that commerce, in turn, provides the infrastructure that enables competition between the opinions, passions, and interests in society so that the outcome is as close to the preservation of liberty and the securing of justice as are possible to expect. Now this economic or commercial foundation where we have the competition of economic, political, and religious interests in an "extended orbit," is the necessary condition for securing liberty, but we need government. Free government, in contrast to good government or a general will government, is characterized by the *rule of law*. According to the Founders, a political and legal system that *constrains the excesses of popular government,* while retaining the essence of popular government, is said to exhibit the rule of law. But we need to remember that the rule of law is not the same as the law of rules. In a Republic, the rule of law is typically embodied in a Constitution, which provides protection for rights within the very structure of government, and a Bill of Rights that specifies those rights against the overreach of government. And thus the rule of law involves the right of the people to elect their representatives, and it also includes the separation of powers and checks and balances on a majority that is motivated and activated to tyrannize over an economic, political, or religious minority.

The rule of law has evolved jurisprudentially into meaning a legal system that *constrains government.*[7] Typically the powers of government are divided among separate branches, with an independent judiciary. Due process and the equal protection of the law protect the rights of individuals by constitutional

---

6. Public Choice economics in the work of James Buchanan and others helps to explain the structure of that degeneration.

7. See F. A. Hayek, *Law, Legislation, and Liberty* (London: Taylor & Francis, 1982) and *The Road to Serfdom*, (Chicago: University of Chicago Press, 1994), Chapter Six "Planning and the Rule of Law"; M. Oakeshott, "The Rule of Law," in *On History and Other Essays* (Indianapolis: Liberty Fund, 1999), pp. 119–164; Supplement (*On Human Conduct* (Oxford: Oxford University Press, 1991), pp. 119, 139, 181, 153–58, 234–5, 286, and 315). 56pp.

means. It is a system of rules designed to allow individuals to pursue their self-defined interests without interfering with that same pursuit on the part of others. As Hayek was to express it, *the rule of law provides the rules of the game without determining the outcome of the game.*

As elaborated by Michael Oakeshott, the rule of law exists only in a modern state that is a civil association, that is, one in which there is no collective good, only the goods of its individual members. The laws prescribe conditions to be observed by individuals who pursue their own purposes, alone or with others. The laws are neutral or indifferent with regard to whether the purposes are achieved. Once the law is construed as an instrument for achieving particular economic or political objectives, the rule of law is violated or disappears.

It is a government of laws and not of men, but in the sense that we can't simply trust men in power to do the right thing and expect liberty to prevail, unless precautions are place on their conduct. As Madison put it not so delicately: "if all men were angels, no government would be necessary." But we add with swiftness: if all men were beasts, free government would be impossible. And that means free government in all three spheres of liberty—political, economic, and religious—supposes the ability of individuals to govern themselves, at least most of the time on the most important matters pertaining to their life, liberty, and pursuit of happiness. And through the give and take of competition, "the deliberative sense of the community" should prevail. There is no temptation in the liberty narrative to turn men into angels and thus eliminate the cause of government. That would mean that no government would be necessary, and it would mean the end to the liberty narrative.

In the Madison model, there is no *collective* good to be imposed by an outside authority of experts or central planners, but there is a *common* good that emerges from the deliberative process. The common good consists of what happens when the conditions (e.g., rule of law, toleration, protection of individual rights, reliance on markets, separation of powers, etc.) are right for the expression of liberty and within which individuals pursue their self-interest. This is similar to Adam Smith's invisible hand and Hayek's theory of spontaneous order: if you leave people alone to pursue their own self interest—within the confines of the rule of law—then the common good is more likely to emerge than if imposed from the outside by an all-knowing expert.

Perhaps the most insightful critic of an early version of the equality narrative was David Hume, life-long friend of Adam Smith, one-time friend of Rousseau, and the inspiration for Madison's writings. In one prescient paragraph in the *Enquiry Concerning the Principles of Morals*, Hume stated the entire case against it. First, there was no agreement on what things should be equalized, i.e., there was no consensus on which universal facts about human nature entailed normative social arrangements. Second, given that lack of agreement, demands for equality would remain nothing more than rhetorical masks for private political agendas. Third, even if it were possible to redistribute everything so that we all started out equal, differences in ability and circumstances (luck, e.g.) would soon lead to inequalities. Fourth, and finally, in order to overcome inegalitarian recidivism, it would be necessary to maintain the most all-encompassing social tyranny.

Notice that Hume is not objecting to equality before the law or equality of opportunity, forms of equality he supported. He supported them because they were part and parcel of a market economy in a commercial republic, that is, what we have called liberal culture. What he objected to was the allegedly scientific open-ended egalitarianism of the Enlightenment Project. Something new was also introduced in Hume's argument. The point of encouraging equality of opportunity is to maximize growth and the creation of greater opportunities, economic and otherwise, for everyone. The secular concern for growth has become identified with (or replaced) the Reformation notion of doing God's work.

Attempts to promote direct democracy as a basic form of organization—a form of government more compatible with the equality narrative than the liberty narrative—and criticisms of those attempts—it encourages people to discover their nastiness and to act on them directly—are as old as the Greeks, as for example, Aristotle's critique in Bk. VI of the *Politics*. The Framers of the United States Constitution followed the 18th century fashion of decrying direct democracy and placing their faith, instead, in the idea of a "Republic." In the nineteenth century, Tocqueville in his *Democracy in America* (1835) warned about the "tyranny of the majority," a theme taken up by J. S. Mill in his essay *On Liberty* (1859). And the twentieth century has also found thinkers like Hoover, Hayek, and Friedman who have defended the liberty narrative over against the equality narrative because of their concern that an overbearing majority encouraged by egalitarian supporting intellectuals and bureaucrats will undermine the rule of law and thus the empire of liberty.

In order for a government to remain limited and not become either authoritarian-totalitarian or subject to mob-rule or the tyranny of the majority, it is necessary that there be a larger supportive culture where the citizens are educated, or given incentives, to become a special or exceptional kind of people. *Autonomous individuals* are those who rule themselves (i.e., they impose order on their lives through self-discipline in order to achieve goals that they have set for themselves). Autonomous people are inner-directed and therefore capable of participating in the Technological Project in a creative and constructive way. In fact, the ultimate purpose of the Technological Project is not to create wealth *per se*, but to allow autonomous people to express their freedom because they are no longer in a condition of dependency. Wealth is a means to freely pursue happiness and not an end in itself.

The Equality Narrative Expanded

Rousseau represented an important and often overlooked and misunderstood counter-current to the Lockean Enlightenment Project. The kind of equality that counted, for him, was moral equality. He recognized that this kind of equality could be threatened by economic inequality (*Discourse on the Origin of Inequality* in 1754) and in the *Social Contract* of 1762 where he urged that no one be "so rich as to be able to buy another, and none so poor as to have to sell himself" (II, 11). His *Political Economy* introduced the concept of the general will that is vital for the collectivist political project presented in the Social Contract.

The French Revolution reflected all of the competing conceptions of equality we have identified. *The Declaration of Rights* of 1789 rejected privileges and opportunities based on birth and advocated equality of opportunity (access to public office should depend only on "virtues and talents"). It abolished feudalism, provided for equality of rights, equality before the law, equality of opportunity (abolished the inheritance of rank and public office), equality of punishment, equality of taxation. The abolition of slavery was proclaimed in 1794. All of this reflects the relative egalitarianism associated with a commercial Republic, and this in turn reflected a secularized version of the Protestant Reformation within a market economy. But it also pointed in a direction away from the Lockean liberty narrative of individual rights and toward the Rousseau equality narrative of the collective or general will. How would this Locke-Rousseau disagreement be resolved?

In the *Discourse on the Arts and Sciences*, Rousseau critiqued what we have called the Technological Project. Instead of satisfying genuine human needs, the arts and sciences are expressions of pride (promoting invidious self-comparison), and they have led to luxury and the introduction of human inequality. In the *Discourse on Inequality*, Rousseau suggests that the division of labor and the institution of private property are antagonistic to the perfection of human beings because, to anticipate the theory of justice propounded by John Rawls, not everyone enters the social contract "naked" as it were or with a "veil of ignorance." Interestingly, Rousseau moves from the critique of the liberty narrative in the two discourses to the introduction of the general will as THE principle of political economy, in his *Discourse on Political Economy*, to a robust political account of the general will in his *Social Contract*, in which will is implemented and sustained by an appeal to civil religion.

The Lockean social contract, as seen from the *Rousseau-through-Rawls* lens in the twentieth century, is a fraud, if it ever actually took place at all! It is a kind of double swindle. It is a fraud, first, because the few who were rich and powerful coerced—or *forced*—the less fortunate many into institutionalizing inequality. Rousseau's own social contract is meant to remedy this political and social inequality, by requiring everybody to give up everything when, again anticipating John Rawls, they enter civil society not knowing what is in store for them ahead of time. And it is a fraud, secondly, because no such event has actually taken place in empirical reality. This notion that certain privileged folks out there are putting one huge something over on us innocent and victimized many is central to the equality narrative.

The Rousseau version of the Enlightenment Project transforms the Lockean conception of rights from the rights of the individual to the rights of the community. Instead of the Lockean model where individuals retain rights upon entering society, and thus government is limited, under the Rousseau model each individual gives up each and all rights upon entering society. Each person enters stripped of rights, and naked, abandons all attachment to a previous and stunted private self and acquires a new and grander public self. The general will replaces individual choice. Obedience becomes total rather than conditional. If you "fall back" into the old way of thinking, namely, a yearning for individual identity and personal autonomy, then it is the appropriate role of government "to force you to be free." In other words, to require you to live up to what you freely willed. Following in the footsteps of the Rousseau version of the enlightenment, individual rights are only *prima facie*, may be overridden, and may be possessed by any entity, not just individual human beings. Such rights can be welfare rights, i.e., they may be such that others have a positive obligation to provide such goods, benefits or means.

Rousseau's critique of modern society, especially the idea that private property was theft and that limited government is contrary to true and pure democracy and the general will, was adapted and broadened in the 19th century (Robert Owen, Charles Fourier, Pierre-Joseph Proudhon, Louis Blanc, Saint-Simon, Marx, etc.), mainly by writers we now identify generically as "socialist." These writers, unlike Rousseau, were more willing to embrace technology, but they criticized the poverty, inequality, alienation and degradation, which they alleged, were consequences of the Industrial Revolution. They focused on the unfairness—the inequality—of the distribution of the goods and services generated by the new technological world. They advocated the abolition of private property, which they asserted had unfairly concentrated power and wealth among a few, exacerbated inequality, and did not provide equal opportunities for everyone. But they sought not merely more equal opportunity; rather they defended more equality of outcome. And they articulated a scientific basis for this moral critique: just as capitalism came into being, it shall go away either as a result of some immanent law of evolution, with the revolutionary conduct of the united working class. All will be well in the end; no government will be necessary because all men will have become angels.

We no longer have to manage faction because liberty to pursue happiness is the supreme value. We can eliminate faction because equality to secure fraternity is the supreme value.

Despite the claim to be scientific, the equality narrative has been criticized for its romanticism, something that we have hinted at in the previous paragraph. In *The Roots of Romanticism*, Sir Isaiah Berlin identifies the romantic roots of this equality narrative: "[Romanticism] introduces for the first time...a crucial note in the history of human thought, namely that ideals, ends, objectives are not to be discovered by intuition, by scientific means, by reading sacred texts, by listening to experts or to authoritative persons; that ideals are not to be discovered at all, they are to be invented."[8] He notes further, that the fundamental basis of romanticism is will, "the fact that there is no structure to things, that you can mould things as you will—they come into being only as a result of your molding activity—and therefore opposition to any view which tried to represent reality as having some kind of form which could be studied, written down, learnt, communicated to others, and in other respects treated in a scientific manner."[9] Again, as Berlin writes, "there is even such a thing as romantic economics…where the purpose of economics, the purpose of money and trade, is the spiritual self-perfection of man, and does not obey the so-called unbreakable laws of economics…. Romantic economics is the precise opposite of [laissez-faire economics]. All economic institutions must be bent toward some kind of ideal of living together in a spiritually progressive manner."[10]

The Rousseau narrative has been expanded in many different directions. It was obviously used in the 18th century by small landowners and agricultural workers against large feudal landowners, and in 19th century by worker movements against employers who owned factories. It has been used by inhabitants of former colonies who were educated in the West, against former colonial powers.[11] It has been used by some feminists against perceived domination by white males.

Reflections on the Two Narratives

The proponents of the equality narrative yearn for a return to the collective identity of the ancient polis, or what Oakeshott came to call the view that society is an enterprise association. In a strange way, there is also a strong, and even unintentional, connection between the mercantilist policies of the countries of Europe and the later components of the equality narrative. The early mercantilists that Adam Smith was opposing in the name of the system of natural liberty can hardly be said to be strong promoters of the equality narrative. The mercantilists were interested in a strong role for government because, deep down, they believed that individuals were incapable of making the choices needed to pursue happiness. But they did make the strong case for a positive role for government control over everyday life in the name of the national interest. In a sense, the equality narrative depends on the case for the acceptance of strong government and for the very same reason: a general will generates communal fraternity and this trumps an individual pursuit of happiness.

Thus whether (1) in the Marxist and strong socialist form of government ownership of the means of production, or (2) the softer socialism and

8. Isiah Berlin, Roots of Romanticism (1965), (London: Chatto & Windus, 1999), p. 87.
9. Ibid., p. 127.
10. Ibid., p. 126.
11. See Ian Buruma and Avishai Margalit, *Occidentalism* (New York: Penguin 2005).

Progressive agenda of greater government regulation of the private sphere of life especially the relationship between capital and labor, or (3) planning for a more rational and fairer society, following FDR and the Great Society programs, the equality narrative relies on government being the solution rather the problem, and the non-governmental sphere is the problem rather than the solution.

To be sure, the equality narrative contains a liberty component, namely, liberation from insecurity, fear, disease, hunger, and misery that is compatible with the emphasis of the equality narrative on equality of outcome as a normative goal and empirical reality. And this task will, for a variety of legitimate reasons, produce restraints on individual liberty.

So for both hard and soft Marxist versions of the equality narrative, a collective good was to be realized in a planned and centrally organized economy. However, for Marx, true equality meant the advent of a "classless society," not simply equality of income or function. "The real content of the proletarian demand for equality is the *abolition of classes*. Any demand for equality which goes beyond that, of necessity passes into absurdity" (*Anti-Dühring*). There is no sentimental notion of equality in Marx, but it is a form of absolute egalitarianism. The workers would clearly not be equal to the planners, but it was assumed that this appearance of inequality would not be onerous or invidious in light of the collective good because the workers and the planners have a common bond. Somehow or other differences of function would not translate into differences of status in light of the collective good.

And this leads us to the phenomenon of the American Progressives who are clearly not Marxists. They are what Marx and Engels derisively call "the utopian socialists." True, along with Marx and Engels, they took Darwin's evolutionary theory rather than Newton's mechanical theory as their point of departure. They also thought that a regime dedicated to the preservation of property was an undemocratic regime because private property is only owned by the few. And, yes, they also were influenced by the Hegelian quest for government under the guidance of disinterested, or neutral, leaders. And, also yes, they wanted to separate politics from administration and rely on the latter rather than the former. But they were not revolutionary nor did they endorse the idea of "inevitability" concerning the case for equality. There was to be no end to the history of Progressivism.

The Progressives thought that through cooperation, rather than competition, in the fields of both politics and economics, we could settle the disputes between labor and capital without having a revolution or ignoring the issue of social justice. If we could just rid politics of the influence of special interests, rid economics of the influence of economic royalists, turn voluntary charity and turn the government over individuals into "the administration of things" then all would be well. It wasn't inevitable, and that is why we need experts. We could replace the world of unbridled self-interested competition with the world of detached public interest administrators. We can replace the old narrative of liberty (which was only for the few anyway) with the new narrative of equality (which is for the public good).

The New Deal and the Great Society programs build on the Progressive approach to "the social question." And this social question is not simply that the market economy is inefficient and not delivering food and shelter to the public. At the core of these problems is a concern with the fundamental fairness of life. The unforgotten man, the ordinary folk, has been the victim of the greed of the unrestrained few. This majority got a raw deal. It is the role of government to initiate recovery and reform and invite the people to engage in a rendezvous with destiny. The liberty narrative has failed the promise of democracy and it is the duty of government to overcome this crisis. Apparently the liberty narrative is no longer defensible or relevant. And just in case one is wondering where religion fits into what seems to be a political and economic concern, just take a look at FDR's speeches as well as LBJ's Michigan Address on the Great Society. Both are presented as crusades to eliminate domestic evils and both appeal to the sense of social justice: in the name of equality and fraternity, we are morally outraged by the depressed and unfulfilled nature of the American regime.

But back to the liberty narrative. The increasing call in the nineteenth and twentieth centuries for an absolute equality, now understood as the call for the recognition of a collective good—equality and fraternity—that subsumed the individual good, raised the same alarm that it had in the eighteenth century. Critics such as Tocqueville and Mill, left a set of writings that warned of a conflict between equality and liberty.

Tocqueville, for example, urged that serious attention must be given to the inclination of modern man to choose equality with slavery over liberty with inequality. In part, this is due to the desire of modern man to "belong" given that the hierarchical connections of the ancient world have been leveled and each man has been turned into an isolated individual. Tocqueville recommended the encouragement of intermediate communities, and he lists political, economic, and religious associations, that actually support the goal of individual liberty. This is what he calls self interest rightly understood: by helping others, you help yourself. Self interest wrongly understood is by helping myself, I help others. There is a third and worse alternative: by not caring about myself at all, I surrender all attachment to individual liberty. And he warned that modern man also had a great inclination to support the centralization of government which, given the history of the French Revolutions of 1789, 1830, and 1848, is the way to tyranny. This is what Hayek, later, called the road to serfdom.

The belief in, and advocacy, of a collective good in which individual good is subsumed does not see the necessity for preserving liberty because the purpose of liberty is to lay the foundation for equality-as-fraternity. Rather it insists upon controlling any institution and practice that contributes to individual fulfillment within the collective good. And that last point is vital: liberty is the necessary condition for equality, which is the avenue to fraternity.

Defenders of liberty justify removing or relaxing external constraints because they presume that there is some kind of basic internal psychological need for something like personal autonomy. The defenders of liberty are reasserting in secular fashion the Christian doctrine of the dignity of the individual soul. This is what is behind J. S. Mill's defense of individuality. The case for individual liberty is that it is the condition for the individual pursuit of happiness.

The argument in favor of individual liberty and against absolute equality is otherwise presented as an argument in favor of freedom or autonomy (understood here as self-rule or self-governance). Even if there were no net economic loss, there would be an end to freedom of speech and eventually freedom of thought and freedom of religion and the right to choose the government under which we live. We would see the triumph of mediocrity or a narrow public opinion imposing the same capricious and arbitrary standards on everything and everyone. These things are considered good because they are instrumental to self-expression and personal autonomy, and the pursuit of happiness. For theorists like Tocqueville and Mill, freedom trumps efficiency and that is why they are often, incorrectly, identified with the egalitarian narrative. In other words, they argue that the defense of liberty requires more than the case for efficiency. Just as the more humane and gentler side of the equality narrative requires more than the claim that capitalism will inevitably collapse.

On the other hand, for Tocqueville and Mill—just as it had been for Locke, Smith, and the Founders before, and forthcoming from Hoover, Hayek, and Friedman after, freedom of choice trumps fraternal equality. *The Declaration of Independence* sees equality as the necessary condition for liberty, and in this respect we have turned away from outcome egalitarianism pointing toward fraternity and returned to foundational egalitarianism pointing toward individual liberty. Autonomy is an intrinsic end, along with the pursuit of happiness, for foundational egalitarians. Autonomy and liberty are not intrinsic ends for absolute or outcome egalitarians. Collectivist Fraternity trumps the pursuit of personal (bourgeois) happiness.

Wealth is important not as an end in itself nor as a means to consumerism but because it serves as the means for personal accomplishment. This is the argument of the liberty narrative. Wealth maximization and efficiency considerations are important because in the end we need to know if such policies are maximizing opportunities for more and more people to become autonomous. Public policies that redistribute wealth are permissible to the extent that they ultimately promote autonomy. Redistribution is not a priori objectionable, but the redistribution must be judged on whether it promotes autonomy as well as efficiency.

The efficiency argument on its own has been under attack since the early 19th century. Constant in his famous essay *The Liberty of the Ancients Compared to that of the Moderns* voiced this concern before Tocqueville. Constant deplored the fact that so many intellectuals were mistakenly hostile to religion, taking what he considered the perversion of religion to be the essence of religion. Constant opposed Rousseau's idea of a civic religion and advocated religious toleration. He did so not only to check centralized power, but because he also believed that the truths individuals would find within religion, if not coerced, were essential both to true human fulfillment and to the preservation of liberal culture as a whole. A liberal state had to be both secular and tolerant; a liberal culture needed to be deeply religious. Similar arguments are to be found in the work of Daniel Bell, Irving Kristol, Peter Burger, and even in Catholic Social Thought.[12]

The major assumptions of the Liberty narrative in the contemporary scene are (1) that growth is potentially infinite, (2) that absolute poverty will be overcome by growth, (3) that autonomous individuals are focused on self-defined achievement and self-respect—do not define themselves in terms of others, and therefore 'relative' income is a non-issue, (4) that 'dysfunctional' members of a free society, including its intellectual critics, lack the courage and self-discipline to become autonomous, and (5) that once they choose to become autonomous there is no going back.

The major assumptions of the Equality narrative in the contemporary scene are (1) that there are limits to growth being ignored by those who are despoiling the environment and that the economic focus should be on sustainability, (2) that sustainability requires "fair," "rational," and politically responsible rationing and regulation, (3) that all individuals are entitled to self-esteem and this is not possible without considering who we are relative to others within a social context, (4) that the pursuit of autonomy leads to anomie or is a mask for private self-aggrandizement, and (5) that true fulfillment is only possible within a larger social context.

Ten Defining Questions

We suggest, further, that there are ten defining questions, with several subparts, that both join and separate these two narratives. And we encourage the reader to ponder these questions while working through the original material.

1. What is the status of private property and free markets? Is private property reward or theft? Under what circumstances can the right to private property be constrained or curtailed?

2. Where does each narrative stand on limited government, separation of powers, and institutional checks and balances? What is the basis of "the stand?"

12. Daniel Bell, *The Cultural Contradictions of Capitalism* (New York: Basic Books, 1976); Irving Kristol, *Two Cheers for Capitalism* (New York: Mentor, 1978); Peter Burger, *The Capitalist Revolution* (New York: Basic Books, 1988).

3. Should government be "democratic," and in what way? Is the liberty narrative more compatible with the deliberation of indirect democracy, whereas the equality narrative is more likely to endorse the action of direct democracy?

4. What should the government do with respect to economic and social questions, and which level should do it, and which branch of which level should do it?

5. Do we need a certain personal and social moral code to support the classical liberal model, or liberty narrative? And do we also need a certain personal and social moral code to support the modern welfare, or egalitarian narrative?

6. What is the "invisible hand?" What is "dialectical materialism?" Are these "mere" metaphors, or are they two competing myths or a vital part of a truth generating methodology? Or are both a sort of "sin against science?"

7. Is the division of labor beneficial or detrimental? And to whom—to the individual or to the society? Do we live with the downside of the division of labor or do we do "something" about it? Does doing "something" amount to "throwing the baby out with the bath water?"

8. What happens when political economy becomes "scientific" and we drop the political component? And are we then following a version of the Newtonian mechanical science or the Darwinian organic science? Must there be more than Newton and Darwin?

9. Is selfishness the same as self-interest and is a "sense of community" the same as collectivism?

10. What changes do the two narratives undergo with the passage of three centuries? How does going back to come back help us?

Conclusion: Two Narratives of Political Economy

The two competing narratives are the **Lockean (liberty)** narrative (but made canonical by Smith) and the **Rousseauean (equality)** narrative (but made canonical by Marx). The first narrative, originating with John Locke, sings the *praises* of technology, markets, private property and individual rights understood "negatively." It is concerned with personal autonomy, avoiding tyranny, and promoting liberty both political and economic. The second narrative, originating with J. J. Rousseau, focuses on the *problems* generated by technology, markets, private property, and supports individual rights understood "positively," and certainly places conditions and restrictions on individual autonomy. It is concerned with the social good, avoiding exploitation and alienation, and promoting equality both political and economic.

Since the Renaissance, the modern western world has endorsed the Technological Project. Instead of seeing nature as an organic process to which we as individuals conform, as did the ancients, Descartes proclaimed the modern vision of controlling nature for human benefit. It is the same project that Bacon had in mind when he observed that knowledge is power. It is only with the Technological Project that knowledge of political economy becomes possible and necessary. But shall this technology be used to advance the cause of liberty or the cause of equality? To advance the latter, the Newton-Descartes mechanical methodology must be replaced by a modern version of the understanding of the organic process, one that is grounded in the historicism of Hegel and the biology of Darwin. Instead of the ancient organic model where what goes around, comes around and the greatest human virtue is moderation, the modern organism model is open ended and so the organism can evolve and transform itself in a linear direction.

And with this transformation of the organic model from antiquity to modernity, we get the substitution of the ideal of human perfection for the virtue of human moderation. Accordingly, there is a clash WITHIN modernity, and not just a clash between a homogeneous modernity over against a homogeneous antiquity that needs to be discussed. We suggest that the battle of the moderns concerns the normative and empirical dimensions of *human progress*. The liberty narrative argues that human progress and human improvement go together. It is the *pursuit* of happiness that ought to be promoted. The equality narrative argues that human progress and human perfection go together. It is the *securing* of happiness that ought to be promoted.

PART ONE

The Emergence of Political Economy: Economic Activity Leaves the Household

Introduction

The Three Pillars of Liberty and Equality

This initial chapter examines the origins of the liberty, or autonomy, narrative with John Locke and the origins of the equality, or fraternity, narrative with J. J. Rousseau. We begin with Locke and Rousseau, rather than the classical thinkers or Church fathers because (1) the economic questions had to be removed from the confines, and the laws (nomos), of the household (oikos) and be made public or political (politea) before we can have a serious talk about political economy, and (2) these two thinkers did just that and thus set the stage for the two narratives that have prevailed over the last four centuries.

We don't mean to imply that Locke is not interested in equality or community, nor do we mean that Rousseau is not interested in liberty and individualism. But the dominant theme in Locke is that the best way of life deals with the individual pursuit of happiness. There is a rejection of the ancient view that one finds happiness by belonging or being with others. And Rousseau has an individualist streak in him. One wonders how he ever became attached to the communitarian spirit given his critique of modern civilization in *The Two Discourses*. But there is more to Rousseau than these two discourses—just as there is more to Locke than *The Two Treatises*.

To what extent is Locke's understanding of religious toleration in *Toleration* linked to his case for limited government and the case for private property? What is the role of money in Locke? We can anticipate his view on money when we look at Chapter 5 on property in the *Second Treatise*. To what extent is Locke's understanding in *Money* a contribution to our notions of political economy? We suggest that Locke is making the case for liberty broadly understood, and this case rests on the three pillars of liberty: political liberty, economic liberty, and cultural liberty.

Rousseau is known for his *Two Discourses* where he criticizes the development of the arts and sciences in modernity and, in this development, he locates the origin of inequality. Whether it is physical inequality, or material inequality, or intellectual inequality, he takes the presence of the inequality of condition as the point of departure in the "real" world of society. And he questions whether the inequality we see around us can be justified. His answer seems to be that we cannot do so on the grounds provided by Locke.

But Rousseau also wrote a book on political economy. What is the content of Rousseau's *Political Economy* and how does he help us tell a good political economy from a bad one? It is in this work that Rousseau introduces the concept of the "general will." We find it instructive and fascinating that Rousseau introduces the general will—a concept central to the equality narrative—in *Political Economy*.

This concept becomes central in Rousseau's *Social Contract* where the general will becomes *the* standard by which all action is judged. Everyone gives up everything—especially private property—when leaving the state of nature entering Rousseau's social contract. As a result, the atomistic individual is transformed into a communal citizen whose transformation is reinforced by quasi-religious festivals on behalf of the secular good. We suggest that Rousseau offers three pillars of equality: political equality, economic equality, and cultural equality.

John Locke and the Liberty Narrative

John Locke is most famous for his critique of Robert Filmer's divine right of kings justification of monarchical rule (*The First Treatise*) and the case for the alternative, namely, that legitimate government is grounded in the consent of the governed (*The Second Treatise*). So compelling has Locke's argument become on behalf of the right of the people to choose, alter, and abolish the form of government under which they live, that we forget that Locke actually had to make the case for that proposition.

We have included Locke's essential arguments concerning the political liberty narrative: individuals endowed with certain natural rights who, in order to make them more secure, first enter into civil society and then, second, choose a government that secures these rights to life, liberty, property, and later in the hands of the American founders, the pursuit of happiness. This chosen government turns out to be a representative form in which the neutral rule of law replaces the biased rule of men. The rule of law is made manifest in the institutional arrangement of the separation of the branches of government and the teaching of self imposed limits on both the people and their chosen rulers. But corruption will occur and the rulers, although elected by the people, will succumb to the temptation of political power, ignore the rule of law, and pass tyrannical laws. After a long train of these abuses, it is the right of the people to overthrow these tyrants, and to create a new form of government that will secure their safety and happiness.

Embedded in this political liberty narrative is a strong hint that there is an economic liberty and a religious liberty dimension to Locke's project. Both hints occur in the chapter on private property in the *Second Treatise*, the chapter that has generated the most controversy in Locke scholarship. There, Locke associates the quest of the individual for material improvement with a mandate from God to cultivate the earth and enclose the commons.

When Locke says that God favors the "rational and industrious" man who acquires private property, is Locke suggesting that it is the few or the many who are industrious and thus is it the many or the few who are unthinking and lazy? We suggest that Locke's "rational and industrious" are the many and thus the right to private property is a democratic right based in effort rather than aristocratic right of the few based in the accident of inheritance. Thus private property is not theft, nor is a government dedicated to the preservation of property an antidemocratic regime.

When Locke says that there are limits, from religious teachings it would seem, on the right of an individual to the accumulation of private property, is he being sincere or cynical? After all, doesn't the introduction of money remove all the restraints that Locke imposes on individual conduct of appropriation as "history" moves from the underdeveloped stage of barter to the civilized stage of commerce? Isn't Locke, according to some scholars, really a warm advocate of economic greed under that pretentious veil of religious restraint?

Locke certainly has a different view of both the intrinsic content of religion and the utility of religion than those who walked the halls of Parliament and Westminster. In order to better appreciate Locke's views on religion, especially Protestant Christianity, we have included excerpts from his *Toleration*. We suggest that Locke is opposed to a government created and supported religious monopoly.

The conventional wisdom is that Locke was an economic mercantilist and this is, it is claimed, clearly shown in his *Interest and Money*. After all, Locke seems to equate the wealth of a nation with the quantity of gold and silver and, thus, economic policy seems to have an international trade emphasis and that international focus demands, in turn, that a country should export more commodities than it imports so that more coin and bullion flow into the country from foreigners than flow from our countrymen abroad. These claims have some merit, but actually miss the point that Locke is addressing.

We suggest that Locke is actually criticizing rather than defending the Mercantilist agenda. He is interested in money as a medium of exchange and a measure of wealth rather than confusing money with wealth itself. Locke, in effect, is trying to demystify the status of money. And at one point in his argument he laments those who equate the accumulation of money with the accumulation of wealth.

Locke's central question in *Interest and Money* is stated in his opening sentence: "whether the price of the hire of money can be regulated by law?" His answer, after an excursion of more than fifty pages, is "'tis manifest it cannot." In order to show why such a policy leads to unintended consequences, Locke covers the whole range of political economy questions central to the mercantilist project of government regulation of the economy. And at the end of these detailed explanations, Locke comes back to his main theme, namely, the compelling case against the government establishing and enforcing a rate of interest for borrowing and lending that deviates from the natural or market price. In the process, he outlines the rudiments of a quantity theory of money where government is limited to providing the amount of money needed to facilitate the "real" economy, namely, the production and consumption of goods and services.

Why Locke wrote and distributed the *Second Treatise* anonymously a decade before he acknowledged authorship in 1691, why he went to Holland as a religious dissenter only returning to England after the 1689 Bill of Rights secured a Protestant succession, and why he published *Interest and Money* in 1691 on economic liberty is beyond the scope of this introduction. Suffice it to suggest that the "judicious Locke" thought that a bold and transparent defense of political liberty, religious liberty, and economic liberty was imprudent and even dangerous in the late seventeenth century. Algernon Sidney was executed for similar beliefs. By the late eighteenth century, however, Adam Smith and James Madison could openly defend the case for the three liberties.

J. J. Rousseau and the Equality Narrative

Unlike Locke whose three dimensions of the liberty narrative seemed to emerge on the scene at the same time, Rousseau's contribution to the equality narrative emerged over several years.

Rousseau is well known for his audacious essay, known as *The First Discourse*, where he emphasizes the huge costs to society from the development of the arts and sciences. Rousseau laments that the arts and sciences have promoted hypocrisy in dress, pretentiousness in manners, and absence of authenticity in demeanor. He makes the case for the simple life of the noble savage over against the complicated existence of city slickers and court pretenders.

The Second Discourse carries his criticism of the liberty narrative one step further. Private property is theft, declares Rousseau in the opening paragraph of Part II. For Rousseau, the inequality that emerges as a result of the arts and sciences is a product of that original theft where the few who are rich bamboozle the many who are poor into agreeing to a social contract that benefit the few who are rich. Thus the liberty narrative is no more than a fraud.

But what are we to do if men are/were born free and are everywhere in chains? Can we do something to transform this condition? These questions lead Rousseau first to write *Political Economy* and then the *Social Contract*. At the heart of both pieces is the claim that the Lockean liberty narrative is actually a narrative of contractual slavery for the vast bulk of the population. And that the only way to have a just society is for everyone upon entering civil society to give up everything and retain nothing. They enter naked and innocent without the clothing of calculation and property. Rousseau's "correction" of Locke destroys the notion of unalienable rights because everyone alienates everything when entering society. The individual is transformed to a Rousseauean willing citizen rather than a Lockean calculating individual. Moreover, this general will for Rousseau is the foundation for political economy. In turn, this general economic and political will is reinforced and uplifted by a civil religion that favors communal orthodoxy over individual dissent.

John Locke

The Second Treatise

The Purpose of Politics

§3. POLITICAL POWER, then, I take to be a RIGHT of making laws with penalties of death, and consequently all less penalties, for the regulating and preserving of property, and of employing the force of the community, in the
execution of such laws, and in the defense of the common-wealth from foreign
injury; and all this only for the public good.

The State of Nature

§4. To understand Political Power right, and derive it from its Original, we
must consider what State all Men are naturally in, and that is, a State of perfect
Freedom to order their Actions, and dispose of their Possessions, and Persons
as they think fit, within the bounds of the Law of Nature, without asking leave,
or depending upon the Will of any other Man.

A State also of Equality, wherein all the Power and Jurisdiction is reciprocal, no one having more than another, there being nothing more evident, than
that Creatures of the same species and rank promiscuously born to all the
same advantages of Nature, and the use of the same faculties, should also be

equal one amongst another without Subordination or Subjection, unless the Lord and Master of them all, should by any manifest Declaration of his Will set one above another, and confer on him by an evident and clear appointment an undoubted Right to Dominion and Sovereignty.

§6. But though this be a State of Liberty, yet it is not a State of Licence, though Man in that State have an uncontrollable Liberty, to dispose of his Person or Possessions, yet he has not Liberty to destroy himself, or so much as any Creature in his Possession, but where some nobler use, than its bare Preservation calls for it. The State of Nature, has a Law of Nature to govern [it] which obliges every one, and Reason, which is that Law, teaches all Mankind, who will but consult it; That being all equal and independent, no one ought to harm another in his Life, Health, Liberty, or Possessions; for Men being all the Workmanship of one Omnipotent, and infinitely wise maker; All the Servants of one Sovereign Master, sent into the World by his order and about his business, they are his Property, whose Workmanship they are, made to last during his, not one anothers Pleasure. And being Furnished with like Faculties, sharing all in one Community of Nature, there cannot be supposed any such Subordination among us, that may Authorize us to destroy one another, as if we were made for one anothers uses, as the inferior ranks of Creatures are for ours, every one as he is bound to preserve himself, and not to quit his Station willfully; so by the like reason when his own Preservation comes not in competition, ought he as much as he can to preserve the rest of Mankind, and may not unless it be to do Justice on an offender, take away, or impair the life, or what tends to the Preservation of the Life, Liberty, Health, Limb or Goods of another.

§7. And that all Men may be restrained from invading others Rights, and from doing hurt to one another, and the Law of Nature be observed, which willeth the Peace and Preservation of all Mankind, the Execution of the Law of Nature is in that State, put into every Mans hands, whereby everyone has a right to punish the transgressors of that Law to such a Degree, as may hinder its Violation. For the Law of Nature would as all other Laws that concern Men in this World be in vain, if there were no body that in the State of Nature, had a Power to Execute that Law, and thereby preserve the innocent and restrain offenders, and if any one in the State of Nature may punish another, for any evil he has done, every one may do so. For in that State of perfect Equality, where naturally there is no superiority or jurisdiction of one, over another, what any may do in Prosecution of that Law, every one must needs have a Right to do.

§13. To this strange Doctrine, viz. That in the State of Nature, every one has the Executive Power of the Law of Nature, I doubt not but it will be objected. That it is unreasonable for Men to be Judges in their own Cases, that self-love will make Men partial to themselves and their Friends. And on the other side, that Ill Nature, Passion and Revenge will carry them too far in punishing others. And hence nothing but Confusion and Disorder will follow, and that therefore God hath certainly appointed Government to restrain the partiality and violence of Men. I easily grant, that Civil Government is the proper

Remedy for the Inconveniences of the State of Nature, which must certainly be Great, where Men may be Judges in their own Case, since 'tis easy to be imagined, that he who was so unjust as to do his Brother an Injury, will scarce be so just as to condemn himself for it: But I shall desire those who make this Objection, to remember that Absolute Monarchs are but Men, and if Government is to be the Remedy of those Evils, which necessarily follow from Mens being Judges in their Own Cases, and the State of Nature is therefore not to be endured, I desire to know what kind of Government that is, and how much better it is than the State of Nature, where one Man commanding a multitude, has the Liberty to be Judge in his own Case, and may do to all his Subjects whatever he pleases, without the least question or control those who Execute his Pleasure? And in whatsoever he doth, whether led by Reason, Mistake or Passion, must be submitted to? Which men in the State of Nature are not bound to do one to another. And if he, he that Judges, Judges amiss in his own, or any other Case, he is answerable for it to the rest of Mankind.

"There Were Never Any Men In The State Of Nature"

§14. 'Tis often asked as a mighty Objection, Where are, or ever were, there any Men in such a State of Nature? To which it may suffice as an answer at present; That since all Princes and Rulers of *Independent* Governments all through the World, are in a State of Nature, 'tis plain the World never was, nor never will be, without Numbers of Men in that State. I have named all Governors of *Independent* Communities, whether they are, or are not, in League with others; For 'tis not every Compact that puts an end to the State of Nature between Men, but only this one of agreeing together mutually to enter into one Community, and make one Body Politick; other Promises and Compacts, Men may make one with another, and yet still be in the State of Nature. The Promises and Bargains for Truck, &c. between the two Men in the Desert Island, mentioned by *Garcilasso De la Vega*, in his *History of Peru*, or between a *Swiss* and an *Indian*, in the *Woods of America*, are binding to them, though they are perfectly in a State of Nature, in reference to one another. For Truth and keeping of Faith belongs to Men, as Men, and not as Members of Society.

§15. To those that say, There were never any Men in the State of Nature; I will not only oppose the Authority of the Judicious *Hooker, Eccl. Pol. Lib. I. Sect 10*…But I moreover affirm, That all Men are naturally in that State, and remain so, till by their own Consents they make themselves Members of some Politick Society; And I doubt not in the Sequel of this Discourse, to make it very clear.

The Right To Private Property

§25. Whether we consider natural reason, which tells us, that men, being once born, have a right to their preservation, and consequently to meat and drink, and such other things as nature affords for their subsistence: or revelation, which gives us an account of those grants God made of the world to Adam, and to Noah, and his sons, it is very clear, that God, as king David says (Psalm. cxv. 16) has given the earth to the children of men; given it to mankind in common. But this being supposed, it seems to some a very great difficulty, how any one should ever come to have a property in any thing: I will not content myself to answer, that if it be difficult to make out property, upon a supposition that God gave the world to Adam, and his posterity in common, it is impossible that any man, but one universal monarch, should have any property upon a supposition, that God gave the world to Adam, and his heirs in succession, exclusive of all the rest of his posterity. But I shall endeavor to show, how men might come to have a property in several parts of that which God gave to mankind in common, and that without any express compact of all the commoners.

§26. God, who hath given the world to men in common, hath also given them reason to make use of it to the best advantage of life, and convenience. The earth, and all that is therein, is given to men for the support and comfort of their being. And though' all the fruits it naturally produces, and beasts it feeds, belong to mankind in common, as they are produced by the spontaneous hand of nature; and no body has originally a private dominion, exclusive of the rest of mankind, in any of them, as they are thus in their natural state: yet being given for the use of men, there must of necessity be a means to appropriate them some way or other, before they can be of any use, or at all beneficial to any particular man. The fruit, or venison, which nourishes the wild Indian, who knows no enclosure, and is still a tenant in common, must be his, and so his, i.e. a part of him, that another can no longer have any right to it, before it can do him any good for the support of his life.

§27. Though the earth, and all inferior creatures, be common to all men, yet every man has a property in his own person: this no body has any right to but himself. The labor of his body, and the work of his hands, we may say, are properly his. Whatsoever then he removes out of the state that nature hath provided, and left it in, he hath mixed his labor with, and joined to it something that is his own, and thereby makes it his property. It being by him removed from the common state nature hath placed it in, it hath by this labor something annexed to it, that excludes the common right of other men: for this labor being the unquestionable property of the laborer, no man but he can have a right to what that is once joined to, at least where there is enough, and as good, left in common for others.

§28. He that is nourished by the acorns he picked up under an oak, or the apples he gathered from the trees in the wood, has certainly appropriated them to himself. No body can deny but the nourishment is his. I ask then, when did they begin to be his? when he digested? or when he eat? or when he boiled? or when he brought them home? or when he picked them up? And it is plain, if the first gathering made them not his, nothing else could. That labor put a distinction between them and common: that added something to them more than nature, the common mother of all, had done; and so they became his private right. And will any one say, he had no right to those acorns or apples, he thus appropriated, because he had not the consent of all mankind to make them his? Was it a robbery thus to assume to himself what belonged to all in common? If such a consent as that was necessary, man had starved, notwithstanding the plenty God had given him. We see in commons, which remain so by compact, that it is the taking any part of what is common, and removing it out of the state nature leaves it in, which begins the property; without which the common is of no use. And the taking of this or that part, does not depend on the express consent of all the commoners. Thus the grass my horse has bit; the turfs my servant has cut; and the ore I have digged in any place, where I have a right to them in common with others, become my property, without the assignation or consent of any body. The labor that was mine, removing them out of that common state they were in, hath fixed my property in them.

§29. By making an explicit consent of every commoner, necessary to any one's appropriating to himself any part of what is given in common, children or servants could not cut the meat, which their father or master had provided for them in common, without assigning to every one his peculiar part. Though the water running in the fountain be every one's, yet who can doubt, but that in the pitcher is his only who drew it out? His labor hath taken it out of the hands of nature, where it was common, and belonged equally to all her children, and hath thereby appropriated it to himself.

§30. Thus this law of reason makes the deer that Indian's who hath killed it; it is allowed to be his goods, who hath bestowed his labor upon it, though before it was the common right of every one. And amongst those who are counted the civilized part of mankind, who have made and multiplied positive laws to determine property, this original law of nature, for the beginning of property, in what was before common, still takes place; and by virtue thereof, what fish any one catches in the ocean, that great and still remaining common of mankind; or what ambergrise any one takes up here, is by the labor that removes it out of that common state nature left it in, made his property who takes that pains about it. And even amongst us, the hare that any one is hunting, is thought his who pursues her during the chase: for being a beast that is still looked upon as common, and no man's private possession; whoever has employed so much labor about any of that kind, as to find and pursue her, has thereby removed her from the state of nature, wherein she was common, and hath begun a property.

§31. It will perhaps be objected to this, that if gathering the acorns, or other fruits of the earth, &c. makes a right to them, then any one may engross as much as he will. To which I answer, Not so. The same law of nature, that does by this means give us property, does also bound that property too. God has given us all things richly (1 Tim. vi. 1) is the voice of reason confirmed by inspiration. But how far has he given it us? To enjoy. As much as any one can make use of to any advantage of life before it spoils, so much he may by his labor fix a property in: whatever is beyond this, is more than his share, and belongs to others. Nothing was made by God for man to spoil or destroy. And thus, considering the plenty of natural provisions there was a long time in the world, and the few spenders; and to how small a part of that provision the industry of one man could extend itself, and engross it to the prejudice of others; especially keeping within the bounds, set by reason, of what might serve for his use; there could be then little room for quarrels or contentions about property so established.

§32. But the chief matter of Property being now not the Fruits of the Earth, and the Beasts that subsist on it, but the Earth itself; as that which takes in and carries with it all the rest: I think it is plain, that Property in that too is acquired as the former. As much Land as a Man Tills, Plants, Improves, Cultivates, and can use the Product of, so much is his Property. He by his Labor does, as it were, enclose it from the Common. Nor will it invalidate his right to say, Everybody else has an equal Title to it; and therefore he cannot appropriate, he cannot enclose, without the Consent of all his Fellow-Commoners, all Mankind. God, when he gave the World in common to all Mankind, commanded Man also to labor, and penury of his Condition required it of him. God and his Reason commanded him to subdue the Earth, *i.e.* improve it for the benefit of Life, and therein lay out something upon it that was his own, his labor. He that in Obedience to this Command of God, subdued, tilled and sowed any part of it, thereby annexed to it something that was his *Property*, which another had no Title to, nor could without injury take from him.

§33. Nor was this appropriation of any parcel of Land, by improving it, any prejudice to any other Man, since there was still enough, and as good left; and more than the yet unprovided could use. So that in effect, there was never the less left for others because of his enclosure for himself. For he that leaves as much as another can make use of, does as good as take nothing at all. No Body could think himself injured by the drinking of another Man, though he took a good Draught, who had a whole River of the same Water left him to quench his thirst. And the Case of Land and Water, where there is enough of both, is perfectly the same.

God's Intention

§34. God gave the World to Men in Common; but since he gave it them for their benefit, and the greatest Conveniences of Life they were capable to draw from it, it cannot be supposed he meant it should always remain common and uncultivated. He gave it to the use of the Industrious and Rational, (and Labor was to be his Title to it;) not to the Fancy or Covetousness of the Quarrelsome and Contentious. He that had as good left for his Improvement, as was already taken up, needed not complain, ought not to meddle with what was already improved by another's Labor: If he did, 'tis plain he desired the benefit of another's Pains which he had no right to, and not the Ground which God had given him in common with others to labor on, and whereof there was as good left, as that already possessed, and more than he knew what to do with, or his Industry could reach to.

§35. Tis true, in Land that is common in England, or any other country, where there is Plenty of People under Government, who have Money and Commerce, no one can enclose or appropriate any part, without the consent of all his Fellow-Commoners: Because this is left common by Compact, i.e. by the Law of the Land, which is not to be violated. And though it be Common, in respect of some Men, it is not so to all Mankind; but is the joint property of this Country, or this Parish. Besides, the remainder, after such enclosure, would not be as good to the rest of the Commoners as the whole was, when they could all make use of the whole: whereas in the beginning and first peopling of the great Common of the World, it was quite otherwise. The Law man was under, was rather for appropriating. God Commanded, and his Wants forced him to labor. That was his Property which could not be taken from him wherever he had fixed it. And hence subduing or cultivating the Earth, and having Dominion, we see are joined together. The one gave Title to the other. So that God, by commanding to subdue, gave Authority so far to appropriate. And the Condition of Humane Life, which requires Labor and Materials to work on, necessarily introduces private Possessions.

The Labor Theory of Value

§36. The measure of Property, Nature has well set, by the Extent of Mens Labor, and the Conveniences of Life: No Man's Labor could subdue, or appropriate all; nor could his Enjoyment consume more than a small part; so that it was impossible for any Man, this way, to entrench upon the right of another, or acquire, to himself, a Property, to the Prejudice of his Neighbor, who would still have room, for as good, and as large a Possession (after the other had taken out his) as before it was appropriated, which measure did confine every Man's Possession, to a very moderate Proportion, and such as he might appropriate to himself, without Injury to any Body, in the first Ages of the World, when Men were more in danger to be lost, by wandering from their Company, in the then vast Wilderness of the Earth, than to be straitened for want of room to plant in. And the same measure may be allowed still, without prejudice to any Body, as full as the World seems. For supposing a Man, or Family, in the state they were at first peopling of the World by the Children of *Adam*, or *Noah*; let him plant in some inland, vacant places of *America*, we shall find that the *Possessions* he could make himself upon the measures we have given, would not be very large, nor, even to this day, prejudice the rest of Mankind, or give them reason to complain, or think themselves injured by this Man's encroachment, though the Race of Men have now spread themselves to all the corners of the World, and do infinitely exceed the small number was at the beginning.

Nay, the extent of Ground is of so little value, without labor, that, I have heard it affirmed, that in *Spain* it self, a Man may be permitted to plough, sow, and reap, without being disturbed, upon Land he has no other Title to, but only his making use of it. But, on the contrary, the Inhabitants think themselves beholden to him, who, by his Industry on neglected, and consequently waste Land, has increased the stock of Corn, which they wanted. But be this as it will, which I lay no stress on; this I dare boldly affirm, That the same Rule of Propriety, (*viz.*) that every Man should have as much as he could make use of, would hold still in the World, without straitening any body, since there is Land enough in the World to suffice double the Inhabitants, had not the Invention of Money, and the tacit Agreement of Men, to put a value on it, introduced (by Consent) larger Possessions, and a Right to them; which, how it has done, I shall, by and by, show more at large.

§37. This is certain, That in the beginning, before the desire of having more than Man needed, had altered the intrinsic value of things, which depends only on their usefulness to the Life of Man; or had agreed, that a little piece of yellow Metal, which would keep without wasting or decay, should be worth a great piece of Flesh, or a whole heap of Corn; though Men had a Right to appropriate, by their Labor, each one to himself, as much of the things of Nature, as he could use: Yet this could not be much, nor to the Prejudice of others, where the same plenty was still left, to those who would use the same Industry.

§38. The same measures governed the possession of land too: whatsoever he tilled and reaped, laid up and made use of, before it spoiled, that was his peculiar right; whatsoever he enclosed, and could feed, and make use of, the cattle and product was also his. But if either the grass of his enclosure rotted on the ground, or the fruit of his planting perished without gathering, and laying up, this part of the earth, notwithstanding his enclosure, was still to be looked on as waste, and might be the possession of any other. Thus, at the beginning, Cain might take as much ground as he could till, and make it his own land, and yet leave enough to Abel's sheep to feed on; a few acres would serve for both their possessions. But as families increased, and industry enlarged their stocks, their possessions enlarged with the need of them; but yet it was commonly without any fixed property in the ground they made use of, till they incorporated, settled themselves together, and built cities; and then, by consent, they came in time, to set out the bounds of their distinct territories, and agree on limits between them and their neighbors; and by laws within themselves, settled the properties of those of the same society: for we see, that in that part of the world which was first inhabited, and therefore like to be best peopled, even as low down as Abraham's time, they wandered with their flocks, and their herds, which was their substance, freely up and down; and this Abraham did, in a country where he was a stranger.

Whence it is plain, that at least a great part of the land lay in common; that the inhabitants valued it not, nor claimed property in any more than they made use of. But when there was not room enough in the same place, for their herds to feed together, they by consent, as Abraham and Lot did (Gen. xiii. 5) separated and enlarged their pasture, where it best liked them. And for the same reason Esau went from his father, and his brother, and planted in Mount Seir (Gen. xxxvi. 6).

§39. And thus, without supposing any private dominion, and property in Adam, over all the world, exclusive of all other men, which can no way be proved, nor any one's property be made out from it; but supposing the world given, as it was, to the children of men in common, we see how labor could make men distinct titles to several parcels of it, for their private uses; wherein there could be no doubt of right, no room for quarrel.

§40. Nor is it so strange, as perhaps before consideration it may appear, that the property of labor should be able to over-balance the community of land: for it is labor indeed that puts the difference of value on every thing; and let any one consider what the difference is between an acre of land planted with tobacco or sugar, sown with wheat or barley, and an acre of the same land lying in common, without any husbandry upon it, and he will find, that the improvement of labor makes the far greater part of the value. I think it will be but a very modest computation to say, that of the products of the earth useful to the life of man nine tenths are the effects of labor: nay, if we will rightly estimate things as they come to our use, and cast up the several expenses about them, what in them is purely owing to nature, and what to labor, we shall find, that in most of them ninety-nine hundredths are wholly to be put on the account of labor.

The American Situation

§41. There cannot be a clearer demonstration of any thing, than several nations of the Americans are of this, who are rich in land, and poor in all the comforts of life; whom nature having furnished as liberally as any other people, with the materials of plenty, i.e. a fruitful soil, apt to produce in abundance, what might serve for food, raiment, and delight; yet for want of improving it by labor, have not one hundredth part of the conveniences we enjoy: and a king of a large and fruitful territory there, feeds, lodges, and is clad worse than a day-laborer in England.

§42. To make this a little clearer, let us but trace some of the ordinary provisions of life, through their several progresses, before they come to our use, and see how much they receive of their value from human industry. Bread, wine and cloth, are things of daily use, and great plenty; yet notwithstanding, acorns, water and leaves, or skins, must be our bread, drink and clothing, did not labor furnish us with these more useful commodities: for whatever bread is more worth than acorns, wine than water, and cloth or silk, than leaves, skins or moss, that is wholly owing to labor and industry; the one of these being the food and raiment which unassisted nature furnishes us with; the other, provisions which our industry and pains prepare for us, which how much they exceed the other in value, when any one hath computed, he will then see how much labor makes the far greatest part of the value of things we enjoy in this world: and the ground which produces the materials, is scarce to be reckoned in, as any, or at most, but a very small part of it; so little, that even amongst us, land that is left wholly to nature, that hath no improvement of pasturage, tillage, or planting, is called, as indeed it is, waste; and we shall find the benefit of it amount to little more than nothing.

This shows how much numbers of men are to be preferred to largeness of dominions; and that the increase of lands, and the right employing of them, is the great art of government: and that prince, who shall be so wise and godlike, as by established laws of liberty to secure protection and encouragement to the honest industry of mankind, against the oppression of power and narrowness of party, will quickly be too hard for his neighbors: but this by the by. To return to the argument in hand.

§43. An acre of land, that bears here twenty bushels of wheat, and another in America, which, with the same husbandry, would do the like, are, without doubt, of the same natural intrinsic value: but yet the benefit mankind receives from the one in a year, is worth 5 pounds and from the other possibly not worth a penny, if all the profit an Indian received from it were to be valued, and sold here; at least, I may truly say, not one thousandth. It is labor then which puts the greatest part of value upon land, without which it would scarcely be worth any thing: it is to that we owe the greatest part of all its useful products; for all that the straw, bran, bread, of that acre of wheat, is more worth than the product of an acre of as good land, which lies waste, is all the effect of labor: for it is not barely the ploughman's pains, the reaper's and thresher's toil, and the baker's sweat, is to be counted into the bread we eat; the labor of those who broke the oxen, who digged and wrought the iron and stones, who felled and framed the timber employed about the plough, mill, oven, or any other utensils, which are a vast number, requisite to this corn, from its being feed to be sown to its being made bread, must all be charged on the account of labor, and received as an effect of that: nature and the earth furnished only the almost worthless materials, as in themselves.

It would be a strange catalogue of things, that industry provided and made use of, about every loaf of bread, before it came to our use, if we could trace them; iron, wood, leather, bark, timber, stone, bricks, coals, lime, cloth, dying drugs, pitch, tar, masts, ropes, and all the materials made use of in the ship, that brought any of the commodities made use of by any of the workmen, to any part of the work; all which it would be almost impossible, at least too long, to reckon up.

§44. From all which it is evident, that though the things of nature are given in common, yet man, by being master of himself, and proprietor of his own person, and the actions or labor of it, had still in himself the great foundation of property; and that, which made up the great part of what he applied to the support or comfort of his being, when invention and arts had improved the conveniences of life, was perfectly his own, and did not belong in common to others.

"Labor, In the Beginning, Gave a Right of Property"

§45. Thus labor, in the beginning, gave a right of property, wherever any one was pleased to employ it upon what was common, which remained a long while the far greater part, and is yet more than mankind makes use of. Men, at first, for the most part, contented themselves with what unassisted nature offered to their necessities: and though afterwards, in some parts of the world, (where the increase of people and stock, with the use of money, had made land scarce, and so of some value) the several communities settled the bounds of their distinct territories, and by laws within themselves regulated the properties of the private men of their society, and so, by compact and agreement, settled the property which labor and industry began; and the leagues that have been made between several states and kingdoms, either expressly or tacitly disowning all claim and right to the land in the others possession, have, by common consent, given up their pretences to their natural common right, which originally they had to those countries, and so have, by positive agreement, settled a property amongst themselves, in distinct parts and parcels of the earth; yet there are still great tracts of ground to be found, which (the inhabitants thereof not having joined with the rest of mankind, in the consent of the use of their common money) lie waste, and are more than the people who dwell on it do, or can make use of, and so still lie in common; though this can scarce happen amongst that part of mankind that have consented to the use of money.

§46. The greatest part of things really useful to the life of man, and such as the necessity of subsisting made the first commoners of the world look after, as it clothe the Americans now, are generally things of short duration; such as, if they are not consumed by use, will decay and perish of themselves: gold, silver and diamonds, are things that fancy or agreement hath put the value on, more than real use, and the necessary support of life. Now of those good things which nature hath provided in common, every one had a right (as hath been said) to as much as he could use, and property in all that he could effect with his labor; all that his industry could extend to, to alter from the state nature had put it in, was his. He that gathered a hundred bushels of acorns or apples, had thereby a property in them, they were his goods as soon as gathered. He was only to look, that he used them before they spoiled, else he took more than his share, and robbed others.

And indeed it was a foolish thing, as well as dishonest, to hoard up more than he could make use of. If he gave away a part to any body else, so that it perished not uselessly in his possession, these he also made use of. And if he also bartered away plums, that would have rotted in a week, for nuts that would last good for his eating a whole year, he did no injury; he wasted not the common stock; destroyed no part of the portion of goods that belonged to others, so long as nothing perished uselessly in his hands. Again, if he would give his nuts for a piece of metal, pleased with its color; or exchange his sheep for shells, or wool for a sparkling pebble or a diamond, and keep those by him all his life he invaded not the right of others, he might heap up as much of these durable things as he pleased; the exceeding of the bounds of his just property not lying in the largeness of his possession, but the perishing of any thing uselessly in it.

The Introduction of Money

§47. And thus came in the use of money, some lasting thing that men might keep without spoiling, and that by mutual consent men would take in exchange for the truly useful, but perishable supports of life.

§48. And as different degrees of industry were apt to give men possessions in different proportions, so this invention of money gave them the opportunity to continue and enlarge them: for supposing an island, separate from all possible commerce with the rest of the world, wherein there were but an hundred families, but there were sheep, horses and cows, with other useful animals, wholesome fruits, and land enough for corn for a hundred thousand times as many, but nothing in the island, either because of its commonness, or perishableness, fit to supply the place of money; what reason could any one have there to enlarge his possessions beyond the use of his family, and a plentiful supply to its consumption, either in what their own industry produced, or they could barter for like perishable, useful commodities, with others? Where there is not some thing, both lasting and scarce, and so valuable to be hoarded up, there men will not be apt to enlarge their possessions of land, were it never so rich, never so free for them to take: for I ask, what would a man value ten thousand, or an hundred thousand acres of excellent land, ready cultivated, and well stocked too with cattle, in the middle of the inland parts of America, where he had no hopes of commerce with other parts of the world, to draw money to him by the sale of the product? It would not be worth the enclosing, and we should see him give up again to the wild common of nature, whatever was more than would supply the conveniences of life to be had there for him and his family.

§49. Thus in the beginning all the world was America, and more so than that is now; for no such thing as money was any where known. Find out something that hath the use and value of money amongst his neighbors, you shall see the same man will begin presently to enlarge his possessions.

§50. But since gold and silver, being little useful to the life of man in pro-portion to food, raiment, and carriage, has its value only from the consent of men, whereof labor yet makes, in great part, the measure, it is plain, that men have agreed to a disproportionate and unequal possession of the earth, they having, by a tacit and voluntary consent, found out, a way how a man may fairly possess more land than he himself can use the product of, by receiving in exchange for the overplus gold and silver, which may be hoarded up with-out injury to any one; these metals not spoiling or decaying in the hands of the possessor. This partage of things in an inequality of private possessions, men have made practicable out of the bounds of society, and without compact, only by putting a value on gold and silver, and tacitly agreeing in the use of money: for in governments, the laws regulate the right of property, and the possession of land is determined by positive constitutions.

§51. And thus, I think, it is very easy to conceive, without any difficulty, how labor could at first begin a title of property in the common things of nature, and how the spending it upon our uses bounded it. So that there could then be no reason of quarrelling about title, nor any doubt about the largeness of possession it gave. Right and conveniency went together; for as a man had a right to all he could employ his labor upon, so he had no temptation to labor for more than he could make use of. This left no room for controversy about the title, nor for encroachment on the right of others; what portion a man carved to himself, was easily seen; and it was useless, as well as dishonest, to carve himself too much, or take more than they needed.

Origin of Political Society

§87. Man being born, as has been proved, with a Title to perfect Freedom, and an uncontrolled enjoyment of all the Rights and Privileges of the Law of Nature, equally with any other Man, or Number of Men in the World, hath by Nature a Power, not only to preserve his Property, that is, his Life, Liberty and Estate, against the Injuries and Attempts of other Men; but to judge of, and punish the breaches of that Law in others, as he is persuaded the Offence deserves, even with Death it self, in Crimes where the heinousness of the fact, in his Opinion, requires it. But because no Political Society can be, nor subsist without having in it self the Power to preserve the Property, and in order thereunto punish the Offences of all those of that Society: There, and there only is Political Society, where every one of the Members hath quitted this natural Power, resigned it up into the hands of the Community in all cases that exclude him not from appealing for Protection to the Law established by it. And thus all private judgment of every particular Member being excluded, the Community comes to be Umpire, by settled standing Rules, indifferent, and the same to all Parties; And by Men having Authority from the Community, for the execution of those Rules, decides all the differences that may happen between any Members of that Society, concerning any matter of right, and punishes those Offences which any Member hath committed against the Society with such Penalties as the Law has established; whereby it is easy to discern who are, and who are not, in Political Society together. Those who are united into one Body, and have a common established Law and Judicature to appeal to, with Authority to decide Controversies between them, and punish Offenders, are in Civil Society one with another; but those who have no such common Appeal, I mean on Earth, are still in the state of Nature, each being, where there is no other, Judge for himself, and Executioner; which is, as I have before showed it, the perfect state of Nature.

§88. And thus the Commonwealth comes by a power to set down what punishment shall belong to the several transgressions which they think worthy of it, committed amongst the Members of that Society, (which is the power of making Laws) as well as it has the power to punish any Injury done unto any of its Members, by any one that is not of it, (which is the power of War and Peace;) and all this for the preservation of the property of all the Members of that Society, as far as is possible. But though every Man entered into civil Society, has quitted his power to punish Offences against the Law of Nature, in prosecution of his own private Judgment; yet with the Judgment of Offences which he has given up to the Legislative in all Cases where he can Appeal to the Magistrate, he has given up a Right to the Commonwealth to employ his force for the Execution of the Judgments of the Commonwealth, whenever he shall be called to it, which indeed are his own Judgments, they being made by himself, or his Representative. And herein we have the original of the Legislative and Executive Power of Civil Society, which is to judge by standing Laws how far Offences are to be punished when committed within the Commonwealth; and also by occasional Judgments founded on the present Circumstances of the Fact, how far Injuries from without are to be vindicated, and in both these to employ all the force of all the Members when there shall be need.

§89. Wherever therefore any number of Men are so united into one Society, as to quit every one his Executive Power of the Law of Nature, and to resign it to the public, there and there only is a Political, or Civil Society. And this is done wherever any number of Men, in the State of Nature, enter into Society to make one People, one Body Politick under one Supreme Government, or else when any one joins himself to, and incorporates with any Government already made. For hereby he authorizes the Society, or which is all one, the Legislative thereof to make Laws for him as the public good of the Society shall require; to the Execution whereof, his own assistance (as to his own decrees) is due. And this puts Men out of a State of Nature into that of a Commonwealth, by setting up a Judge on Earth, with Authority to determine all the Controversies, and redress the injuries, that may happen to any Member of the Commonwealth; which Judge is the Legislative, or Magistrates appointed by it. And wherever there are any number of Men, however associated, that have no such decisive power to appeal to, there they are still in the state of Nature.

§90. And hence it is evident, that Absolute Monarchy which by some Men is counted for the only Government in the World, is indeed inconsistent with Civil Society, and so can be no Form of Civil Government at all. For the end of Civil Society, being to avoid and remedy those inconveniencies of the State of Nature which necessarily follow from every Man's being Judge in his own Case, by setting up a known Authority, to which every one of that Society may Appeal upon any injury received, or Controversy that may arise, and which every one of the Society ought to obey; where ever any persons are, who have not such an Authority to Appeal to, for the decision of any difference between them, there those persons are still in the state of Nature. And so is every Absolute Prince in respect of those who are under his *Dominion*.

§99. Whosoever therefore out of a State of Nature unite into a Community, must be understood to give up all the power necessary to the ends for which they unite into Society, to the majority of the Community, unless they expressly agreed in any number greater than the majority. And this is done by barely agreeing to unite into one Political Society, which is all the Compact that is, or needs be, between the Individuals that enter into or make up a Commonwealth. And thus that which begins and actually constitutes any Political Society, is nothing but the consent of any number of Freemen capable of a majority to unite and incorporate into such a Society. And this is that, and that only which did or could give beginning to any lawful Government in the World.

The Purpose of Government

§123. If Man in the State of Nature be so free, as has been said; If he be absolute Lord of his own Person and Possessions, equal to the greatest, and subject to no Body, why will he part with his Freedom? Why will he give up this Empire, and subject himself to the Dominion and Control of any other Power? To which 'tis obvious to Answer, that though in the state of Nature he hath such a right, yet the Enjoyment of it is very uncertain, and constantly exposed to the Invasion of others; for all being Kings as much as he, every Man his Equal, and the greater part no strict Observers of Equity and Justice, the enjoyment of the property he has in this state is very unsafe, very unsecure. This makes him willing to quit this Condition, which however free, is full of fears and continual dangers: And 'tis not without reason, that he seeks out, and is willing to join in Society with others who are already united, or have a mind to unite for the mutual Preservation of their Lives, Liberties, and Estates, which I call by the general Name, Property.

§124. The great and chief end therefore, of Mens uniting into Commonwealths, and putting themselves under Government, is the Preservation of their Property. To which in the state of Nature there are many things wanting.

The Three Defects of the State of Nature

First, There wants an established, settled, known Law, received and allowed by common consent to be the Standard of Right and Wrong, and the common measure to decide all Controversies between them. For though the Law of Nature be plain and intelligible to all rational Creatures; yet Men being biased by their Interest, as well as ignorant for want of study of it, are not apt to allow of it as a Law binding to them in the application of it to their particular Cases.

§125. *Secondly,* In the State of Nature there wants a known and indifferent Judge, with Authority to determine all differences according to the established Law. For every one in the state being both Judge and Executioner of the Law of Nature, Men being partial to themselves, Passion and Revenge is very apt to carry them too far, and with too much heat in their own Cases, as well as negligence, and unconcernedness, make them too remiss, in other Mens.

§126. *Thirdly,* In the state of Nature there often wants Power to back and support the Sentence when right, and to give it due Execution. They who by any Injustice offended, will seldom fail, where they are able, by force to make good their Injustice, such resistance many times makes the punishment dangerous, and frequently destructive, to those who attempt it.

§127. Thus Mankind, notwithstanding all the Privileges of the state of Nature, being but in an ill condition while they remain in it, are quickly driven into Society. Hence it comes to pass, that we seldom find any number of Men live any time together in this State. The inconveniencies that they are therein exposed to, by the irregular and uncertain exercise of the Power every Man has of punishing the transgressions of others, make them take Sanctuary under the established Laws of Government, and therein seek the preservation of their Property. 'Tis this makes them so willingly give up every one his single power of punishing to be exercised by such alone as shall be appointed to it amongst them; and by such Rules as the Community, or those authorized by it to them to that purpose shall agree on. And in this we have the original right and rise of both the Legislative and Executive Power, as well as of the Governments and Societies themselves.

The Two Powers of Man in the State of Nature

§128. For in the State of Nature, to omit the liberty he has of innocent Delights, a Man has two Powers.

The first is to do whatsoever he thinks fit for the preservation of himself and others within the permission of the Law of Nature: by which Law common to them all, he and all the rest of Mankind are one Community, make up one Society distinct from all other Creatures, and were it not for the corruption and viciousness of degenerate Men, there would be no need of any other, no necessity that Men should separate from this great and associate into less Combinations.

The other power a Man has in the State of Nature, is the power to punish the Crimes committed against that Law. Both these he gives up when he joins in a private, if I may so call it, or particular Political Society, and incorporates into any Commonwealth, separate from the rest of Mankind.

§129. The first Power, *viz* of doing whatsoever he thought fit for the preservation of himself, and the rest of Mankind, he gives up to be regulated by Laws made by the Society, so far forth as the preservation of himself, and the rest of that Society shall require; which Laws of the Society in many things confine the liberty he had by the Law of Nature.

§130. *Secondly*, the Power of punishing he wholly gives up, and engages his natural force, (which he might before employ in the Execution of the Law of Nature, by his own single Authority, as he thought fit) to assist the Executive Power of the Society, as the Law thereof shall require. For being now in a new State, wherein he is to enjoy many Conveniences from the labor, assistance and society of others in the same Community, as well as protection from its whole strength; he is to part also with as much of his natural liberty in providing for himself, as the good, prosperity and safety of the Society shall require; which is not only necessary but just, since the other Members of the Society do the like.

The Rule of Law

§131. But though Men when they enter into Society, give up the Equality, Liberty, and Executive Power they had in the State of Nature, into the hands of the Society, to be so far disposed of by the Legislative, as the good of the Society shall require; yet it being only with an intention in every one the better to preserve himself his Liberty and Property; (For no rational Creature can be supposed to change his condition with an intention to be worse) the power of the Society, or Legislative constituted by them, can never be supposed to extend farther than the common good; but is obliged to secure every ones Property by providing against those three defects above-mentioned, that made the State of Nature so unsafe and uneasy. And so whoever has the Legislative or supreme Power of any Common-wealth, is bound to govern by established standing Laws, promulgated and known to the People, and not by Extemporary Decrees; by indifferent and upright Judges, who are to decide Controversies by those Laws; and to employ the force of the Community sat home, only in the Execution of such Laws, or abroad to prevent or redress Foreign Injuries, and secure the Community from Inroads and Invasion. And all this to be directed to no other end, but the Peace, Safety, and public good of the People.

§142. These are the Bounds which the trust that is put in them by the Society, and the Law of God and Nature, have set to the Legislative Power of every Commonwealth, in all Forms of Government.

First, They are to govern by promulgated established Laws, not to be varied in particular Cases, but to have one Rule for the Rich and Poor, for the Favorite at Court, and the Country Man at Plough.

Secondly, These Laws also ought to be designed for no other end ultimately but the good of the People.

Thirdly, they must not raise Taxes on the Property of the People, without the Consent of the People, given by themselves, or their Deputies. And this properly concerns only such Governments where the Legislative is always in being, or at least where the People have not reserved any part of the Legislative to Deputies, to be from time to time chosen by themselves.

Fourthly, The Legislative neither must nor can transfer the Power of making Laws to any Body else, or place it anywhere but where the People have.

The Right to Revolution: "A Long Train of Abuses"

§222. The Reason why Men enter into Society, is the preservation of their Property; and the end why they choose and authorize a Legislative, is, that there may be Laws made, and Rules set as Guards and Fences to the Properties of all the Members of the Society, to limit the Power, and moderate the Dominion of every Part and Member of the Society. For since it can never be supposed to be the Will of the Society, that the Legislative should have a Power to destroy that which every one designs to secure, by entering into Society, and for which the People submitted themselves to Legislators of their own making; whenever the Legislators endeavor to take away, and destroy the Property of the People, or to reduce them to Slavery under Arbitrary Power, they put themselves into a state of War with the People, who are thereupon absolved from any farther Obedience, and are left to the common Refuge, which God hath provided for all Men, against Force and Violence.

When so ever therefore the Legislative shall transgress this fundamental Rule of Society; and either by Ambition, Fear, Folly or Corruption, endeavor to grasp themselves, or put into the hands of any other and Absolute Power over the Lives, Liberties, and Estates of the People: By this breach of Trust they forfeit the Power, the People had put into their hands for quite contrary ends, and it devolves to the People; who have a Right to resume their original Liberty, and, by the Establishment of a new Legislative (such as they shall think fit) provide for their own Safety and Security, which is the end for which they are in Society. What I have said here, concerning the Legislative in general, holds true also concerning the supreme Executor, who having a double trust put in him, both to have a part in the Legislative, and the supreme Execution of the Law, acts against both, when he goes about to set up his own Arbitrary Will, as the Law of the Society. He acts also contrary to his Trust, when he either employs the Force, Treasure, and Offices of the Society, to corrupt the Representatives, and gain them to his purposes: When he openly pre-engages the Electors, and prescribes to their choice, such, whom he has by Solicitations, Threats, Promises, or otherwise won to his designs; and employs them to bring in such, who have promised before-hand, what to Vote, and what to Enact. Thus to regulate Candidates and Electors, and new model the ways of Election what is it but to cut up the Government by the Roots, and poison the very Fountain of public Security?

For the People having reserved to themselves the Choice of Representatives, as the Fence to their Properties, could do it for no other end, but that they might always be freely chosen, and so chosen, freely act and advise, as the necessity of the Commonwealth, and the public Good should, upon examination, and mature debate, be judged to require. This, those who give their Votes before they hear the Debate, and have weighed the Reasons on all sides, are not capable of doing. To prepare such an Assembly as this, and endeavor to set up the declared Abettors of his own Will, for the true Representatives of the People, and the Law-makers of the Society, is certainly as great a breach of trust, and as perfect a Declaration of a design to subvert the Government, as is possible to be met with. To which, if one shall add Rewards and Punishments visibly employed to the same end, and all the Arts of perverted Law made use of to take off and destroy all that stand in the way of such a design, and will not comply and consent to betray the Liberties of their Country, 'twill be past doubt what is doing. What Power they ought to have in the Society, who thus employ it contrary to the trust went along with it in its first Institution, is easy to determine; and one cannot but see, that he who has once attempted any such thing as this, cannot any longer be trusted.

§223. To this perhaps it will be said, that the People being ignorant and always discontented, to lay the Foundation of Government in the unsteady Opinion and uncertain Humor of the People, is to expose it to certain ruin: And no Government will be able long to subsist, if the People may set up a new Legislative whenever they take offense at the old one. To this I Answer quite the contrary. People are not so easily got out of their old Forms, as some are apt to suggest. They are hardly to be prevailed with to amend the acknowledged Faults in the Frame they have been accustomed to. And if there be any Original defects, or adventitious ones introduced by time or corruption; 'tis not an easy thing to get them changed, even when all the World sees there is an opportunity for it. This slowness and aversion in the People to quit their old Constitutions, has in the many Revolutions which have been seen in this Kingdom, in this and former Ages, still kept us to, or after some interval of fruitless attempts, still brought us back again to our old Legislative of King, Lords and Commons: And whatever provocations have made the Crown be taken from some of our Princes Heads, they never carried the People so far as to place it in another Line.

§224. But 'twill be said, this Hypothesis lays a ferment for frequent Rebellion. To which I Answer, First, No more than any other Hypothesis. For when the People are made miserable, and find themselves exposed to the ill usage of Arbitrary Power; cry up their Governors as much as you will for Sons of Jupiter, let them be Sacred and Divine, descended or authorized from Heaven; give them out for whom or what you please the same will happen. The People generally ill-treated, and contrary to right, will be ready upon any occasion to ease themselves of a burden that sits heavy upon them. They will wish and seek for the opportunity, which in the change, weakness and accidents of humane affairs seldom delays long to offer it self. He must have lived but a little while in the World, who has not seen Examples of this in his time; and he must have read very little, who cannot produce Examples of it in all sorts of Governments in the World.

§225. Secondly, I Answer, such Revolutions happen not upon every little mismanagement in public affairs. Great mistakes in the ruling part, many wrong and inconvenient Laws, and all the slips of human frailty will be born by the People, without mutiny or murmur. But if a long train of Abuses, Prevarications and Artifices, all tending the same way, make the design visible to the People, and they cannot but feel what they lie under, and see whither they are going; 'tis not to be wondered that they should then rouse themselves, and endeavor to put the rule into such hands, which may secure to them the ends for which Government was at first erected; and without which, ancient Name, and specious Forms, are so far from being better, that they are much worse than the state of Nature, or pure Anarchy; the inconveniencies being all as great and as near, but the remedy farther off and more difficult.

§226. Thirdly, I Answer, That this Power in the People of providing for their safety a-new, by a new Legislative, when their Legislators have acted contrary to their trust, by invading their Property, is the best fence against Rebellion, and the probablest means to hinder it. For Rebellion being an Opposition, not to Persons, but Authority, which is founded only in the Constitutions and Laws of the Government; those, whoever they be, who by force break through, and by force justify their violation of them, are truly and properly Rebels. For when Men by entering into Society and Civil Government, have excluded force, and introduced Laws for the preservation of Property Peace and Unity amongst themselves; those who set up force again in opposition to the Laws, do *Rebellare*, that is, bring back again the state of War, and are properly Rebels: Which they who are in Power, by the pretence they have to Authority, the temptation of force they have in their hands, and the Flattery of those about them being likeliest to do; the properest way to prevent the evil, is to show them the danger and injustice of it, who are under the greatest temptation to run into it.

§227. In both the fore mentioned Cases, when either the Legislative is changed, or the Legislators act contrary to the end for which they were constituted; those who are guilty are guilty of Rebellion. For if any one by force takes away the established Legislative of any Society, and the Laws by them made, pursuant to their trust, he thereby takes away the Umpirage which every one had consented to, for a peaceable decision of all their Controversies, and a bar to the state of War amongst them. They who remove, or change the Legislative, take away this decisive power, which no Body can have, but by the appointment and consent of the People; and so destroying the Authority which the People did, and no Body else can set up, and introducing a Power which the People hath not authorized; actually introduce a state of War, which is that of Force without Authority: And thus by removing the Legislative established by the Society, in whose decisions the People acquiesced and united, as to that of their own will; they untie the Knot, and expose the People a new to the state of War. And if those, who by force take away the Legislative, are Rebels, the Legislators themselves, as has been shown, can be no less esteemed so; when they who were set up for the protection and preservation of the People, their Liberties and Properties shall by force invade and endeavor to take them away; and so they putting themselves into a state of War with those who made them the Protectors and Guardians of their Peace, are properly, and with the greatest aggravation, *Rebellantes* Rebels.

§228. But if they who say it lays a foundation for Rebellion, mean that it may occasion Civil Wars, or Intestine Broils, to tell the People they are absolved from Obedience, when illegal attempts are made upon their Liberties or Properties, and may oppose the unlawful violence of those who were their Magistrates when they invade their Properties contrary to the trust put in them; and that therefore this Doctrine is not to be allowed, being so destructive to the Peace of the World. They may as well say upon the same ground, that honest Men may not oppose Robbers or Pirates, because this may occasion disorder or bloodshed. If any mischief come in such Cases, it is not to be charged upon him who defends his own right, but on him that invades his Neighbors. If the innocent honest Man must quietly quit all he has for Peace sake, to him who will lay violent hands upon it, I desire it may be considered, what a kind of Peace there will be in the World, which consists only in Violence and Rapine; and which is to be maintained only for the benefit of Robbers and Oppressors. Who would not think it an admirable Peace betwixt the Mighty and the Mean, when the Lamb, without resistance, yielded his Throat to be torn by the imperious Wolf? *Polyphemus's* Den gives us a perfect Pattern of such a Peace. Such a Government wherein *Ulysses* and his Companions had nothing to do, but quietly to suffer themselves to be devoured. And no doubt, *Ulysses* who was a prudent Man, preached up Passive Obedience, and exhorted them to a quiet Submission, by representing to them of what concernment Peace was to Mankind; and by showing the inconveniencies might happen, if they should offer to resist Polyphemus, who had now the power over them.

§229. The end of Government is the good of Mankind; and which is best for Mankind, that the People should be always exposed to the boundless will of Tyranny, or that the Rulers should be sometimes liable to be opposed, when they grow exorbitant in the use of their Power, and employ it for the destruction, and not the preservation of the Properties of their People?

§230. Nor let any one say, that mischief can arise from hence, as often as it shall please a busy head or turbulent spirit to desire the alteration of the Government. 'Tis true, such Men may stir whenever they please, but it will be only to their own just ruin and perdition. For till the mischief be grown general, and the ill designs of the Rulers become visible, or their attempts sensible to the greater part, the People, who are more disposed to suffer, than right themselves by Resistance, are not apt to stir. The examples of particular Injustice, or Oppression of here and there an unfortunate Man, moves them not. But if they universally have a persuasion grounded upon manifest evidence, that designs are carrying on against their Liberties, and the general course and tendency of things cannot but give them strong suspicions of the evil intention of their Governors, who is to be blamed for it? Who can help it, if they, who might avoid it, bring themselves into suspicion?

Are the People to be blamed, if they have the sense of rational Creatures, and can think of things no otherwise than as they find and feel them? And is it not rather their fault who puts things in such a posture that they would not have them thought as they are? I grant, that the Pride, Ambition, and Turbulency of private Men have sometimes caused great Disorders in Commonwealths, and Factions have been fatal to States and Kingdoms. But whether the mischief hath oftner begun in the Peoples Wantonness, and a Desire to cast off the lawful Authority of their Rulers; or in the Rulers Insolence, and Endeavors to get, and exercise an Arbitrary Power over their People; whether Oppression, or Disobedience gave the first rise to the Disorder, I leave it to impartial History to determine. This I am sure, whoever, either Ruler or Subject, by force goes about to invade the Rights of either Prince or People, and lays the foundation for overturning the Constitution and Frame of any Just Government; he is guilty of the greatest Crime, I think, a Man is capable of, being to answer for all those mischiefs of Blood, Rapine, and Desolation, which the breaking to pieces of Governments bring on a Country. And he who does it, is justly to be esteemed the common Enemy and Pest of Mankind; and is to be treated accordingly.

"Who Shall be Judge?"

§240. Here, 'tis like, the common Question will be made, Who shall be Judge whether the Prince or Legislative act contrary to their Trust? This, perhaps, ill affected and factious Men may spread amongst the People, when the Prince only makes use of his due Prerogative. To this I reply; The People shall be Judge; for who shall be Judge whether his Trustee or Deputy acts well, and according to the Trust reposed in him, but he who deputes him, and must, by having deputed him have still a Power to discard him, when he fails in his Trust? If this be reasonable in particular Cases of private Men, why should it be otherwise in that of the greatest moment, where the Welfare of Millions is concerned, and also where the evil, if not prevented, is greater, and the Redress very difficult, dear, and dangerous?

§241. But farther, this Question, (Who shall be Judge?) cannot mean, that there is no Judge at all. For where there is no Judicature on Earth, to decide Controversies amongst Men, God in Heaven is Judge: He alone, 'tis true, is Judge of the Right. But every Man is Judge for himself, as in all other Cases, so in this, whether another hath put himself into a State of War with him, and whether he should appeal to the Supreme Judge, as *Jeptha* did.

Conclusion

§243. To conclude, The Power that every individual gave the Society, when he entered into it, can never revert to the Individuals again, as long as the Society lasts, but will always remain in the Community; because without this, there can be no Community, no Commonwealth, which is contrary to the original Agreement: So also when the Society hath placed the Legislative in any Assembly of Men, to continue in them and their Successors, with Direction and Authority for providing such Successors, the Legislative can never revert to the People whilst that Government lasts: Because having provided a Legislative with Power to continue for ever, they have given up their Political Power to the Legislative, and cannot resume it. But if they have set Limits to the Duration of their Legislative, and made this Supreme Power in any Person, or Assembly, only temporary: Or else when by the Miscarriages of those in Authority, it is forfeited; upon the Forfeiture of their Rulers, or at the Determination of the Time set, it reverts to the Society, and the People have a Right to act as Supreme, and continue the Legislative in themselves, or place in it a new Form, or new hands, as they think good.

John Locke

A Letter Concerning Toleration

Purpose of Letter

Since you are pleased to inquire what are my thoughts about the mutual toleration of Christians in their different professions of religion, I must needs answer you freely that I esteem that toleration to be the chief characteristic mark of the true Church. For whatsoever some people boast of the antiquity of places and names, or of the pomp of their outward worship; others, of the reformation of their discipline; all, of the orthodoxy of their faith—for everyone is orthodox to himself—these things, and all others of this nature, are much rather marks of men striving for power and empire over one another than of the Church of Christ....

That any man should think fit to cause another man—whose salvation he heartily desires—to expire in torments, and that even in an unconverted state, would, I confess, seem very strange to me, and I think, to any other also. But nobody, surely, will ever believe that such a carriage can proceed from charity, love, or goodwill. If anyone maintain that men ought to be compelled by fire and sword to profess certain doctrines, and conform to this or that exterior worship, without any regard had unto their morals; if anyone endeavor to convert those that are erroneous unto the faith, by forcing them to profess things that they do not believe and allowing them to practice things that the

Gospel does not permit, it cannot be doubted indeed but such a one is desirous to have a numerous assembly joined in the same profession with himself; but that he principally intends by those means to compose a truly Christian Church is altogether incredible. It is not, therefore, to be wondered at if those who do not really contend for the advancement of the true religion, and of the Church of Christ, make use of arms that do not belong to the Christian warfare....

Separation of Civil Government and Religion

I esteem it above all things necessary to distinguish exactly the business of civil government from that of religion and to settle the just bounds that lie between the one and the other. If this be not done, there can be no end put to the controversies that will be always arising between those that have, or at least pretend to have, on the one side, a concernment for the interest of men's souls, and, on the other side, a care of the commonwealth.

The commonwealth seems to me to be a society of men constituted only for the procuring, preserving, and advancing their own civil interests.

Civil interests I call life, liberty, health, and indolency of body; and the posses-sion of outward things, such as money, lands, houses, furniture, and the like.

It is the duty of the civil magistrate, by the impartial execution of equal laws, to secure unto all the people in general and to every one of his subjects in particular the just possession of these things belonging to this life. If anyone presume to violate the laws of public justice and equity, established for the preservation of those things, his presumption is to be checked by the fear of punishment, consisting of the deprivation or diminution of those civil inter-ests, or goods, which otherwise he might and ought to enjoy. But seeing no man does willingly suffer himself to be punished by the deprivation of any part of his goods, and much less of his liberty or life, therefore, is the magis-trate armed with the force and strength of all his subjects, in order to the pun-ishment of those that violate any other man's rights.

Now that the whole jurisdiction of the magistrate reaches only to these civil concernments, and that all civil power, right and dominion, is bounded and confined to the only care of promoting these things; and that it neither can nor ought in any manner to be extended to the salvation of souls, these follow-ing considerations seem unto me abundantly to demonstrate.

First, because the care of souls is not committed to the civil magistrate, any more than to other men....

In the second place, the care of souls cannot belong to the civil magistrate, because his power consists only in outward force; but true and saving religion consists in the inward persuasion of the mind, without which nothing can be acceptable to God....

In the third place, the care of the salvation of men's souls cannot belong to the magistrate; because, though the rigor of laws and the force of penalties were capable to convince and change men's minds, yet would not that help at all to the salvation of their souls....

The Church as a Voluntary Society

A church, then, I take to be a voluntary society of men, joining themselves together of their own accord in order to the public worshipping of God in such manner as they judge acceptable to Him, and effectual to the salvation of their souls.

I say it is a free and voluntary society. Nobody is born a member of any church; otherwise the religion of parents would descend unto children by the same right of inheritance as their temporal estates, and everyone would hold his faith by the same tenure he does his lands, than which nothing can be imagined more absurd. Thus, therefore, that matter stands. No man by nature is bound unto any particular church or sect, but everyone joins himself voluntarily to that society in which he believes he has found that profession and worship which is truly acceptable to God....

The Power and Limitations of the Church

What is the power of this church and unto what laws it is subject?...

Since the joining together of several members into this church-society, as has already been demonstrated, is absolutely free and spontaneous, it necessarily follows that the right of making its laws can belong to none but the society itself; or, at least (which is the same thing), to those whom the society by common consent has authorized thereunto.

Some, perhaps, may object that no such society can be said to be a true church unless it have in it a bishop or presbyter, with ruling authority derived from the very apostles, and continued down to the present times by an uninterrupted succession.

To these I answer:

In the first place, let them show me the edict by which Christ has imposed that law upon His Church. And let not any man think me impertinent, if in a thing of this consequence I require that the terms of that edict be very express and positive; for the promise He has made us, that "where so ever two or three are gathered together" in His name, He will be in the midst of them, seems to imply the contrary. Whether such an assembly want anything necessary to a true church, pray do you consider. Certain I am that nothing can be there wanting unto the salvation of souls, which is sufficient to our purpose.

Next, pray observe how great have always been the divisions amongst even those who lay so much stress upon the Divine institution and continued succession of a certain order of rulers in the Church. Now, their very dissension unavoidably puts us upon a necessity of deliberating and, consequently, allows a liberty of choosing that which upon consideration we prefer.

And, in the last place, I consent that these men have a ruler in their church, established by such a long series of succession as they judge necessary, provided I may have liberty at the same time to join myself to that society in which I am persuaded those things are to be found which are necessary to the salvation of my soul. In this manner ecclesiastical liberty will be preserved on all sides, and no man will have a legislator imposed upon him but whom himself has chosen....

The Extent and Duty of Toleration by the Church

These things being thus determined, let us inquire, in the next place: How far the duty of toleration extends, and what is required from everyone by it?

And, first, I hold that no church is bound, by the duty of toleration, to retain any such person in her bosom as, after admonition, continues obstinately to offend against the laws of the society. For, these being the condition of communion and the bond of the society, if the breach of them were permitted without any animadversion the society would immediately be thereby dissolved. But, nevertheless, in all such cases care is to be taken that the sentence of excommunication, and the execution thereof, carry with it no rough usage of word or action whereby the ejected person may any wise be damnified in body or estate.... Excommunication neither does, nor can, deprive the excommunicated person of any of those civil goods that he formerly possessed. All those things belong to the civil government and are under the magistrate's protection....

Secondly, no private person has any right in any manner to prejudice another person in his civil enjoyments because he is of another church or religion. All the rights and franchises that belong to him as a man, or as a denizen, are inviolably to be preserved to him. These are not the business of religion....

This is the fundamental and immutable right of a spontaneous society—that it has power to remove any of its members who transgress the rules of its institution; but it cannot, by the accession of any new members, acquire any right of jurisdiction over those that are not joined with it. And therefore peace, equity, and friendship are always mutually to be observed by particular churches, in the same manner as by private persons, without any pretence of superiority or jurisdiction over one another....

Nobody, therefore, in fine, neither single persons nor churches, nay, nor even commonwealths, have any just title to invade the civil rights and worldly goods of each other upon pretence of religion. Those that are of another opinion would do well to consider with themselves how pernicious a seed of discord and war, how powerful a provocation to endless hatreds, rapines, and slaughters they thereby furnish unto mankind. No peace and security, no, not so much as common friendship, can ever be established or preserved amongst men so long as this opinion prevails, that dominion is founded in grace and that religion is to be propagated by force of arms.

In the third place, let us see what the duty of toleration requires from those who are distinguished from the rest of mankind (from the laity, as they please to call us) by some ecclesiastical character and office; whether they be bishops, priests, presbyters, ministers, or however else dignified or distinguished. It is not my business to inquire here into the original of the power or dignity of the clergy. This only I say, that, when so ever their authority be sprung, since it is ecclesiastical, it ought to be confined within the bounds of the Church, nor can it in any manner be extended to civil affairs, because the Church itself is a thing absolutely separate and distinct from the commonwealth. The boundaries on both sides are fixed and immovable....

But this is not all. It is not enough that ecclesiastical men abstain from violence and rapine and all manner of persecution. He that pretends to be a successor of the apostles, and takes upon him the office of teaching, is obliged also to admonish his hearers of the duties of peace and goodwill towards all men, as well towards the erroneous as the orthodox; towards those that differ from them in faith and worship as well as towards those that agree with them therein. And he ought industriously to exhort all men, whether private persons or magistrates (if any such there be in his church), to charity, meekness, and toleration, and diligently endeavor to ally and temper all that heat and unreasonable averseness of mind which either any man's fiery zeal for his own sect or the craft of others has kindled against dissenters....

In private domestic affairs, in the management of estates, in the conservation of bodily health, every man may consider what suits his own convenience and follow what course he likes best. No man complains of the ill management of his neighbor's affairs. No man is angry with another for an error committed in sowing his land or in marrying his daughter. Nobody corrects a spendthrift for consuming his substance in taverns. Let any man pull down, or build, or make whatsoever expenses he pleases, nobody murmurs, nobody controls him; he has his liberty. But if any man does not frequent the church, if he do not there conform his behavior exactly to the accustomed ceremonies, or if he brings not his children to be initiated in the sacred mysteries of this or the other congregation, this immediately causes an uproar. The neighborhood is filled with noise and clamor. Everyone is ready to be the avenger of so great a crime, and the zealots hardly have the patience to refrain from violence and rapine so long till the cause be heard and the poor man be, according to form, condemned to the loss of liberty, goods, or life....

The Extent and Duty of Toleration by the Magistrate

Let us now consider what is the magistrate's duty in the business of toleration, which certainly is very considerable.

We have already proved that the care of souls does not belong to the magistrate. Not a magisterial care, I mean (if I may so call it), which consists in prescribing by laws and compelling by punishments. But a charitable care, which consists in teaching, admonishing, and persuading, cannot be denied unto any man. The care, therefore, of every man's soul belongs unto himself and is to be left unto himself. But what if he neglect the care of his soul? I answer: What if he neglect the care of his health or of his estate, which things are [more closely] related to the government of the magistrate than the other? Will the magistrate provide by an express law that such a one shall not become poor or sick?

Laws provide, as much as is possible, that the goods and health of subjects be not injured by the fraud and violence of others; they do not guard them from the negligence or ill husbandry of the possessors themselves. No man can be forced to be rich or healthful whether he will or no. Nay, God Himself will not save men against their wills....

But let us grant unto these zealots, who condemn all things that are not of their mode, that from these circumstances are different ends. What shall we conclude from thence? There is only one of these which is the true way to eternal happiness: but in this great variety of ways that men follow, it is still doubted which is the right one. Now, neither the care of the commonwealth, nor the right enacting of laws, does discover this way that leads to heaven more certainly to the magistrate than every private man's search and study discovers it unto himself. I have a weak body, sunk under a languishing disease, for which (I suppose) there is one only remedy, but that unknown. Does it therefore belong unto the magistrate to prescribe me a remedy, because there is but one, and because it is unknown? Because there is but one way for me to escape death, will it therefore be safe for me to do whatsoever the magistrate ordains? Those things that every man ought sincerely to inquire into himself, and by meditation, study, search, and his own endeavors, attain the knowledge of, cannot be looked upon as the peculiar possession of any sort of men. Princes, indeed, are born superior unto other men in power, but in nature equal. Neither the right nor the art of ruling does necessarily carry along with it the certain knowledge of other things, and least of all of true religion....

Perhaps some will say that they do not suppose this infallible judgment, that all men are bound to follow in the affairs of religion, to be in the civil magistrate, but in the Church.... I answer: Who sees not how frequently the name of the Church, which was venerable in time of the apostles, has been made use of to throw dust in the people's eyes in the following ages? But, however, in the present case it helps us not. The one only narrow way which leads to heaven is not better known to the magistrate than to private persons, and therefore I cannot safely take him for my guide, who may probably be as ignorant of the way as myself, and who certainly is less concerned for my salvation than I myself am....

But, after all, the principal consideration, and which absolutely determines this controversy, is this: Although the magistrate's opinion in religion be sound, and the way that he appoints be truly Evangelical, yet, if I be not thoroughly persuaded thereof in my own mind, there will be no safety for me in following it. No way whatsoever that I shall walk in against the dictates of my conscience will ever bring me to the mansions of the blessed. I may grow rich by an art that I take not delight in; I may be cured of some disease by remedies that I have not faith in; but I cannot be saved by a religion that I distrust and by a worship that I abhor. It is in vain for an unbeliever to take up the outward show of another man's profession. Faith only and inward sincerity are the things that procure acceptance with God. The most likely and most approved remedy can have no effect upon the patient, if his stomach reject it as soon as taken; and you will in vain cram a medicine down a sick man's throat, which his particular constitution will be sure to turn into poison.

In a word, whatsoever may be doubtful in religion, yet this at least is certain, that no religion which I believe not to be true can be either true or profitable unto me. In vain, therefore, do princes compel their subjects to come into their Church communion, under pretence of saving their souls. If they believe, they will come of their own accord, if they believe not, their coming will nothing avail them. How great so ever, in fine, may be the pretence of good-will and charity, and concern for the salvation of men's souls, men cannot be forced to be saved whether they will or no. And therefore, when all is done, they must be left to their own consciences....

The Concept of "Indifferent Things"

But perhaps it may be concluded from hence that I deny unto the magistrate all manner of power about indifferent things, which, if it be not granted, the whole subject matter of law making is taken away. No, I readily grant that indifferent things, and perhaps none but such, are subjected to the legislative power. But it does not therefore follow that the magistrate may ordain whatsoever he pleases concerning anything that is indifferent. The public good is the rule and measure of all law making. If a thing be not useful to the commonwealth, though it be never so indifferent, it may not presently be established by law.

And further, things never so indifferent in their own nature, when they are brought into the Church and worship of God, are removed out of the reach of the magistrate's jurisdiction, because in that use they have no connection at all with civil affairs. The only business of the Church is the salvation of souls, and it no way concerns the commonwealth, or any member of it, that this or the other ceremony be there made use of. Neither the use nor the omission of any ceremonies in those religious assemblies does either advantage or prejudice the life, liberty, or estate of any man....

In the next place: As the magistrate has no power to impose by his laws the use of any rites and ceremonies in any Church, so neither has he any power to forbid the use of such rites and ceremonies as are already received, approved, and practiced by any Church; because, if he did so, he would destroy the Church itself: the end of whose institution is only to worship God with freedom after its own manner.

You will say, by this rule, if some congregations should have a mind to sacrifice infants, or (as the primitive Christians were falsely accused) lustfully pollute themselves in promiscuous uncleanness, or practice any other such heinous enormities, is the magistrate obliged to tolerate them, because they are committed in a religious assembly? I answer: No. These things are not lawful in the ordinary course of life, nor in any private house; and therefore neither are they so in the worship of God, or in any religious meeting.

But, indeed, if any people congregated upon account of religion should be desirous to sacrifice a calf, I deny that that ought to be prohibited by a law. Meliboeus, whose calf it is, may lawfully kill his calf at home, and burn any part of it that he thinks fit. For no injury is thereby done to any one, no prejudice to another man's goods. And for the same reason he may kill his calf also in a religious meeting. Whether the doing so be well pleasing to God or no, it is their part to consider that do it.

The part of the magistrate is only to take care that the commonwealth receive no prejudice, and that there be no injury done to any man, either in life or estate. And thus what may be spent on a feast may be spent on a sacrifice. But if peradventure such were the state of things that the interest of the commonwealth required all slaughter of beasts should be forborne for some while, in order to the increasing of the stock of cattle that had been destroyed by some extraordinary murrain, who sees not that the magistrate, in such a case, may forbid all his subjects to kill any calves for any use whatsoever? Only it is to be observed that, in this case, the law is not made about a religious, but a political matter; nor is the sacrifice, but the slaughter of calves, thereby prohibited.

By this we see what difference there is between the Church and the Commonwealth. Whatsoever is lawful in the Commonwealth cannot be prohibited by the magistrate in the Church. Whatsoever is permitted unto any of his subjects for their ordinary use, neither can nor ought to be forbidden by him to any sect of people for their religious uses. If any man may lawfully take bread or wine, either sitting or kneeling in his own house, the law ought not to abridge him of the same liberty in his religious worship; though in the Church the use of bread and wine be very different and be there applied to the mysteries of faith and rites of Divine worship. But those things that are prejudicial to the commonweal of a people in their ordinary use and are, therefore, forbidden by laws, those things ought not to be permitted to Churches in their sacred rites. Only the magistrate ought always to be very careful that he do not misuse his authority to the oppression of any Church, under pretence of public good....

The Magistrate and "an Idolatrous Church"

It may be said: "What if a Church be idolatrous, is that also to be tolerated by the magistrate?" I answer: What power can be given to the magistrate for the suppression of an idolatrous Church, which may not in time and place be made use of to the ruin of an orthodox one?... Not even Americans, subjected unto a Christian prince, are to be punished either in body or goods for not embracing our faith and worship. If they are persuaded that they please God in observing the rites of their own country and that they shall obtain happiness by that means, they are to be left unto God and themselves....

Now whosoever maintains that idolatry is to be rooted out of any place by laws, punishments, fire, and sword, may apply this story to himself. For the reason of the thing is equal, both in America and Europe. And neither Pagans there, nor any dissenting Christians here, can, with any right, be deprived of their worldly goods by the predominating faction of a court-church; nor are any civil rights to be either changed or violated upon account of religion in one place more than another.

But idolatry, say some, is a sin and therefore not to be tolerated. If they said it were therefore to be avoided, the inference were good. But it does not follow that because it is a sin it ought therefore to be punished by the magistrate. For it does not belong unto the magistrate to make use of his sword in punishing everything, indifferently, that he takes to be a sin against God.

Covetousness, uncharitableness, idleness, and many other things are sins by the consent of men, which yet no man ever said were to be punished by the magistrate. The reason is because they are not prejudicial to other men's rights, nor do they break the public peace of societies. Nay, even the sins of lying and perjury are nowhere punishable by laws; unless, in certain cases, in which the real turpitude of the thing and the offence against God are not considered, but only the injury done unto men's neighbors and to the commonwealth. And what if in another country, to a Mahometan or a Pagan prince, the Christian religion seem false and offensive to God; may not the Christians for the same reason, and after the same manner, be extirpated there?...

The Magistrate and "Articles of Faith"

The articles of religion are some of them practical and some speculative. Now, though both sorts consist in the knowledge of truth, yet these terminate simply in the understanding, those influence the will and manners. Speculative opinions, therefore, and articles of faith (as they are called) which are required only to be believed, cannot be imposed on any Church by the law of the land. For it is absurd that things should be enjoined by laws which are not in men's power to perform. And to believe this or that to be true does not depend upon our will. But of this enough has been said already. "But." will some say; "let men at least profess that they believe." A sweet religion, indeed, that obliges men to dissemble and tell lies, both to God and man, for the salvation of their souls! If the magistrate thinks to save men thus, he seems to understand little of the way of salvation. And if he does it not in order to save them, why is he so solicitous about the articles of faith as to enact them by a law?

Further, the magistrate ought not to forbid the preaching or professing of any speculative opinions in any Church because they have no manner of relation to the civil rights of the subjects. If a Roman Catholic believe that to be really the body of Christ which another man calls bread, he does no injury thereby to his neighbor. If a Jew do not believe the New Testament to be the Word of God, he does not thereby alter anything in men's civil rights. If a heathen doubt of both Testaments, he is not therefore to be punished as a pernicious citizen. The power of the magistrate and the estates of the people may be equally secure whether any man believe these things or no. I readily grant that these opinions are false and absurd. But the business of laws is not to provide for the truth of opinions, but for the safety and security of the commonwealth and of every particular man's goods and person. And so it ought to be.

For the truth certainly would do well enough if she were once left to shift for herself. She seldom has received and, I fear, never will receive much assistance from the power of great men, to whom she is but rarely known and more rarely welcome. She is not taught by laws, nor has she any need of force to procure her entrance into the minds of men. Errors, indeed, prevail by the assistance of foreign and borrowed succors. But if Truth makes not her way into the understanding by her own light, she will be but the weaker for any borrowed force violence can add to her. Thus much for speculative opinions. Let us now proceed to practical ones.

The Importance of the Temporal Life

A good life, in which consist not the least part of religion and true piety, concerns also the civil government; and in it lies the safety both of men's souls and of the commonwealth. Moral actions belong, therefore, to the jurisdiction both of the outward and inward court; both of the civil and domestic governor; I mean both of the magistrate and conscience. Here, therefore, is great danger, lest one of these jurisdictions entrench upon the other, and discord arise between the keeper of the public peace and the overseers of souls. But if what has been already said concerning the limits of both these governments be rightly considered, it will easily remove all difficulty in this matter.

Every man has an immortal soul, capable of eternal happiness or misery; whose happiness depending upon his believing and doing those things in this life which are necessary to the obtaining of God's favor, and are prescribed by God to that end.... Any one may employ as many exhortations and arguments as he pleases, towards the promoting of another man's salvation. But all force and compulsion are to be forborne. Nothing is to be done imperiously. Nobody is obliged in that matter to yield obedience unto the admonitions or injunctions of another, further than he himself is persuaded. Every man in that has the supreme and absolute authority of judging for himself. And the reason is because nobody else is concerned in it, nor can receive any prejudice from his conduct therein.

But besides their souls, which are immortal, men have also their temporal lives here upon earth; the state whereof being frail and fleeting, and the duration uncertain, they have need of several outward conveniences to the support thereof, which are to be procured or preserved by pains and industry. For those things that are necessary to the comfortable support of our lives are not the spontaneous products of nature, nor do offer themselves fit and prepared for our use. This part, therefore, draws on another care and necessarily gives another employment. But the depravity of mankind being such that they had rather injuriously prey upon the fruits of other men's labors than take pains to provide for themselves, the necessity of preserving men in the possession of what honest industry has already acquired and also of preserving their liberty and strength, whereby they may acquire what they farther want, obliges men to enter into society with one another, that by mutual assistance and joint force they may secure unto each other their properties, in the things that contribute to the comfort and happiness of this life, leaving in the meanwhile to every man the care of his own eternal happiness, the attainment whereof can neither be facilitated by another man's industry, nor can the loss of it turn to another man's prejudice, nor the hope of it be forced from him by any external violence....

These things being thus explained, it is easy to understand to what end the legislative power ought to be directed and by what measures regulated; and that is the temporal good and outward prosperity of the society; which is the sole reason of men's entering into society, and the only thing they seek and aim at in it. And it is also evident what liberty remains to men in reference to their eternal salvation, and that is that every one should do what he in his conscience is persuaded to be acceptable to the Almighty, on whose good pleasure and acceptance depends their eternal happiness. For obedience is due, in the first place, to God and, afterwards to the laws....

Who Shall Be Judge?

As the private judgment of any particular person, if erroneous, does not exempt him from the obligation of law, so the private judgment (as I may call it) of the magistrate does not give him any new right of imposing laws upon his subjects, which neither was in the constitution of the government granted him, nor ever was in the power of the people to grant, much less if he make it his business to enrich and advance his followers and fellow-sectaries with the spoils of others. But what if the magistrate believe that he has a right to make such laws and that they are for the public good, and his subjects believe the contrary? Who shall be judge between them? I answer: God alone. For there is no judge upon earth between the supreme magistrate and the people. God, I say, is the only judge in this case, who will retribute unto every one at the last day according to his deserts; that is, according to his sincerity and uprightness in endeavoring to promote piety, and the public weal, and peace of mankind....

Liberty of Conscience as a Natural Right

It remains that I say something concerning those assemblies which, being vulgarly called and perhaps having sometimes been conventicles and nurseries of factions and seditions, are thought to afford against this doctrine of toleration. But this has not happened by anything peculiar unto the genius of such assemblies, but by the unhappy circumstances of an oppressed or ill-settled liberty. These accusations would soon cease if the law of toleration were once so settled that all Churches were obliged to lay down toleration as the foundation of their own liberty, and teach that liberty of conscience is every man's natural right, equally belonging to dissenters as to themselves; and that nobody ought to be compelled in matters of religion either by law or force. The establishment of this one thing would take away all ground of complaints and tumults upon account of conscience; and these causes of discontents and animosities being once removed, there would remain nothing in these assemblies that were not more peaceable and less apt to produce disturbance of state than in any other meetings whatsoever. But let us examine particularly the heads of these accusations.

You will say that assemblies and meetings endanger the public peace and threaten the commonwealth. I answer: If this be so, why are there daily such numerous meetings in markets and Courts of Judicature? Why are crowds upon the Exchange and a concourse of people in cities suffered? You will reply: "Those are civil assemblies, but these we object against are ecclesiastical." I answer: It is a likely thing, indeed, that such assemblies as are altogether remote from civil affairs should be most apt to embroil them. Oh, but civil assemblies are composed of men that differ from one another in matters of religion, but these ecclesiastical meetings are of persons that are all of one opinion. As if an agreement in matters of religion were in effect a conspiracy against the commonwealth; or as if men would not be so much the more warmly unanimous in religion the less liberty they had of assembling.

But it will be urged still that civil assemblies are open and free for any one to enter into, whereas religious conventicles are more private and thereby give opportunity to clandestine machinations. I answer that this is not strictly true, for many civil assemblies are not open to everyone. And if some religious meetings be private, who are they (I beseech you) that are to be blamed for it, those that desire, or those that forbid there being public! Again, you will say that religious communion does exceedingly unite men's minds and affections to one another and is therefore the more dangerous. But if this be so, why is not the magistrate afraid of his own Church; and why does he not forbid their assemblies as things dangerous to his Government? You will say because he himself is a part and even the head of them. As if he were not also a part of the commonwealth, and the head of the whole people!...

Freedom of Conscience and Separation of Church and State

The sum of all we drive at is that every man may enjoy the same rights that are granted to others. Is it permitted to worship God in the Roman manner? Let it be permitted to do it in the Geneva form also. Is it permitted to speak Latin in the market place? Let those that have a mind to it be permitted to do it also in the Church. Is it lawful for any man in his own house to kneel, stand, sit, or use any other posture; and to clothe him in white or black, in short or in long garments? Let it not be made unlawful to eat bread, drink wine, or wash with water in the church. In a word, whatsoever things are left free by law in the common occasions of life let them remain free unto every Church in divine worship. Let no man's life, or body, or house, or estate, suffer any manner of prejudice upon these accounts. Can you allow of the Presbyterian discipline? Why should not the Episcopal also have what they like? Ecclesiastical authority, whether it be administered by the hands of a single person or many, is everywhere the same; and neither has any jurisdiction in things civil, nor any manner of power of compulsion, nor anything at all to do with riches and revenues. Ecclesiastical assemblies...ought not to be sanctuaries for factious and flagitious fellows.

Nor ought it to be less lawful for men to meet in churches than in halls; nor is one part of the subjects to be esteemed more blamable for their meeting together than others. Every one is to be accountable for his own actions, and no man is to be laid under a suspicion or odium for the fault of another. Those that are seditious, murderers, thieves, robbers, adulterers, slanderers, etc., of whatsoever Church, whether national or not, ought to be punished and suppressed. But those whose doctrine is peaceable and whose manners are pure and blameless ought to be upon equal terms with their fellow-subjects. Thus if solemn assemblies, observations of festivals, public worship be permitted to any one sort of professors, all these things ought to be permitted to the Presbyterians, Independents, Anabaptists, Arminians, Quakers, and others, with the same liberty.

Nay, if we may openly speak the truth, and as becomes one man to another, neither Pagan nor Mahometan, nor Jew, ought to be excluded from the civil rights of the commonwealth because of his religion. The Gospel commands no such thing. The Church which "judgeth not those that are without" wants it not. And the commonwealth, which embraces indifferently all men that are honest, peaceable, and industrious, requires it not. Shall we suffer a Pagan to deal and trade with us, and shall we not suffer him to pray unto and worship God? If we allow the Jews to have private houses and dwellings amongst us, why should we not allow them to have synagogues? Is their doctrine more false, their worship more abominable, or is the civil peace more endangered by their meeting in public than in their private houses? But if these things may be granted to Jews and Pagans, surely the condition of any Christians ought not to be worse than theirs in a Christian commonwealth....

It is not the diversity of opinions (which cannot be avoided), but the refusal of toleration to those that are of different opinions (which might have been granted), that has produced all the bustles and wars that have been in the Christian world upon account of religion. The heads and leaders of the Church, moved by avarice and insatiable desire of dominion, making use of the immoderate ambition of magistrates and the credulous superstition of the giddy multitude, have incensed and animated them against those that dissent from themselves, by preaching unto them, contrary to the laws of the Gospel and to the precepts of charity, that schismatics and heretics are to be ousted of their possessions and destroyed....

That this has been hitherto the ordinary course of things is abundantly evident in history, and that it will continue to be so hereafter is but too apparent in reason. It cannot indeed, be otherwise so long as the principle of persecution for religion shall prevail, as it has done hitherto, with magistrate and people, and so long as those that ought to be the preachers of peace and concord shall continue with all their art and strength to excite men to arms and sound the trumpet of war. But that magistrates should thus suffer these incendiaries and disturbers of the public peace might justly be wondered at if it did not appear that they have been invited by them unto a participation of the spoil, and have therefore thought fit to make use of their covetousness and pride as means whereby to increase their own power. For who does not see that these good men are, indeed, more ministers of the government than ministers of the Gospel and that, by flattering the ambition and favoring the dominion of princes and men in authority, they endeavor with all their might to promote that tyranny in the commonwealth which otherwise they should not be able to establish in the Church? This is the unhappy agreement that we see between the Church and State.

Whereas if each of them would contain itself within its own bounds—the one attending to the worldly welfare of the commonwealth, the other to the salvation of souls—it is impossible that any discord should ever have happened between them.

John Locke

Some Considerations of the Lowering of Interest and the Raising the Value of Money

Can "the Price of the Hire of Money…be regulated?"

The first thing to be considered, is, Whether the Price of the Hire of Money can be regulated by Law. And to that I think, generally speaking, one may say, 'tis manifest it cannot. For since it's impossible, to make a Law that shall hinder a Man from giving away his Money or Estate to whom he pleases, it will be impossible, by any Contrivance of Law, to hinder Men, skilled in the Power they have over their own Goods, and the ways of Conveying them to others, to purchase Money to be Lent them at what Rate so ever their Occasions shall make it necessary for them to have it.

For it is to be Remembered, That no Man borrows Money, or pays Use, out of mere Pleasure: 'Tis the want of Money drives Men to that Trouble and Charge of Borrowing: And proportionally to this Want, so will every one have it, whatever Price it cost him. Wherein the Skilful, I say, will always so manage it, as to avoid the Prohibition of your Law, and keep out of its Penalty, do what you can.

"The Unavoidable Consequences of such a Law"

1. It will make the Difficulty of Borrowing and Lending much greater; whereby Trade (the Foundation of Riches) will be obstructed.

2. It will be a Prejudice to none but those who most need Assistance and Help, I mean Widows and Orphans, and others uninstructed in the Arts and Managements of more skilful Men; whose Estates lying in Money, they will be sure, especially Orphans, to have no more Profit of their Money, than what Interest the Law barely allows.

3. It will mightily increase the Advantage of Bankers and Scriveners, and other such expert Brokers: Who skilled in the Arts of putting out Money according to the true and natural Value, which the present State of Trade, Money and Debts, shall always raise Interest to, they will infallibly get, what the true Value of Interest shall be, above the Legal. For Men finding the Convenience of Lodging their Money in Hands, where they can be sure of it at short Warning, the Ignorant and Lazy will be (the most) forward to put it into these Men's hands, who are known willingly to receive it, and where they can readily have the whole, or a part, upon any sudden Occasion, that may call for it.

4. I may reckon it as one of the probable Consequences of such a Law, That it is likely to cause great Perjury in the Nation; a Crime, than which nothing is more carefully to be prevented by Lawmakers, not only by Penalties, that shall attend apparent and proved Perjury; but by avoiding and lessening, as much as may be, the Temptations to it....

'Tis in vain therefore to go about effectually to reduce the price of Interest by a Law; and you may as rationally hope to set a fixed Rate upon the Hire of Houses, or Ships, as of Money. He that wants a Vessel, rather than lose his Market, will not stick to have it at the Market Rate, and find ways to do it, with security to the Owner, though the Rate were limited by a Law: And he that wants Money, rather than lose his Voyage, or his Trade, will pay the Natural Interest for it; and submit to such ways of Conveyance, as shall keep the Lender out of the reach of the Law.

So that your Act, at best, will serve only to increase the Arts of Lending, but not at all lessen the Charge of the Borrower: He 'tis likely shall with more trouble, and going farther about, pay also the more for his Money; unless you intend to break in only upon Mortgages and Contracts already made, and (which is not to be supposed) by a Law, *post factum*, void Bargains lawfully made, and give to Richard what is Peters Due, for no other Reason, but because one was Borrower, and the other Lender....

"What will be the Consequences of such a Law?"

1. It will be a loss to Widows, Orphans, and all those who have their Estate in Money, one third of their Estates: which will be a very hard case upon a

great number of People, and it is warily to be considered by the Wisdom of the Nation, whether they will thus at one blow, fine and impoverish a great and innocent part of the People, who having their Estates in Money, have as much Right to make as much of their Money, as it is worth, (for more they cannot) as the Landlord has to let his Land for as much as it will yield. To Fine Men one Third of their Estates, without any Crime or Offence committed, seems very hard.

2. As it will be a considerable Loss and Injury to the moneyed Man, so it will be no Advantage at all to the Kingdom....

3. It will be a Gain to the Borrowing Merchant, For if he Borrow at Four per Cent. and his Returns be Twelve per Cent. He will have Eight Per Cent and the Lender Four: Whereas now they divide the profit equally at Six Per Cent....

4. It will hinder Trade. For there being a certain proportion of Money necessary for driving such a proportion of Trade, so much Money of this as lies still, lessens so much of the Trade.... Trade as is lost, so much of our Riches must necessarily go with it; and the over-balancing of Trade between us and our Neighbors, must inevitably carry away our Money, and quickly leave us Poor, and exposed. Gold and Silver though they serve for few yet they command all the conveniences of life; and therefore in a plenty of them consists Riches.

Riches do not consist in having more Gold and Silver, but in having more in proportion, than the rest of the World, or than our Neighbors, whereby we are enabled to procure to our selves a greater Plenty of the Conveniences of Life than comes within the reach of Neighboring kingdoms and States, who, sharing the Gold and Silver of the World in a less proportion, want the means of Plenty and Power, and so are Poorer.

"There are but Two Ways of Growing Rich"

In a Country not furnished with Mines there are but two ways of growing Rich, either Conquest, or Commerce....

Commerce therefore is the only way left to us, either for Riches or Subsistence, for this the advantages of our Situation, as well as the Industry and Inclination of our People, bold and skilful at Sea, do Naturally fit us: By this the Nation of England has been hitherto Supported, and Trade left almost to it self, and assisted only by the Natural Advantages above-mentioned, brought us in Plenty and Riches, and always set this kingdom in a rank equal, if not superior to any of its Neighbors: And would no doubt without any difficulty have continued it so, if the more enlarged, and better understood Interest of Trade, since the Improvement of Navigation, had not raised us many Rivals; and the amazing Politicks of some late Reigns, let in other Competitors with us for the Sea, who will be sure to seize to themselves whatever parts of Trade our mismanagement, or want of Money, shall let slip out of our Hands....

Trade then is necessary to the producing of Riches, and Money necessary to the carrying on of Trade. This is principally to be looked after and taken Care of....

And so the reducing of Money, to Four per Cent which will discourage Men from Lending, will be a Loss to the Kingdom, in stopping so much of the Current Of Money, which turns the Wheels of Trade.

The Farmer and the Kingdom Analogy

A kingdom grows Rich, or Poor just as a Farmer doth, and no otherwise. Let us suppose the whole Isle of Portland one Farm; and that the Owner, besides what serves his Family, carries to Market to Weymouth and Dorchester, &c. Cattle, Corn, Butter, Cheese, Wool, or Cloth, Lead and Tin, all Commodities produced and wrought within his Farm of Portland, to the value of a Thousand Pounds; yearly; and for this, brings home in Salt, Wine, Oil, Spice, Linen and Silks, to the value of Nine hundred Pounds, and the remaining Hundred Pounds in Money....

A Farm and a kingdom in this respect differ no more than as greater and less. We may Trade, and be busy, and grow Poor by it, unless we regulate our Expenses; If to this we are Idle, Negligent, Dishonest, Malicious, and disturb the Sober and Industrious in their Business, let it be upon what pretence it will, we shall Ruin the faster....

The Necessity of a certain Proportion of Money to Trade, (I conceive) lies in this, That Money in its Circulation driving the several Wheels of Trade, whilst it keeps in that Channel (for some of it will unavoidably be drained into standing Pools) is all shared between the Landholder, whose Land affords the Materials; The Laborer, who works them; The Broker, (i.e.) Merchant and Shopkeeper, who distributes them to those, that want them; And the Consumer, who spends them. Now Money is necessary to all these sorts of Men, as serving both for Counters and for Pledges, and so carrying with it even Reckoning, and Security, that he, that receives it, shall have the same Value for it again, of other things that he wants, whenever he pleases. The one of these it does by its Stamp and Denomination; the other by its intrinsic Value, which is its Quantity....

Money and Trade

To return to the business in hand, and show the necessity of a Proportion of Money to Trade. Every Man must have at least so much Money, or so timely Recruits, as may in hand, or in a short distance of time, satisfy his Creditor who supplies him with the necessaries of Life, or of his Trade. For no body has any longer these necessary Supplies, than he has Money, or Credit, which is nothing else but an Assurance of Money in some short time. So that it is requisite to Trade that there should be so much Money, as to keep up the Landholders, Laborers and Brokers Credit: And therefore ready Money must be constantly exchanged for Wares and Labor, or follow within a short time after.

This shows the necessity of some Proportion of Money to Trade: But what Proportion that is, is hard to determine; because it depends not barely on the quantity of Money, but the quickness of its Circulation....

By what has been said, we may see what Injury the Lowering of Interest is like to do us by hindering Trade, when it shall either make the Foreigner call home his Money, or your own People backward to Lend, the Reward not being judged proportional to the risk....

"Industrious and Thriving Men"

All Things that are Bought and Sold, raise and fall their price in proportion, as there are more Buyers or Sellers. Where there are a great many Sellers to a few Buyers, there use what Art you will, the thing to be Sold will be cheap. On the other side, turn the Tables, and raise up a great many Buyers for a few Sellers, and the same thing will immediately grow dear. This Rule holds in Land as well as all other Commodities, and is the Reason, why in England at the same time, that Land in some places is at seventeen or eighteen Years Purchase, it is about others, where there are profitable Manufactures, at two or three and twenty Years Purchase: Because there (Men thriving and getting Money by their Industry, and willing to leave their Estates to their Children in Land, as the surest, and most lasting Provision, and not so liable to Casualties as Money in untrading or unskillful Hands) there are many Buyers ready always to Purchase, but few Sellers.

For the Land thereabout being already possessed by that sort of Industrious and Thriving Men, they have neither need, nor will, to Sell. In such places of Manufacture, the Riches of the one not arising from the squandering and waste of another, (as it doth in other places where Men live lazily upon the product of the Land) the Industry of the People bringing in increase of Wealth from remote Parts, makes plenty of Money there without the impoverishing of their Neighbors. And when the thriving Tradesman has got more, than he can well employ in Trade, his next Thoughts are to look out for a Purchase, but it must be a Purchase in the Neighborhood, where the Estate may be under his Eye, and within convenient distance, that the Care and Pleasure of his Farm may not take him off from the Engagements of his Calling, nor remove his Children too far from him, or the Trade he breeds them up in....

"Should there be no Law at all to Regulate Interest?"

If this be so, that Interest cannot be regulated by Law, or that if it could, yet the reducing of it to Four per cent would do more harm than good: What then should there (will you say) be no Law at all to regulate Interest? I say not so. For,

1. It is necessary that there should be a stated Rate of Interest, that in Debts and Forbearances, where Contract has not settled it between the Parties, the Law might give a Rule, and Courts of Judicature might know what Damages to allow. This may, and therefore should, be Regulated.

2. That in the present current of running Cash, which now takes its course almost all to London, and is Engrossed by a very few Hands in Comparison, young Men, and those in Want, might not too easily be exposed to Extortion and Oppression; and the dexterous and combining Money Jobbers not have too great and unbounded a Power, to Prey upon the Ignorance or Necessity of Borrowers. There would not be much danger of this, if Money were more equally distributed into the several quarters of England, and into a greater number of Hands, according to the Exigencies of Trade....

The Example of Holland

To this I hear some say, That the Dutch, Skilful in all Arts of promoting Trade, to out-do us in this, as well as all other Advancements of it, have observed this Rule, viz, That when we fell Interest in England from Ten to Eight, they presently sunk Interest in Holland to Four per Cent and again, when we lowered it to Six they fell it to Three per Cent thereby to keep the Advantage which the lowness of Interest gives to Trade. From whence these Men readily conclude, That the falling of Interest will advance Trade in England. To which I answer,

1. That this looks like an Argument, rather made for the present Occasion, to mislead those who are credulous enough to swallow it, than arising from true Reason, and matter of Fact. For if lowering of Interest were so advantageous to Trade, why did the Dutch so constancy take their measures only by us, and not as well by some other of their Neighbors, with whom they have as great or greater Commerce than with us? This is enough at first sight to make one suspect this, to be Dust only raised, to throw in Peoples eyes, and a Suggestion made to serve a Purpose.

2. It will not be found true, That when we abated Interest here in England to Eight, the Dutch sunk it in Holland to Four per Cent by Law; or that there was any Law made in Holland to limit the Rate of Interest to Three per Cent when we reduced it in England to Six. It is true, John de Witt, when he managed the Affairs of Holland, setting himself to lessen the public Debt, and having actually paid some, and getting Money in a readiness to Pay others,

sent notice to all the Creditors, That those who would not take Four per Cent should come and receive their Money....

Interest, I grant these Men, is low in Holland: But it is so not as an effect of Law, or the politick Contrivance of the Government, to promote Trade; but as the Consequence of great Plenty of ready Money, when their Interest first fell. I say when it first fell: For being once brought low, and the Public having borrowed a great part of private Men's Money, and continuing in Debt, it must continue so though the Plenty of Money, which first brought Interest low, were very much decayed, and a great part of their Wealth were really gone....

The Case of the Landholder

I have heard it brought for a reason, why Interest should be reduced to Four per Cent That thereby the Landholder, who bears the burthen of the Public Charge, may be, in some degree eased by falling of Interest.

This Argument will be put right, if you say it will ease the Borrower, and lay the loss on the Lender: But it concerns not the Land in general, unless you will suppose all Landholders in Debt. But I hope, we may yet think that Men in England, who have Land, have Money too; and that Landed Men, as well as others, by their providence and good Husbandry, accommodating their Expenses to their Income, keep themselves from going backwards in the World.

That which is urged, as most deserving consideration and remedy in the case, is, That it is hard and unreasonable, that one, who has Mortgaged half his Land, should yet pay Taxes for the whole, whilst the Mortgagee goes away with the clear profit of an high Interest. To this I answer,

1. That if any Man has run himself in Debt, for the Service of his Country, 'tis fit the Public should reimburse him, and set him free. This is a care, that becomes the Public Justice; That Men, if they receive no Rewards, should, at least, be kept from Suffering, in having Served their Country.... Men's paying Taxes of Mortgaged Lands, is a punishment for ill husbandry, which ought to be discouraged: But it concerns very little the Frugal and the Thrifty.

2. Another thing to be said in reply to this, is, That it is with Gentlemen in the Country, as with Tradesmen in the City. If they will own Titles to greater Estates than really they have, it is their own faults, and there is no way left to help them from Paying for them. The Remedy is in their own hands, to discharge themselves when they please....

"Money is the Measure of Commerce"

Being now upon the Consideration of Interest and Money, give me leave to say one Word more on this occasion, which may not be wholly unseasonable at this time. I hear a Talk up and down of raising our Money, as a means to retain our Wealth, and keep our Money from being carried away. I wish those that use the Phrase of raising our Money, had some clear Notion annexed to it; and that then they would examine, Whether, that being true, it would at all serve to those Ends, for which is proposed....

Money is the measure of Commerce, and of the rate of everything, and therefore ought to be kept (as all other measures) as steady and invariable as may be. But this cannot be, if your Money be made of two Metals, whose proportion, and consequently whose price, constantly varies in respect of one another. Silver, for many Reasons, is the fittest of all metals to be this measure, and therefore generally made use of for Money. But then it is very unfit and inconvenient, that Gold, or any other Metal, should be made current Legal Money, at a standing settled Rate.

This is to set a Rate upon the varying value of Things by Law, which justly cannot be done; and is, as I have showed, as far as it prevails, a constant damage and prejudice to the Country, where it is practiced. Suppose Fifteen to one be now the exact Par between Gold and Silver. What Law can make it lasting; and establish it so, that next Year, or twenty Years hence, this shall be the just value of Gold to Silver, and that one Ounce of Gold shall be just worth fifteen Ounces of Silver, neither more nor less? 'Tis possible, the East-India Trade sweeping away great Sums of Gold, may make it scarcer in Europe. Perhaps the Guinea Trade, and Mines of Peru, affording it in greater abundance, may make it more plentiful; and so its value in respect of Silver, come on the one side to be as sixteen, or on the other as fourteen to one.

And can any Law you shall make alter this proportion here, when it is so every where else round about you? If your Law set it at fifteen, when it is at the free Market Rate, in the Neighboring Countries, as sixteen to one; Will they not send hither their Silver to fetch away your Gold at One sixteen loss to you? Or if you will keep its Rate to Silver, as fifteen to one, when in Holland, France, and Spain, its Market value is but fourteen; Will they not send hither their Gold, and fetch away your Silver at One fifteen loss to you? This is unavoidable, if you will make Money of both Gold and Silver at the same time, and set Rates upon them by Law in respect of one another....

Removing the "Great Mystery" of Money

This business of Money and Coinage is by some Men, and amongst them some very Ingenious Persons, thought a great Mystery, and very hard to be understood. Not that truly in it self it is so: But because interested People that treat of it, wrap up the Secret they make advantage of in mystical, obscure, and unintelligible ways of Talking; Which Men, from a preconceived opinion of the difficulty of the subject, taking for Sense, in a matter not easy to be penetrated, but by the Men of Art, let pass for Current without Examination. Whereas, would they look into those Discourses, enquire what meaning their Words have, they would find, for the most part, either their Positions to be false; their Deductions to be wrong; or (which often happens) their words to have no distinct meaning at all. Where none of these be, there their plain, true, honest Sense, would prove very easy and intelligible, if expressed in ordinary and direct Language....

Jean-Jacques Rousseau

The Two Discourses

The First Discourse

Preface

I foresee that I shall not readily be forgiven for having taken up the position I have adopted. Setting myself up against all that is nowadays most admired, I can expect no less than a universal outcry against me: nor is the approbation of a few sensible men enough to make me count on that of the public. But I have taken my stand, and I shall be at no pains to please either intellectuals or men of the world. There are in all ages men born to be in bondage to the opinions of the society in which they live. There are not a few, who to-day play the free-thinker and the philosopher, who would, if they had lived in the time of the League, have been no more than fanatics. No author, who has a mind to outlive his own age, should write for such readers.

A word more and I have done. As I did not expect the honor conferred on me, I had, since sending in my Discourse, so altered and enlarged it as almost to make it a new work; but in the circumstances I have felt bound to publish it just as it was when it received the prize. I have only added a few notes, and left two alterations which are easily recognizable, of which the Academy possibly might not have approved. The respect, gratitude and even justice I owe to that body seemed to me to demand this acknowledgment.

A Discourse on the Moral Effects of the Arts and Sciences

The question before me is, "Whether the Restoration of the arts and sciences has had the effect of purifying or corrupting morals." Which side am I to take? That, gentlemen, which becomes an honest man, who is sensible of his own ignorance, and thinks himself none the worse for it.

I feel the difficulty of treating this subject fittingly, before the tribunal which is to judge of what I advance. How can I presume to belittle the sciences before one of the most learned assemblies in Europe, to commend ignorance in a famous Academy, and reconcile my contempt for study with the respect due to the truly learned?

I was aware of these inconsistencies, but not discouraged by them. It is not science, I said to myself, that I am attacking; it is virtue that I am defending, and that before virtuous men—and goodness is even dearer to the good than learning to the learned....

The First Part

It is a noble and beautiful spectacle to see man raising himself, so to speak, from nothing by his own exertions; dissipating, by the light of reason, all the thick clouds in which he was by nature enveloped; mounting above himself; soaring in thought even to the celestial regions; like the sun, encompassing with giant strides the vast extent of the universe; and, what is still grander and more wonderful, going back into himself, there to study man and get to know his own nature, his duties and his end. All these miracles we have seen renewed within the last few generations.

Europe had relapsed into the barbarism of the earliest ages; the inhabitants of this part of the world, which is at present so highly enlightened, were plunged, some centuries ago, in a state still worse than ignorance. A scientific jargon, more despicable than mere ignorance, had usurped the name of knowledge, and opposed an almost invincible obstacle to its restoration....

So long as government and law provide for the security and well-being of men in their common life, the arts, literature and the sciences, less despotic though perhaps more powerful, fling garlands of flowers over the chains which weigh them down. They stifle in men's breasts that sense of original liberty, for which they seem to have been born; cause them to love their own slavery, and so make of them what is called a civilized people.

Necessity raised up thrones; the arts and sciences have made them strong. Powers of the earth, cherish all talents and protect those who cultivate them. Civilized peoples, cultivate such pursuits: to them, happy slaves, you owe that delicacy and exquisiteness of taste, which is so much your boast, that sweetness of disposition and urbanity of manners which make intercourse so easy and agreeable among you—in a word, the appearance of all the virtues, without being in possession of one of them....

Richness of apparel may proclaim the man of fortune, and elegance the man of taste; but true health and manliness are known by different signs. It is under the homespun of the laborer, and not beneath the gilt and tinsel of the courtier, that we should look for strength and vigor of body.

External ornaments are no less foreign to virtue, which is the strength and activity of the mind. The honest man is an athlete, who loves to wrestle stark naked; he scorns all those vile trappings, which prevent the exertion of his strength, and were, for the most part, invented only to conceal some deformity.

Before art had molded our behavior, and taught our passions to speak an artificial language, our morals were rude but natural; and the different ways in which we behaved proclaimed at the first glance the difference of our dispositions. Human nature was not at bottom better then than now; but men found their security in the ease with which they could see through one another, and this advantage, of which we no longer feel the value, prevented their having many vices.

In our day, now that more subtle study and a more refined taste have reduced the art of pleasing to a system, there prevails in modern manners a servile and deceptive conformity; so that one would think every mind had been cast in the same mould. Politeness requires this thing; decorum that; ceremony has its forms, and fashion its laws, and these we must always follow, never the promptings of our own nature.

We no longer dare seem what we really are, but lie under a perpetual restraint; in the meantime the herd of men, which we call society, all act under the same circumstances exactly alike, unless very particular and powerful motives prevent them. Thus we never know with whom we have to deal; and even to know our friends we must wait for some critical and pressing occasion; that is, till it is too late; for it is on those very occasions that such knowledge is of use to us.

What a train of vices must attend this uncertainty! Sincere friendship, real esteem, and perfect confidence are banished from among men. Jealousy, suspicion, fear, coldness, reserve, hate and fraud lie constantly concealed under that uniform and deceitful veil of politeness; that boasted candor and urbanity, for which we are indebted to the light and leading of this age. We shall no longer take in vain by our oaths the name of our Creator; but we shall insult Him with our blasphemies, and our scrupulous ears will take no offence. We have grown too modest to brag of our own deserts; but we do not scruple to decry those of others. We do not grossly outrage even our enemies, but artfully calumniate them. Our hatred of other nations diminishes, but patriotism dies with it. Ignorance is held in contempt; but a dangerous skepticism has succeeded it. Some vices indeed are condemned and others grown dishonorable; but we have still many that are honored with the names of virtues, and it is become necessary that we should either have, or at least pretend to have them. Let who will extol the moderation of our modern sages, I see nothing in it but a refinement of intemperance as unworthy of my commendation as their artificial simplicity.

Such is the purity to which our morals have attained; this is the virtue we have made our own. Let the arts and sciences claim the share they have had in this salutary work. I shall add but one reflection more; suppose an inhabitant of some distant country should endeavor to form an idea of European morals from the state of the sciences, the perfection of the arts, the propriety of our public entertainments, the politeness of our behavior, the affability of our conversation, our constant professions of benevolence, and from those tumultuous assemblies of people of all ranks, who seem, from morning till night, to have no other care than to oblige one another. Such a stranger, I maintain, would arrive at a totally false view of our morality.

Where there is no effect, it is idle to look for a cause: but here the effect is certain and the depravity actual; our minds have been corrupted in proportion as the arts and sciences have improved. Will it be said, that this is a misfortune peculiar to the present age? No, gentlemen, the evils resulting from our vain curiosity are as old as the world. The daily ebb and flow of the tides are not more regularly influenced by the moon, than the morals of a people by the progress of the arts and sciences. As their light has risen above our horizon, virtue has taken flight, and the same phenomenon has been constantly observed in all times and places....

Contrast with these instances the morals of those few nations which, being preserved from the contagion of useless knowledge, have by their virtues become happy in themselves and afforded an example to the rest of the world. Such were the first inhabitants of Persia, a nation so singular that virtue was taught among them in the same manner as the sciences are with us. They very easily subdued Asia, and possess the exclusive glory of having had the history of their political institutions regarded as a philosophical romance. Such were the Scythians, of whom such wonderful eulogies have come down to us. Such were the Germans, whose simplicity, innocence and virtue, afforded a most delightful contrast to the pen of an historian, weary of describing the baseness and villainies of an enlightened, opulent and voluptuous nation. Such had been even Rome in the days of its poverty and ignorance. And such has shown itself to be, even in our own times, that rustic nation, whose justly renowned courage not even adversity could conquer, and whose fidelity no example could corrupt....

Can it be forgotten that, in the very heart of Greece, there arose a city as famous for the happy ignorance of its inhabitants, as for the wisdom of its laws; a republic of demi-gods rather than of men, so greatly superior their virtues seemed to those of mere humanity? Sparta, eternal proof of the vanity of science, while the vices, under the conduct of the fine arts, were being introduced into Athens, even while its tyrant was carefully collecting together the works of the prince of poets, was driving from her walls artists and the arts, the learned and their learning!...

It is true that, among the Athenians, there were some few wise men who withstood the general torrent, and preserved their integrity even in the company of the muses. But hear the judgment which the principal, and most unhappy of them, passed on the artists and learned men of his day.

"I have considered the poets," says he, "and I look upon them as people whose talents impose both on themselves and on others; they give themselves out for wise men, and are taken for such; but in reality they are anything sooner than that."

"From the poets," continues Socrates, "I turned to the artists. Nobody was more ignorant of the arts than myself; nobody was more fully persuaded that the artists were possessed of amazing knowledge. I soon discovered, however, that they were in as bad a way as the poets, and that both had fallen into the same misconception. Because the most skilful of them excel others in their particular jobs, they think themselves wiser than all the rest of mankind. This arrogance spoilt all their skill in my eyes, so that, putting myself in the place of the oracle, and asking myself whether I would rather be what I am or what they are, know what they know, or know that I know nothing, I very readily answered, for myself and the god, that I had rather remain as I am.

"None of us, neither the sophists, nor the poets, nor the orators, nor the artists, nor I, know what is the nature of the *true*, the *good*, or the *beautiful*. But there is this difference between us; that, though none of these people know anything, they all think they know something; whereas for my part, if I know nothing, I am at least in no doubt of my ignorance. So the superiority of wisdom, imputed to me by the oracle, is reduced merely to my being fully convinced that I am ignorant of what I do not know."

Thus we find Socrates, the wisest of men in the judgment of the god, and the most learned of all the Athenians in the opinion of all Greece, speaking in praise of ignorance. Were he alive now, there is little reason to think that our modern scholars and artists would induce him to change his mind. No, gentlemen, that honest man would still persist in despising our vain sciences. He would lend no aid to swell the flood of books that flows from every quarter: he would leave to us, as he did to his disciples, only the example and memory of his virtues; that is the noblest method of instructing mankind....

But let pass the distance of time and place, and let us see what has happened in our own time and country; or rather let us banish odious descriptions that might offend our delicacy, and spare ourselves the pains of repeating the same things under different names. It was not for nothing that I invoked the Manes of Fabricius; for what have I put into his mouth, that might not have come with as much propriety from Louis the Twelfth or Henry the Fourth? It is true that in France Socrates would not have drunk the hemlock, but he would have drunk of a potion infinitely more bitter, of insult, mockery and contempt a hundred times worse than death.

Thus it is that luxury, profligacy and slavery, have been, in all ages, the scourge of the efforts of our pride to emerge from that happy state of ignorance, in which the wisdom of providence had placed us. That thick veil with which it has covered all its operations seems to be a sufficient proof that it never designed us for such fruitless researches. But is there, indeed, one lesson it has taught us, by which we have rightly profited, or which we have neglected with impunity? Let men learn for once that nature would have preserved them from science, as a mother snatches a dangerous weapon from the hands of her child. Let them know that all the secrets she hides are so many evils from which she protects them, and that the very difficulty they find in acquiring knowledge is not the least of her bounty towards them. Men are perverse; but they would have been far worse, if they had had the misfortune to be born learned.

How humiliating are these reflections to humanity, and how mortified by them our pride should be! What! it will be asked, is uprightness the child of ignorance? Is virtue inconsistent with learning? What consequences might not be drawn from such suppositions? But to reconcile these apparent contradictions, we need only examine closely the emptiness and vanity of those pompous titles, which are so liberally bestowed on human knowledge, and which so blind our judgment. Let us consider, therefore, the arts and sciences in themselves. Let us see what must result from their advancement, and let us not hesitate to admit the truth of all those points on which our arguments coincide with the inductions we can make from history.

The Second Part

What a variety of dangers surrounds us! What a number of wrong paths present themselves in the investigation of the sciences! Through how many errors, more perilous than truth itself is useful, must we not pass to arrive at it? The disadvantages we lie under are evident; for falsehood is capable of an infinite variety of combinations; but the truth has only one manner of being. Besides, where is the man who sincerely desires to find it? Or even admitting his good will, by what characteristic marks is he sure of knowing it? Amid the infinite diversity of opinions where is the criterion by which we may certainly judge of it? Again, what is still more difficult, should we even be fortunate enough to discover it, who among us will know how to make right use of it?

If our sciences are futile in the objects they propose, they are no less dangerous in the effects they produce. Being the effect of idleness, they generate idleness in their turn; and an irreparable loss of time is the first prejudice which they must necessarily cause to society. To live without doing some good is a great evil as well in the political as in the moral world; and hence every useless citizen should be regarded as a pernicious person. Tell me then, illustrious philosophers, of whom we learn the ratios in which attraction acts in vacuum; and in the revolution of the planets, the relations of spaces traversed in equal times; by whom we are taught what curves have conjugate points, points of inflexion, and cusps; how the soul and body correspond, like two clocks, without actual communication; what planets may be inhabited; and what insects reproduce in an extraordinary manner. Answer me, I say, you from whom we receive all this sublime information, whether we should have been less numerous, worse governed, less formidable, less flourishing, or more perverse, supposing you had taught us none of all these fine things.

Reconsider therefore the importance of your productions; and, since the labors of the most enlightened of our learned men and the best of our citizens are of so little utility, tell us what we ought to think of that numerous herd of obscure writers and useless littérateurs, who devour without any return the substance of the State.

Useless, do I say? Would God they were! Society would be more peaceful, and morals less corrupt. But these vain and futile declaimers go forth on all sides, armed with their fatal paradoxes, to sap the foundations of our faith, and nullify virtue. They smile contemptuously at such old names as patriotism and religion, and consecrate their talents and philosophy to the destruction and defamation of all that men hold sacred. Not that they bear any real hatred to virtue or dogma; they are the enemies of public opinion alone; to bring them to the foot of the altar, it would be enough to banish them to a land of atheists. What extravagancies will not the rage of singularity induce men to commit!

The waste of time is certainly a great evil; but still greater evils attend upon literature and the arts. One is luxury, produced like them by indolence and vanity. Luxury is seldom unattended by the arts and sciences; and they are always attended by luxury. I know that our philosophy, fertile in paradoxes, pretends, in contradiction to the experience of all ages, that luxury contributes to the splendor of States. But, without insisting on the necessity of sumptuary laws, can it be denied that rectitude of morals is essential to the duration of empires, and that luxury is diametrically opposed to such rectitude?

Let it be admitted that luxury is a certain indication of wealth; that it even serves, if you will, to increase such wealth: what conclusion is to be drawn from this paradox, so worthy of the times? And what will become of virtue if riches are to be acquired at any cost? The politicians of the ancient world were always talking of morals and virtue; ours speak of nothing but commerce and money....

It is thus that the dissolution of morals, the necessary consequence of luxury, brings with it in its turn the corruption of taste. Further, if by chance there be found among men of average ability, an individual with enough strength of mind to refuse to comply with the spirit of the age, and to debase himself by puerile productions, his lot will be hard. He will die in indigence and oblivion. This is not so much a prediction, as a fact already confirmed by experience!...

We cannot reflect on the morality of mankind without contemplating with pleasure the picture of the simplicity which prevailed in the earliest times. This image may be justly compared to a beautiful coast, adorned only by the hands of nature; towards which our eyes are constantly turned, and which we see receding with regret. While men were innocent and virtuous and loved to have the gods for witnesses of their actions, they dwelt together in the same huts; but when they became vicious, they grew tired of such inconvenient onlookers, and banished them to magnificent temples. Finally, they expelled their deities even from these, in order to dwell there themselves; or at least the temples of the gods were no longer more magnificent than the palaces of the citizens. This was the height of degeneracy; nor could vice ever be carried to greater lengths than when it was seen, supported, as it were, at the doors of the great, on columns of marble, and graven on Corinthian capitals.

As the conveniences of life increase, as the arts are brought to perfection, and luxury spreads, true courage flags, the virtues disappear; and all this is the effect of the sciences and of those arts which are exercised in the privacy of men's dwellings. When the Goths ravaged Greece, the libraries only escaped the flames owing to an opinion that was set on foot among them, that it was best to leave the enemy with a possession so calculated to divert their attention from military exercises, and keep them engaged in indolent and sedentary occupations....

Our gardens are adorned with statues and our galleries with pictures. What would you imagine these masterpieces of art, thus exhibited to public admiration, represent? The great men, who have defended their country, or the still greater men who have enriched it by their virtues? Far from it. They are the images of every perversion of heart and mind, carefully selected from ancient mythology, and presented to the early curiosity of our children, doubtless that they may have before their eyes the representations of vicious actions, even before they are able to read.

Whence arise all those abuses, unless it be from that fatal inequality introduced among men by the difference of talents and the cheapening of virtue? This is the most evident effect of all our studies, and the most dangerous of all their consequences. The question is no longer whether a man is honest, but whether he is clever. We do not ask whether a book is useful, but whether it is well-written. Rewards are lavished on with and ingenuity, while virtue is left unhonored. There are a thousand prizes for fine discourses, and none for good actions. I should be glad, however, to know whether the honor attaching to the best discourse that ever wins the prize in this Academy is comparable with the merit of having founded the prize.

A wise man does not go in chase of fortune; but he is by no means insensible to glory, and when he sees it so ill distributed, his virtue, which might have been animated by a little emulation, and turned to the advantage of society, droops and dies away in obscurity and indigence. It is for this reason that the agreeable arts must in time everywhere be preferred to the useful; and this truth has been but too much confirmed since the revival of the arts and sciences. We have physicists, geometricians, chemists, astronomers, poets, musicians, and painters in plenty; but we have no longer a citizen among us; or if there be found a few scattered over our abandoned countryside, they are left to perish there unnoticed and neglected. Such is the condition to which we are reduced, and such are our feelings towards those who give us our daily bread, and our children milk....

But if the progress of the arts and sciences has added nothing to our real happiness; if it has corrupted our morals, and if that corruption has vitiated our taste, what are we to think of the herd of text-book authors, who have removed those impediments which nature purposely laid in the way to the Temple of the Muses, in order to guard its approach and try the powers of those who might be tempted to seek knowledge? What are we to think of those compilers who have indiscreetly broken open the door of the sciences, and introduced into their sanctuary a populace unworthy to approach it, when it was greatly to be wished that all who should be found incapable of making a considerable progress in the career of learning should have been repulsed at the entrance, and thereby cast upon those arts which are useful to society.

A man who will be all his life a bad versifier, or a third-rate geometrician, might have made nevertheless an excellent clothier. Those whom nature intended for her disciples have not needed masters. Bacon, Descartes and Newton, those teachers of mankind, had themselves no teachers. What guide indeed could have taken them so far as their sublime genius directed them? Ordinary masters would only have cramped their intelligence, by confining it within the narrow limits of their own capacity. It was from the obstacles they met with at first, that they learned to exert themselves, and bestirred themselves to traverse the vast field which they covered. If it be proper to allow some men to apply themselves to the study of the arts and sciences, it is only those who feel themselves able to walk alone in their footsteps and to outstrip them. It belongs only to these few to raise monuments to the glory of the human understanding....

But so long as power alone is on one side, and knowledge and understanding alone on the other, the learned will seldom make great objects their study, princes will still more rarely do great actions, and the peoples will continue to be, as they are, mean, corrupt and miserable.

As for us, ordinary men, on whom Heaven has not been pleased to bestow such great talents; as we are not destined to reap such glory, let us remain in our obscurity. Let us not covet a reputation we should never attain, and which, in the present state of things, would never make up to us for the trouble it would have cost us, even if we were fully qualified to obtain it. Why should we build our happiness on the opinions of others, when we can find it in our own hearts? Let us leave to others the task of instructing mankind in their duty, and confine ourselves to the discharge of our own. We have no occasion for greater knowledge than this.

Virtue! sublime science of simple minds, are such industry and preparation needed if we are to know you? Are not your principles graven on every heart? Need we do more, to learn your laws, than examine ourselves, and listen to the voice of conscience, when the passions are silent?

This is the true philosophy, with which we must learn to be content, without envying the fame of those celebrated men, whose names are immortal in the republic of letters. Let us, instead of envying them, endeavor to make, between them and us, that honorable distinction which was formerly seen to exist between two great peoples, that the one knew how to speak, and the other how to act, aright.

The Second Discourse

The Second Part

"This Is Mine"
The first man who, having enclosed a piece of ground, bethought himself of saying *This is mine,* and found people simple enough to believe him, was the real founder of civil society. From how many crimes, wars and murders, from how many horrors and misfortunes might not any one have saved mankind, by pulling up the stakes, or filling up the ditch, and crying to his fellows, "Beware of listening to this impostor; you are undone if you once forget that the fruits of the earth belong to us all, and the earth itself to nobody." But there is great probability that things had then already come to such a pitch, that they could no longer continue as they were; for the idea of property depends on many prior ideas, which could only be acquired successively, and cannot have been formed all at once in the human mind. Mankind must have made very considerable progress, and acquired considerable knowledge and industry which they must also have transmitted and increased from age to age, before they arrived at this last point of the state of nature. Let us then go farther back, and endeavor to unify under a single point of view that slow succession of events and discoveries in the most natural order.

"The Condition of Infant Man"

Man's first feeling was that of his own existence, and his first care that of self-preservation. The produce of the earth furnished him with all he needed, and instinct told him how to use it. Hunger and other appetites made him at various times experience various modes of existence; and among these was one which urged him to propagate his species—a blind propensity that, having nothing to do with the heart, produced a merely animal act. The want once gratified, the two sexes knew each other no more; and even the offspring was nothing to its mother, as soon as it could do without her.

Such was the condition of infant man; the life of an animal limited at first to mere sensations, and hardly profiting by the gifts nature bestowed on him, much less capable of entertaining a thought of forcing anything from her. But difficulties soon presented themselves, and it became necessary to learn how to surmount them: the height of the trees, which prevented him from gathering their fruits, the competition of other animals desirous of the same fruits, and the ferocity of those who needed them for their own preservation, all obliged him to apply himself to bodily exercises. He had to be active, swift of foot, and vigorous in fight. Natural weapons, stones and sticks, were easily found: he learnt to surmount the obstacles of nature, to contend in case of necessity with other animals, and to dispute for the means of subsistence even with other men, or to indemnify himself for what he was forced to give up to a stronger.

The Development of the Human Race

In proportion as the human race grew more numerous, men's cares increased. The difference of soils, climates and seasons, must have introduced some differences into their manner of living. Barren years, long and sharp winters, scorching summers which parched the fruits of the earth, must have demanded a new industry. On the seashore and the banks of rivers, they invented the hook and line, and became fishermen and eaters of fish. In the forests they made bows and arrows, and became huntsmen and warriors. In cold countries they clothed themselves with the skins of the beasts they had slain. The lightning, a volcano, or some lucky chance acquainted them with fire, a new resource against the rigors of winter: they next learned how to preserve this element, then how to reproduce it, and finally how to prepare with it the flesh of animals which before they had eaten raw.

This repeated relevance of various beings to himself, and one to another, would naturally give rise in the human mind to the perceptions of certain relations between them. Thus the relations which we denote by the terms, great, small, strong, weak, swift, slow, fearful, bold, and the like, almost insensibly compared at need, must have at length produced in him a kind of reflection, or rather a mechanical prudence, which would indicate to him the precautions most necessary to his security.

The new intelligence which resulted from this development increased his superiority over other animals, by making him sensible of it. He would now endeavor, therefore, to ensnare them, would play them a thousand tricks, and though many of them might surpass him in swiftness or in strength, would in time become the master of some and the scourge of others. Thus, the first time he looked into himself, he felt the first emotion of pride; and, at a time when he scarce knew how to distinguish the different orders of beings, by looking upon his species as of the highest order, he prepared the way for assuming pre-eminence as an individual....

"The Love of Well-Being...[becomes]...the Sole Motive of Human Action"

Taught by experience that the love of well-being is the sole motive of human actions, he found himself in a position to distinguish the few cases, in which mutual interest might justify him in relying upon the assistance of his fellows; and also the still fewer cases in which a conflict of interests might give cause to suspect them. In the former case, he joined in the same herd with them, or at most in some kind of loose association, that laid no restraint on its members, and lasted no longer than the transitory occasion that formed it. In the latter case, every one sought his own private advantage, either by open force, if he thought himself strong enough, or by address and cunning, if he felt himself the weaker.

In this manner, men may have insensibly acquired some gross ideas of mutual undertakings, and of the advantages of fulfilling them: that is, just so far as their present and apparent interest was concerned: for they were perfect strangers to foresight, and were so far from troubling themselves about the distant future, that they hardly thought of the morrow. If a deer was to be taken, every one saw that, in order to succeed, he must abide faithfully by his post: but if a hare happened to come within the reach of any one of them, it is not to be doubted that he pursued it without scruple, and, having seized his prey, cared very little, if by so doing he caused his companions to miss theirs. It is easy to understand that such intercourse would not require a language much more refined than that of rooks or monkeys, who associate together for much the same purpose....

These first advances enabled men to make others with greater rapidity. In proportion as they grew enlightened, they grew industrious. They ceased to fall asleep under the first tree, or in the first cave that afforded them shelter; they invented several kinds of implements of hard and sharp stones, which they used to dig up the earth, and to cut wood; they then made huts out of branches, and afterwards learnt to plaster them over with mud and clay. This was the epoch of a first revolution, which established and distinguished families, and introduced a kind of property, in itself the source of a thousand quarrels and conflicts. As, however, the strongest were probably the first to build themselves huts which they felt themselves able to defend, it may be concluded that the weak found it much easier and safer to imitate, than to attempt to dislodge them: and of those who were once provided with huts, none could have any inducement to appropriate that of his neighbor; not indeed so much because it did not belong to him, as because it could be of no use, and he could not make himself master of it without exposing himself to a desperate battle with the family which occupied it.

"How the Use of Speech Became Established"

The simplicity and solitude of man's life in this new condition, the paucity of his wants, and the implements he had invented to satisfy them, left him a great deal of leisure, which he employed to furnish himself with many conveniences unknown to his fathers: and this was the first yoke he inadvertently imposed on himself, and the first source of the evils he prepared for his descendants. For, besides continuing thus to enervate both body and mind, these conveniences lost with use almost all their power to please, and even degenerated into real needs, till the want of them became far more disagreeable than the possession of them had been pleasant. Men would have been unhappy at the loss of them, though the possession did not make them happy.

We can here see a little better how the use of speech became established, and insensibly improved in each family, and we may form a conjecture also concerning the manner in which various causes may have extended and accelerated the progress of language, by making it more and more necessary. Floods or earthquakes surrounded inhabited districts with precipices or waters: revolutions of the globe tore off portions from the continent, and made them islands. It is readily seen that among men thus collected and compelled to live together, a common idiom must have arisen much more easily than among those who still wandered through the forests of the continent. Thus it is very possible that after their first essays in navigation the islanders brought over the use of speech to the continent: and it is at least very probable that communities and languages were first established in islands, and even came to perfection there before they were known on the mainland.

Everything now begins to change its aspect. Men, who have up to now been roving in the woods, by taking to a more settled manner of life, come gradually together, form separate bodies, and at length in every country arises a distinct nation, united in character and manners, not by regulations or laws, but by uniformity of life and food, and the common influence of climate. Permanent neighborhood could not fail to produce, in time, some connection between different families. Among young people of opposite sexes, living in neighboring huts, the transient commerce required by nature soon led, through mutual intercourse, to another kind not less agreeable, and more permanent. Men began now to take the difference between objects into account, and to make comparisons; they acquired imperceptibly the ideas of beauty and merit, which soon gave rise to feelings of preference. In consequence of seeing each other often, they could not do without seeing each other constantly. A tender and pleasant feeling insinuated itself into their souls, and the least opposition turned it into an impetuous fury: with love arose jealousy; discord triumphed, and human blood was sacrificed to the gentlest of all passions.

Laying Aside "Their Original Wildness"

As ideas and feelings succeeded one another, and heart and head were brought into play, men continued to lay aside their original wildness; their private connections became every day more intimate as their limits extended. They accustomed themselves to assemble before their huts round a large tree; singing and dancing, the true offspring of love and leisure, became the amusement, or rather the occupation, of men and women thus assembled together with nothing else to do. Each one began to consider the rest, and to wish to be considered in turn; and thus a value came to be attached to public esteem. Whoever sang or danced best, whoever was the handsomest, the strongest, the most dexterous, or the most eloquent, came to be of most consideration; and this was the first step towards inequality, and at the same time towards vice. From these first distinctions arose on the one side vanity and contempt and on the other shame and envy: and the fermentation caused by these new leavens ended by producing combinations fatal to innocence and happiness.

As soon as men began to value one another, and the idea of consideration had got a footing in the mind, every one put in his claim to it, and it became impossible to refuse it to any with impunity. Hence arose the first obligations of civility even among savages; and every intended injury became an affront; because, besides the hurt which might result from it, the party injured was certain to find in it a contempt for his person, which was often more insupportable than the hurt itself.

Thus, as every man punished the contempt shown him by others, in proportion to his opinion of himself, revenge became terrible, and men bloody and cruel. This is precisely the state reached by most of the savage nations known to us: and it is for want of having made a proper distinction in our ideas, and see how very far they already are from the state of nature, that so many writers have hastily concluded that man is naturally cruel, and requires civil institutions to make him more mild; whereas nothing is more gentle than man in his primitive state, as he is placed by nature at an equal distance from the stupidity of brutes, and the fatal ingenuity of civilized man. Equally confined by instinct and reason to the sole care of guarding himself against the mischiefs which threaten him, he is restrained by natural compassion from doing any injury to others, and is not led to do such a thing even in return for injuries received. For, according to the axiom of the wise Locke, *There can be no injury, where there is no property....*

"Equality Disappeared, Property was Introduced, Work Became Indispensable"

So long as men remained content with their rustic huts, so long as they were satisfied with clothes made of the skins of animals and sewn together with thorns and fish-bones, adorned themselves only with feathers and shells, and continued to paint their bodies different colors, to improve and beautify their bows and arrows and to make with sharp-edged stones fishing boats or clumsy musical instruments; in a word, so long as they undertook only what a single person could accomplish, and confined themselves to such arts as did not require the joint labor of several hands, they lived free, healthy, honest and happy lives, so long as their nature allowed, and as they continued to enjoy the pleasures of mutual and independent intercourse. But from the moment one man began to stand in need of the help of another; from the moment it appeared advantageous to any one man to have enough provisions for two, equality disappeared, property was introduced, work became indispensable, and vast forests became smiling fields, which man had to water with the sweat of his brow, and where slavery and misery were soon seen to germinate and grow up with the crops.

Metallurgy and agriculture were the two arts which produced this great revolution. The poets tell us it was gold and silver, but, for the philosophers, it was iron and corn, which first civilized men, and ruined humanity. Thus both were unknown to the savages of America, who for that reason are still savage: the other nations also seem to have continued in a state of barbarism while they practiced only one of these arts. One of the best reasons, perhaps, why Europe has been, if not longer, at least more constantly and highly civilized than the rest of the world, is that it is at once the most abundant in iron and the most fertile in corn....

The invention of the other arts must therefore have been necessary to compel mankind to apply themselves to agriculture. No sooner were artificers wanted to smelt and forge iron, than others were required to maintain them; the more hands that were employed in manufactures, the fewer were left to provide for the common subsistence, though the number of mouths to be furnished with food remained the same: and as some required commodities in exchange for their iron, the rest at length discovered the method of making iron serve for the multiplication of commodities. By this means the arts of husbandry and agriculture were established on the one hand, and the art of working metals and multiplying their uses on the other.

"The Cultivation of the Earth"

The cultivation of the earth necessarily brought about its distribution; and property, once recognized, gave rise to the first rules of justice; for, to secure each man his own, it had to be possible for each to have something. Besides, as men began to look forward to the future, and all had something to lose, every one had reason to apprehend that reprisals would follow any injury he might do to another. This origin is so much the more natural, as it is impossible to conceive how property can come from anything but manual labor: for what else can a man add to things which he does not originally create, so as to make them his own property? It is the husbandman's labor alone that, giving him a title to the produce of the ground he has tilled, gives him a claim also to the land itself, at least till harvest, and so, from year to year, a constant possession which is easily transformed into property. When the ancients, says Grotius, gave to Ceres the title of Legislatrix, and to a festival celebrated in her honor the name of Thesmophoria, they meant by that that the distribution of lands had produced a new kind of right: that is to say, the right of property, which is different from the right deducible from the law of nature.

In this state of affairs, equality might have been sustained, had the talents of individuals been equal, and had, for example, the use of iron and the consumption of commodities always exactly balanced each other; but, as there was nothing to preserve this balance, it was soon disturbed; the strongest did most work; the most skilful turned his labor to best account; the most ingenious devised methods of diminishing his labor: the husbandman wanted more iron, or the smith more corn, and, while both labored equally, the one gained a great deal by his work, while the other could hardly support himself. Thus natural inequality unfolds itself insensibly with that of combination, and the difference between men, developed by their different circumstances, becomes more sensible and permanent in its effects, and begins to have an influence, in the same proportion, over the lot of individuals.

"Mankind in this New Situation"

I shall ...[now]...confine myself to a glance at mankind in this new situation.

Behold then all human faculties developed, memory and imagination in full play, egoism interested, reason active, and the mind almost at the highest point of its perfection. Behold all the natural qualities in action, the rank and condition of every man assigned him; not merely his share of property and his power to serve or injure others, but also his wit, beauty, strength or skill, merit or talents: and these being the only qualities capable of commanding respect, it soon became necessary to possess or to affect them.

It now became the interest of men to appear what they really were not. To be and to seem became two totally different things; and from this distinction sprang insolent pomp and cheating trickery, with all the numerous vices that go in their train. On the other hand, free and independent as men were before, they were now, in consequence of a multiplicity of new wants, brought into subjection, as it were, to all nature, and particularly to one another; and each became in some degree a slave even in becoming the master of other men: if rich, they stood in need of the services of others; if poor, of their assistance; and even a middle condition did not enable them to do without one another.

Man must now, therefore, have been perpetually employed in getting others to interest themselves in his lot, and in making them, apparently at least, if not really, find their advantage in promoting his own. Thus he must have been sly and artful in his behavior to some, and imperious and cruel to others; being under a kind of necessity to ill-use all the persons of whom he stood in need, when he could not frighten them into compliance, and did not judge it his interest to be useful to them. Insatiable ambition, the thirst of raising their respective fortunes, not so much from real want as from the desire to surpass others, inspired all men with a vile propensity to injure one another, and with a secret jealousy, which is the more dangerous, as it puts on the mask of benevolence, to carry its point with greater security.

In a word, there arose rivalry and competition on the one hand, and conflicting interests on the other, together with a secret desire on both of profiting at the expense of others. All these evils were the first effects of property, and the inseparable attendants of growing inequality.

"All Ran Headlong to their Chains"

Thus, as the most powerful or the most miserable considered their might or misery as a kind of right to the possessions of others, equivalent, in their opinion, to that of property, the destruction of equality was attended by the most terrible disorders. Usurpations by the rich, robbery by the poor, and the unbridled passions of both, suppressed the cries of natural compassion and the still feeble voice of justice, and filled men with avarice, ambition and vice. Between the title of the strongest and that of the first occupier, there arose perpetual conflicts, which never ended but in battles and bloodshed. The newborn state of society thus gave rise to a horrible state of war; men thus harassed and depraved were no longer capable of retracing their steps or renouncing the fatal acquisitions they had made, but, laboring by the abuse of the faculties which do them honor, merely to their own confusion, brought themselves to the brink of ruin.

It is impossible that men should not at length have reflected on so wretched a situation, and on the calamities that overwhelmed them. The rich, in particular, must have felt how much they suffered by a constant state of war, of which they bore all the expense; and in which, though all risked their lives, they alone risked their property. Besides, however speciously they might disguise their usurpations, they knew that they were founded on precarious and false titles; so that, if others took from them by force what they themselves had gained by force, they would have no reason to complain. Even those who had been enriched by their own industry, could hardly base their proprietorship on better claims. It was in vain to repeat, "I built this well; I gained this spot by my industry."

Who gave you your standing, it might be answered, and what right have you to demand payment of us for doing what we never asked you to do? Do you not know that numbers of your fellow-creatures are starving, for want of what you have too much of? You ought to have had the express and universal consent of mankind, before appropriating more of the common subsistence than you needed for your own maintenance. Destitute of valid reasons to justify and sufficient strength to defend himself, able to crush individuals with ease, but easily crushed himself by a troop of bandits, one against all, and incapable, on account of mutual jealousy, of joining with his equals against numerous enemies united by the common hope of plunder, the rich man, thus urged by necessity, conceived at length the profoundest plan that ever entered the mind of man: this was to employ in his favor the forces of those who attacked him, to make allies of his adversaries, to inspire them with different maxims, and to give them other institutions as favorable to himself as the law of nature was unfavorable.

With this view, after having represented to his neighbors the horror of a situation which armed every man against the rest, and made their possessions as burdensome to them as their wants, and in which no safety could be expected either in riches or in poverty, he readily devised plausible arguments to make them close with his design. "Let us join," said he, "to guard the weak from oppression, to restrain the ambitious, and secure to every man the possession of what belongs to him: let us institute rules of justice and peace, to which all without exception may be obliged to conform; rules that may in some measure make amends for the caprices of fortune, by subjecting equally the powerful and the weak to the observance of reciprocal obligations. Let us, in a word, instead of turning our forces against ourselves, collect them in a supreme power which may govern us by wise laws, protect and defend all the members of the association, repulse their common enemies, and maintain eternal harmony among us."

Far fewer words to this purpose would have been enough to impose on men so barbarous and easily seduced; especially as they had too many disputes among themselves to do without arbitrators, and too much ambition and avarice to go long without masters. All ran headlong to their chains, in hopes of securing their liberty; for they had just wit enough to perceive the advantages of political institutions, without experience enough to enable them to foresee the dangers. The most capable of foreseeing the dangers were the very persons who expected to benefit by them; and even the most prudent judged it not inexpedient to sacrifice one part of their freedom to ensure the rest; as a wounded man has his arm cut off to save the rest of his body.

Such was, or may well have been, the origin of society and law, which bound new fetters on the poor, and gave new powers to the rich; which irretrievably destroyed natural liberty, eternally fixed the law of property and inequality, converted clever usurpation into unalterable right, and, for the advantage of a few ambitious individuals, subjected all mankind to perpetual labor, slavery and wretchedness. It is easy to see how the establishment of one community made that of all the rest necessary, and how, in order to make head against united forces, the rest of mankind had to unite in turn. Societies soon multiplied and spread over the face of the earth, till hardly a corner of the world was left in which a man could escape the yoke, and withdraw his head from beneath the sword which he saw perpetually hanging over him by a thread. Civil right having thus become the common rule among the members of each community, the law of nature maintained its place only between different communities, where, under the name of the right of nations, it was qualified by certain tacit conventions, in order to make commerce practicable, and serve as a substitute for natural compassion, which lost, when applied to societies, almost all the influence it had over individuals, and survived no longer except in some great cosmopolitan spirits, who, breaking down the imaginary barriers that separate different peoples, follow the example of our Sovereign Creator, and include the whole human race in their benevolence....

"The Progress of Inequality"

The different forms of government owe their origin to the differing degrees of inequality which existed between individuals at the time of their institution. If there happened to be any one man among them pre-eminent in power, virtue, riches or personal influence, he became sole magistrate, and the State assumed the form of monarchy. If several, nearly equal in point of eminence, stood above the rest, they were elected jointly, and formed an aristocracy. Again, among a people who had deviated less from a state of nature, and between whose fortune or talents there was less disproportion, the supreme administration was retained in common, and a democracy was formed. It was discovered in process of time which of these forms suited men the best. Some peoples remained altogether subject to the laws; others soon came to obey their magistrates. The citizens labored to preserve their liberty; the subjects, irritated at seeing others enjoying a blessing they had lost, thought only of making slaves of their neighbors. In a word, on the one side arose riches and conquests, and on the other happiness and virtue....

If we follow the progress of inequality in these various revolutions, we shall find that the establishment of laws and of the right of property was its first term, the institution of magistracy the second, and the conversion of legitimate into arbitrary power the third and last; so that the condition of rich and poor was authorized by the first period; that of powerful and weak by the second; and only by the third that of master and slave, which is the last degree of inequality, and the term at which all the rest remain, when they have got so far, till the government is either entirely dissolved by new revolutions, or brought back again to legitimacy....

If this were the place to go into details, I could readily explain how, even without the intervention of government, inequality of credit and authority became unavoidable among private persons, as soon as their union in a single society made them compare themselves one with another, and take into account the differences which they found out from the continual intercourse every man had to have with his neighbors. These differences are of several kinds; but riches, nobility or rank, power and personal merit being the principal distinctions by which men form an estimate of each other in society, I could prove that the harmony or conflict of these different forces is the surest indication of the good or bad constitution of a State.

I could show that among these four kinds of inequality, personal qualities being the origin of all the others, wealth is the one to which they are all reduced in the end; for, as riches tend most immediately to the prosperity of individuals, and are easiest to communicate, they are used to purchase every other distinction. By this observation we are enabled to judge pretty exactly how far a people has departed from its primitive constitution, and of its progress towards the extreme term of corruption. I could explain how much this universal desire for reputation, honors and advancement, which inflames us all, exercises and holds up to comparison our faculties and powers; how it excites and multiplies our passions, and, by creating universal competition and rivalry, or rather enmity, among men, occasions numberless failures, successes and disturbances of all kinds by making so many aspirants run the same course. I could show that it is to this desire of being talked about, and this unremitting rage of distinguishing ourselves, that we owe the best and the worst things we possess, both our virtues and our vices, our science and our errors, our conquerors and our philosophers; that is to say, a great many bad things, and a very few good ones.

In a word, I could prove that, if we have a few rich and powerful men on the pinnacle of fortune and grandeur, while the crowd grovels in want and obscurity, it is because the former prize what they enjoy only in so far as others are destitute of it; and because, without changing their condition, they would cease to be happy the moment the people ceased to be wretched....

From great inequality of fortunes and conditions, from the vast variety of passions and of talents, of useless and pernicious arts, of vain sciences, would arise a multitude of prejudices equally contrary to reason, happiness and virtue. We should see the magistrates fomenting everything that might weaken men united in society, by promoting dissension among them; everything that might sow in it the seeds of actual division, while it gave society the air of harmony; everything that might inspire the different ranks of people with mutual hatred and distrust, by setting the rights and interests of one against those of another, and so strengthen the power which comprehended them all.

"The Savage and the Civilized Man"

The savage and the civilized man differ so much in the bottom of their hearts and in their inclinations, that what constitutes the supreme happiness of one would reduce the other to despair. The former breathes only peace and liberty; he desires only to live and be free from labor; even the *ataraxia* of the Stoic falls far short of his profound indifference to every other object. Civilized man, on the other hand, is always moving, sweating, toiling and racking his brains to find still more laborious occupations: he goes on in drudgery to his last moment, and even seeks death to put himself in a position to live, or renounces life to acquire immortality. He pays his court to men in power, whom he hates, and to the wealthy, whom he despises; he stops at nothing to have the honor of serving them; he is not ashamed to value himself on his own meanness and their protection; and, proud of his slavery, he speaks with disdain of those, who have not the honor of sharing it.

What a sight would the perplexing and envied labors of a European minister of State present to the eyes of a Caribbean! How many cruel deaths would not this indolent savage prefer to the horrors of such a life, which is seldom even sweetened by the pleasure of doing good! But, for him to see into the motives of all this solicitude, the words *power* and *reputation*, would have to bear some meaning in his mind; he would have to know that there are men who set a value on the opinion of the rest of the world; who can be made happy and satisfied with themselves rather on the testimony of other people than on their own. In reality, the source of all these differences is, that the savage lives within himself, while social man lives constantly outside himself, and only knows how to live in the opinion of others, so that he seems to receive the consciousness of his own existence merely from the judgment of others concerning him.

It is not to my present purpose to insist on the indifference to good and evil which arises from this disposition, in spite of our many fine works on morality, or to show how, everything being reduced to appearances, there is but art and mummery in even honor, friendship, virtue, and often vice itself, of which we at length learn the secret of boasting; to show, in short, how, always asking others what we are, and never daring to ask ourselves, in the midst of so much philosophy, humanity and civilization, and of such sublime codes of morality, we have nothing to show for ourselves but a frivolous and deceitful appearance, honor without virtue, reason without wisdom, and pleasure without happiness. It is sufficient that I have proved that this is not by any means the original state of man, but that it is merely the spirit of society, and the inequality which society produces, that thus transform and alter all our natural inclinations.

Conclusion: Inequality and the Arts and Sciences

I have endeavored to trace the origin and progress of inequality, and the institution and abuse of political societies, as far as these are capable of being deduced from the nature of man merely by the light of reason, and independently of those sacred dogmas which give the sanction of divine right to sovereign authority. It follows from this survey that, as there is hardly any inequality in the state of nature, all the inequality which now prevails owes its strength and growth to the development of our faculties and the advance of the human mind, and becomes at last permanent and legitimate by the establishment of property and laws. Secondly, it follows that moral inequality, authorized by positive right alone, clashes with natural right, whenever it is not proportionate to physical inequality; a distinction which sufficiently determines what we ought to think of that species of inequality which prevails in all civilized countries; since it is plainly contrary to the law of nature, however defined, that children should command old men, fools wise men, and that the privileged few should gorge themselves with superfluities, while the starving multitude are in want of the bare necessities of life.

Jean-Jacques Rousseau

A Discourse on Political Economy

The Definition of Political Economy

The word Economy, or OEconomy, is derived from oikos, a house, and nomos, law, and meant originally only the wise and legitimate government of the house for the common good of the whole family. The meaning of the term was then extended to the government of that great family, the State. To distinguish these two senses of the word, the latter is called general or political economy, and the former domestic or particular economy....

From all that has just been said, it follows that public economy, which is my subject, has been rightly distinguished from private economy, and that, the State having nothing in common with the family except the obligations which their heads lie under of making both of them happy, the same rules of conduct cannot apply to both....

The General Will and Political Economy

The body politic, therefore, is also a moral being possessed of a will; and this general will, which tends always to the preservation and welfare of the whole and of every part, and is the source of the laws, constitutes for all the members of the State, in their relations to one another and to it, the rule of what is just or unjust....

Every political society is composed of other smaller societies of different kinds, each of which has its interests and its rules of conduct: but those societies which everybody perceives, because they have an external and authorized form, are not the only ones that actually exist in the State: all individuals who are united by a common interest compose as many others, either transitory or permanent, whose influence is none the less real because it is less apparent, and the proper observation of whose various relations is the true knowledge of public morals and manners. The influence of all these tacit or formal associations causes, by the influence of their will, as many different modifications of the public will.

The will of these particular societies has always two relations; for the members of the association, it is a general will; for the great society, it is a particular will; and it is often right with regard to the first object, and wrong as to the second.... It is true that particular societies being always subordinate to the general society in preference to others, the duty of a citizen takes precedence of that of a senator, and a man's duty of that of a citizen: but unhappily personal interest is always found in inverse ratio to duty, and increases in proportion as the association grows narrower, and the engagement less sacred; which irrefragably proves that the most general will is always the most just also, and that the voice of the people is in fact the voice of God....

"The General Will [is] the First Principle of Public Economy"

The first and most important rule of legitimate or popular government, that is to say, of government whose object is the good of the people, is therefore, as I have observed, to follow in everything the general will. But to follow this will it is necessary to know it, and above all to distinguish it from the particular will, beginning with one's self: this distinction is always very difficult to make, and only the most sublime virtue can afford sufficient illumination for it....

I conclude, therefore, that, as the first duty of the legislator is to make the laws conformable to the general will, the first rule of public economy is that the administration of justice should be conformable to the laws. It will even be enough to prevent the State from being ill governed, that the Legislator shall have provided, as he should, for every need of place, climate, soil, custom, neighborhood, and all the rest of the relations peculiar to the people he had to institute. Not but what there still remains an infinity of details of administration and economy, which are left to the wisdom of the government: but there are two infallible rules for its good conduct on these occasions; one is, that the spirit of the law ought to decide in every particular case that could not be foreseen; the other is that the general will, the source and supplement of all laws, should be consulted wherever they fail.

But how, I shall be asked, can the general will be known in cases in which it has not expressed itself? Must the whole nation be assembled together at every unforeseen event? Certainly not. It ought the less to be assembled, because it is by no means certain that its decision would be the expression of the general will; besides, the method would be impractible in a great people, and is hardly ever necessary where the government is well-intentioned: for the rulers well know that the general will is always on the side which is most favorable to the public interest, that is to say, most equitable; so that it is needful only to act justly, to be certain of following the general will....

The Second Rule of Political Economy

The second essential rule of public economy is no less important than the first. If you would have the general will accomplished, bring all the particular wills into conformity with it; in other words, as virtue is nothing more than this conformity of the particular wills with the general will, establish the reign of virtue....

When the citizens love their duty, and the guardians of the public authority sincerely apply themselves to the fostering of that love by their own example and assiduity, every difficulty vanishes; and government becomes so easy that it needs none of that art of darkness, whose blackness is its only mystery....

It is not enough to say to the citizens, be good; they must be taught to be so; and even example, which is in this respect the first lesson, is not the sole means to be employed; patriotism is the most efficacious: for, as I have said already, every man is virtuous when his particular will is in all things conformable to the general will, and we voluntarily will what is willed by those whom we love....

Do we wish men to be virtuous? Then let us begin by making them love their country: but how can they love it, if their country be nothing more to them than to strangers, and afford them nothing but what it can refuse nobody? It would be still worse, if they did not enjoy even the privilege of social security.... It must not be imagined that a man can break or lose an arm, without the pain being conveyed to his head: nor is it any more credible that the general will should consent that any one member of the State, whoever he might be, should wound or destroy another, than it is that the fingers of a man in his senses should willfully scratch his eyes out....

In fact, does not the undertaking entered into by the whole body of the nation bind it to provide for the security of the least of its members with as much care as for that of all the rest? Is the welfare of a single citizen any less the common cause than that of the whole State?

It is therefore one of the most important functions of government to prevent extreme inequality of fortunes; not by taking away wealth from its possessors, but by depriving all men of means to accumulate it; not by building hospitals for the poor, but by securing the citizens from becoming poor. The unequal distribution of inhabitants over the territory, when men are crowded together in one place, while other places are depopulated; the encouragement of the arts that minister to luxury and of purely industrial arts at the expense of useful and laborious crafts; the sacrifice of agriculture to commerce; the necessitation of the tax-farmer by the mal-administration of the funds of the State; and in short, venality pushed to such an extreme that even public esteem is reckoned at a cash value, and virtue rated at a market price: these are the most obvious causes of opulence and of poverty, of public interest, of mutual hatred among citizens, of indifference to the common cause, of the corruption of the people, and of the weakening of all the springs of government. Such are the evils, which are with difficulty cured when they make themselves felt, but which a wise administration ought to prevent, if it is to maintain, along with good morals, respect for the laws, patriotism, and the influence of the general will.

Political Economy and Public Education

But all these precautions will be inadequate, unless rulers go still more to the root of the matter. I conclude this part of public economy where I ought to have begun it.... To form citizens is not the work of a day; and in order to have men it is necessary to educate them when they are children....

If, for example, they were early accustomed to regard their individuality only in its relation to the body of the State, and to be aware, so to speak, of their own existence merely as a part of that of the State, they might at length come to identify themselves in some degree with this greater whole, to feel themselves members of their country, and to love it with that exquisite feeling which no isolated person has save for himself; to lift up their spirits perpetually to this great object, and thus to transform into a sublime virtue that dangerous disposition which gives rise to all our vices....

From the first moment of life, men ought to begin learning to deserve to live; and, as at the instant of birth we partake of the rights of citizenship, that instant ought to be the beginning of the exercise of our duty. If there are laws for the age of maturity, there ought to be laws for infancy, teaching obedience to others: and as the reason of each man is not left to be the sole arbiter of his duties, government ought the less indiscriminately to abandon to the intelligence and prejudices of fathers the education of their children, as that education is of still greater importance to the State than to the fathers: for, according to the course of nature, the death of the father often deprives him of the final fruits of education; but his country sooner or later perceives its effects. Families dissolve, but the State remains....

Public education, therefore, under regulations prescribed by the government, and under magistrates established by the Sovereign, is one of the fundamental rules of popular or legitimate government. If children are brought up in common in the bosom of equality; if they are imbued with the laws of the State and the precepts of the general will; if they are taught to respect these above all things; if they are surrounded by examples and objects which constantly remind them of the tender mother who nourishes them, of the love she bears them, of the inestimable benefits they receive from her, and of the return they owe her, we cannot doubt that they will learn to cherish one another mutually as brothers, to will nothing contrary to the will of society, to substitute the actions of men and citizens for the futile and vain babbling of sophists, and to become in time defenders and fathers of the country of which they will have been so long the children....

Thus a careful and well-intentioned government, vigilant incessantly to maintain or restore patriotism and morality among the people, provides beforehand against the evils which sooner or later result from the indifference of the citizens to the fate of the Republic, keeping within narrow bounds that personal interest which so isolates the individual that the State is enfeebled by his power, and has nothing to hope from his good-will. Wherever men love their country, respect the laws, and live simply, little remains to be done in order to make them happy; and in public administration, where chance has less influence than in the lot of individuals, wisdom is so nearly allied to happiness, that the two objects are confounded.

Third Rule of Political Economy

It is not enough to have citizens and to protect them, it is also necessary to consider their subsistence. Provision for the public wants is an obvious inference from the general will, and the third essential duty of government.....

But apart from the public demesne, which is of service to the State in proportion to the uprightness of those who govern, any one sufficiently acquainted with the whole force of the general administration, especially when it confines itself to legitimate methods, would be astonished at the resources the rulers can make use of for guarding against public needs, without trespassing on the goods of individuals.

As they are masters of the whole commerce of the State, nothing is easier for them than to direct it into such channels as to provide for every need, without appearing to interfere. The distribution of provisions, money, and merchandise in just proportions, according to times and places, is the true secret of finance and the source of wealth, provided those who administer it have foresight enough to suffer a present apparent loss, in order really to obtain immense profits in the future. When we see a government paying bounties, instead of receiving duties, on the exportation of corn in time of plenty, and on its importation in time of scarcity, we must have such facts before our eyes if we are to be persuaded of their reality....

"The Distinction between Necessaries and Superfluities"

He who possesses only the common necessaries of life should pay nothing at all, while the tax on him who is in possession of superfluities may justly be extended to everything he has over and above mere necessaries. To this he will possibly object that, when his rank is taken into account, what may be superfluous to a man of inferior station is necessary for him. But this is false: for a grandee has two legs just like a cowherd, and, like him again, but one belly. Besides, these pretended necessaries are really so little necessary to his rank, that if he should renounce them on any worthy occasion, he would only be the more honored. The populace would be ready to adore a Minister who went to Council on foot, because he had sold off his carriages to supply a pressing need of the State. Lastly, to no man does the law prescribe magnificence; and propriety is no argument against right....

Cui Bono? Rich or Poor?

Are not all the advantages of society for the rich and powerful? Are not all lucrative posts in their hands? Are not all privileges and exemptions reserved for them alone? Is not the public authority always on their side? If a man of eminence robs his creditors, or is guilty of other knaveries, is he not always assured of impunity? Are not the assaults, acts of violence, assassinations, and even murders committed by the great, matters that are hushed up in a few months, and of which nothing more is thought?

But if a great man himself is robbed or insulted, the whole police force is immediately in motion, and woe even to innocent persons who chance to be suspected. If he has to pass through any dangerous road, the country is up in arms to escort him. If the axle-tree of his chaise breaks, everybody flies to his assistance. If there is a noise at his door, he speaks but a word, and all is silent. If he is incommoded by the crowd, he waves his hand and every one makes way. If his coach is met on the road by a wagon, his servants are ready to beat the driver's brains out, and fifty honest pedestrians going quietly about their business had better be knocked on the head than an idle jackanapes be delayed in his coach. Yet all this respect costs him not a farthing: it is the rich man's right, and not what he buys with his wealth.

How different is the case of the poor man! The more humanity owes him, the more society denies him. Every door is shut against him, even when he has a right to its being opened: and if ever he obtains justice, it is with much greater difficulty than others obtain favors. If the militia is to be raised or the highway to be mended, he is always given the preference; he always bears the burden which his richer neighbor has influence enough to get exempted from. On the least accident that happens to him, everybody avoids him: if his cart be overturned in the road, so far is he from receiving any assistance, that he is lucky if he does not get horse-whipped by the impudent lackeys of some young Duke; in a word, all gratuitous assistance is denied to the poor when they need it, just because they cannot pay for it. I look upon any poor man as totally undone, if he has the misfortune to have an honest heart, a fine daughter, and a powerful neighbor.

Another no less important fact is that the losses of the poor are much harder to repair than those of the rich, and that the difficulty of acquisition is always greater in proportion as there is more need for it. "Nothing comes out of nothing," is as true of life as in physics: money is the seed of money, and the first guinea is sometimes more difficult to acquire than the second million. Add to this that what the poor pay is lost to them for ever, and remains in, or returns to, the hands of the rich: and as, to those who share in the government or to their dependents, the whole produce of the taxes must sooner or later pass, although they pay their share, these persons have always a sensible interest in increasing them.

The terms of the social compact between these two estates of men may be summed up in a few words. "You have need of me, because I am rich and you are poor. We will therefore come to an agreement. I will permit you to have the honor of serving me, on condition that you bestow on me the little you have left, in return for the pains I shall take to command you."

Putting all these considerations carefully together, we shall find that, in order to levy taxes in a truly equitable and proportionate manner, the imposition ought not to be in simple ratio to the property of the contributors, but in compound ratio to the difference of their conditions and the superfluity of their possessions....

"Heavy Taxes" on "Superfluous Expenses"

Heavy taxes should be laid on servants in livery, on equipages, rich furniture, fine clothes, on spacious courts and gardens, on public entertainments of all kinds, on useless professions, such as dancers, singers, players, and in a word, on all that multiplicity of objects of luxury, amusement and idleness, which strike the eyes of all, and can the less be hidden, as their whole purpose is to be seen, without which they would be useless.

We need be under no apprehension of the produce of these taxes being arbitrary, because they are laid on things not absolutely necessary. They must know but little of mankind who imagine that, after they have been once seduced by luxury, they can ever renounce it: they would a hundred times sooner renounce common necessaries, and had much rather die of hunger than of shame. The increase in their expense is only an additional reason for supporting them, when the vanity of appearing wealthy reaps its profit from the price of the thing and the charge of the tax. As long as there are rich people in the world, they will be desirous of distinguishing themselves from the poor, nor can the State devise a revenue less burdensome or more certain than what arises from this distinction.

For the same reason, industry would have nothing to suffer from an economic system which increased the revenue, encouraged agriculture by relieving the husbandman, and insensibly tended to bring all fortunes nearer to that middle condition which constitutes the genuine strength of the State. These taxes might, I admit, bring certain fashionable articles of dress and amusement to an untimely end; but it would be only to substitute others, by which the artificer would gain, and the exchequer suffer no loss.

In a word, suppose the spirit of government was constantly to tax only the superfluities of the rich, one of two things must happen: either the rich would convert their superfluous expenses into useful ones, which would redound to the profit of the State, and thus the imposition of taxes would have the effect of the best sumptuary laws, the expenses of the State would necessarily diminish with those of individuals, and the treasury would not receive so much less as it would gain by having less to pay; or, if the rich did not become less extravagant, the exchequer would have such resources in the product of taxes on their expenditure as would provide for the needs of the State. In the first case the treasury would be the richer by what it would save, from having the less to do with its money; and in the second, it would be enriched by the useless expenses of individuals.

Jean-Jacques Rousseau

The Social Contract

Book I: "What Can Make It Legitimate?"

Subject of the First Book

MAN is born free; and everywhere he is in chains. One thinks himself the master of others, and still remains a greater slave than they. How did this change come about? I do not know. What can make it legitimate? That question I think I can answer.

The Social Compact

I SUPPOSE men to have reached the point at which the obstacles in the way of their preservation in the state of nature show their power of resistance to be greater than the resources at the disposal of each individual for his maintenance in that state. That primitive condition can then subsist no longer; and the human race would perish unless it changed its manner of existence.

But, as men cannot engender new forces, but only unite and direct existing ones, they have no other means of preserving themselves than the formation, by aggregation, of a sum of forces great enough to overcome the resistance.

These they have to bring into play by means of a single motive power, and cause to act in concert.

This sum of forces can arise only where several persons come together: but, as the force and liberty of each man are the chief instruments of his self-preservation, how can he pledge them without harming his own interests, and neglecting the care he owes to himself? This difficulty, in its bearing on my present subject, may be stated in the following terms:

> "The problem is to find a form of association which will defend and protect with the whole common force the person and goods of each associate, and in which each, while uniting himself with all, may still obey himself alone, and remain as free as before."

This is the fundamental problem of which the Social Contract provides the solution.

The clauses of this contract are so determined by the nature of the act that the slightest modification would make them vain and ineffective; so that, although they have perhaps never been formally set forth, they are everywhere the same and everywhere tacitly admitted and recognized, until, on the violation of the social compact, each regains his original rights and resumes his natural liberty, while losing the conventional liberty in favor of which he renounced it.

These clauses, properly understood, may be reduced to one—the total alienation of each associate, together with all his rights, to the whole community; for, in the first place, as each gives himself absolutely, the conditions are the same for all; and, this being so, no one has any interest in making them burdensome to others.

Moreover, the alienation being without reserve, the union is as perfect as it can be, and no associate has anything more to demand: for, if the individuals retained certain rights, as there would be no common superior to decide between them and the public, each, being on one point his own judge, would ask to be so on all; the state of nature would thus continue, and the association would necessarily become inoperative or tyrannical.

Finally, each man, in giving himself to all, gives himself to nobody; and as there is no associate over whom he does not acquire the same right as he yields others over himself, he gains an equivalent for everything he loses, and an increase of force for the preservation of what he has.

If then we discard from the social compact what is not of its essence, we shall find that it reduces itself to the following terms:

> "Each of us puts his person and all his power in common under the supreme direction of the general will, and, in our corporate capacity, we receive each member as an indivisible part of the whole."

At once, in place of the individual personality of each contracting party, this act of association creates a moral and collective body, composed of as many members as the assembly contains votes, and receiving from this act its unity, its common identity, its life and its will. This public person, so formed by the union of all other persons formerly took the name of city, and now takes that of Republic or body politic; it is called by its members State when passive. Sovereign when active, and Power when compared with others like itself. Those who are associated in it take collectively the name of people, and severally are called citizens, as sharing in the sovereign power, and subjects, as being under the laws of the State. But these terms are often confused and taken one for another: it is enough to know how to distinguish them when they are being used with precision.

The Sovereign

Each individual, as a man, may have a particular will contrary or dissimilar to the general will which he has as a citizen. His particular interest may speak to him quite differently from the common interest: his absolute and naturally independent existence may make him look upon what he owes to the common cause as a gratuitous contribution, the loss of which will do less harm to others than the payment of it is burdensome to himself; and, regarding the moral person which constitutes the State as a *persona ficta*, because not a man, he may wish to enjoy the rights of citizenship without being ready to fulfill the duties of a subject. The continuance of such an injustice could not but prove the undoing of the body politic.

In order then that the social compact may not be an empty formula, it tacitly includes the undertaking, which alone can give force to the rest, that whoever refuses to obey the general will shall be compelled to do so by the whole body. This means nothing less than that he will be forced to be free; for this is the condition which, by giving each citizen to his country, secures him against all personal dependence. In this lies the key to the working of the political machine; this alone legitimizes civil undertakings, which, without it, would be absurd, tyrannical, and liable to the most frightful abuses.

The Civil State

The passage from the state of nature to the civil state produces a very remarkable change in man, by substituting justice for instinct in his conduct, and giving his actions the morality they had formerly lacked. Then only, when the voice of duty takes the place of physical impulses and right of appetite, does man, who so far had considered only himself, find that he is forced to act on different principles, and to consult his reason before listening to his inclinations. Although, in this state, he deprives himself of some advantages which he got from nature, he gains in return others so great, his faculties are so stimulated and developed, his ideas so extended, his feelings so ennobled, and his whole soul so uplifted, that, did not the abuses of this new condition often degrade him below that which he left, he would be bound to bless continually the happy moment which took him from it for ever, and, instead of a stupid and unimaginative animal, made him an intelligent being and a man.

Let us draw up the whole account in terms easily commensurable. What man loses by the social contract is his natural liberty and an unlimited right to everything he tries to get and succeeds in getting; what he gains is civil liberty and the proprietorship of all he possesses. If we are to avoid mistake in weighing one against the other, we must clearly distinguish natural liberty, which is bounded only by the strength of the individual, from civil liberty, which is limited by the general will; and possession, which is merely the effect of force or the right of the first occupier, from property, which can be founded only on a positive title.

We might, over and above all this, add, to what man acquires in the civil state, moral liberty, which alone makes him truly master of himself; for the mere impulse of appetite is slavery, while obedience to a law which we pre-scribe to ourselves is liberty. But I have already said too much on this head, and the philosophical meaning of the word liberty does not now concern us.

Book II: Sovereignty

Sovereignty is Inalienable

The first and most important deduction from the principles we have so far laid down is that the general will alone can direct the State according to the object for which it was instituted, i.e., the common good: for if the clashing of par-ticular interests made the establishment of societies necessary, the agreement of these very interests made it possible. The common element in these differ-ent interests is what forms the social tie; and, were there no point of agreement between them all, no society could exist. It is solely on the basis of this com-mon interest that every society should be governed.

I hold then that Sovereignty, being nothing less than the exercise of the general will, can never be alienated, and that the Sovereign, who is no less than a collective being, cannot be represented except by himself: the power indeed may be transmitted, but not the will.

In reality, if it is not impossible for a particular will to agree on some point with the general will, it is at least impossible for the agreement to be lasting and constant; for the particular will tends, by its very nature, to partiality, while the general will tends to equality....

Sovereignty is Indivisible

Sovereignty, for the same reason as makes it inalienable, is indivisible; for will either is, or is not, general; it is the will either of the body of the people, or only of a part of it. In the first case, the will, when declared, is an act of Sovereignty and constitutes law: in the second, it is merely a particular will, or act of magistracy—at the most a decree.

If we examined the other divisions in the same manner, we should find that, whenever Sovereignty seems to be divided, there is an illusion: the rights which are taken as being part of Sovereignty are really all subordinate, and always imply supreme wills of which they only sanction the execution....

The General Will is Infallible

It follows from what has gone before that the general will is always right and tends to the public advantage; but it does not follow that the deliberations of the people are always equally correct. Our will is always for our own good, but we do not always see what that is; the people is never corrupted, but it is often deceived, and on such occasions only does it seem to will what is bad.

There is often a great deal of difference between the will of all and the general will; the latter considers only the common interest, while the former takes private interest into account, and is no more than a sum of particular wills: but take away from these same wills the pluses and minuses that cancel one another, and the general will remains as the sum of the differences.

If, when the people, being furnished with adequate information, held its deliberations, the citizens had no communication one with another, the grand total of the small differences would always give the general will, and the decision would always be good. But when factions arise, and partial associations are formed at the expense of the great association, the will of each of these associations becomes general in relation to its members, while it remains particular in relation to the State: it may then be said that there are no longer as many votes as there are men, but only as many as there are associations. The differences become less numerous and give a less general result. Lastly, when one of these associations is so great as to prevail over all the rest, the result is no longer a sum of small differences, but a single difference; in this case there is no longer a general will, and the opinion which prevails is purely particular....

The Limits of The Sovereign Power

If the State is a moral person whose life is in the union of its members, and if the most important of its cares is the care for its own preservation, it must have a universal and compelling force, in order to move and dispose each part as may be most advantageous to the whole. As nature gives each man absolute power over all his members, the social compact gives the body politic absolute power over all its members also; and it is this power which, under the direction of the general will, bears, as I have said, the name of Sovereignty....

Why is it that the general will is always in the right, and that all continually will the happiness of each one, unless it is because there is not a man who does not think of "each" as meaning him, and consider himself in voting for all? This proves that equality of rights and the idea of justice which such equality creates originate in the preference each man gives to himself, and accordingly in the very nature of man. It proves that the general will, to be really such, must be general in its object as well as its essence; that it must both come from all and apply to all; and that it loses its natural rectitude when it is directed to some particular and determinate object, because in such a case we are judging of something foreign to us, and have no true principle of equity to guide us....

It should be seen from the foregoing that what makes the will general is less the number of voters than the common interest uniting them; for, under this system, each necessarily submits to the conditions he imposes on others: and this admirable agreement between interest and justice gives to the common deliberations an equitable character which at once vanishes when any particular question is discussed, in the absence of a common interest to unite and identify the ruling of the judge with that of the party.

From whatever side we approach our principle, we reach the same conclusion, that the social compact sets up among the citizens an equality of such a kind, that they all bind themselves to observe the same conditions and should therefore all enjoy the same rights.

Thus, from the very nature of the compact, every act of Sovereignty, i.e., every authentic act of the general will, binds or favors all the citizens equally; so that the Sovereign recognizes only the body of the nation, and draws no distinctions between those of whom it is made up. What, then, strictly speaking, is an act of Sovereignty? It is not a convention between a superior and an inferior, but a convention between the body and each of its members. It is legitimate, because based on the social contract, and equitable, because common to all; useful, because it can have no other object than the general good, and stable, because guaranteed by the public force and the supreme power. So long as the subjects have to submit only to conventions of this sort, they obey no-one but their own will; and to ask how far the respective rights of the Sovereign and the citizens extend, is to ask up to what point the latter can enter into undertakings with themselves, each with all, and all with each.

Book IV: Civil Religion

The Disadvantages of the Separation of Church and State

Of all Christian writers, the philosopher Hobbes alone has seen the evil and how to remedy it, and has dared to propose the reunion of the two heads of the eagle, and the restoration throughout of political unity, without which no State or government will ever be rightly constituted. But he should have seen that the masterful spirit of Christianity is incompatible with his system, and that the priestly interest would always be stronger than that of the State. It is not so much what is false and terrible in his political theory, as what is just and true, that has drawn down hatred on it....

Religion...which gives men two codes of legislation, two rulers, and two countries, renders them subject to contradictory duties, and makes it impossible for them to be faithful both to religion and to citizenship. Such are the religions of the Lamas and of the Japanese, and such is Roman Christianity, which may be called the religion of the priest. It leads to a sort of mixed and anti-social code which has no name....

Is a "Christian Republic" Possible?

We are told that a people of true Christians would form the most perfect society imaginable. I see in this supposition only one great difficulty: that a society of true Christians would not be a society of men....Christianity as a religion is entirely spiritual, occupied solely with heavenly things; the country of the Christian is not of this world. He does his duty, indeed, but does it with profound indifference to the good or ill success of his cares. Provided he has nothing to reproach himself with, it matters little to him whether things go well or ill here on earth. If the State is prosperous, he hardly dares to share in the public happiness, for fear he may grow proud of his country's glory; if the State is languishing, he blesses the hand of God that is hard upon His people....

But I am mistaken in speaking of a Christian republic; the terms are mutually exclusive. Christianity preaches only servitude and dependence. Its spirit is so favorable to tyranny that it always profits by such a régime. True Christians are made to be slaves, and they know it and do not much mind: this short life counts for too little in their eyes....

"A Purely Civil Profession of Faith"

But, setting aside political considerations, let us come back to what is right, and settle our principles on this important point. The right which the social compact gives the Sovereign over the subjects does not, we have seen, exceed the limits of public expediency. The subjects then owe the Sovereign an account of their opinions only to such an extent as they matter to the community. Now, it matters very much to the community that each citizen should have a religion. That will make him love his duty; but the dogmas of that religion concern the State and its members only so far as they have reference to morality and to the duties which he who professes them is bound to do to others....

There is therefore a purely civil profession of faith of which the Sovereign should fix the articles, not exactly as religious dogmas, but as social sentiments without which a man cannot be a good citizen or a faithful subject. While it can compel no one to believe them, it can banish from the State whoever does not believe them—it can banish him, not for impiety, but as an anti-social being, incapable of truly loving the laws and justice, and of sacrificing, at need, his life to his duty. If any one, after publicly recognizing these dogmas, behaves as if he does not believe them, let him be punished by death: he has committed the worst of all crimes, that of lying before the law.

The dogmas of civil religion ought to be few, simple, and exactly worded, without explanation or commentary. The existence of a mighty, intelligent and beneficent Divinity, possessed of foresight and providence, the life to come, the happiness of the just, the punishment of the wicked, the sanctity of the social contract and the laws: these are its positive dogmas....

PART TWO

The Arrival of Political Economy: Liberty, Property, and Equality

Introduction

Adam Smith and the System of Natural Liberty

There are four themes in Adam Smith's *Wealth of Nations*. (1) In Book I, Smith presents what he calls the System of Natural Liberty where he asks the reader to first imagine and second to understand what would happen to an economy if left to its own "natural" devices. (2) Book III provides a non-Marxist account of what we might call a natural theory of economic growth. (3) Book IV looks at the competing theories of political economy with special emphasis on the Mercantilists and their vast range of public policy tools which they use to intervene in the economy both at home and abroad. (4) Book V examines the legitimate role of government, namely, those activities that are consistent with the natural system described in the earlier books. We suggest that an important key to grasping Smith's work is to trace his various uses of the word "nature." Like Hume, Smith espoused a kind of natural history wherein growth moves through various organic and historical stages. It is not a classical teleology found in Plato and Aristotle, nor is it like the rigid mechanism found in the "scientific socialism" of Marx and Engels.

In Book I, Smith espouses what we have called the technological project. Echoing Locke, Smith maintains that wealth and growth are the result of the labor that human beings put into nature. Specifically, he sees that the division of labor leads to the invention of labor-saving devices. This is manifest in his famous example of the pin factory (now represented on the present £20 pound note). Moreover, like his friend Hume, who had written an essay "On Commerce" to rebut Rousseau's charges that science and technology ruin society, Smith thinks that technology and growth are on the whole better than living in a primitive agricultural society.

Smith argues as well that the wealth of a nation ought to be measured by the total amount of the necessities and conveniences of life produced divided by the total population. Today, we might call this the per capita Gross National Product. Smith contrasts this natural measure with the balance of trade and accumulation of gold measures of the Mercantilists. And he focuses exclusively on increasing the numerator, or production of wealth, rather than decreasing the denominator or size of the population to be fed, clothed, and housed by the wealth. The cause of the wealth of nations thus depends on increasing the output of the nation and this depends on the productivity of labor, which depends on the division of labor and which, in turn, depends on the extent of the market. Both here and later, Smith claims that natural inclinations and accidental geographical discoveries are more important in the story of human liberty than "human wisdom."

Also central to the productivity of the process of wealth creation is the natural capacity of human beings to "truck, barter, and exchange" with the butcher, baker, and brewer for their daily beef, bread, and beer. Is Smith advocating selfishness as opposed to benevolence, or is he putting forth a doctrine that Tocqueville would later call self-interest rightly understood? According to Smith, the exchange of surpluses among human beings is natural and this sociability is sown in human nature. Does this amount to a sort of correction of Locke's understanding that sociability is more a calculation than instinctive? And does it matter for an understanding of this stage of classical liberalism? According to Smith, in a commercial society, we all become merchants. But doesn't he also say that merchants prefer monopoly to competition? Is it a sufficient response to critics to say, as Smith does, that while the worker in a market-oriented system is not as well off as "the captains of industry," they are better off than those who hold absolute power in underdeveloped countries?

Like Locke, Smith argues that the process of exchange is facilitated by the invention of money which, properly understood, is a medium of exchange rather than wealth itself. It is instructive that both Locke and Smith only introduce money into the discussion after they have talked about what is *real* in the process. What Smith is less clear about is whether or not there is a natural distribution of this naturally produced output among the factors of production—land, labor, and capital—so that the reward is commensurate with the contribution to production.

Book III supports a natural theory of economic growth over against a planned theory of economic growth. There is a natural pattern to progress: food, then clothing, and then shelter. The domestic market first and then exchange internationally. All this seems so obvious, but the twentieth century is full of examples where countries have engaged in forced growth by the planned skipping of a stage or two.

Book IV contains, among other things, Smith's discussion of the invisible hand. This concept is also present in the *Theory of Moral Sentiments*, and we have included this brief passage for comparative purposes. (Smith has a third reference in the *Astronomy* where he is dismissive of "the invisible hand of Jupiter"). What does this concept mean and how central are these couple of pages to Smith's overall project? Can we dismiss these pages and not lose anything in Smith? Is it a metaphor or does it have a supernatural quality? Is he articulating an early version of the doctrine of unintended consequences? Does it make any difference if we read the passage to be saying "led *as if* by an invisible hand," rather than "led by *an* invisible hand?" Is this proto-cybernetics or just a mystical explanation? And does the use of the indefinite article, "an," rather than the definite article, "the," make a difference? We are thinking of references in the Smith literature to his apparent reliance on "*the* invisible hand of the market*."

In Book V, Smith outlines three major areas where government has an important part to play in a market orientated system: defense, justice, and public works which last mentioned is broken down into the facilitation of commerce, the education of youth, and the instruction of all ages especially in the area of religion. Among other things, Smith encourages the government to be involved in overcoming the negative effects to the individual of a life defined by the division of labor. So we have a paradox: the division of labor is central to the well-being of the nation, but contributes to the degradation of the individual. How do we resolve this paradox? Also, is Smith "giving away the store" with his rather robust role for government in the areas of defense, public works, and the regulation of religion? Or is he arguing that the government has an obligation to defend the country and that countries that are well off will face increasing defense costs due to international jealousies? Is Smith arguing that it is legitimate for government to promote (a) economic liberty by extending the market and (b) religious liberty by encouraging competition among religious sects?

The American Founding

According to James Madison, in *Federalist* 10, "the most common and durable sources of faction" are the "various and unequal distribution of property." As we shall see, Karl Marx also considers the distribution of property as the great divide in modern society. But Madison and Marx differ over whether the Madisonian distinction between the "various" distribution of property and the "unequal" distribution of property is relevant. Madison does not deny Marx's claim that the battle between the few who are rich and the many who are poor—the unequal distribution issue—is at the core of class war and factious politics, and thus the "mortal disease" of every regime. He does, however, take seriously the possibility that economic disagreements can be framed in terms of the more manageable differences of degree, or variety, of property ownership. These differences of degree, in turn, are linked to an income or flow distribution of property concept rather than the more dangerous distinctions of wealth distribution or ownership of the means of production concept of property.

Is Madison arguing that the harsher aspects of the distribution of property question can be tamed if we incorporate the distribution question into the larger issue of the purpose of political economy? Is he within the Smith tradition when he argues that we need to focus more on the production side of the economic question and let the distribution issue fall in line? In other words, it is better for free governments to tolerate unequal distribution of income because it is a byproduct of a system of human improvement whose core value is individual liberty and the pursuit of happiness. By increasing the overall quantity and variety of the necessities and conveniences of life, then we can increase the size of the pie and avoid the nasty politics of redistributing the slices of a fixed size pie. The improvement in the human condition, which includes the preservation of liberty, requires an increase in the wealth of the nation so that we can avoid the negative impact on liberty and justice of a zero sum game condition.

Madison's adaptation of Smith can be expressed thus: the well-being of the nation depends on the control of faction, and this depends on the productivity of labor which depends on generating a division of labor and multiplicity of interests which, finally, depends on "the enlargement of the orbit," or what Smith called the extent of the market. Competition, over against monopoly, is at the core of Madison's solution to the problems of faction that emerge of necessity in every civilized society. With competition comes prosperity which is vital for the enhancement of political liberty.

Madison continues his theme of controlling the effects of faction in *Federalist* 51. We know from *Federalist* 10 that faction is sown in human nature. But it is impossible and undesirable to eliminate faction by (1) transforming humans into angels and (2) eliminating the very liberty that leads to the division of opinions, passions, and interests in the community. Is Madison articulating a doctrine of realism or is he selling short the human possibility of transformation? Is he too quick to acknowledge the fact that "enlightened statesmen" will not always be at the helm, and that government officials will not always be angels? Madison says experience has taught us to supplement a dependence of the government on the people with "auxiliary precautions," or "inventions of prudence." Thus, the separation of powers is an auxiliary to aid regular elections in the effort to oblige the government to control itself. He supplements this competition between the three branches of the federal government with the advantages of a "compound republic" where competition between the different levels of government makes the formation of a tyrannical majority unlikely.

"Let ambition counteract ambition," in a system of "opposite and rival interests." That seems to be Madison's theory of politics and economics. Madison, consistent with the teachings of Smith in the *Wealth of Nations*, adds one last word in favor of competition facilitated by the extended orbit or extended market: it provides the infrastructure for the development of a multiplicity of religious sects which is the prerequisite for the preservation of religious liberty. And thus, like Smith, he underscores the interrelationship between political liberty, economic liberty, and religious liberty.

We have also included an edited version of the *Declaration of Independence*, the *Constitution*, and the *Bill of Rights*. (The version of the Declaration combines Jefferson's original draft—see the underlined portions—with those parts that were added to the final draft—see the words in parenthesis in the text.)

We do so to (1) raise the issue of the continuity between the Founding and Locke on the one hand and (2) show the compatibility between the *Constitution* and the development of a commercial republic.

With regard to the *Declaration*, it is important to note the emphasis on the natural right of the individual to life, liberty, and the pursuit of happiness with (natural) equality as a point of departure rather than as a social outcome to be secured. And, by liberty, the *Declaration* means economic liberty—the right to the fruits of one's labor in the form of private property—political liberty—the right to choose the form of government under which one shall live—and religious liberty—the right to worship God according to one's conscience. We have also included extracts from Madison's *Memorial and Remonstrance* written between the Declaration (1776) and the Constitution (1787). Like Locke, Madison was aware of the interrelationship between the three pillars of liberty.

The *Constitution* and the *Bill of Rights* also demonstrate the interconnection between the three pillars. Note that (a) all the representatives of the federal government are to be paid an income for their services, (b) the powers of Congress extend to the regulation of (regularizing of) international and interstate commerce and the promotion of "the sciences and useful arts," (c) private property is protected by due process of law, (d) Congress shall pass no law with respect to the establishment of religion or abridging the free exercise of religion, and that (e) the powers not granted to the general government are reserved to the states or to the people.

Tocqueville and the Two Narratives

One might wonder why we include three entries from Alex Tocqueville, 1805-1859, in our anthology of political economy. The answer is because he makes the insightful claim in the early part of the 19th century that "the love of equality" rather than "the love of liberty" is the ruling passion of modernity. Tocqueville wrote a scathing critique of Rousseau's *Second Discourse* in his own *MEMOIR ON PAUPERISM: Does Public Charity Produce an Idle and Dependent Class of Society?* And, moreover, that passion for equality manifested itself in the violent unfolding of the French Revolution where "the economic question" not only came out of the household and into the polity, but made its way into the society at large. Humans in modernity, he continued, prefer equality in slavery to inequality in liberty. In short, and in conformity with the theme of this reader, equality and not liberty is the default position of modernity. Thus, liberty is in constant need of being defended and equality is in constant need of being moderated. He thought he saw this defense in America.

The task of statesmen and educators in modernity then, says Tocqueville, is not to do battle with the inevitable march of equality and democracy by longing for the good old days of inequality and aristocracy. Rather, the task is to first discover, and then keep, the "mores" and institutions of liberty alive and well. Again, he thought he saw the answers in the aftermath of the American Revolution in the new world.

Our first entry, his Introduction to a later edition of the two volume *Democracy in America*, was written when the specter of communism was haunting Europe and France was experiencing its second revolution in 1848. This entry links this phase of the story of the two narratives to the final phase, which focuses on J.S. Mill and Marx and Engels, and it also points back to Smith. (Is Tocqueville's the "Creator's hand" the same as Smith's "invisible hand?") The second and third entries are from the later parts of the second volume of *Democracy in America* published in 1840 where he is very critical of the materialist approach to history and the reliance of revolutionaries on the centralization of administration. Is Tocqueville's attachment to intermediary institutions, such as the local newspaper, no longer relevant in the twenty-first century? He noted that "on the seventh day of every week," Americans suspend trading and making money. Has this disappeared from American life and with what consequences? Does his recommendation that in order to avoid the softer despotism of modernity we must "lay down extensive but distinct and settled limits to the action of the government" still make sense? Are they part of what has become known as "American exceptionalism?" Are the American restraints on the centralized administrative state exportable?

Central to Tocqueville's project is the distinction between self-interest rightly understood and self-interest wrongly understood. This, in turn, is linked to what we shall call the distinction between liberty properly understood and liberty improperly understood.

His project seems to be this: What we need is a prudent attachment to intermediate institutions, such as civic associations and religious sects, and the defense of the non-sublime morality that being virtuous and helpful to others can be useful to the advancement of ones own interests. Is this what Smith is getting at in the butcher, the baker, and the brewer story? Is this what Madison means by a system of rival and opposite interests? Or are Smith and Madison suggesting that by helping myself, I help others? Is it good enough that religion be reduced to the politically and economically useful? Is that also what Smith and Madison are calling for? Is he articulating the need for, and sufficiency of, what are often called "the bourgeois virtues?" In pointing out the need for religion that supports a commercial society, Tocqueville warns that the alternatives are either an atheism that ends up doubting the centrality of all values of restraint and an unreasonable religion that fills the soul with an extreme rejection of the secular world.

He ends the second entry with what has been referred to as his "Marxist chapter" about the return of aristocracy. But could it not be also called his "Smithian chapter" that points out the dangers associated with the progress of the division of labor. He warns that if ever aristocracy were to return to the modern world it would be in the form of an industrial aristocracy. He thinks that statesmen should be on the alert to the corrosive effects of this development.

He also warns about what happens to those who are workers in this system. So how fair is it to call this warning a sort of Marxist prediction rather than a Smithian recommendation? In the final entry, Tocqueville warns of the dangers of a new kind of despotism which he calls soft and enervating rather than harsh and cruel. Has his prediction come true?

The French Revolution and the Equality Narrative

We suggest that the French Revolution was the decisive event for the next stage in the development of the equality narrative just as the American Revolution provided the next step in the liberty narrative. Compared to the American scene, which emerged in a fairly smooth fashion from the *Declaration of Independence* through the *Constitution* and beyond, the French situation went far less smoothly. We have included edited versions of the *Declaration of the Rights of Man and the Citizen* and the *French Constitutions* of 1791, 1793, and 1795. How is the French *Declaration* similar to and different from the American *Declaration*? What are the implications for political economy of these similarities and differences? How do the French Constitutions differ form the United States Constitution? What is it about the "Constitution of '93" that is so attractive to the radical wing of the equality narrative?

We suggest further that while Locke, Smith, and the American Revolution brought the economic question out of the household and made it a political question—and thus gave birth to political economy—Rousseau, The French Revolution, and European authors of the early nineteenth century brought the economic question out of the polity and made it a social question. They gave birth to the equality narrative of socialism that understands itself in opposition to the liberty narrative of political economy.

The equality narrative challenges political economy on behalf of "social economy." Poverty replaces profit as the central category of the scope and method of economic inquiry. What do "we" do with the poor? What do "we" do with the marginalized? Where is "our" social conscience? What is the cause of the poverty of a nation rather than what is the cause of the wealth of a nation becomes the focus of attention. Besides, isn't there something greater than the individual? How about the national good or the common good or the class good or the social good? Should we replace the profit-seeking entrepreneur with the scientifically trained administrative expert?

There are a number of similarities between the 1776 American *Declaration of Independence* and the 1789 French *Declaration of the Rights of Man and the Citizen*. We are struck, however, by the following three differences. The French *Declaration* (1) is far shorter and less particular than the American *Declaration*, confining itself to 22 abstract principles and omitting even a brief list of particular grievances against the French monarchy and aristocracy. (Tocqueville thinks that liberty is preserved by an appeal to particulars, where as the passion for equality is revealed in the attachment to general principles. (2) Announces, in the fashion of Rousseau's *Social Contract*, that "Men are born free and equal in rights. Social distinctions may be based only on common utility." The point of departure is liberty and the goal is equality. The American *Declaration*, by contrast, announces that all "Men are created equal," and proceeds to state that the purpose of government is to protect the individual right to the pursuit of life, liberty, and happiness. The point of departure is equality and the goal is liberty. How important is the difference between "born" and "created" as a point of departure? (3) States, again in Rousseauean *Social Contract* fashion, that "the law is the expression of the general will." How "sacred" are individual natural rights, if the "general will" of the citizen becomes the voice of God?

Equally revealing are the similarities and differences between the American *Constitution* of 1787, as amended in 1791 with the addition of a *Bill of Rights*, with the three French *Constitutions* of 1791, 1793, and 1795. We are struck, once again by the potentiality of the differences for the future of political economy.

Suffice it to note that the 1791 French *Constitution* attempts to restrain, but not abolish, the monarchy. And the 1795 *Constitution* attempts to restrain, but not abolish, the republic created in 1793. We have provided excerpts from these documents. The 1791 *Constitution* contains within its very Preamble a confrontation between the past and the present rather than, as in the Preamble to the United States *Constitution*, a promise between the present and the future. What are we to make of the "guarantee" of the right to "public relief" and the institutions of "national festivals?" The word "guarantee," is absent from the American *Constitution*, bur very present in 21st Century America? We note that the monarch is referred to as "King of the French." Also interesting is that the 1795 *Constitution* leads off not with the Legislative powers or a statement of purposes but the construction of the Executive Power in the form of an Executive Directory. Does this move toward a Directory, and the restrictions on intermediate institutions, anticipate and confirm the arrival of the Administrative State?

We suggest that it is the 1793 *Constitution*, also known as the "Montagnard Constitution," which is the central contribution of the French Revolution to the equality narrative. It repeats the tension between the "sanctity of property" and the "right to subsistence." But it removes the monarchy entirely from the picture much to the delight of the Jacobins. We have reproduced all 124 sections of this *Constitution*. How is the republican *Constitution* of France similar to and different from the republican *Constitution* of the United States and with what implications for the future of political economy? Does the 1793 Constitution (1) represent a direct democracy version of republicanism and (2) "guarantee" social and economic equality? The "guarantee of rights" is entrusted "to the care of all the virtues." What virtues could these be? Are they the sort that are compatible with Tocqueville's non-sublime mores of an individualistically based, but corrected, self interest rightly understood or is a sense of self sacrifice on behalf of the general will involved?

We rely on the Rousseau inspired Jacobin, Maximilien Robespierre, born in 1758 and executed in 1794 for an explanation of the virtues. In his Justification of the Reign of Terror speech in February 1794, officially called, "On the Principles of Morality," he says that the "fundamental principle of the democratic or popular government...is virtue which is nothing other than the love of country and ...the love of country necessarily includes the love of equality." Moreover, "terror is nothing other than justice...it is an emanation of virtue."

Robert Owen and the Application of Rousseau's Project

For both Rousseau and Owen, 1771–1858, the individual is not responsible for his miserable condition. Fortunately, his nature is malleable and thus if we transform society, we can change human nature. Where they differ, however, is in the identification of the cause of the misery. Rousseau saw the cause as the result of the development of the useful arts and practical sciences. For Owen, the cause is ignorance about what education can achieve and a lack of Christian conscience. For both, there is a collective responsibility to apply the general will to removing the blight of poverty from the body politic. But Owen "corrects" Rousseau's reliance on innocence and ignorance.

What are we to make of Owen's claim that human nature can be transformed if we transform the environment in which humans live, play, and work? Are the arts and sciences beneficial? Is it odd that an industrial business man like Owen would adopt a sense of social justice and urge reform of the Child Labor Laws and Poor Laws in Britain as well as set up agrarian reform communities in Scotland and America? What role do religion, education, and philanthropy play in Owen's analysis of, and solution to, the poverty problem? Does he ultimately advocate a national government plan to deal with the problem of poverty? Is he correct that poverty is the cause of crime and that public policy is better off fighting poverty through education than punishing crime through incarceration? Is Owen suggesting that fighting poverty is the moral equivalent of fighting slavery?

We have reproduced two short pieces from Owen's work that capture his (1) critique of the liberty narrative as individualistic and selfish and (2) hope for the success of what he portrays as the more humanitarian equality narrative. The first entry is an excerpt from the First Essay in *New View of Society* from the second edition of 1816. The second entry is from the Second Essay.

Again, we have kept editorial intrusions to a minimum. It might be useful for the reader to know, however, that Andrew Bell and Joseph Lancaster mentioned in the First Essay, were Christians active in the late eighteenth and early nineteenth centuries who opened schools for the poor in India and London respectively. (The first edition of the First Essay was dedicated to William Wilberforce.) David Dale, mentioned in the Second Essay, was Owen's father in law and also a philanthropic businessman.

Saint-Simon and the Birth of Socialism

We have included one edited piece of Saint Simon, 1760–1825, often referred to as the "Father of French Socialism," or the "Father of Christian Socialism." His work, like Owens's work, raises an interesting paradox in the equality narrative: the main focus is on alleviating poverty, but this is to be accomplished by a managerial class of (scientific) experts infused by a renewed attachment to a "true" religion.

In his *Geneva Letters* (1803), cited favorably by Engels in *Socialism: Utopian and Scientific*, but not included in our collection, Saint-Simon attempts to persuade the three classes of society—he actually addresses the lower or third class as "my friends"—to adopt his project, namely, to select "men of genius" who will make decisions in the "collective interest." On the surface, this seems more of a call for elitism than it does for egalitarianism. But is he not suggesting that there is an important alliance, even community of interests, between the intellectual and scientist and the mass of the people on the other hand? This reliance on well trained neutral experts, men of science is a "correction" of Rousseau and marks the importance of planning in an administrative state for the accomplishment of the equality narrative. But this detached expertise is also infused with a religious zeal!

In *Nouveau Christianisme* (1825) he proclaims "that it is the duty of religion to direct society to the great end of ameliorating as rapidly as possible the lot of the poorest class." The market can't accomplish this amelioration. Most of the argument is replete with accusations. "J'accuse," he says "les papes," and "les Lutherans" of being "heritiques." But he claims to have discovered the true meaning of Christianity: social justice implemented by caring officials. Are we seeing here the emergence of Christian Socialism? Is Saint-Simon anticipating a new direction in political economy where the government takes an active role in eliminating poverty in the name of divine justice or secular fairness? In other words, is political economy becoming social economy? Is economics acquiring a social conscience? Does he also represent the joining of the equality narrative with the nationalist narrative in the form of state socialism?

Friedrich List and the Critique of Adam Smith

Friedrich List is an important transitional figure in the conversation over the scope and method of political economy. We suggest he is important because he accuses Smith of limiting the role of government to a minimal level in his pursuit of a system suitable for shopkeepers engaged in the freedom of international trade. In other words, for political economy to be truly political, it must be governmental economy. Does he accurately portray Smith's system? Is his reliance on Stewart, Smith's biographer, effective? Does it makes sense to call Smith a Physiocrat, or a Mercantilist when Book IV of the *Wealth of Nations* criticizes these two systems? Is it fair to say that while not a clear proponent of the equality narrative, List is opposed to all political economy systems that do not give credit to the centrality of the nation and the role of human wisdom at the helm guiding the public interest? Does he deny the central premise of classical political economy, namely, that if left to their own devices individuals will make wise choices?

P. J. Proudhon and the Fulfillment of Rousseau

Like Rousseau before him, Proudhon proclaimed in the opening paragraph of *What is Property?* that "Property is Robbery." (We have retained the original translation by Tucker "Property is Robbery" rather than the more popular version that Proudhon actually said, "Property is Theft.") The full title of the work is *What is Property? Or an Inquiry into the Principle of Right and of Government*. It is also called his *First Memoir*.

Proudhon's point is that the pursuit of equality of conditions ought to be the principle of right and the project of government. This equation of property and robbery is also significant because he refers to "Property is Robbery... [as]...the war cry of '93" thus suggesting a remarkable continuity to the equality narrative beginning with Rousseau in the mid eighteenth century to the French Revolution and beyond. And that the purpose of the French Revolution, as expressed in the Constitution of '93, is to establish the "equality of condition."

Also interesting is that he quickly tempers his opening remarks in the *First Memoir* with the comment that "I am no agent of discord." It is as if he anticipated a critical response to his bold challenge to the established order. Suffice it to note, that this *First Memoir*, originally published in 1840, caused considerable controversy. Proudhon, in a prefatory dedication, praised the Academy of Besancon which, in turn, distanced itself from the "bold defender of the principle of equality of conditions." He was defended in this confrontation by Blanqui. Proudhon responded to Blanqui and this became his *Second Memoir on Property* in 1841. There, Proudhon adopts a more gradualist approach.

But let's return to the *First Memoir*. How does Proudhon see the relationship between economics, politics, and religion? Is his call for "science," a call to replace religion or are they in harmony? How central are the presence of classes and estates—how French in other words—to Proudhon's articulation of the alternative equality narrative? Is Proudhon suggesting that justice and property are in an antagonistic relationship? In other words, is private property unjust?

Proudhon begins *The Philosophy of Poverty* with an affirmation: "I affirm the reality of an economic science." He contrasts this with the non-science of "political economy." Is Proudhon anticipating the claim of Marx and Engels that socialism is scientific, and thus fair, but political economy is "the glorification of selfishness?" Or is he seeking a third way for the equality narrative beyond political economy and socialism suggesting that even socialism is insufficiently scientific? Is political economy "absurd" and socialism "utopian?" Isn't this the same as the criticism found in Marx and Engels? Yet they are not supportive of Proudhon's contribution. Marx, for example, wrote an essay called *The Poverty of Philosophy*!

Adam Smith

Wealth of Nations

Book I: Of The Causes Of Improvement In The Productive Powers of Labor, And of The Order According To Which Its Produce Is Naturally Distributed Among The Different Ranks of The People

Chapter I: Of The Division of Labor

The greatest improvement in the productive powers of labor, and the greater part of the skill, dexterity, and judgment with which it is anywhere directed, or applied, seem to have been the effects of the division of labor.

The effects of the division of labor, in the general business of society, will be more easily understood by considering in what manner it operates in some particular manufactures. It is commonly supposed to be carried furthest in some very trifling ones; not perhaps that it really is carried further in them than in others of more importance: but in those trifling manufactures which are destined to supply the small wants of but a small number of people, the whole number of workmen must necessarily be small; and those employed in every different branch of the work can often be collected into the same work-house, and placed at once under the view of the spectator. In those great manufactures, on the contrary, which are destined to supply the great wants of the great body of the people, every different branch of the work employs so great a number of workmen that it is impossible to collect them all into the same workhouse. We can seldom see more, at one time, than those employed in one single branch. Though in such manufactures, therefore, the work may really be divided into a much greater number of parts than in those of a more trifling nature, the division is not near so obvious, and has accordingly been much less observed.

To take an example, therefore, from a very trifling manufacture; but one in which the division of labor has been very often taken notice of, the trade of the pin-maker; a workman not educated to this business (which the division of labor has rendered a distinct trade), nor acquainted with the use of the machinery employed in it (to the invention of which the same division of labor has probably given occasion), could scarce, perhaps, with his utmost industry, make one pin in a day, and certainly could not make twenty. But in the way in which this business is now carried on, not only the whole work is a peculiar trade, but it is divided into a number of branches, of which the greater part are likewise peculiar trades. One man draws out the wire, another straights it, a third cuts it, a fourth points it, a fifth grinds it at the top for receiving, the head; to make the head requires two or three distinct operations; to put it on is a peculiar business, to whiten the pins is another; it is even a trade by itself to put them into the paper; and the important business of making a pin is, in this manner, divided into about eighteen distinct operations, which, in some manufactories, are all performed by distinct hands, though in others the same man will sometimes perform two or three of them.

I have seen a small manufactory of this kind where ten men only were employed, and where some of them consequently performed two or three distinct operations. But though they were very poor, and therefore but indifferently accommodated with the necessary machinery, they could, when they exerted themselves, make among them about twelve pounds of pins in a day. There are in a pound upwards of four thousand pins of a middling size. Those ten persons, therefore, could make among them upwards of forty-eight thousand pins in a day. Each person, therefore, making a tenth part of forty-eight thousand pins, might be considered as making four thousand eight hundred pins in a day. But if they had all wrought separately and independently, and without any of them having been educated to this peculiar business, they certainly could not each of them have made twenty, perhaps not one pin in a day; that is, certainly, not the two hundred and fortieth, perhaps not the four thousand eight hundredth part of what they are at present capable of performing, in consequence of a proper division and combination of their different operations.

In every other art and manufacture, the effects of the division of labor are similar to what they are in this very trifling one; though, in many of them, the labor can neither be so much subdivided, nor reduced to so great a simplicity of operation. The division of labor, however, so far as it can be introduced, occasions, in every art, a proportionable increase of the productive powers of labor. The separation of different trades and employments from one another seems to have taken place in consequence of this advantage. This separation, too, is generally called furthest in those countries which enjoy the highest degree of industry and improvement; what is the work of one man in a rude state of society being generally that of several in an improved one. In every improved society, the farmer is generally nothing but a farmer; the manufacturer, nothing but a manufacturer. The labor, too, which is necessary to produce any one complete manufacture is almost always divided among a great number of hands. How many different trades are employed in each branch of the linen and woolen manufactures from the growers of the flax and the wool, to the bleachers and smoothers of the linen, or to the dyers and dressers of the cloth!

The nature of agriculture, indeed, does not admit of so many subdivisions of labor, nor of so complete a separation of one business from another, as manufactures. It is impossible to separate so entirely the business of the grazer from that of the corn-farmer as the trade of the carpenter is commonly separated from that of the smith. The spinner is almost always a distinct person from the weaver; but the ploughman, the harrower, the sower of the seed, and the reaper of the corn, are often the same. The occasions for those different sorts of labor returning with the different seasons of the year, it is impossible that one man should be constantly employed in any one of them. This impossibility of making so complete and entire a separation of all the different branches of labor employed in agriculture is perhaps the reason why the improvement of the productive powers of labor in this art does not always keep pace with their improvement in manufactures. The most opulent nations, indeed, generally excel all their neighbors in agriculture as well as in manufactures; but they are commonly more distinguished by their superiority in the latter than in the former. Their lands are in general better cultivated, and having more labor and expense bestowed upon them, produce more in proportion to the extent and natural fertility of the ground.

But this superiority of produce is seldom much more than in proportion to the superiority of labor and expense. In agriculture, the labor of the rich country is not always much more productive than that of the poor; or, at least, it is never so much more productive as it commonly is in manufactures. The corn of the rich country, therefore, will not always, in the same degree of goodness, come cheaper to market than that of the poor. The corn of Poland, in the same degree of goodness, is as cheap as that of France, notwithstanding the superior opulence and improvement of the latter country. The corn of France is, in the corn provinces, fully as good, and in most years nearly about the same price with the corn of England, though, in opulence and improvement, France is perhaps inferior to England. The corn-lands of England, however, are better cultivated than those of France, and the corn-lands of France are said to be much better cultivated than those of Poland. But though the poor country, notwithstanding the inferiority of its cultivation, can, in some measure, rival the rich in the cheapness and goodness of its corn, it can pretend to no such competition in its manufactures; at least if those manufactures suit the soil, climate, and situation of the rich country. The silks of France are better and cheaper than those of England, because the silk manufacture, at least under the present high duties upon the importation of raw silk, does not so well suit the climate of England as that of France. But the hardware and the coarse woolens of England are beyond all comparison superior to those of France, and much cheaper too in the same degree of goodness. In Poland there are said to be scarce any manufactures of any kind, a few of those coarser household manufactures excepted, without which no country can well subsist.

This great increase of the quantity of work which, in consequence of the division of labor, the same number of people are capable of performing, is owing to three different circumstances; first, to the increase of dexterity in every particular workman; secondly, to the saving of the time which is commonly lost in passing from one species of work to another; and lastly, to the invention of a great number of machines which facilitate and abridge labor, and enable one man to do the work of many.

First, the improvement of the dexterity of the workman necessarily increases the quantity of the work he can perform; and the division of labor, by reducing every man's business to some one simple operation, and by making this operation the sole employment of his life, necessarily increased very much dexterity of the workman. A common smith, who, though accustomed to handle the hammer, has never been used to make nails, if upon some particular occasion he is obliged to attempt it, will scarce, I am assured, be able to make above two or three hundred nails in a day, and those too very bad ones. A smith who has been accustomed to make nails, but whose sole or principal business has not been that of a nailer, can seldom with his utmost diligence make more than eight hundred or a thousand nails in a day. I have seen several boys under twenty years of age who had never exercised any other trade but that of making nails, and who, when they exerted themselves, could make, each of them, upwards of two thousand three hundred nails in a day. The making of a nail, however, is by no means one of the simplest operations.

The same person blows the bellows, stirs or mends the fire as there is occasion, heats the iron, and forges every part of the nail: in forging the head too he is obliged to change his tools. The different operations into which the making of a pin, or of a metal button, is subdivided, are all of them much more simple, and the dexterity of the person, of whose life it has been the sole business to perform them, is usually much greater. The rapidity with which some of the operations of those manufacturers are performed, exceeds what the human hand could, by those who had never seen them, be supposed capable of acquiring.

Secondly, the advantage which is gained by saving the time commonly lost in passing from one sort of work to another is much greater than we should at first view be apt to imagine it. It is impossible to pass very quickly from one kind of work to another that is carried on in a different place and with quite different tools. A country weaver, who cultivates a small farm, must lose a good deal of time in passing from his loom to the field, and from the field to his loom. When the two trades can be carried on in the same workhouse, the loss of time is no doubt much less. It is even in this case, however, very considerable. A man commonly saunters a little in turning his hand from one sort of employment to another. When he first begins the new work he is seldom very keen and hearty; his mind, as they say, does not go to it, and for some time he rather trifles than applies to good purpose. The habit of sauntering and of indolent careless application, which is naturally, or rather necessarily acquired by every country workman who is obliged to change his work and his tools every half hour, and to apply his hand in twenty different ways almost every day of his life, renders him almost always slothful and lazy, and incapable of any vigorous application even on the most pressing occasions. Independent, therefore, of his deficiency in point of dexterity, this cause alone must always reduce considerably the quantity of work which he is capable of performing.

Thirdly, and lastly, everybody must be sensible how much labor is facilitated and abridged by the application of proper machinery. It is unnecessary to give any example. I shall only observe, therefore, that the invention of all those machines by which labor is so much facilitated and abridged seems to have been originally owing to the division of labor. Men are much more likely to discover easier and readier methods of attaining any object when the whole attention of their minds is directed towards that single object than when it is dissipated among a great variety of things. But in consequence of the division of labor, the whole of every man's attention comes naturally to be directed towards some one very simple object. It is naturally to be expected, therefore, that some one or other of those who are employed in each particular branch of labor should soon find out easier and readier methods of performing their own particular work, wherever the nature of it admits of such improvement.

A great part of the machines made use of in those manufactures in which labor is most subdivided, were originally the inventions of common workmen, who, being each of them employed in some very simple operation, naturally turned their thoughts towards finding out easier and readier methods of performing it. Whoever has been much accustomed to visit such manufactures must frequently have been shown very pretty machines, which were the inventions of such workmen in order to facilitate and quicken their particular part of the work. In the first fire-engines, a boy was constantly employed to open and shut alternately the communication between the boiler and the cylinder, according as the piston either ascended or descended. One of those boys, who loved to play with his companions, observed that, by tying a string from the handle of the valve which opened this communication to another part of the machine, the valve would open and shut without his assistance, and leave him at liberty to divert himself with his playfellows. One of the greatest improvements that has been made upon this machine, since it was first invented, was in this manner the discovery of a boy who wanted to save his own labor.

All the improvements in machinery, however, have by no means been the inventions of those who had occasion to use the machines. Many improvements have been made by the ingenuity of the makers of the machines, when to make them became the business of a peculiar trade; and some by that of those who are called philosophers or men of speculation, whose trade it is not to do anything, but to observe everything; and who, upon that account, are often capable of combining together the powers of the most distant and dissimilar objects. In the progress of society, philosophy or speculation becomes, like every other employment, the principal or sole trade and occupation of a particular class of citizens. Like every other employment too, it is subdivided into a great number of different branches, each of which affords occupation to a peculiar tribe or class of philosophers; and this subdivision of employment in philosophy, as well as in every other business, improves dexterity, and saves time. Each individual becomes more expert in his own peculiar branch, more work is done upon the whole, and the quantity of science is considerably increased by it.

It is the great multiplication of the productions of all the different arts, in consequence of the division of labor, which occasions, in a well-governed society, that universal opulence which extends itself to the lowest ranks of the people. Every workman has a great quantity of his own work to dispose of beyond what he himself has occasion for; and every other workman being exactly in the same situation, he is enabled to exchange a great quantity of his own goods for a great quantity, or, what comes to the same thing, for the price of a great quantity of theirs. He supplies them abundantly with what they have occasion for, and they accommodate him as amply with what he has occasion for, and a general plenty diffuses itself through all the different ranks of the society.

Observe the accommodation of the most common artificer or day-laborer in a civilized and thriving country, and you will perceive that the number of people of whose industry a part, though but a small part, has been employed in procuring him this accommodation, exceeds all computation. The woolen coat, for example, which covers the day-laborer, as coarse and rough as it may appear, is the produce of the joint labor of a great multitude of workmen. The shepherd, the sorter of the wool, the wool-comber or carder, the dyer, the scribbler, the spinner, the weaver, the fuller, the dresser, with many others, must all join their different arts in order to complete even this homely production. How many merchants and carriers, besides, must have been employed in transporting the materials from some of those workmen to others who often live in a very distant part of the country!

How much commerce and navigation in particular, how many shipbuilders, sailors, sail-makers, rope-makers, must have been employed in order to bring together the different drugs made use of by the dyer, which often come from the remotest corners of the world! What a variety of labor, too, is necessary in order to produce the tools of the meanest of those workmen! To say nothing of such complicated machines as the ship of the sailor, the mill of the fuller, or even the loom of the weaver, let us consider only what a variety of labor is requisite in order to form that very simple machine, the shears with which the shepherd clips the wool. The miner, the builder of the furnace for smelting the ore, the seller of the timber, the burner of the charcoal to be made use of in the smelting-house, the brick maker, the brick-layer, the workmen who attend the furnace, the mill-wright, the forger, the smith, must all of them join their different arts in order to produce them.

Were we to examine, in the same manner, all the different parts of his dress and household furniture, the coarse linen shirt which he wears next his skin, the shoes which cover his feet, the bed which he lies on, and all the different parts which compose it, the kitchen-grate at which he prepares his victuals, the coals which he makes use of for that purpose, dug from the bowels of the earth, and brought to him perhaps by a long sea and a long land carriage, all the other utensils of his kitchen, all the furniture of his table, the knives and forks, the earthen or pewter plates upon which he serves up and divides his victuals, the different hands employed in preparing his bread and his beer, the glass window which lets in the heat and the light, and keeps out the wind and the rain, with all the knowledge and art requisite for preparing that beautiful and happy invention, without which these northern parts of the world could scarce have afforded a very comfortable habitation, together with the tools of all the different workmen employed in producing those different conveniences; if we examine, I say, all these things, and consider what a variety of labor is employed about each of them, we shall be sensible that, without the assistance and co-operation of many thousands, the very meanest person in a civilized country could not be provided, even according to what we very falsely imagine the easy and simple manner in which he is commonly accommodated. Compared, indeed, with the more extravagant luxury of the great, his accommodation must no doubt appear extremely simple and easy; and yet it may be true, perhaps, that the accommodation of a European prince does not always so much exceed that of an industrious and frugal peasant as the accommodation of the latter exceeds that of many an African king, the absolute master of the lives and liberties of ten thousand naked savages.

Chapter II: Of The Principle Which Gives Occasion To The Division of Labor

This division of labor, from which so many advantages are derived, is not originally the effect of any human wisdom, which foresees and intends that general opulence to which it gives occasion. It is the necessary, though very slow and gradual consequence of a certain propensity in human nature which has in view no such extensive utility; the propensity to truck, barter, and exchange one thing for another.

Whether this propensity be one of those original principles in human nature of which no further account can be given; or whether, as seems more probable, it be the necessary consequence of the faculties of reason and speech, it belongs not to our present subject to inquire. It is common to all men, and to be found in no other race of animals, which seem to know neither this nor any other species of contracts.

Two greyhounds, in running down the same hare, have sometimes the appearance of acting in some sort of concert. Each turns her towards his companion, or endeavors to intercept her when his companion turns her towards himself. This, however, is not the effect of any contract, but of the accidental concurrence of their passions in the same object at that particular time. Nobody ever saw a dog make a fair and deliberate exchange of one bone for another with another dog. Nobody ever saw one animal by its gestures and natural cries signify to another, this is mine, that yours; I am willing to give this for that. When an animal wants to obtain something either of a man or of another animal, it has no other means of persuasion but to gain the favor of those whose service it requires. A puppy fawns upon its dam, and a spaniel endeavors by a thousand attractions to engage the attention of its master who is at dinner, when it wants to be fed by him.

Man sometimes uses the same arts with his brethren, and when he has no other means of engaging them to act according to his inclinations, endeavors by every servile and fawning attention to obtain their good will. He has not time, however, to do this upon every occasion. In civilized society he stands at all times in need of the cooperation and assistance of great multitudes, while his whole life is scarce sufficient to gain the friendship of a few persons. In almost every other race of animals each individual, when it is grown up to maturity, is entirely independent, and in its natural state has occasion for the assistance of no other living creature. But man has almost constant occasion for the help of his brethren, and it is in vain for him to expect it from their benevolence only. He will be more likely to prevail if he can interest their self-love in his favor, and show them that it is for their own advantage to do for him what he requires of them.

Whoever offers to another a bargain of any kind, proposes to do this. Give me that which I want, and you shall have this which you want, is the meaning of every such offer; and it is in this manner that we obtain from one another the far greater part of those good offices which we stand in need of. It is not from the benevolence of the butcher, the brewer, or the baker that we expect our dinner, but from their regard to their own interest. We address ourselves, not to their humanity but to their self-love, and never talk to them of our own necessities but of their advantages. Nobody but a beggar chooses to depend chiefly upon the benevolence of his fellow-citizens.

Even a beggar does not depend upon it entirely. The charity of well-disposed people, indeed, supplies him with the whole fund of his subsistence. But though this principle ultimately provides him with all the necessaries of life which he has occasion for, it neither does nor can provide him with them as he has occasion for them. The greater part of his occasional wants are supplied in the same manner as those of other people, by treaty, by barter, and by purchase. With the money which one man gives him he purchases food. The old clothes which another bestows upon him he exchanges for other old clothes which suit him better, or for lodging, or for food, or for money, with which he can buy either food, clothes, or lodging, as he has occasion.

As it is by treaty, by barter, and by purchase that we obtain from one another the greater part of those mutual good offices which we stand in need of, so it is this same trucking disposition which originally gives occasion to the division of labor. In a tribe of hunters or shepherds a particular person makes bows and arrows, for example, with more readiness and dexterity than any other. He frequently exchanges them for cattle or for venison with his companions; and he finds at last that he can in this manner get more cattle and venison than if he himself went to the field to catch them. From a regard to his own interest, therefore, the making of bows and arrows grows to be his chief business, and he becomes a sort of armourer. Another excels in making the frames and covers of their little huts or movable houses. He is accustomed to be of use in this way to his neighbors, who reward him in the same manner with cattle and with venison, till at last he finds it his interest to dedicate himself entirely to this employment, and to become a sort of house-carpenter. In the same manner a third becomes a smith or a brazier, a fourth a tanner or dresser of hides or skins, the principal part of the nothing of savages. And thus the certainty of being able to exchange all that surplus part of the produce of his own labor, which is over and above his own consumption, for such parts of the produce of other men's labor as he may have occasion for, encourages every man to apply himself to a particular occupation, and to cultivate and bring to perfection whatever talent or genius he may possess for that particular species of business.

The difference of natural talents in different men is, in reality, much less than we are aware of; and the very different genius which appears to distinguish men of different professions, when grown up to maturity, is not upon many occasions so much the cause as the effect of the division of labor. The difference between the most dissimilar characters, between a philosopher and a common street porter, for example, seems to arise not so much from nature as from habit, custom, and education. When they came into the world, and for the first six or eight years of their existence, they were perhaps very much alike, and neither their parents nor playfellows could perceive any remarkable difference. About that age, or soon after, they come to be employed in very different occupations. The difference of talents comes then to be taken notice of, and widens by degrees, till at last the vanity of the philosopher is willing to acknowledge scarce any resemblance. But without the disposition to truck,

barter, and exchange, every man must have procured to himself every necessary and conveniency of life which he wanted. All must have had the same
duties to perform, and the same work to do, and there could have been no
such difference of employment as could alone give occasion to any great difference of talents.

As it is this disposition which forms that difference of talents, so remarkable
among men of different professions, so it is this same disposition which renders
that difference useful. Many tribes of animals acknowledged to be all of the
same species derive from nature a much more remarkable distinction of genius,
than what, antecedent to custom and education, appears to take place among
men. By nature a philosopher is not in genius and disposition half so different
from a street porter, as a mastiff is from a greyhound, or a greyhound from a
spaniel, or this last from a shepherd's dog. Those different tribes of animals,
however, though all of the same species, are of scarce any use to one another.
The strength of the mastiff is not, in the least, supported either by the swiftness
of the greyhound, or by the sagacity of the spaniel, or by the docility of the
shepherd's dog. The effects of those different geniuses and talents, for want of
the power or disposition to barter and exchange, cannot be brought into a common stock, and do not in the least contribute to the better accommodation and
conveniency of the species. Each animal is still obliged to support and defend
itself, separately and independently, and derives no sort of advantage from that
variety of talents with which nature has distinguished its fellows.

Among men, on the contrary, the most dissimilar geniuses are of use to one
another; the different produces of their respective talents, by the general disposition to truck, barter, and exchange, being brought, as it were, into a common stock, where every man may purchase whatever part of the produce of
other men's talents he has occasion for.

Chapter III: The Division Of Labor Is Limited By The Extent Of The Market

As it is the power of exchanging that gives occasion to the division of labor, so
the extent of this division must always be limited by the extent of that power,
or, in other words, by the extent of the market. When the market is very small,
no person can have any encouragement to dedicate himself entirely to one
employment, for want of the power to exchange all that surplus part of the
produce of his own labor, which is over and above his own consumption, for
such parts of the produce of other men's labor as he has occasion for.

There are some sorts of industry, even of the lowest kind, which can be carried on nowhere but in a great town. A porter, for example, can find employment and subsistence in no other place. A village is by much too narrow a
sphere for him; even an ordinary market town is scarce large enough to afford
him constant occupation. In the lone houses and very small villages which are
scattered about in so desert a country as the Highlands of Scotland, every

farmer must be butcher, baker and brewer for his own family. In such situations we can scarce expect to find even a smith, a carpenter, or a mason, within less than twenty miles of another of the same trade. The scattered families that live at eight or ten miles distance from the nearest of them must learn to perform themselves a great number of little pieces of work, for which, in more populous countries, they would call in the assistance of those workmen.

Country workmen are almost everywhere obliged to apply themselves to all the different branches of industry that have so much affinity to one another as to be employed about the same sort of materials. A country carpenter deals in every sort of work that is made of wood: a country smith in every sort of work that is made of iron. The former is not only a carpenter, but a joiner, a cabinet-maker, and even a carver in wood, as well as a wheel-wright, a plough-wright, a cart and wagon maker. The employments of the latter are still more various. It is impossible there should be such a trade as even that of a nailer in the remote and inland parts of the Highlands of Scotland. Such a workman at the rate of a thousand nails a day, and three hundred working days in the year, will make three hundred thousand nails in the year. But in such a situation it would be impossible to dispose of one thousand, that is, of one day's work in the year.

As by means of water-carriage a more extensive market is opened to every sort of industry than what land-carriage alone can afford it, so it is upon the sea-coast, and along the banks of navigable rivers, that industry of every kind naturally begins to subdivide and improve itself, and it is frequently not till a long time after that those improvements extend themselves to the inland parts of the country. A broad-wheeled wagon, attended by two men, and drawn by eight horses, in about six weeks' time carries and brings back between London and Edinburgh near four ton weight of goods. In about the same time a ship navigated by six or eight men, and sailing between the ports of London and Leith, frequently carries and brings back two hundred ton weight of goods. Six or eight men, therefore, by the help of water-carriage, can carry and bring back in the same time the same quantity of goods between London and Edinburgh, as fifty broad-wheeled wagons, attended by a hundred men, and drawn by four hundred horses. Upon two hundred tons of goods, therefore, carried by the cheapest land-carriage from London to Edinburgh, there must be charged the maintenance of a hundred men for three weeks, and both the maintenance, and, what is nearly equal to the maintenance, the wear and tear of four hundred horses as well as of fifty great wagons. Whereas, upon the same quantity of goods carried by water, there is to be charged only the maintenance of six or eight men, and the wear and tear of a ship of two hundred tons burden, together with the value of the superior risk, or the difference of the insurance between land and water-carriage.

Were there no other communication between those two places, therefore, but by land-carriage, as no goods could be transported from the one to the other, except such whose price was very considerable in proportion to their weight, they could carry on but a small part of that commerce which at present subsists between them, and consequently could give but a small part of that encouragement which they at present mutually afford to each other's industry. There could be little or no commerce of any kind between the distant parts of the world. What goods could bear the expense of land-carriage between London and Calcutta? Or if there were any so precious as to be able to support this expense, with what safety could they be transported through the territories of so many barbarous nations? Those two cities, however, at present carry on a very considerable commerce with each other, and by mutually affording a market, give a good deal of encouragement to each other's industry.

Since such, therefore, are the advantages of water-carriage, it is natural that the first improvements of art and industry should be made where this conveniency opens the whole world for a market to the produce of every sort of labor, and that they should always be much later in extending themselves into the inland parts of the country. The inland parts of the country can for a long time have no other market for the greater part of their goods, but the country which lies round about them, and separates them from the sea-coast, and the great navigable rivers. The extent of their market, therefore, must for a long time be in proportion to the riches and populousness of that country, and consequently their improvement must always be posterior to the improvement of that country. In our North American colonies the plantations have constantly followed either the sea-coast or the banks of the navigable rivers, and have scarce anywhere extended themselves to any considerable distance from both....

Chapter IV: The Origin And Use of Money

When the division of labor has been once thoroughly established, it is but a very small part of a man's wants which the produce of his own labor can supply. He supplies the far greater part of them by exchanging that surplus part of the produce of his own labor, which is over and above his own consumption, for such parts of the produce of other men's labor as he has occasion for. Every man thus lives by exchanging, or becomes in some measure a merchant, and the society itself grows to be what is properly a commercial society.

But when the division of labor first began to take place, this power of exchanging must frequently have been very much clogged and embarrassed in its operations. One man, we shall suppose, has more of a certain commodity than he himself has occasion for, while another has less. The former consequently would be glad to dispose of, and the latter to purchase, a part of this superfluity. But if this latter should chance to have nothing that the former stands in need of, no exchange can be made between them. The butcher has more meat in his shop than he himself can consume, and the brewer and the baker would each of them be willing to purchase a part of it. But they have nothing to offer in exchange, except the different productions of their respective trades, and the butcher is already provided with all the bread and beer which he has immediate occasion for. No exchange can, in this case, be made between them. He cannot be their merchant, nor they his customers; and they are all of them thus mutually less serviceable to one another. In order to avoid the inconveniency of such situations, every prudent man in every period of society, after the first establishment of the division of labor, must naturally have endeavored to manage his affairs in such a manner as to have at all times by him, besides the peculiar produce of his own industry, a certain quantity of some one commodity or other, such as he imagined few people would be likely to refuse in exchange for the produce of their industry.

Chapter VI: Of The Component Parts Of The Price Of Commodities

In that early and rude state of society which precedes both the accumulation of stock and the appropriation of land, the proportion between the quantities of labor necessary for acquiring different objects seems to be the only circumstance which can afford any rule for exchanging them for one another. If among a nation of hunters, for example, it usually costs twice the labor to kill a beaver which it does to kill a deer, one beaver should naturally exchange for or be worth two deer. It is natural that what is usually the produce of two days' or two hours' labor, should be worth double of what is usually the produce of one day's or one hour's labor....

In this state of things, the whole produce of labor belongs to the laborer; and the quantity of labor commonly employed in acquiring or producing any commodity is the only circumstance which can regulate the quantity exchange for which it ought commonly to purchase, command, or exchange for.

As soon as stock has accumulated in the hands of particular persons, some of them will naturally employ it in setting to work industrious people, whom they will supply with materials and subsistence, in order to make a profit by the sale of their work, or by what their labor adds to the value of the materials. In exchanging the complete manufacture either for money, for labor, or for other goods, over and above what may be sufficient to pay the price of the materials, and the wages of the workmen, something must be given for the profits of the undertaker of the work who hazards his stock in this adventure. The value which the workmen add to the materials, therefore, resolves itself in this ease into two parts, of which the one pays their wages, the other the profits of their employer upon the whole stock of materials and wages which he advanced. He could have no interest to employ them, unless he expected from the sale of their work something more than what was sufficient to replace his stock to him; and he could have no interest to employ a great stock rather than a small one, unless his profits were to bear some proportion to the extent of his stock....

In this state of things, the whole produce of labor does not always belong to the laborer. He must in most cases share it with the owner of the stock which employs him. Neither is the quantity of labor commonly employed in acquiring or producing any commodity, the only circumstance which can regulate the quantity which it ought commonly to purchase, command, or exchange for. An additional quantity, it is evident, must be due for the profits of the stock which advanced the wages and furnished the materials of that labor.

As soon as the land of any country has all become private property, the landlords, like all other men, love to reap where they never sowed, and demand a rent even for its natural produce. The wood of the forest, the grass of the field, and all the natural fruits of the earth, which, when land was in common, cost the laborer only the trouble of gathering them, come, even to him, to have an additional price fixed upon them. He must then pay for the license to gather them; and must give up to the landlord a portion of what his labor either collects or produces. This portion, or, what comes to the same thing, the price of this portion, constitutes the rent of land, and in the price of the greater part of commodities makes a third component part.

The real value of all the different component parts of price, it must be observed, is measured by the quantity of labor which they can, each of them, purchase or command. Labor measures the value not only of that part of price which *resolves itself* [italics added] into labor, but of that which *resolves itself* [italics added] into rent, and of that which *resolves itself* [italics added] into profit.

In every society the price of every commodity finally *resolves itself* [italics added] into some one or other, or all of those three parts; and in every improved society, all the three enter more or less, as component parts, into the price of the far greater part of commodities....

As any particular commodity comes to be more manufactured, that part of the price which *resolves itself* into wages and profit comes to be greater in proportion to that which resolves itself into rent. In the progress of the manufacture, not only the number of profits increase, but every subsequent profit is greater than the foregoing; because the capital from which it is derived must always be greater. The capital which employs the weavers, for example, must be greater than that which employs the spinners; because it not only replaces that capital with its profits, but pays, besides, the wages of the weavers; and the profits must always bear some proportion to the capital.

In the most improved societies, however, there are always a few commodities of which the price *resolves itself* into two parts only, the wages of labor, and the profits of stock; and a still smaller number, in which it consists altogether in the wages of labor. In the price of sea-fish, for example, one part pays the labor of the fishermen, and the other the profits of the capital employed in the fishery. Rent very seldom makes any part of it, though it does sometimes, as I shall show hereafter. It is otherwise, at least through the greater part of Europe, in river fisheries. A salmon fishery pays a rent, and rent, though it cannot well be called the rent of land, makes a part of the price of a salmon as well as wages and profit. In some parts of Scotland a few poor people make a trade of gathering, along the sea-shore, those little variegated stones commonly known by the name of Scotch Pebbles. The price which is paid to them by the stone-cutter is altogether the wages of their labor; neither rent nor profit make any part of it.

But the whole price of any commodity must still finally *resolve itself* into some one or other, or all of those three parts; as whatever part of it remains after paying the rent of the land, and the price of the whole labor employed in raising, manufacturing, and bringing it to market, must necessarily be profit to somebody.

As the price or exchangeable value of every particular commodity, taken separately, *resolves itself* into some one or other or all of those three parts; so that of all the commodities which compose the whole annual produce of the labor of every country, taken complexly, must resolve itself into the same three parts, and be parceled out among different inhabitants of the country, either as the wages of their labor, the profits of their stock, or the rent of their land. The whole of what is annually either collected or produced by the labor of every society, or what comes to the same thing, the whole price of it, is in this manner originally distributed among some of its different members. Wages, profit, and rent, are the three original sources of all revenue as well as of all exchangeable value. All other revenue is ultimately derived from some one or other of these....

As in a civilized country there are but few commodities of which the exchangeable value arises from labor only, rent and profit contributing largely to that of the far greater part of them, so the annual produce of its labor will always be sufficient to purchase or command a much greater quantity of labor than what employed in raising, preparing, and bringing that produce to market. If the society were annually to employ all the labor which it can annually purchase, as the quantity of labor would increase greatly every year, so the produce of every succeeding year would be of vastly greater value than that of the foregoing. But there is no country in which the whole annual produce is employed in maintaining the industrious. The idle everywhere consume a great part of it; and according to the different proportions in which it is annually divided between those two different orders of people, its ordinary or average value must either annually increase, or diminish, or continue the same from one year to another.

Chapter X: Conclusion

The whole annual produce of the land and labor of every country, or what comes to the same thing, the whole price of that annual produce, naturally divides itself, it has already been observed, into three parts; the rent of land, the wages of labor, and the profits of stock; and constitutes a revenue to three different orders of people; to those who live by rent, to those who live by wages, and to those who live by profit. These are the three great, original, and constituent orders of every civilized society, from whose revenue that of every other order is ultimately derived.

The interest of the first of those three great orders, it appears from what has been just now said, is strictly and inseparably connected with the general interest of the society. Whatever either promotes or obstructs the one, necessarily promotes or obstructs the other. When the public deliberates concerning any regulation of commerce or police, the proprietors of land never can mislead it, with a view to promote the interest of their own particular order; at least, if they have any tolerable knowledge of that interest. They are, indeed, too often defective in this tolerable knowledge. They are the only one of the three orders whose revenue costs them neither labor nor care, but comes to them, as it were, of its own accord, and independent of any plan or project of their own. That indolence, which is the natural effect of the ease and security of their situation, renders them too often, not only ignorant, but incapable of that application of mind which is necessary in order to foresee and understand the consequences of any public regulation.

The interest of the second order, that of those who live by wages, is as strictly connected with the interest of the society as that of the first. The wages of the laborer, it has already been shown, are never so high as when the demand for labor is continually rising, or when the quantity employed is every year increasing considerably. When this real wealth of the society becomes stationary, his wages are soon reduced to what is barely enough to enable him to bring up a family, or to continue the race of laborers. When the society declines, they fall even below this. The order of proprietors may, perhaps, gain more by the prosperity of the society than that of laborers: but there is no order that suffers so cruelly from its decline. But though the interest of the laborer is strictly connected with that of the society, he is incapable either of comprehending that interest or of understanding its connection with his own. His condition leaves him no time to receive the necessary information, and his education and habits are commonly such as to render him unfit to judge even though he was fully informed. In the public deliberations, therefore, his voice is little heard and less regarded, except upon some particular occasions, when his clamor is animated, set on and supported by his employers, not for his, but their own particular purposes.

His employers constitute the third order, that of those who live by profit. It is the stock that is employed for the sake of profit which puts into motion the greater part of the useful labor of every society. The plans and projects of the employers of stock regulate and direct all the most important operations of labor, and profit is the end proposed by all those plans and projects. But the rate of profit does not, like rent and wages, rise with the prosperity and fall with the declension of the society. On the contrary, it is naturally low in rich and high in poor countries, and it is always highest in the countries which are going fastest to ruin.

The interest of this third order, therefore, has not the same connection with the general interest of the society as that of the other two. Merchants and master manufacturers are, in this order, the two classes of people who commonly employ the largest capitals, and who by their wealth draw to themselves the greatest share of the public consideration. As during their whole lives they are engaged in plans and projects, they have frequently more acuteness of understanding than the greater part of country gentlemen. As their thoughts, however, are commonly exercised rather about the interest of their own particular branch of business, than about that of the society, their judgment, even when given with the greatest candor (which it has not been upon every occasion) is much more to be depended upon with regard to the former of those two objects than with regard to the latter. Their superiority over the country gentleman is not so much in their knowledge of the public interest, as in their having a better knowledge of their own interest than he has of his. It is by this superior knowledge of their own interest that they have frequently imposed upon his generosity, and persuaded him to give up both his own interest and that of the public, from a very simple but honest conviction that their interest, and not his, was the interest of the public.

The interest of the dealers, however, in any particular branch of trade or manufactures, is always in some respects different from, and even opposite to, that of the public. To widen the market and to narrow the competition, is always the interest of the dealers. To widen the market may frequently be agreeable enough to the interest of the public; but to narrow the competition must always be against it, and can serve only to enable the dealers, by raising their profits above what they naturally would be, to levy, for their own benefit, an absurd tax upon the rest of their fellow-citizens....

Book III: Of The Different Progress of Opulence In Different Nations

Chapter I: Of The Natural Progress Of Opulence

As subsistence is, in the nature of things, prior to conveniency and luxury, so the industry which procures the former must necessarily be prior to that which ministers to the latter. The cultivation and improvement of the country, therefore, which affords subsistence, must, necessarily, be prior to the increase of the town, which furnishes only the means of conveniency and luxury. It is the surplus produce of the country only, or what is over and above the maintenance of the cultivators, that constitutes the subsistence of the town, which can therefore increase only with the increase of this surplus produce. The town, indeed, may not always derive its whole subsistence from the country in its neighborhood, or even from the territory to which it belongs, but from very distant countries; and this, though it forms no exception from the general rule, has occasioned considerable variations in the progress of opulence in different ages and nations.

That order of things which necessity imposes in general, though not in every particular country, is, in every particular country, promoted by the natural inclinations of man. If human institutions had never thwarted those natural inclinations, the towns could nowhere have increased beyond what the improvement and cultivation of the territory in which they were situated could support; till such time, at least, as the whole of that territory was completely cultivated and improved. Upon equal, or nearly equal profits, most men will choose to employ their capitals rather in the improvement and cultivation of land than either in manufactures or in foreign trade. The man who employs his capital in land has it more under his view and command, and his fortune is much less liable to accidents than that of the trader, who is obliged frequently to commit it, not only to the winds and the waves, but to the more uncertain elements of human folly and injustice, by giving great credits in distant countries to men with whose character and situation he can seldom be thoroughly acquainted. The capital of the landlord, on the contrary, which is fixed in the improvement of his land, seems to be as well secured as the nature of human affairs can admit of. The beauty of the country besides, the pleasures of a country life, the tranquility of mind which it promises, and wherever the injustice of human laws does not disturb it, the independency which it really affords, have charms that more or less attract everybody; and as to cultivate the ground was the original destination of man, so in every stage of his existence he seems to retain a predilection for this primitive employment....

In seeking for employment to a capital, manufactures are, upon equal or nearly equal profits, naturally preferred to foreign commerce, for the same reason that agriculture is naturally preferred to manufactures. As the capital of the landlord or farmer is more secure than that of the manufacturer, so the capital of the manufacturer, being at all times more within his view and command, is more secure than that of the foreign merchant. In every period, indeed, of every society, the surplus part both of the rude and manufactured produce, or that for which there is no demand at home, must be sent abroad in order to be exchanged for something for which there is some demand at home. But whether the capital, which carries this surplus produce abroad, be a foreign or a domestic one is of very little importance. If the society has not acquired sufficient capital both to cultivate all its lands, and to manufacture in the (most) complete manner the whole of its rude produce, there is even a considerable advantage that rude produce should be exported by a foreign capital, in order that the whole stock of the society may be employed in more useful purposes. The wealth of ancient Egypt, that of China and Indostan, sufficiently demonstrate that a nation may attain a very high degree of opulence though the greater part of its exportation trade be carried on by foreigners. The progress of our North American and West Indian colonies would have been much less rapid had no capital but what belonged to themselves been employed in exporting their surplus produce.

According to the natural course of things, therefore, the greater part of the capital of every growing society is, first, directed to agriculture, afterwards to manufactures, and last of all to foreign commerce. This order of things is so very natural that in every society that had any territory it has always, I believe, been in some degree observed. Some of their lands must have been cultivated before any considerable towns could be established, and some sort of coarse industry of the manufacturing kind must have been carried on in those towns, before they could well think of employing themselves in foreign commerce.

But though this natural order of things must have taken place in some degree in every such society, it has, in all the modern states of Europe, been, in many respects, entirely inverted. The foreign commerce of some of their cities has introduced all their finer manufactures, or such as were fit for distant sale; and manufactures and foreign commerce together have given birth to the principal improvements of agriculture. The manners and customs which the nature of their original government introduced, and which remained after that government was greatly altered, necessarily forced them into this unnatural and retrograde order.

Chapter II: Of The Discouragement of Agriculture In The Ancient State of Europe

When land, like movables, is considered as the means only of subsistence and enjoyment, the natural law of succession divides it, like them, among all the children of the family; of an of whom the subsistence and enjoyment may be supposed equally dear to the father....

The law of primogeniture, therefore, came to take place, not immediately, indeed, but in process of time, in the succession of landed estates, for the same reason that it has generally taken place in that of monarchies, though not always at their first institution. That the power, and consequently the security of the monarchy, may not be weakened by division, it must descend entire to one of the children. To which of them so important a preference shall be given must be determined by some general rule, founded not upon the doubtful distinctions of personal merit, but upon some plain and evident difference which can admit of no dispute. Among the children of the same family, there can be no indisputable difference but that of sex, and that of age. The male sex is universally preferred to the female; and when all other things are equal, the elder everywhere takes place of the younger. Hence the origin of the right of primogeniture, and of what is called lineal succession.

Laws frequently continue in force long after the circumstances which first gave occasion to them, and which could alone render them reasonable, are no more. In the present state of Europe, the proprietor of a single acre of land is as perfectly secure of his possession as the proprietor of a hundred thousand. The right of primogeniture, however, still continues to be respected, and as of all institutions it is the fittest to support the pride of family distinctions, it is still likely to endure for many centuries. In every other respect, nothing can be more contrary to the real interest of a numerous family than a right which, in order to enrich one, beggars all the rest of the children.

Entails are the natural consequences of the law of primogeniture. They were introduced to preserve a certain lineal succession, of which the law of primogeniture first gave the idea, and to hinder any part of the original estate from being carried out of the proposed line either by gift, or devise, or alienation; either by the folly, or by the misfortune of any of its successive owners....

To improve land with profit, like all other commercial projects, requires an exact attention to small savings and small gains, of which a man born to a great fortune, even though naturally frugal, is very seldom capable. The situation of such a person naturally disposes him to attend rather to ornament which pleases his fancy than to profit for which he has so little occasion. The elegance of his dress, of his equipage, of his house, and household furniture, are objects which from his infancy he has been accustomed to have some anxiety about. The turn of mind which this habit naturally forms follows him when he comes to think of the improvement of land. He embellishes perhaps four or five hundred acres in the neighborhood of his house, at ten times the expense which the land is worth after all his improvements; and finds that if he was to improve his whole estate in the same manner, and he has little taste for any other, he would be a bankrupt before he had finished the tenth part of it. There still remain in both parts of the United Kingdom some great estates which have continued without interruption in the hands of the same family since the times of feudal anarchy. Compare the present condition of those estates with the possessions of the small proprietors in their neighborhood, and you will require no other argument to convince you how unfavorable such extensive property is to improvement....

But if great improvements are seldom to be expected from great proprietors, they are least of all to be expected when they employ slaves for their workmen. The experience of all ages and nations, I believe, demonstrates that the work done by slaves, though it appears to cost only their maintenance, is in the end the dearest of any. A person who can acquire no property, can have no other interest but to eat as much, and to labor as little as possible. Whatever work he does beyond what is sufficient to purchase his own maintenance can be squeezed out of him by violence only, and not by any interest of his own. In ancient Italy, how much the cultivation of corn degenerated, how unprofitable it became to the master when it fell under the management of slaves, is remarked by both Pliny and Columella. In the time of Aristotle it had not been much better in ancient Greece. Speaking of the ideal republic described in the laws of Plato, to maintain five thousand idle men (the number of warriors supposed necessary for its defense) together with their women and servants, would require, he says, a territory of boundless extent and fertility, like the plains of Babylon.

The pride of man makes him love to domineer, and nothing mortifies him so much as to be obliged to condescend to persuade his inferiors. Wherever the law allows it, and the nature of the work can afford it, therefore, he will generally prefer the service of slaves to that of freemen. The planting of sugar and tobacco can afford the expense of slave-cultivation. The raising of corn, it seems, in the present times, cannot. In the English colonies, of which the principal produce is corn, the far greater part of the work is done by freemen. The late resolution of the Quakers in Pennsylvania to set at liberty all their negro slaves may satisfy us that their number cannot be very great. Had they made any considerable part of their property, such a resolution could never have been agreed to. In our sugar colonies, on the contrary, the whole work is done by slaves, and in our tobacco colonies a very great part of it. The profits of a sugar-plantation in any of our West Indian colonies are generally much greater than those of any other cultivation that is known either in Europe or America; and the profits of a tobacco plantation, though inferior to those of sugar, are superior to those of corn, as has already been observed. Both can afford the expense of slave-cultivation, but sugar can afford it still better than tobacco. The number of negroes accordingly is much greater, in proportion to that of whites, in our sugar than in our tobacco colonies....

Chapter IV: The Commerce of The Town [and] The Improvement of The Country

The increase and riches of commercial and manufacturing towns contributed to the improvement and cultivation of the countries to which they belonged in three different ways.

First, by affording a great and ready market for the rude produce of the country, they gave encouragement to its cultivation and further improvement. This benefit was not even confined to the countries in which they were situated, but extended more or less to all those with which they had any dealings. To all of them they afforded a market for some part either of their rude or manufactured produce, and consequently gave some encouragement to the industry and improvement of all. Their own country, however, on account of its neighborhood, necessarily derived the greatest benefit from this market. Its rude produce being charged with less carriage, the traders could pay the growers a better price for it, and yet afford it as cheap to the consumers as that of more distant countries.

Secondly, the wealth acquired by the inhabitants of cities was frequently employed in purchasing such lands as were to be sold, of which a great part would frequently be uncultivated. Merchants are commonly ambitious of becoming country gentlemen, and when they do, they are generally the best of all improvers. A merchant is accustomed to employ his money chiefly in profitable projects, whereas a mere country gentleman is accustomed to employ it chiefly in expense. The one often sees his money go from him and return to him again with a profit; the other, when once he parts with it, very seldom expects to see any more of it. Those different habits naturally affect their temper and disposition in every sort of business. A merchant is commonly a bold, a country gentleman a timid undertaker. The one is not afraid to lay out at once a large capital upon the improvement of his land when he has a probable prospect of raising the value of it in proportion to the expense. The other, if he has any capital, which is not always the case, seldom ventures to employ it in this manner. If he improves at all, it is commonly not with a capital, but with what he can save out of his annual revenue. Whoever has had the fortune to live in a mercantile town situated in an unimproved country must have frequently observed how much more spirited the operations of merchants were in this way than those of mere country gentlemen. The habits, besides, of order, economy, and attention, to which mercantile business naturally forms a merchant, render him much fitter to execute, with profit and success, any project of improvement.

Thirdly, and lastly, commerce and manufactures gradually introduced order and good government, and with them, the liberty and security of individuals, among the inhabitants of the country, who had before lived almost in a continual state of war with their neighbors and of servile dependency upon their superiors. This, though it has been the least observed, is by far the most important of all their effects. Mr. Hume is the only writer who, so far as I know, has hitherto taken notice of it....

But what all the violence of the feudal institutions could never have effected, the silent and insensible operation of foreign commerce and manufactures gradually brought about. These gradually furnished the great proprietors with something for which they could exchange the whole surplus produce of their lands, and which they could consume themselves without sharing it either with tenants or retainers. All for ourselves and nothing for other people, seems, in every age of the world, to have been the vile maxim of the masters of mankind. As soon, therefore, as they could find a method of consuming the whole value of their rents themselves, they had no disposition to share them with any other persons. For a pair of diamond buckles, perhaps, or for something as frivolous and useless, they exchanged the maintenance, or what is the same thing, the price of the maintenance of a thousand men for a year, and with it the whole weight and authority which it could give them. The buckles, however, were to be all their own, and no other human creature was to have any share of them; whereas in the more ancient method of expense they must have shared with at least a thousand people. With the judges that were to determine the preference this difference was perfectly decisive; and thus, for the gratification of the most childish, the meanest, and the most sordid of all vanities, they gradually bartered their whole power and authority.

In a country where there is no foreign commerce, nor any of the finer manufactures, a man of ten thousand a year cannot well employ his revenue in any other way than in maintaining, perhaps, a thousand families, who are all of them necessarily at his command. In the present state of Europe, a man of ten thousand a year can spend his whole revenue, and he generally does so, without directly maintaining twenty people, or being able to command more than ten footmen not worth the commanding. Indirectly, perhaps, he maintains as great or even a greater number of people than he could have done by the ancient method of expense. For though the quantity of precious productions for which he exchanges his whole revenue be very small, the number of workmen employed in collecting and preparing it must necessarily have been very great. Its great price generally arises from the wages of their labor, and the profits of all their immediate employers. By paying that price he indirectly pays all those wages and profits and thus indirectly contributes to the maintenance of all the workmen and their employers. He generally contributes, however, but a very small proportion to that of each, to very few perhaps a tenth, to many not a hundredth, and to some not a thousandth, nor even a ten-thousandth part of their whole annual maintenance. Though he contributes, therefore, to the maintenance of them all, they are all more or less independent of him, because generally they can all be maintained without him.

When the great proprietors of land spend their rents in maintaining their tenants and retainers, each of them maintains entirely all his own tenants and all his own retainers. But when they spend them in maintaining tradesmen and artificers, they may, all of them taken together, perhaps, maintain as great, or, on account of the waste which attends rustic hospitality, a greater number of people than before. Each of them, however, taken singly, contributes often but a very small share to the maintenance of any individual of this greater number. Each tradesman or artificer derives his subsistence from the employment, not of one, but of a hundred or a thousand different customers. Though in some measure obliged to them all, therefore, he is not absolutely dependent upon any one of them.

The personal expense of the great proprietors having in this manner gradually increased, it was impossible that the number of their retainers should not as gradually diminish till they were at last dismissed altogether. The same cause gradually led them to dismiss the unnecessary part of their tenants. Farms were enlarged, and the occupiers of land, notwithstanding the complaints of depopulation, reduced to the number necessary for cultivating it, according to the imperfect state of cultivation and improvement in those times. By the removal of the unnecessary mouths, and by exacting from the farmer the full value of the farm, a greater surplus, or what is the same thing, the price of a greater surplus, was obtained for the proprietor, which the merchants and manufacturers soon furnished him with a method of spending upon his own person in the same manner as he had done the rest. The same cause continuing to operate, he was desirous to raise his rents above what his lands, in the actual state of their improvement, could afford. His tenants could agree to this upon one condition only, that they should be secured in their possession for such a term of years as might give them time to recover with profit whatever they should lay out in the further improvement of the land. The expensive vanity of the landlord made him willing to accept of this condition; and hence the origin of long leases....

A revolution of the greatest importance to the public happiness was in this manner brought about by two different orders of people who had not the least intention to serve the public. To gratify the most childish vanity was the sole motive of the great proprietors. The merchants and artificers, much less ridiculous, acted merely from a view to their own interest, and in pursuit of their own peddler principle of turning a penny wherever a penny was to be got. Neither of them had either knowledge or foresight of that great revolution which the folly of the one, and the industry of the other, was gradually bringing about....

The capital, however, that is acquired to any country by commerce and manufactures is all a very precarious and uncertain possession till some part of it has been secured and realized in the cultivation and improvement of its lands. A merchant, it has been said very properly, is not necessarily the citizen of any particular country. It is in a great measure indifferent to him from what place he carries on his trade; and a very trifling disgust will make him remove his capital, and together with it all the industry which it supports, from one country to another. No part of it can be said to belong to any particular country, till it has been spread as it were over the face of that country, either in buildings or in the lasting improvement of lands....

Book IV: Systems of Political Economy

Introduction: (Definition of Political Economy)

Political economy, considered as a branch of the science of a statesman or legislator, proposes two distinct objects: first, to provide a plentiful revenue or subsistence for the people, or more properly to enable them to provide such a revenue or subsistence for themselves; and secondly, to supply the state or commonwealth with a revenue sufficient for the public services. It proposes to enrich both the people and the sovereign.

The different progress of opulence in different ages and nations has given occasion to two different systems of political economy with regard to enriching the people. The one may be called the system of commerce, the other that of agriculture. I shall endeavor to explain both as fully and distinctly as I can, and shall begin with the system of commerce. It is the modern system, and is best understood in our own country and in our own times.

Chapter I: The Principle of The Commercial or Mercantile System

That wealth consists in money, or and silver, is a popular notion which naturally arises from the double function of money, as the instrument of commerce and as the measure of value. In consequence of its being the instrument of commerce, when we have money we can more readily obtain whatever else we have occasion for than by means of any other commodity. The great affair, we always find, is to get money. When that is obtained, there is no difficulty in making any subsequent purchase. In consequence of its being the measure of value, we estimate that of all other commodities by the quantity of money which they will exchange for. We say of a rich man that he is worth a great deal, and of a poor man that he is worth very little money. A frugal man, or a man eager to be rich, is said to love money; and a careless, a generous, or a profuse man, is said to be indifferent about it. To grow rich is to get money; and wealth and money, in short, are, in common language, considered as in every respect synonymous.

A rich country, in the same manner as a rich man, is supposed to be a country abounding in money; and to heap up gold and saver in any country is supposed to be the readiest way to enrich it....

The two principles being established, however, that wealth consisted in gold and silver, and that those metals could be brought into a country which had no mines only by the balance of trade, or by exporting to a greater value than it imported, it necessarily became the great object of political economy to diminish as much as possible the importation of foreign goods for home consumption, and to increase as much as possible the exportation of the produce of domestic industry. Its two great engines for enriching the country, therefore, were restraints upon importation, and encouragements to exportation.

The restraints upon importation were of two kinds.

First, restraints upon the importation of such foreign goods for home consumption as could be produced at home, from whatever country they were imported.

Secondly, restraints upon the importation of goods of almost all kinds from those particular countries with which the balance of trade was supposed to be disadvantageous....

By advantageous treaties of commerce, particular privileges were procured in some foreign state for the goods and merchants of the country, beyond what were granted to those other countries.

By established establishment of colonies in distant countries, not only particular privileges, but a monopoly was frequently procured for the goods and merchants of the country which established them.

The two sorts of restraints upon importation above-mentioned, together with these four encouragements to exportation, constitute the six principal means by which the commercial system proposes to increase the quantity of gold and silver in any country by turning the balance of trade in its favor. I shall consider each of them in a particular chapter....

Chapter II: Of Restraints Upon The Importation From Foreign Countries Of Such Goods As Can Be Produced At Home

By restraining, either by high duties or by absolute prohibitions, the importation of such goods from foreign countries as can be produced at home, the monopoly of the home market is more or less secured to the domestic industry employed in producing them. Thus the prohibition of importing either live cattle or salt provisions from foreign countries secures to the grazers of Great Britain the monopoly of the home market for butcher's meat. The high duties upon the importation of corn, which in times of moderate plenty amount to a prohibition, give a like advantage to the growers of that commodity. The prohibition of the importation of foreign woolens is equally favorable to the woolen manufacturers. The silk manufacture, though altogether employed upon foreign materials, has lately obtained the same advantage. The linen manufacture has not yet obtained it, but is making great strides towards it. Many other sorts of manufacturers have, in the same manner, obtained in Great Britain, either altogether or very nearly, a monopoly against their countrymen. The variety of goods of which the importation into Great Britain is prohibited, either absolutely, or under certain circumstances, greatly exceeds what can easily be suspected by those who are not well acquainted with the laws of the customs.

That this monopoly of the home-market frequently gives great encouragement to that particular species of industry which enjoys it, and frequently turns towards that employment a greater share of both the labor and stock of the society than would otherwise have gone to it, cannot be doubted. But whether it tends either to increase the general industry of the society, or to give it the most advantageous direction, is not, perhaps, altogether so evident.

The general industry of the society never can exceed what the capital of the society can employ. As the number of workmen that can be kept in employment by any particular person must bear a certain proportion to his capital, so the number of those that can be continually employed by all the members of a great society must bear a certain proportion to the whole capital of that society, and never can exceed that proportion. No regulation of commerce can increase the quantity of industry in any society beyond what its capital can maintain. It can only divert a part of it into a direction into which it might not otherwise have gone; and it is by no means certain that this artificial direction is likely to be more advantageous to the society than that into which it would have gone of its own accord.

Every individual is continually exerting himself to find out the most advantageous employment for whatever capital he can command. It is his own advantage, indeed, and not that of the society, which he has in view. But the study of his own advantage naturally, or rather necessarily, leads him to prefer that employment which is most advantageous to the society.

First, every individual endeavors to employ his capital as near home as he can, and consequently as much as he can in the support of domestic industry; provided always that he can thereby obtain the ordinary, or not a great deal less than the ordinary profits of stock.

Thus, upon equal or nearly equal profits, every wholesale merchant naturally prefers the home-trade to the foreign trade of consumption, and the foreign trade of consumption to the carrying trade. In the home-trade his capital is never so long out of his sight as it frequently is in the foreign trade of consumption. He can know better the character and situation of the persons whom he trusts, and if he should happen to be deceived, he knows better the laws of the country from which he must seek redress. In the carrying trade, the capital of the merchant is, as it were, divided between two foreign countries, and no part of it is ever necessarily brought home, or placed under his own immediate view and command. The capital which an Amsterdam merchant employs in carrying corn from Konigsberg to Lisbon, and fruit and wine from Lisbon to Konigsberg, must generally be the one half of it at Konigsberg and the other half at Lisbon. No part of it need ever come to Amsterdam. The natural residence of such a merchant should either be at Konigsberg or Lisbon, and it can only be some very particular circumstances which can make him prefer the residence of Amsterdam.

The uneasiness, however, which he feels at being separated so far from his capital generally determines him to bring part both of the Konigsberg goods which he destines for the market of Lisbon, and of the Lisbon goods which he destines for that of Konigsberg, to Amsterdam: and though this necessarily subjects him to a double charge of loading and unloading, as well as to the payment of some duties and customs, yet for the sake of having some part of his capital always under his own view and command, he willingly submits to this extraordinary charge; and it is in this manner that every country which has any considerable share of the carrying trade becomes always the emporium, or general market, for the goods of all the different countries whose trade it carries on. The merchant, in order to save a second loading and unloading, endeavors always to sell in the home-market as much of the goods of all those different countries as he can, and thus, so far as he can, to convert his carrying trade into a foreign trade of consumption.

A merchant, in the same manner, who is engaged in the foreign trade of consumption, when he collects goods for foreign markets, will always be glad, upon equal or nearly equal profits, to sell as great a part of them at home as he can. He saves himself the risk and trouble of exportation, when, so far as he can, he thus converts his foreign trade of consumption into a home-trade. Home is in this manner the centre, if I may say so, round which the capitals of the inhabitants of every country are continually circulating, and towards which they are always tending, though by particular causes they may sometimes be driven off and repelled from it towards more distant employments. But a capital employed in the home-trade, it has already been shown, necessarily puts into motion a greater quantity of domestic industry, and gives revenue and employment to a greater number of the inhabitants of the country, than an equal capital employed in the foreign trade of consumption: and one employed in the foreign trade of consumption has the same advantage over an equal capital employed in the carrying trade. Upon equal, or only nearly equal profits, therefore, every individual naturally inclines to employ his capital in the manner in which it is likely to afford the greatest support to domestic industry, and to give revenue and employment to the greatest number of people of his own country.

Secondly, every individual who employs his capital in the support of domestic industry, necessarily endeavors so to direct that industry that its produce may be of the greatest possible value.

The produce of industry is what it adds to the subject or materials upon which it is employed. In proportion as the value of this produce is great or small, so will likewise be the profits of the employer. But it is only for the sake of profit that any man employs a capital in the support of industry; and he will always, therefore, endeavor to employ it in the support of that industry of which the produce is likely to be of the greatest value, or to exchange for the greatest quantity either of money or of other goods.

But the annual revenue of every society is always precisely equal to the exchangeable value of the whole annual produce of its industry, or rather is precisely the same thing with that exchangeable value. As every individual, therefore, endeavors as much as he can both to employ his capital in the support of domestic industry, and so to direct that industry that its produce may be of the greatest value; every individual necessarily labors to render the annual revenue of the society as great as he can. He generally, indeed, neither intends to promote the public interest, nor knows how much he is promoting it. By preferring the support of domestic to that of foreign industry, he intends only his own security; and by directing that industry in such a manner as its produce may be of the greatest value, he intends only his own gain, and he is in this, as in many other cases, led by an invisible hand to promote an end which was no part of his intention. Nor is it always the worse for the society that it was no part of it. By pursuing his own interest he frequently promotes that of the society more effectually than when he really intends to promote it. I have never known much good done by those who affected to trade for the public good. It is an affectation, indeed, not very common among merchants, and very few words need be employed in dissuading them from it.

What is the species of domestic industry which his capital can employ, and of which the produce is likely to be of the greatest value, every individual, it is evident, can, in his local situation, judge much better than any statesman or lawgiver can do for him. The statesman who should attempt to direct private people in what manner they ought to employ their capitals would not only load himself with a most unnecessary attention, but assume an authority which could safely be trusted, not only to no single person, but to no council or senate whatever, and which would nowhere be so dangerous as in the hands of a man who had folly and presumption enough to fancy himself fit to exercise it....

What is prudence in the conduct of every private family can scarce be folly in that of a great kingdom. If a foreign country can supply us with a commodity cheaper than we ourselves can make it, better buy it of them with some part of the produce of our own industry employed in a way in which we have some advantage. The general industry of the country, being always in proportion to the capital which employs it, will not thereby be diminished, no more than that of the above-mentioned artificers; but only left to find out the way in which it can be employed with the greatest advantage. It is certainly not employed to the greatest advantage when it is thus directed towards an object which it can buy cheaper than it can make. The value of its annual produce is certainly more or less diminished when it is thus turned away from producing commodities evidently of more value than the commodity which it is directed to produce. According to the supposition, that commodity could be purchased from foreign countries cheaper than it can be made at home. It could, therefore, have been purchased with a part only of the commodities, or, what is the same thing, with a part only of the price of the commodities, which the industry employed by an equal capital would have produced at home, had it been left to follow its natural course. The industry of the country, therefore, is thus turned away from a more to a less advantageous employment, and the exchangeable value of its annual produce, instead of being increased, according to the intention of the lawgiver, must necessarily be diminished by every such regulation.

By means of such regulations, indeed, a particular manufacture may sometimes be acquired sooner than it could have been otherwise, and after a certain time may be made at home as cheap or cheaper than in the foreign country. But though the industry of the society may be thus carried with advantage into a particular channel sooner than it could have been otherwise, it will by no means follow that the sum total, either of its industry, or of its revenue, can ever be augmented by any such regulation. The industry of the society can augment only in proportion as its capital augments, and its capital can augment only in proportion to what can be gradually saved out of its revenue. But the immediate effect of every such regulation is to diminish its revenue, and what diminishes its revenue is certainly not very likely to augment its capital faster than it would have augmented of its own accord had both capital and industry been left to find out their natural employments.

Though for want of such regulations the society should never acquire the proposed manufacture, it would not, upon that account, necessarily be the poorer in any one period of its duration. In every period of its duration its whole capital and industry might still have been employed, though upon different objects, in the manner that was most advantageous at the time. In every period its revenue might have been the greatest which its capital could afford, and both capital and revenue might have been augmented with the greatest possible rapidity.

The natural advantages which one country has over another in producing particular commodities are sometimes so great that it is acknowledged by all the world to be in vain to struggle with them. By means of glasses, hotbeds, and hot walls, very good grapes can be raised in Scotland, and very good wine too can be made of them at about thirty times the expense for which at least equally good can be brought from foreign countries. Would it be a reasonable law to prohibit the importation of all foreign wines merely to encourage the making of claret and burgundy in Scotland? But if there would be a manifest absurdity in turning towards any employment thirty times more of the capital and industry of the country than would be necessary to purchase from foreign countries an equal quantity of the commodities wanted, there must be an absurdity, though not altogether so glaring, yet exactly of the same kind, in turning towards any such employment a thirtieth, or even a three-hundredth part more of either. Whether the advantages which one country has over another be natural or acquired is in this respect of no consequence. As long as the one country has those advantages, and the other wants them, it will always be more advantageous for the latter rather to buy of the former than to make. It is an acquired advantage only, which one artificer has over his neighbor, who exercises another trade; and yet they both find it more advantageous to buy of one another than to make what does not belong to their particular trades....

There seem, however, to be two cases in which it will generally be advantageous to lay some burden upon foreign for the encouragement of domestic industry.

The first is, when some particular sort of industry is necessary for the defense of the country. The defense of Great Britain, for example, depends very much upon the number of its sailors and shipping. The act of navigation, therefore, very properly endeavors to give the sailors and shipping of Great Britain the monopoly of the trade of their own country in some cases by absolute prohibitions and in others by heavy burdens upon the shipping of foreign countries....

The act of navigation, it is true, lays no burden upon foreign ships that come to export the produce of British industry. Even the ancient aliens duty, which used to be paid upon all goods exported as well as imported, has, by several subsequent acts, been taken off from the greater part of the articles of exportation. But if foreigners, either by prohibitions or high duties, are hindered from coming to sell, they cannot always afford to come to buy; because coming without a cargo, they must lose the freight from their own country to Great Britain. By diminishing the number of sellers, therefore, we necessarily diminish that of buyers, and are thus likely not only to buy foreign goods dearer, but to sell our own cheaper, than if there was a more perfect freedom of trade. As defined, however it is of much more importance than opulence, the act of navigation is, perhaps, the wisest of all the commercial regulations of England.

The second case, in which it will generally be advantageous to lay some burden upon foreign for the encouragement of domestic industry is, when some tax is imposed at home upon the produce of the latter. In this case, it seems reasonable that an equal tax should be imposed upon the like produce of the former. This would not give the monopoly of the home market to domestic industry, nor turn towards a particular employment a greater share of the stock and labor of the country than what would naturally go to it. It would only hinder any part of what would naturally go to it from being turned away by the tax into a less natural direction, and would leave the competition between foreign and domestic industry, after the tax, as nearly as possible upon the same footing as before it. In Great Britain, when any such tax is laid upon the produce of domestic industry, it is usual at the same time, in order to stop the clamorous complaints of our merchants and manufacturers that they will be undersold at home, to lay a much heavier duty upon the importation of all foreign goods of the same kind.

This second limitation of the freedom of trade according to some people should, upon some occasions, be extended much farther than to the precise foreign commodities which could come into competition with those which had been taxed at home. When the necessaries of life have been taxed any country, it becomes proper, they pretend, to tax not only the like necessaries of life imported from other countries, but all sorts of foreign goods which can come into competition with anything that is the produce of domestic industry. Subsistence, they say, becomes necessarily dearer in consequence of such taxes; and the price of labor must always rise with the price of the laborers' subsistence. Every commodity, therefore, which is the produce of domestic industry, though not immediately taxed itself, becomes dearer in consequence of such taxes, because the labor which produces it becomes so. Such taxes, therefore, are really equivalent, they say, to a tax upon every particular commodity produced at home. In order to put domestic upon the same footing with foreign industry, therefore, it becomes necessary, they think, to lay some duty upon every foreign commodity equal to this enhancement of the price of the home commodities with which it can come into competition.

Whether taxes upon the necessaries of life, such as those in Great Britain upon soap, salt, leather, candles, &c. necessarily raise the price of labor, and consequently that of all other commodities, I shall consider hereafter, when I come to treat of taxes. Supposing, however, in the meantime, that they have this effect, and they have it undoubtedly, this general enhancement of the price of all commodities, in consequence of that of labor, is a case which differs in the two following respects from that of a particular commodity of which the price was enhanced by a particular tax immediately imposed upon it.

First, it might always be known with great exactness how far the price of such a commodity could be enhanced by such a tax: but how far the general enhancement of the price of labor might affect that of every different commodity about which labor was employed could never be known with any tolerable exactness. It would be impossible, therefore, to proportion with any tolerable exactness the tax upon every foreign to this enhancement of the price of every home commodity.

Secondly, taxes upon the necessaries of life have nearly the same effect upon the circumstances of the people as a poor soil and a bad climate. Provisions are thereby rendered dearer in the same manner as if it required extraordinary labor and expense to raise them....

As there are two cases in which it will generally be advantageous to lay some burden upon foreign for the encouragement of domestic industry, so there are two others in which it may sometimes be a matter of deliberation; in the one, how far it is proper to continue the free importation of certain foreign goods; and in the other, how far, or in what manner, it may be proper to restore that free importation after it has been for some time interrupted....

There may be good policy in retaliations of this kind, when there is a probability that they will procure the repeal of the high duties or prohibitions complained of. The recovery of a great foreign market will generally more than compensate the transitory inconveniency of paying dearer during a short time for some sorts of goods. To judge whether such retaliations are likely to produce such an effect does not, perhaps, belong so much to the science of a legislator, whose deliberations ought to be governed by general principles which are always the same, as to the skill of that insidious and crafty animal, vulgarly called a statesman or politician, whose councils are directed by the momentary fluctuations of affairs. When there is no probability that any such repeal can be procured, it seems a bad method of compensating the injury done to certain classes of our people to do another injury ourselves, not only to those classes, but to almost all the other classes of them. When our neighbors prohibit some manufacture of ours, we generally prohibit, not only the same, for that alone would seldom affect them considerably, but some other manufacture of theirs. This may no doubt give encouragement to some particular class of workmen among ourselves, and by excluding some of their rivals, may enable them to raise their price in the home-market. Those workmen, however, who suffered by our neighbors prohibition will not be benefited by ours. On the contrary, they and almost all the other classes of our citizens will thereby be obliged to pay dearer than before for certain goods. Every such law, therefore, imposes a real tax upon the whole country, not in favor of that particular class of workmen who were injured by our neighbors prohibition, but of some other class.

The case in which it may sometimes be a matter of deliberation, how far, or in what manner, it is proper to restore the free importation of foreign goods, after it has been for some time interrupted, is, when particular manufactures, by means of high duties or prohibitions upon all foreign goods which can come into competition with them, have been so far extended as to employ a great multitude of hands. Humanity may in this case require that the freedom of trade should be restored only by slow gradations, and with a good deal of reserve and circumspection. Were those high duties and prohibitions taken away all at once, cheaper foreign goods of the same kind might be poured so fast into the home-market as to deprive all at once many thousands of our people of their ordinary employment and means of subsistence. The disorder which this would occasion might no doubt be very considerable. It would in all probability, however, be much less than is commonly imagined, for the two following reasons:

First, all those manufactures, of which any part is commonly exported to other European countries without a bounty, could be very little affected by the freest importation of foreign goods. Such manufactures must be sold as cheap abroad as any other foreign goods of the same quality and kind, and consequently must be sold cheaper at home. They would still, therefore, keep possession of the home-market, and though a capricious man of fashion might sometimes prefer foreign wares, merely because they were foreign, to cheaper and better goods of the same kind that were made at home, this folly could, from the nature of things, extend to so few that it could make no sensible impression upon the general employment of the people. But a great part of all the different branches of our woolen manufacture, of our tanned leather, and of our hardware, are annually exported to other European countries without any bounty, and these are the manufactures which employ the greatest number of hands. The silk, perhaps, is the manufacture which would suffer the most by this freedom of trade, and after it the linen, though the latter much less than the former.

Secondly, though a great number of people should, by thus restoring the freedom of trade, be thrown all at once out of their ordinary employment and common method of subsistence, it would by no means follow that they would thereby be deprived either of employment or subsistence. By the reduction of the army and navy at the end of the late war, more than a hundred thousand soldiers and seamen, a number equal to what is employed in the greatest manufactures, were all at once thrown out of their ordinary employment; but, though they no doubt suffered some inconveniency, they were not thereby deprived of all employment and subsistence. The greater part of the seamen, it is probable, gradually betook themselves to the merchant-service as they could find occasion, and in the meantime both they and the soldiers were absorbed in the great mass of the people, and employed in a great variety of occupations. Not only no great convulsion, but no sensible disorder arose from so great a change in the situation of more than a hundred thousand men, all accustomed to the use of arms, and many of them to rapine and plunder. The number of vagrants was scarce any-where sensibly increased by it, even the wages of labor were not reduced by it in any occupation, so far as I have been able to learn, except in that of seamen in the merchant-service....

Let the same natural liberty of exercising what species of industry they please, be restored to all his Majesty's subjects, in the same manner as to soldiers and seamen; that is, break down the exclusive privileges of corporations, and repeal the statute of apprenticeship, both which are real encroachments upon natural liberty, and add to these the repeal of the law of settlements, so that a poor workman, when thrown out of employment either in one trade or in one place, may seek for it in another trade or in another place without the fear either of a prosecution or of a removal, and neither the public nor the individuals will suffer much more from the occasional disbanding some particular classes of manufacturers than from that of soldiers. Our manufacturers have no doubt great merit with their country, but they cannot have more than those who defend it with their blood, nor deserve to be treated with more delicacy.

To expect, indeed, that the freedom of trade should ever be entirely restored in Great Britain is as absurd as to expect that an Oceana or Utopia should ever be established in it. Not only the prejudices of the public, but what is much more unconquerable, the private interests of many individuals, irresistibly oppose it....

BOOK V

Chapter I: Of The Expenses Of The Sovereign Or Commonwealth

(Part) I Of The Expense of Defense
The first duty of the sovereign, that of protecting the society from the violence and invasion of other independent societies, can be performed only by means of a military force. But the expense both of preparing this military force in time of peace, and of employing it in time of war, is very different in the different states of society, in the different periods of improvement....

In a more advanced state of society, two different causes contribute to render it altogether impossible that they who take the field should maintain themselves at their own expense. Those two causes are, the progress of manufactures, and the improvement in the art of war.

Though a husbandman should be employed in an expedition, provided it begins after seed-time and ends before harvest, the interruption of his business will not always occasion any considerable diminution of his revenue. Without the intervention of his labor, nature does herself the greater part of the work which remains to be done. But the moment that an artificer, a smith, a carpenter, or a weaver, for example, quits his workhouse, the sole source of his revenue is completely dried up. Nature does nothing for him, he does all for himself. When he takes the field, therefore, in defense of the public, as he has no revenue to maintain himself, he must necessarily be maintained by the public. But in a country of which a great part of the inhabitants are artificers and manufacturers, a great part of the people who go to war must be drawn from those classes, and must therefore be maintained by the public as long as they are employed in its service.

When the art of war, too, has gradually grown up to be a very intricate and complicated science, when the event of war ceases to be determined, as in the first ages of society, by a single irregular skirmish or battle, but when the contest is generally spun out through several different campaigns, each of which lasts during the greater part of the year, it becomes universally necessary that the public should maintain those who serve the public in war, at least while they are employed in that service. Whatever in time of peace might be the ordinary occupation of those who go to war, so very tedious and expensive a service would otherwise be far too heavy a burden upon them. After the second Persian war, accordingly, the armies of Athens seem to have been generally composed of mercenary troops, consisting, indeed, partly of citizens, but partly too of foreigners, and all of them equally hired and paid at the expense of the state. From the time of the siege of Veii, the armies of Rome received pay for their service during the time which they remained in the field. Under the feudal governments the military service both of the great lords and of their immediate dependants was, after a certain period, universally exchanged for a payment in money, which was employed to maintain those who served in their stead.

The number of those who can go to war, in proportion to the whole number of the people, is necessarily much smaller in a civilized than in a rude state of society. In a civilized society, as the soldiers are maintained altogether by the labor of those who are not soldiers, the number of the former can never exceed what the latter can maintain, over and above maintaining, in a manner suitable to their respective stations, both themselves and the other officers of government and law whom they are obliged to maintain. In the little agrarian states of ancient Greece, a fourth or a fifth part of the whole body of the people considered themselves as soldiers, and would sometimes, it is said, take a field. Among the civilized nations of modern Europe, it is commonly computed that not more than one-hundredth part of the inhabitants in any country can be employed as soldiers without ruin to the country which pays the expenses of their service....

The art of war, however, as it is certainly the noblest of all arts, so in the progress of improvement it necessarily becomes one of the most complicated among them. The state of the mechanical, as well as of some other arts, with which it is necessarily connected, determines the degree of perfection to which it is capable of being carried at any particular time. But in order to carry it to this degree of perfection, it is necessary that it should become the sole or principal occupation of a particular class of citizens, and the division of labor is as necessary for the improvement of this, as of every other art. Into other arts the division of labor is naturally introduced by the prudence of individuals, who find that they promote their private interest better by confining themselves to a particular trade than by exercising a great number. But it is the wisdom of the state only which can render the trade of a soldier a particular trade separate and distinct from all others. A private citizen who, in time of profound peace, and without any particular encouragement from the public, should spend the greater part of his time in military exercises, might, no doubt, both improve himself very much in them, and amuse himself very well; but he certainly would not promote his own interest. It is the wisdom of the state only which can render it for his interest to give up the greater part of his time to this peculiar occupation: and states have not always had this wisdom, even when their circumstances had become such that the preservation of their existence required that they should have it.

An industrious, and upon that account a wealthy nation, is of all nations the most likely to be attacked; and unless the state takes some new measures for the public defense, the natural habits of the people render them altogether incapable of defending themselves.

In these circumstances there seem to be but two methods by which the state can make any tolerable provision for the public defense.

It may either, first, by means of a very rigorous police, and in spite of the whole bent of the interest, genius, and inclinations of the people, enforce the practice of military exercises, and oblige either all the citizens of the military age, or a certain number of them, to join in some measure the trade of a soldier to whatever other trade or profession they may happen to carry on.

Or, secondly, by maintaining and employing a certain number of citizens in the constant practice of military exercises, it may render the trade of a soldier a particular trade, separate and distinct from all others....

Regularity, order, and prompt obedience to command are qualities which, in modern armies, are of more importance towards determining the fate of battles than the dexterity and skill of the soldiers in the use of their arms. But the noise of fire-arms, the smoke, and the invisible death to which every man feels himself every moment exposed as soon as he comes within cannon-shot, and frequently a long time before the battle can be well said to be engaged, must render it very difficult to maintain any considerable degree of this regularity, order, and prompt obedience, even in the beginning of a modern battle. In an ancient battle there was no noise but what arose from the human voice; there was no smoke, there was no invisible cause of wounds or death. Every man, till some mortal weapon actually did approach him, saw clearly that no such weapon was near him. In these circumstances, and among troops who had some confidence in their own skill and dexterity in the use of their arms, it must have been a good deal less difficult to preserve some degree regularity and order, not only in the beginning, but through the whole progress of an ancient battle, and till one of the two armies was fairly defeated. But the habits of regularity, order, and prompt obedience to command can be acquired only by troops which are exercised in great bodies....

As it is only by means of a well-regulated standing army that a civilized country can be defended, so it is only by means of it that a barbarous country can be suddenly and tolerably civilized. A standing army establishes, with an irresistible force, the law of the sovereign through the remotest provinces of the empire, and maintains some degree of regular government in countries which could not otherwise admit of any. Whoever examines, with attention, the improvements which Peter the Great introduced into the Russian empire, will find that they almost all resolve themselves into the establishment of a well-regulated standing army. It is the instrument which executes and maintains all his other regulations. That degree of order and internal peace which that empire has ever since enjoyed is altogether owing to the influence of that army.

Men of republican principles have been jealous of a standing army as dangerous to liberty. It certainly is so wherever the interest of the general and that of the principal officers are not necessarily connected with the support of the constitution of the state. The standing army of Cæsar destroyed the Roman republic. The standing army of Cromwell turned the long parliament out of doors. But where the sovereign is himself the general, and the principal nobility and gentry of the country the chief officers of the army, where the military force is placed under the command of those who have the greatest interest in the support of the civil authority, because they have themselves the greatest share of that authority, a standing army can never be dangerous to liberty. On the contrary, it may in some cases be favorable to liberty. The security which it gives to the sovereign renders unnecessary that troublesome jealousy, which, in some modern republics, seems to watch over the minutest actions, and to be at all times ready to disturb the peace of every citizen....

The first duty of the sovereign, therefore, that of defending the society from the violence and injustice of other independent societies, grows gradually more and more expensive as the society advances in civilization. The military force of the society, which originally cost the sovereign no expense either in time of peace or in time of war, must, in the progress of improvement, first be maintained by him in time of war, and afterwards even in time of peace.

The great change introduced into the art of war by the invention of fire-arms has enhanced still further both the expense of exercising and disciplining any particular number of soldiers in time of peace, and that of employing them in time of war. Both their arms and their ammunition are become more expensive. A musket is a more expensive machine than a javelin or a bow and arrows; a cannon or a mortar than a ballista or a catapult. The powder which is spent in a modern review is lost irrecoverably, and occasions a very considerable expense. The javelins and arrows which were thrown or shot in an ancient one, could easily be picked up again, and were besides of very little value. The cannon and the mortar are not only much dearer, but much heavier machines than the ballista or catapult, and require a greater expense, not only to prepare them for the field, but to carry them to it. As the superiority of the modern artillery too over that of the ancients is very great, it has become much more difficult, and consequently much more expensive, to fortify a town so as to resist even for a few weeks the attack of that superior artillery. In modern times many different causes contribute to render the defense of the society more expensive. The unavoidable effects of the natural progress of improvement have, in this respect, been a good deal enhanced by a great revolution in the art of war, to which a mere accident, the invention of gunpowder, seems to have given occasion.

In modern war the great expense of firearms gives an evident advantage to the nation which can best afford that expense, and consequently to an opulent and civilized over a poor and barbarous nation. In ancient times the opulent and civilized found it difficult to defend themselves against the poor and barbarous nations. In modern times the poor and barbarous find it difficult to defend themselves against the opulent and civilized. The invention of fire-arms, an invention which at first sight appears to be so pernicious, is certainly favorable both to the permanency and to the extension of civilization.

(Part) II Of the Expense of Justice
The second duty of the sovereign, that of protecting, as far as possible, every member of the society from the injustice or oppression of every other member of it, or the duty of establishing an exact administration of justice, requires, too, very different degrees of expense in the different periods of society....

Wherever there is great property there is great inequality. For one very rich man there must be at least five hundred poor, and the affluence of the few sup-poses the indigence of the many. The affluence of the rich excites the indigna-tion of the poor, who are often both driven by want, and prompted by envy, to invade his possessions. It is only under the shelter of the civil magistrate that the owner of that valuable property, which is acquired by the labor of many years, or perhaps of many successive generations, can sleep a single night in security. He is at all times surrounded by unknown enemies, whom, though he never provoked, he can never appease, and from whose injustice he can be protected only by the powerful arm of the civil magistrate continually held up to chastise it. The acquisition of valuable and extensive property, therefore, necessarily requires the establishment of civil government. Where there is no property, or at least none that exceeds the value of two or three days labor, civil government is not so necessary.

Civil government supposes a certain subordination. But as the necessity of civil government gradually grows up with the acquisition of valuable prop-erty, so the principal causes which naturally introduce subordination gradu-ally grow up with the growth of that valuable property.

The causes or circumstances which naturally introduce subordination, or which naturally, and antecedent to any civil institution, give some men some superiority over the greater part of their brethren, seem to be four in number.

The first of those causes or circumstances is the superiority of personal qualifications, of strength, beauty, and agility of body; of wisdom and virtue, of prudence, justice, fortitude, and moderation of mind. The qualifications of the body, unless supported by those of the mind, can give little authority in any period of society. He is a very strong man, who, by mere strength of body, can force two weak ones to obey him. The qualifications of the mind can alone give a very great authority. They are, however, invisible qualities; always dis-putable, and generally disputed. No society, whether barbarous or civilized, has ever found it convenient to settle the rules of precedency of rank and sub-ordination according to those invisible qualities; but according to something that is more plain and palpable.

The second of those causes or circumstances is the superiority of age....The third of those causes or circumstances is the superiority of fortune....The fourth of those causes or circumstances is the superiority of birth....

It is in the age of shepherds, in the second period of society, that the inequality of fortune first begins to take place, and introduces among men a degree of authority and subordination which could not possibly exist before....The rich, in particular, are necessarily interested to support that order of things which can alone secure them in the possession of their own advantages. Men of inferior wealth combine to defend those of superior wealth in the possession of their property, in order that men of superior wealth may combine to defend them in the possession of theirs. All the inferior shepherds and herdsmen feel that the security of their own herds and flocks depends upon the security of those of the great shepherd or herdsman; that the maintenance of their lesser authority depends upon that of his greater authority, and that upon their subordination to him depends his power of keeping their inferiors in subordination to them. They constitute a sort of little nobility, who feel themselves interested to defend the property and to support the authority of their own little sovereign in order that he may be able to defend their property and to support their authority. Civil government, so far as it is instituted for the security of property, is in reality instituted for the defense of the rich against the poor, or of those who have some property against those who have none at all....

(Part) III The Expense of Public Works And Public Institutions
The third and last duty of the sovereign or commonwealth is that of erecting and maintaining those public institutions and those public works, which, though they may be in the highest degree advantageous to a great society, are, however, of such a nature that the profit could never repay the expense to any individual or small number of individuals, and which it therefore cannot be expected that any individual or small number of individuals should erect or maintain. The performance of this duty requires, too, very different degrees of expense in the different periods of society.

After the public institutions and public works necessary for the defense of the society, and for the administration of justice, both of which have already been mentioned, the other works and institutions of this kind are chiefly those for facilitating the commerce of the society, and those for promoting the instruction of the people. The institutions for instruction are of two kinds: those for the education of youth, and those for the instruction of people of all ages. The consideration of the manner in which the expense of those different sorts of public, works and institutions may be most properly defrayed will divide this third part of the present chapter into three different articles.

Article I A Of The Public Works And Institutions For Facilitating the Commerce of The Society. And, First, Of Those Which Are Necessary For Facilitating Commerce In General

That the erection and maintenance of the public works which facilitate the commerce of any country, such as good roads, bridges, navigable canals, harbors, &c. must require very different degrees of expense in the different periods of society is evident without any proof. The expense of making and maintaining the public roads of any country must evidently increase with the annual produce of the land and labor of that country, or with the quantity and weight of the goods which it becomes necessary to fetch and carry upon those roads. The strength of a bridge must be suited to the number and weight of the carriages which are likely to pass over it. The depth and the supply of water for a navigable canal must be proportioned to the number and tonnage of the lighters which are likely to carry goods upon it; the extent of a harbor to the number of the shipping which are likely to take shelter in it.

It does not seem necessary that the expense of those public works should be defrayed from that public revenue, as it is commonly called, of which the collection and application are in most countries assigned to the executive power. The greater part of such public works may easily be so managed as to afford a particular revenue sufficient for defraying their own expense, without bringing any burden upon the general revenue of the society.

A highway, a bridge, a navigable canal, for example, may in most cases be both made and maintained by a small toll upon the carriages which make use of them: a harbor, by a moderate port-duty upon the tonnage of the shipping which load or unload in it. The coinage, another institution for facilitating commerce, in many countries, not only defrays its own expense, but affords a small revenue or seignorage to the sovereign. The post-office, another institution for the same purpose, over and above defraying its own expense, affords in almost all countries a very considerable revenue to the sovereign.

When the carriages which pass over a highway or a bridge, and the lighters which sail upon a navigable canal, pay toll in proportion to their weight or their tonnage, they pay for the maintenance of those public works exactly in proportion to the wear and tear which they occasion of them. It seems scarce possible to invent a more equitable way of maintaining such works. This tax or toll too, though it is advanced by the carrier, is finally paid by the consumer, to whom it must always be charged in the price of the goods. As the expense of carriage, however, is very much reduced by means of such public works, the goods, notwithstanding the toll come cheaper to the consumer than the; could otherwise have done; their price not being so much raised by the toll as it is lowered by the cheapness of the carriage. The person who finally pays this tax, therefore, gains by the application more than he loses by the payment of it. His payment is exactly in proportion to his gain. It is in reality no more than a part of that gain which he is obliged to give up in order to get the rest. It seems impossible to imagine a more equitable method of raising a tax.

When the toll upon carriages of luxury, upon coaches, post-chaises, &c. is made somewhat higher in proportion to their weight, than upon carriages of necessary use, such as carts, wagons, &c. the indolence and vanity of the rich is made to contribute in a very easy manner to the relief of the poor, by rendering cheaper the transportation of heavy goods to all the different parts of the country.

When high roads, bridges, canals, &c. are in this manner made and supported by the commerce which is carried on by means of them, they can be made only where that commerce requires them, and consequently where it is proper to make them. Their expenses too, their grandeur and magnificence, must be suited to what that commerce can afford to pay. They must be made consequently as it is proper to make them. A magnificent high road cannot be made through a desert country where there is little or no commerce, or merely because it happens to lead to the country villa of the intendant of the province, or to that of some great lord to whom the intendant finds it convenient to make his court. A great bridge cannot be thrown over a river at a place where nobody passes, or merely to embellish the view from the windows of a neighboring palace: things which sometimes happen in countries where works of this kind are carried on by any other revenue than that which they themselves are capable of affording....

The tolls for the maintenance of a high road cannot with any safety be made the property of private persons. A high road, though entirely neglected, does not become altogether impassable, though a canal does. The proprietors of the tolls upon a high road, therefore, might neglect altogether the repair of the road, and yet continue to levy very nearly the same tolls. It is proper, therefore, that the tolls for the maintenance of such a work should be put under the management of commissioners or trustees....

That a considerable revenue might be gained in this manner I have no doubt, though probably not near so much as the projectors of this plan have supposed. The plan itself, however, seems liable to several very important objections.

First, if the tolls which are levied at the turnpikes should ever be considered as one of the resources for supplying the exigencies of the state, they would certainly be augmented as those exigencies were supposed to require....

Secondly, a tax upon carriages in proportion to their weight, though a very equal tax when applied to the sole purpose of repairing the roads, is a very unequal one when applied to any other purpose, or to supply the common exigencies of the state. When it is applied to the sole purpose above mentioned, each carriage is supposed to pay exactly for the wear and tear which that carriage occasions of the roads. But when it is applied to any other purpose, each carriage is supposed to pay for more than that wear and tear, and contributes to the supply of some other exigency of the state. But as the turnpike toll raises the price of goods in proportion to their weight, and not to their value, it is chiefly paid by the consumers of coarse and bulky, not by those of precious and light, commodities. Whatever exigency of the state therefore this tax might be intended to supply, that exigency would be chiefly supplied at the expense of the poor, not the rich; at the expense of those who are least able to supply it, not of those who are most able.

Thirdly, if government should at any time neglect the reparation of the high roads, it would be still more difficult than it is at present to compel the proper application of any part of the turnpike tolls. A large revenue might thus be levied upon the people without any part of it being applied to the only purpose to which a revenue levied in this manner ought ever to be applied. If the meanness and poverty of the trustees of turnpike roads render it sometimes difficult at present to oblige them to repair their wrong, their wealth and greatness would render it ten times more so in the case which is here supposed....

Even those public works which are of such a nature that they cannot afford any revenue for maintaining themselves, but of which the conveniency is nearly confined to some particular place or district, are always better maintained by a local or provincial revenue, under the management of a local or provincial administration, than by the general revenue of the state, of which the executive power must always have the management. Were the streets of London to be lighted and paved at the expense of the treasury, is there any probability that they would be so well lighted and paved as they are at present, or even at so small an expense? The expense, besides, instead of being raised by a local tax upon the inhabitants of each particular street, parish, or district in London, would, in this case, be defrayed out of the general revenue of the state, and would consequently be raised by a tax upon all the inhabitants of the kingdom, of whom the greater part derive no sort of benefit from the lighting and paving of the streets of London.

The abuses which sometimes creep into the local and provincial administration of a local and provincial revenue, how enormous sever they may appear, are in reality, however, almost always very trifling in comparison of those which commonly take place in the administration and expenditure of the revenue of a great empire. They are, besides, much more easily corrected....

Article I B Of The Public Works And Institutions Which Are Necessary For Facilitating Particular Branches Of Commerce

The object of the public works and institutions above mentioned is to facilitate commerce in general. But in order to facilitate some particular branches of it, particular institutions are necessary, which again require a particular and extraordinary expense....

It seems not unreasonable that the extraordinary expense which the protection of any particular branch of commerce may occasion should be defrayed by a moderate tax upon that particular branch; by a moderate fine, for example, to be paid by the traders when they first enter into it, or, what is more equal, by a particular duty of so much per cent. upon the goods which they either import into, or export out of, the particular countries with which it is carried on. The protection of trade in general, from pirates and free-booters, is said to have given occasion to the first institution of the duties of customs. But, if it was thought reasonable to lay a general tax upon trade, in order to defray the expense of protecting trade in general, it should seem equally reasonable to lay a particular tax upon a particular branch of trade, in order to defray the extraordinary expense of protecting that branch....

Regulated companies resemble, in every respect, the corporations of trades so common in the cities and towns of all the different countries of Europe, and are a sort of enlarged monopolies of the same kind.... The usual corporation spirit, wherever the law does not restrain it, prevails in all regulated companies. When they have been allowed to act according to their natural genius, they have always, in order to confine the competition to as small a number of persons as possible, endeavored to subject the trade to many burden some regulations. When the law has restrained them from doing this, they have become altogether useless and insignificant....

Article II Of The Expense of The Institutions For The Education of Youth

The institutions for the education of the youth may, in the same manner, furnish a revenue sufficient for defraying their own expense. The fee or honorary which the scholar pays to the master naturally constitutes a revenue of this kind.

Even where the reward of the master does not arise altogether from this natural revenue, it still is not necessary that it should be derived from that general revenue of the society, of which the collection and application are, in most countries, assigned to the executive power. Through the greater part of Europe, accordingly, the endowment of schools and colleges makes either no charge upon that general revenue, or but a very small one. It every where arises chiefly from some local or provincial revenue, from the rent of some landed estate, or from the interest of some sum of money allotted and put under the management of trustees for this particular purpose, sometimes by the sovereign himself, and sometimes by some private donor.

Have those public endowments contributed in general to promote the end of their institution? Have they contributed to encourage the diligence and to improve the abilities of the teachers? Have they directed the course of education towards objects more useful, both to the individual and to the public, than those to which it would naturally have gone of its own accord? It should not seem very difficult to give at least a probable answer to each of those questions.

In every profession, the exertion of the greater part of those who exercise it is always in proportion to the necessity they are under of making that exertion. This necessity is greatest with those to whom the emoluments of their profession are the only source from which they expect their fortune, or even their ordinary revenue and subsistence. In order to acquire this fortune, or even to get this subsistence, they must, in the course of a year, execute a certain quantity of work of a known value; and, where the competition is free, the rivalship of competitors, who are all endeavoring to jostle one another out of employment, obliges every man to endeavor to execute his work with a certain degree of exactness. The greatness of the objects which are to be acquired by success in some particular professions may, no doubt, sometimes animate the exertion of a few men of extraordinary spirit and ambition. Great objects, however, are evidently not necessary in order to occasion the greatest exertions. Rivalship and emulation render excellency, even in mean professions, an object of ambition, and frequently occasion the very greatest exertions. Great objects, on the contrary, alone and unsupported by the necessity of application, have seldom been sufficient to occasion any considerable exertion. In England, success in the profession of the law leads to some very great objects of ambition; and yet how few men, born to easy fortunes, have ever in this country been eminent in that profession?

The endowments of schools and colleges have necessarily diminished more or less the necessity of application in the teachers. Their subsistence, so far as it arises from their salaries, is evidently derived from a fund altogether independent of their success and reputation in their particular professions.

In some universities the salary makes but a part, and frequently but a small part, of the emoluments of the teacher, of which the greater part arises from the honoraries or fees of his pupils. The necessity of application, though always more or less diminished, is not in this case entirely taken away. Reputation in his profession is still of some importance to him, and he still has some dependency upon the affection, gratitude, and favorable report of those who have attended upon his instructions; and these favorable sentiments he is likely to gain in no way so well as by deserving them, that is, by the abilities and diligence with which he discharges every part of his duty.

In other universities the teacher is prohibited from receiving any honorary or fee from his pupils, and his salary constitutes the whole of the revenue which he derives from his office. His interest is, in this case, set as directly in opposition to his duty as it is possible to set it. It is the interest of every man to live as much at his ease as he can; and if his emoluments are to be precisely the same, whether he does or does not perform some very laborious duty, it is certainly his interest, at least as interest is vulgarly understood, either to neglect it altogether, or, if he is subject to some authority which will not suffer him to do this, to perform it in as careless and slovenly a manner as that authority will permit. If he is naturally active and a lover of labor, it is his interest to employ that activity in any way from which he can derive some advantage, rather than in the performance of his duty, from which he can derive none....

In England it becomes every day more and more the custom to send young people to travel in foreign countries immediately upon their leaving school, and without sending them to any university. Our young people, it is said, generally return home much improved by their travels. A young man who goes abroad at seventeen or eighteen, and returns home at one and twenty, returns three or four years older than he was when he went abroad; and at that age it is very difficult not to improve a good deal in three or four years. In the course of his travels he generally acquires some knowledge of one or two foreign languages; a knowledge, however, which is seldom sufficient to enable him either to speak or write them with propriety. In other respects he commonly returns home more conceited, more unprincipled, more dissipated, and more incapable of any serious application either to study or to business than he could well have become in so short a time had he lived at home. By travelling so very young, by spending in the most frivolous dissipation the most precious years of his life, at a distance from the inspection and control of his parents and relations, every useful habit which the earlier parts of his education might have had some tendency to form in him, instead of being riveted and confirmed, is almost necessarily either weakened or effaced. Nothing but the discredit into which the universities are allowing themselves to fall could ever have brought into repute so very absurd a practice as that of travelling at this early period of life. By sending his son abroad, a father delivers himself at least for some time, from so disagreeable an object as that of a son unemployed, neglected, and going to ruin before his eyes.

Such have been the effects of some of the modern institutions for education....

There are no public institutions for the education of women, and there is accordingly nothing useless, absurd, or fantastical in the common course of their education. They are taught what their parents or guardians judge it necessary or useful for them to learn, and they are taught nothing else. Every part of their education tends evidently to some useful purpose; either to improve the natural attractions of their person, or to form their mind to reserve, to modesty, to chastity, and to economy; to render them both likely to become the mistresses of a family, and to behave properly when they have become such. In every part of her life a woman feels some conveniency or advantage from every part of her education. It seldom happens that a man, in any part of his life, derives any conveniency or advantage from some of the most laborious and troublesome parts of his education.

Ought the public, therefore, to give no attention, it may be asked, to the education of the people? Or if it ought to give any, what are the different parts of education which it ought to attend to in the different orders of the people? And in what manner ought it to attend to them?

In some cases the state of the society necessarily places the greater part of individuals in such situations as naturally form in them, without any attention of government, almost all the abilities and virtues which that state requires, or perhaps can admit of. In other cases the state of the society does not place the part of individuals in such situations, and some attention of government is necessary in order to prevent the almost entire corruption and degeneracy of the great body of the people.

In the progress of the division of labor, the employment of the far greater part of those who live by labor, that is, of the great body of the people, comes to be confined to a few very simple operations, frequently to one or two. But the understandings of the greater part of men are necessarily formed by their ordinary employments. The man whose whole life is spent in performing a few simple operations, of which the effects are perhaps always the same, or very nearly the same, has no occasion to exert his understanding or to exercise his invention in finding out expedients for removing difficulties which never occur. He naturally loses, therefore, the habit of such exertion, and generally becomes as stupid and ignorant as it is possible for a human creature to become. The torpor of his mind renders him not only incapable of relishing or bearing a part in any rational conversation, but of conceiving any generous, noble, or tender sentiment, and consequently of forming any just judgment concerning many even of the ordinary duties of private life. Of the great and extensive interests of his country he is altogether incapable of judging, and unless very particular pains have been taken to render him otherwise, he is equally incapable of defending his country in war. The uniformity of his stationary life naturally corrupts the courage of his mind, and makes him regard with abhorrence the irregular, uncertain, and adventurous life of a soldier. It corrupts even the activity of his body, and renders him incapable of exerting his strength with vigor and perseverance in any other employment than that to which he has been bred. His dexterity at his own particular trade seems, in this manner, to be acquired at the expense of his intellectual, social, and martial virtues. But in every improved and civilized society this is the state into which the laboring poor, that is, the great body of the people, must necessarily fall, unless government takes some pains to prevent it....

The education of the common people requires, perhaps, in a civilized and commercial society the attention of the public more than that of people of some rank and fortune....They have little time to spare for education. Their parents can scarce afford to maintain them even in infancy. As soon as they are able to work they must apply to some trade by which they can earn their subsistence. That trade, too, is generally so simple and uniform as to give little exercise to the understanding, while, at the same time, their labor is both so constant and so severe, that it leaves them little leisure and less inclination to apply to, or even to think of, anything else.

But though the common people cannot, in any civilized society, be so well instructed as people of some rank and fortune, the most essential parts of education, however, to read, write, and account, can be acquired at so early a period of life that the greater part even of those who are to be bred to the lowest occupations have time to acquire them before they can be employed in those occupations. For a very small expense the public can facilitate, can encourage, and can even impose upon almost the whole body of the people the necessity of acquiring those most essential parts of education.

The public can facilitate this acquisition by establishing in every parish or district a little school, where children may be taught for a reward so moderate that even a common laborer may afford it; the master being partly, but not wholly, paid by the public, because, if he was wholly, or even principally, paid by it, he would soon learn to neglect his business. In Scotland the establishment of such parish schools has taught almost the whole common people to read, and a very great proportion of them to write and account. In England the establishment of charity schools has had an effect of the same kind, though not so universally, because the establishment is not so universal. If in those little schools the books, by which the children are taught to read, were a little more instructive than they commonly are, and if, instead of a little smattering of Latin, which the children of the common people are sometimes taught there, and which can scarce ever be of any use to them, they were instructed in the elementary parts of geometry and mechanics, the literary education of this rank of people would perhaps be as complete as it can be. There is scarce a common trade which does not afford some opportunities of applying to it the principles of geometry and mechanics, and which would not therefore gradually exercise and improve the common people in those principles, the necessary introduction to the most sublime as well as to the most useful sciences.

The public can encourage the acquisition of those most essential parts of education by giving small premiums, and little badges of distinction, to the children of the common people who excel in them.

The public can impose upon almost the whole body of the people the necessity of acquiring those most essential parts of education, by obliging every man to undergo an examination or probation in them before he can obtain the freedom in any corporation, or be allowed to set up any trade either in a village or town corporate....

The same thing may be said of the gross ignorance and stupidity which, in a civilized society, seem so frequently to benumb the understandings of all the inferior ranks of people. A man without the proper use of the intellectual faculties of a man, is, if possible, more contemptible than even a coward, and seems to be mutilated and deformed in a still more essential part of the character of human nature. Though the state was to derive no advantage from the instruction of the inferior ranks of people, it would still deserve its attention that they should not be altogether uninstructed. The state, however, derives no inconsiderable advantage from their instruction. The more they are instructed the less liable they are to the delusions of enthusiasm and superstition, which, among ignorant nations, frequently occasion the most dreadful disorders. An instructed and intelligent people, besides, are always more decent and orderly than an ignorant and stupid one. They feel themselves, each individually, more respectable and more likely to obtain the respect of their lawful superiors, and they are therefore more disposed to respect those superiors. They are more disposed to examine, and more capable of seeing through, the interested complaints of faction and sedition, and they are, upon that account, less apt to be misled into any wanton or unnecessary opposition to the measures of government. In free countries, where the safety of government depends very much upon the favorable judgment which the people may form of its conduct, it must surely be of the highest importance that they should not be disposed to judge rashly or capriciously concerning it.

Article III The Expense of the Institutions for the Instruction of People of All Ages

The institutions for the instruction of people of all ages are chiefly those for religious instruction. This is a species of instruction of which the object is not so much to render the people good citizens in this world, as to prepare them for another and a better world in a life to come. The teachers of the doctrine which contains this instruction, in the same manner as other teachers, may either depend altogether for their subsistence upon the voluntary contributions of their hearers, or they may derive it from some other fund to which the law of their country may entitle them; such as a landed estate, a tithe or land-tax, an established salary or stipend. Their exertion, their zeal and industry, are likely to be much greater in the former situation than in the latter....

But if politics had never called in the aid of religion, had the conquering party never adopted the tenets of one sect more than those of another when it had gained the victory, it would probably have dealt equally and impartially with all the different sects, and have allowed every man to choose his own priest and his own religion as he thought proper. There would in this case, no doubt have been a great multitude of religious sects. Almost every different congregation might probably have made a little sect by itself, or have entertained some peculiar tenets of its own. Each teacher would no doubt have felt himself under the necessity of making the utmost exertion and of using every art both to preserve and to increase the number of his disciples. But as every other teacher would have felt himself under the same necessity, the success of no one teacher, or sect of teachers, could have been very great. The interested and active zeal of religious teachers can be dangerous and troublesome only where there is either but one sect tolerated in the society, or where the whole of a large society is divided into two or three great sects; the teachers of each acting by concert, and under a regular discipline and subordination. But that zeal must be altogether innocent where the society is divided into two or three hundred, or perhaps into as many thousand small sects, of which no one could be considerable enough to disturb the public tranquility....

This plan of ecclesiastical government, or more properly of no ecclesiastical government, was what the sect called Independents, a sect no doubt of very wild enthusiasts, proposed to establish in England towards the end of the civil war. If it had been established, though of a very unphilosophical origin, it would probably by this time have been productive of the most philosophical good temper and moderation with regard to every sort of religious principle. It has been established in Pennsylvania, where, though the Quakers happen to be the most numerous, the law in reality favors no one sect more than another, and it is there said to have been productive of this philosophical good temper and moderation.

But though this equality of treatment should not be productive of this good temper and moderation in all, or even in the greater part of the religious sects of a particular country, yet provided those sects were sufficiently numerous, and each of them consequently too small to disturb the public tranquility, the excessive zeal of each for its particular tenets could not well be productive of any very harmful effects, but, on the contrary, of several good ones: and if the government was perfectly decided both to let them all alone, and to oblige them all to let alone one another, there is little danger that they would not of their own accord subdivide themselves fast enough so as soon to become sufficiently numerous.

In every civilized society, in every society where the distinction of ranks has once been completely established, there have been always two different schemes or systems of morality current at the same time; of which the one may be called the strict or austere; the other the liberal, or, if you will, the loose system. The former is generally admired and revered by the common people: the latter is commonly more esteemed and adopted by what are called people of fashion. The degree of disapprobation with which we ought to mark the vices of levity, the vices which are apt to arise from great prosperity, and from the excess of gaiety and good humor, seems to constitute the principal distinction between those two opposite schemes or systems. In the liberal or loose system, luxury, wanton and even disorderly mirth, the pursuit of pleasure to some degree of intemperance, the breach of chastity, at least in one of the two sexes, &c. provided they are not accompanied with gross indecency, and do not lead to falsehood or injustice, are generally treated with a good deal of indulgence, and are easily either excused or pardoned altogether....

There are two very easy and effectual remedies, however, by whose joint operation the state might, without violence, correct whatever was unsocial or disagreeably rigorous in the morals of all the little sects into which the country was divided.

The first of those remedies is the study of science and philosophy, which the state might render almost universal among all people of middling or more than middling rank and fortune; not by giving salaries to teachers in order to make them negligent and idle, but by instituting some sort of probation, even in the higher and more difficult sciences, to be undergone by every person before he was permitted to exercise any liberal profession, or before he could be received as a candidate for any honorable office of trust or profit.... Science is the great antidote to the poison of enthusiasm and superstition; and where all the superior ranks of people were secured from it, the inferior ranks could not be much exposed to it.

The second of those remedies is the frequency and gaiety of public diversions. The state, by encouraging, that is by giving entire liberty to all those who for their own interest would attempt without scandal or indecency, to amuse and divert the people by painting, poetry, music, dancing; by all sorts of dramatic representations and exhibitions, would easily dissipate, in the greater part of them, that melancholy and gloomy humor which is almost always the nurse of popular superstition and enthusiasm....

In a country where the law favored the teachers of no one religion more than those of another, it would not be necessary that any of them should have any particular or immediate dependency upon the sovereign or executive power; or that he should have anything to do either in appointing or in dismissing them from their offices. In such a situation he would have no occasion to give himself any concern about them, further than to keep the peace among them in the same manner as among the rest of his subjects; that is, to hinder them from persecuting, abusing, or oppressing one another. But it is quite otherwise in countries where there is an established or governing religion. The sovereign can in this case never be secure unless he has the means of influencing in a considerable degree the greater part of the teachers of that religion.

The clergy of every established church constitute a great incorporation. They can act in concert, and pursue their interest upon one plan and with one spirit, as much as if they were under the direction of one man; and they are frequently, too, under such direction. Their interest as an incorporated body is never the same with that of the sovereign, and is sometimes directly opposite to it. Their great interest is to maintain their authority with the people; and this authority depends upon the supposed certainty and importance of the whole doctrine which they inculcate, and upon the supposed necessity of adopting every part of it with the most implicit faith, in order to avoid eternal misery....When the authorized teachers of religion propagate through the great body of the people doctrines subversive of the authority of the sovereign, it is by violence only, or by the force of a standing army, that he can maintain his authority....

Articles of faith, as well as all other spiritual matters, it is evident enough, are not within the proper department of a temporal sovereign, who, though he may be very well qualified for protecting, is seldom supposed to be so for instructing the people. With regard to such matters, therefore, his authority can seldom be sufficient to counterbalance the united authority of the clergy of the established church. The public tranquility, however, and his own security, may frequently depend upon the doctrines which they may think proper to propagate concerning such matters. As he can seldom directly oppose their decision, therefore, with proper weight and authority, it is necessary that he should be able to influence it; and be can influence it only by the fears and expectations which he may excite in the greater part of the individuals of the order. Those fears and expectations may consist in the fear of deprivation or other punishment, and in the expectation of further preferment. ...

The gradual improvements of arts, manufactures, and commerce, the same causes which destroyed the power of the great barons, destroyed in the same manner, through the greater part of Europe, the whole temporal power of the clergy. In the produce of arts, manufactures, and commerce, the clergy, like the great barons, found something for which they could exchange their rude produce, and thereby discovered the means of spending their whole revenues upon their own persons, without giving any considerable share of them to other people. Their charity became gradually less extensive, their hospitality less liberal or less profuse. Their retainers became consequently less numerous, and by degrees dwindled away altogether. The clergy too, like the great barons, wished to get a better rent from their landed estates, in order to spend it, in the same manner, upon the gratification of their own private vanity and folly. But this increase of rent could be got only by granting leases to their tenants, who thereby became in a great measure independent of them....

(Part) IV Of The Expense of Supporting the Dignity of the Sovereign

In an opulent and improved society, where all the different orders of people are growing every day more expensive in their houses, in their furniture, in their tables, in their dress, and in their equipage, it cannot well be expected that the sovereign should alone hold out against the fashion. He naturally, therefore, or rather necessarily, becomes more expensive in all those different articles too. His dignity even seems to require that he should become so.

The expense of defending the society, and that of supporting the dignity of the chief magistrate, are both laid out for the general benefit of the whole society. It is reasonable, therefore, that they should be defrayed by the general contribution of the whole society, all the different members contributing, as nearly as possible, in proportion to their respective abilities.

The expense of the administration of justice, too, may, no doubt, be considered as laid out for the benefit of the whole society. There is no impropriety, therefore, in its being defrayed by the general contribution of the whole society. The persons, however, who gave occasion to this expense are those who, by their injustice in one way or another, make it necessary to seek redress or protection from the courts of justice. The persons again most immediately benefited by this expense are those whom the courts of justice either restore to their rights or maintain in their rights. The expense of the administration of justice, therefore, may very properly be defrayed by the particular contribution of one or other, or both, of those two different sets of persons, according as different occasions may require, that is, by the fees of court. It cannot be necessary to have recourse to the general contribution of the whole society, except for the conviction of those criminals who have not themselves any estate or fund sufficient for paying those fees.

Those local or provincial expenses of which the benefit is local or provincial (what is laid out, for example, upon the police of a particular town or district) ought to be defrayed by a local or provincial revenue, and ought to be no burden upon the general revenue of the society. It is unjust that the whole society should contribute towards an expense of which the benefit is confined to a part of the society.

The expense of maintaining good roads and communications is, no doubt, beneficial to the whole society, and may, therefore, without any injustice. be defrayed by the general contribution of the whole society. This expense, however, is most immediately and directly beneficial to those who travel or carry goods from one place to another, and to those who consume such goods. The turnpike tolls in England, and the duties called peages in other countries, lay it altogether upon those two different sets of people, and thereby discharge the general revenue of the society from a very considerable burden.

The expense of the institutions for education and religious instruction is likewise, no doubt, beneficial to the whole society, and may, therefore, without injustice, be defrayed by the general contribution of the whole society. This expense, however, might perhaps with equal propriety, and even with some advantage, be defrayed altogether by those who receive the immediate benefit of such education and instruction, or by the voluntary contribution of those who think they have occasion for either the one or the other.

When the institutions or public works which are beneficial to the whole society either cannot be maintained altogether, or are not maintained altogether by the contribution of such particular members of the society as are most immediately benefited by them, the deficiency must in most cases be made up by the general contribution of the whole society. The general revenue of the society, over and above defraying the expense of defending the society, and of supporting the dignity of the chief magistrate, must make up for the deficiency of many particular branches of revenue. The sources of this general or public revenue I shall endeavor to explain in the following chapter.

Adam Smith

The Theory of Moral Sentiments

Part IV, Chapter I, Paragraph 10

The Invisible Hand

And it is well that nature imposes upon us in this manner. It is this deception which rouses and keeps in continual motion the industry of mankind. It is this which first prompted them to cultivate the ground, to build houses, to found cities and commonwealths, and to invent and improve all the sciences and arts, which ennoble and embellish human life; which have entirely changed the whole face of the globe, have turned the rude forests of nature into agreeable and fertile plains, and made the trackless and barren ocean a new fund of subsistence, and the great high road of communication to the different nations of the earth.

The earth by these labors of mankind has been obliged to redouble her natural fertility, and to maintain a greater multitude of inhabitants. It is to no purpose, that the proud and unfeeling landlord views his extensive fields, and without a thought for the wants of his brethren, in imagination consumes himself the whole harvest that grows upon them. The homely and vulgar proverb, that the eye is larger than the belly, never was more fully verified than with regard to him. The capacity of his stomach bears no proportion to the immensity of his desires, and will receive no more than that of the meanest peasant. The rest he is obliged to distribute among those, who prepare, in the nicest manner, that little which he himself makes use of, among those who fit up the palace in which this little is to be consumed, among those who provide and keep in order all the different baubles and trinkets, which are employed in the economy of greatness; all of whom thus derive from his luxury and caprice, that share of the necessaries of life, which they would in vain have expected from his humanity or his justice. The produce of the soil maintains at all times nearly that number of inhabitants which it is capable of maintaining. The rich only select from the heap what is most precious and agreeable. They consume little more than the poor, and in spite of their natural selfishness and rapacity, though they mean only their own conveniency, though the sole end which they propose from the labors of all the thousands whom they employ, be the gratification of their own vain and insatiable desires, they divide with the poor the produce of all their improvements.

They are led by an invisible hand to make nearly the same distribution of the necessaries of life, which would have been made, had the earth been divided into equal portions among all its inhabitants, and thus without intending it, without knowing it, advance the interest of the society, and afford means to the multiplication of the species. When Providence divided the earth among a few lordly masters, it neither forgot nor abandoned those who seemed to have been left out in the partition. These last too enjoy their share of all that it produces. In what constitutes the real happiness of human life, they are in no respect inferior to those who would seem so much above them. In ease of body and peace of mind, all the different ranks of life are nearly upon a level, and the beggar, who suns himself by the side of the highway, possesses that security which kings are fighting for.

The American Founding

The Declaration of Independence

When, in the course of human events, it becomes necessary for one people to dissolve the political bands which have connected them with another, and to assume among the powers of the earth the separate and equal station to which the laws of nature and of nature's God entitle them, a decent respect to the opinions of mankind requires that they should declare the causes which impel them to the separation.

We hold these truths to be self evident: that all men are created equal; that they are endowed by their creator with (certain) inherent and inalienable rights; that among these are life, liberty and the pursuit of happiness; that to secure these rights, governments are instituted among men, deriving their just powers from the consent of the governed; that whenever any form of government becomes destructive of these ends, it is the right of the people to alter or to abolish it, and to institute new government, laying its foundation on such principles, and organizing its powers in such form, as to them shall seem most likely to effect their safety and happiness. Prudence, indeed, will dictate that governments long established should not be changed for light and transient causes; and accordingly all experience hath shown that mankind are more disposed to suffer while evils are sufferable, than to right themselves by abolishing the forms to which they are accustomed.

But when a long train of abuses and usurpations, <u>begun at a distinguished period and</u> pursuing invariably the same object, evinces a design to reduce them under absolute despotism, it is their right, it is their duty to throw off such government, and to provide new guards for their future security. Such has been the patient sufferance of these colonies; and such is now the necessity which constrains them to (alter) <u>expunge</u> their former systems of government. The history of the present king of Great Britain is a history of (repeated) <u>unremitting</u> injuries and usurpations, <u>among which appears no solitary fact to contradict the uniform tenor of the rest but all have</u> (all having) in direct object the establishment of an absolute tyranny over these states. To prove this let facts be submitted to a candid world <u>for the truth of which we pledge a faith yet unsullied by falsehood.</u>

He has refused his assent to laws the most wholesome and necessary for the public good....

He has dissolved representative houses repeatedly <u>and continually</u> for opposing with manly firmness his invasions on the rights of the people....

He has (obstructed) <u>suffered</u> the administration of justice <u>totally to cease in some of these states</u> (by) refusing his assent to laws for establishing judiciary powers.

He has made <u>our</u> judges dependant on his will alone for the tenure of their offices, and the amount and payment of their salaries.

He has erected a multitude of new offices <u>by a self assumed power</u> and sent hither swarms of new officers to harass our people and eat our their substance.

He has combined with others to subject us to a jurisdictions foreign to our constitutions and unacknowledged by our laws, giving his assent to their acts of pretended legislation for quartering large bodies of armed troops among us; for protecting them by a mock trial from punishment for any murders which they should commit on the inhabitants of these states; for cutting off our trade with all parts of the world; for imposing taxes on us without our consent; for depriving us (in many cases) of the benefits of trial by jury; for transporting us beyond seas to be tried for pretended offences; for abolishing the free system of English laws in a neighboring province, establishing therein an arbitrary government, and enlarging its boundaries, so as to render it at once an example and fit instrument for introducing the same absolute rule into these (colonies) <u>states</u>; for taking away our charters, abolishing our most valuable laws, and altering fundamentally the forms of our governments; for suspending our own legislatures, and declaring themselves invested with power to legislate for us in all cases whatsoever.

He has incited treasonable insurrections of our fellow citizens, with the allurements of forfeiture and confiscation of our property.

He has waged cruel war against human nature itself, violating its most sacred rights of life and liberty in the persons of a distant people who never offended him, captivating and carrying them into slavery in another hemisphere or to incur miserable death in their transportation thither. This piratical warfare, the opprobrium of INFIDEL powers, is the warfare of the CHRISTIAN king of Great Britain. Determined to keep open a market where MEN should be bought and sold, he has prostituted his negative for suppressing every legislative attempt to prohibit or to restrain this execrable commerce. And that this assemblage of horrors might want no fact of distinguished die, he is now exciting those very people to rise in arms among us, and to purchase that liberty of which he has deprived them, by murdering the people on whom he also obtruded them: thus paying off former crimes committed against the LIBERTIES of one people, with crimes which he urges them to commit against the LIVES of another.

In every stage of these oppressions we have petitioned for redress in the most humble terms: our repeated petitions have been answered only by repeated injuries. A prince whose character is thus marked by every act which may define a tyrant is unfit to be the ruler of a (free) people who mean to be free. Future ages will scarcely believe that the hardiness of one man adventured, within the short compass of twelve years only, to lay a foundation so broad and so undisguised for tyranny over a people fostered and fixed in principle of freedom.

The Virginia Declaration of Rights

16. That religion, or the duty which we owe to our CREATOR, and the manner of discharging it, can be directed only by reason and conviction, not by force or violence, and therefore all men are equally entitled to the free exercise of religion, according to the dictates of conscience; and that it is the mutual duty of all to practice Christian forbearance, love, and charity, towards each other.

James Madison's Memorial and Remonstrance

1. Because we hold it for a fundamental and undeniable truth, "that Religion, or the duty which we owe to our Creator, and the manner of discharging it, can be directed only by reason and conviction, not by force or violence." The Religion, then, of every man must be left to the conviction and conscience of every man; and it is the right of every man to exercise it, as these may dictate. This right is in its nature an unalienable right. It is unalienable, because the opinions of men, depending only on the evidence contemplated by their own minds, cannot follow the dictates of other men. It is unalienable, also, because what is here a right towards men is a duty towards the Creator. It is the duty of every man to render to the Creator such homage, and such only, as he believes to be acceptable to him. This duty is precedent, both in order of time and in degree of obligation, to the claims of Civil Society. Before any man can be considered as a member of Civil society, he must be considered as a subject

of the Governor of the Universe, and if a member of Civil Society who enters into any subordinate Association must always do it with a reservation of his duty to the General Authority, much more must every man who becomes a member of any particular Civil Society do it with a saving of his allegiance to the Universal Sovereign. We maintain, therefore, that in matters of Religion, no man's right is abridged by the institution of Civil Society, and that Religion is wholly exempt from its cognizance. True it is, that no other rule exists by which any question which may divide a Society can be ultimately determined than the will of the majority; but it is also true that the majority may trespass on the rights of the minority....

3. Because it is proper to take alarm at the first experiment on our liberties. We hold this prudent jealousy to be the first duty of citizens, and one of the noblest characteristics of the late Revolution. The freemen of America did not wait till usurped power had strengthened itself by exercise, and entangled the question in precedents. They saw all the consequences in the principle, and they avoided the consequences by denying the principle. We revere this lesson too much soon to forget it. Who does not see that the same authority which can establish Christianity, in exclusion of all other Religions, may establish, with the same ease, any particular sect of Christians, in exclusion of all other sects? That the same authority which can force a citizen to contribute three pence only of his property for the support of any one establishment, may force him to conform to any other establishment in all cases whatsoever?

4. "If all men are by nature equally free and independent," all men are to be considered as entering into Society on equal conditions; as relinquishing no more, and therefore retaining no less, one than another, of their natural rights. Above all are they to be considered as retaining an "equal title to the free exercise of Religion according to the dictates of Conscience." Whilst we assert for ourselves a freedom to embrace, to profess, and to observe, the Religion which we believe to be of divine origin, we cannot deny an equal freedom to them whose minds have not yet yielded to the evidence which has convinced us. If this freedom be abused, it is an offence against God, not against man. To God, therefore, not to man, must an account of it be rendered....

8. Because the establishment in question is not necessary for the support of Civil Government. If it be urged as necessary for the support of Civil Government only as it is a means of supporting Religion, and it be not necessary for the latter purpose, it cannot be necessary for the former. If Religion be not within the cognizance of Civil Government, how can its legal establishment be necessary to Civil Government? What influence, in fact, have ecclesiastical establishments had on Civil Society? In some instances they have been seen to erect a spiritual tyranny on the ruins of the civil authority; in many instances they have been seen upholding the thrones of political tyranny; in no instance have they been seen the guardians of the liberties of the people. Rulers who wished to subvert the public liberty may have found an established Clergy convenient auxiliaries. A just Government, instituted to secure and perpetuate

it, needs them not. Such a Government will be best supported by protecting every citizen in the enjoyment of his Religion with the same equal hand which protects his person and his property; by neither invading the equal rights of any sect, nor suffering any Sect to invade those of another....

The very appearance of the Bill has transformed "that Christian forbearance, love and charity," which of late mutually prevailed, into animosities and jealousies, which may not soon be appeased. What mischiefs may not be dreaded, should this enemy to the public quiet be armed with the force of a law?

Because the policy of the Bill is adverse to the diffusion of the light of Christianity. The first wish of those who enjoy this precious gift ought to be, that it may be imparted to the whole race of mankind. Compare the number of those who have as yet received it with the number still remaining under the dominion of false Religions, and how small is the former! Does the policy of the Bill tend to lessen the disproportion? No; it at once discourages those who are strangers to the light of revelation from coming into the Region of it, and countenances by example the nations who continue in darkness in shutting out those who might convey it to them. Instead of Leveling as far as possible, every obstacle to the victorious progress of truth, the Bill, with an ignoble and unchristian timidity, would circumscribe it with a wall of defense against the encroachments of error....

Because, finally, "the equal right of every Citizen to the free exercise of his Religion, according to the dictates of conscience," is held by the same tenure with all our other rights. If we recur to its origin, it is equally the gift of nature; if we weigh its importance, it cannot be less dear to us; if we consult the Declaration of those rights "which pertain to the good people of Virginia as the basis and foundation of Government," it is enumerated with equal solemnity, or rather studied emphasis. Either, then, we must say, that the will of the Legislature is the only measure of their authority, and that in the plenitude of that authority they may sweep away all our fundamental rights, or, that they are bound to leave this particular right untouched and sacred. Either we must say, that they may control the freedom of the press, may abolish the trial by jury, may swallow up the Executive and Judiciary powers of the State; nay, that they may despoil us of our very right of suffrage, and erect themselves into an independent and hereditary Assembly; or we must say, that they have no authority to enact into law the Bill under consideration.

The Constitution and Political Economy

Article I.
Section 6. The Senators and Representatives shall receive a Compensation for their Services, to be ascertained by Law, and paid out of the Treasury of the United States.

Section 7. All Bills for raising Revenue shall originate in the House of Representatives; but the Senate may propose or concur with Amendments as on other Bills.

Section 8. The Congress shall have Power To lay and collect Taxes, Duties, Imposts and Excises, to pay the Debts and provide for the common Defense and general Welfare of the United States; but all Duties, Imposts and Excises shall be uniform throughout the United States;

To borrow Money on the credit of the United States;

To regulate Commerce with foreign Nations, and among the several States, and with the Indian Tribes;

To establish an uniform Rule of Naturalization, and uniform Laws on the subject of Bankruptcies throughout the United States;

To coin Money, regulate the Value thereof, and of foreign Coin, and fix the Standard of Weights and Measures;

To provide for the Punishment of counterfeiting the Securities and current Coin of the United States;

To establish Post Offices and Post Roads;

To promote the Progress of Science and useful Arts, by securing for limited Times to Authors and Inventors the exclusive Right to their respective Writings and Discoveries;

To make all Laws which shall be necessary and proper for carrying into Execution the foregoing Powers, and all other Powers vested by this Constitution in the Government of the United States, or in any Department or Officer thereof.

Section 9. No Capitation, or other direct, Tax shall be laid, unless in Proportion to the Census or Enumeration herein before directed to be taken.

No Tax or Duty shall be laid on Articles exported from any State.

No Preference shall be given by any Regulation of Commerce or Revenue to the Ports of one State over those of another: nor shall Vessels bound to, or from, one State, be obliged to enter, clear, or pay Duties in another.

No Money shall be drawn from the Treasury, but in Consequence of Appropriations made by Law; and a regular Statement and Account of the Receipts and Expenditures of all public Money shall be published from time to time.

No Title of Nobility shall be granted by the United States: And no Person holding any Office of Profit or Trust under them, shall, without the Consent of the Congress, accept of any present, Emolument, Office, or Title, of any kind whatever, from any King, Prince, or foreign State.

Section 10. No State shall enter into any Treaty, Alliance, or Confederation; grant Letters of Marque and Reprisal; coin Money; emit Bills of Credit; make any Thing but gold and silver Coin a Tender in Payment of Debts; pass any Bill of Attainder, ex post facto Law, or Law impairing the Obligation of Contracts, or grant any Title of Nobility.

No State shall, without the Consent of the Congress, lay any Imposts or Duties on Imports or Exports, except what may be absolutely necessary for executing it's [sic] inspection Laws: and the net Produce of all Duties and

Imposts, laid by any State on Imports or Exports, shall be for the Use of the Treasury of the United States; and all such Laws shall be subject to the Revision and Control of the Congress.

No State shall, without the Consent of Congress, lay any Duty of Tonnage, keep Troops, or Ships of War in time of Peace, enter into any Agreement or Compact with another State, or with a foreign Power, or engage in War, unless actually invaded, or in such imminent Danger as will not admit of delay.

Article II
Section 1. The executive Power shall be vested in a President of the United States of America. He shall hold his Office during the Term of four Years, and, together with the Vice The President shall, at stated Times, receive for his Services, a Compensation, which shall neither be increased nor diminished during the Period for which he shall have been elected, and he shall not receive within that Period any other Emolument from the United States, or any of them.

Article III
Section 1. The judicial Power of the United States, shall be vested in one supreme Court, and in such inferior Courts as the Congress may from time to time ordain and establish. The Judges, both of the supreme and inferior Courts, shall hold their Offices during good Behavior, and shall, at stated Times, receive for their Services, a Compensation, which shall not be diminished during their Continuance in Office.

Article VI
All Debts contracted and Engagements entered into, before the Adoption of this Constitution, shall be as valid against the United States under this Constitution, as under the Confederation....But no religious test shall ever be required as a qualification to any office or public trust under the United States.

Federalist 10

By a faction, I understand a number of citizens, whether amounting to a majority or a minority of the whole, who are united and actuated by some common impulse of passion, or of interest, adverse to the rights of other citizens, or to the permanent and aggregate interests of the community.

There are two methods of curing the mischiefs of faction: the one, by removing its causes; the other, by controlling its effects.

There are again two methods of removing the causes of faction: the one, by destroying the liberty which is essential to its existence; the other, by giving to every citizen the same opinions, the same passions, and the same interests.

It could never be more truly said than of the first remedy, that it was worse than the disease. Liberty is to faction what air is to fire, an aliment without which it instantly expires. But it could not be less folly to abolish liberty, which is essential to political life, because it nourishes faction, than it would be to wish the annihilation of air, which is essential to animal life, because it imparts to fire its destructive agency.

The second expedient is as impracticable as the first would be unwise. As long as the reason of man continues fallible, and he is at liberty to exercise it, different opinions will be formed. As long as the connection subsists between his reason and his self-love, his opinions and his passions will have a reciprocal influence on each other; and the former will be objects to which the latter will attach themselves. The diversity in the faculties of men, from which the rights of property originate, is not less an insuperable obstacle to a uniformity of interests. The protection of these faculties is the first object of government. From the protection of different and unequal faculties of acquiring property, the possession of different degrees and kinds of property immediately results; and from the influence of these on the sentiments and views of the respective proprietors, ensues a division of the society into different interests and parties.

The latent causes of faction are thus sown in the nature of man; and we see them everywhere brought into different degrees of activity, according to the different circumstances of civil society. A zeal for different opinions concerning religion, concerning government, and many other points, as well of speculation as of practice; an attachment to different leaders ambitiously contending for pre-eminence and power; or to persons of other descriptions whose fortunes have been interesting to the human passions, have, in turn, divided mankind into parties, inflamed them with mutual animosity, and rendered them much more disposed to vex and oppress each other than to co-operate for their common good. So strong is this propensity of mankind to fall into mutual animosities, that where no substantial occasion presents itself, the most frivolous and fanciful distinctions have been sufficient to kindle their unfriendly passions and excite their most violent conflicts. But the most common and durable source of factions has been the various and unequal distribution of property. Those who hold and those who are without property have ever formed distinct interests in society. Those who are creditors, and those who are debtors, fall under a like discrimination. A landed interest, a manufacturing interest, a mercantile interest, a moneyed interest, with many lesser interests, grow up of necessity in civilized nations, and divide them into different classes, actuated by different sentiments and views. The regulation of these various and interfering interests forms the principal task of modern legislation, and involves the spirit of party and faction in the necessary and ordinary operations of the government.

No man is allowed to be a judge in his own cause, because his interest would certainly bias his judgment, and, not improbably, corrupt his integrity. With equal, nay with greater reason, a body of men are unfit to be both judges and parties at the same time; yet what are many of the most important acts of legislation, but so many judicial determinations, not indeed concerning the rights of single persons, but concerning the rights of large bodies of citizens?

And what are the different classes of legislators but advocates and parties to the causes which they determine? Is a law proposed concerning private debts? It is a question to which the creditors are parties on one side and the debtors on the other. Justice ought to hold the balance between them. Yet the parties are, and must be, themselves the judges; and the most numerous party, or, in other words, the most powerful faction must be expected to prevail. Shall domestic manufactures be encouraged, and in what degree, by restrictions on foreign manufactures are questions which would be differently decided by the landed and the manufacturing classes, and probably by neither with a sole regard to justice and the public good. The apportionment of taxes on the various descriptions of property is an act which seems to require the most exact impartiality; yet there is, perhaps, no legislative act in which greater opportunity and temptation are given to a predominant party to trample on the rules of justice. Every shilling with which they overburden the inferior number, is a shilling saved to their own pockets.

It is in vain to say that enlightened statesmen will be able to adjust these clashing interests, and render them all subservient to the public good. Enlightened statesmen will not always be at the helm. Nor, in many cases, can such an adjustment be made at all without taking into view indirect and remote considerations, which will rarely prevail over the immediate interest which one party may find in disregarding the rights of another or the good of the whole.

The inference to which we are brought is, that the causes of faction cannot be removed, and that relief is only to be sought in the means of controlling its effects.

If a faction consists of less than a majority, relief is supplied by the republican principle, which enables the majority to defeat its sinister views by regular vote. It may clog the administration, it may convulse the society; but it will be unable to execute and mask its violence under the forms of the Constitution. When a majority is included in a faction, the form of popular government, on the other hand, enables it to sacrifice to its ruling passion or interest both the public good and the rights of other citizens. To secure the public good and private rights against the danger of such a faction, and at the same time to preserve the spirit and the form of popular government, is then the great object to which our inquiries are directed. Let me add that it is the great desideratum by which this form of government can be rescued from the opprobrium under which it has so long labored, and be recommended to the esteem and adoption of mankind.

By what means is this object attainable? Evidently by one of two only. Either the existence of the same passion or interest in a majority at the same time must be prevented, or the majority, having such coexistent passion or interest, must be rendered, by their number and local situation, unable to concert and carry into effect schemes of oppression. If the impulse and the opportunity be suffered to coincide, we well know that neither moral nor religious motives can be relied on as an adequate control. They are not found to be such on the injustice and violence of individuals, and lose their efficacy in proportion to the number combined together, that is, in proportion as their efficacy becomes needful.

From this view of the subject it may be concluded that a pure democracy, by which I mean a society consisting of a small number of citizens, who assemble and administer the government in person, can admit of no cure for the mischiefs of faction. A common passion or interest will, in almost every case, be felt by a majority of the whole; a communication and concert result from the form of government itself; and there is nothing to check the inducements to sacrifice the weaker party or an obnoxious individual. Hence it is that such democracies have ever been spectacles of turbulence and contention; have ever been found incompatible with personal security or the rights of property; and have in general been as short in their lives as they have been violent in their deaths. Theoretic politicians, who have patronized this species of government, have erroneously supposed that by reducing mankind to a perfect equality in their political rights, they would, at the same time, be perfectly equalized and assimilated in their possessions, their opinions, and their passions.

A republic, by which I mean a government in which the scheme of representation takes place, opens a different prospect, and promises the cure for which we are seeking. Let us examine the points in which it varies from pure democracy, and we shall comprehend both the nature of the cure and the efficacy which it must derive from the Union.

The two great points of difference between a democracy and a republic are: first, the delegation of the government, in the latter, to a small number of citizens elected by the rest; secondly, the greater number of citizens, and greater sphere of country, over which the latter may be extended.

The effect of the first difference is, on the one hand, to refine and enlarge the public views, by passing them through the medium of a chosen body of citizens, whose wisdom may best discern the true interest of their country, and whose patriotism and love of justice will be least likely to sacrifice it to temporary or partial considerations. Under such a regulation, it may well happen that the public voice, pronounced by the representatives of the people, will be more consonant to the public good than if pronounced by the people themselves, convened for the purpose. On the other hand, the effect may be inverted. Men of factious tempers, of local prejudices, or of sinister designs, may, by intrigue, by corruption, or by other means, first obtain the suffrages, and then betray the interests, of the people. The question resulting is, whether small or extensive republics are more favorable to the election of proper guardians of the public weal; and it is clearly decided in favor of the latter by two obvious considerations:

In the first place, it is to be remarked that, however small the republic may be, the representatives must be raised to a certain number, in order to guard against the cabals of a few; and that, however large it may be, they must be limited to a certain number, in order to guard against the confusion of a multitude. Hence, the number of representatives in the two cases not being in proportion to that of the two constituents, and being proportionally greater in the small republic, it follows that, if the proportion of fit characters be not less in the large than in the small republic, the former will present a greater option, and consequently a greater probability of a fit choice.

In the next place, as each representative will be chosen by a greater number of citizens in the large than in the small republic, it will be more difficult for unworthy candidates to practice with success the vicious arts by which elections are too often carried; and the suffrages of the people being more free, will be more likely to centre in men who possess the most attractive merit and the most diffusive and established characters.

It must be confessed that in this, as in most other cases, there is a mean, on both sides of which inconveniences will be found to lie. By enlarging too much the number of electors, you render the representatives too little acquainted with all their local circumstances and lesser interests; as by reducing it too much, you render him unduly attached to these, and too little fit to comprehend and pursue great and national objects. The federal Constitution forms a happy combination in this respect; the great and aggregate interests being referred to the national, the local and particular to the State legislatures.

The other point of difference is, the greater number of citizens and extent of territory which may be brought within the compass of republican than of democratic government; and it is this circumstance principally which renders factious combinations less to be dreaded in the former than in the latter. The smaller the society, the fewer probably will be the distinct parties and interests composing it; the fewer the distinct parties and interests, the more frequently will a majority be found of the same party; and the smaller the number of individuals composing a majority, and the smaller the compass within which they are placed, the more easily will they concert and execute their plans of oppression. Extend the sphere, and you take in a greater variety of parties and interests; you make it less probable that a majority of the whole will have a common motive to invade the rights of other citizens; or if such a common motive exists, it will be more difficult for all who feel it to discover their own strength, and to act in unison with each other. Besides other impediments, it may be remarked that, where there is a consciousness of unjust or dishonorable purposes, communication is always checked by distrust in proportion to the number whose concurrence is necessary.

Hence, it clearly appears, that the same advantage which a republic has over a democracy, in controlling the effects of faction, is enjoyed by a large over a small republic—is enjoyed by the Union over the States composing it. Does the advantage consist in the substitution of representatives whose enlightened views and virtuous sentiments render them superior to local prejudices and schemes of injustice? It will not be denied that the representation of the Union will be most likely to possess these requisite endowments. Does it consist in the greater security afforded by a greater variety of parties, against the event of any one party being able to outnumber and oppress the rest? In an equal degree does the increased variety of parties comprised within the Union, increase this security. Does it, in fine, consist in the greater obstacles opposed to the concert and accomplishment of the secret wishes of an unjust and interested majority? Here, again, the extent of the Union gives it the most palpable advantage.

The influence of factious leaders may kindle a flame within their particular States, but will be unable to spread a general conflagration through the other States. A religious sect may degenerate into a political faction in a part of the Confederacy; but the variety of sects dispersed over the entire face of it must secure the national councils against any danger from that source. A rage for paper money, for an abolition of debts, for an equal division of property, or for any other improper or wicked project, will be less apt to pervade the whole body of the Union than a particular member of it; in the same proportion as such a malady is more likely to taint a particular county or district, than an entire State.

In the extent and proper structure of the Union, therefore, we behold a republican remedy for the diseases most incident to republican government. And according to the degree of pleasure and pride we feel in being republicans ought to be our zeal in cherishing the spirit and supporting the character of federalists.

Federalist 51

But the great security against a gradual concentration of the several powers in the same department, consists in giving to those who administer each department the necessary constitutional means and personal motives to resist encroachments of the others. The provision for defense must in this, as in all other cases, be made commensurate to the danger of attack. Ambition must be made to counteract ambition. The interest of the man must be connected with the constitutional rights of the place. It may be a reflection on human nature, that such devices should be necessary to control the abuses of government. But what is government itself, but the greatest of all reflections on human nature? If men were angels, no government would be necessary. If angels were to govern men, neither external nor internal controls on government would be necessary. In framing a government which is to be administered by men over men, the great difficulty lies in this: you must first enable the government to control the governed; and in the next place oblige it to control itself. A dependence on the people is, no doubt, the primary control on the government; but experience has taught mankind the necessity of auxiliary precautions.

This policy of supplying, by opposite and rival interests, the defect of better motives, might be traced through the whole system of human affairs, private as well as public. We see it particularly displayed in all the subordinate distributions of power, where the constant aim is to divide and arrange the several offices in such a manner as that each may be a check on the other that the private interest of every individual may be a sentinel over the public rights. These inventions of prudence cannot be less requisite in the distribution of the supreme powers of the State.

But it is not possible to give to each department an equal power of self-defense. In republican government, the legislative authority necessarily predominates. The remedy for this inconveniency is to divide the legislature into different branches; and to render them, by different modes of election and different principles of action, as little connected with each other as the nature of their common functions and their common dependence on the society will admit. It may even be necessary to guard against dangerous encroachments by still further precautions. As the weight of the legislative authority requires that it should be thus divided, the weakness of the executive may require, on the other hand, that it should be fortified....

There are, moreover, two considerations particularly applicable to the federal system of America, which place that system in a very interesting point of view.

First. In a single republic, all the power surrendered by the people is submitted to the administration of a single government; and the usurpations are guarded against by a division of the government into distinct and separate departments. In the compound republic of America, the power surrendered by the people is first divided between two distinct governments, and then the portion allotted to each subdivided among distinct and separate departments. Hence a double security arises to the rights of the people. The different governments will control each other, at the same time that each will be controlled by itself.

Second. It is of great importance in a republic not only to guard the society against the oppression of its rulers, but to guard one part of the society against the injustice of the other part. Different interests necessarily exist in different classes of citizens. If a majority be united by a common interest, the rights of the minority will be insecure. There are but two methods of providing against this evil: the one by creating a will in the community independent of the majority that is, of the society itself; the other, by comprehending in the society so many separate descriptions of citizens as will render an unjust combination of a majority of the whole very improbable, if not impracticable. The first method prevails in all governments possessing an hereditary or self-appointed authority. This, at best, is but a precarious security; because a power independent of the society may as well espouse the unjust views of the major, as the rightful interests of the minor party, and may possibly be turned against both parties. The second method will be exemplified in the federal republic of the United States. Whilst all authority in it will be derived from and dependent on the society, the society itself will be broken into so many parts, interests, and classes of citizens, that the rights of individuals, or of the minority, will be in little danger from interested combinations of the majority.

In a free government the security for civil rights must be the same as that for religious rights. It consists in the one case in the multiplicity of interests, and in the other in the multiplicity of sects. The degree of security in both cases will depend on the number of interests and sects; and this may be presumed to depend on the extent of country and number of people comprehended under the same government. This view of the subject must particularly recommend a proper federal system to all the sincere and considerate friends of republican government, since it shows that in exact proportion as the territory of the Union may be formed into more circumscribed Confederacies, or States oppressive combinations of a majority will be facilitated: the best security, under the republican forms, for the rights of every class of citizens, will be diminished: and consequently the stability and independence of some member of the government, the only other security, must be proportionately increased. Justice is the end of government. It is the end of civil society. It ever has been and ever will be pursued until it be obtained, or until liberty be lost in the pursuit. In a society under the forms of which the stronger faction can readily unite and oppress the weaker, anarchy may as truly be said to reign as in a state of nature, where the weaker individual is not secured against the violence of the stronger; and as, in the latter state, even the stronger individuals are prompted, by the uncertainty of their condition, to submit to a government which may protect the weak as well as themselves; so, in the former state, will the more powerful factions or parties be gradually induced, by a like motive, to wish for a government which will protect all parties, the weaker as well as the more powerful....

In the extended republic of the United States, and among the great variety of interests, parties, and sects which it embraces, a coalition of a majority of the whole society could seldom take place on any other principles than those of justice and the general good; whilst there being thus less danger to a minor from the will of a major party, there must be less pretext, also, to provide for the security of the former, by introducing into the government a will not dependent on the latter, or, in other words, a will independent of the society itself. It is no less certain than it is important, notwithstanding the contrary opinions which have been entertained, that the larger the society, provided it lie within a practical sphere, the more duly capable it will be of self-government. And happily for the republican cause, the practicable sphere may be carried to a very great extent, by a judicious modification and mixture of the federal principle.

The Amendments of 1791

First
Congress shall make no law respecting an establishment of religion, or prohibiting the free exercise thereof; or abridging the freedom of speech, or of the

press; or the right of the people peaceably to assembly, and to petition the Government for a redress of grievances.

Fifth

No person shall be held to answer for a capital, or otherwise infamous crime, unless on a presentment or indictment of a Grand Jury, except in cases arising in the land or naval forces, or in the Militia, when in actual service in time of War or public danger; nor shall any person be subject for the same offence to be twice put in jeopardy of life or limb; nor shall be compelled in any criminal case to be a witness against himself, nor be deprived of life, liberty, or property, without due process of law; nor shall private property be taken for public use, without just compensation.

Eighth

Excessive bail shall not be required, nor excessive fines imposed, nor cruel and unusual punishments inflicted.

Ninth

The enumeration in the Constitution, of certain rights, shall not be construed to deny or disparage others retained by the people.

Tenth

The powers not delegated to the United States by the Constitution, nor prohibited by it to the States, are reserved to the States respectively, or to the people.

Alexis De Tocqueville

Democracy in America

Author's Introduction

It is evident to all alike that a great democratic revolution is going on among us, but all do not look at it in the same light. To some it appears to be novel but accidental, and, as such, they hope it may still be checked; to others it seems irresistible, because it is the most uniform, the most ancient, and the most permanent tendency that is to be found in history....

The gradual development of the principle of equality is, therefore, a providential fact. It has all the chief characteristics of such a fact: it is universal, it is lasting, it constantly eludes all human interference, and all events as well as all men contribute to its progress.

Would it, then, be wise to imagine that a social movement the causes of which lie so far back can be checked by the efforts of one generation? Can it be believed that the democracy which has overthrown the feudal system and vanquished kings will retreat before tradesmen and capitalists? Will it stop now that it has grown so strong and its adversaries so weak?

Whither, then, are we tending? No one can say, for terms of comparison already fail us. There is greater equality of condition in Christian countries at the present day than there has been at any previous time, in any part of the world, so that the magnitude of what already has been done prevents us from foreseeing what is yet to be accomplished.

The whole book that is here offered to the public has been written under the influence of a kind of religious awe produced in the author's mind by the view of that irresistible revolution which has advanced for centuries in spite of every obstacle and which is still advancing in the midst of the ruins it has caused. It is not necessary that God himself should speak in order that we may discover the unquestionable signs of his will. It is enough to ascertain what is the habitual course of nature and the constant tendency of events. I know, without special revelation, that the planets move in the orbits traced by the Creator's hand.

If the men of our time should be convinced, by attentive observation and sincere reflection, that the gradual and progressive development of social equality is at once the past and the future of their history, this discovery alone would confer upon the change the sacred character of a divine decree. To attempt to check democracy would be in that case to resist the will of God; and the nations would then be constrained to make the best of the social lot awarded to them by Providence.

The Christian nations of our day seem to me to present a most alarming spectacle; the movement which impels them is already so strong that it cannot be stopped, but it is not yet so rapid that it cannot be guided. Their fate is still in their own hands; but very soon they may lose control.

The first of the duties that are at this time imposed upon those who direct our affairs is to educate democracy, to reawaken, if possible, its religious beliefs; to purify its morals; to mold its actions; to substitute a knowledge of statecraft for its inexperience, and an awareness of its true interest for its blind instincts, to adapt its government to time and place, and to modify it according to men and to conditions. A new science of politics is needed for a new world.

This, however, is what we think of least; placed in the middle of a rapid stream, we obstinately fix our eyes on the ruins that may still be descried upon the shore we have left, while the current hurries us away and drags us backward towards the abyss.

In no country in Europe has the great social revolution that I have just described made such rapid progress as in France; but it has always advanced without guidance....

The phenomena which the intellectual world presents are not less deplorable. The democracy of France, hampered in its course or abandoned to its lawless passions, has overthrown whatever crossed its path and has shaken all that it has not destroyed. Its empire has not been gradually introduced or peaceably established, but it has constantly advanced in the midst of the disorders and the agitations of a conflict. In the heat of the struggle each partisan is hurried beyond the natural limits of his opinions by the doctrines and the excesses of his opponents, until he loses sight of the end of his exertions, and holds forth in a way which does not correspond to his real sentiments or secret instincts. Hence arises the strange confusion that we are compelled to witness.

I can recall nothing in history more worthy of sorrow and pity than the scenes which are passing before our eyes. It is as if the natural bond that unites the opinions of man to his tastes, and his actions to his principles, was now broken; the harmony that has always been observed between the feelings and the ideas of mankind appears to be dissolved and all the laws of moral analogy to be abolished....

Where are we, then?

The religionists are the enemies of liberty, and the friends of liberty attack religion; the high-minded and the noble advocate bondage, and the meanest and most servile preach independence; honest and enlightened citizens are opposed to all progress, while men without patriotism and without principle put themselves forward as the apostles of civilization and intelligence.

Has such been the fate of the centuries which have preceded our own? And has man always inhabited a world like the present, where all things are not in their proper relationships, where virtue is without genius, and genius without honor; where the love of order is confused with a taste for oppression, and the holy cult of freedom with a contempt of law; where the light thrown by conscience on human actions is dim, and where nothing seems to be any longer forbidden or allowed, honorable or shameful, false or true?

I cannot believe that the Creator made man to leave him in an endless struggle with the intellectual wretchedness that surrounds us. God destines a calmer and a more certain future to the communities of Europe. I am ignorant of his designs, but I shall not cease to believe in them because I cannot fathom them, and I had rather mistrust my own capacity than his justice.

There is one country in the world where the great social revolution that I am speaking of seems to have nearly reached its natural limits. It has been effected with ease and simplicity; say rather that this country is reaping the fruits of the democratic revolution which we are undergoing, without having had the revolution itself.

The emigrants who colonized the shores of America in the beginning of the seventeenth century somehow separated the democratic principle from all the principles that it had to contend with in the old communities of Europe, and transplanted it alone to the New World. It has there been able to spread in perfect freedom and peaceably to determine the character of the laws by influencing the manners of the country. It appears to me beyond a doubt that, sooner or later, we shall arrive, like the Americans, at an almost complete equality of condition. But I do not conclude from this that we shall ever be necessarily led to draw the same political consequences which the Americans have derived from a similar social organization. I am far from supposing that they have chosen the only form of government which a democracy may adopt; but as the generating cause of laws and manners in the two countries is the same, it is of immense interest for us to know what it has produced in each of them.

Volume Two: Part Two – Influence Of Democracy On The Feelings Of The Americans

Chapter I: Why Democratic Nations Show a More Ardent and Enduring Love of Equality than of Liberty

The first and most intense passion that is produced by equality of condition is, I need hardly say, the love of that equality. My readers will therefore not be surprised that I speak of this feeling before all others.

Everybody has remarked that in our time, and especially in France, this passion for equality is every day gaining ground in the human heart. It has been said a hundred times that our contemporaries are far more ardently and tenaciously attached to equality than to freedom; but as I do not find that the causes of the fact have been sufficiently analyzed, I shall endeavour to point them out....

The taste which men have for liberty and that which they feel for equality are, in fact, two different things; and I am not afraid to add that among democratic nations they are two unequal things.

Upon close inspection it will be seen that there is in every age some peculiar and preponderant fact with which all others are connected; this fact almost always gives birth to some pregnant idea or some ruling passion, which attracts to itself and bears away in its course all the feelings and opinions of the time; it is like a great stream towards which each of the neighboring rivulets seems to flow.

Freedom has appeared in the world at different times and under various forms; it has not been exclusively bound to any social condition, and it is not confined to democracies. Freedom cannot, therefore, form the distinguishing characteristic of democratic ages. The peculiar and preponderant fact that marks those ages as its own is the equality of condition; the ruling passion of men in those periods is the love of this equality. Do not ask what singular charm the men of democratic ages find in being equal, or what special reasons they may have for clinging so tenaciously to equality rather than to the other advantages that society holds out to them: equality is the distinguishing characteristic of the age they live in; that of itself is enough to explain that they prefer it to all the rest.

But independently of this reason there are several others which will at all times habitually lead men to prefer equality to freedom.

If a people could ever succeed in destroying, or even in diminishing, the equality that prevails in its own body, they could do so only by long and laborious efforts. Their social condition must be modified, their laws abolished, their opinions superseded, their habits changed, their manners corrupted. But political liberty is more easily lost; to neglect to hold it fast is to allow it to escape. Therefore not only do men cling to equality because it is dear to them; they also adhere to it because they think it will last forever.

That political freedom in its excesses may compromise the tranquility, the property, the lives of individuals is obvious even to narrow and unthinking minds. On the contrary, none but attentive and clear-sighted men perceive the perils with which equality threatens us, and they commonly avoid pointing them out. They know that the calamities they apprehend are remote and flatter themselves that they will only fall upon future generations, for which the present generation takes but little thought. The evils that freedom sometimes brings with it are immediate; they are apparent to all, and all are more or less affected by them. The evils that extreme equality may produce are slowly disclosed; they creep gradually into the social frame; they are seen only at intervals; and at the moment at which they become most violent, habit already causes them to be no longer felt.

The advantages that freedom brings are shown only by the lapse of time, and it is always easy to mistake the cause in which they originate. The advantages of equality are immediate, and they may always be traced from their source.

Political liberty bestows exalted pleasures from time to time upon a certain number of citizens. Equality every day confers a number of small enjoyments on every man. The charms of equality are every instant felt and are within the reach of all; the noblest hearts are not insensible to them, and the most vulgar souls exult in them. The passion that equality creates must therefore be at once strong and general. Men cannot enjoy political liberty unpurchased by some sacrifices, and they never obtain it without great exertions. But the pleasures of equality are self-proffered; each of the petty incidents of life seems to occasion them, and in order to taste them, nothing is required but to live....

I think that democratic communities have a natural taste for freedom; left to themselves, they will seek it, cherish it, and view any privation of it with regret. But for equality their passion is ardent, insatiable, incessant, invincible; they call for equality in freedom; and if they cannot obtain that, they still call for equality in slavery. They will endure poverty, servitude, barbarism, but they will not endure aristocracy....

Chapter II: Of Individualism in Democratic Countries

Individualism is a novel expression, to which a novel idea has given birth. Our fathers were only acquainted with egoisme (selfishness). Selfishness is a passionate and exaggerated love of self, which leads a man to connect everything with himself and to prefer himself to everything in the world. Individualism is a mature and calm feeling, which disposes each member of the community to sever himself from the mass of his fellows and to draw apart with his family and his friends, so that after he has thus formed a little circle of his own, he willingly leaves society at large to itself. Selfishness originates in blind instinct; individualism proceeds from erroneous judgment more than from depraved feelings; it originates as much in deficiencies of mind as in perversity of heart.

Selfishness blights the germ of all virtue; individualism, at first, only saps the virtues of public life; but in the long run it attacks and destroys all others and is at length absorbed in downright selfishness. Selfishness is a vice as old as the world, which does not belong to one form of society more than to another; individualism is of democratic origin, and it threatens to spread in the same ratio as the equality of condition....

Among democratic nations new families are constantly springing up, others are constantly falling away, and all that remain change their condition; the woof of time is every instant broken and the track of generations effaced. Those who went before are soon forgotten; of those who will come after, no one has any idea: the interest of man is confined to those in close propinquity to himself. As each class gradually approaches others and mingles with them, its members become undifferentiated and lose their class identity for each other. Aristocracy had made a chain of all the members of the community, from the peasant to the king; democracy breaks that chain and severs every link of it.

As social conditions become more equal, the number of persons increases who, although they are neither rich nor powerful enough to exercise any great influence over their fellows, have nevertheless acquired or retained sufficient education and fortune to satisfy their own wants. They owe nothing to any man, they expect nothing from any man; they acquire the habit of always considering themselves as standing alone, and they are apt to imagine that their whole destiny is in their own hands.

Thus not only does democracy make every man forget his ancestors, but it hides his descendants and separates his contemporaries from him; it throws him back forever upon himself alone and threatens in the end to confine him entirely within the solitude of his own heart.

Chapter IV: The Americans Combat the Effects of Individualism by Free Institutions

Despotism which by its nature is suspicious, sees in the separation among men the surest guarantee of its continuance, and it usually makes every effort to keep them separate. No vice of the human heart is so acceptable to it as selfishness: a despot easily forgives his subjects for not loving him, provided they do not love one another. He does not ask them to assist him in governing the state; it is enough that they do not aspire to govern it themselves. He stigmatizes as turbulent and unruly spirits those who would combine their exertions to promote the prosperity of the community; and, perverting the natural meaning of words, he applauds as good citizens those who have no sympathy for any but themselves.

Thus the vices which despotism produces are precisely those which equality fosters. These two things perniciously complete and assist each other. Equality places men side by side, unconnected by any common tie; despotism raises barriers to keep them asunder; the former predisposes them not to consider their fellow creatures, the latter makes general indifference a sort of public virtue.

Despotism, then, which is at all times dangerous, is more particularly to be feared in democratic ages. It is easy to see that in those same ages men stand most in need of freedom. When the members of a community are forced to attend to public affairs, they are necessarily drawn from the circle of their own interests and snatched at times from self-observation. As soon as a man begins to treat of public affairs in public, he begins to perceive that he is not so independent of his fellow men as he had at first imagined, and that in order to obtain their support he must often lend them his co-operation....

The Americans have combated by free institutions the tendency of equality to keep men asunder, and they have subdued it. The legislators of America did not suppose that a general representation of the whole nation would suffice to ward off a disorder at once so natural to the frame of democratic society and so fatal; they also thought that it would be well to infuse political life into each portion of the territory in order to multiply to an infinite extent opportunities of acting in concert for all the members of the community and to make them constantly feel their mutual dependence. The plan was a wise one. The general affairs of a country engage the attention only of leading politicians, who assemble from time to time in the same places; and as they often lose sight of each other afterwards, no lasting ties are established between them. But if the object be to have the local affairs of a district conducted by the men who reside there, the same persons are always in contact, and they are, in a manner, forced to be acquainted and to adapt themselves to one another.

It is difficult to draw a man out of his own circle to interest him in the destiny of the state, because he does not clearly understand what influence the destiny of the state can have upon his own lot. But if it is proposed to make a road cross the end of his estate, he will see at a glance that there is a connection between this small public affair and his greatest private affairs; and he will discover, without its being shown to him, the close tie that unites private to general interest. Thus far more may be done by entrusting to the citizens the administration of minor affairs than by surrendering to them in the control of important ones, towards interesting them in the public welfare and convincing them that they constantly stand in need of one another in order to provide for it. A brilliant achievement may win for you the favor of a people at one stroke; but to earn the love and respect of the population that surrounds you, a long succession of little services rendered and of obscure good deeds, a constant habit of kindness, and an established reputation for disinterestedness will be required. Local freedom, then, which leads a great number of citizens to value the affection of their neighbors and of their kindred, perpetually brings men together and forces them to help one another in spite of the propensities that sever them.

In the United States the more opulent citizens take great care not to stand aloof from the people; on the contrary, they constantly keep on easy terms with the lower classes: they listen to them, they speak to them every day. They know that the rich in democracies always stand in need of the poor, and that in democratic times you attach a poor man to you more by your manner than by benefits conferred. The magnitude of such benefits, which sets off the difference of condition, causes a secret irritation to those who reap advantage from them, but the charm of simplicity of manners is almost irresistible; affability carries men away, and even want of polish is not always displeasing. This truth does not take root at once in the minds of the rich. They generally resist it as long as the democratic revolution lasts, and they do not acknowledge it immediately after that revolution is accomplished. They are very ready to do good to the people, but they still choose to keep them at arm's length; they think that is sufficient, but they are mistaken. They might spend fortunes thus without warming the hearts of the population around them; that population does not ask them for the sacrifice of their money, but of their pride.

It would seem as if every imagination in the United States were upon the stretch to invent means of increasing the wealth and satisfying the wants of the public. The best-informed inhabitants of each district constantly use their information to discover new truths that may augment the general prosperity; and if they have made any such discoveries, they eagerly surrender them to the mass of the people....

When the vices and weaknesses frequently exhibited by those who govern in America are closely examined, the prosperity of the people occasions, but improperly occasions, surprise. Elected magistrates do not make the American democracy flourish; it flourishes because the magistrates are elective.

Many people in France consider equality of condition as one evil and political freedom as a second. When they are obliged to yield to the former, they strive at least to escape from the latter. But I contend that in order to combat the evils which equality may produce, there is only one effectual remedy: namely, political freedom.

Chapter V: The Use which the Americans Make of Public Associations

Americans of all ages, all conditions, and all dispositions constantly form associations. They have not only commercial and manufacturing companies, in which all take part, but associations of a thousand other kinds, religious, moral, serious, futile, general or restricted, enormous or diminutive. The Americans make associations to give entertainments, to found seminaries, to build inns, to construct churches, to diffuse books, to send missionaries to the antipodes; in this manner they found hospitals, prisons, and schools. If it is proposed to inculcate some truth or to foster some feeling by the encouragement of a great example, they form a society. Wherever at the head of some new undertaking you see the government in France, or a man of rank in England, in the United States you will be sure to find an association....

Thus the most democratic country on the face of the earth is that in which men have, in our time, carried to the highest perfection the art of pursuing in common the object of their common desires and have applied this new science to the greatest number of purposes. Is this the result of accident, or is there in reality any necessary connection between the principle of association and that of equality?...

Among democratic nations...all the citizens are independent and feeble; they can do hardly anything by themselves, and none of them can oblige his fellow men to lend him their assistance. They all, therefore, become powerless if they do not learn voluntarily to help one another. If men living in democratic countries had no right and no inclination to associate for political purposes, their independence would be in great jeopardy, but they might long preserve their wealth and their cultivation: whereas if they never acquired the habit of forming associations in ordinary life, civilization itself would be endangered. A people among whom individuals lost the power of achieving great things single-handed, without acquiring the means of producing them by united exertions, would soon relapse into barbarism....

As soon as several of the inhabitants of the United States have taken up an opinion or a feeling which they wish to promote in the world, they look out for mutual assistance; and as soon as they have found one another out, they combine. From that moment they are no longer isolated men, but a power seen from afar, whose actions serve for an example and whose language is listened to.

The first time I heard in the United States that a hundred thousand men had bound themselves publicly to abstain from spirituous liquors, it appeared to me more like a joke than a serious engagement, and I did not at once perceive why these temperate citizens could not content themselves with drinking water by their own firesides. I at last understood that these hundred thousand Americans, alarmed by the progress of drunkenness around them, had made up their minds to patronize temperance.

They acted in just the same way as a man of high rank who should dress very plainly in order to inspire the humbler orders with a contempt of luxury. It is probable that if these hundred thousand men had lived in France, each of them would singly have memorialized the government to watch the public houses all over the kingdom.

Nothing, in my opinion, is more deserving of our attention than the intellectual and moral associations of America. The political and industrial associations of that country strike us forcibly; but the others elude our observation, or if we discover them, we understand them imperfectly because we have hardly ever seen anything of the kind. It must be acknowledged, however, that they are as necessary to the American people as the former, and perhaps more so. In democratic countries the science of association is the mother of science; the progress of all the rest depends upon the progress it has made.

Among the laws that rule human societies there is one which seems to be more precise and clear than all others. If men are to remain civilized or to become so, the art of associating together must grow and improve in the same ratio in which the equality of conditions is increased.

Chapter VI: Of the Relation Between Public Associations and the Newspapers

When men are no longer united among themselves by firm and lasting ties, it is impossible to obtain the co-operation of any great number of them unless you can persuade every man whose help you require that his private interest obliges him voluntarily to unite his exertions to the exertions of all the others. This can be habitually and conveniently effected only by means of a newspaper; nothing but a newspaper can drop the same thought into a thousand minds at the same moment. A newspaper is an adviser that does not require to be sought, but that comes of its own accord and talks to you briefly every day of the common weal, without distracting you from your private affairs.

Newspapers therefore become more necessary in proportion as men become more equal and individualism more to be feared. To suppose that they only serve to protect freedom would be to diminish their importance: they maintain civilization. I shall not deny that in democratic countries newspapers frequently lead the citizens to launch together into very ill-digested schemes; but if there were no newspapers there would be no common activity. The evil which they produce is therefore much less than that which they cure....

This connection between the number of newspapers and that of associations leads us to the discovery of a further connection between the state of the periodical press and the form of the administration in a country, and shows that the number of newspapers must diminish or increase among a democratic people in proportion as its administration is more or less centralized. For among democratic nations the exercise of local powers cannot be entrusted to the principal members of the community as in aristocracies. Those powers must be either abolished or placed in the hands of very large numbers of men, who then in fact constitute an association permanently established by law for the purpose of administering the affairs of a certain extent of territory; and they require a journal to bring to them every day, in the midst of their own minor concerns, some intelligence of the state of their public weal. The more numerous local powers are, the greater is the number of men in whom they are vested by law; and as this want is hourly felt, the more profusely do newspapers abound....

Chapter VII: Relation of Civil to Political Associations

There is only one country on the face of the earth where the citizens enjoy unlimited freedom of association for political purposes. This same country is the only one in the world where the continual exercise of the right of association has been introduced into civil life and where all the advantages which civilization can confer are procured by means of it.

In all the countries where political associations are prohibited, civil associations are rare. It is hardly probable that this is the result of accident, but the inference should rather be that there is a natural and perhaps a necessary connection between these two kinds of associations. Certain men happen to have a common interest in some concern; either a commercial undertaking is to be managed, or some speculation in manufactures to be tried: they meet, they combine, and thus, by degrees, they become familiar with the principle of association. The greater the multiplicity of small affairs, the more do men, even without knowing it, acquire facility in prosecuting great undertakings in common.

Civil associations, therefore, facilitate political association; but, on the other hand, political association singularly strengthens and improves associations for civil purposes. In civil life every man may, strictly speaking, fancy that he can provide for his own wants; in politics he can fancy no such thing. When a people, then, have any knowledge of public life, the notion of association and the wish to coalesce present themselves every day to the minds of the whole community; whatever natural repugnance may restrain men from acting in concert, they will always be ready to combine for the sake of a party. Thus political life makes the love and practice of association more general; it imparts a desire of union and teaches the means of combination to numbers of men who otherwise would have always lived apart....

When you see the Americans freely and constantly forming associations for the purpose of promoting some political principle, of raising one man to the head of affairs, or of wresting power from another, you have some difficulty in understanding how men so independent do not constantly fall into the abuse of freedom. If, on the other hand, you survey the infinite number of trading companies in operation in the United States, and perceive that the Americans are on every side unceasingly engaged in the execution of important and difficult plans, which the slightest revolution would throw into confusion, you will readily comprehend why people so well employed are by no means tempted to perturb the state or to destroy that public tranquility by which they all profit....

Chapter VIII: How the Americans Combat Individualism by the Principle of Self-Interest Rightly Understood

I have already shown, in several parts of this work, by what means the inhabitants of the United States almost always manage to combine their own advantage with that of their fellow citizens; my present purpose is to point out the general rule that enables them to do so. In the United States hardly anybody talks of the beauty of virtue, but they maintain that virtue is useful and prove it every day. The American moralists do not profess that men ought to sacrifice themselves for their fellow creatures because it is noble to make such sacrifices, but they boldly aver that such sacrifices are as necessary to him who imposes them upon himself as to him for whose sake they are made.

They have found out that, in their country and their age, man is brought home to himself by an irresistible force; and, losing all hope of stopping that force, they turn all their thoughts to the direction of it. They therefore do not deny that every man may follow his own interest, but they endeavor to prove that it is the interest of every man to be virtuous. I shall not here enter into the reasons they allege, which would divert me from my subject; suffice it to say that they have convinced their fellow countrymen.

Montaigne said long ago: "Were I not to follow the straight road for its straightness, I should follow it for having found by experience that in the end it is commonly the happiest and most useful track." The doctrine of self-interest rightly understood is not then new, but among the Americans of our time it finds universal acceptance; it has become popular there; you may trace it at the bottom of all their actions, you will remark it in all they say. It is as often asserted by the poor man as by the rich. In Europe the principle of interest is much grosser than it is in America, but it is also less common and especially it is less avowed; among us, men still constantly feign great abnegation which they no longer feel.

The Americans, on the other hand, are fond of explaining almost all the actions of their lives by the principle of self-interest rightly understood; they show with complacency how an enlightened regard for themselves constantly prompts them to assist one another and inclines them willingly to sacrifice a portion of their time and property to the welfare of the state. In this respect I think they frequently fail to do themselves justice, for in the United States as well as elsewhere people are sometimes seen to give way to those disinterested and spontaneous impulses that are natural to man; but the Americans seldom admit that they yield to emotions of this kind; they are more anxious to do honor to their philosophy than to themselves.

I might here pause without attempting to pass a judgment on what I have described. The extreme difficulty of the subject would be my excuse, but I shall not avail myself of it; and I had rather that my readers, clearly perceiving my object, would refuse to follow me than that I should leave them in suspense.

The principle of self-interest rightly understood is not a lofty one, but it is clear and sure. It does not aim at mighty objects, but it attains without excessive exertion all those at which it aims. As it lies within the reach of all capacities, everyone can without difficulty learn and retain it. By its admirable conformity to human weaknesses it easily obtains great dominion; nor is that dominion precarious, since the principle checks one personal interest by another, and uses, to direct the passions, the very same instrument that excites them.

The principle of self-interest rightly understood produces no great acts of self-sacrifice, but it suggests daily small acts of self-denial. By itself it cannot suffice to make a man virtuous; but it disciplines a number of persons in habits of regularity, temperance, moderation, foresight, self-command; and if it does not lead men straight to virtue by the will, it gradually draws them in that direction by their habits. If the principle of interest rightly understood were to sway the whole moral world, extraordinary virtues would doubtless be more rare; but I think that gross depravity would then also be less common. The principle of interest rightly understood perhaps prevents men from rising far above the level of mankind, but a great number of other men, who were falling far below it, are caught and restrained by it. Observe some few individuals, they are lowered by it; survey mankind, they are raised.

I am not afraid to say that the principle of self-interest rightly understood appears to me the best suited of all philosophical theories to the wants of the men of our time, and that I regard it as their chief remaining security against themselves. Towards it, therefore, the minds of the moralists of our age should turn; even should they judge it to be incomplete, it must nevertheless be adopted as necessary.

I do not think, on the whole, that there is more selfishness among us than in America; the only difference is that there it is enlightened, here it is not. Each American knows when to sacrifice some of his private interests to save the rest; we want to save everything, and often we lose it all. Everybody I see about me seems bent on teaching his contemporaries, by precept and example, that what is useful is never wrong Will nobody undertake to make them understand how what is right may be useful?...

I do not think that the system of self-interest as it is professed in America is in all its parts self-evident, but it contains a great number of truths so evident that men, if they are only educated, cannot fail to see them. Educate, then, at any rate, for the age of implicit self-sacrifice and instinctive virtues is already flitting far away from us, and the time is fast approaching when freedom, public peace, and social order itself will not be able to exist without education.

Chapter IX: That the Americans Apply the Principle of Self-Interest Rightly Understood to Religious Matters

If the principle of self-interest rightly understood had nothing but the present world in view, it would be very insufficient, for there are many sacrifices that can find their recompense only in another; and whatever ingenuity may be put forth to demonstrate the utility of virtue, it will never be an easy task to make that man live aright who has no thought of dying.

The founders of almost all religions have held to the same language. The track they point out to man is the same, only the goal is more remote; instead of placing in this world the reward of the sacrifices they impose, they transport it to another.

Nevertheless, I cannot believe that all those who practice virtue from religious motives are actuated only by the hope of a recompense. I have known zealous Christians who constantly forgot themselves to work with greater ardor for the happiness of their fellow men, and I have heard them declare that all they did was only to earn the blessings of a future state. I cannot but think that they deceive themselves; I respect them too much to believe them.

Christianity, indeed, teaches that a man must prefer his neighbor to himself in order to gain eternal life; but Christianity also teaches that men ought to benefit their fellow creatures for the love of God. A sublime expression! Man searches by his intellect into the divine conception and sees that order is the purpose of God; he freely gives his own efforts to aid in prosecuting this great design and, while he sacrifices his personal interests to this consummate order of all created things, expects no other recompense than the pleasure of contemplating it.

I do not believe that self-interest is the sole motive of religious men, but I believe that self-interest is the principal means that religions themselves employ to govern men, and I do not question that in this way they strike the multitude and become popular. I do not see clearly why the principle of interest rightly understood should undermine the religious opinions of men; it seems to me more easy to show why it should strengthen them. Let it be supposed that in order to attain happiness in this world, a man combats his instincts on all occasions and deliberately calculates every action of his life; that instead of yielding blindly to the impetuosity of first desires, he has learned the art of resisting them, and that he has accustomed himself to sacrifice without an effort the pleasure of a moment to the lasting interest of his whole life. If such a man believes in the religion that he professes, it will cost him but little to submit to the restrictions it may impose....

Not only do the Americans follow their religion from interest, but they often place in this world the interest that makes them follow it. In the Middle Ages the clergy spoke of nothing but a future state; they hardly cared to prove that a sincere Christian may be a happy man here below. But the American preachers are constantly referring to the earth, and it is only with great difficulty that they can divert their attention from it. To touch their congregations, they always show them how favorable religious opinions are to freedom and public tranquility; and it is often difficult to ascertain from their discourses whether the principal object of religion is to procure eternal felicity in the other world or prosperity in this.

Chapter X: Of the Taste for Physical Well-Being in America

If I were to inquire what passion is most natural to men who are stimulated and circumscribed by the obscurity of their birth or the mediocrity of their fortune, I could discover none more peculiarly appropriate to their condition than this love of physical prosperity. The passion for physical comforts is essentially a passion of the middle classes; with those classes it grows and spreads, with them it is preponderant. From them it mounts into the higher orders of society and descends into the mass of the people.

I never met in America any citizen so poor as not to cast a glance of hope and envy on the enjoyments of the rich or whose imagination did not possess itself by anticipation of those good things that fate still obstinately withheld from him.

On the other hand, I never perceived among the wealthier inhabitants of the United States that proud contempt of physical gratifications which is sometimes to be met with even in the most opulent and dissolute aristocracies. Most of these wealthy persons were once poor; they have felt the sting of want; they were long a prey to adverse fortunes; and now that the victory is won, the passions which accompanied the contest have survived it; their minds are, as it were, intoxicated by the small enjoyments which they have pursued for forty years.

Not but that in the United States, as elsewhere, there is a certain number of wealthy persons who, having come into their property by inheritance, possess without exertion an opulence they have not earned. But even these men are not less devotedly attached to the pleasures of material life. The love of well-being has now become the predominant taste of the nation; the great current of human passions runs in that channel and sweeps everything along in its course.

Chapter XI: Peculiar Effects of the Love of Physical Gratification in Democratic Times

The taste for physical gratifications leads a democratic people into no such excesses [as in aristocratic nations]. The love of well-being is there displayed as a tenacious, exclusive, universal passion, but its range is confined. To build enormous palaces, to conquer or to mimic nature, to ransack the world in order to gratify the passions of a man, is not thought of, but to add a few yards of land to your field, to plant an orchard, to enlarge a dwelling, to be always making life more comfortable and convenient, to avoid trouble, and to satisfy the smallest wants without effort and almost without cost. These are small objects, but the soul clings to them; it dwells upon them closely and day by day, till they at last shut out the rest of the world and sometimes intervene between itself and heaven....

The reproach I address to the principle of equality is not that it leads men away in the pursuit of forbidden enjoyments, but that it absorbs them wholly in quest of those which are allowed. By these means a kind of virtuous materialism may ultimately be established in the world, which would not corrupt, but enervate, the soul and noiselessly unbend its springs of action.

Chapter XIII: Why the Americans are so Restless in the Midst of their Prosperity

In the United States a man builds a house in which to spend his old age, and he sells it before the roof is on; he plants a garden and lets it just as the trees are coming into bearing; he brings a field into tillage and leaves other men to gather the crops; he embraces a profession and gives it up; he settles in a place, which he soon afterwards leaves to carry his changeable longings elsewhere.

If his private affairs leave him any leisure, he instantly plunges into the vortex of politics; and if at the end of a year of unremitting labor he finds he has a few days' vacation, his eager curiosity whirls him over the vast extent of the United States, and he will travel fifteen hundred miles in a few days to shake off his happiness. Death at length overtakes him, but it is before he is weary of his bootless chase of that complete felicity which forever escapes him.

At first sight there is something surprising in this strange unrest of so many happy men, restless in the midst of abundance. The spectacle itself, however, is as old as the world; the novelty is to see a whole people furnish an exemplification of it.

Their taste for physical gratifications must be regarded as the original source of that secret disquietude which the actions of the Americans betray and of that inconstancy of which they daily ford fresh examples. He who has set his heart exclusively upon the pursuit of worldly welfare is always in a hurry, for he has but a limited time at his disposal to reach, to grasp, and to enjoy it. The recollection of the shortness of life is a constant spur to him. Besides the good things that he possesses, he every instant fancies a thousand others that death will prevent him from trying if he does not try them soon. This thought fills him with anxiety, fear, and regret and keeps his mind in ceaseless trepidation, which leads him perpetually to change his plans and his abode. If in addition to the taste for physical well-being a social condition be added in which neither laws nor customs retain any person in his place, there is a great additional stimulant to this restlessness of temper. Men will then be seen continually to change their track for fear of missing the shortest cut to happiness....

Chapter XIV: How the Taste of Physical Gratification in America is United to Love of Freedom and Attention to Public Affairs

I have already shown that men who live in ages of equality have a continual need of forming associations in order to procure the things they desire; and, on the other hand, I have shown how great political freedom improves and diffuses the art of association. Freedom in these ages is therefore especially favorable to the production of wealth; nor is it difficult to perceive that despotism is especially adverse to the same result.

The nature of despotic power in democratic ages is not to be fierce or cruel, but minute and meddling. Despotism of this kind though it does not trample on humanity, is directly opposed to the genius of commerce and the pursuits of industry.

Thus the men of democratic times require to be free in order to procure more readily those physical enjoyments for which they are always longing. It sometimes happens, however, that the excessive taste they conceive for these same enjoyments makes them surrender to the first master who appears. The passion for worldly welfare then defeats itself and, without their perceiving it, throws the object of their desires to a greater distance.

There is, indeed, a most dangerous passage in the history of a democratic people. When the taste for physical gratifications among them has grown more rapidly than their education and their experience of free institutions, the time will come when men are carried away and lose all self-restraint at the sight of the new possessions they are about to obtain. In their intense and exclusive anxiety to make a fortune they lose sight of the close connection that exists between the private fortune of each and the prosperity of all. It is not necessary to do violence to such a people in order to strip them of the rights they enjoy; they themselves willingly loosen their hold.

The discharge of political duties appears to them to be a troublesome impediment which diverts them from their occupations and business. If they are required to elect representatives, to support the government by personal service, to meet on public business, they think they have no time, they cannot waste their precious hours in useless engagements; such idle amusements are unsuited to serious men who are engaged with the more important interests of life. These people think they are following the principle of self-interest, but the idea they entertain of that principle is a very crude one; and the better to look after what they call their own business, they neglect their chief business, which is to remain their own masters.

As the citizens who labor do not care to attend to public affairs, and as the class which might devote its leisure to these duties has ceased to exist, the place of the government is, as it were, unfilled. If at that critical moment some able and ambitious man grasps the supreme power, he will find the road to every kind of usurpation open before him. If he attends for some time only to the material prosperity of the country, no more will be demanded of him. Above all, he must ensure public tranquility: men who are possessed by the passion for physical gratification generally find out that the turmoil of freedom disturbs their welfare before they discover how freedom itself serves to promote it. If the slightest rumor of public commotion intrudes into the petty pleasures of private life, they are aroused and alarmed by it. The fear of anarchy perpetually haunts them, and they are always ready to fling away their freedom at the first disturbance.

I readily admit that public tranquility is a great good, but at the same time I cannot forget that all nations have been enslaved by being kept in good order. Certainly it is not to be inferred that nations ought to despise public tranquility, but that state ought not to content them. A nation that asks nothing of its government but the maintenance of order is already a slave at heart, the slave of its own well-being, awaiting only the hand that will bind it. By such a nation the despotism of faction is not less to be dreaded than the despotism of an individual. When the bulk of the community are engrossed by private concerns, the smallest parties need not despair of getting the upper hand in public affairs. At such times it is not rare to see on the great stage of the world, as we see in our theaters, a multitude represented by a few players, who alone speak in the name of an absent or inattentive crowd: they alone are in action, while all others are stationary; they regulate everything by their own caprice; they change the laws and tyrannize at will over the manners of the country, and then men wonder to see into how small a number of weak and worthless hands a great people may fall.

Hitherto the Americans have fortunately escaped all the perils that I have just pointed out, and in this respect they are really deserving of admiration. Perhaps there is no country in the world where fewer idle men are to be met with than in America, or where all who work are more eager to promote their own welfare. But if the passion of the Americans for physical gratifications is vehement, at least it is not indiscriminate; and reason, though unable to restrain it, still directs its course....

Chapter XV: How Religious Belief Sometimes Turns the Thoughts of Americans to Immaterial Pleasures

In the United States on the seventh day of every week the trading and working life of the nation seems suspended; all noises cease; a deep tranquility, say rather the solemn calm of meditation, succeeds the turmoil of the week, and the soul resumes possession and contemplation of itself. On this day the marts of traffic are deserted; every member of the community, accompanied by his children, goes to church, where he listens to strange language which would seem unsuited to his ear. He is told of the countless evils caused by pride and covetousness; he is reminded of the necessity of checking his desires, of the finer pleasures that belong to virtue alone, and of the true happiness that attends it. On his return home he does not turn to the ledgers of his business, but he opens the book of Holy Scripture; there he meets with sublime and affecting descriptions of the greatness and goodness of the Creator, of the infinite magnificence of the handiwork of God, and of the lofty destinies of man, his duties, and his immortal privileges.

Thus it is that the American at times steals an hour from himself, and, laying aside for a while the petty passions which agitate his life, and the ephemeral interests which engross it, he strays at once into an ideal world, where all is great, eternal, and pure.

I have endeavored to point out, in another part of this work, the causes to which the maintenance of the political institutions of the Americans is attributable, and religion appeared to be one of the most prominent among them. I am now treating of the Americans in an individual capacity, and I again observe that religion is not less useful to each citizen than to the whole state. The Americans show by their practice that they feel the high necessity of imparting morality to democratic communities by means of religion, What they think of themselves in this respect is a truth of which every democratic nation ought to be thoroughly persuaded....

But while man takes delight in this honest and lawful pursuit of his own well-being, it is to be apprehended that in the end he may lose the use of his sublimest faculties, and that while he is busied in improving all around him, he may at length degrade himself. Here, and here only, does the peril lie. It should therefore be the unceasing object of the legislators of democracies and of all the virtuous and enlightened men who live there to raise the souls of their fellow citizens and keep them lifted up towards heaven. It is necessary that all who feel an interest in the future destinies of democratic society should unite, and that all should make joint and continual efforts to diffuse the love of the infinite, lofty aspirations, and a love of pleasures not of earth. If among the opinions of a democratic people any of those pernicious theories exist which tend to inculcate that all perishes with the body, let men by whom such theories are professed be marked as the natural foes of the whole people.

The materialists are offensive to me in many respects; their doctrines I hold to be pernicious, and I am disgusted at their arrogance. If their system could be of any utility to man, it would seem to be by giving him a modest opinion of himself; but these reasoners show that it is not so; and when they think they have said enough to prove that they are brutes, they appear as proud as if they had demonstrated that they are gods.

Materialism, among all nations, is a dangerous disease of the human mind; but it is more especially to be dreaded among a democratic people because it readily amalgamates with that vice which is most familiar to the heart under such circumstances. Democracy encourages a taste for physical gratification; this taste, if it become excessive, soon disposes men to believe that all is matter only; and materialism, in its turn, hurries them on with mad impatience to these same delights; such is the fatal circle within which democratic nations are driven round. It were well that they should see the danger and hold back.

Most religions are only general, simple, and practical means of teaching men the doctrine of the immortality of the soul. That is the greatest benefit which a democratic people derives from its belief, and hence belief is more necessary to such a people than to all others. When, therefore, any religion has struck its roots deep into a democracy, beware that you do not disturb it; but rather watch it carefully, as the most precious bequest of aristocratic ages. Do not seek to supersede the old religious opinions of men by new ones, lest in the passage from one faith to another, the soul being left for a while stripped of all belief, the love of physical gratifications should grow upon it and fill it wholly.

The doctrine of metempsychosis is assuredly not more rational than that of materialism; nevertheless, if it were absolutely necessary that a democracy should choose one of the two, I should not hesitate to decide that the community would run less risk of being brutalized by believing that the soul of man will pass into the carcass of a hog than by believing that the soul of man is nothing at all. The belief in a super sensual and immortal principle, united for a time to matter is so indispensable to man's greatness that its effects are striking even when it is not united to the doctrine of future reward and punishment, or even when it teaches no more than that after death the divine principle contained in man is absorbed in the Deity or transferred to animate the frame of some other creature. Men holding so imperfect a belief will still consider the body as the secondary and inferior portion of their nature, and will despise it even while they yield to its influence; whereas they have a natural esteem and secret admiration for the immaterial part of man, even though they sometimes refuse to submit to its authority. That is enough to give a lofty cast to their opinions and their tastes, and to bid them tend, with no interested motive, and as it were by impulse, to pure feelings and elevated thoughts....

What means then remain in the hands of constituted authorities to bring men back to spiritual opinions or to hold them fast to the religion by which those opinions are suggested?

My answer will do me harm in the eyes of politicians. I believe that the sole effectual means which governments can employ in order to have the doctrine of the immortality of the soul duly respected is always to act as if they believed in it themselves; and I think that it is only by scrupulous conformity to religious morality in great affairs that they can hope to teach the community at large to know, to love, and to observe it in the lesser concerns of life.

Chapter XVIII: Why Among the Americans all Honest Callings are Considered Honorable

Among a democratic people, where there is no hereditary wealth, every man works to earn a living, or has worked, or is born of parents who have worked. The notion of labor is therefore presented to the mind, on every side, as the necessary, natural, and honest condition of human existence. Not only is labor not dishonorable among such a people, but it is held in honor; the prejudice is not against it, but in its favor. In the United States a wealthy man thinks that he owes it to public opinion to devote his leisure to some kind of industrial or commercial pursuit or to public business. He would think himself in bad repute if he employed his life solely in living. It is for the purpose of escaping this obligation to work that so many rich Americans come to Europe, where they find some scattered remains of aristocratic society, among whom idleness is still held in honor....

Chapter XIX: What Causes Almost All Americans to Follow Industrial Callings

The United States of America has only been emancipated for half a century from the state of colonial dependence in which it stood to Great Britain; the number of large fortunes there is small and capital is still scarce. Yet no people in the world have made such rapid progress in trade and manufactures as the Americans; they constitute at the present day the second maritime nation in the world, and although their manufactures have to struggle with almost insurmountable natural impediments, they are not prevented from making great and daily advances.

In the United States the greatest undertakings and speculations are executed without difficulty, because the whole population are engaged in productive industry, and because the poorest as well as the most opulent members of the commonwealth are ready to combine their efforts for these purposes. The consequence is that a stranger is constantly amazed by the immense public works executed by a nation which contains, so to speak, no rich men. The Americans arrived but as yesterday on the territory which they inhabit, and they have already changed the whole order of nature for their own advantage. They have joined the Hudson to the Mississippi and made the Atlantic Ocean communicate with the Gulf of Mexico, across a continent of more than five hundred leagues in extent which separates the two seas. The longest railroads that have been constructed up to the present time are in America.

But what most astonishes me in the United States is not so much the marvelous grandeur of some undertakings as the innumerable multitude of small ones. Almost all the farmers of the United States combine some trade with agriculture; most of them make agriculture itself a trade. It seldom happens that an American farmer settles for good upon the land which he occupies; especially in the districts of the Far West, he brings land into tillage in order to sell it again, and not to farm it: he builds a farmhouse on the speculation that, as the state of the country will soon be changed by the increase of population, a good price may be obtained for it....

The Americans make immense progress in productive industry, because they all devote themselves to it at once; and for this same reason they are exposed to unexpected and formidable embarrassments. As they are all engaged in commerce, their commercial affairs are affected by such various and complex causes that it is impossible to foresee what difficulties may arise. As they are all more or less engaged in productive industry, at the least shock given to business all private fortunes are put in jeopardy at the same time, and the state is shaken. I believe that the return of these commercial panics is an endemic disease of the democratic nations of our age. It may be rendered less dangerous, but it cannot be cured, because it does not originate in accidental circumstances, but in the temperament of these nations.

Chapter XX: How an Aristocracy May be Created by Manufactures

It is acknowledged that when a workman is engaged every day upon the same details, the whole commodity is produced with greater ease, speed, and economy. It is likewise acknowledged that the cost of production of manufactured goods is diminished by the extent of the establishment in which they are made and by the amount of capital employed or of credit. These truths had long been imperfectly discerned, but in our time they have been demonstrated. They have been already applied to many very important kinds of manufactures, and the humblest will gradually be governed by them. I know of nothing in politics that deserves to fix the attention of the legislator more closely than these two new axioms of the science of manufactures.

When a workman is unceasingly and exclusively engaged in the fabrication of one thing, he ultimately does his work with singular dexterity; but at the same time he loses the general faculty of applying his mind to the direction of the work. He every day becomes more adroit and less industrious; so that it may be said of him that in proportion as the workman improves, the man is degraded. What can be expected of a man who has spent twenty years of his life in making heads for pins? And to what can that mighty human intelligence which has so often stirred the world be applied in him except it be to investigate the best method of making pins' heads? When a workman has spent a considerable portion of his existence in this manner, his thoughts are forever set upon the object of his daily toil; his body has contracted certain fixed habits, which it can never shake off; in a word, he no longer belongs to himself, but to the calling that he has chosen.

It is in vain that laws and manners have been at pains to level all the barriers round such a man and to open to him on every side a thousand different paths to fortune; a theory of manufactures more powerful than customs and laws binds him to a craft, and frequently to a spot, which he cannot leave; it assigns to him a certain place in society, beyond which he cannot go; in the midst of universal movement it has rendered him stationary.

In proportion as the principle of the division of labor is more extensively applied, the workman becomes more weak, more narrow-minded, and more dependent. The art advances, the artisan recedes. On the other hand, in proportion as it becomes more manifest that the productions of manufactures are by so much the cheaper and better as the manufacture is larger and the amount of capital employed more considerable, wealthy and educated men come forward to embark in manufactures, which were heretofore abandoned to poor or ignorant handicraftsmen. The magnitude of the efforts required and the importance of the results to be obtained attract them. Thus at the very time at which the science of manufactures lowers the class of workmen, it raises the class of masters.

While the workman concentrates his faculties more and more upon the study of a single detail, the master surveys an extensive whole, and the mind of the latter is enlarged in proportion as that of the former is narrowed. In a short time the one will require nothing but physical strength without intelligence; the other stands in need of science, and almost of genius, to ensure success. This man resembles more and more the administrator of a vast empire; that man, a brute.

The master and the workman have then here no similarity, and their differences increase every day. They are connected only like the two rings at the extremities of a long chain. Each of them fills the station which is made for him, and which he does not leave; the one is continually, closely, and necessarily dependent upon the other and seems as much born to obey as that other is to command. What is this but aristocracy?

As the conditions of men constituting the nation become more and more equal, the demand for manufactured commodities becomes more general and extensive, and the cheapness that places these objects within the reach of slender fortunes becomes a great element of success. Hence there are every day more men of great opulence and education who devote their wealth and knowledge to manufactures and who seek, by opening large establishments and by a strict division of labor, to meet the fresh demands which are made on all sides. Thus, in proportion as the mass of the nation turns to democracy, that particular class which is engaged in manufactures becomes more aristocratic. Men grow more alike in the one, more different in the other; and inequality increases in the less numerous class in the same ratio in which it decreases in the community. Hence it would appear, on searching to the bottom, that aristocracy should naturally spring out of the bosom of democracy.

But this kind of democracy by no means resembles those kinds which preceded it. It will be observed at once that, as it applies exclusively to manufactures and to some manufacturing callings, it is a monstrous exception in the general aspect of society. The small aristocratic societies that are formed by some manufacturers in the midst of the immense democracy of our age contain, like the great aristocratic societies of former ages, some men who are very opulent and a multitude who are wretchedly poor. The poor have few means of escaping from their condition and becoming rich, but the rich are constantly becoming poor, or they give up business when they have realized a fortune. Thus the elements of which the class of poor is composed are fixed, but the elements of which the class of the rich is composed are not so. To tell the truth, though there are rich men, the class of rich men does not exist; for these rich individuals have no feelings or purposes, no traditions or hopes, in common; there are individuals, therefore, but no definite class.

Not only are the rich not compactly united among themselves, but there is no real bond between them and the poor. Their relative position is not a permanent one; they are constantly drawn together or separated by their interests. The workman is generally dependent on the master, but not on any particular master; these two men meet in the factory, but do not know each other elsewhere; and while they come into contact on one point, they stand very far apart on all others. The manufacturer asks nothing of the workman but his labor; the workman expects nothing from him but his wages. The one contracts no obligation to protect nor the other to defend, and they are not permanently connected either by habit or by duty. The aristocracy created by business rarely settles in the midst of the manufacturing population which it directs; the object is not to govern that population, but to use it. An aristocracy thus constituted can have no great hold upon those whom it employs, and even if it succeeds in retaining them at one moment, they escape the next; it knows not how to will, and it cannot act....

I am of the opinion, on the whole, that the manufacturing aristocracy which is growing up under our eyes is one of the harshest that ever existed in the world; but at the same time it is one of the most confined and least dangerous. Nevertheless, the friends of democracy should keep their eyes anxiously fixed in this direction; for if ever a permanent inequality of conditions and aristocracy again penetrates into the world, it may be predicted that this is the gate by which they will enter.

Volume Two: Part Four – Influence of Democratic Opinions on Political Society

Chapter II: The Opinions of Democratic Nations about Government are Naturally Favorable to the Concentration of Power

As the conditions of men become equal among a people, individuals seem of less and society of greater importance; or rather every citizen, being assimilated to all the rest, is lost in the crowd, and nothing stands conspicuous but the great and imposing image of the people at large. This naturally gives the men of democratic periods a lofty opinion of the privileges of society and a very humble notion of the rights of individuals; they are ready to admit that the interests of the former are everything and those of the latter nothing. They are willing to acknowledge that the power which represents the community has far more information and wisdom than any of the members of that community; and that it is the duty, as well as the right, of that power to guide as well as govern each private citizen....

In France, where the revolution of which I am speaking has gone further than in any other European country, these opinions have got complete hold of the public mind. If we listen attentively to the language of the various parties in France, we find that there is not one which has not adopted them. Most of these parties censure the conduct of the government, but they all hold that the government ought perpetually to act and interfere in everything that is done. Even those which are most at variance are nevertheless agreed on this head. The unity, the ubiquity, the omnipotence of the supreme power, and the uniformity of its rules constitute the principal characteristics of all the political systems that have been put forward in our age. They recur even in the wildest visions of political regeneration; the human mind pursues them in its dreams....

Our contemporaries are therefore much less divided than is commonly supposed; they are constantly disputing as to the hands in which supremacy is to be vested, but they readily agree upon, the duties and the rights of that supremacy. The notion they all form of government is that of a sole, simple, providential, and creative power.

Chapter III: The Sentiments of Democratic Nations accord with their Opinions in Leading them to Concentrate Political Power

It frequently happens that the members of the community promote the influence of the central power without intending to. Democratic eras are periods of experiment, innovation, and adventure. There is always a multitude of men engaged in difficult or novel undertakings, which they follow by themselves without shackling themselves to their fellows. Such persons will admit, as a general principle, that the public authority ought not to interfere in private concerns; but, by an exception to that rule, each of them craves its assistance in the particular concern on which he is engaged and seeks to draw upon the influence of the government for his own benefit, although he would restrict it on all other occasions. If a large number of men applies this particular exception to a great variety of different purposes, the sphere of the central power extends itself imperceptibly in all directions, although everyone wishes it to be circumscribed.

Thus a democratic government increases its power simply by the fact of its permanence. Time is on its side, every incident befriends it, the passions of individuals unconsciously promote it; and it may be asserted that the older a democratic community is, the more centralized will its government become.

This may more completely explain what frequently takes place in democratic countries, where the very men who are so impatient of superiors patiently submit to a master, exhibiting at once their pride and their servility.

The hatred that men bear to privilege increases in proportion as privileges become fewer and less considerable, so that democratic passions would seem to burn most fiercely just when they have least fuel. I have already given the reason for this phenomenon. When all conditions are unequal, no inequality is so great as to offend the eye, whereas the slightest dissimilarity is odious in the midst of general uniformity; the more complete this uniformity is, the more insupportable the sight of such a difference becomes. Hence it is natural that the love of equality should constantly increase together with equality itself, and that it should grow by what it feeds on.

This never dying, ever kindling hatred which sets a democratic people against the smallest privileges is peculiarly favorable to the gradual concentration of all political rights in the hands of the representative of the state alone. The sovereign, being necessarily and incontestably above all the citizens, does not excite their envy, and each of them thinks that he strips his equals of the prerogative that he concedes to the crown. The man of a democratic age is extremely reluctant to obey his neighbor, who is his equal; he refuses to acknowledge superior ability in such a person; he mistrusts his justice and is jealous of his power; he fears and he despises him; and he loves continually to remind him of the common dependence in which both of them stand to the same master.

Every central power, which follows its natural tendencies, courts and encourages the principle of equality; for equality singularly facilitates, extends, and secures the influence of a central power. In like manner it may be said that every central government worships uniformity; uniformity relieves it from inquiry into an infinity of details, which must be attended to if rules have to be adapted to different men, instead of indiscriminately subjecting all men to the same rule....

Thus by two separate paths I have reached the same conclusion. I have shown that the principle of equality suggests to men the notion of a sole, uniform, and strong government; I have now shown that the principle of equality imparts to them a taste for it. To governments of this kind the nations of our age are therefore tending. They are drawn thither by the natural inclination of mind and heart; and in order to reach that result, it is enough that they do not check themselves in their course.

I am of the opinion that, in the democratic ages which are opening upon us, individual independence and local liberties will ever be the products of art; that centralization will be the natural government.

Chapter V: That Amongst the European Nations of Our Time the Sovereign Power is Increasing, Although the Persons Who Govern Are Less Stable

In the course of the last half-century Europe has endured many revolutions and counter-revolutions, which have agitated it in opposite directions; but all these perturbations resemble each other in one respect: they have all shaken or destroyed the secondary powers of government. The local privileges which the French did not abolish in the countries they conquered have finally succumbed to the policy of the princes who conquered the French. Those princes rejected all the innovations of the French Revolution except centralization; that is the only principle they consented to receive from such a source.

My object is to remark that all these various rights which have been successively wrested, in our time, from classes, guilds, and individuals have not served to raise new secondary powers on a more democratic basis, but have uniformly been concentrated in the hands of the sovereign. Everywhere the state acquires more and more direct control over the humblest members of the community and a more exclusive power of governing each of them in his smallest concerns....

I assert that there is no country in Europe in which the public administration has not become, not only more centralized, but more inquisitive and more minute: it everywhere interferes in private concerns more than it did; it regulates more undertakings, and undertakings of a lesser kind; and it gains a firmer footing every day about, above, and around all private persons, to assist, to advise, and to coerce them....

Chapter VI: What Sort of Despotism Democratic Nations Have to Fear

It would seem that if despotism were to be established among the democratic nations of our day, it might assume a different character; it would be more extensive and more mild; it would degrade men without tormenting them. I do not question that, in an age of instruction and equality like our own, sovereigns might more easily succeed in collecting all political power into their own hands and might interfere more habitually and decidedly with the circle of private interests than any sovereign of antiquity could ever do. But this same principle of equality which facilitates despotism tempers its rigor....

I think, then, that the species of oppression by which democratic nations are menaced is unlike anything that ever before existed in the world; our contemporaries will find no prototype of it in their memories. I seek in vain for an expression that will accurately convey the whole of the idea I have formed of it; the old words despotism and tyranny are inappropriate: the thing itself is new, and since I cannot name, I must attempt to define it.

I seek to trace the novel features under which despotism may appear in the world. The first thing that strikes the observation is an innumerable multitude of men, all equal and alike, incessantly endeavoring to procure the petty and paltry pleasures with which they glut their lives. Each of them, living apart, is as a stranger to the fate of all the rest; his children and his private friends constitute to him the whole of mankind. As for the rest of his fellow citizens, he is close to them, but he does not see them; he touches them, but he does not feel them; he exists only in himself and for himself alone; and if his kindred still remain to him, he may be said at any rate to have lost his country.

Above this race of men stands an immense and tutelary power, which takes upon itself alone to secure their gratifications and to watch over their fate. That power is absolute, minute, regular, provident, and mild. It would be like the authority of a parent if, like that authority, its object was to prepare men for manhood; but it seeks, on the contrary, to keep them in perpetual childhood: it is well content that the people should rejoice, provided they think of nothing but rejoicing. For their happiness such a government willingly labors, but it chooses to be the sole agent and the only arbiter of that happiness; it provides for their security, foresees and supplies their necessities, facilitates their pleasures, manages their principal concerns, directs their industry, regulates the descent of property, and subdivides their inheritances: what remains, but to spare them all the care of thinking and all the trouble of living?

Thus it every day renders the exercise of the free agency of man less useful and less frequent; it circumscribes the will within a narrower range and gradually robs a man of all the uses of himself. The principle of equality has prepared men for these things; it has predisposed men to endure them and often to look on them as benefits.

After having thus successively taken each member of the community in its powerful grasp and fashioned him at will, the supreme power then extends its arm over the whole community. It covers the surface of society with a network of small complicated rules, minute and uniform, through which the most original minds and the most energetic characters cannot penetrate, to rise above the crowd. The will of man is not shattered, but softened, bent, and guided; men are seldom forced by it to act, but they are constantly restrained from acting. Such a power does not destroy, but it prevents existence; it does not tyrannize, but it compresses, enervates, extinguishes, and stupefies a people, till each nation is reduced to nothing better than a flock of timid and industrious animals, of which the government is the shepherd....

Chapter VII: Continuation of the Preceding Chapters

I shall conclude with one general idea, which comprises not only all the particular ideas that have been expressed in the present chapter, but also most of those of which it is the object of this book to treat.

Among the greater part of modern nations the government, whatever may be its origin, its constitution, or its name, has become almost omnipotent, and private persons are falling more and more into the lowest stage of weakness and dependence. In olden society everything was different; unity and uniformity were nowhere to be met with. In modern society everything threatens to become so much alike that the peculiar characteristics of each individual will soon be entirely lost in the general aspect of the world. Our forefathers were always prone to make an improper use of the notion that private rights ought to be respected; and we are naturally prone, on the other hand, to exaggerate the idea that the interest of a private individual ought always to bend to the interest of the many.

The political world is metamorphosed; new remedies must henceforth be sought for new disorders. To lay down extensive but distinct and settled limits to the action of the government; to confer certain rights on private persons, and to secure to them the undisputed enjoyment of those rights; to enable individual man to maintain whatever independence, strength, and original power he still possesses; to raise him by the side of society at large, and uphold him in that position; these appear to me the main objects of legislators in the ages upon which we are now entering. It would seem as if the rulers of our time sought only to use men in order to make things great; I wish that they would try a little more to make great men; that they would set less value on the work and more upon the workman; that they would never forget that a nation cannot long remain strong when every man belonging to it is individually weak; and that no form or combination of social polity has yet been devised to make an energetic people out of a community of pusillanimous and enfeebled citizens.

I trace among our contemporaries two contrary notions which are equally injurious. One set of men can perceive nothing in the principle of equality but the anarchical tendencies that it engenders; they dread their own free agency, they fear themselves. Other thinkers, less numerous but more enlightened, take a different view: beside that track which starts from the principle of equality to terminate in anarchy, they have at last discovered the road that seems to lead men to inevitable servitude. They shape their souls beforehand to this necessary condition; and, despairing of remaining free, they already do obeisance in their hearts to the master who is soon to appear. The former abandon freedom because they think it dangerous; the latter, because they hold it to be impossible....

The men who live in the democratic ages upon which we are entering have naturally a taste for independence; they are naturally impatient of regulation, and they are wearied by the permanence even of the condition they themselves prefer. They are fond of power, but they are prone to despise and hate those who wield it, and they easily elude its grasp by their own mobility and insignificance.

These propensities will always manifest themselves, because they originate in the groundwork of society, which will undergo no change; for a long time they will prevent the establishment of any despotism, and they will furnish fresh weapons to each succeeding generation that struggles in favor of the liberty of mankind. Let us, then, look forward to the future with that salutary fear which makes men keep watch and ward for freedom, not with that faint and idle terror which depresses and enervates the heart.

The French Revolution

Declaration of the Rights of Man and Citizen, 1789

The representatives of the French people, constituted as a National Assembly, and considering that ignorance, neglect, or contempt of the rights of man are the sole causes of public misfortunes and governmental corruption, have resolved to set forth in a solemn declaration the natural, inalienable and sacred rights of man: so that by being constantly present to all the members of the social body this declaration may always remind them of their rights and duties; so that by being liable at every moment to comparison with the aim of any and all political institutions the acts of the legislative and executive powers may be the more fully respected; and so that by being founded henceforward on simple and incontestable principles the demands of the citizens may always tend toward maintaining the constitution and the general welfare.

In consequence, the National Assembly recognizes and declares, in the presence and under the auspices of the Supreme Being, the following rights of man and the citizen:

1. Men are born and remain free and equal in rights. Social distinctions may be based only on common utility.

2.   The purpose of all political association is the preservation of the natural and imprescriptible rights of man. These rights are liberty, property, security, and resistance to oppression.

3.   The principle of all sovereignty rests essentially in the nation. No body and no individual may exercise authority which does not emanate expressly from the nation.

4.   Liberty consists in the ability to do whatever does not harm another; hence the exercise of the natural rights of each man has no other limits than those which assure to other members of society the enjoyment of the same rights. These limits can only be determined by the law.

5.   The law only has the right to prohibit those actions which are injurious to society. No hindrance should be put in the way of anything not prohibited by the law, nor may any one be forced to do what the law does not require.

6.   The law is the expression of the general will. All citizens have the right to take part, in person or by their representatives, in its formation. It must be the same for everyone whether it protects or penalizes. All citizens being equal in its eyes are equally admissible to all public dignities, offices, and employments, according to their ability, and with no other distinction than that of their virtues and talents.

7.   No man may be indicted, arrested, or detained except in cases determined by the law and according to the forms which it has prescribed. Those who seek, expedite, execute, or cause to be executed arbitrary orders should be punished; but citizens summoned or seized by virtue of the law should obey instantly, and render themselves guilty by resistance.

8.   Only strictly and obviously necessary punishments may be established by the law, and no one may be punished except by virtue of a law established and promulgated before the time of the offense, and legally applied.

9.   Every man being presumed innocent until judged guilty, if it is deemed indispensable to arrest him, all rigor unnecessary to securing his person should be severely repressed by the law.

10.   No one should be disturbed for his opinions, even in religion, provided that their manifestation does not trouble public order as established by law.

11.   The free communication of thoughts and opinions is one of the most precious of the rights of man. Every citizen may therefore speak, write, and print freely, if he accepts his own responsibility for any abuse of this liberty in the cases set by the law.

12. The safeguard of the rights of man and the citizen requires public powers. These powers are therefore instituted for the advantage of all, and not for the private benefit of those to whom they are entrusted.

13. For maintenance of public authority and for expenses of administration, common taxation is indispensable. It should be apportioned equally among all the citizens according to their capacity to pay.

14. All citizens have the right, by themselves or through their representatives, to have demonstrated to them the necessity of public taxes, to consent to them freely, to follow the use made of the proceeds, and to determine the means of apportionment, assessment, and collection, and the duration of them.

15. Society has the right to hold accountable every public agent of the administration.

16. Any society in which the guarantee of rights is not assured or the separation of powers not settled has no constitution.

17. Property being an inviolable and sacred right, no one may be deprived of it except when public necessity, certified by law, obviously requires it, and on the condition of a just compensation in advance.

The French Constitution, 1791

The National Assembly, wishing to establish the French Constitution upon the principles it has just recognized and declared, abolishes irrevocably the institutions which were injurious to liberty and equality of rights.

Neither nobility, nor peerage, nor hereditary distinctions, nor distinctions of orders, nor feudal regime, nor patrimonial courts, nor any titles, denominations, or prerogatives derived there from, nor any order of knighthood, nor any corporations or decorations requiring proofs of nobility or implying distinctions of birth, nor any superiority other than that of public functionaries in the performance of their duties any longer exists.

Neither venality nor inheritance of any public office any longer exists.

Neither privilege nor exception to the law common to all Frenchmen any longer exists for any part of the nation or for any individual.

Neither jurandes nor corporations of professions, arts, and crafts any longer exist.

The law no longer recognizes religious vows or any other obligation contrary to natural rights or the Constitution.

Title I: Fundamental Provisions Guaranteed by the Constitution
1st, That all citizens are admissible to offices and employments, without other distinction than virtues and talents;

2nd, That all taxes shall be assessed equally upon all citizens, in proportion to their means;

3rd, That similar offences shall be punished with similar penalties, without any distinction of persons. The Constitution guarantees likewise as natural and civil rights:

Liberty to every man to come and go without being subject to arrest or detention, except according to the forms determined by the Constitution;

Liberty to every man to speak, write, print, and publish his opinions without having his writings subject to any censorship or inspection before their publication, and to worship as he pleases;

Liberty to citizens to assemble peaceably and without arms in accordance with police regulations;

Liberty to address individually signed petitions to the constituted authorities.

The legislative power may not make any laws which infringe upon or obstruct the exercise of the natural and civil rights recorded in the present title and guaranteed by the Constitution; but, since liberty consists of being able to do only whatever is not injurious to the rights of others or to public security, the law may establish penalties for acts which, assailing either public security or the rights of others, might be injurious to society.

The Constitution guarantees the inviolability of property, or a just and previous indemnity for that of which a legally established public necessity requires the sacrifice.

Property reserved for the expenses of worship and for all services of public benefit belongs to the nation, and is at its disposal at all times....Citizens have the right to elect or choose the ministers of their religions.

A general establishment for public relief shall be created and organized to raise foundlings, relieve the infirm poor, and furnish work for the able-bodied poor who have been unable to procure it for themselves.

Public instruction for all citizens, free of charge in those branches of education which are indispensable to all men, shall be constituted and organized, and the establishments thereof shall be apportioned gradually, in accordance with the division of the kingdom.

National festivals shall be instituted to preserve the memory of the French Revolution, to maintain fraternity among the citizens, and to bind them to the Constitution, the Patrie, and the laws.

A code of civil law common to the entire kingdom shall be drafted.

Title III: Of Public Works
1. Sovereignty is one, indivisible, inalienable, and imprescriptible. It appertains to the nation; no section of the people nor any individual may assume the exercise thereof.

2. The nation, from which alone all powers emanate, may exercise such powers only by delegation. The French Constitution is representative; the representatives are the legislative body and the King.

3.   The legislative power is delegated to a National Assembly, composed of temporary representatives freely elected by the people, to be exercised by it, with the sanction of the King, in the manner hereinafter determined.

4.   The government is monarchical; the executive power is delegated to the King, to be exercised, under his authority, by ministers and other responsible agents in the manner herein after determined.

5.   The judicial power is delegated to judges who are elected at stated times by the people.

The French Constitution, 1793

1.   The French Republic is one and indivisible.

2.   The French people is, for the purpose of exercising its sovereignty, divided into primary assemblies according to cantons.

3.   For the purpose of administration and justice, it is divided into departments, districts, and municipalities.

4.   Every man born and living in France, of twenty-one years of age, and every alien, who has attained the age of twenty-one, and has been domiciled in France one year, and lives from his labor;

or has acquired property;

or has married a French woman;

or has adopted a child;

or supports an aged man;

and finally every alien whom the legislative body has declared as one well deserving of the human race, are admitted to exercise the rights of a French citizen.

5.   The right of exercising the rights of citizen is lost:

by being naturalized in a foreign state;

by accepting offices of state, or favors which do not proceed from a democratic government;

by being sentenced to dishonorable or corporal punishments, till reinstated in the former state.

6.   The exercise of the rights of citizen is suspended:

by being in a state of accusation;

by a sentence in contumaciam, so long as this sentence has not been rescinded.

7.   The sovereign people embraces the whole of French citizens.

8.   It chooses its deputies directly.

9.   It delegates to electors the choice of administrators, public civil judges, penal judges, and judges of cassation.

10. It deliberates on laws.

11. The primary assemblies are formed of the citizens who have resided six months in a canton.

12. They consist of no less than 200 and no more than 600 citizens, called together for the purpose of voting.

13. They are organized, after a president, secretaries and collectors of votes have been appointed.

14. They exercise their own police.

15. No one is allowed to appear there with arms.

16. The elections are made either by secret or loud voting, at the pleasure of each voter.

17. A primary meeting can in no case prescribe more than one manner of voting.

18. The collectors of votes note down the votes of those citizens who cannot write, and yet prefer to vote secretly.

19. The votes on laws are given by "Yes," and "No."

20. The elections of primary assemblies are published in the following manner:

    The united citizens in the primary assembly at—, numbering—votes, vote for, or vote against, by a majority of—.

21. Population is the only basis of national representation.

22. For every 40,000 individuals, one deputy is chosen.

23. Every primary assembly which is formed of from 39,000 to 41,000 individuals, chooses directly a deputy.

24. The choice is effected by an absolute majority of votes.

25. Every assembly makes an abstract of the votes, and sends a commissioner to the appointed central place of general record.

26. If at the first voting, no absolute majority be effected, a second meeting shall be held, and those two citizens who had the most votes, shall be voted for again.

27. In case of an equal division of votes, the oldest person has the preference, no matter whether he was voted for, or whether he was chosen without it. In case of an equality of age, the casting of lots shall decide.

28. Every Frenchman, who enjoys the rights of a citizen, is eligible throughout the whole republic.

29. Every deputy belongs to the whole nation.

30. In case of non-acceptance, of abdication, or expiration of office, or of the death of a deputy, the primary assembly which had chosen him shall choose a substitute.

31. A deputy who hands in his resignation, cannot leave his post till his successor shall have been appointed.

32. The French people assembles every year on the 1st of May for election.

33. It proceeds thereto, whatever the number of citizens [present] may be, who have a right to vote.

34. Extraordinary primary meetings are held at the demand of one-fifth of the eligible citizens.

35. The meeting is, in this case, called by the municipal authority of the usual place of assembly.

36. These extraordinary meetings can transact business only when at least more than one-half of the qualified voters are present.

37. The citizens, united in primary assemblies, nominate in proportion of 200 citizens, (they may be present or not,) one elector; two, for from 301 to 400;three, for from 501 to 600.

38. The holding of election meetings, and the manner of election, are the same as in the primary meetings.

39. The legislative body is one, indivisible and continual.

40. Its session lasts one year.

41. It assembles on the 1st of July.

42. The national assembly cannot be organized, unless at least one more than one-half of the deputies are present.

43. The deputies can, at no time, be held answerable, accused or condemned on account of opinions uttered within the legislative body.

44. In criminal cases, they may be arrested if caught in the act; but the warrant of arrest and the warrant of committal can be issued only by the legislative body.

45. The sessions of the national assembly are public.

46. The debates in their sessions shall be printed.

47. It cannot deliberate, unless it consist of 200 members.

48. It cannot refuse to members the floor, in the order in which they demand the same.

49. It decides by a majority of those present.

50. Fifty members have the right to demand a call by names.

51. It has the right of censorship on the conduct of the members in its midst.

52. It exercises the power of police at the place of its sessions, and within the whole extent of its environs.

53.   The legislative body proposes laws, and issues decrees.

54.   By the general name of law, are understood the provisions of the legislative body which concern:

the civil and penal legislation;

the general administration of revenues and of the ordinary expenditures of the republic;

the national domains;

the inscription, alloy, stamp and names of coins; declaration of war;

every new general division of the French territory; public instruction;

public demonstrations of honor to the memory of great men.

55.   By the particular name of decrees are understood those enactments of the legislative body, which concern:

the annual establishment of the land and marine forces; the permission or refusal of the marching of foreign troops through the French territory; the admission of foreign vessels of war into the ports of the republic;

the measures for the common peace and safety; the distribution of annual and momentary relief and of public works;

the orders for the stamping of coins of every description; the unforeseen and extraordinary expenses;

the local and particular orders for an administration, a commune, and any kind of public works;

the defense of the territory;

the ratification of treaties;

the nomination and removal of the commander-in-chief of the army;

the carrying into effect the responsibility of members of the executive council, and of public officers;

the accusation of discovered conspiracies against the common safety of the republic;

every alteration in the division of the French territory; the national rewards.

56.   A notice must precede the introduction of a bill.

57.   Not till after a fortnight from the giving of notice can the debate begin, and the law be temporarily accepted.

58.   The proposed law is printed and sent to all the communes of the republic, under the address of, Proposed law.

59.   If, forty days after the sending in of the proposed law, of the absolute majority of departments, one-tenth of all the primary meetings, legally

assembled by the departments, have not protested, the bill is accepted and becomes a law.

60. If protest be made, the legislative body calls together the primary meetings.

61. The laws, decrees, sentences, and all public transactions are superscribed:

In the name of the French people, in the—year of the French Republic.

62. There shall be an executive council, consisting of twenty-four members.

63. The electoral assembly of each department nominates a candidate. The legislative body chooses from this general list the members of the executive council.

64. It shall be renewed each half session of every legislature, in the last months of its session.

65. The executive council has the management and supervision of the general administration. Its activity is limited to the execution of laws and decrees of the legislative body.

66. It appoints, but not out of its midst, the highest agents of the general administration of the republic.

67. The legislative body establishes the number of these agents, and their business.

68. These agents form no council. They are separated one from the other, and have no relation among themselves. They exercise no personal power.

69. The executive council chooses, but not from its midst, the foreign agents of the republic.

70. It negotiates treaties.

71. The members of the executive council are, in case of violation of duties, accused by the legislative body.

72. The executive council is responsible for the non-execution of the laws and decrees, and the abuses, of which it does not give notice.

73. It recalls and substitutes the agents at pleasure.

74. It is obliged, if possible, to inform the judicial authorities regarding them.

75. The executive council shall have its seat near the legislative body. It shall have admittance to, and a special seat at the place of session.

76. It shall every time be heard, when it shall have to give account.

77. The legislative body shall call it into its midst, in whole or in part, when it is thought necessary.

78.   There shall be a municipal authority in each commune of the republic; and in each district an intermediate administration; and in each department a central administration.

79.   The municipal officers are chosen by the assemblies of the commune.

80.   The administrators are chosen by the electoral assemblies of the departments and of the district.

81.   The municipalities and the administrative authorities are annually renewed one-half.

82.   The administrative authorities and municipal officers have not a representative character. They can, in no case, limit the resolves of the legislative body, nor the execution of them.

83.   The legislative body assigns the business of the municipal officers and of the administrative authorities, the rules regarding their subordination, and the punishments to which they may become liable.

84.   The sessions of the municipalities and of the administrative authorities are held in public.

85.   The civil and penal code is the same for the whole republic.

86.   No encroachment can be made upon the right of citizens to have their matters in dispute decided on by arbitrators of their own choice.

87.   The decision of these arbitrators is final, unless the citizens have reserved the right of protesting.

88.   There shall be justices of the peace, chosen by the citizens of the districts, appointed by law.

89.   They shall conciliate and hold court without fees.

90.   Their number and extent of power shall be established by the legislative body.

91.   There shall be public judges of arbitration, who are chosen by electoral assemblies.

92.   Their number and districts are fixed by the legislative body.

93.   They shall decide on matters in controversy, which have not been brought to a final decision by private arbitrators or by the justices of the peace.

94.   They shall deliberate publicly. They shall vote with loud voice.

    They shall decide in the last resort on oral pleadings, or on a simple petition, without legal forms and without cost. They shall assign the reasons of their decisions.

95.   The justices of the peace and the public arbitrators are chosen annually.

96.   In criminal cases, no citizen can be put on trial, except a true bill of complaint be found by a jury, or by the legislative body. The accused shall have advocates, either chosen by themselves, or appointed officially. The proceedings are in public. The state of facts and the intention are passed upon by a jury. The punishment is executed by a criminal authority.

97.   The criminal judges are chosen annually by the electoral assemblies.

98.   There is a court of cassation for the whole republic.

99.   This court takes no cognizance of the state of facts.

It decides on the violation of matters of form, and on transgressions expressed by law.

100.   The members of this court are appointed annually through the electoral assemblies.

101.   No citizen is excluded from the honorable obligation to contribute towards the public expenses.

102.   The national treasury is the central point of the revenues and expenses of the republic.

103.   It is managed by public accountants, whom the legislative body shall elect.

104.   These agents are supervised by officers of account, whom the legislative body shall elect, but who cannot be taken from their own body: they are responsible for abuses of which they do not give legal notice to the courts.

105.   The accounts of the agents of the national treasury, and those of the administrators of public moneys are taken annually, by responsible commissioners appointed by the executive council.

106.   Those persons appointed to revise the accounts are under the supervision of commissioners, who are elected by the legislative body, not out of their own number; and they are responsible for the frauds and mistakes of accounts, of which they do not give notice. The legislative body preserves the accounts.

107.   The general military power of the republic consists of the whole people.

108.   The republic supports, also, in times of peace, a paid land and marine force.

109.   All Frenchmen are soldiers; all shall be exercised in the use of arms.

110.   There is no generalissimo.

111.   The distinction of grade, the military marks of distinction and subordination, exist only in service and in time of its duration.

112.   The general military force is used for the preservation of order and peace in the interior; it acts only on a written requisition of the constituted authorities.

113.   The general military force against foreign enemies is under the command of the executive council.

114.   No armed body can deliberate.

115.   If of the absolute majority of departments, the tenth part of their regularly formed primary assemblies demand a revision of the constitution, or an alteration of some of its articles; the legislative body is obliged to call together all primary assemblies of the republic, in order to ascertain whether a national convention shall be called.

116.   The national convention is formed in like manner as the legislatures, and unites in itself the highest power.

117.   It is occupied, as regards the constitution, only with those subjects which caused its being called together.

118.   The French nation is the friend and natural ally of free nations.

119.   It does not interfere with the affairs of government of other nations. It suffers no interference of other nations with its own.

120.   It serves as a place of refuge for all who, on account of liberty, are banished from their native country. These it refuses to deliver up to tyrants.

121.   It concludes no peace with an enemy that holds possession of its territory.

122.   The constitution guarantees to all Frenchmen equality, liberty, security, property, the public debt, free exercise of religion, general instruction, public assistance, absolute liberty of the press, the right of petition, the right to hold popular assemblies, and the enjoyment of all the rights of man.

123.   The French republic respects loyalty, courage, age, filial love, misfortune. It places the constitution under the guaranty of all virtues.

124.   The declaration of the rights of man and the constitution shall be engraven on tables, to be placed in the midst of the legislative body, and in public places.

The French Constitution, 1795

The Executive Power shall be delegated to a Directory of five members appointed by the Legislative Body, which for such purpose performs the functions of an electoral body, in the name of the nation.

The Council of Five-Hundred shall prepare, by secret ballot, a list of ten times the number of members of the Directory to be appointed, and shall present it to the Council of Elders, which shall choose, also by secret ballot, from said list.

The members of the Directory must be at least forty years of age.

They may be chosen only from among citizens who have been ministers or members of the Legislative Body.

The present article shall be observed only dating from the ninth year of the Republic.

Dating from the first day of Year V of the Republic, members of the Legislative Body may not be elected members of the Directory or ministers, either during the continuance of their legislative functions or during the first year after the expiration of same.

The Directory shall be renewed in part by the election of one new member annually.

During the first four years, the order of retirement of those first elected shall be determined by lot.

None of the retiring members may be reelected until after an interval of five years.

Ancestors and descendants in direct line, brothers, uncles and nephews, first cousins, and those related by marriage in said several degrees may not be members of the Directory at one and the same time, or succeed one another therein until after an interval of five years.

In case of the removal of one of the members of the Directory by death, resignation, or otherwise, his successor shall be elected by the Legislative Body within ten days at the latest.

The Council of Five-Hundred shall be required to propose candidates within the first five days, and the Council of Elders shall complete the election within the last five days.

The new member shall be elected only for the term of office remaining to the one to be replaced.

Nevertheless, if such time does not exceed six months, the person elected shall remain in office until the end of the fifth year following.

Each member of the Directory shall preside over it in turn for three months only.

The president shall possess the right of signature, and shall have custody of the seal.

Laws and acts of the Legislative Body shall be addressed to the Directory in the person of its president.

The Executive Directory may not deliberate unless at least three of its members are present.

It shall choose for itself, from outside its own membership, a secretary who shall countersign dispatches and record deliberations in a register, in which every member has the right to have his motivated opinion inscribed.

When it deems expedient, the Directory may deliberate without the presence of its secretary; in such case, the deliberations shall be recorded in a special register by one of the members of the Directory.

The Directory shall provide, according to law, for the external and internal security of the Republic.

It may issue proclamations in conformity with the laws, and for the execution thereof.

It shall dispose the armed force, but neither the Directory collectively nor any one of its members may, under any circumstances, command same while in office or during the two years immediately following the expiration of his term.

If the Directory is informed that a conspiracy is being plotted against the external or internal security of the State, it may issue warrants of apprehension and arrest against those who are presumed to be the authors or accomplices thereof; it may question them; but it shall be required, under the penalties provided for the crime of arbitrary detention, to send them before the police officer within two days, in order to proceed according to law.

The Directory shall appoint the generals in chief; it may not choose them from among the blood or marriage relations of its members in the degrees stated in article 139.

It shall supervise and ensure the execution of laws in the administrations and courts, through commissioners of its own appointment.

It shall appoint the ministers, from outside its own membership, and may dismiss them when it thinks it advisable.

It may not select anyone under the age of thirty years, or from among the blood or marriage relations of its members in the degrees stated in article 139.

The ministers shall correspond directly with the authorities that are subordinate to them.

The Legislative Body shall determine the number of the ministers and their prerogatives.

Such number may not be fewer than six or more than eight.

The ministers do not constitute a council.

The ministers shall be jointly and severally responsible for non-execution of laws, as well as for non-execution of orders of the Directory.

The Directory shall appoint the collector of direct taxes in each and every department.

It shall appoint the superintendents-in-chief for the administration of indirect taxes and the national domains.

Until peace has been made, all public functionaries in the French colonies, except in the departments of the Île de France and the Île de la Réunion, shall be appointed by the Directory.

The Legislative Body may authorize the Directory to send to all French colonies, as occasion may require, one or more special agents appointed by it for a limited time.

Such special agents shall perform the same duties as the Directory, and shall be subordinate thereto.

There shall be no superiority among citizens other than that of public functionaries, and that only in relation to the performance of their duties.

The law shall recognize neither religious vows nor any obligation contrary to the natural rights of man.

No one may be prevented from speaking, writing, printing, or publishing his ideas.

Writings may not be subjected to any censorship before their publication.

No one may be held responsible for what he has written or published, except in cases provided for by law.

No one may be prevented from performing the worship of his choice, so long as he complies with the laws.

No one may be forced to contribute to the expenses of a religion. The Republic does not pay for any. There shall be neither privilege, nor mastership, nor wardenship, nor limitation on the liberty of the press, of commerce, or of the practice of industry or arts of any kind.

When circumstances render such prohibitive laws necessary, they shall be essentially provisional, and shall be effective for one year only, unless formally renewed.

The law shall watch particularly over the professions which affect public morals and the security and health of citizens; but admission to the practice of such professions may not be made conditional upon any pecuniary payment.

The law shall provide for the compensation of inventors, or for the maintenance of the exclusive ownership of their discoveries or productions.

The Constitution guarantees the inviolability of all property, or just indemnification for that of which legally established public necessity requires the sacrifice.

The house of every citizen is an inviolable asylum; during the night no one shall have the right to enter except in case of fire, flood, or a call proceeding from inside the house.

During the day, orders of the constituted authorities may be executed therein.

No domiciliary visit may take place except by virtue of a law, and for the person or object expressly designated in the warrant ordering such visit.

Corporations and associations which are contrary to public order may not be formed.

No assembly of citizens may call itself a popular society.

No private society which concerns itself with political questions may correspond with another, or affiliate therewith, or hold public sessions composed of the members of the societies and of associates distinguished from one another, or impose conditions of admission and eligibility, or arrogate to itself rights of exclusion, or cause its members to wear any external insignia of their association.

Citizens may exercise their political rights only in the primary or communal assemblies.

All citizens shall be free to address petitions to the public authorities, but they must be individual ones; no association may present them collectively, except the constituted authorities, and only for matters within their competence.

The petitioners must never forget the respect due the constituted authorities.

Every armed gathering is an attack upon the Constitution; it shall be dispersed immediately by force.

Every unarmed gathering, likewise, shall be dispersed, at first by verbal command, and, if necessary, by the deployment of armed force.

Several constituted authorities may never unite for the purpose of deliberating together; no instrument emanating from such a union may be executed.

No one may wear distinctive symbols indicative of duties formerly performed or services rendered.

The members of the Legislative Body, and all public functionaries, shall wear, in the performance of their duties, the costume or insignia of the authority with which they are invested; the form thereof shall be determined by law.

No citizen may renounce, in whole or in part, the indemnity or salary assigned to him by law because of public duties.

There shall be uniformity of weights and measures throughout the Republic.

The French era shall date from 22 September 1792, the day of the establishment of the Republic.

The French nation declares that under no circumstances will it permit the return of Frenchmen who, having abandoned their homeland since 15 July 1789, are not included in the exceptions provided in the laws against émigrés; and it forbids the Legislative Body to make new exceptions in such connection.

The property of émigrés is irrevocably acquired for the benefit of the Republic.

The French nation likewise proclaims, as a guarantee of public faith, that after a legally consummated auction of national property, whatever its origin, the lawful acquirer may not be dispossessed thereof; reserving to third claimants, if need be, indemnification by the National Treasury.

None of the powers instituted by the Constitution shall have the right to change it in its entirety, or in any of its parts, except for reforms which may be effected by way of revision in conformity with the provisions of Title XIII.

The citizens shall always remember that the duration, preservation, and prosperity of the Republic depend principally upon the wisdom of elections in the primary and electoral assemblies.

The French people entrust the present Constitution to the fidelity of the Legislative Body, the Executive Directory, the administrators, and the judges; to the vigilance of fathers of families, to wives and mothers, to the affection of young citizens, to the courage of all Frenchmen.

Robespierre: On the Principles of Political Morality

Citizens, Representatives of the People:

A sudden change in the success of the nation announced to Europe the regeneration which was operated in the national representation. But to this point of time, even now that I address you, it must be allowed that we have been impelled through the tempest of a revolution, rather by a love of right and a feeling of the wants of our country, than by an exact theory, and precise rules of conduct, which we had not even leisure to sketch.

It is time to designate clearly the purposes of the revolution and the point which we wish to attain: It is time we should examine ourselves the obstacles which yet are between us and our wishes, and the means most proper to realize them: A consideration simple and important which appears not yet to have been contemplated. Indeed, how could a base and corrupt government have dared to view themselves in the mirror of political rectitude? A king, a proud senate, a Caesar, a Cromwell; of these the first care was to cover their dark designs under the cloak of religion, to covenant with every vice, caress every party, destroy men of probity, oppress and deceive the people in order to attain the end of their perfidious ambition. If we had not had a task of the first magnitude to accomplish; if all our concern had been to raise a party or create a new aristocracy, we might have believed, as certain writers more ignorant than wicked asserted, that the plan of the French revolution was to be found written in the works of Tacitus and of Machiavel; we might have sought the duties of the representatives of the people in the history of Augustus, of Tiberius, or of Vespasian, or even in that of certain French legislators; for tyrants are substantially alike and only differ by trifling shades of perfidy and cruelty.

For our part we now come to make the whole world partake in your political secrets, in order that all friends of their country may rally at the voice of reason and public interest, and that the French nation and her representatives be respected in all countries which may attain a knowledge of their true principles; and that intriguers who always seek to supplant other intriguers may be judged by public opinion upon settled and plain principles.

Every precaution must early be used to place the interests of freedom in the hands of truth, which is eternal, rather than in those of men who change; so that if the government forgets the interests of the people or falls into the hands of men corrupted, according to the natural course of things, the light of acknowledged principles should unmask their treasons, and that every new faction may read its death in the very thought of a crime.

Happy the people that attains this end; for, whatever new machinations are plotted against their liberty, what resources does not public reason present when guaranteeing freedom!

What is the end of our revolution? The tranquil enjoyment of liberty and equality; the reign of that eternal justice, the laws of which are graven, not on marble or stone, but in the hearts of men, even in the heart of the slave who has forgotten them, and in that of the tyrant who disowns them.

We wish that order of things where all the low and cruel passions are enchained, all the beneficent and generous passions awakened by the laws; where ambition subsists in a desire to deserve glory and serve the country: where distinctions grow out of the system of equality, where the citizen submits to the authority of the magistrate, the magistrate obeys that of the people, and the people are governed by a love of justice; where the country secures the comfort of each individual, and where each individual prides himself on the prosperity and glory of his country; where every soul expands by a free communication of republican sentiments, and by the necessity of deserving the esteem of a great people: where the arts serve to embellish that liberty which gives them value and support, and commerce is a source of public wealth and not merely of immense riches to a few individuals.

We wish in our country that morality may be substituted for egotism, probity for false honor, principles for usages, duties for good manners, the empire of reason for the tyranny of fashion, a contempt of vice for a contempt of misfortune, pride for insolence, magnanimity for vanity, the love of glory for the love of money, good people for good company, merit for intrigue, genius for wit, truth for tinsel show, the attractions of happiness for the ennui of sensuality, the grandeur of man for the littleness of the great, a people magnanimous, powerful, happy, for a people amiable, frivolous and miserable; in a word, all the virtues and miracles of a Republic instead of all the vices and absurdities of a Monarchy.

We wish, in a word, to fulfill the intentions of nature and the destiny of man, realize the promises of philosophy, and acquit providence of a long reign of crime and tyranny. That France, once illustrious among enslaved nations, may, by eclipsing the glory of all free countries that ever existed, become a model to nations, a terror to oppressors, a consolation to the oppressed, an ornament of the universe and that, by sealing the work with our blood, we may at least witness the dawn of the bright day of universal happiness. This is our ambition, this is the end of our efforts....

What kind of government can realize these marvels? Only a democratic or republican government.

But what is the fundamental principle of the democratic or popular government, that is to say, the essential strength that sustains it and makes it move? It is virtue: I am speaking of the public virtue which brought about so many marvels in Greece and Rome and which must bring about much more astonishing ones yet in republican France; of that virtue which is nothing more than love of the fatherland and of its laws.

If the strength of popular government in peacetime is virtue, the strength of popular government in revolution is both virtue and terror; terror without virtue is disastrous, virtue without terror is powerless. Terror is nothing but prompt, severe, and inflexible justice; it is thus an emanation of virtue; it is less a particular principle than a consequence of the general principle of democracy applied to the most urgent needs of the fatherland. It is said that terror is the strength of despotic government. Does ours then resemble the one with which the satellites of tyranny are armed. Let the despot govern his brutalized subjects through terror; he is right as a despot. Subdue the enemies of liberty through terror and you will be right as founders of the Republic. The government of revolution is the despotism of liberty against tyranny...,

Since virtue and equality are the soul of the republic, and that your aim is to found, to consolidate the republic, it follows, that the first rule of your political conduct should be, to let all your measures tend to maintain equality and encourage virtue, for the first care of the legislator should be to strengthen the principles on which the government rests. Hence all that tends to excite a love of country, to purify manners, to exalt the mind, to direct the passions of the human heart towards the public good, you should adopt and establish. All that tends to concenter and debase them into selfish egotism, to awaken an infatuation for littlenesses, and a disregard for greatness, you should reject or repress. In the system of the French revolution that which is immoral is impolitic, and what tends to corrupt is counter-revolutionary. Weaknesses, vices, prejudices are the road to monarchy.

Carried away, too often perhaps, by the force of ancient habits, as well as by the innate imperfection of human nature, to false ideas and pusillanimous sentiments, we have more to fear from the excesses of weakness, than from excesses of energy. The warmth of zeal is not perhaps the most dangerous rock that we have to avoid; but rather that languor which ease produces and a distrust of our own courage. Therefore continually wind up the sacred spring of republican government, instead of letting it run down. I need not say that I am not here justifying any excess. Principles the most sacred may be abused: the wisdom of government should guide its operations according to circumstances, it should time its measures, choose its means; for the manner of bringing about great things is an essential part of the talent of producing them, just as wisdom is an essential attribute of virtue....

Republican virtue may be considered as it respects the people and as it respects the government. It is necessary in both. When however, the government alone want it, there exists a resource in that of the people; but when the people themselves are corrupted liberty is already lost.

Happily virtue is natural in the people....If virtue be the spring of a popular government in times of peace, the spring of that government during a revolution is virtue combined with terror: virtue, without which terror is destructive; terror, without which virtue is impotent. Terror is only justice prompt, severe and inflexible; it is then an emanation of virtue; it is less a distinct principle than a natural consequence of the general principle of democracy, applied to the most pressing wants of the country.

It has been said that terror is the spring of despotic government. Does yours then resemble despotism? Yes, as the steel that glistens in the hands of the heroes of liberty resembles the sword with which the satellites of tyranny are armed. Let the despot govern by terror his debased subjects; he is right as a despot: conquer by terror the enemies of liberty and you will be right as founders of the republic. The government in a revolution is the despotism of liberty against tyranny. Is force only intended to protect crime? Is not the lightning of heaven made to blast vice exalted?

The law of self-preservation, with every being whether physical or moral, is the first law of nature. Crime butchers innocence to secure a throne, and innocence struggles with all its might against the attempts of crime. If tyranny reigned one single day not a patriot would survive it. How long yet will the madness of despots be called justice, and the justice of the people barbarity or rebellion? How tenderly oppressors and how severely the oppressed are treated! Nothing more natural: whoever does not abhor crime cannot love virtue. Yet one or the other must be crushed. Let mercy be shown the royalists exclaim some men. Pardon the villains! No: be merciful to innocence, pardon the unfortunate, show compassion for human weakness.

The protection of government is only due to peaceable citizens; and all citizens in the republic are republicans. The royalists, the conspirators, are strangers, or rather enemies. Is not this dreadful contest, which liberty maintains against tyranny, indivisible? Are not the internal enemies the allies of those in the exterior? The assassins who lay waste the interior; the intriguers who purchase the consciences of the delegates of the people: the traitors who sell them; the mercenary libelists paid to dishonor the cause of the people, to smother public virtue, to fan the flame of civil discord, and bring about a political counter revolution by means of a moral one; all these men, are they less culpable or less dangerous than the tyrants whom they serve?...

To punish the oppressors of humanity is clemency; to forgive them is cruelty. The severity of tyrants has barbarity for its principle; that of a republican government is founded on beneficence. Therefore let him beware who should dare to influence the people by that terror which is made only for their enemies! Let him beware, who, regarding the inevitable errors of civism in the same light, with the premeditated crimes of perfidiousness, or the attempts of conspirators, suffers the dangerous intriguer to escape and pursues the peaceable citizen! Death to the villain who dares abuse the sacred name of liberty or the powerful arms intended for her defense, to carry mourning or death to the patriotic heart....

Robert Owen

A New View of Society

First Essay

"The Chief Object of these Essays"

According to the last returns under the Population Act, the poor and working classes of Great Britain and Ireland have been found to exceed fifteen millions of persons, or nearly three-fourths of the population of the British Islands.

The characters of these persons are now permitted to be very generally formed without proper guidance or direction, and, in many cases, under circumstances which directly impel them to a course of extreme vice and misery; thus rendering them the worst and most dangerous subjects in the empire; while the far greater part of the remainder of the community are educated upon the most mistaken principles of human nature, such, indeed, as cannot fail to produce a general conduct throughout society, totally unworthy of the character of rational beings.

The first thus unhappily situated are the poor and the uneducated profligate among the working classes, who are now trained to commit crimes, for the commission of which they are afterwards punished.

The second is the remaining mass of the population, who are now instructed to believe, or at least to acknowledge, that certain principles are unerringly true, and to act as though they were grossly false; thus filling the world with folly and inconsistency, and making society, throughout all its ramifications, a scene of insincerity and counteraction.

In this state the world has continued to the present time; its evils have been and are continually increasing; they cry aloud, for efficient corrective measures, which if we longer delay, general disorder must ensue.

Based on the fundamental principle that character formation can be governed, non-sectarian, non-partisan attempts must he made to improve society: The chief object of these Essays is to assist and forward investigations of such vital importance to the well being of this country, and of society in general.

"To Contend for a Principle Regarding Man"

The view of the subject which is about to be given has arisen from extensive experience for upwards of twenty years, during which period its truth and importance have been proved by multiplied experiments.

That the writer may not be charged with precipitation or presumption, he has had the principle and its consequences examined, scrutinized, and fully canvassed, by some of the most learned, intelligent, and competent characters of the present day: who, on every principle and duty as well as of interest, if they had discovered error in either, would have exposed it; but who, on the contrary, have fairly acknowledged their incontrovertible truth and practical importance.

Assured, therefore, this his principles are true, he proceeds with confidence, and courts the most ample and free discussion of the subject; courts it for the sake of humanity—for the sake of his fellow creatures—millions of whom experience sufferings which, were they to be unfolded, would compel those who govern the world to exclaim—"Can these things exist, and we have no knowledge of them?" But they do exist—and even the heartrending statements which were made known to the public during the discussions upon Negro slavery, do not exhibit more afflicting scenes, than those which, in various parts of the world, daily arise from the injustice of society towards itself; from the inattention of mankind to the circumstances which incessantly surround them; and from the want of a correct knowledge of human nature in those who govern and control the affairs of men.

If these circumstances did not exist to an extent almost incredible, it would be unnecessary now to contend for a principle regarding Man, which scarcely requires more than to be fairly stated to make it self-evident.

This principle is, that "Any general character, from the best to the worst, front the most ignorant to the most enlightened, may be given to any community, even to the world at large, by the application of proper means; which means are to a great extent at the command and under the control of those who have influence in the affairs of men."

The principle as now stated is a broad one, and, if it should be found to be true, cannot fail to give a new character to legislative proceedings, and such a character as will be most favorable to the well-being of society.

The principles on which this knowledge is founded must universally prevail.

In preparing the way for the introduction of these principles, it cannot now be necessary to enter into the detail of facts to prove that children can be trained to acquire "any language, sentiments, belief, or any bodily habits and manners, not contrary to human nature."

The Duty of Man to Society

The lessons of history show man his duty to society—the promotion of common happiness, which self-evidently lies within his power, must be the inevitable goal:

Possessing, then, the knowledge of a power so important, which, when understood, is capable of being wielded with the certainty of a law of nature, and which would gradually remove the evils which now chiefly afflict mankind, shall we permit it to remain dormant and useless, and suffer the plagues of society perpetually to exist and increase?

No: the time is now arrived when the public mind of this country and the general state of the world, call imperatively for the introduction of this all-pervading principle, not only in theory, but into practice.

Nor can any human power now impede its rapid progress. Silence will not retard its course, and opposition will give increased celerity to its movements. The commencement of the work will, in fact, ensure its accomplishment; henceforth all the irritating angry passions arising from ignorance of the true cause of bodily and mental character, will gradually subside, and be replaced by the most frank and conciliating confidence and good will.

Nor will it be possible hereafter for comparatively a few individuals, unintentionally to occasion the rest of mankind to be surrounded by circumstances which inevitably form such characters as they afterwards deem it a duty and a right to punish even to death; and that, too, while they themselves have been the instruments of forming those characters.

Such proceedings not only create innumerable evils to the directing few, but essentially retard them and the great mass of society from attaining the enjoyment of a high degree of positive happiness. Instead of punishing crimes after they have permitted the human character to be formed so as to commit them, they will adopt the only means which can be adopted to prevent the existence of those crimes; means by which they may be most easily prevented.

"The Power Which Governs...the Universe"

Happily for poor traduced and degraded human nature, the principle for which we now contend will speedily divest it of all the ridiculous and absurd mystery with which it has been hitherto enveloped by the ignorance of preceding times: and all the complicated and counteracting motives for good conduct, which have been multiplied almost to infinity, will be reduced to one single principle of action, which, by its evident operation and sufficiency, shall render this intricate system unnecessary, and ultimately supersede it in ail parts of the earth. That principle is the happiness of self, clearly understood and uniformly practiced; which can only he attained by conduct that must promote the happiness of the community.

For that Power which governs and pervades the universe has evidently so formed man, that he must progressively pass from a state of ignorance to intelligence, the limits of which it is not for man himself to define; and in that progress to discover, that his individual happiness can be increased and extended only in proportion as he actively endeavors to increase and extend the happiness of all around him. For this state of matters, and for all the gradual changes contemplated, the extraordinary events of the present times have essentially contributed to prepare the way.

The Impact of the French Revolution

Even the late Ruler of France, although immediately influenced by the most mistaken principles of ambition, has contributed to this happy result, by shaking to its foundation that mass of superstition and bigotry, which on the continent of Europe had been accumulating for ages, until it had so overpowered and depressed the human intellect, that to attempt improvement without its removal would have been most unavailing.

These transactions, in which millions have been immolated, or con-signed to poverty and bereft of friends, will be preserved in the records of time, and impress future ages with a just estimation of the principles now about to be introduced into practice; and will thus prove perpetually useful to all succeeding generations.

For the direful effects of Napoleon's government have created the most deep-rooted disgust at notions which could produce a belief that such conduct was glorious, or calculated to increase the happiness of even the individual by whom it was pursued.

The Important Discoveries of Bell and Lancaster

The late discoveries of the Rev. Dr Bell and Mr. Joseph Lancaster have also been preparing the way...by directing the public attention to the beneficial effects, on the young and unresisting mind, of even the limited education which their system embrace.

They have already effected enough to prove that all which is now in contemplation respecting the raining of youth may be accomplished without fear of disappointment. And by so doing, as the consequences of their of their improvements cannot be confined within the British Isles, they will forever be ranked among the most important benefactors of the human race, but henceforward to contend for any new exclusive system will be in vain: the public mind is already too well informed, and has too far passed the possibility of retrogression, much longer to permit the continuance of any such evil.

For it is now obvious that such a system must be destructive of the happiness of the excluded, by their seeing others enjoy what they are not permitted to possess; and also that it tends, by creating opposition, from the justly injured feelings of the excluded, in proportion to the extent of the exclusion, to diminish the happiness even of the privileged: the former therefore can have no rational motive for its continuance.

It will therefore be the essence of wisdom in the privileged class to co-operate sincerely and cordially with those who desire not to touch one iota of the supposed advantages which they now possess; and whose first and last wish is to increase the particular happiness of those classes, as well as the general happiness of society. Society has hitherto been ignorant of the true means by which the most useful and valuable character may be formed.

Establish "Rational Plans" of Education

This ignorance being removed, experience will soon teach us how to form character, individually and generally, so as to give the greatest sum of happiness to the individual and to mankind.

These principles require only to be known in order to establish themselves; the outline of our future proceedings then becomes clear and defined, nor will they permit us henceforth to wander from the right path. They direct that the governing powers of all countries should establish rational plans for the education and general formation of the characters of their subjects. These plans must he devised to train children from their earliest infancy in good habits of every description (which will of course prevent them from acquiring those of falsehood and deception). They must afterwards be rationally educated, and their labor be usefully directed. Such habits and education will impress them with an active and ardent desire to promote the happiness of every individual, and that without the shadow of exception for sect, or party, or country, or climate. They will also ensure, with the fewest possible exceptions, health, strength, and vigor of body; for the happiness of man can be erected only on the foundations of health of body and peace of mind....

Eliminate Ignorance and Poverty and You Eliminate Crime

The present Essays, therefore, are not brought forward as mere matter of speculation, to amuse the idle visionary who thinks in his closet, and never acts in the world; but to create universal activity, pervade society with a knowledge of its true interests, and direct the public mind to the most important object to which it can be directed—to a national proceeding for rationally forming the character of that immense mass of population which is now allowed to be so formed as to fill the world with crimes.

Shall questions of merely local and temporary interest, whose ultimate results are calculated only to withdraw pecuniary profits from one set of individuals and give them to others, engage day after day the attention of politicians and ministers; call forth petitions and delegates from the widely spread agricultural and commercial interests of the empire—and shall the well-being of millions of the poor, half-naked, half-famished, untaught, and untrained hourly increasing to a most alarming extent in these islands, not call forth one petition, one delegate, or one rational effective legislative measure?

No! for such has been our education, that we hesitate not to devote years and expend millions in the detection and punishment of crimes, and in the attainment of objects whose ultimate results are, in comparison with this, insignificancy itself: and yet we have not moved one step in the true path to prevent crimes, and to diminish the innumerable evils with which mankind are now afflicted.

Are these false principles of conduct in those who govern the world to influence mankind permanently? And if not, how, and when is the change to commence?

These important considerations shall form the subject of the next Essay.

Second Essay

General principles only were developed in the First Essay. In this an attempt will be made to show the advantages which may be derived from the adoption of those principles into practice, and to explain the mode by which the practice may, without inconvenience, be generally introduced.

The Rational Molding of Children

Society's aim must be for "each man to have charity for all men."

No feeling short of this can indeed find place in any mind which has been taught clearly to understand that children in all parts of the earth have been, are, and everlastingly will be, impressed with habits and sentiments similar to those of their parents and instructors; modified, however, by the circumstances in which they have been, are, or may be placed, and by the peculiar organization of each individual.

Yet not one of these causes of character is at the command, or in any manner under the control, of infants, who (whatever absurdity we may have been taught to the contrary) cannot possibly be accountable for the sentiments and manners which may be given to them. And here lies the fundamental error of society; and from hence have proceeded, and do proceed, most of the miseries of mankind.

Children are, without exception, passive and wonderfully contrived compounds; which, by an accurate previous and subsequent attention, founded on a correct knowledge of the subject, may be formed collectively to have any human character. And although these compounds, like all the other works of nature, possess endless varieties, yet they partake of that plastic quality, which, by perseverance under judicious management, may be ultimately molded into the very image of rational wishes and desires.

Attaining True Moral and Religious Instruction

In the next place, these principles cannot fail to create feelings which, without force or the production of any counteracting motive, will irresistibly lead those who posses them to make due allowance for the difference of sentiments and manners, not only among their friends and countrymen, but also among the inhabitants of every region of every region of the earth, even including their enemies. With this insight into the formation of character, there is no conceivable foundation for private displeasure or public enmity.

He will then also strongly entertain the desire "to do good to all men," and even to those who think themselves his enemies.

Thus shortly, directly, and certainly may mankind be taught the essence, and to attain the ultimate object, of all former moral and religious instruction.

These Essays, however, are intended to explain that which is true, and not to attack that which is false. For to explain that which is true may permanently improve, without creating even temporary evil; whereas to attack that, which is false, is often productive of very fatal consequences.

The principles developed in this *New View of Society* will point out a remedy which is almost simplicity itself, possessing no more practical difficulties than many of the common employments of life; and such as are readily overcome by men of very ordinary practical talents.

The Challenge of New Lanark

That such a remedy is easily practicable, may be collected from the account of the following very partial experiment.

In the year 1784, the late Mr. Dale, of Glasgow, founded a manufactory for spinning of cotton, near the falls of the Clyde, in the county of Lanark, in Scotland; and about that period cotton mills were first introduced into the northern part of the kingdom.

It was the power which could be obtained from the falls of water that induced Mr. Dale to erect his mills in this situation; for in other respects it was not well chosen. The country around was uncultivated; the inhabitants were poor and few in number; and the roads in the neighborhood were so bad, that the Falls, now so celebrated, were then unknown to strangers.

It was therefore necessary to collect a new population to supply the infant establishment with laborers. This, however, was no light task; for all the regularly trained Scotch peasantry disdained the idea of working early and late, day after day, within cotton mills.

Two modes then only remained of obtaining these laborers; the one, to procure children from the various public charities of the country; and the other, to induce families to settle around the works.

To accommodate the first, a large house was erected, which ultimately contained about five hundred children, who were procured chiefly from workhouses and charities in Edinburgh. These children were to be fed, clothed, and educated: and these duties Mr. Dale performed with the unwearied benevolence which it is well known he possessed.

To obtain the second, a village was built; and the houses were let at a low rent to such families as could be induced to accept employment in the mills; but such was the general dislike to that occupation at the time, that, with a few exceptions, only persons destitute of friends, employment, and character, were found willing to try the experiment; and of these a sufficient number to supply a constant increase of the manufactory could not be obtained. It was therefore deemed a favor on the part even of such individuals to reside at the village, and, when taught the business, they grew so valuable to the establishment, that they became agents not to be governed contrary to their own inclinations....

"The Manager Formed his Plans"

Here then was a fair field on which to try the efficacy in practice of principles supposed capable of altering any characters. The manager formed his plans accordingly. He spent some time in finding out the full extent of the evil against which he had to contend, and in tracing the true causes which had produced and were continuing those effects. He found that all was distrust, disorder, and disunion; and he wished to introduce confidence, regularity, and harmony. He therefore began to bring forward his various expedients to withdraw the unfavorable circumstances by which they had hitherto been surrounded, and to replace them by others calculated to produce a more happy result. He soon discovered that theft was extended through almost all the ramifications of the community, and the receipt of stolen goods through all the country around.

To remedy this evil, not one legal punishment was inflicted, not one individual imprisoned, even for an hour; but checks and other regulations of prevention were introduced, a short plain explanation of the immediate benefits they would derive from a different conduct was inculcated by those instructed for the purpose, who had the best powers of reasoning among themselves. They were at the same time instructed how to direct their industry in legal and useful occupations, by which, without danger or disgrace, they could really earn more than they had previously obtained by dishonest practices. Thus the difficulty of committing the crime was increased, the detection afterwards rendered more easy, the habit of honest industry formed, and the pleasure of good conduct experienced.

The Attack on Drunkenness, Deception, and Dissension

Drunkenness was attacked in the same manner; it was discountenanced on every occasion by those who had charge of any department: its destructive and pernicious effects were frequently stated by his own more prudent comrades, at the proper moment when the individual was soberly suffering from the effects of his previous excess; pot and public houses were gradually removed from the immediate vicinity of their dwellings; the health and comfort of temperance were made familiar to them: by degrees drunkenness disappeared, and many who were habitual bacchanalians are now conspicuous for undeviating sobriety.

Falsehood and deception met with a similar fate: they were held in disgrace: their practical evils were shortly explained; and every countenance was given to truth and open conduct. The pleasure and substantial advantages derived from the latter soon overcame the impolicy, error, and consequent misery, which the former mode of acting had created.

Dissensions and quarrels were undermined by analogous expedients. When they could not be readily adjusted between the parties themselves, they were stated to the manager; and as in such cases both disputants were usually more or less in the wrong, that wrong was in as few words as possible explained, forgiveness and friendship recommended, and one simple and easily remembered precept inculcated, as the most valuable rule for their whole conduct, and the advantages of "which they would experience every moment of their lives; viz—That in future they should endeavor to use the same active exertions to make each other happy and comfortable, as they had hitherto done to make each other miserable; and by carrying this short memorandum in their mind, and applying it on all occasions, they would soon render that place a paradise, which, from the most mistaken principle, of action, they now made the abode of misery." The experiment was tried: the parties enjoyed the gratification of this new mode of conduct; references rapidly subsided; and now serious differences are scarcely known....

The Treatment of Children

The practice of employing children in the mills, of six, seven, and eight years of age, was discontinued, and their parents advised to allow them to acquire health and education until they were ten years old. (It may be remarked, that even this age is too early to keep them at constant employment in manufactories, from six in the morning to seven in the evening. Far better would it be for the children, their parents, and for society, that the first should not commence employment until they attain the age of twelve, when their education might be finished, and their bodies would be more competent to undergo the fatigue and exertions required of them. When parents can be trained to afford this additional time to their children without inconvenience, they will, of course, adopt the practice now recommended.)

The children were taught reading, writing, and arithmetic, during five years, that is, from five to ten, in the village school, without expense to their parents. All the modern improvements in education have been adopted, or are in process of adoption. (To avoid the inconveniences which must ever arise from the introduction of a particular creed into a school, the children are taught to read in such books as inculcate those precepts of the Christian religion which are common to all denominations.) They may therefore be taught and well-trained before they engage in any regular employment....

"The Domestic Arrangements of the Community"

During the period that these changes were going forward, attention was given to the domestic arrangements of the community. Their houses were rendered more comfortable, their streets were improved, the best provisions were purchased, and sold to them at low rates, yet covering the original expense, and under such regulations as taught them how to proportion their expenditure to their income. Fuel and clothes were obtained for them in the same manner; and no advantage was attempted to be taken of them, or means used to deceive them. In consequence, their animosity and opposition to the stranger subsided, their full confidence was obtained, and they became satisfied that no evil was intended them; they were convinced that a real desire existed to increase their happiness upon those grounds alone on which it could be permanently increased. All difficulties in the way of future improvement vanished. They were taught to be rational, and they acted rationally.

Thus both parties experienced the incalculable advantages of the system which had been adopted. Those employed became industrious, temperate, healthy, faithful to their employers and kind to each other; while the proprietors were deriving services from their attachment, almost without inspection, far beyond those which could be obtained by any other means than those of mutual confidence and kindness. Such was the effect of these principles on the adults; on those whose previous habits had been as ill-formed as habits could be: and certainly the application of the principles to practice was made under the most unfavorable circumstances.

Advancing the Narrative of Renovation Worldwide

I have thus given a detailed account of this experiment, although a partial application of the principles is of far less importance than a clear and accurate account of the principles themselves, in order that they may be so well understood as to be easily rendered applicable to practice in any community and under any circumstances.

Without this, particular facts may indeed amuse or astonish, but they would not contain that substantial value which the principles will be found to possess. But if the relation of the narrative shall forward this object, the experiment cannot fail to prove the certain means of renovating the moral and religious principles of the world, by showing whence arise the various opinions, manners, vices, and virtues of mankind, and how the best or the worst of them may, with mathematical precision, be taught to the rising generation.

Let it not, therefore, be longer said that evil or injurious actions cannot be prevented, or that the most rational habits in the rising generation cannot be universally formed. In those characters which now exhibit crime, the fault is obviously not in the individual, but the defects proceed from the system in which the individual was trained. Withdraw those circumstances which tend to create crime in the human character, and crime will not be created. Replace them with such as are calculated to form habits or order, regularity, temperance, industry; and these qualities will be formed. Adopt measures of fair equity and justice, and you will readily acquire the full and complete confidence of the lower orders.

Proceed systematically on principles of undeviating persevering kindness, yet retaining and using, with the least possible severity, the means of restraining crime from immediately injuring society; and by degrees even the crimes now existing in the adults will also gradually disappear: for the worst former disposition, short of incurable insanity will not long resist a firm, determined, well-directed, persevering kindness. Such a proceeding, whenever practiced, will be found the most powerful and effective corrector of crime, and of all injurious and improper habits.

The experiment narrated shows that this is not hypothesis and theory. The principles may be with confidence stated to be universal, and applicable to all times, persons, and circumstances.

These principles, applied to the community at New Lanark, at first under many of the most discouraging circumstances, but persevered in for sixteen years, effected a complete change in the general character of the village, containing upwards of two thousand inhabitants, and into which, also, there was a constant influx of new-comers. But as the promulgation of new miracles is not for present times, it is not pretended that under such circumstances one and all are become wise and good; or that they are free from error. But it may be truly stated, that they now constitute a very improved society; that their worst habits are gone, and that their minor ones will soon disappear under a continuance of the application of the same principles; that during the period mentioned, punishment has been inflicted, or an application been made for parish funds by any individual among them. Drunkenness is not seen in their streets; and the children are taught and trained in the institution for forming their character without any punishment.

The community exhibits the general appearance of industry, temperance, comfort, health, and happiness. These are and ever will be the sure and certain effects of the adoption of the principles explained; and these principles, applied with judgment, will effectually reform the most vicious community existing, and train the younger part of it to any character which may be desired; and that, too, much more easily on an extended than on a limited scale.

"A National, Well-Digested, Unexclusive System"

To apply these principles, however, successfully to practice, both a comprehensive and a minute view must be taken of the existing state of the society on which they are intended to operate. If the introduction of change is gradual, even barely perceptible, it will be readily accepted and the resulting improvement will in turn be rapid. Further, since ignorance of the principles must have been the sole barrier to their national application by Church and State, reform must be inevitable.

For some time to come there can be but one practicable, and therefore one rational reform, which without danger can be attempted in these realms; a reform in which all men and all parties may join—that is, a reform in the training and in the management of the poor, the ignorant, the untaught and untrained, or ill-taught and ill-trained, among the whole mass of British population; and a plain, simple, practicable plan which would not contain the least danger to any individual, or to any part of society, may be devised for that purpose.

That plan is a national, well-digested, unexclusive system for the formation of character and general amelioration of the lower orders. On the experience of a life devoted to the subject, I hesitate not to say, that the members of any community may by degrees be trained to live without idleness, without poverty, without crime, and without punishment; for each of these is the effect of error in the various systems prevalent throughout the world. They are all necessary consequences of ignorance.

Train any population rationally, and they will be rational. Furnish honest and useful employments to those so trained, and such employments they will greatly prefer to dishonest or injurious occupations. It is beyond all calculation the interest of every government to provide that training and that employment; and to provide both is easily practicable.

Comte De Saint-Simon

Nouveau Christianisme

The Religions

The New Christianity will be composed of parties resembling those that today comprise the diverse heretical associations in Europe and America.

The New Christianity, like the heretical associations, will have its morality, worship, and dogma; it will have its clergy, and the clergy its leadership.

But despite this similarity in organization, the New Christianity will be purged of all the existing heresies. But the doctrine of morality will be considered the most important feature. The worship and dogma (le culte et le dogma) will be only regarded as accessories to the object of fixing the moral attention of the faithful of all classes.

In The New Christianity, all morality will be derived directly from this principle: "*Men should conduct themselves to one another as brothers.*" [Italics in original.] And this principle, which harkens back to primitive Christianity, will be proven a *transfiguration* [italics in original] to be announced every day as the goal of all religious action.

This regenerated principle will be presented in the following manner: *Religion should direct the society toward the great aim of ameliorating as soon as possible the condition of the poorest class.* [Italics in original.]

Those who are to be the founders of The New Christianity and constituted as leaders of the New Church, ought to be men most capable of contributing by their hard work to the well-being of the poorest class. The functions of the clergy will be focused on the areas of the New Christian Doctrine, and to perfecting relentlessly the work of leaders of the Church.

Thus, briefly, is the manner, under present circumstances, that True Christianity should develop. We shall next compare this [true] conception of the religious institution with the religions that exist in Europe and America; this comparison will show that the pretended Christian religions practiced today are heresies; in other words, they do not tend directly at the most rapid amelioration of the well-being of the poorest class, which is the essential goal [le but unique] of Christianity.

Friedrich List

The National System of Political Economy

Chapter 31: The System of Values of Exchange (Falsely Termed by the School, The "Industrial" System)—Adam Smith

Adam Smith's doctrine is, in respect to national and international conditions, merely a continuation of the physiocratic system. Like the latter, it ignores the very nature of nationalities, seeks almost entirely to exclude politics and the power of the State, presupposes the existence of a state of perpetual peace and of universal union, underrates the value of a national manufacturing power, and the means of obtaining it, and demands absolute freedom of trade.

Adam Smith fell into these fundamental errors in exactly the same way as the physiocrats had done before him, namely, by regarding absolute freedom in international trade as an axiom assent to which is demanded by common sense, and by not investigating to the bottom how far history supports this idea.

Dugald Stewart (Adam Smith's able biographer) informs us that Smith, at a date twenty-one years before his work was published in 1776 (viz. in 1755), claimed priority in conceiving the idea of universal freedom of trade, at a literary party at which he was present, in the following words:

> "Man is usually made use of by statesmen and makers of projects, as the material for a sort of political handiwork. The project makers, in their operations on

243

human affairs, disturb Nature, whereas people ought simply to leave her to herself to act freely; in order that she may accomplish her objects. In order to raise a State from the lowest depth of barbarism to the highest degree of wealth, all that is requisite is peace, moderate taxation, and good administration of justice; everything else will follow of its own accord in the natural course of things. All governments which act in a contrary spirit to this natural course, which seek to divert capital into other channels, or to restrict the progress of the community in its spontaneous course, act contrary to nature, and, in order to maintain their position, become oppressive and tyrannical."

Adam Smith set out from this fundamental idea, and to prove it and to illustrate it was the sole object of all his later works. He was confirmed in this idea by Quesnay, Turgot, and the other coryphaei of the physiocratic school, whose acquaintance he had made in a visit to France in the year 1765.

Smith evidently considered the idea of freedom of trade as an intellectual discovery which would constitute the foundation of his literary fame. How natural, therefore, it was that he should endeavor in his work to put aside and to refute everything that stood in the way of that idea; that he should consider himself as the professed advocate of absolute freedom of trade, and that he thought and wrote in that spirit.

How could it be expected, that with such preconceived opinions, Smith should judge of men and of things, of history and statistics, of political measures and of their authors, in any other light than as they confirmed or contradicted his fundamental principle?

In the passage above quoted from Dugald Stewart, Adam Smith's whole system is comprised as in a nutshell. The power of the State can and ought to do nothing, except to allow justice to be administered, to impose as little taxation as possible. Statesmen who attempt to found a manufacturing power, to promote navigation, to extend foreign trade, to protect it by naval power, and to found or to acquire colonies, are in his opinion project makers who only hinder the progress of the community. For him no nation exists, but merely a community, i.e. a number of individuals dwelling together.

These individuals know best for themselves what branches of occupation are most to their advantage, and they can best select for themselves the means which promote their prosperity. This entire nullification of nationality and of State power, this exaltation of individualism to the position of author of all effective power, could be made plausible only by making the main object of investigation to be not the power which effects, but the thing effected, namely, material wealth, or rather the value in exchange which the thing effected possesses. Materialism must come to the aid of individualism, in order to conceal what an enormous amount of power accrues to individuals from nationality, from national unity, and from the national confederation of the productive powers. A bare theory of values must be made to pass current as national economy, because individuals alone produce values, and the State, incapable of creating values, must limit its operations to calling into activity, protecting, and promoting the productive powers of individuals. In this combination, the quintessence of political economy may be stated as follows, viz.:

Wealth consists in the possession of objects of exchangeable value; objects of exchangeable value are produced by the labor of individuals in combination with the powers of nature and with capital. By the division of labor, the productiveness of the labor is increased; capital is accumulated by savings, by production exceeding consumption. The greater the total amount of capital, so much the greater is the division of labor, and hence the capacity to produce. Private interest is the most effectual stimulus to labor and to economy. Therefore the highest wisdom of statecraft consists in placing no obstacle in the way of private industry, and in caring only for the good administration of justice. And hence also it is folly to induce the subjects of a State, by means of State legislative measures, to produce for themselves anything which they can buy cheaper from abroad....

This system regards everything from the shopkeeper's point of view. The value of anything is wealth, according to it, so its sole object is to gain values. The establishment of powers of production, it leaves to chance, to nature, or to the providence of God (whichever you please), only the State must have nothing at all to do with it, nor must politics venture to meddle with the business of accumulating exchangeable values. It is resolved to buy wherever it can find the cheapest articles—that the home manufactories are ruined by their importation, matters not to it. If foreign nations give a bounty on the export of their manufactured goods, so much the better; it can buy them so much the cheaper. In its view no class is productive save those who actually produce things valuable in exchange. It well recognizes how the division of labor promotes the success of a business in detail, but it has no perception of the effect of the division of labor as affecting a whole nation. It knows that only by individual economy can it increase its capital, and that only in proportion to the increase in its capital can it extend its individual trades; but it sets no value on the increase of the productive power, which results from the establishment of native manufactories, or on the foreign trade and national power which arise out of that increase.

What may become of the entire nation in the future, is to it a matter of perfect indifference, so long as private individuals can gain wealth. It takes notice merely of the rent yielded by land, but pays no regard to the value of landed property; it does not perceive that the greatest part of the wealth of a nation consists in the value of its land and its fixed property. For the influence of foreign trade on the value and price of landed property, and for the fluctuations and calamities thence arising; it cares not a straw.

In short, this system is the strictest and most consistent "mercantile system," and it is incomprehensible how that term could have been applied to the system of Colbert, the main tendency of which is towards an "industrial system"—i.e. a system which has solely in view the founding of a national industry—a national commerce—without regarding the temporary gains or losses of values in exchange.

Notwithstanding, we would by no means deny the great merits of Adam Smith. He was the first who successfully applied the analytical method to political economy. By means of that method and an unusual degree of sagacity, he threw light on the most important branches of the science, which were previously almost wholly obscure. Before Adam Smith only a practice existed; his works rendered it possible to constitute a science of political economy, and he has contributed a greater amount of materials for that object than all his predecessors or successors.

But that very peculiarity of his mind by which, in analyzing the various constituent parts of political economy, he rendered such important service, was the cause why he did not take a comprehensive view of the community in its entirety; that he was unable to combine individual interests in one harmonious whole; that he would not consider the nation in preference to mere individuals; that out of mere anxiety for the freedom of action of the individual producers, he lost sight of the interests of the entire nation. He who so clearly perceived the benefits of the division of labor in a single manufactory, did not perceive that the same principle is applicable with equal force to entire provinces and nations.

With this opinion, that which Dugald Stewart says of him exactly agrees. Smith could judge individual traits of character with extraordinary acuteness; but if an opinion was needed as to the entire character of a man or of a book, one could not be sufficiently astonished at the narrowness and obliquity of his views. Nay, he was incapable of forming a correct estimate of the character of those with whom he had lived for many years in the most intimate friendship. "The portrait," says his biographer, "was ever full of life and expression, and had a strong resemblance to the original if one compared it with the original from a certain point of view; but it never gave a true and perfect representation according to all its dimensions and circumstances."

P. J. Proudhon

The Philosophy of Poverty

Chapter I: Of the Economic Science

Opposition Between FACT and RIGHT in Social Economy

I affirm the reality of an economic science.

This proposition, which few economists now dare to question, is the boldest, perhaps, that a philosopher ever maintained; and the inquiries to follow will prove, I hope, that its demonstration will one day be deemed the greatest effort of the human mind.

I affirm, on the other hand, the absolute certainty as well as the progressive nature of economic science, of all the sciences in my opinion the most comprehensive, the purest, the best supported by facts: a new proposition, which alters this science into logic or metaphysics *in concreto*, and radically changes the basis of ancient philosophy. In other words, economic science is to me the objective form and realization of metaphysics; it is metaphysics in action, metaphysics projected on the vanishing plane of time; and whoever studies the laws of labor and exchange is truly and specially a metaphysician.

After what I have said in the introduction, there is nothing in this which should surprise any one. The labor of man continues the work of God, who, in creating all beings, did but externally realize the eternal laws of reason.

Economic science is, then, necessarily and at once a theory of ideas, a natural theology, and a psychology. This general outline alone would have sufficed to explain why, having to treat of economic matters, I was obliged previously to suppose the existence of God, and by what title I, a simple economist, aspire to solve the problem of certainty.

But I hasten to say that I do not regard as a science the incoherent ensemble of theories to which the name political economy has been officially given for almost a hundred years, and which, in spite of the etymology of the name, is after all but the code, or immemorial routine, of property. These theories offer us only the rudiments, or first section, of economic science; and that is why, like property, they are all contradictory of each other, and half the time inapplicable. The proof of this assertion, which is, in one sense, a denial of political economy as handed down to us by Adam Smith, Ricardo, Malthus, and J. B. Say, and as we have known it for half a century, will be especially developed in this treatise.

The inadequacy of political economy has at all times impressed thoughtful minds, who, too fond of their dreams for practical investigation, and confining themselves to the estimation of apparent results, have constituted from the beginning a party of opposition to the status quo, and have devoted themselves to persevering, and systematic ridicule of civilization and its customs. Property, on the other hand, the basis of all social institutions, has never lacked zealous defenders, who, proud to be called practical, have exchanged blow for blow with the traducers of political economy, and have labored with a courageous and often skilful hand to strengthen the edifice which general prejudice and individual liberty have erected in concert. The controversy between conservatives and reformers, still pending, finds its counterpart, in the history of philosophy, in the quarrel between realists and nominalists; it is almost useless to add that, on both sides, right and wrong are equal, and that the rivalry, narrowness, and intolerance of opinions have been the sole cause of the misunderstanding.

Thus two powers are contending for the government of the world, and cursing each other with the fervor of two hostile religions: political economy, or tradition; and socialism, or utopia.

What is "Political Economy? What is Socialism?"

What is, then, in more explicit terms, political economy? What is socialism?

Political economy is a collection of the observations thus far made in regard to the phenomena of the production and distribution of wealth; that is, in regard to the most common, most spontaneous, and therefore most genuine, forms of labor and exchange.

The economists have classified these observations as far as they were able; they have described the phenomena, and ascertained their contingencies and relations; they have observed in them, in many cases, a quality of necessity which has given them the name of laws; and this ensemble of information, gathered from the simplest manifestations of society, constitutes political economy.

Political economy is, therefore, the natural history of the most apparent and most universally accredited customs, traditions, practices, and methods of humanity in all that concerns the production and distribution of wealth. By this title, political economy considers itself legitimate in fact and in right: in fact, because the phenomena which it studies are constant, spontaneous, and universal; in right, because these phenomena rest on the authority of the human race, the strongest authority possible. Consequently, political economy calls itself a science; that is, a rational and systematic knowledge of regular and necessary facts.

Socialism, which, like the god Vishnu, ever dying and ever returning to life, has experienced within a score of years its ten-thousandth incarnation in the persons of five or six revelators,—socialism affirms the irregularity of the present constitution of society, and, consequently, of all its previous forms. It asserts, and proves, that the order of civilization is artificial, contradictory, inadequate; that it engenders oppression, misery, and crime; it denounces, not to say calumniates, the whole past of social life, and pushes on with all its might to a reformation of morals and institutions.

Socialism concludes by declaring political economy a false and sophistical hypothesis, devised to enable the few to exploit the many; and applying the maxim *A fructibus cognoscetis*, it ends with a demonstration of the impotence and emptiness of political economy by the list of human calamities for which it makes it responsible.

But if political economy is false, jurisprudence, which in all countries is the science of law and custom, is false also; since, founded on the distinction of thine and mine, it supposes the legitimacy of the facts described and classified by political economy. The theories of public and international law, with all the varieties of representative government, are also false, since they rest on the principle of individual appropriation and the absolute sovereignty of wills.

All these consequences socialism accepts. To it, political economy, regarded by many as the physiology of wealth, is but the organization of robbery and poverty; just as jurisprudence, honored by legalists with the name of written reason, is, in its eyes, but a compilation of the rubrics of legal and official spoliation, in a word, of property.

Considered in their relations, these two pretended sciences, political economy and law, form, in the opinion of socialism, the complete theory of iniquity and discord. Passing then from negation to affirmation, socialism opposes the principle of property with that of association, and makes vigorous efforts to reconstruct social economy from top to bottom; that is, to establish a new code, a new political system, with institutions and morals diametrically opposed to the ancient forms.

Thus the line of demarcation between socialism and political economy is fixed, and the hostility flagrant.

Political economy tends toward the glorification of selfishness; socialism favors the exaltation of communism.

The economists, saving a few violations of their principles, for which they deem it their duty to blame governments, are optimists with regard to accomplished facts; the socialists, with regard to facts to be accomplished.

The first affirm that that which ought to be is; the second, that that which ought to be is not. Consequently, while the first are defenders of religion, authority, and the other principles contemporary with, and conservative of, property, — although their criticism, based solely on reason, deals frequent blows at their own prejudices, — the second reject authority and faith, and appeal exclusively to science, — although a certain religiosity, utterly illiberal, and an unscientific disdain for facts, are always the most obvious characteristics of their doctrines.

For the rest, neither party ever ceases to accuse the other of incapacity and sterility.

The socialists ask their opponents to account for the inequality of conditions, for those commercial debaucheries in which monopoly and competition, in monstrous union, perpetually give birth to luxury and misery; they reproach economic theories, always modeled after the past, with leaving the future hopeless; in short, they point to the regime of property as a horrible hallucination, against which humanity has protested and struggled for four thousand years.

The economists, on their side, defy socialists to produce a system in which property, competition, and political organization can be dispensed with; they prove, with documents in hand, that all reformatory projects have ever been nothing but rhapsodies of fragments borrowed from the very system that socialism sneers at, — plagiarisms, in a word, of political economy, outside of which socialism is incapable of conceiving and formulating an idea.

Every day sees the proofs in this grave suit accumulating, and the question becoming confused.

While society has traveled and stumbled, suffered and thrived, in pursuing the economic routine, the socialists, since Pythagoras, Orpheus, and the unfathomable Hermes, have labored to establish their dogma in opposition to political economy. A few attempts at association in accordance with their views have even been made here and there: but as yet these exceptional undertakings, lost in the ocean of property, have been without result; and, as if destiny had resolved to exhaust the economic hypothesis before attacking the socialistic utopia, the reformatory party is obliged to content itself with pocketing the sarcasms of its adversaries while waiting for its own turn to come.

This, then, is the state of the cause: socialism incessantly denounces the crimes of civilization, verifies daily the powerlessness of political economy to satisfy the harmonic attractions of man, and presents petition after petition; political economy fills its brief with socialistic systems, all of which, one after another, pass away and die, despised by common sense. The persistence of evil nourishes the complaint of the one, while the constant succession of reformatory checks feeds the malicious irony of the other. When will judgment be given? The tribunal is deserted; meanwhile, political economy improves its opportunities, and, without furnishing bail, continues to lord it over the world; *possideo quia possideo.*

"The Realities of the World"

When, in these recent years, socialism, instigated by prolonged convulsions, made its fantastic appearance in our midst, men whom all controversy had found until then indifferent and lukewarm went back in fright to monarchical and religious ideas; democracy, which was charged with being developed at last to its ultimate, was cursed and driven back. This accusation of the conservatives against the democrats was a libel. Democracy is by nature as hostile to the socialistic idea as incapable of filling the place of royalty, against which it is its destiny endlessly to conspire. This soon became evident, and we are witnesses of it daily in the professions of Christian and proprietary faith by democratic publicists, whose abandonment by the people began at that moment.

On the other hand, philosophy proves no less distinct from socialism, no less hostile to it, than politics and religion.

For just as in politics the principle of democracy is the sovereignty of numbers, and that of monarchy the sovereignty of the prince; just as likewise in affairs of conscience religion is nothing but submission to a mystical being, called God, and to the priests who represent him; just as finally in the economic world property—that is, exclusive control by the individual of the instruments of labor—is the point of departure of every theory, —so philosophy, in basing itself upon the a priori assumptions of reason, is inevitably led to attribute to the "me" alone, the generation and autocracy of ideas, and to deny the metaphysical value of experience; that is, universally to substitute, for the objective law, absolutism, despotism.

Now, a doctrine which, springing up suddenly in the heart of society, without antecedents and without ancestors, rejected from every department of conscience and society the arbitrary principle, in order to substitute as sole truth the relation of facts; which broke with tradition, and consented to make use of the past only as a point from which to launch forth into the future—such a doctrine could not fail to stir up against it the established AUTHORITIES; and we can see today how, in spite of their internal discords, the said AUTHORITIES, which are but one, combine to fight the monster that is ready to swallow them.

To the workingmen who complain of the insufficiency of wages and the uncertainty of labor, political economy opposes the liberty of commerce; to the citizens who are seeking for the conditions of liberty and order, the ideologists respond with representative systems; to the tender souls who, having lost their ancient faith, ask the reason and end of their existence, religion proposes the unfathomable secrets of Providence, and philosophy holds doubt in reserve. Subterfuges always; complete ideas, in which heart and mind find rest, never! Socialism cries that it is time to set sail for the mainland, and to enter port: but, say the antisocialists, there is no port; humanity sails onward in God's care, under the command of priests, philosophers, orators, economists, and our circumnavigation is eternal.

Thus society finds itself, at its origin, divided into two great parties: the one traditional and essentially hierarchical, which, according to the object it is considering, calls itself by turns royalty or democracy, philosophy or religion, in short, property; the other socialism, which, coming to life at every crisis of civilization, proclaims itself preeminently anarchical and atheistic; that is, rebellious against all authority, human and divine.

Now, modern civilization has demonstrated that in a conflict of this nature the truth is found, not in the exclusion of one of the opposites, but wholly and solely in the reconciliation of the two; it is, I say, a fact of science that every antagonism, whether in Nature or in ideas, is resolvable in a more general fact or in a complex formula, which harmonizes the opposing factors by absorbing them, so to speak, in each other. Can we not, then, men of common sense, while awaiting the solution which the future will undoubtedly bring forth, prepare ourselves for this great transition by an analysis of the struggling powers, as well as their positive and negative qualities? Such a work, performed with accuracy and conscientiousness, even though it should not lead us directly to the solution, would have at least the inestimable advantage of revealing to us the conditions of the problem, and thereby putting us on our guard against every form of utopia.

What is there, then, in political economy that is necessary and true; whither does it tend; what are its powers; what are its wishes? It is this which I propose to determine in this work. What is the value of socialism? The same investigation will answer this question also.

For since, after all, socialism and political economy pursue the same end— namely, liberty, order, and well-being among men—it is evident that the conditions to be fulfilled—in other words, the difficulties to be overcome—to attain this end, are also the same for both, and that it remains only to examine the methods attempted or proposed by either party. But since, moreover, it has been given thus far to political economy alone to translate its ideas into acts, while socialism has scarcely done more than indulge in perpetual satire, it is no less clear that, in judging the works of economy according to their merit, we at the same time shall reduce to its just value the invective of the socialists: so that our criticism, though apparently special, will lead to absolute and definitive conclusions.

This it is necessary to make clearer by a few examples, before entering fully upon the examination of political economy.

Is Political Economy a Science?

We will record first an important observation: the contending parties agree in acknowledging a common authority, whose support each claims, SCIENCE.

Plato, a utopian, organized his ideal republic in the name of science, which, through modesty and euphemism, he called philosophy. Aristotle, a practical man, refuted the Platonic utopia in the name of the same philosophy. Thus the social war has continued since Plato and Aristotle. The modern socialists refer all things to science one and indivisible, but without power to agree either as to its content, its limits, or its method; the economists, on their side, affirm that social science in no wise differs from political economy.

It is our first business, then, to ascertain what a science of society must be.

Science, in general, is the logically arranged and systematic knowledge of that which IS.

Applying this idea to society, we will say: Social science is the logically arranged and systematic knowledge, not of that which society has been, nor of that which it will be, but of that which it IS in its whole life; that is, in the sum total of its successive manifestations: for there alone can it have reason and system. Social science must include human order, not alone in such or such a period of duration, nor in a few of its elements; but in all its principles and in the totality of its existence: as if social evolution, spread throughout time and space, should find itself suddenly gathered and fixed in a picture which, exhibiting the series of the ages and the sequence of phenomena, revealed their connection and unity. Such must be the science of every living and progressive reality; such social science indisputably is.

It may be, then, that political economy, in spite of its individualistic tendency and its exclusive affirmations, is a constituent part of social science, in which the phenomena that it describes are like the starting-points of a vast triangulation and the elements of an organic and complex whole. From this point of view, the progress of humanity, proceeding from the simple to the complex, would be entirely in harmony with the progress of science; and the conflicting and so often desolating facts, which are today the basis and object of political economy, would have to be considered by us as so many special hypotheses, successively realized by humanity in view of a superior hypothesis, whose realization would solve all difficulties, and satisfy socialism without destroying political economy. For, as I said in my introduction, in no case can we admit that humanity, however it expresses itself, is mistaken.

Let us now make this clearer by facts.

"The Organization of Labor"

The question now most disputed is unquestionably that of the organization of labor.

As John the Baptist preached in the desert, "Repent Ye," so the socialists go about proclaiming everywhere this novelty old as the world, Organize labor, though never able to tell what, in their opinion, this organization should be. However that may be, the economists have seen that this socialistic clamor was damaging their theories: it was, indeed, a rebuke to them for ignoring that which they ought first to recognize, — labor. They have replied, therefore, to the attack of their adversaries, first by maintaining that labor is organized, that there is no other organization of labor than liberty to produce and exchange, either on one's own personal account, or in association with others, — in which case the course to be pursued has been prescribed by the civil and commercial codes. Then, as this argument served only to make them the laughing-stock of their antagonists, they assumed the offensive; and, showing that the socialists understood nothing at all themselves of this organization that they held up as a scarecrow, they ended by saying that it was but a new socialistic chimera, a word without sense, — an absurdity. The latest writings of the economists are full of these pitiless conclusions.

Nevertheless, it is certain that the phrase organization of labor contains as clear and rational a meaning as these that follow: organization of the work-shop, organization of the army, organization of police, organization of charity, organization of war. In this respect, the argument of the economists is deplor-ably irrational. No less certain is it that the organization of labor cannot be a utopia and chimera; for at the moment that labor, the supreme condition of civilization, begins to exist, it follows that it is already submitted to an organi-zation, such as it is, which satisfies the economists, but which the socialists think detestable.

There remains, then, relative to the proposal to organize labor formulated by socialism, this objection—that labor is organized. Now, this is utterly unten-able, since it is notorious that in labor, supply, demand, division, quantity, proportion, price, and security, nothing, absolutely nothing is regulated; on the contrary, everything is given up to the caprices of free-will; that is, to chance.

As for us, guided by the idea that we have formed of social science, we shall affirm, against the socialists and against the economists, not that labor must he organized, nor that it is organized but that it is being organized.

Labor, we say, is being organized: that is, the process of organization has been going on from the beginning of the world, and will continue till the end. Political economy teaches us the primary elements of this organization; but socialism is right in asserting that, in its present form, the organization is inad-equate and transitory; and the whole mission of science is continually to ascer-tain, in view of the results obtained and the phenomena in course of development, what innovations can be immediately effected.

Socialism and political economy, then, while waging a burlesque war, pur-sue in reality the same idea—the organization of labor.

But both are guilty of disloyalty to science and of mutual calumny, when on the one hand political economy, mistaking for science its scraps of theory, denies the possibility of further progress; and when socialism, abandoning tradition, aims at reestablishing society on undiscoverable bases.

Thus socialism is nothing but a profound criticism and continual develop-ment of political economy; and, to apply here the celebrated aphorism of the school, *Nihil est in intellectu, quod non prius fuerit in sensu*, there is nothing in the socialistic hypotheses which is not duplicated in economic practice. On the other hand, political economy is but an impertinent rhapsody, so long as it affirms as absolutely valid the facts collected by Adam Smith and J. B. Say.

Usury or "Lending at Interest"

Another question, no less disputed than the preceding one, is that of usury, or lending at interest.

Usury, or in other words the price of use, is the emolument, of whatever nature, which the proprietor derives from the loan of his property. *Quid sorti accrescit usura est*, say the theologians. Usury, the foundation of credit, was one of the first of the means which social spontaneity employed in its work of organization, and whose analysis discloses the profound laws of civilization. The ancient philosophers, and the Fathers of the Church, who must be regarded here as the representatives of socialism in the early centuries of the Christian era, by a singular fallacy—which arose however from the paucity of economic knowledge in their day—allowed farm-rent and condemned interest on money, because, as they believed, money was unproductive. They distinguished consequently between the loan of things which are consumed by us—among which they included money and the loan of things which, without being consumed, yield a product to the user.

The economists had no difficulty in showing, by generalizing the idea of rent, that in the economy of society the action of capital, or its productivity, was the same whether it was consumed in wages or retained the character of an instrument; that, consequently, it was necessary either to prohibit the rent of land or to allow interest on money, since both were by the same title payment for privilege, indemnity for loan. It required more than fifteen centuries to get this idea accepted, and to reassure the consciences that had been terrified by the anathemas pronounced by Catholicism against usury. But finally the weight of evidence and the general desire favored the usurers: they won the battle against socialism; and from this legitimization of usury, society gained some immense and unquestionable advantages. Under these circumstances, socialism, which had tried to generalize the law enacted by Moses for the Israelites alone, *Non foeneraberis proximo tuo, sed alieno*, was beaten by an idea which it had accepted from the economic routine, namely, farm-rent, elevated into the theory of the productivity of capital.

But the economists in their turn were less fortunate, when they were afterwards called upon to justify farm-rent in itself, and to establish this theory of the product of capital. It may be said that, on this point, they have lost all the advantage they had at first gained against socialism.

Undoubtedly—and I am the first to recognize it—the rent of land, like that of money and all personal and real property, is a spontaneous and universal fact, which has its source in the depths of our nature, and which soon

becomes, by its natural development, one of the most potent means of organization. I shall prove even that interest on capital is but the materialization
of the aphorism, All Labor Should Leave an Excess. But in the face of this
theory, or rather this fiction, of the productivity of capital, arises another
thesis no less certain, which in these latter days has struck the ablest economists: it is that all value is born of labor, and is composed essentially of
wages; in other words, that no wealth has its origin in privilege, or acquires
any value except through work; and that, consequently, labor alone is the
source of revenue among men. How, then, reconcile the theory of farm-rent
or productivity of capital—a theory confirmed by universal custom, which
conservative political economy is forced to accept but cannot justify—with
this other theory which shows that value is normally composed of wages,
and which inevitably ends, as we shall demonstrate, in an equality in society
between net product and raw product?

The Clash between Political Economy and Socialism

The socialists have not wasted the opportunity. Starting with the principle that
labor is the source of all income, they began to call the holders of capital to
account for their farm-rents and emoluments; and, as the economists won the
first victory by generalizing under a common expression farm-rent and usury,
so the socialists have taken their revenge by causing the seigniorial rights of
capital to vanish before the still more general principle of labor. Property has
been demolished from top to bottom: the economists could only keep silent;
but, powerless to arrest itself in this new descent, socialism has slipped clear
to the farthest boundaries of communistic utopia, and, for want of a practical
solution, society is reduced to a position where it can neither justify its tradition, nor commit itself to experiments in which the least mistake would drive
it backward several thousand years.

In such a situation what is the mandate of science?

Certainly not to halt in an arbitrary, inconceivable, and impossible *juste
milieu*; it is to generalize further, and discover a third principle, a fact, a superior law, which shall explain the fiction of capital and the myth of property,
and reconcile them with the theory which makes labor the origin of all wealth.
This is what socialism, if it wishes to proceed logically, must undertake. In fact,
the theory of the real productivity of labor, and that of the fictitious productivity of capital, are both essentially economical: socialism has endeavored only
to show the contradiction between them, without regard to experience or logic;
for it appears to be as destitute of the one as of the other. Now, in law, the liti-
gant who accepts the authority of a title in one particular must accept it in all;
it is not allowable to divide the documents and proofs. Had socialism the right
to decline the authority of political economy in relation to usury, when it
appealed for support to this same authority in relation to the analysis of value?
By no means. All that socialism could demand in such a case was, either that

political economy should be directed to reconcile its theories, or that it might be itself entrusted with this difficult task.

The more closely we examine these solemn discussions, the more clearly we see that the whole trouble is due to the fact that one of the parties does not wish to see, while the other refuses to advance.

It is a principle of our law that no one can be deprived of his property except for the sake of general utility, and in consideration of a fair indemnity payable in advance.

This principle is eminently an economic one; for, on the one hand, it assumes the right of eminent domain of the citizen expropriated, whose consent, according to the democratic spirit of the social compact, is necessarily presupposed. On the other hand, the indemnity, or the price of the article taken, is fixed, not by the intrinsic value of the article, but by the general law of commerce, by supply and demand; in a word, by opinion. Expropriation in the name of society may be likened to a contract of convenience, agreed to by each with all; not only then must the price be paid, but the convenience also must be paid for: and it is thus, in reality, that the indemnity is estimated. If the Roman legists had seen this analogy, they undoubtedly would have hesitated less over the question of expropriation for the sake of public utility. Such, then, is the sanction of the social right of expropriation: indemnity.

Now, practically, not only is the principle of indemnity not applied in all cases where it ought to be, but it is impossible that it should be so applied. Thus, the law which established railways provided indemnity for the lands to be occupied by the rails; it did nothing for the multitude of industries dependent upon the previous method of conveyance, whose losses far exceeded the value of the lands whose owners received compensation. Similarly, when the question of indemnifying the manufacturers of beet-root sugar was under consideration, it occurred to no one that the State ought to indemnify also the large number of laborers and employees who earned their livelihood in the beet-root industry, and who were, perhaps, to be reduced to want. Nevertheless, it is certain, according to the idea of capital and the theory of production, that as the possessor of land, whose means of labor is taken from him by the railroad, has a right to be indemnified, so also the manufacturer, whose capital is rendered unproductive by the same railroad, is entitled to indemnification. Why, then, is he not indemnified? Alas! because to indemnify him is impossible. With such a system of justice and impartiality society would be, as a general thing, unable to act, and would return to the fixedness of Roman justice. There must be victims. The principle of indemnity is consequently abandoned; to one or more classes of citizens the State is inevitably bankrupt.

At this point the socialists appear. They charge that the sole object of political economy is to sacrifice the interests of the masses and create privileges; then, finding in the law of expropriation the rudiment of an agrarian law, they suddenly advocate universal expropriation; that is, production and consumption in common.

But here socialism relapses from criticism into utopia, and its incapacity becomes freshly apparent in its contradictions. If the principle of expropriation for the sake of public utility, carried to its logical conclusion, leads to a complete reorganization of society, before commencing the work the character of this new organization must be understood; now, socialism, I repeat, has no science save a few bits of physiology and political economy. Further, it is necessary in accordance with the principle of indemnity, if not to compensate citizens, at least to guarantee to them the values which they part with; it is necessary, in short, to insure them against loss. Now, outside of the public fortune, the management of which it demands, where will socialism find security for this same fortune?

It is impossible, in sound and honest logic, to escape this circle. Consequently the communists, more open in their dealings than certain other sectarians of flowing and pacific ideas, decide the difficulty; and promise, the power once in their hands, to expropriate all and indemnify and guarantee none. At bottom, that would be neither unjust nor disloyal. Unfortunately, to burn is not to reply, as the interesting Desmoulins said to Robespierre; and such a discussion ends always in fire and the guillotine. Here, as everywhere, two rights, equally sacred, stand in the presence of each other, the right of the citizen and the right of the State; it is enough to say that there is a superior formula which reconciles the socialistic utopias and the mutilated theories of political economy, and that the problem is to discover it. In this emergency what are the contending parties doing? Nothing. We might say rather that they raise questions only to get an opportunity to redress injuries. What do I say? The questions are not even understood by them; and, while the public is considering the sublime problems of society and human destiny, the professors of social science, orthodox and heretics, do not agree on principles. Witness the question which occasioned these inquiries, and which its authors certainly understand no better than its disparagers, the relation of profits and wages.

What! an Academy of economists has offered for competition a question the terms of which it does not understand! How, then, could it have conceived the idea?

Well! I know that my statement is astonishing and incredible; but it is true. Like the theologians, who answer metaphysical problems only by myths and allegories, which always reproduce the problems but never solve them, the economists reply to the questions which they ask only by relating how they were led to ask them: should they conceive that it was possible to go further, they would cease to be economists.

For example, what is profit? That which remains for the manager after he has paid all the expenses. Now, the expenses consist of the labor performed and the materials consumed; or, in fine, wages. What, then, is the wages of a workingman? The least that can be given him; that is, we do not know. What should be the price of the merchandise put upon the market by the manager? The highest that he can obtain; that is, again, we do not know. Political economy prohibits the supposition that the prices of merchandise and labor can be fixed, although it admits that they can be estimated; and that for the reason, say the economists, that estimation is essentially an arbitrary operation, which never can lead to sure and certain conclusions. How, then, shall we find the relation between two unknowns which, according to political economy, cannot be determined? Thus political economy proposes insolvable problems; and yet we shall soon see that it must propose them, and that our century must solve them. That is why I said that the Academy of Moral Sciences, in offering for competition the question of the relation of profits and wages, spoke unconsciously, spoke prophetically.

But it will be said, Is it not true that, if labor is in great demand and laborers are scarce, wages will rise, while profits on the other hand will decrease; that if, in the press of competition, there is an excess of production, there will be a stoppage and forced sales, consequently no profit for the manager and a danger of idleness for the laborer; that then the latter will offer his labor at a reduced price; that, if a machine is invented, it will first extinguish the fires of its rivals; then, a monopoly established, and the laborer made dependent on the employer, profits and wages will be inversely proportional? Cannot all these causes, and others besides, be studied, ascertained, counterbalanced, etc.?

Oh, monographs, histories! We have been saturated with them since the days of Adam Smith and J. B. Say, and they are scarcely more than variations of these authors' words.

But it is not thus that the question should be understood, although the Academy has given it no other meaning. The relation of profits and wages should be considered in an absolute sense, and not from the inconclusive point of view of the accidents of commerce and the division of interests: two things which must ultimately receive their interpretation. Let me explain myself.

Considering producer and consumer as a single individual, whose recompense is naturally equal to his product; then dividing this product into two parts, one which rewards the producer for his outlay, another which represents his profit, according to the axiom that all labor should leave an excess—we have to determine the relation of one of these parts to the other. This done, it will be easy to deduce the ratio of the fortunes of these two classes of men, employers and wage-laborers, as well as account for all commercial oscillations. This will be a series of corollaries to add to the demonstration.

Now, that such a relation may exist and be estimated, there must necessarily be a law, internal or external, which governs wages and prices; and since, in the present state of things, wages and prices vary and oscillate continually, we must ask what are the general facts, the causes, which make value vary and oscillate, and within what limits this oscillation takes place.

But this very question is contrary to the accepted principles; for whoever says oscillation necessarily supposes a mean direction toward which value's center of gravity continually tends; and when the Academy asks that we determine the oscillations of profit and wages, it asks thereby that we determine value. Now that is precisely what the gentlemen of the Academy deny: they are unwilling to admit that, if value is variable, it is for that very reason determinable; that variability is the sign and condition of determinability. They pretend that value, ever varying, can never be determined. This is like maintaining that, given the number of oscillations of a pendulum per second, their amplitude, and the latitude and elevation of the spot where the experiment is performed, the length of the pendulum cannot be determined because the pendulum is in motion. Such is political economy's first article of faith.

As for socialism, it does not appear to have understood the question, or to be concerned about it. Among its many organs, some simply and merely put aside the problem by substituting division for distribution, that is by banishing number and measure from the social organism: others relieve themselves of the embarrassment by applying universal suffrage to the wages question. It is needless to say that these platitudes find dupes by thousands and hundreds of thousands.

The Contribution of Thomas Malthus to Political Economy

The condemnation of political economy has been formulated by Malthus in this famous passage: —

A man who is born into a world already occupied, his family unable to support him, and society not requiring his labor, such a man, I say, has not the least right to claim any nourishment whatever: he is really one too many on the earth. At the great banquet of Nature there is no plate laid for him. Nature commands him to take himself away, and she will not be slow to put her order into execution.

This then is the necessary, the fatal, conclusion of political economy, a conclusion which I shall demonstrate by evidence hitherto unknown in this field of inquiry. Death to him who does not possess!

In order better to grasp the thought of Malthus, let us translate it into philosophical propositions by stripping it of its rhetorical gloss: —

"Individual liberty, and property, which is its expression, are economical data; equality and solidarity are not."

"Under this system, each one by himself, each one for himself: labor, like all merchandise, is subject to fluctuation: hence the risks of the proletariat."

"Whoever has neither income nor wages has no right to demand anything of others: his misfortune falls on his own head; in the game of fortune, luck has been against him."

From the point of view of political economy these propositions are irrefutable; and Malthus, who has formulated them with such alarming exactness, is secure against all reproach. From the point of view of the conditions of social science, these same propositions are radically false, and even contradictory.

The error of Malthus, or rather of political economy, does not consist in saying that a man who has nothing to eat must die; or in maintaining that, under the system of individual appropriation, there is no course for him who has neither labor nor income but to withdraw from life by suicide, unless he prefers to be driven from it by starvation: such is, on the one hand, the law of our existence; such is, on the other, the consequence of property; and M. Rossi has taken altogether too much trouble to justify the good sense of Malthus on this point. I suspect, indeed, that M. Rossi, in making so lengthy and loving an apology for Malthus, intended to recommend political economy in the same way that his fellow-countryman Machiavelli, in his book entitled *The Prince*, recommended despotism to the admiration of the world. In pointing out misery as the necessary condition of industrial and commercial absolutism, M. Rossi seems to say to us: There is your law, your justice, your political economy; there is property.

But Gallic simplicity does not understand artifice; and it would have been better to have said to France, in her immaculate tongue: The error of Malthus, the radical vice of political economy, consists, in general terms, in affirming as a definitive state a transitory condition, namely, the division of society into patricians and *proletaires*; and, particularly, in saying that in an organized, and consequently *solidaire*, society, there may be some who possess, labor, and consume, while others have neither possession, nor labor, nor bread. Finally Malthus, or political economy, reasons erroneously when seeing in the faculty of indefinite reproduction—which the human race enjoys in neither greater nor less degree than all animal and vegetable species—a permanent danger of famine; whereas it is only necessary to show the necessity, and consequently the existence, of a law of equilibrium between population and production.

In short, the theory of Malthus—and herein lies the great merit of this writer, a merit which none of his colleagues has dreamed of attributing to him—is a *reductio ad absurdum* of all political economy.

Socialism is "Utopia, that is, No-Place, a Chimera"

As for socialism, that was summed up long since by Plato and Thomas More in a single word, UTOPIA, that is, no-place, a chimera.

Nevertheless, for the honor of the human mind and that justice may be done to all, this must be said: neither could economic and legislative science have had any other beginning than they did have, nor can society remain in this original position.

Every science must first define its domain, produce and collect its materials: before system, facts; before the age of art, the age of learning. The economic science, subject like every other to the law of time and the conditions of experience, before seeking to ascertain how things ought to take place in society, had to tell us how things do take place; and all these processes which the authors speak of so pompously in their books as laws, principles, and theories, in spite of their incoherence and inconsistency, had to be gathered up with scrupulous diligence, and described with strict impartiality. The fulfillment of this task called for more genius perhaps, certainly for more self-sacrifice, than will be demanded by the future progress of the science.

If, then, social economy is even yet rather an aspiration towards the future than a knowledge of reality, it must be admitted that the elements of this study are all included in political economy; and I believe that I express the general sentiment in saying that this opinion has become that of the vast majority of minds. The present finds few defenders, it is true; but the disgust with utopia is no less universal: and everybody understands that the truth lies in a formula which shall reconcile these two terms: CONSERVATION and MOTION.

Thus, thanks to Adam Smith, J. B. Say, Ricardo, and Malthus, as well as their rash opponents, the mysteries of fortune, *atria Ditis*, are uncovered; the power of capital, the oppression of the laborer, the machinations of monopoly, illumined at all points, shun the public gaze. Concerning the facts observed and described by the economists, we reason and conjecture: abusive laws, iniquitous customs, respected so long as the obscurity which sustained their life lasted, with difficulty dragged to the daylight, are expiring beneath the general reprobation; it is suspected that the government of society must be learned no longer from an empty ideology, after the fashion of the Contrat Social, but, as Montesquieu foresaw, from the relation of things; and already a Left of eminently socialistic tendencies, composed of savants, magistrates, legists, professors, and even capitalists and manufacturers—all born representatives and defenders of privilege—and of a million of adepts, is forming in the nation above and outside of parliamentary opinions, and seeking, by an analysis of economic facts, to capture the secrets of the life of societies.

Let us represent political economy, then, as an immense plain, strewn with materials prepared for an edifice. The laborers await the signal, full of ardor, and burning to commence the work: but the architect has disappeared without leaving the plan. The economists have stored their memories with many things: unhappily they have not the shadow of an estimate. They know the origin and history of each piece; what it cost to make it; what wood makes the best joists, and what clay the best bricks; what has been expended in tools and carts; how much the carpenters earned, and how much the stone-cutters: they do not know the destination and the place of anything. The economists cannot deny that they have before them the fragments, scattered pell-mell, of a chef-d'oeuvre, *disjecti membra poetae*; but it has been impossible for them as yet to recover the general design, and, whenever they have attempted any comparisons, they have met only with incoherence. Driven to despair at last by their fruitless combinations, they have erected as a dogma the architectural incongruity of the science, or, as they say, the inconveniences of its principles; in a word, they have denied the science.

Thus the division of labor, without which production would be almost nothing, is subject to a thousand inconveniences, the worst of which is the demoralization of the laborer; machinery causes, not only cheapness, but obstruction of the market and stoppage of business; competition ends in oppression; taxation, the material bond of society, is generally a scourge dreaded equally with fire and hail; credit is necessarily accompanied by bankruptcy; property is a swarm of abuses; commerce degenerates into a game of chance, in which it is sometimes allowable even to cheat: in short, disorder existing everywhere to an equal extent with order, and no one knowing how the latter is to banish the former, *taxis ataxien diokein*, the economists have decided that all is for the best, and regard every reformatory proposition as hostile to political economy.

The social edifice, then, has been abandoned; the crowd has burst into the wood-yard; columns, capitals, and plinths, wood, stone, and metal, have been distributed in portions and drawn by lot: and, of all these materials collected for a magnificent temple, property, ignorant and barbarous, has built huts. The work before us, then, is not only to recover the plan of the edifice, but to dislodge the occupants, who maintain that their city is superb, and, at the very mention of restoration, appear in battle-array at their gates. Such confusion was not seen of old at Babel: happily we speak French, and are more courageous than the companions of Nimrod.

But enough of allegory: the historical and descriptive method, successfully employed so long as the work was one of examination only, is henceforth useless: after thousands of monographs and tables, we are no further advanced than in the age of Xenophon and Hesiod. The Phenicians, the Greeks, the Italians, labored in their day as we do in ours: they invested their money, paid their laborers, extended their domains, made their expeditions and recoveries, kept their books, speculated, dabbled in stocks, and ruined themselves according to all the rules of economic art; knowing as well as ourselves how to gain monopolies and fleece the consumer and laborer. Of all this accounts are only too numerous; and, though we should rehearse forever our statistics and our figures, we should always have before our eyes only chaos—chaos constant and uniform.

The Contribution of Christianity to the General Welfare

It is thought, indeed, that from the era of mythology to the present year 57 of our great revolution, the general welfare has improved: Christianity has long been regarded as the chief cause of this amelioration, but now the economists claim all the honor for their own principles. For after all, they say, what has been the influence of Christianity upon society? Thoroughly utopian at its birth, it has been able to maintain and extend itself only by gradually adopting all the economic categories: labor, capital, farm-rent, usury, traffic, property; in short, by consecrating the Roman law, the highest expression of political economy.

Christianity, a stranger in its theological aspect to the theories of production and consumption, has been to European civilization what the trades-unions and free-masons were not long since to itinerant workmen—a sort of insurance company and mutual aid society; in this respect, it owes nothing to political economy, and the good which it has done cannot be invoked by the latter in its own support. The effects of charity and self-sacrifice are outside of the domain of economy, which must bring about social happiness through justice and the organization of labor. For the rest, I am ready to admit the beneficial effects of the system of property; but I observe that these effects are entirely balanced by the misery which it is the nature of this system to produce; so that, as an illustrious minister recently confessed before the English Parliament, and as we shall soon show, the increase of misery in the present state of society is parallel and equal to the increase of wealth—which completely annuls the merits of political economy.

Thus political economy is justified neither by its maxims nor by its works; and, as for socialism, its whole value consists in having established this fact. We are forced, then, to resume the examination of political economy, since it alone contains, at least in part, the materials of social science; and to ascertain whether its theories do not conceal some error, the correction of which would reconcile fact and right, reveal the organic law of humanity, and give the positive conception of order.

P. J. Proudhon

What is Property?

Chapter I: Method Pursued in this Work. The Idea of Revolution

Property as Robbery

If I were asked to answer the following question: WHAT IS SLAVERY? and I should answer in one word, IT IS MURDER, my meaning would be understood at once. No extended argument would be required to show that the power to take from a man his thought, his will, his personality, is a power of life and death; and that to enslave a man is to kill him. Why, then, to this other question: WHAT IS PROPERTY! may I not likewise answer, IT IS ROBBERY, without the certainty of being misunderstood; the second proposition being no other than a transformation of the first?

I undertake to discuss the vital principle of our government and our institutions, property: I am in my right. I may be mistaken in the conclusion which shall result from my investigations: I am in my right. I think best to place the last thought of my book first: still am I in my right.

Such an author teaches that property is a civil right, born of occupation and sanctioned by law; another maintains that it is a natural right, originating in labor,—and both of these doctrines, totally opposed as they may seem, are encouraged and applauded. I contend that neither labor, nor occupation, nor law, can create property; that it is an effect without a cause: am I censurable?

But murmurs arise!

PROPERTY IS ROBBERY! That is the war cry of '93! That is the signal of revolutions!

Reader, calm yourself: I am no agent of discord, no firebrand of sedition. I anticipate history by a few days; I disclose a truth whose development we may try in vain to arrest; I write the preamble of our future constitution. This proposition which seems to you blasphemous—PROPERTY IS ROBBERY—would, if our prejudices allowed us to consider it, be recognized as the lightning-rod to shield us from the coming thunderbolt; but too many interests stand in the way!... Alas! philosophy will not change the course of events: destiny will fulfill itself regardless of prophecy. Besides, must not justice be done and our education be finished?

PROPERTY IS ROBBERY!...What a revolution in human ideas! PROPRIETOR and ROBBER have been at all times expressions as contradictory as the beings whom they designate are hostile; all languages have perpetuated this opposition. On what authority, then, do you venture to attack universal consent, and give the lie to the human race? Who are you, that you should question the judgment of the nations and the ages?...

"Why is there so much Sorrow and Misery in Society?"

One day I asked myself: Why is there so much sorrow and misery in society? Must man always be wretched? And not satisfied with the explanations given by the reformers,—these attributing the general distress to governmental cowardice and incapacity, those to conspirators and emeutes, still others to ignorance and general corruption,—and weary of the interminable quarrels of the tribune and the press, I sought to fathom the matter myself. I have consulted the masters of science; I have read a hundred volumes of philosophy, law, political economy, and history: would to God that I had lived in a century in which so much reading had been useless! I have made every effort to obtain exact information, comparing doctrines, replying to objections, continually constructing equations and reductions from arguments, and weighing thousands of syllogisms in the scales of the most rigorous logic. In this laborious work, I have collected many interesting facts which I shall share with my friends and the public as soon as I have leisure. But I must say that I recognized at once that we had never understood the meaning of these words, so common and yet so sacred: JUSTICE, EQUITY, LIBERTY; that concerning each of these principles our ideas have been utterly obscure; and, in fact, that this ignorance was the sole cause, both of the poverty that devours us, and of all the calamities that have ever afflicted the human race.

My mind was frightened by this strange result: I doubted my reason. What! said I, that which eye has not seen, nor ear heard, nor insight penetrated, you have discovered! Wretch, mistake not the visions of your diseased brain for the truths of science! Do you not know (great philosophers have said so) that in points of practical morality universal error is a contradiction?

I resolved then to test my arguments; and in entering upon this new labor I sought an answer to the following questions: Is it possible that humanity can have been so long and so universally mistaken in the application of moral principles? How and why could it be mistaken? How can its error, being universal, be capable of correction?...

All men believe and repeat that equality of conditions is identical with equality of rights; that PROPERTY and ROBBERY are synonymous terms; that every social advantage accorded, or rather usurped, in the name of superior talent or service, is iniquity and extortion. All men in their hearts, I say, bear witness to these truths; they need only to be made to understand it.

A Methodological Issue

Before entering directly upon the question before me, I must say a word of the road that I shall traverse. When Pascal approached a geometrical problem, he invented a method of solution; to solve a problem in philosophy a method is equally necessary. Well, by how much do the problems of which philosophy treats surpass in the gravity of their results those discussed by geometry! How much more imperatively, then, do they demand for their solution a profound and rigorous analysis!

It is a fact placed forever beyond doubt, say the modern psychologists, that every perception received by the mind is determined by certain general laws which govern the mind; is molded, so to speak, in certain types pre-existing in our understanding, and which constitutes its original condition. Hence, say they, if the mind has no innate IDEAS, it has at least innate FORMS. Thus, for example, every phenomenon is of necessity conceived by us as happening in TIME and SPACE,—that compels us to infer a CAUSE of its occurrence; every thing which exists implies the ideas of SUBSTANCE, MODE, RELATION, NUMBER, &c.; in a word, we form no idea which is not related to some one of the general principles of reason, independent of which nothing exists.

These axioms of the understanding, add the psychologists, these fundamental types, by which all our judgments and ideas are inevitably shaped, and which our sensations serve only to illuminate, are known in the schools as CATEGORIES. Their primordial existence in the mind is today demonstrated; they need only to be systematized and catalogued. Aristotle recognized ten; Kant increased the number to fifteen; M. Cousin has reduced it to three, to two, to one; and the indisputable glory of this professor will be due to the fact that, if he has not discovered the true theory of categories, he has, at least, seen more clearly than any one else the vast importance of this question,—the greatest and perhaps the only one with which metaphysics has to deal.

I confess that I disbelieve in the innateness, not only of IDEAS, but also of FORMS or LAWS of our understanding; and I hold the metaphysics of Reid and Kant to be still farther removed from the truth than that of Aristotle. However, as I do not wish to enter here into a discussion of the mind, a task which would demand much labor and be of no interest to the public, I shall admit the hypothesis that our most general and most necessary ideas—such as time, space, substance, and cause—exist originally in the mind; or, at least, are derived immediately from its constitution.

But it is a psychological fact none the less true, and one to which the philosophers have paid too little attention, that habit, like a second nature, has the power of fixing in the mind new categorical forms derived from the appearances which impress us, and by them usually stripped of objective reality, but whose influence over our judgments is no less predetermining than that of the original categories. Hence we reason by the ETERNAL and ABSOLUTE laws of our mind, and at the same time by the secondary rules, ordinarily faulty, which are suggested to us by imperfect observation. This is the most fecund source of false prejudices, and the permanent and often invincible cause of a multitude of errors. The bias resulting from these prejudices is so strong that often, even when we are fighting against a principle which our mind thinks false, which is repugnant to our reason, and which our conscience disapproves, we defend it without knowing it, we reason in accordance with it, and we obey it while attacking it. Enclosed within a circle, our mind revolves about itself, until a new observation, creating within us new ideas, brings to view an external principle which delivers us from the phantom by which our imagination is possessed.

Thus, we know today that, by the laws of a universal magnetism whose cause is still unknown, two bodies (no obstacle intervening) tend to unite by an accelerated impelling force which we call GRAVITATION. It is gravitation which causes unsupported bodies to fall to the ground, which gives them weight, and which fastens us to the earth on which we live. Ignorance of this cause was the sole obstacle which prevented the ancients from believing in the antipodes. "Can you not see," said St. Augustine after Lactantius, "that, if there were men under our feet, their heads would point downward, and that they would fall into the sky?" The bishop of Hippo, who thought the earth flat because it appeared so to the eye, supposed in consequence that, if we should connect by straight lines the zenith with the nadir in different places, these lines would be parallel with each other; and in the direction of these lines he traced every movement from above to below. Thence he naturally concluded that the stars were rolling torches set in the vault of the sky; that, if left to themselves, they would fall to the earth in a shower of fire; that the earth was one vast plain, forming the lower portion of the world, &c. If he had been asked by what the world itself was sustained, he would have answered that he did not know, but that to God nothing is impossible. Such were the ideas of St. Augustine in regard to space and movement, ideas fixed within him by a prejudice derived from an appearance, and which had become with him a general and categorical rule of judgment. Of the reason why bodies fall his mind knew nothing; he could only say that a body falls because it falls.

With us the idea of a fall is more complex: to the general ideas of space and movement which it implies, we add that of attraction or direction towards a centre, which gives us the higher idea of cause. But if physics has fully corrected our judgment in this respect, we still make use of the prejudice of St. Augustine; and when we say that a thing has FALLEN, we do not mean simply and in general that there has been an effect of gravitation, but specially and in particular that it is towards the earth, and FROM ABOVE TO BELOW, that this movement has taken place. Our mind is enlightened in vain; the imagination prevails, and our language remains forever incorrigible. To DESCEND FROM HEAVEN is as incorrect an expression as to MOUNT TO HEAVEN; and yet this expression will live as long as men use language.

All these phrases—FROM ABOVE TO BELOW; TO DESCEND FROM HEAVEN; TO FALL FROM THE CLOUDS, &C.—are henceforth harmless, because we know how to rectify them in practice; but let us deign to consider for a moment how much they have retarded the progress of science. If, indeed, it be a matter of little importance to statistics, mechanics, hydrodynamics, and ballistics, that the true cause of the fall of bodies should be known, and that our ideas of the general movements in space should be exact, it is quite otherwise when we undertake to explain the system of the universe, the cause of tides, the shape of the earth, and its position in the heavens: to understand these things we must leave the circle of appearances. In all ages there have been ingenious mechanicians, excellent architects, skilful artillerymen: any error, into which it was possible for them to fall in regard to the rotundity of the earth and gravitation, in no wise retarded the development of their art; the solidity of their buildings and accuracy of their aim was not affected by it. But sooner or later they were forced to grapple with phenomena, which the supposed parallelism of all perpendiculars erected from the earth's surface rendered inexplicable: then also commenced a struggle between the prejudices, which for centuries had sufficed in daily practice, and the unprecedented opinions which the testimony of the eyes seemed to contradict.

Thus, on the one hand, the falsest judgments, whether based on isolated facts or only on appearances, always embrace some truths whose sphere, whether large or small, affords room for a certain number of inferences, beyond which we fall into absurdity. The ideas of St. Augustine, for example, contained the following truths: that bodies fall towards the earth, that they fall in a straight line, that either the sun or the earth moves, that either the sky or the earth turns, &c. These general facts always have been true; our science has added nothing to them. But, on the other hand, it being necessary to account for every thing, we are obliged to seek for principles more and more comprehensive: that is why we have had to abandon successively, first the opinion

that the world was flat, then the theory which regards it as the stationary centre of the universe, &c.

If we pass now from physical nature to the moral world, we still find ourselves subject to the same deceptions of appearance, to the same influences of
spontaneity and habit. But the distinguishing feature of this second division of
our knowledge is, on the one hand, the good or the evil which we derive from
our opinions; and, on the other, the obstinacy with which we defend the prejudice which is tormenting and killing us.

Whatever theory we embrace in regard to the shape of the earth and the
cause of its weight, the physics of the globe does not suffer; and, as for us, our
social economy can derive there from neither profit nor damage. But it is in us
and through us that the laws of our moral nature work; now, these laws cannot
be executed without our deliberate aid, and, consequently, unless we know
them. If, then, our science of moral laws is false, it is evident that, while desiring
our own good, we are accomplishing our own evil; if it is only incomplete, it
may suffice for a time for our social progress, but in the long run it will lead us
into a wrong road, and will finally precipitate us into an abyss of calamities.
Then it is that we need to exercise our highest judgments; and, be it said to our
glory, they are never found wanting: but then also commences a furious struggle
between old prejudices and new ideas. Days of conflagration and anguish! We
are told of the time when, with the same beliefs, with the same institutions, all the
world seemed happy: why complain of these beliefs; why banish these institutions? We are slow to admit that that happy age served the precise purpose of
developing the principle of evil which lay dormant in society; we accuse men
and gods, the powers of earth and the forces of Nature. Instead of seeking the
cause of the evil in his mind and heart, man blames his masters, his rivals, his
neighbors, and himself; nations arm themselves, and slay and exterminate each
other, until equilibrium is restored by the vast depopulation, and peace again
arises from the ashes of the combatants. So loath is humanity to touch the customs of its ancestors, and to change the laws framed by the founders of communities, and confirmed by the faithful observance of the ages.

Nihil motum ex antiquo probabile est: Distrust all innovations, wrote Titus
Livius. Undoubtedly it would be better were man not compelled to change:
but what! because he is born ignorant, because he exists only on condition of
gradual self-instruction, must he abjure the light, abdicate his reason, and
abandon himself to fortune? Perfect health is better than convalescence: should
the sick man, therefore, refuse to be cured? Reform, reform! cried, ages since,
John the Baptist and Jesus Christ. Reform, reform! cried our fathers, fifty years
ago; and for a long time to come we shall shout, Reform, reform!

A Principle as "Old as Humanity"

Seeing the misery of my age, I said to myself: Among the principles that support society, there is one which it does not understand, which its ignorance has

vitiated, and which causes all the evil that exists. This principle is the most ancient of all; for it is a characteristic of revolutions to tear down the most modern principles, and to respect those of long-standing. Now the evil by which we suffer is anterior to all revolutions. This principle, impaired by our ignorance, is honored and cherished; for if it were not cherished it would harm nobody, it would be without influence.

But this principle, right in its purpose, but misunderstood: this principle, as old as humanity, what is it? Can it be religion?

All men believe in God: this dogma belongs at once to their conscience and their mind. To humanity God is a fact as primitive, an idea as inevitable, a principle as necessary as are the categorical ideas of cause, substance, time, and space to our understanding. God is proven to us by the conscience prior to any inference of the mind; just as the sun is proven to us by the testimony of the senses prior to all the arguments of physics. We discover phenomena and laws by observation and experience; only this deeper sense reveals to us existence. Humanity believes that God is; but, in believing in God, what does it believe? In a word, what is God?

The nature of this notion of Divinity—this primitive, universal notion, born in the race,—the human mind has not yet fathomed. At each step that we take in our investigation of Nature and of causes, the idea of God is extended and exalted; the farther science advances, the more God seems to grow and broaden. Anthropomorphism and idolatry constituted of necessity the faith of the mind in its youth, the theology of infancy and poesy. A harmless error, if they had not endeavored to make it a rule of conduct, and if they had been wise enough to respect the liberty of thought. But having made God in his own image, man wished to appropriate him still farther; not satisfied with disfiguring the Almighty, he treated him as his patrimony, his goods, his possessions. God, pictured in monstrous forms, became throughout the world the property of man and of the State. Such was the origin of the corruption of morals by religion, and the source of pious feuds and holy wars.

Thank Heaven! We have learned to allow every one his own beliefs; we seek for moral laws outside the pale of religion. Instead of legislating as to the nature and attributes of God, the dogmas of theology, and the destiny of our souls, we wisely wait for science to tell us what to reject and what to accept. God, soul, religion—eternal objects of our unwearied thought and our most fatal aberrations, terrible problems whose solution, for ever attempted, for ever remains unaccomplished—concerning all these questions we may still be mistaken, but at least our error is harmless. With liberty in religion, and the separation of the spiritual from the temporal power, the influence of religious ideas upon the progress of society is purely negative; no law, no political or civil institution being founded on religion. Neglect of duties imposed by religion may increase the general corruption, but it is not the primary cause; it is only an auxiliary or result. It is universally admitted, and especially in the matter which now engages our attention, that the cause of the inequality of

conditions among men—of pauperism, of universal misery, and of governmental embarrassments—can no longer be traced to religion: we must go farther back, and dig still deeper.

But what is there in man older and deeper than the religious sentiment?

There is man himself; that is, volition and conscience, free will and law,
eternally antagonistic. Man is at war with himself: why?

"Man," say the theologians, "transgressed in the beginning; our race is
guilty of an ancient offence. For this transgression humanity has fallen; error
and ignorance have become its sustenance. Read history, you will find universal proof of this necessity for evil in the permanent misery of nations. Man
suffers and always will suffer; his disease is hereditary and constitutional. Use
palliatives, employ emollients; there is no remedy."

Nor is this argument peculiar to the theologians; we find it expressed in
equivalent language in the philosophical writings of the materialists, believers
in infinite perfectibility. Destutt de Tracy teaches formally that poverty, crime,
and war are the inevitable conditions of our social state; necessary evils, against
which it would be folly to revolt. So, call it NECESSITY OF EVIL or ORIGI-
NAL DEPRAVITY, it is at bottom the same philosophy.

"The first man transgressed." If the votaries of the Bible interpreted it faithfully, they would say: MAN ORIGINALLY TRANSGRESSED, that is, made a
mistake; for TO TRANSGRESS, TO FAIL, TO MAKE A MISTAKE, all mean the
same thing.

"The consequences of Adam's transgression are inherited by the race; the
first is ignorance." Truly, the race, like the individual, is born ignorant; but, in
regard to a multitude of questions, even in the moral and political spheres, this
ignorance of the race has been dispelled: who says that it will not depart altogether? Mankind makes continual progress toward truth, and light ever tri-
umphs over darkness. Our disease is not, then, absolutely incurable, and the
theory of the theologians is worse than inadequate; it is ridiculous, since it is
reducible to this tautology: "Man errs, because he errs." While the true statement is this: "Man errs, because he learns."

Now, if man arrives at a knowledge of all that he needs to know, it is reasonable to believe that, ceasing to err, he will cease to suffer.

But if we question the doctors as to this law, said to be engraved upon the
heart of man, we shall immediately see that they dispute about a matter of
which they know nothing; that, concerning the most important questions,
there are almost as many opinions as authors; that we find no two agreeing as
to the best form of government, the principle of authority, and the nature of
right; that all sail haphazard upon a shoreless and bottomless sea, abandoned
to the guidance of their private opinions which they modestly take to be right
reason. And, in view of this medley of contradictory opinions, we say: "The
object of our investigations is the law, the determination of the social principle.
Now, the politicians, that is, the social scientists, do not understand each other;
then the error lies in themselves; and, as every error has a reality for its object,

we must look in their books to find the truth which they have unconsciously deposited there."

Now, of what do the lawyers and the publicists treat? Of JUSTICE, EQUITY, LIBERTY, NATURAL LAW, CIVIL LAWS, &c. But what is justice? What is its principle, its character, its formula? To this question our doctors evidently have no reply; for otherwise their science, starting with a principle clear and well defined, would quit the region of probabilities, and all disputes would end.

"What is Justice?"

What is justice? The theologians answer: "All justice comes from God." That is true; but we know no more than before.

The philosophers ought to be better informed: they have argued so much about justice and injustice! Unhappily, an examination proves that their knowledge amounts to nothing, and that with them—as with the savages whose every prayer to the sun is simply O! O!—it is a cry of admiration, love, and enthusiasm; but who does not know that the sun attaches little meaning to the interjection O! That is exactly our position toward the philosophers in regard to justice. Justice, they say, is a DAUGHTER OF HEAVEN; A LIGHT WHICH ILLUMINES EVERY MAN THAT COMES INTO THE WORLD; THE MOST BEAUTIFUL PREROGATIVE OF OUR NATURE; THAT WHICH DISTINGUISHES US FROM THE BEASTS AND LIKENS US TO GOD—and a thousand other similar things. What, I ask, does this pious litany amount to? To the prayer of the savages: O!

All the most reasonable teachings of human wisdom concerning justice are summed up in that famous adage: DO UNTO OTHERS THAT WHICH YOU WOULD THAT OTHERS SHOULD DO UNTO YOU; DO NOT UNTO OTHERS THAT WHICH YOU WOULD NOT THAT OTHERS SHOULD DO UNTO YOU. But this rule of moral practice is unscientific: what have I a right to wish that others should do or not do to me? It is of no use to tell me that my duty is equal to my right, unless I am told at the same time what my right is.

"Justice is the Central Star"

Let us try to arrive at something more precise and positive.

Justice is the central star which governs societies, the pole around which the political world revolves, the principle and the regulator of all transactions. Nothing takes place between men save in the name of RIGHT; nothing without the invocation of justice. Justice is not the work of the law: on the contrary, the law is only a declaration and application of JUSTICE in all circumstances where men are liable to come in contact. If, then, the idea that we form of justice and right were ill-defined, if it were imperfect or even false, it is clear that all our legislative applications would be wrong, our institutions vicious, our politics erroneous: consequently there would be disorder and social chaos.

This hypothesis of the perversion of justice in our minds, and, as a necessary result, in our acts, becomes a demonstrated fact when it is shown that the opinions of men have not borne a constant relation to the notion of justice and its applications; that at different periods they have undergone modifications: in a word, that there has been progress in ideas. Now, that is what history proves by the most overwhelming testimony.

Eighteen Hundred years ago, the world, under the rule of the Caesars, exhausted itself in slavery, superstition, and voluptuousness. The people—intoxicated and, as it were, stupefied by their long-continued orgies—had lost the very notion of right and duty: war and dissipation by turns swept them away; usury and the labor of machines (that is of slaves), by depriving them of the means of subsistence, hindered them from continuing the species. Barbarism sprang up again, in a hideous form, from this mass of corruption, and spread like a devouring leprosy over the depopulated provinces. The wise foresaw the downfall of the empire, but could devise no remedy. What could they think indeed? To save this old society it would have been necessary to change the objects of public esteem and veneration, and to abolish the rights affirmed by a justice purely secular; they said: "Rome has conquered through her politics and her gods; any change in theology and public opinion would be folly and sacrilege. Rome, merciful toward conquered nations, though binding them in chains, spared their lives; slaves are the most fertile source of her wealth; freedom of the nations would be the negation of her rights and the ruin of her finances. Rome, in fact, enveloped in the pleasures and gorged with the spoils of the universe, is kept alive by victory and government; her luxury and her pleasures are the price of her conquests: she can neither abdicate nor dispossess herself." Thus Rome had the facts and the law on her side. Her pretensions were justified by universal custom and the law of nations. Her institutions were based upon idolatry in religion, slavery in the State, and epicurism in private life; to touch those was to shake society to its foundations, and, to use our modern expression, to open the abyss of revolutions. So the idea occurred to no one; and yet humanity was dying in blood and luxury.

All at once a man appeared, calling himself The Word of God. It is not known to this day who he was, whence he came, nor what suggested to him his ideas. He went about proclaiming everywhere that the end of the existing society was at hand, that the world was about to experience a new birth; that the priests were vipers, the lawyers ignoramuses, and the philosophers hypocrites and liars; that master and slave were equals, that usury and every thing akin to it was robbery, that proprietors and idlers would one day burn, while the poor and pure in heart would find a haven of peace.

This man—The Word of God—was denounced and arrested as a public enemy by the priests and the lawyers, who well understood how to induce the people to demand his death. But this judicial murder, though it put the finishing stroke to their crimes, did not destroy the doctrinal seeds which The Word of God had sown. After his death, his original disciples travelled about in all directions, preaching what they called the GOOD NEWS, creating in their turn millions of missionaries; and, when their task seemed to be accomplished, dying by the sword of Roman justice. This persistent agitation, the war of the executioners and martyrs, lasted nearly three centuries, ending in the conversion of the world. Idolatry was destroyed, slavery abolished, dissolution made room for a more austere morality, and the contempt for wealth was sometimes pushed almost to privation. Society was saved by the negation of its own principles, by a revolution in its religion, and by violation of its most sacred rights. In this revolution, the idea of justice spread to an extent that had not before been dreamed of, never to return to its original limits. Heretofore justice had existed only for the masters; it then commenced to exist for the slaves.

Nevertheless, the new religion at that time had borne by no means all its fruits. There was a perceptible improvement of the public morals, and a partial release from oppression; but, other than that, the SEEDS SOWN BY THE SON OF MAN, having fallen into idolatrous hearts, had produced nothing save innumerable discords and a quasi-poetical mythology. Instead of developing into their practical consequences the principles of morality and government taught by The Word of God, his followers busied themselves in speculations as to his birth, his origin, his person, and his actions; they discussed his parables, and from the conflict of the most extravagant opinions upon unanswerable questions and texts which no one understood, was born THEOLOGY—which may be defined as the SCIENCE OF THE INFINITELY ABSURD.

The truth of CHRISTIANITY did not survive the age of the apostles; the GOSPEL, commented upon and symbolized by the Greeks and Latins, loaded with pagan fables, became literally a mass of contradictions; and to this day the reign of the INFALLIBLE CHURCH has been a long era of darkness. It is said that the GATES OF HELL will not always prevail, that THE WORD OF GOD will return, and that one day men will know truth and justice; but that will be the death of Greek and Roman Catholicism, just as in the light of science disappeared the caprices of opinion.

The monsters which the successors of the apostles were bent on destroying, frightened for a moment, reappeared gradually, thanks to the crazy fanaticism, and sometimes the deliberate connivance, of priests and theologians. The history of the enfranchisement of the French communes offers constantly the spectacle of the ideas of justice and liberty spreading among the people, in spite of the combined efforts of kings, nobles, and clergy. In the year 1789 of the Christian era, the French nation, divided by caste, poor and oppressed, struggled in the triple net of royal absolutism, the tyranny of nobles and parliaments, and priestly intolerance. There was the right of the king and the right of the priest, the right of the patrician and the right of the plebeian; there were the privileges of birth, province, communes, corporations, and trades; and, at the bottom of all, violence, immorality, and misery. For some time they talked of reformation; those who apparently desired it most favoring it only for their own profit, and the people who were to be the gainers expecting little and saying nothing. For a long time these poor people, either from distrust, incredulity, or despair, hesitated to ask for their rights: it is said that the habit of serving had taken the courage away from those old communes, which in the middle ages were so bold.

"A Sudden Revelation"

Finally a book appeared, summing up the whole matter in these two propositions: WHAT IS THE THIRD ESTATE?—NOTHING. WHAT OUGHT IT TO BE?—EVERY THING. Some one added by way of comment: WHAT IS THE KING?—THE SERVANT OF THE PEOPLE.

This was a sudden revelation: the veil was torn aside, a thick bandage fell from all eyes. The people commenced to reason thus:

If the king is our servant, he ought to report to us;

If he ought to report to us, he is subject to control;

If he can be controlled, he is responsible;

If he is responsible, he is punishable;

If he is punishable, he ought to be punished according to his merits;

If he ought to be punished according to his merits, he can be punished with death.

Five years after the publication of the brochure of Sieyes, the third estate was every thing; the king, the nobility, the clergy, were no more. In 1793, the nation, without stopping at the constitutional fiction of the inviolability of the sovereign, conducted Louis XVI. to the scaffold; in 1830, it accompanied Charles X. to Cherbourg. In each case, it may have erred, in fact, in its judgment of the offence; but, in right, the logic which led to its action was irreproachable. The people, in punishing their sovereign, did precisely that which the government of July was so severely censured for failing to do when it refused to execute Louis Bonaparte after the affair of Strasburg: they struck the true culprit. It was an application of the common law, a solemn decree of justice enforcing the penal laws.

The spirit which gave rise to the movement of '89 was a spirit of negation; that, of itself, proves that the order of things which was substituted for the old system was not methodical or well-considered; that, born of anger and hatred, it could not have the effect of a science based on observation and study; that its foundations, in a word, were not derived from a profound knowledge of the laws of Nature and society. Thus the people found that the republic, among the so-called new institutions, was acting on the very principles against which they had fought, and was swayed by all the prejudices which they had intended to destroy. We congratulate ourselves, with inconsiderate enthusiasm, on the glorious French Revolution, the regeneration of 1789, the great changes that have been effected, and the reversion of institutions: a delusion, a delusion!

When our ideas on any subject, material, intellectual, or social, undergo a thorough change in consequence of new observations, I call that movement of the mind REVOLUTION. If the ideas are simply extended or modified, there is only PROGRESS. Thus the system of Ptolemy was a step in astronomical progress, that of Copernicus was a revolution. So, in 1789, there was struggle and progress; revolution there was none. An examination of the reforms which were attempted proves this.

The nation, so long a victim of monarchical selfishness, thought to deliver itself for ever by declaring that it alone was sovereign. But what was monarchy? The sovereignty of one man. What is democracy? The sovereignty of the nation, or, rather, of the national majority. But it is, in both cases, the sovereignty of man instead of the sovereignty of the law, the sovereignty of the will instead of the sovereignty of the reason; in one word, the passions instead of justice. Undoubtedly, when a nation passes from the monarchical to the democratic state, there is progress, because in multiplying the sovereigns we increase the opportunities of the reason to substitute itself for the will; but in reality there is no revolution in the government, since the principle remains the same. Now, we have the proof today that, with the most perfect democracy, we cannot be free.

Nor is that all. The nation-king cannot exercise its sovereignty itself; it is obliged to delegate it to agents: this is constantly reiterated by those who seek to win its favor. Be these agents five, ten, one hundred, or a thousand, of what consequence is the number; and what matters the name? It is always the government of man, the rule of will and caprice. I ask what this pretended revolution has revolutionized?

We know, too, how this sovereignty was exercised; first by the Convention, then by the Directory, afterwards confiscated by the Consul. As for the Emperor, the strong man so much adored and mourned by the nation, he never wanted to be dependent on it; but, as if intending to set its sovereignty at defiance, he dared to demand its suffrage: that is, its abdication, the abdication of this inalienable sovereignty; and he obtained it.

But what is sovereignty? It is, they say, the POWER TO MAKE LAW. Another absurdity, a relic of despotism. The nation had long seen kings issuing their commands in this form: FOR SUCH IS OUR PLEASURE; it wished to taste in its turn the pleasure of making laws. For fifty years it has brought them forth by myriads; always, be it understood, through the agency of representatives. The play is far from ended.

The definition of sovereignty was derived from the definition of the law. The law, they said, is THE EXPRESSION OF THE WILL OF THE SOVEREIGN: then, under a monarchy, the law is the expression of the will of the king; in a republic, the law is the expression of the will of the people. Aside from the difference in the number of wills, the two systems are exactly identical: both share the same error, namely, that the law is the expression of a will; it ought to be the expression of a fact. Moreover they followed good leaders: they took the citizen of Geneva for their prophet, and the Contrat Social for their Koran.

Bias and prejudice are apparent in all the phrases of the new legislators. The nation had suffered from a multitude of exclusions and privileges; its representatives issued the following declaration: ALL MEN ARE EQUAL BY NATURE AND BEFORE THE LAW; an ambiguous and redundant declaration. MEN ARE EQUAL BY NATURE: does that mean that they are equal in size, beauty, talents, and virtue? No; they meant, then, political and civil equality. Then it would have been sufficient to have said: ALL MEN ARE EQUAL BEFORE THE LAW.

But what is equality before the law? Neither the constitution of 1790, nor that of '93, nor the granted charter, nor the accepted charter, have defined it accurately. All imply an inequality in fortune and station incompatible with even a shadow of equality in rights. In this respect it may be said that all our constitutions have been faithful expressions of the popular will: I am going, to prove it.

Formerly the people were excluded from civil and military offices; it was considered a wonder when the following high-sounding article was inserted in the Declaration of Rights: "All citizens are equally eligible to office; free nations know no qualifications in their choice of officers save virtues and talents."

They certainly ought to have admired so beautiful an idea: they admired a piece of nonsense. Why! the sovereign people, legislators, and reformers, see in public offices, to speak plainly, only opportunities for pecuniary advancement. And, because it regards them as a source of profit, it decrees the eligibility of citizens. For of what use would this precaution be, if there were nothing to gain by it? No one would think of ordaining that none but astronomers and geographers should be pilots, nor of prohibiting stutterers from acting at the theatre and the opera. The nation was still aping the kings: like them it wished to award the lucrative positions to its friends and flatterers. Unfortunately, and this last feature completes the resemblance, the nation did not control the list of livings; that was in the hands of its agents and representatives. They, on the other hand, took care not to thwart the will of their gracious sovereign.

This edifying article of the Declaration of Rights, retained in the charters of 1814 and 1830, implies several kinds of civil inequality; that is, of inequality before the law: inequality of station, since the public functions are sought only for the consideration and emoluments which they bring; inequality of wealth, since, if it had been desired to equalize fortunes, public service would have been regarded as a duty, not as a reward; inequality of privilege, the law not stating what it means by TALENTS and VIRTUES. Under the empire, virtue and talent consisted simply in military bravery and devotion to the emperor; that was shown when Napoleon created his nobility, and attempted to connect it with the ancients. To-day, the man who pays taxes to the amount of two hundred francs is virtuous; the talented man is the honest pickpocket: such truths as these are accounted trivial.

The people finally legalized property. God forgive them, for they knew not what they did! For fifty years they have suffered for their miserable folly. But how came the people, whose voice, they tell us, is the voice of God, and whose conscience is infallible,—how came the people to err? How happens it that, when seeking liberty and equality, they fell back into privilege and slavery? Always through copying the ancient regime.

Formerly, the nobility and the clergy contributed towards the expenses of the State only by voluntary aid and gratuitous gift; their property could not be seized even for debt,—while the plebeian, overwhelmed by taxes and statute-labor, was continually tormented, now by the king's tax-gatherers, now by those of the nobles and clergy. He whose possessions were subject to mort-main could neither bequeath nor inherit property; he was treated like the animals, whose services and offspring belong to their master by right of accession. The people wanted the conditions of OWNERSHIP to be alike for all; they thought that every one should ENJOY AND FREELY DISPOSE OF HIS POSSESSIONS HIS INCOME AND THE FRUIT OF HIS LABOR AND INDUSTRY. The people did not invent property; but as they had not the same privileges in regard to it, which the nobles and clergy possessed, they decreed that the right should be exercised by all under the same conditions. The more obnoxious forms of property—statute-labor, mortmain, maitrise, and exclusion from public office—have disappeared; the conditions of its enjoyment have been modified: the principle still remains the same. There has been progress in the regulation of the right; there has been no revolution.

These, then, are the three fundamental principles of modern society, established one after another by the movements of 1789 and 1830: 1. SOVEREIGNTY OF THE HUMAN WILL; in short, DESPOTISM. 2. INEQUALITY OF WEALTH AND RANK. 3. PROPERTY—above JUSTICE, always invoked as the guardian angel of sovereigns, nobles, and proprietors; JUSTICE, the general, primitive, categorical law of all society.

We must ascertain whether the ideas of DESPOTISM, CIVIL INEQUALITY and PROPERTY, are in harmony with the primitive notion of JUSTICE, and necessarily follow from it,—assuming various forms according to the condition, position, and relation of persons; or whether they are not rather the illegitimate result of a confusion of different things, a fatal association of ideas. And since justice deals especially with the questions of government, the condition of persons, and the possession of things, we must ascertain under what conditions, judging by universal opinion and the progress of the human mind, government is just, the condition of citizens is just, and the possession of things is just; then, striking out every thing which fails to meet these conditions, the result will at once tell us what legitimate government is, what the legitimate condition of citizens is, and what the legitimate possession of things is; and finally, as the last result of the analysis, what JUSTICE is.

What isn't Justice?

Is the authority of man over man just?

Everybody answers, "No; the authority of man is only the authority of the law, which ought to be justice and truth." The private will counts for nothing in government, which consists, first, in discovering truth and justice in order to make the law; and, second, in superintending the execution of this law. I do not now inquire whether our constitutional form of government satisfies these conditions; whether, for example, the will of the ministry never influences the declaration and interpretation of the law; or whether our deputies, in their debates, are more intent on conquering by argument than by force of numbers: it is enough for me that my definition of a good government is allowed to be correct. This idea is exact. Yet we see that nothing seems more just to the Oriental nations than the despotism of their sovereigns; that, with the ancients and in the opinion of the philosophers themselves, slavery was just; that in the middle ages the nobles, the priests, and the bishops felt justified in holding slaves; that Louis XIV. thought that he was right when he said, "The State! I am the State;" and that Napoleon deemed it a crime for the State to oppose his will. The idea of justice, then, applied to sovereignty and government, has not always been what it is to-day; it has gone on developing and shaping itself by degrees, until it has arrived at its present state. But has it reached its last phase? I think not: only, as the last obstacle to be overcome arises from the institution of property which we have kept intact, in order to finish the reform in government and consummate the revolution, this very institution we must attack.

Is political and civil inequality just?

Some say yes; others no. To the first I would reply that, when the people abolished all privileges of birth and caste, they did it, in all probability, because it was for their advantage; why then do they favor the privileges of fortune more than those of rank and race? Because, say they, political inequality is a result of property; and without property society is impossible: thus the question just raised becomes a question of property. To the second I content myself with this remark: If you wish to enjoy political equality, abolish property; otherwise, why do you complain?

Is property just?

Everybody answers without hesitation, "Yes, property is just." I say everybody, for up to the present time no one who thoroughly understood the meaning of his words has answered no. For it is no easy thing to reply understandingly to such a question; only time and experience can furnish an answer. Now, this answer is given; it is for us to understand it. I undertake to prove it.

Property and Justice

In fact, property being defensible on no ground save that of justice, the idea, or at least the intention, of justice must of necessity underlie all the arguments that have been made in defense of property; and, as on the other hand the right of property is only exercised over those things which can be appreciated by the senses, justice, secretly objectifying itself, so to speak, must take the shape of an algebraic formula...

Property, then, being of necessity conceived as existing only in connection with equality, it remains to find out why, in spite of this necessity of logic, equality does not exist....

Probing man's nature to the bottom, we shall disclose the principle of JUSTICE—its formula and character; we shall state with precision the organic law of society; we shall explain the origin of property, the causes of its establishment, its long life, and its approaching death; we shall definitively establish its identity with robbery. And, after having shown that these three prejudices—THE SOVEREIGNTY OF MAN, THE INEQUALITY OF CONDITIONS, AND PROPERTY—are one and the same; that they may be taken for each other, and are reciprocally convertible—we shall have no trouble in inferring there from, by the principle of contradiction, the basis of government and right. There our investigations will end, reserving the right to continue them in future works.

The importance of the subject which engages our attention is recognized by all minds.

"Property," says M. Hennequin, "is the creative and conservative principle of civil society. Property is one of those basic institutions, new theories concerning which cannot be presented too soon; for it must not be forgotten, and the publicist and statesman must know, that on the answer to the question whether property is the principle or the result of social order, whether it is to be considered as a cause or an effect, depends all morality, and, consequently, all the authority of human institutions."

These words are a challenge to all men of hope and faith; but, although the cause of equality is a noble one, no one has yet picked up the gauntlet thrown down by the advocates of property; no one has been courageous enough to enter upon the struggle. The spurious learning of haughty jurisprudence, and the absurd aphorisms of a political economy controlled by property have puzzled the most generous minds; it is a sort of password among the most influential friends of liberty and the interests of the people that EQUALITY IS A CHIMERA! So many false theories and meaningless analogies influence minds otherwise keen, but which are unconsciously controlled by popular prejudice. Equality advances every day—*fit aequalitas*. Soldiers of liberty, shall we desert our flag in the hour of triumph?

A defender of equality, I shall speak without bitterness and without anger; with the independence becoming a philosopher, with the courage and firmness of a free man. May I, in this momentous struggle, carry into all hearts the light with which I am filled; and show, by the success of my argument, that equality failed to conquer by the sword only that it might conquer by the pen!

PART THREE

The Maturation of the Two Narratives: The Challenge of Social Economy

Introduction

John Stuart Mill, Karl Marx and the Maturation of Political Economy

We remind the reader of the full titles of John Stuart Mill's *Principles of Political Economy* and Karl Marx's *Das Kapital*. The full title of the former is *Principles of Political Economy with some of their applications to Social Philosophy*. The full title of the latter is *Das Kapital: Krtik der politeschen Oekonomic*. In short, Mill and Marx were aware that the content and method of political economy were under close scrutiny. Mill realized that a "correction" to Adam Smith was needed; he had to (1) address the social question raised by the vast and growing socialist literature and (2) restate the case for individual liberty on different intellectual grounds. Thus his turn to utilitarianism, albeit understood in a way different from that originally introduced by Jeremy Bentham and James Mill, and his attention to the distribution question. Marx, with the assistance of Engels, on the other hand, criticized what he saw as the (1) abstract method of classical political economy, with its reliance on stories about the fictitious Robinson Crusoe and other illusionary phenomenon, and (2) the utopian, and thus equally abstract, alternatives being offered by Owen and Proudhon, *et al*. He turned, instead, to what has been variously called "the materialist concept of history," "dialectical materialism," and "historical materialism." *Reality* was to be found in the unfolding of concrete historical material circumstances and not in self-evident truths concocted by the human mind per se. And this understanding was to be grounded in historical science. Both Mill and Marx presume the demise of the doctrine of natural rights espoused by Locke and Rousseau.

We aren't going to cover such important economists as David Ricardo, Thomas Malthus, James Mill, and Jeremy Bentham whose work forms a bridge between Smith and John Stuart Mill on the one hand and Marx and Engels on the other hand. Rather we are going directly to Mill and Marx/Engels.

Suffice it to note, that Ricardo embraced the labor theory of value articulated by Locke and Smith but in such a way that made that theory easier to appropriate by Marx and the equality narrative. For all his criticism of the Robinson Crusoe model as an illusory abstraction, Marx thought that Robinson, as he called Crusoe, represented the critical insight into the creation of use value over against the "fetishism" of value in exchange. In part, the labor theory of value in the liberty narrative was a way of calling attention to the technological project and the promise of growth. How ironic that the labor theory of value, the foundation and departure of the liberty narrative, becomes with Marx the new foundation and departure for the equality narrative.

Malthus reminds the reader that the wealth of a nation not only increases by the division of labor but also by control over the size of the population. Recall that Adam Smith defined the objective measure of the wealth of a nation as the amount of the necessities and conveniences of life divided by the number of people to which this product is to be consumed. As an early classical liberal, Smith placed his emphasis on increasing production—the numerator—rather than controlling population, or the denominator. Malthus's "dismal" message is that the optimism of classical liberalism is misplaced because the denominator—size of the population—will increase exponentially even though the numerator—size of the total production—will increase arithmetically.

And yet there is an irony in Malthus's turn toward the *distribution* of production within the community and away from the *production* of commodities for the improvement of well-being. Despite the criticism of Malthus by Marx and Engels as a "shameless and mechanical" thinker guilty of "plagiarism," Malthus helped to give credence to the equality narrative of distribution over the liberty narrative of production.

Bentham and James Mill are probably best known for moving the study of economics away from Locke's natural right and Smith's natural history Scottish enlightenment principles. They are the popular initiators of what became known as "utilitarianism," a doctrine that the standard of value for measuring the wealth of a nation was the greatest good for the greatest number. And they also severed the classical liberal portion of political economy from any connection with the labor theory of value. Utility, and not labor, became the measure of value.

John Stuart Mill abandoned natural right and the labor theory of value. He made both the increase in production and the control of population vital aspects of his approach to political economy. And Mill provided a richer and deeper understanding of utilitarianism, one that had a much greater impact on the subsequent development of the liberty narrative. Marx, on the other hand, held the classical liberals to the implications of the labor theory of value and moved political economy even further toward social economy and a concern with poverty rather than property.

Mill and the Liberty Narrative

Does Mill's claim that the "production of wealth" in Books II and III of *Political Economy* can be subject to scientific analysis where as the "distribution of wealth" is "a matter of human institution solely" make sense? Does he place too little reliance on the forces of competition and too much emphasis on the persistence of custom in what actually determines distribution? Is Mill's rather sympathetic treatment of the socialistic critique of private property just another example of Mill's intellectual approach which gives a fair hearing to all arguments or is Mill actually "dabbling" with adopting one or more of the socialistic alternatives? Is Mill's willingness to support a "liberal" version of the inheritance laws surprising? For example, Milton Friedman, among the leading proponents of classical liberalism in the late twentieth century, is in favor of the abolition of inheritance taxes. See Friedman's *Capitalism and Freedom*. And yet, if one can make the distinction between the deserving and undeserving poor—which Mill and other classical liberals do make—is it not also reasonable to make the distinction between the deserving and undeserving rich? Is it reasonable to distinguish, as Mill does, between various degrees of the "sacredness of property?"

This leads us back to the question: Why did Locke and Smith pay so much attention to a real measure of value or worth and locate that standard in turn in a labor theory of value? One of the themes of our anthology has been how the next generation understand themselves to be correcting or modifying the contribution of the earlier generations. So another question is: how does Mill correct Locke and Smith? Has Mill abandoned a reliance on the labor theory of value? Has he provided a more coherent account of wealth distribution than Smith's "resolves" itself account? Is he more interested in the distribution question and the fate of "the laboring classes" than Smith? Mill was at an early point in his career influenced by the writings of St. Simon. Is it surprising that he uses the terminology "the laborers and the capitalists" with such ease whereas these terms are absent from Locke and Smith? Similarly Mill's two predecessors never used the French term *laisser faire*.

Nor did Locke and Smith use the term "Catallactics." But Mill does in the opening pages of Book III indicating that many economists claim there is a similarity between Catallactics and political economy and "one eminent writer has proposed as a name for Political Economy, 'Catallactics,' or the science of exchanges; by others it has been called the Science of Values." In the twentieth century, we find the eminent James Buchanan proposing that political economy is preferable to economics, but Catallactics is preferable to political economy. See his *What Should Economists Do?* What is fascinating is that Buchanan locates the roots of Catallactics in Adam Smith's the "invisible hand." Mill, on the other hand, claims the Catallactics "view of the nature of Political Economy is too confined." Thus, he says, his postponement of the subject to Book III is the result of a conscious decision concerning its lack of importance.

In Book IV, Mill distinguishes between the "theory of dependence and protection," and the "theory of self-dependence," when considering "the probable futurity of the laboring poor." He claims that the laboring poor will love the taste of liberty that comes with self-dependence (or self-reliance) and will reject government paternalism associated with the theory of dependence. How is this interpretation similar to, and different from, Tocqueville's prognosis for the future and the viability of intermediate institutions? Is Mill more opti-mistic about the future of liberty than is Tocqueville?

Is Mill seriously exploring what has come to be known as "workplace democracy"—a central feature of the equality narrative—as a natural exten-sion of the liberty narrative? Or is he simply saying that labor and capital need not be locked in mortal combat and that through "the co-operative principle" their mutual goals can be met? Is he being naïve, that we can have both coop-eration and competition?

Does Mill seem more willing, or less willing, than Smith to provide a greater role for government in the conduct of the everyday affairs of human beings? In other words, does he provide, in Book V, more exceptions or fewer exceptions, than Smith does, in his Book V, to the *laisser faire* maxim, or "the voluntary system," that if left to their own devices, individuals will make bet-ter decisions than outside government experts? Does Mill, for example, think that the consumer is always right, particularly in the area of education and the making of long term contracts, including "until death do us part" contracts? Should there be special protection for children, but not for women?

Which leads us to the next set of questions. Does his *Political Economy* antic-ipate his *On Liberty* and *Subjection of Women*? Does Mill make a connection between the competition for goods and services with competition on the mar-ket place of ideas? How is Mill's critique of the theory of the dependence of the poor on the rich, for example, related to his critique of the dependence of women on men? Or to what extent is the liberation of women an economic argument linked to "the theory of self-dependence" or what we have called the liberty narrative? How valuable for the liberty narrative is Mill's distinc-tion in *Political Economy* between authoritative and advisory interference by government in the economy? To what extent does this argument anticipate his case for "individuality" in *On Liberty*? To what extent does the inviolable circle around an individual make sense anymore? And does his concept of "harm" also have relevance in the twenty-first century. His "very simple principle" of *laisser faire*, let competition not custom decide matters, doesn't seem quite so simple in the twenty-first century. Yet Mill insists that the onus for presenting arguments for regulation has to be put on those who propose the regulation. Liberty is his default position.

In *On Liberty*, Mill says he does not rely on "the idea of abstract right," and contract theory in his defense of liberty. Rather, he turns to what he calls the idea of "utility in the largest sense." Does this utilitarian argument apply to his case for what we might call the freedom of markets and the freedom of women? Although he tries to stay away from all versions of natural rights, he does have an understanding that humans have natures. Does he not have a sort of organic idea of human nature as a growing or decaying organism? And he has a theory of social contracts that is critical of long-term contracts, including marriage. His utilitarianism addresses "the mental well-being of mankind." Does this con-scious "correction" of Locke and Smith from an appeal to nature, long-term contracts, and material well-being, mark an improvement in the liberty narrative? Or does this reliance on utilitarianism put Mill, despite his protestations to the contrary, on the slippery slope to the relativism of the "Open Society" suggested by his famous First Footnote in Chapter 2 of *On Liberty*?

In *On the Subjection of Women*, Mill makes the argument that competition and not custom should hold sway in the relationship between men and women. He also claims that he is not asking for "protective duties and bounties in favor of women; it is only asked that the present bounties and protective duties in favor of men should be recalled." Would this place Mill in the non-affirmative action camp in terms of twentieth century politics and economics? He also equates the status of women with the status of slaves. The writers of the equality narrative in the French Revolution tradition equate the status of the poor with the status of slaves. Is that a critical difference between the two narratives?

Marx and Engels and the Equality Narrative

In his1883 Graveside Speech, Engels suggested that Marx made three important scientific "discoveries." (1) "Just as Darwin discovered the law of development or organic nature, so Marx discovered the law of development of human history: the simple fact, hitherto concealed by an overgrowth of ideology, that mankind must first of all eat, drink, have shelter and clothing, before it can pursue politics, science, art, religion, etc." (2) "Marx also discovered the special law of motion governing the present-day capitalist mode of production and the bourgeois society that this mode of production has created." This discovery was the doctrine of surplus value. "The discovery of surplus value suddenly threw light on the problem, in trying to solve which all previous investigations, of both bourgeois economists and socialist critics, had been groping in the dark." Engels, harkening back no doubt to Marx's third "discovery," or what we have earlier referred to as a "correction" of the earlier tradition, expressed clearly in *The Eleventh Thesis on Feuerbach* that "the philosophers have only interpreted the world, in various ways; the point, however, is to change it," concludes his speech: (3) "Science was for Marx a historically dynamic, revolutionary force.... Marx was before all else a revolutionist. His real mission in life was to contribute, in one way or another, to the overthrow of capitalist society and of the state institutions which it had brought into being."

We have captured these three dimensions of the Marx-Engels contribution to the equality narrative with excerpts from three of their works: *The Communist Manifesto, Das Kapital, and Socialism: Utopian and Scientific*. In the last mentioned work, Engels says that with the first two discoveries—"the materialist conception of history and the revelation of the secret of capitalistic production through surplus value...Socialism became a science. The next thing was to work out all its details and relations." That's where revolutionary politics fits in.

We gave careful consideration to the inclusion of several other pieces in the Marx-Engels tradition, including selections from the *Economic and Philosophical Manuscripts*, also known as the *Paris Manuscripts*, *The Jewish Question*, and *The German Ideology* all of which preceded the *Communist Manifesto* of 1848. Of particular interest is the critique of (1) private property (2) the division of labor and (3) toleration of religion along with the rare articulation of what the fulfillment of the equality narrative might look like. In the *Manuscripts*, Marx speaks about the "alienation" or "estrangement" of labor from the end product and the process of production under a system of private property. It is as if he were making central what Smith made peripheral in his warning about the downside to the division of labor in Book V of *The Wealth of Nations*. He also offers a glimpse of life without the division of labor in *The German Ideology*: "In communist society, where nobody has one exclusive sphere of activity but each can become accomplished in any branch he wishes, society regulates the general production and thus makes it possible for me to do one thing today and another tomorrow, to hunt in the morning, fish in the afternoon, rear cattle in the evening, criticize after dinner, just as I have a mind, without ever becoming hunter, fisherman, herdsman or critic." Also important is his substitution of freedom from religion for freedom of religion as a solution to the question: What to do with the question of the Jews in a Christian state? He specifically rejects Tocqueville's answer of religious toleration in favor of the abolition of religion. And there is the lingering question of what does Marx owe to Hegel with respect to the dialectical movement of history and whether or not there is an end to history.

In the end, however, we decided to summarize these arguments here rather than add yet more material, especially since (a) they emerged as critical features of basically an intra-Marxist scholarship over the status of Engels and only in the mid twentieth-century, (b) the arguments are included in the three main texts mentioned above—see, for example, the three discoveries of Marx and the problematic nature of German Idealism mentioned by Engels in *Socialism: Utopian and Scientific*—and the reader can find them once alerted, and (c) this early phase of Marx's critique is very close to the approach articulated by Proudhon and included in our coverage of the second phase of the development of the equality narrative. Marx himself seems to land a telling blow in *The Communist Manifesto* when he talks critically about the abstract categories of the German intellectuals, and in *Das Kapital* where he announces that he found the dialectic with Hegel standing on its head. "It must be turned right side up again, if you would discover the rational kernel within the mystical shell."

In *Das Kapital*, Marx incorporates his earlier comments about alienation without an appeal to Hegel. So, in Volume 1, Part III we learn that "the elementary factors of the labor-process are 1, the personal activity of man, i.e., work itself, 2, the subject of that work, and 3, its instruments." In Part IV, Chapter 12, we learn further that this process leads to "the cheapening of labor itself." There is also his sarcastic reference in Part IV, Chapter 14 to Adam

Smith's solution of "homeopathic doses" of State education to what both agree are the dehumanizing effects of the division of labor. Substantial portions of Parts IV and V are devoted to a critique of Political Economy especially its apparent lack of concern for the "crippled" worker "mutilated" by the division of labor and mechanization in the modern factory system.

What Engels called the three discoveries of Marx can be found in the three texts we have included. There are glimpses of a Communist Society free from the "dehumanizing" and "alienating" features of the division of labor in the *Communist Manifesto* and *Das Kapital*. The revolutionary agenda and its relation to the materialist concept of history appear in the *Communist Manifesto* and *Socialism: Utopian and Scientific*. Similarly, we decided not to include in the readings the "corrections" of Marx and Engels made by such influential twentieth century articulators as Lenin, Mao, the Frankfurt School, and the New Left in America. We hope, however, readers will explore the vast literature on these "corrections" and their place in the next phase of the equality narrative.

We invite the reader to explore the following questions which appear in the *Communist Manifesto* and *Socialism: Utopian and Scientific*. What is the materialist conception of history? Does it have any "wiggle room," or is this an all-linear and inevitable concept? Is there any evidence that one can skip a stage from feudalism to socialism or is the rise and fall of capitalism intrinsic to the Marx-Engels account? Can we have proletarians without having capitalists? How are economics, politics, and religion joined together, if they are joined together, by Marx and Engels? Does the advancement of the equality narrative require that the world be viewed as a class struggle to end class divisions in contrast to a liberty narrative that sees life as an individual struggle to retain autonomy? Is the theory of surplus value a "scientific" way of explaining "alienation" and exploitation? How revolutionary is *The Communist Manifesto*? Is the Ten Point Program still, today, a revolutionary program? What do Marx and Engels mean by "science" and how is this science related to (a) the historical understanding of economics and (b) the dialectical unfolding of the world? Do they provide a convincing response to Madison's argument that faction should not be eliminated and Tocqueville's claim that self interest rightly understood should be the central component of the new mores for the new age? How have Marx and Engels modified the scope and content of the equality narrative? Engels introduces two interesting concepts near the end of *Socialism*. One is that the state will wither away. Does this mean that the equality narrative has come to an end because equality has been fulfilled? The other is that the government of the people has been replaced by the administration of things. What does this mean?

We suggest that *Das Kapital* be broken down into ten sections. The mysterious, even cultish, reputation of this work can at least be partially dispelled if we keep a few basic questions and points in mind. What does this work tell us about the status of political economy? How would Marx like to see the scope and method of political economy change? Does he change political economy into social economy? In what sense is *Das Kapital* a work that "corrects" the equality narrative? Is there a moral dimension to the work or is the core doctrine of surplus value a breakthrough in economics as a science?

1. Marx accepts the distinction between use value and exchange value that we saw in both Smith and Mill, but he places a higher worth on use value than exchange value. In fact, we get the impression that exchange value neither measures true value nor adds value. Use value has true value because the commodities are produced to satisfy human needs and value is created by labor power. Every commodity has a true value that is measured by the socially necessary labor time it takes to bring the commodity to market. Apparently, Robinson Crusoe makes sense after all! Marx seems to have "corrected" Locke and Smith by showing that only a pure labor theory of value uncontaminated by the false claims of landlords and capitalists to a share in the product of labor is a true measure of worth or value. Isn't this an argument that property is theft by another means? But don't landlords and capitalists contribute to the creation of the product? Would it be fair to say that a pure labor theory of value makes sense only in the most primitive society or one where the production problem has been solved?

2. We don't think it is stretching Marx's approach to suggest that the ideal communist society would be in accordance with formula C-M-C where M is money used as a medium of exchange to facilitate the circulation of commodities that meet human needs. This C-M-C ideal is the alternative to his harsh version of an exchange economy based on manipulation and greed, or M-C-M'.

3. Marx's version of an actual capitalistic economy is the M-C-M' formula where M' is greater than M and thus money has been turned into capital by the buying and selling of commodities, and the creation of capital is equivalent to the creation of profit. So it doesn't matter, in the end, what the commodity is since turning money into capital is the alpha and omega of the exchange system. We suggest, in other words, that there is a strong moral side to this formulation. And this becomes even clearer when we realize that the production of commodities is actually determined by those who own the means of commodity production. Property is not an expression of personal autonomy or to be measured in income earned. Rather property is the stock of industrial wealth owned by the captains of modern industry.

4. C-M-C is praised by Marx for meeting human needs and M-C-M' is criticized for creating profit through the marketing of commodities. This is the equivalent of saying that exchange value is "fetish" value, or illusionary value, or, to adopt the language of the earlier *Economic Manuscripts*, exchange value is alienated or estranged value. Put differently, we

suggest that the fetishism of commodities articulated through the M-C-M′ formula is Marx's more scientific way of articulating his earlier philosophical concept of the alienation or estrangement of labor. For the next step in the argument is to show precisely how this takes place.

5.   It turns out that one of the commodities in the M-C-M′ formula is labor whose labor power is bought and sold like any other commodity. And thus as a commodity, there must be socially necessary labor time needed to bring that commodity to market. In other words, what time in the laboring day would it take for the laborer to spend to feed, house, and clothe his family? Let's say four hours. But the capitalist determines the length of the working day. Let's say 10 hours. It turns out that the capitalist gets these 6 hours for free. This surplus value is profit and is based on force and fraud. Again the equality narrative is fortified by the notion that property is theft.

6.   The irony here is that the worker is and is not paid what he is worth and that is the ultimate "contradiction" of capitalism. He should be getting ten hours pay but he is getting, according to the labor theory of value, and the socially necessary labor time concept, the four he needs to preserve his family!

7.   Marx's discovery of the doctrine of absolute surplus value has had a profound impact on the work place aspects of public policy and the strategy of trade unions. No wonder so many disputes between management and labor turn on the length of the working day.

8.   But Marx also discovered the doctrine of relative surplus value. If the length of the working day is shortened—say from 10 hours to 8 hours—as a result of union activity and/or government policy, the capitalist's absolute surplus value has declined from 6 hours to four hours. He introduces machinery that does two things: (a) it reduces the socially necessary labor time for the worker to cover the cost of the necessities of life from say 4 hours to 3 hours and (b) he can fire several workers who have been made redundant by the machinery.

9.   Marx does not see the capacity to truck, barter, and exchange as part of the natural way humans improve their condition. Instead, he considers exchange as the mechanism by which one set of humans—the owners of the means of production—exploit other humans—the many who have only their labor to sell on the market. And far from seeing the natural course of the economy being toward (1) growth and equilibrium and (2) the improvement in the condition of the working class—as do Locke, Smith, and Mill—Marx predicts the collapse of capitalism and the decline in the condition of the working class.

10.   With Marx, the established equality narrative takes on a new and revolutionary tone. In fact it is difficult to distinguish between the equality

narrative and the revolutionary narrative in Marx. And here is where the link with the other readings by Marx and Engels come together. There is a strong dismissive tone in their writings to previous articulators of the equality narrative. The French Socialists were utopian, or reactionary, or opportunists. Is this dismissal of the religious dimension of Owen and St-Simon, for example, warranted? What if it is possible to advance the equality narrative by reform rather than revolution? They see politics, in fact all ideas, as the mere plaything of those with power and this is defined as those who own economic property. Accordingly, all politics and ideas are the result of the dictatorial imposition by the few over the many. Thus one is tempted to think that winning the battle for democracy is no more, and no less, than the dictatorship of the many over the few; that justice is simply the advantage of the stronger. But does this position not raise some serious questions about the sense of social justice and fundamental fairness that undergirds the equality narrative?

John Stuart Mill

The Principles of Political Economy

BOOK II: Distribution

Chapter I: Of Property

1. The principles which have been set forth in the first part of this Treatise, are, in certain respects, strongly distinguished from those, on the consideration of which we are now about to enter. The laws and conditions of the production of wealth partake of the character of physical truths. There is nothing optional or arbitrary in them. Whatever mankind produce, must be produced in the modes, and under the conditions, imposed by the constitution of external things, and by the inherent properties of their own bodily and mental structure. Whether they like it or not, their productions will be limited by the amount of their previous accumulation, and, that being given, it will be proportional to their energy, their skill, the perfection of their machinery, and their judicious use of the advantages of combined labor. Whether they like it or not, a double quantity of labor will not raise, on the same land, a double quantity of food, unless some improvement takes place in the processes of cultivation. Whether they like it or not, the unproductive expenditure of individuals will *pro tanto* tend to impoverish the community, and only their productive expenditure will enrich it. The opinions, or the wishes, which may exist on these

different matters, do not control the things themselves. We cannot, indeed, foresee to what extent the modes of production may be altered, or the productiveness of labor increased, by future extensions of our knowledge of the laws of nature, suggesting new processes of industry of which we have at present no conception. But howsoever we may succeed in making for ourselves more space within the limits set by the constitution of things, we know that there must be limits. We cannot alter the ultimate properties either of matter or mind, but can only employ those properties more or less successfully, to bring about the events in which we are interested.

It is not so with the Distribution of Wealth. That is a matter of human institution solely. The things once there, mankind, individually or collectively, can do with them as they like. They can place them at the disposal of whomsoever they please, and on whatever terms. Further, in the social state, in every state except total solitude, any disposal whatever of them can only take place by the consent of society, or rather of those who dispose of its active force. Even what a person has produced by his individual toil, unaided by any one, he cannot keep, unless by the permission of society. Not only can society take it from him, but individuals could and would take it from him, if society only remained passive; if it did not either interfere en masse, or employ and pay people for the purpose of preventing him from being disturbed in the possession. The distribution of wealth, therefore, depends on the laws and customs of society. The rules by which it is determined, are what the opinions and feelings of the ruling portion of the community make them, and are very different in different ages and countries; and might be till more different, if mankind so chose.

The opinions and feelings of mankind, doubtless, are not a matter of chance. They are consequences of the fundamental laws of human nature, combined with the existing state of knowledge and experience, and the existing condition of social institutions and intellectual and moral culture. But the laws of the generation of human opinions are not within our present subject. They are part of the general theory of human progress, a far larger and more difficult subject of inquiry than political economy. We have here to consider, not the causes, but the consequences, of the rules according to which wealth may be distributed. Those, at least, are as little arbitrary, and have as much the character of physical laws, as the laws of production. Human beings can control their own acts, but not the consequences of their acts neither to themselves or to others. Society can subject the distribution of wealth to whatever rules it thinks best: but what practical results will flow from the operation of those rules, must be discovered, like any other physical or mental truths, by observation and reasoning.

We proceed, then, to the consideration of the different modes of distributing the produce of land and labor, which have been adopted in practice, or may be conceived in theory. Among these, our attention is first claimed by that primary and fundamental institution, on which, unless in some exceptional and very limited cases, the economical arrangements of society have always rested, though in its secondary features it has varied, and is liable to vary. I mean, of course, the institution of individual property.

2. Private property, as an institution, did not owe its origin to any of those considerations of utility, which plead for the maintenance of it when established. Enough is known of rude ages, both from history and from analogous states of society in our own time, to show, that tribunals (which always precede laws) were originally established, not to determine rights, but to repress violence and terminate quarrels. With this object chiefly in view, they naturally enough gave legal effect to first occupancy, by treating as the aggressor the person who first commenced violence, by turning, or attempting to turn, another out of possession. The preservation of the peace, which was the original object of civil government, was thus attained; while by confirming, to those who already possessed it, even what was not the fruit of personal exertion, a guarantee was incidentally given to them and others that they would be protected in what was so.

In considering the institution of property as a question in social philosophy, we must leave out of consideration its actual origin in any of the existing nations of Europe. We may suppose a community unhampered by any previous possession; a body of colonists, occupying for the first time an uninhabited country; bringing nothing with them but what belonged to them in common, and having a clear field for the adoption of the institutions and polity which they judged most expedient; required, therefore, to choose whether they would conduct the work of production on the principle of individual property, or on some system of common ownership and collective agency.

If private property were adopted, we must presume that it would be accompanied by none of the initial inequalities and injustices which obstruct the beneficial operation of the principle in old societies. Every full grown man or woman, we must suppose, would be secured in the unfettered use and disposal of his or her bodily and mental faculties; and the instruments of production, the land and tools, would be divided fairly among them, so that all might start, in respect to outward appliances, on equal terms. It is possible also to conceive that in this original apportionment, compensation might be made for the injuries of nature, and the balance redressed by assigning to the less robust members of the community advantages in the distribution, sufficient to put them on a par with the rest.

But the division, once made, would not again be interfered with; individuals would be left to their own exertions and to the ordinary chances, for making an advantageous use of what was assigned to them. If individual property, on the contrary, were excluded, the plan which must be adopted would be to hold the land and all instruments of production as the joint property of the community, and to carry on the operations of industry on the common account. The direction of the labor of the community would devolve upon a magistrate or magistrates, whom we may suppose elected by the suffrages of the community, and whom we must assume to be voluntarily obeyed by them. The division of the produce would in like manner be a public act. The principle might either be that of complete equality, or of apportionment to the necessities or deserts of individuals, in whatever manner might be conformable to the ideas of justice or policy prevailing in the community....

The assailants of the principle of individual property may be divided into two classes: those whose scheme implies absolute equality in the distribution of the physical means of life and enjoyment, and those who admit inequality, but grounded on some principle, or supposed principle, of justice or general expediency, and not, like so many of the existing social inequalities, dependent on accident alone. At the head of the first class, as the earliest of those belonging to the present generation, must be placed Mr. Owen and his followers. M. Louis Blanc and M. Cabet have more recently become conspicuous as apostles of similar doctrines (though the former advocates equality of distribution only as a transition to a still higher standard of justice, that all should work according to their capacity, and receive according to their wants). The characteristic name for this economical system is Communism, a word of continental origin, only of late introduced into this country. The word Socialism, which originated among the English Communists, and was assumed by them as a name to designate their own doctrine, is now, on the Continent, employed in a larger sense; not necessarily implying Communism, or the entire abolition of private property, but applied to any system which requires that the land and the instruments of production should be the property, not of individuals, but of communities or associations, or of the government. Among such systems, the two of highest intellectual pretension are those which, from the names of their real or reputed authors, have been called St. Simonism and Fourierism; the former defunct as a system, but which during the few years of its public promulgation, sowed the seeds of nearly all the Socialist tendencies which have since spread so widely in France: the second, still flourishing in the number, talent, and zeal of its adherents.

3. The objection ordinarily made to a system of community of property and equal distribution of the produce, that each person would be incessantly occupied in evading his fair share of the work, points, undoubtedly, to a real difficulty. But those who urge this objection, forget to how great an extent the same difficulty exists under the system on which nine-tenths of the business of society is now conducted. The objection supposes, that honest and efficient labor is only to be had from those who are themselves individually to reap the benefit of their own exertions. But how small a part of all the labor performed in England, from the lowest-paid to the highest, is done by persons working for their own benefit....

It will no doubt be said, that though the laborers themselves have not, in most cases, a personal interest in their work, they are watched and superintended, and their labor directed, and the mental part of the labor performed, by persons who have. Even this, however, is far from being universally the fact. In all public, and many of the largest and most successful private undertakings, not only the labors of detail but the control and superinten-dence are entrusted to salaried officers. And though the "master's eye," when the master is vigilant and intelligent, is of proverbial value, it must be remem-bered that in a Socialist farm or manufactory, each laborer would be under the eye not of one master, but of the whole community. In the extreme case of obstinate perseverance in not performing the due share of work, the commu-nity would have the same resources which society now has for compelling conformity to the necessary conditions of the association. Dismissal, the only remedy at present, is no remedy when any other laborer who may be engaged does no better than his predecessor: the power of dismissal only enables an employer to obtain from his workmen the customary amount of labor, but that customary labor may be of any degree of inefficiency. Even the laborer who loses his employment by idleness or negligence, has nothing worse to suffer, in the most unfavorable case, than the discipline of a workhouse, and if the desire to avoid this be a sufficient motive in the one system, it would be suffi-cient in the other.

I am not undervaluing the strength of the incitement given to labor when the whole or a large share of the benefit of extra exertion belongs to the laborer. But under the present system of industry this incitement, in the great majority of cases, does not exist. If Communistic labor might be less vigorous than that of a peasant proprietor, or a workman laboring on his own account, it would probably be more energetic than that of a laborer for hire, who has no personal interest in the matter at all. The neglect by the uneducated classes of laborers for hire, of the duties which they engage to perform, is in the present state of society most flagrant. Now it is an admitted condition of the Communist scheme that all shall be educated: and this being supposed, the duties of the members of the association would doubtless be as diligently performed as those of the generality of salaried officers in the middle or higher classes; who are not supposed to be necessarily unfaithful to their trust, because so long as they are not dismissed, their pay is the same in however lax a manner their duty is fulfilled. Undoubtedly, as a general rule, remuneration by fixed sala-ries does not in any class of functionaries produce the maximum of zeal: and this is as much as can be reasonably alleged against Communistic labor.

That even this inferiority would necessarily exist, is by no means so certain as is assumed by those who are little used carry to their minds beyond the state of things with which they are familiar. Mankind are capable of a far greater amount of public spirit than the present age is accustomed to suppose possible. History bears witness to the success with which large bodies of human beings may be trained to feel the public interest their own. And no soil could be more favorable to the growth of such a feeling, than a Communist association, since all the ambition, and the bodily and mental activity, which are now exerted in the pursuit of separate and self-regarding interests, would require another sphere of employment, and would naturally find it in the pur-suit of the general benefit of the community. The same cause, so often assigned in explanation of the devotion of the Catholic priest or monk to the interest of his order—that he has no interest apart from it—would, under Communism, attach the citizen to the community. And independently of the public motive, every member of the association would be amenable to the most universal, and one of the strongest, of personal motives, that of public opinion. The force of this motive in deterring from any act or omission positively reproved by the community, no one is likely to deny; but the power also of emulation, in exciting to the most strenuous exertions for the sake of the approbation and admiration of others, is borne witness to by experience in every situation in which human beings publicly compete with one another, even if it be in things frivolous, or from which the public derive no benefit. A contest, who can do most for the common good, is not the kind of competition which Socialists repudiate. To what extent, therefore, the energy of labor would be diminished by Communism, or whether in the long run it would be diminished at all, must be considered for the present an undecided question.

Another of the objections to Communism is similar to that, so often urged against poor-laws: that if every member of the community were assured of subsistence for himself and any number of children, on the sole condition of willingness to work, prudential restraint on the multiplication of mankind would be at an end, and population would start forward at a rate which would reduce the community, through successive stages of increasing discomfort, to actual starvation. There would certainly be much ground for this apprehension if Communism provided no motives to restraint, equivalent to those which it would take away. But Communism is precisely the state of things m which opinion might be expected to declare itself with greatest intensity against this kind of selfish intemperance. Any augmentation of numbers which diminished the comfort or increased the toil of the mass, would then cause (which now it does not) immediate and unmistakable inconvenience to every individual in the association; inconvenience which could not then be imputed to the avarice of employers, or the unjust privileges of the rich. In such altered circumstances opinion could not fail to reprobate, and if reprobation did not suffice, to repress by penalties of some description, this or any other culpable self-indulgence at the expense of the community. The Communistic scheme, instead of being peculiarly open to the objection drawn from danger of over-population, has the recommendation of tending in an especial degree to the prevention of that evil.

A more real difficulty is that of fairly apportioning the labor of the community among its members. There are many kinds of work, and by what standard are they to be measured one against another? Who is to judge how much cotton spinning, or distributing goods from the stores, or bricklaying, or chimney sweeping, is equivalent to so much ploughing? The difficulty of making the adjustment between different qualities of labor is so strongly felt by Communist writers, that they have usually thought it necessary to provide that all should work by turns at every description of useful labor, an arrangement which, by putting an end to the division of employments, would sacrifice so much of the advantage of co-operative production as greatly to diminish the productiveness of labor. Besides, even in the same kind of work, nominal equality of labor would be so great a real inequality, that the feeling of justice would revolt against its being enforced. All persons are not equally fit for all labor; and the same quantity of labor is an unequal burthen on the weak and the strong, the hardy and the delicate, the quick and the slow, the dull and the intelligent.

But these difficulties, though real, are not necessarily insuperable. The apportionment of work to the strength and capacities of individuals, the mitigation of a general rule to provide for cases in which it would operate harshly, are not problems to which human intelligence, guided by a sense of justice, would be inadequate. And the worst and most unjust arrangement which could be made of these points, under a system aiming at equality, would be so far short of the inequality and injustice with which labor (not to speak of remuneration) is now apportioned, as to be scarcely worth counting in comparison. We must remember too, that Communism, as a system of society, exists only in idea; that its difficulties, at present, are much better understood than its resources; and that the intellect of mankind is only beginning to contrive the means of organizing it in detail, so as to overcome the one and derive the greatest advantage from the other.

If, therefore, the choice were to be made between Communism with all its chances, and the present state of society with all its sufferings and injustices; if the institution of private property necessarily carried with it as a consequence, that the produce of labor should be apportioned as we now see it, almost in an inverse ratio to the labor—the largest portions to those who have never worked at all, the next largest to those whose work is almost nominal, and so in a descending scale, the remuneration dwindling as the work grows harder and more disagreeable, until the most fatiguing and exhausting bodily labor cannot count with certainty on being able to earn even the necessaries of life; if this or Communism were the alternative, all the difficulties, great or small, of Communism would be but as dust in the balance. But to make the comparison applicable, we must compare Communism at its best, with the regime of individual property, not as it is, but as it might be made.

The principle of private property has never yet had a fair trial in any country; and less so, perhaps, in this country than in some others. The social arrangements of modern Europe commenced from a distribution of property which was the result, not of just partition, or acquisition by industry, but of conquest and violence: and notwithstanding what industry has been doing for many centuries to modify the work of force, the system still retains many and large traces of its origin. The laws of property have never yet conformed to the principles on which the justification of private property rests. They have made property of things which never ought to be property, and absolute property where only a qualified property ought to exist. They have not held the balance fairly between human beings, but have heaped impediments upon some, to give advantage to others; they have purposely fostered inequalities, and prevented all from starting fair in the race. That all should indeed start on perfectly equal terms, is inconsistent with any law of private property: but if as much pains as has been taken to aggravate the inequality of chances arising from the natural working of the principle, had been taken to temper that inequality by every means not subversive of the principle itself; if the tendency of legislation had been to favor the diffusion, instead of the concentration of wealth—to encourage the subdivision of the large masses, instead of striving to keep them together; the principle of individual property would have been found to have no necessary connection with the physical and social evils which almost all Socialist writers assume to be inseparable from it.

Private property, in every defense made of it, is supposed to mean, the guarantee to individuals of the fruits of their own labor and abstinence. The guarantee to them of the fruits of the labor and abstinence of others, transmitted to them without any merit or exertion of their own, is not of the essence of the institution, but a mere incidental consequence, which, when it reaches a certain height, does not promote, but conflicts with, the ends which render private property legitimate. To judge of the final destination of the institution of property, we must suppose everything rectified, which causes the institution to work in a manner opposed to that equitable principle, of proportion between remuneration and exertion, on which in every vindication of it that will bear the light, it is assumed to be grounded. We must also suppose two conditions realized, without which neither Communism nor any other laws or institutions could make the condition of the mass of mankind other than degraded and miserable. One of these conditions is, universal education; the other, a due limitation of the numbers of the community. With these, there could be no poverty, even under the present social institutions: and these being supposed, the question of Socialism is not, as generally stated by Socialists, a question of flying to the sole refuge against the evils which now bear down humanity; but a mere question of comparative advantages, which futurity must determine. We are too ignorant either of what individual agency in its best form, or Socialism in its best form, can accomplish, to be qualified to decide which of the two will be the ultimate form of human society.

If a conjecture may be hazarded, the decision will probably depend mainly on one consideration, viz. which of the two systems is consistent with the greatest amount of human liberty and spontaneity. After the means of subsistence are assured, the next in strength of the personal wants of human beings is liberty; and (unlike the physical wants, which as civilization advances become more moderate and more amenable to control) it increases instead of diminishing in intensity, as the intelligence and the moral faculties are more developed. The perfection both of social arrangements and of practical morality would be, to secure to all persons complete independence and freedom of action, subject to no restriction but that of not doing injury to others: and the education which taught or the social institutions which required them to exchange the control of their own actions for any amount of comfort or afflu- ence, or to renounce liberty for the sake of equality, would deprive them of one of the most elevated characteristics of human nature. It remains to be discov- ered how far the preservation of this characteristic would be found compatible with the Communistic organization of society.

No doubt, this, like all the other objections to the Socialist schemes, is vastly exaggerated. The members of the association need not be required to live together more than they do now, nor need they be controlled in the disposal of their individual share of the produce, and of the probably large amount of leisure which, if they limited their production to things really worth produc- ing, they would possess. Individuals need not be chained to an occupation, or to a particular locality. The restraints of Communism would be freedom in comparison with the present condition of the majority of the human race. The generality of laborers in this and most other countries, have as little choice of occupation or freedom of locomotion, are practically as dependent on fixed rules and on the will of others, as they could be on any system short of actual slavery; to say nothing of the entire domestic subjection of one half the species, to which it is the signal honor of Owenism and most other forms of Socialism that they assign equal rights, in all respects, with those of the hitherto domi- nant sex.

But it is not by comparison with the present bad state of society that the claims of Communism can be estimated; nor is it sufficient that it should promise greater personal and mental freedom than is now enjoyed by those who have not enough of either to deserve the name. The question is, whether there would be any asylum left for individuality of character; whether public opinion would not be a tyrannical yoke; whether the absolute dependence of each on all, and surveillance of each by all, would not grind all down into a tame uniformity of thoughts, feelings, and actions. This is already one of the glaring evils of the existing state of society, notwithstanding a much greater diversity of education and pursuits, and a much less absolute dependence of the individual on the mass, than would exist in the Communistic regime. No society in which eccentricity is a matter of reproach, can be in a wholesome state. It is yet to be ascertained whether the Communistic scheme would be consistent with that multiform development of human nature, those manifold unlikenesses, that diversity of tastes and talents, and variety of intellectual points of view, which not only form a great part of the interest of human life, but by bringing intellects into stimulating collision, and by presenting to each innumerable notions that he would not have conceived of himself, are the mainspring of mental and moral progression.

4. The two elaborate forms of non-communistic Socialism known as St. Simonism and Fourierism, are totally free from the objections usually urged against Communism; and though they are open to others of their own, yet by the great intellectual power which in many respects distinguishes them, and

by their large and philosophic treatment of some of the fundamental problems of society and morality, they may justly be counted among the most remarkable productions of the past and present age.

The St. Simonian scheme does not contemplate an equal, but an unequal division of the produce; it does not propose that all should be occupied alike, but differently, according to their vocation or capacity., the function of each being assigned, like grades in a regiment, by the choice of the directing authority, and the remuneration being by salary, proportioned to the importance, in the eyes of that authority, of the function itself, and the merits of the person who fulfils it. For the constitution of the ruling body, different plans might be adopted, consistently with the essentials of the system. It might be appointed by popular suffrage. In the idea of the original authors, the rulers were supposed to be persons of genius and virtue, who obtained the voluntary adhesion of the rest by the force of mental superiority. That the scheme might in some peculiar states of society work with advantage, is not improbable. There is indeed a successful experiment, of a somewhat similar kind, on record, to which I have once alluded; that of the Jesuits in Paraguay. A race of savages, belonging to a portion of mankind more averse to consecutive exertion for a distant object than any other authentically known to us, was brought under the mental dominion of civilized and instructed men who were united among themselves by a system of community of goods. To the absolute authority of these men they reverentially submitted themselves, and were induced by them to learn the arts of civilized life, and to practice labors for the community, which no inducement that could have been offered would have prevailed on them to practice for themselves.

This social system was of short duration, being prematurely destroyed by diplomatic arrangements and foreign force. That it could be brought into action at all was probably owing to the immense distance in point of knowledge and intellect which separated the few rulers from the whole body of the ruled, without any intermediate orders, either social or intellectual. In any other circumstances it would probably have been a complete failure. It supposes an absolute despotism in the heads of the association; which would probably not be much improved if the depositaries of the despotism (contrary to the views of the authors of the system) were varied from time to time according to the result of a popular canvass. But to suppose that one or a few human beings, howsoever selected, could, by whatever machinery of subordinate agency, be qualified to adapt each person's work to his capacity, and proportion each person's remuneration to his merits—to be, in fact, the dispensers of distributive justice to every member of a community; or that any use which they could make of this power would give general satisfaction, or would be submitted to without the aid of force—is a supposition almost too chimerical to be reasoned against. A fixed rule, like that of equality, might be acquiesced in, and so might chance, or an external necessity; but that a handful of human beings should weigh everybody in the balance, and give more to one and less to another at their sole pleasure and judgment would not be borne, unless from persons believed to be more than men, and backed by supernatural terrors.

The most skillfully combined, and with the greatest foresight of objections, of all the forms of Socialism, is that commonly known as Fourierism. This system does not contemplate the abolition of private property, nor even of inheritance; on the contrary, it avowedly takes into consideration, as an element in the distribution of the produce, capital as well as labor. It proposes that the operations of industry should be carried on by associations of about two thousand members, combining their labor on a district of about a square league in extent, under the guidance of chiefs selected by themselves. In the distribution, a certain minimum is first assigned for the subsistence of every member of the community, whether capable or not of labor. The remainder of the produce is shared in certain proportions, to be deterred beforehand, among the three elements, Labor, Capital, and Talent. The capital of the community may be owned in unequal shares by different members, who would in that case receive, as in any other joint-stock company, proportional dividends. The claim of each person on the share of the produce apportioned to talent, is estimated by the grade or rank which the individual occupies in the several groups of laborers to which he or she belongs; these grades being in all cases conferred by the choice of his or her companions. The remuneration, when received, would not of necessity be expended or enjoyed in common; there would be separate ménages for all who preferred them, and no other community of living is contemplated, than that all the members of the association should reside in the same pile of buildings; for saving of labor and expense, not only in building, but in every branch of domestic economy; and in order that, the whole of the buying and selling operations of the community being performed by a single agent, the enormous portion of the produce of industry now carried off by the profits of mere distributors might be reduced to the smallest amount possible.

This system, unlike Communism, does not, in theory at least, withdraw any of the motives to exertion which exist in the present state of society. On the contrary, if the arrangement worked according to the intentions of its contrivers, it would even strengthen those motives; since each person would have much more certainty of reaping individually the fruits of increased skill or energy, bodily or mental, than under the present social arrangements can be felt by any but those who are in the most advantageous positions, or to whom the chapter of accidents is more than ordinarily favorable. The Fourierists, however, have still another resource. They believe that they have solved the great and fundamental problem of rendering labor attractive. That this is not impracticable, they contend by very strong arguments; in particular by one which they have in common with the Owenites, viz., that scarcely any labor, however severe, undergone by human beings for the sake of subsistence, exceeds in intensity that which other human beings, whose subsistence is already provided for, are found ready and even eager to undergo for pleasure....

According to the Fourierists, scarcely any kind of useful labor is naturally and necessarily disagreeable, unless it is either regarded as dishonorable, or is immoderate in degree, or destitute of the stimulus of sympathy and emulation. Excessive toil needs not, they contend, be undergone by any one, in a society in which there would be no idle class, and no labor so enormous an amount of labor is now wasted, in was here useless things; full advantage would be taken of the power of association, both in increasing the efficiency of production, and in economizing consumption. The other requisites for rendering labor attractive would, they think, be found in the execution of all labor by social groups, to any number of which the same individual might simultaneously belong, at his or her own choice: their grade in each being determined by the degree of service which they were found capable of rendering, as appreciated by the suffrages of their comrades. It is inferred from the diversity of tastes and talents, that every member of the community would be attached to several groups, employing themselves in various kinds of occupation, some bodily, others mental, and would be capable of occupying a high place in some one or more; so that a real equality, or something more nearly approaching to it than might at first be supposed, would practically result: not, from the compression, but, on the contrary, from the largest possible development, of the various natural superiorities residing in each individual.

Even from so brief an outline, it must be evident that this system does no violence to any of the general laws by which human action, even in the present imperfect state of moral and intellectual cultivation, is influenced; and that it would be extremely rash to pronounce it incapable of success, or unfitted to realize a great part of the hopes founded on it by its partisans. With regard to this, as to all other varieties of Socialism, the thing to be desired, and to which they have a just claim, is opportunity of trial. They are all capable of being tried on a moderate scale, and at no risk, either personal or pecuniary, to any except those who try them. It is for experience to determine how far or how soon any one or more of the possible systems of community of property will be fitted to substitute itself for the "organization of industry" based on private ownership of land and capital. In the meantime we may, without attempting to limit the ultimate capabilities of human nature, affirm, that the political economist, for a considerable time to come, will be chiefly concerned with the conditions of existence and progress belonging to a society founded on private property and individual competition; and that the object to be principally aimed at in the present stage of human improvement, is not the subversion of the system of individual property, but the improvement of it, and the full participation of every member of the community in its benefits.

Chapter II: "The Idea of private Property"

1. The institution of property, when limited to its essential elements, consists in the recognition, in each person, of a right to the exclusive disposal of what

he or she have produced by their own exertions, or received either by gift or by fair agreement, without force or fraud, from those who produced it. The foundation of the whole is the right of producers to what they themselves have produced. It may be objected, therefore, to the institution as it now exists, that it recognizes rights of property in individuals over things which they have not produced. For example (it may be said) the operatives in a manufactory create, by their labor and skill, the whole produce; yet, instead of its belonging to them, the law gives them only their stipulated hire, and transfers the produce to some one who has merely supplied the funds, without perhaps contributing anything to the work itself, even in the form of superintendence. The answer to this is, that the labor of manufacture is only one of the conditions which must combine for the production of the commodity. The labor cannot be carried on without materials and machinery, nor without a stock of necessaries provided in advance, to maintain the laborers during the production. All these things are the fruits of previous labor. If the laborers were possessed of them, they would not need to divide the produce with any one; but while they have them not, an equivalent must be given to those who have, both for the antecedent labor, and for the abstinence by which the produce of that labor, instead of being expended on indulgences, has been reserved for this use. The capital may not have been, and in most cases was not, created by the labor and abstinence of the present possessor; but it was created by the labor and abstinence of some former person, who may indeed have been wrongfully dispossessed of it, but who, in the present age of the world, much more probably transferred his claims to the present capitalist by gift or voluntary contract: and the abstinence at least must have been continued by each successive owner, down to the present.

If it be said, as it may with truth, that those who have inherited the savings of others have an advantage which they may have in no way deserved, over the industrious whose predecessors have not left them anything; I not only admit, but strenuously contend, that this unearned advantage should be curtailed, as much as is consistent with justice to those who thought fit to dispose of their savings by giving them to their descendants. But while it is true that the laborers are at a disadvantage compared with those whose predecessors have saved, it is also true that the laborers are far better off than if those predecessors had not saved. They share in the advantage, though not to an equal extent with the inheritors. The terms of co-operation between present labor and the fruits of past labor and saving, are a subject for adjustment between the two parties. Each is necessary to the other. The capitalists can do nothing without laborers, nor the laborers without capital.

If the laborers compete for employment, the capitalists on their part compete for labor, to the full extent of the circulating capital of the country. Competition is often spoken of as if it were necessarily a cause of misery and degradation to the laboring class; as if high wages were not precisely as much a product of competition as low wages. The remuneration of labor is as much the result of the law of competition in the United States, as it is in Ireland, and much more completely so than in England.

The right of property includes then, the freedom of acquiring by contract. The right of each to what he has produced, implies a right to what has been produced by others, if obtained by their free consent; since the producers must either have given it from good will, or exchanged it for what they esteemed an equivalent, and to prevent them from doing so would be to infringe their right of property in the product of their own industry.

2. Before proceeding to consider the things which the principle of individual property does not include, we must specify one more thing which it does include: and this is that a title, after a certain period, should be given by prescription. According to the fundamental idea of property, indeed, nothing ought to be treated as such, which has been acquired by force or fraud, or appropriated in ignorance of a prior title vested in some other person; but it is necessary to the security of rightful possessors, that they should not be molested by charges of wrongful acquisition, when by the lapse of time witnesses must have perished or been lost sight of, and the real character of the transaction can no longer be cleared up. Possession which has not been legally questioned within a moderate number of years, ought to be, as by the laws of all nations it is, a complete title. Even when the acquisition was wrongful, the dispossession, after a generation has elapsed, of the probably *bonâ fide* possessors, by the revival of a claim which had been long dormant, would generally be a greater injustice, and almost always a greater private and public mischief, than leaving the original wrong without atonement.

It may seem hard that a claim, originally just, should be defeated by mere lapse of time; but there is a time after which (even looking at the individual case, and without regard to the general effect on the security of possessors), the balance of hardship turns the other way. With the injustices of men, as with the convulsions and disasters of nature, the longer they remain unrepaired, the greater become the obstacles to repairing them, arising from the after-growths which would have to be torn up or broken through. In no human transactions, not even in the simplest and clearest, does it follow that a thing is fit to be done now, because it was fit to be done sixty years ago. It is scarcely needful to remark, that these reasons for not disturbing acts of injustice of old date, cannot apply to unjust systems or institutions; since a bad law or usage is not one bad act, in the remote past, but a perpetual repetition of bad acts, as long as the law or usage lasts.

Such, then, being the essentials of private property, it is now to be considered, to what extent the forms in which the institution has existed in different states of society, or still exists, are necessary consequences of its principle, or are recommended by the reasons on which it is grounded.

3. Nothing is implied in property but the right of each to his (or her) own faculties, to what he can produce by them, and to whatever he can get for them

in a fair market; together with his right to give this to any other person if he chooses, and the right of that other to receive and enjoy it.

It follows, therefore, that although the right of bequest, or gift after death, forms part of the idea of private property, the right of inheritance, as distinguished from bequest, does not. That the property of persons who have made no disposition of it during their lifetime, should pass first to their children, and failing them, to the nearest relations, may be a proper arrangement or not, but is no consequence of the principle of private property. Although there belong to the decision of such questions many considerations besides those of political economy, it is not foreign to the plan of this work to suggest, for the judgment of thinkers, the view of them which most recommends itself to the writer's mind.

No presumption in favor of existing ideas on this subject is to be derived from their antiquity. In early ages, the property of a deceased person passed to his children and nearest relatives by so natural and obvious an arrangement, that no other was likely to be even thought of in competition with it. In the first place, they were usually present on the spot: they were in possession, and if they had no other title, had that, so important in an early state of society, of first occupancy. Secondly, they were already, in a manner, joint owners of his property during his life. If the property was in land, it had generally been conferred by the State on a family rather than on an individual: if it consisted of cattle or moveable goods, it had probably been acquired, and was certainly protected and defended, by the united efforts of all members of the family who were of an age to work or fight. Exclusive individual property in the modern sense, scarcely entered into the ideas of the time; and when the first magistrate of the association died, he really left nothing vacant but his own share in the division, which devolved on the member of the family who succeeded to his authority. To have disposed of the property otherwise, would have been to break up a little commonwealth, united by ideas, interest, and habits, and to cast them adrift on the world. These considerations, though rather felt than reasoned about, had so great an influence on the minds of mankind, as to create the idea of an inherent right in the children to the possessions of their ancestor; a right which it was not competent to himself to defeat. Bequest, in a primitive state of society, was seldom recognized; a clear proof, were there no other, that property was conceived in a manner totally different from the conception of it in the present time.

But the feudal family, the last historical form of patriarchal life, has long perished, and the unit of society is not now the family or clan, composed of all the reputed descendants of a common ancestor, but the individual; or at most a pair of individuals, with their unemancipated children. Property is now inherent in individuals, not in families: the children when grown up do not follow the occupations or fortunes of the parent: if they participate in the parent's pecuniary means it is at his or her pleasure, and not by a voice in the ownership and government of the whole, but generally by the exclusive enjoyment of a part; and in this country at least (except as far as entails or settlements are an obstacle) it is in the power of parents to disinherit even their children, and leave their fortune to strangers. More distant relatives are in general almost as completely detached from the family and its interests as if they were in no way connected with it. The only claim they are supposed to have on their richer relations, is to a preference, *cæteris paribus*, in good offices, and some aid in case of actual necessity.

So great a change in the constitution of society must make a considerable difference in the grounds on which the disposal of property by inheritance should rest. The reasons usually assigned by modern writers for giving the property of a person who dies intestate to the children, or nearest relatives, are, first, the supposition that in so disposing of it, the law is more likely than in any other mode to do what the proprietor would have done, if he had done anything; and secondly, the hardship, to those who lived with their parents and partook in their opulence, of being cast down from the enjoyments of wealth into poverty and privation.

There is some force in both these arguments. The law ought, no doubt, to do for the children or dependents of an intestate, whatever it was the duty of the parent or protector to have done, so far as this can be known by any one besides himself. Since, however, the law cannot decide on individual claims, but must proceed by general rules, it is next to be considered what these rules should be....

The claims of children are of a different nature: they are real, and indefeasible. But even of these, I venture to think that the measure usually taken is an erroneous one: what is due to children is in some respects underrated, in others, as it appears to me, exaggerated. One of the most binding of all obligations, that of not bringing children into the world unless they can be maintained in comfort during childhood, and brought up with a likelihood of supporting themselves when of full age, is both disregarded in practice and made light of in theory in a manner disgraceful to human intelligence. On the other hand, when the parent possesses property, the claims of the children upon it seem to me to be the subject of an opposite error. Whatever fortune a parent may have inherited, or still more, may have acquired, I cannot admit that he owes to his children, merely because they are his children, to leave them rich, without the necessity of any exertion. I could not admit it, even if to be so left were always, and certainly, for the good of the children themselves. But this is in the highest degree uncertain. It depends on individual character. Without supposing extreme cases, it may be affirmed that in a majority of instances the good not only of society but of the individuals would be better consulted by bequeathing to them a moderate, than a large provision. This, which is a commonplace of moralists ancient and modern, is felt to be true by many intelligent parents, and would be acted upon much more frequently, if they did not allow themselves to consider less what really is, than what will be thought by others to be, advantageous to the children....

In order to give the children that fair chance of a desirable existence, to which they are entitled, it is generally necessary that they should not be brought up from childhood in habits of luxury which they will not have the means of indulging in after-life. This, again, is a duty often flagrantly violated by possessors of terminable incomes, who have little property to leave. When the children of rich parents have lived, as it is natural they should do, in habits corresponding to the scale of expenditure in which the parents indulge, it is generally the duty of the parents to make a greater provision for them than would suffice for children otherwise brought up. I say generally, because even here there is another side to the question. It is a proposition quite capable of being maintained, that to a strong nature which has to make its way against narrow circumstances, to have known early some of the feelings and experiences of wealth, is an advantage both in the formation of character and in the happiness of life. But allowing that children have a just ground of complaint, who have been brought up to require luxuries which they are not afterwards likely to obtain, and that their claim, therefore, is good to a provision bearing some relation to the mode of their bringing up; this, too, is a claim which is particularly liable to be stretched further than its reasons warrant. The case is exactly that of the younger children of the nobility and landed gentry, the bulk of whose fortune passes to the eldest son. The other sons, who are usually numerous, are brought up in the same habits of luxury as the future heir, and they receive as a younger brother's portion, generally what the reason of the case dictates, namely, enough to support, in the habits of life to which they are accustomed, themselves, but not a wife or children. It really is no grievance to any man, that for the means of marrying and of supporting a family, he has to depend on his own exertions.

A provision, then, such as is admitted to be reasonable in the case of illegitimate children, for younger children, wherever in short the justice of the case, and the real interests of the individuals and of society, are the only things considered, is, I conceive, all that parents owe to their children, and all, therefore, which the State owes to the children of those who die intestate. The surplus, if any, I hold that it may rightfully appropriate to the general purposes of the community. I would not, however, be supposed to recommend that parents should never do more for their children than what, merely as children, they have a moral right to. In some cases it is imperative, in many laudable, and in all allowable, to do much more. For this, however, the means are afforded by the liberty of bequest. It is due, not to the children but to the parents, that they should have the power of showing marks of affection, of requiting services and sacrifices, and of bestowing their wealth according to their own preferences, or their own judgment of fitness.

4. Whether the power of bequest should itself be subject to limitation, is an ulterior question of great importance. Unlike inheritance *ab intestato*, bequest is one of the attributes of property: the ownership of a thing cannot be looked upon as complete without the power of bestowing it, at death or during life, at

the owner's pleasure: and all the reasons, which recommend that private property should exist, recommend *pro tanto* this extension of it. But property is only a means to an end, not itself the end. Like all other proprietary rights, and even in a greater degree than most, the power of bequest may be so exercised as to conflict with the permanent interests of the human race. It does so, when, not content with bequeathing an estate to A, the testator prescribes that on A's death it shall pass to his eldest son, and to that son's son, and so on for ever. No doubt, persons have occasionally exerted themselves more strenuously to acquire a fortune from the hope of founding a family in perpetuity; but the mischiefs to society of such perpetuities outweigh the value of this incentive to exertion, and the incentives in the case of those who have the opportunity of making large fortunes are strong enough without it. A similar abuse of the power of bequest is committed when a person who does the meritorious act of leaving property for public uses, attempts to prescribe the details of its application in perpetuity; when in founding a place of education (for instance) he dictates, for ever, what doctrines shall be taught. It being impossible that any one should know what doctrines will be fit to be taught after he has been dead for centuries, the law ought not to give effect to such dispositions of property, unless subject to the perpetual revision (after a certain interval has elapsed) of a fitting authority....

By the French law since the Revolution, the parent can only dispose by will, of a portion equal to the share of one child, each of the children taking an equal portion. This entail, as it may be called, of the bulk of every one's property upon the children collectively, seems to me as little defensible in principle as an entail in favor of one child, though it does not shock so directly the idea of justice. I cannot admit that parents should be compelled to leave to their children even that provision which, as children, I have contended that they have a moral claim to. Children may forfeit that claim by general unworthiness, or particular ill-conduct to the parents: they may have other resources or prospects: what has been previously done for them, in the way of education and advancement in life, may fully satisfy their moral claim; or others may have claims superior to theirs.

The extreme restriction of the power of bequest in French law, was adopted as a democratic expedient, to break down the custom of primogeniture, and counteract the tendency of inherited property to collect in large masses. I agree in thinking these objects eminently desirable; but the means used are not, I think, the most judicious. Were I framing a code of laws according to what seems to me best in itself, without regard to existing opinions and sentiments, I should prefer to restrict, not what any one might bequeath, but what any one should be permitted to acquire, by bequest or inheritance. Each person should have power to dispose by will of his or her whole property; but not to lavish it in enriching some one individual, beyond a certain maximum, which should be fixed sufficiently high to afford the means of comfortable independence. The inequalities of property which arise from unequal industry, frugality, perseverance, talents, and to a certain extent even opportunities, are insepa-rable from the principle of private property, and if we accept the principle, we must bear with these consequences of it: but I see nothing objectionable in fix-ing a limit to what any one may acquire by the mere favor of others, without any exercise of his faculties, and in requiring that if he desires any further accession of fortune, he shall work for it.

I do not conceive that the degree of limitation which this would impose on the right of bequest, would be felt as a burthensome restraint by any testator who estimated a large fortune at its true value, that of the pleasures and advan-tages that can be purchased with it: on even the most extravagant estimate of which, it must be apparent to every one, that the difference to the happiness of the possessor between a moderate independence and five times as much, is insignificant when weighed against the enjoyment that might be given, and the permanent benefits diffused, by some other disposal of the four-fifths. So long indeed as the opinion practically prevails, that the best thing which can be done for objects of affection is to heap on them to satiety those intrinsically worthless things on which large fortunes are mostly expended, there might be little use in enacting such a law, even if it were possible to get it passed, since if there were the inclination, there would generally be the power of evading it.

The law would be unavailing unless the popular sentiment went energeti-cally along with it; which (judging from the tenacious adherence of public opinion in France to the law of compulsory division) it would in some states of society and government be very likely to do, however much the contrary may be the fact in England and at the present time. If the restriction could be made practically effectual, the benefit would be great. Wealth which could no longer be employed in over-enriching a few, would either be devoted to objects of public usefulness, or if bestowed on individuals, would be distributed among a larger number. While those enormous fortunes which no one needs for any personal purpose but ostentation or improper power, would become much less numerous, there would be a great multiplication of persons in easy circumstances, with the advantages of leisure, and all the real enjoyments which wealth can give, except those of vanity; a class by whom the services which a nation having leisured classes is entitled to expect from them, either by their direct exertions or by the tone they give to the feelings and tastes of the public, would be rendered in a much more beneficial manner than at pres-ent. A large portion also of the accumulations of successful industry would probably be devoted to public uses, either by direct bequests to the State, or by the endowment of institutions; as is already done very largely in the United States, where the ideas and practice in the matter of inheritance seem to be unusually rational and beneficial.

5. The next point to be considered is, whether the reasons on which the institution of property rests are applicable to all things in which a right of exclusive ownership is at present recognized; and if not, on what other grounds the recognition is defensible.

The essential principle of property being to assure to all persons what they have produced by their labor and accumulated by their abstinence, this principle cannot apply to what is not the produce of labor, the raw material of the earth. If the land derived its productive power wholly from nature, and not at all from industry, or if there were any means of discriminating what is derived from each source, it not only would not be necessary, but it would be the height of injustice, to let the gift of nature be engrossed by individuals. The use of the land in agriculture must indeed, for the time being, be of necessity exclusive; the same person who has ploughed and sown must be permitted to reap: but the land might be occupied for one season only, as among the ancient Germans; or might be periodically redivided as population increased: or the State might be the universal landlord, and the cultivators tenants under it, either on lease or at will.

But though land is not the produce of industry, most of its valuable qualities are so. Labor is not only requisite for using, but almost equally so for fashioning, the instrument. Considerable labor is often required at the commencement, to clear the land for cultivation. In many cases, even when cleared, its productiveness is wholly the effect of labor and art.... Cultivation also requires buildings and fences, which are wholly the produce of labor. The fruits of this industry cannot be reaped in a short period. The labor and outlay are immediate, the benefit is spread over many years, perhaps over all future time. A holder will not incur this labor and outlay when strangers and not himself will be benefited by it. If he undertakes such improvements, he must have a sufficient period before him in which to profit by them: and he is in no way so sure of having always a sufficient period as when his tenure is perpetual.

6. These are the reasons which form the justification in an economical point of view, of property in land. It is seen, that they are only valid, in so far as the proprietor of land is its improver. Whenever, in any country, the proprietor, generally speaking, ceases to be the improver, political economy has nothing to say in defense of landed property, as there established. In no sound theory of private property was it ever contemplated that the proprietor of land should be merely a sinecurist quartered on it....

The truth is, that any very general improvement of land by the landlords is hardly compatible with a law or custom of primogeniture. When the land goes wholly to the heir, it generally goes to him severed from the pecuniary resources which would enable him to improve it, the personal property being absorbed by the provision for younger children, and the land itself often heavily burdened for the same purpose. There is therefore but a small proportion of landlords who have the means of making expensive improvements, unless they do it with borrowed money, and by adding to the mortgages with which in most cases the land was already burdened when they received it....

When the "sacredness of property" is talked of, it should always be remembered, that any such sacredness does not belong in the same degree to landed property. No man made the land. It is the original inheritance of the whole species. Its appropriation is wholly a question of general expediency. When private property in land is not expedient, it is unjust. It is no hardship to any one to be excluded from what others have produced: they were not bound to produce it for his use, and he loses nothing by not sharing in what otherwise would not have existed at all. But it is some hardship to be born into the world and to find all nature's gifts previously engrossed, and no place left for the new-comer. To reconcile people to this, after they have once admitted into their minds the idea that any moral rights belong to them as human beings, it will always be necessary to convince them that the exclusive appropriation is good for mankind on the whole, themselves included. But this is what no sane human being could be persuaded of, if the relation between the landowner and the cultivator were the same everywhere as it has been in Ireland.

Landed property is felt, even by those most tenacious of its rights, to be a different thing from other property; and where the bulk of the community have been disinherited of their share of it, and it has become the exclusive attribute of a small minority, men have generally tried to reconcile it, at least in theory, to their sense of justice, by endeavoring to attach duties to it, and erecting it into a sort of magistracy, either moral or legal. But if the state is at liberty to treat the possessors of land as public functionaries, it is only going one step further to say, that it is at liberty to discard them. The claim of the landowners to the land is altogether subordinate to the general policy of the state. The principle of property gives them no right to the land, but only a right to compensation for whatever portion of their interest in the land it may be the policy of the state to deprive them of....

To me it seems almost an axiom that property in land should be interpreted strictly, and that the balance in all cases of doubt should incline against the proprietor. The reverse is the case with property in moveables, and in all things the product of labor: over these, the owner's power both of use and of exclusion should be absolute, except where positive evil to others would result from it: but in the case of land, no exclusive right should be permitted in any individual, which cannot be shown to be productive of positive good....

7. Besides property in the produce of labor, and property in land, there are other things which are or have been subjects of property, in which no proprietary rights ought to exist at all. But as the civilized world has in general made up its mind on most of these, there is no necessity for dwelling on them in this place. At the head of them, is property in human beings. It is almost superfluous to observe, that this institution can have no place in any society even pretending to be founded on justice, or on fellowship between human creatures. But, iniquitous as it is, yet when the state has expressly legalized it, and human beings, for generations, have been bought, sold, and inherited under sanction of law, it is another wrong, in abolishing the property, not to make full compensation. This wrong was avoided by the great measure of justice in 1833, one of the most virtuous acts, as well as the most practically beneficent, ever done collectively by a nation....

Chapter III: Of The Classes Among Whom The Produce Is Distributed

1. Private property being assumed as a fact, we have next to enumerate the different classes of persons to whom it gives rise; whose concurrence, or at least whose permission, is necessary to production, and who are therefore able to stipulate for a share of the produce. We have to inquire, according to what laws the produce distributes itself among these classes, by the spontaneous action of the interests of those concerned: after which, a further question will be, what effects are or might be produced by laws, institutions, and measures of government, in superseding or modifying that spontaneous distribution.

The three requisites of production, as has been so often repeated, are labor, capital, and land: understanding by capital, the means and appliances which are the accumulated results of previous labor, and by land, the materials and instruments supplied by nature, whether contained in the interior of the earth, or constituting its surface. Since each of these elements of production may be separately appropriated, the industrial community may be considered as divided into landowners, capitalists, and productive laborers. Each of these classes, as such, obtains a share of the produce: no other person or class obtains anything, except by concession from them. The remainder of the community is, in fact, supported at their expense, giving, if any equivalent, one consisting of unproductive services. These three classes, therefore, are considered in political economy as making up the whole community

2. But although these three sometimes exist as separate classes, dividing the produce among them, they do not necessarily or always so exist. The fact is so much otherwise, that there are only one or two communities in which the complete separation of these classes is the general rule. England and Scotland, with parts of Belgium and Holland, are almost the only countries in the world, where the land, capital, and labor employed in agriculture, are generally the property of separate owners. The ordinary case is, that the same person owns either two of these requisites, or all three....

3. The case in which the same person owns all three, embraces the two extremes of existing society, in respect to the independence and dignity of the laboring class. First, when the laborer himself is the proprietor. This is the commonest case in the Northern States of the American Union; one of the commonest in France, Switzerland, the three Scandinavian kingdoms, and parts of Germany; and a common case in parts of Italy and in Belgium. In all these countries there are, no doubt, large landed properties, and a still greater number which, without being large, require the occasional or constant aid of hired laborers. Much, however, of the land is owned in portions too small to require any other labor than that of the peasant and his family, or fully to occupy even that. The capital employed is not always that of the peasant proprietor, many of these small properties being mortgaged to obtain the means of cultivating; but the capital is invested at the peasant's risk, and though he

pays interest for it, it gives to no one any right of interference, except, perhaps, eventually to take possession of the land, if the interest ceases to be paid.

The other case in which the land, labor, and capital, belong to the same person, is the case of slave countries, in which the laborers themselves are owned by the landowner. Our West India colonies before emancipation, and the sugar colonies of the nations by whom a similar act of justice is still unperformed, are examples of large establishments for agricultural and manufacturing labor (the production of sugar and rum is a combination of both) in which the land, the factories (if they may be so called), the machinery, and the degraded laborers, are all the property of a capitalist. In this case, as well as in its extreme opposite, the case of the peasant proprietor, there is no division of the produce.

4. When the three requisites are not all owned by the same person, it often happens that two of them are so. Sometimes the same person owns the capital and the land, but not the labor. The landlord makes his engagement directly with the laborer, and supplies the whole or part of the stock necessary for cultivation. This system is the usual one in those parts of Continental Europe, in which the laborers are neither serfs on the one hand, nor proprietors on the other. It was very common in France before the Revolution, and is still practiced in some parts of that country, when the land is not the property of the cultivator. It prevails generally in the level districts of Italy, except those principally pastoral, such as the Maremma of Tuscany and the Campagna of Rome. On this system the division of the produce is between two classes, the landowner and the laborer....

These are the principal variations in the classification of those among whom the produce of agricultural labor is distributed. In the case of manufacturing industry there never are more than two classes, the laborers and the capitalists. The original artisans in all countries were either slaves, or the women of the family. In the manufacturing establishments of the ancients, whether on a large or on a small scale, the laborers were usually the property of the capitalist. In general, if any manual labor was thought compatible with the dignity of a freeman, it was only agricultural labor.... Where ever the extent of the market admits of it, the distinction is now fully established between the class of capitalists, or employers of labor, and the class of laborers; the capitalists, in general, contributing no other labor than that of direction and superintendence.

Chapter IV: Of Competition And Custom

1. Under the rule of individual property, the division of the produce is the result of two determining agencies: Competition, and Custom. It is important to ascertain the amount of influence which belongs to each of these causes, and in what manner the operation of one is modified by the other.

Political economists generally, and English political economists above others, have been accustomed to lay almost exclusive stress upon the first of these agencies; to exaggerate the effect of competition, and to take into little account the other and conflicting principle. They are apt to express themselves as if they thought that competition actually does, in all cases, whatever it can be shown to be the tendency of competition to do. This is partly intelligible, if we consider that only through the principle of competition has political economy any pretension to the character of a science. So far as rents, profits, wages, prices, are determined by competition, laws may be assigned for them. Assume competition to be their exclusive regulator, and principles of broad generality and scientific precision may be laid down, according to which they will be regulated. The political economist justly deems this his proper business: and as an abstract or hypothetical science, political economy cannot be required to do, and indeed cannot do, anything more.

But it would be a great misconception of the actual course of human affairs, to suppose that competition exercises in fact this unlimited sway. I am not speaking of monopolies, either natural or artificial, or of any interferences of authority with the liberty of production or exchange. Such disturbing causes have always been allowed for by political economists. I speak of cases in which there is nothing to restrain competition; no hindrance to it either in the nature of the case or in artificial obstacles; yet in which the result is not determined by competition, but by custom or usage; competition either not taking place at all, or producing its effect in quite a different manner from that which is ordinarily assumed to be natural to it.

2. Competition, in fact, has only become in any considerable degree the governing principle of contracts, at a comparatively modern period. The farther we look back into history, the more we see all transactions and engagements under the influence of fixed customs. The reason is evident. Custom is the most powerful protector of the weak the strong; their sole protector where there are no laws or government adequate to the purpose. Custom is a barrier which, even in the most oppressed condition of mankind, tyranny is forced in some degree to respect. To the industrious population, in a turbulent military community, freedom of competition is a vain phrase; they are never in a condition to make terms for themselves by it: there is always a master who throws his sword into the scale, and the terms are such as he imposes. But though the law of the strongest decides, it is not the interest nor in general the practice of the strongest to strain that law to the utmost, and every relaxation of it has a tendency to become a custom, and every custom to become a right. Rights thus originating, and not competition in any shape, determine, in a rude state of society, the share of the produce enjoyed by those who produce it. The relations, more especially, between the landowner and the cultivator, and the payments made by the latter to the former, are, in all states of society but the most modern, determined by the usage of the country. Never until late times have the conditions of the occupancy of land been (as a general rule) an affair of

competition. The occupier for the time has very commonly been considered to have a right to retain his holdings, while he fulfils the customary requirements; and thus become, in a certain sense, a co-proprietor of the soil. Even where the holder has not acquired this fixity of tenure, the terms of occupation have often been fixed and invariable....

3. Prices, whenever there was no monopoly, came earlier under the influence of competition, and are much more universally subject to it, than rents: but that influence is by no means, even in the present activity of mercantile competition, so absolute as is sometimes assumed. There is no proposition which meets us in the field of political economy oftener than this—that there cannot be two prices in the same market. Such undoubtedly is the natural effect of unimpeded competition; yet every one knows that there are, almost always, two prices in the same market. Not only are there in every large town, and in almost every trade, cheap shops and dear shops, but the same shop often sells the same article at different prices to different customers: and, as a general rule, each retailer adapts his scale of prices to the class of customers whom he expects. The wholesale trade, in the great articles of commerce, is really under the dominion of competition. There, the buyers as well as sellers are traders or manufacturers, and their purchases are not influenced by indolence or vulgar finery, nor depend on the smaller motives of personal convenience, but are business transactions. In the wholesale markets therefore it is true as a general proposition, that there are not two prices at one time for the same thing: there is at each time and place a market price, which can be quoted in a price-current. But retail price, the price paid by the actual consumer, seems to feel very slowly and imperfectly the effect of competition; and when competition does exist, it often, instead of lowering prices, merely divides the gains of the high price among a greater number of dealers....

All professional remuneration is regulated by custom. The fees of physicians, surgeons, and barristers, the charges of attorneys, are nearly invariable. Not certainly for want of abundant competition in those professions, but because the competition operates by diminishing each competitor's chance of fees, not by lowering the fees themselves....

Book III: Exchange

Chapter I: Of Value

1. The subject on which we are now about to enter fills so important and conspicuous a position in political economy, that in the apprehension of some thinkers its boundaries confound themselves with those of the science itself. One eminent writer has proposed as a name for Political Economy, "Catallactics," or the science of exchanges; by others it has been called the Science of Values. If these denominations had appeared to me logically correct, I must

have placed the discussion of the elementary laws of value at the commence-ment of our inquiry, instead of postponing it to the Third Part; and the possi-bility of so long deferring it is alone a sufficient proof that this view of the nature of Political Economy is too confined.

It is true that in the preceding Books we have not escaped the necessity of anticipating some small portion of the theory of Value, especially as to the value of labor and of land. It is nevertheless evident, that of the two great depart-ments of Political Economy, the production of wealth and its distribution, the consideration of Value has to do with the latter alone; and with that, only so far as competition, and not usage or custom, is the distributing agency. The condi-tions and laws of Production would be the same as they are, if the arrange-ments of society did not depend on Exchange, or did not admit of it. Even in the present system of industrial life, in which employments are minutely subdi-vided, and all concerned in production depend for their remuneration on the price of a particular commodity, exchange is not the fundamental law of the distribution of the produce, no more than roads and carriages are the essential laws of motion, but merely a part of the machinery for effecting it.

To confound these ideas, seems to me, not only a logical, but a practical blunder. It is a case of the error too common in political economy, of not distin-guishing between necessities arising from the nature of things, and those cre-ated by social arrangements: an error, which appears to me to be at all times producing two opposite mischiefs; on the one hand, causing political econo-mists to class the merely temporary truths of their subject among its perma-nent and universal laws; and on the other, leading many persons to mistake the permanent laws of Production (such as those on which the necessity is grounded of restraining population) for temporary accidents arising from the existing constitution of society-which those who would frame a new system of social arrangements, are at liberty to disregard.

In a state of society, however, in which the industrial system is entirely founded on purchase and sale, each individual, for the most part, living not on things in the production of which he himself hears a part, but on things obtained by a double exchange, a sale followed by a purchase-the question of Value is fundamental. Almost every speculation respecting the economical interests of a society thus constituted, implies some theory of Value: the small-est error on that subject infects with corresponding error all our other conclu-sions; and anything vague or misty in our conception of it, creates confusion and uncertainty in everything else. Happily, there is nothing in the laws of Value which remains for the present or any future writer to clear up; the theory of the subject is complete: the only difficulty to be overcome is that of so stat-ing it as to solve by anticipation the chief perplexities which occur in applying it: and to do this, some minuteness of exposition, and considerable demands on the patience of the reader, are unavoidable. He will be amply repaid, how-ever (if a stranger to these inquiries), by the ease and rapidity with which a thorough understanding of this subject will enable him to fathom most of the remaining questions of political economy.

2. We must begin by settling our phraseology. Adam Smith, in a passage often quoted, has touched upon the most obvious ambiguity of the word value; which, in one of its senses, signifies usefulness, in another, power of purchasing; in his own language, value in use and value in exchange. But (as Mr. De Quincey has remarked) in illustrating this double meaning, Adam Smith has himself fallen into another ambiguity. Things (he says) which have the greatest value in use have often little or no value in exchange; which is true, since that which can be obtained without labor or sacrifice will command no price, however useful or needful it may be. But he proceeds to add, that things which have the greatest value in exchange, as a diamond for example, may have little or no value in use. This is employing the word use, not in the sense in which political economy is concerned with it, but in that other sense in which use is opposed to pleasure. Political economy has nothing to do with the comparative estimation of different uses in the judgment of a philosopher or a moralist. The use of a thing, in political economy, means its capacity to satisfy a desire, or serve a purpose. Diamonds have this capacity in a high degree, and unless they had it, would not bear any price. Value in use, or as Mr. De Quincey calls it, teleologic value, is the extreme limit of value in exchange. The exchange value of a thing may fall short, to any amount, of its value in use; but that it can ever exceed the value in use, implies a contradiction; it supposes that persons will give, to possess a thing, more than the utmost value which they themselves put upon it as a means of gratifying their inclinations.

The word Value, when used without adjunct, always means, in political economy, value in exchange; or as it has been called by Adam Smith and his successors, exchangeable value, a phrase which no amount of authority that can be quoted for it can make other than bad English. Mr. De Quincey substitutes the term Exchange Value, which is unexceptionable.

Exchange value requires to be distinguished from Price. The words Value and Price were used as synonymous by the early political economists, and are not always discriminated even by Ricardo. But the most accurate modern writers, to avoid the wasteful expenditure of two good scientific terms on a single idea, have employed Price to express the value of a thing in relation to money; the quantity of money for which it will exchange. By the price of a thing, therefore, we shall henceforth understand its value in money; by the value, or exchange value of a thing, its general power of purchasing; the command which its possession gives over purchasable commodities in general.

Book IV: Influence of Progress

Chapter VII: On The Probable Futurity Of The Laboring Classes

1. When I speak, either in this place or elsewhere, of "the laboring classes," or of laborers as a "class," I use those phrases in compliance with custom, and as descriptive of an existing, but by no means a necessary or permanent, state of

social relations. I do not recognize as either just or salutary, a state of society in which there is any "class" which is not laboring; any human beings, exempt from bearing their share of the necessary labors of human life, except those unable to labor, or who have fairly earned rest by previous toil. So long, however, as the great social evil exists of a non-laboring class, laborers also constitute a class, and may be spoken of, though only provisionally, in that character.

Considered in its moral and social aspect, the state of the laboring people has latterly been a subject of much more speculation and discussion than formerly; and the opinion that it is not now what it ought to be, has become very general. The suggestions which have been promulgated, and the controversies which have been excited, on detached points rather than on the foundations of the subject, have put in evidence the existence of two conflicting theories, respecting the social position desirable for manual laborers. The one may be called the theory of dependence and protection, the other that of self-dependence.

According to the former theory, the lot of the poor, in all things which affect them collectively, should be regulated *for* them, not *by* them. They should not be required or encouraged to think for themselves, or give to their own reflection or forecast an influential voice in the determination of their destiny. It is supposed to be the duty of the higher classes to think for them, and to take the responsibility of their lot, as the commander and officers of an army take that of the soldiers composing it. This function, it is contended, the higher classes should prepare themselves to perform conscientiously, and their whole demeanor should impress the poor with a reliance on it, in order that, while yielding passive and active obedience to the rules prescribed for them, they may resign themselves in all other respects to a trustful *insouciance,* and repose under the shadow of their protectors. The relation between rich and poor, according to this theory (a theory also applied to the relation between men and women) should be only partly authoritative; it should be amiable, moral, and sentimental: affectionate tutelage on the one side, respectful and grateful deference on the other. The rich should be *in loco parentis* to the poor, guiding and restraining them like children. Of spontaneous action on their part there should be no need. They should be called on for nothing but to do their day's work, and to be moral and religious. Their morality and religion should be provided for them by their superiors, who should see them properly taught it, and should do all that is necessary to ensure their being, in return for labor and attachment, properly fed, clothed, housed, spiritually edified, and innocently amused.

This is the ideal of the future, in the minds of those whose dissatisfaction with the Present assumes the form of affection and regret towards the Past. Like other ideals, it exercises an unconscious influence on the opinions and sentiments of numbers who never consciously guide themselves by any ideal. It has also this in common with other ideals, that it has never been historically realized. It makes its appeal to our imaginative sympathies in the character of a restoration of the good times of our forefathers. But no times can be pointed out in which the higher classes of this or any other country performed a part even distantly resembling the one assigned to them in this theory. It is an idealization, grounded on the conduct and character of here and there an individual. All privileged and powerful classes, as such, have used their power in the interest of their own selfishness, and have indulged their self-importance in despising, and not in lovingly caring for, those who were, in their estimation, degraded, by being under the necessity of working for their benefit. I do not affirm that what has always been must always be, or that human improvement has no tendency to correct the intensely selfish fillings engendered by power; but though the evil may be lessened, it cannot be eradicated, until the power itself is withdrawn. This, at least, seems to me undeniable, that long before the superior classes could be sufficiently improved to govern in the tutelary manner supposed, the inferior classes would be too much improved to be so governed....

Of the working men, at least in the more advanced countries of Europe, it may be pronounced certain, that the patriarchal or paternal system of government is one to which they will not again be subject. That question was decided, when they were taught to read, and allowed access to newspapers and political tracts; when dissenting preachers were suffered to go among them, and appeal to their faculties and feelings in opposition to the creeds professed and countenanced by their superiors; when they were brought together in numbers, to work socially under the same roof; when railways enabled them to shift from place to place, and change their patrons and employers as easily as their coats; when they were encouraged to seek a share in the government, by means of the electoral franchise.

The working classes have taken their interests into their own hands, and are perpetually showing that they think the interests of their employers not identical with their own, but opposite to them. Some among the higher classes flatter themselves that these tendencies may be counteracted by moral and religious education: but they have let the time go by for giving an education which can serve their purpose. The principles of the Reformation have reached as low down in society as reading and writing, and the poor will not much longer accept morals and religion of other people's prescribing....

2. It is on a far other basis that the well-being and well-doing of the laboring people must henceforth rest. The poor have come out of leading-strings, and cannot any longer be governed or treated like children. To their own qualities must now be commended the care of their destiny. Modern nations will have to learn the lesson, that the well-being of a people must exist by means of the justice and self-government, and of the individual citizens. The theory of dependence attempts to dispense with the necessity of these qualities in the dependent classes. But now, when even in position they are becoming less and less dependent, and their minds less and less acquiescent in the degree of dependence which remains, the virtues of independence are those which they stand in need of. Whatever advice, exhortation or guidance is held out to the

laboring classes, must henceforth be tendered to them as equals, and accepted by them with their eyes open. The prospect of the future depends on the degree in which they can be made rational beings.

There is no reason to believe that prospect other than hopeful. The progress indeed has hitherto been, and still is, slow. But there is a spontaneous education going on in the minds of the multitude, which may be greatly accelerated and improved by artificial aids. The instruction obtained from newspapers and political tracts may not be the most solid kind of instruction, but it is an immense improvement upon none at all....

In the meantime, the working classes are now part of the public; in all discussions on matters of general interest they, or a portion of them, are now partakers; all who use the press as an instrument may, if it so happens, have them for an audience; the avenues of instruction through which the middle classes acquire such ideas as they have, are accessible to, at least, the operatives in the towns. With these resources, it cannot be doubted that they will increase in intelligence, even by their own unaided efforts; while there is reason to hope that great improvements both in the quality and quantity of school education will be effected by the exertions either of government or of individuals, and that the progress of the mass of the people in mental cultivation, and in the virtues which are dependent on it, will take place more rapidly, and with fewer intermittences and aberrations, than if left to itself....

3. It appears to me impossible but that the increase of intelligence, of education, and of the love of independence among the working classes, must be attended with a corresponding growth of the good sense which manifests itself in provident habits of conduct, and that population, therefore, will bear a gradually diminishing ratio to capital and employment.

This most desirable result would be much accelerated by another change, which lies in the direct line of the best tendencies of the time; the opening of industrial occupations freely to both sexes. The same reasons which make it no longer necessary that the poor should depend on the rich, make it equally unnecessary that women should depend on men; and the least which justice requires is that law and custom should not enforce dependence (when the correlative protection has become superfluous) by ordaining that a woman, who does not happen to have a provision by inheritance, shall have scarcely any means open to her of gaining a livelihood, except as a wife and mother. Let women who prefer that occupation, adopt it; but that there should be no option, no other *carrière* possible for the great majority of women, except in the humbler departments of life, is a flagrant social injustice. The ideas and institutions by which the accident of sex is made the groundwork of an inequality of legal rights, and a forced dissimilarity of social functions, must ere long be recognized as the greatest hindrance to moral, social, and even intellectual improvement. On the present occasion I shall only indicate, among the probable consequences of the industrial and social independence of women, a great diminution of the evil of over-population. It is by devoting one-half of the human species to that exclusive function, by making it fill the entire life of one sex, and interweave itself with almost all the objects of the other, that the animal instinct in question is nursed into the disproportionate preponderance which it has hitherto exercised in human life.

4. The political consequences of the increasing power and importance of the operative classes, and of the growing ascendancy of numbers, which, even in England and under the present institutions, is rapidly giving to the will of the majority at least a negative voice in the acts of government, are too wide a subject to be discussed in this place. But, confining ourselves to economical considerations, and notwithstanding the effect which improved intelligence in the working classes, together with just laws, may have in altering the distribution of the produce to their advantage, I cannot think that they will be permanently contented with the condition of laboring for wages as their ultimate state. They may be willing to pass through the class of servants in their way to that of employers; but not to remain in it all their lives. To begin as hired laborers, then after a few years to work on their own account, and finally employ others, is the normal condition of laborers in a new country, rapidly increasing in wealth and population, like America or Australia....

The aim of improvement should be not solely to place human beings in a condition in which they will be able to do without one another, but to enable them to work with or for one another in relations not involving dependence. Hitherto there has been no alternative for those who lived by their labor, but that of laboring either each for himself alone, or for a master. But the civilizing and improving influences of association, and the efficiency and economy of production on a large scale, may be obtained without dividing the producers into two parties with hostile interests and feelings, the many who do the work being mere servants under the command of the one who supplies the funds, and having no interest of their own in the enterprise except to earn their wages with as little labor as possible.

The speculations and discussions of the last fifty years, and the events of the last thirty, are abundantly conclusive on this point. If the improvement which even triumphant military despotism has only retarded, not stopped, shall continue its course, there can be little doubt that the *status* of hired laborers will gradually tend to confine itself to the description of workpeople whose low moral qualities render them unfit for anything more independent: and that the relation of masters and work-people will be gradually superseded by partnership, in one of two forms: in some cases, association of the laborers with the capitalist; in others, and perhaps finally in all, association of laborers among themselves....

6. The form of association, however, which if mankind continue to improve, must be expected in the end to predominate, is not that which can exist between a capitalist as chief, and work-people without a voice in the management, but the association of the laborers themselves on terms of equality, collectively owning the capital with which they carry on their operations, and working

under managers elected and removable by themselves. So long as this idea remained in a state of theory, in the writings of Owen or of Louis Blanc, it may have appeared, to the common modes of judgment, incapable of being realized, and not likely to be tried unless by seizing on the existing capital, and confiscating it for the benefit of the laborers; which is even now imagined by many persons, and pretended by more, both in England and on the Continent, to be the meaning and purpose of Socialism. But there is a capacity of exertion and self-denial in the masses of mankind, which is never known but on the rare occasions on which it is appealed to in the name of some great idea or elevated sentiment. Such an appeal was made by the French Revolution of 1848.

For the first time it then seemed to the intelligent and generous of the working classes of a great nation, that they had obtained a government who sincerely desired the freedom and dignity of the many, and who did not look upon it as their natural and legitimate state to be instruments of production, worked for the benefit of the possessors of capital. Under this encouragement, the ideas sown by Socialist writers, of an emancipation of labor to be effected by means of association, throve and fructified; and many working people came to the resolution, not only that they would work for one another, instead of working for a master tradesman or manufacturer, but that they would also free themselves, at whatever cost of labor or privation, from the necessity of paying, out of the produce of their industry, a heavy tribute for the use of capital; that they would extinguish this tax, not by robbing the capitalists of what they or their predecessors had acquired by labor and preserved by economy, but by honestly acquiring capital for themselves. If only a few operatives had attempted this arduous task, or if, while many attempted it, a few only had succeeded, their success might have been deemed to furnish no argument for their system as a permanent mode of industrial organization. But, excluding all the instances of failure, there exist, or existed a short time ago, upwards of a hundred successful, and many eminently prosperous, associations of operatives in Paris alone, besides a considerable number in the departments....

The same admirable qualities by which the associations were carried through their early struggles, maintained them in their increasing prosperity. Their rules of discipline, instead of being more lax, are stricter than those of ordinary workshops; but being rules self-imposed, for the manifest good of the community, and not for the convenience of an employer regarded as having an opposite interest, they are far more scrupulously obeyed, and the voluntary obedience carries with it a sense of personal worth and dignity. With wonderful rapidity the associated workpeople have learnt to correct those of the ideas they set out with which are in opposition to the teaching of reason and experience. Almost all the associations, at first, excluded piece-work, and gave equal wages whether the work done was more or less. Almost all have abandoned this system, and after allowing to every one a fixed minimum, sufficient for subsistence, they apportion all further remuneration according to the work done: most of them even dividing the profits at the end of the year, in the same proportion as the earnings....

It is not in France alone that these associations have commenced a career of prosperity. To say nothing at present of Germany, Piedmont, and Switzerland (where the Konsum-Verein of Zürich is one of the most prosperous co-operative associations in Europe), England can produce cases of success rivaling even those which I have cited from France. Under the impulse commenced by Mr. Owen, and more recently propagated by the writings and personal efforts of a band of friends, chiefly clergymen and barristers, to whose noble exertions too much praise can scarcely be given, the good seed was widely sown; the necessary alterations in the English law of partnership were obtained from Parliament, on the benevolent and public-spirited initiative of Mr. Slaney; many industrial associations, and a still greater number of co-operative stores for retail purchases, were founded....

It is hardly possible to take any but a hopeful view of the prospects of mankind, when, in two leading countries of the world, the obscure depths of society contain simple working men whose integrity, good sense, self-command, and honorable confidence in one another, have enabled them to carry these noble experiments to the triumphant issue which the facts recorded in the preceding pages attest.

From the progressive advance of the co-operative movement, a great increase may be looked for even in the aggregate productiveness of industry. The sources of the increase are twofold. In the first place, the class of mere distributors, who are not producers but auxiliaries of production, and whose inordinate numbers, far more than the gains of capitalists, are the cause why so great a portion of the wealth produced does not reach the producers—will be reduced to more modest dimensions. Distributors differ from producers in this, that when producers increase, even though in any given department of industry they may be too numerous, they actually produce more: but the multiplication of distributors does not make more distribution to be done, more wealth to be distributed; it does but divide the same work among a greater number of persons, seldom even cheapening the process. By limiting the distributors to the number really required for making the commodities accessible to the consumers-which is the direct effect of the co-operative system—a vast number of hands will be set free for production, and the capital which feeds and the gains which remunerate them will be applied to feed and remunerate producers. This great economy of the world's resources would be realized even if co-operation stopped at associations for purchase and consumption, without extending to production.

The other mode in which co-operation tends, still more efficaciously, to increase the productiveness of labor, consists in the vast stimulus given to productive energies, by placing the laborers, as a mass, in a relation to their work which would make it their principle and their interest—at present it is neither—to do the utmost, instead of the least possible, in exchange for their remuneration. It is scarcely possible to rate too highly this material benefit, which yet is as nothing compared with the moral revolution in society that would accompany it: the healing of the standing feud between capital and labor; the transformation of human life, from a conflict of classes struggling for opposite interests, to a friendly rivalry in the pursuit of a good common to all; the elevation of the dignity of labor; a new sense of security and independence in the laboring class; and the conversion of each human being's daily occupation into a school of the social sympathies and the practical intelligence....

Under the most favorable supposition, it will be desirable, and perhaps for a considerable length of time, that individual capitalists, associating their work-people in the profits, should coexist with even those co-operative societies which are faithful to the co-operative principle. Unity of authority makes many things possible, which could not or would not be undertaken subject to the chance of divided councils or changes in the management. A private capitalist, exempt from the control of a body, if he is a person of capacity, is considerably more likely than almost any association to run judicious risks, and originate costly improvements. Co-operative societies may be depended on for adopting improvements after they have been tested by success, but individuals are more likely to commence things previously untried. Even in ordinary business, the competition of capable persons who in the event of failure are to have all the loss, and in the case of success the greater part of the gain, will be very useful in keeping the managers of co-operative societies up to the due pitch of activity and vigilance.

When, however, co-operative societies shall have sufficiently multiplied, it is not probable that any but the least valuable work-people will any longer consent to work all their lives for wages merely; both private capitalists and associations will gradually find it necessary to make the entire body of laborers participants in profits. Eventually, and in perhaps a less remote future than may be supposed, we may, through the co-operative principle, see our way to a change in society, which would combine the freedom and independence of the individual, with the moral, intellectual, and economical advantages of aggregate production; and which, without violence or spoliation, or even any sudden disturbance of existing habits and expectations, would realize, at least in the industrial department, the best aspirations of the democratic spirit, by putting an end to the division of society into the industrious and the idle, and effacing all social distinctions but those fairly earned by personal services and exertions.

Associations like those which we have described, by the very process of their success, are a course of education in those moral and active qualities by which alone success can be either deserved or attained. As associations multiplied, they would tend more and more to absorb all work-people, except those who have too little understanding, or too little virtue, to be capable of learning to act on any other system than that of narrow selfishness. As this change proceeded, owners of capital would gradually find it to their advantage, instead of maintaining the struggle of the old system with work-people of only the worst description, to lend their capital to the associations; to do this at a diminishing rate of interest, and at last, perhaps, even to exchange their capital for terminable annuities. In this or some such mode, the existing accumulations of capital might honestly, and by a kind of spontaneous process, become in the end the joint property of all who participate in their productive employment: a transformation which, thus effected, (and assuming of course that both sexes participate equally in the rights and in the government of the association) would be the nearest approach to social justice, and the most beneficial ordering of industrial affairs for the universal good, which it is possible at present to foresee.

7. I agree, then, with the Socialist writers in their conception of the form which industrial operations tend to assume in the advance of improvement; and I entirely share their opinion that the time is ripe for commencing this transformation, and that it should by all just and effectual means be aided and encouraged. But while I agree and sympathize with Socialists in this practical portion of their aims, I utterly dissent from the most conspicuous and vehement part of their teaching, their declamations against competition. With moral conceptions in many respects far ahead of the existing arrangements of society, they have in general very confused and erroneous notions of its actual working; and one of their greatest errors, as I conceive, is to charge upon competition all the economical evils which at present exist. They forget that wherever competition is not, monopoly is; and that monopoly, in all its forms, is the taxation of the industrious for the support of indolence, if not of plunder. They forget, too, that with the exception of competition among laborers, all other competition is for the benefit of the laborers, by cheapening the articles they consume; that competition even in the labor market is a source not of low but of high wages, wherever the competition *for* labor exceeds the competition *of* labor, as in America, in the colonies, and in the skilled trades; and never could be a cause of low wages, save by the overstocking of the labor market through the too great numbers of the laborers' families; while, if the supply of laborers is excessive, not even Socialism can prevent their remuneration from being low. Besides, if association were universal, there would be no competition between laborer and laborer; and that between association and association would be for the benefit of the consumers, that is, of the associations; of the industrious classes generally....

Instead of looking upon competition as the baneful and anti-social principle which it is held to be by the generality of Socialists, I conceive that, even in the present state of society and industry, every restriction of it is an evil, and every extension of it, even if for the time injuriously affecting some class of laborers, is always an ultimate good. To be protected against competition is to be protected in idleness, in mental dullness; to be saved the necessity of being as active and as intelligent as other people; and if it is also to be protected against being underbid for employment by a less highly paid class of laborers, this is only where old custom, or local and partial monopoly, has placed some particular class of artisans in a privileged position as compared with the rest; and the time has come when the interest of universal improvement is no longer promoted by prolonging the privileges of a few....What is now required is not to bolster up old customs, whereby limited classes of laboring people obtain partial gains which interest them in keeping up the present organization of society, but to introduce new general practices beneficial to all; and there is reason to rejoice at whatever makes the privileged classes of skilled artisans feel that they have the same interests, and depend for their remuneration on the same general causes, and must resort for the improvement of their condition to the same remedies, as the less fortunately circumstanced and comparatively helpless multitude.

Book V: Of The Influence of Government

Chapter XI: Of The Grounds And Limits of The Laisser-Faire Principle

1. We have now reached the last part of our undertaking; the discussion, so far as suited to this treatise (that is, so far as it is a question of principle, not detail) of the limits of the province of government: the question, to what objects governmental intervention in the affairs of society may or should extend, over and above those which necessarily appertain to it. No subject has been more keenly contested in the present age: the contest, however, has chiefly taken place round certain select points, with only flying excursions into the rest of the field. Those indeed who have discussed any particular question of government interference, such as state education (spiritual or secular), regulation of hours of labor, a public provision for the poor, &c., have often dealt largely in general arguments, far outstretching the special application made of them, and have shown a sufficiently strong bias either in favor of letting things alone, or in favor of meddling; but have seldom declared, or apparently decided in their own minds, how far they would carry either principle. The supporters of interference have been content with asserting a general right and duty on the part of government to intervene, wherever its intervention would be useful: and when those who have been called the *laisser-faire* school have attempted any definite limitation of the province of government, they have usually restricted it to the protection of person and property against force and fraud; a definition to which neither they nor any one else can deliberately adhere, since it excludes, as has been shown in a preceding chapter, some of the most indispensable and unanimously recognized of the duties of government....

We must set out by distinguishing between two kinds of intervention by the government, which, though they may relate to the same subject, differ widely in their nature and effects, and require, for their justification, motives of a very different degree of urgency. The intervention may extend to controlling the free agency of individuals. Government may interdict all persons from doing certain things; or from doing them without its authorization; or may prescribe to them certain things to be done, or a certain manner of doing things which it is left optional with them to do or to abstain from. This is the *authoritative* interference of government. There is another kind of intervention which is not authoritative: when a government, instead of issuing a command and enforcing it by penalties, adopts the course so seldom resorted to by governments, and of which such important use might be made, that of giving advice and promulgating information; or when, leaving individuals free to use their own means of pursuing any object of general interest, the government, not meddling with them, but not trusting the object solely to their care, establishes, side by side with their arrangements, an agency of its own for a like purpose....

2. It is evident, even at first sight, that the authoritative form of government intervention has a much more limited sphere of legitimate action than the other. It requires a much stronger necessity to justify it in any case; while there are large departments of human life from which it must be unreservedly and imperiously excluded. Whatever theory we adopt respecting the foundation of the social union, and under whatever political institutions we live, there is a circle around every individual human being which no government, be it that of one, of a few, or of the many, ought to be permitted to overstep: there is a part of the life of every person who has come to years of discretion, within which the individuality of that person ought to reign uncontrolled either by any other individual or by the public collectively. That there is, or ought to be, some space in human existence thus entrenched around, and sacred from authoritative intrusion, no one who professes the smallest regard to human freedom or dignity will call in question: the point to be determined is, where the limit should be placed; how large a province of human life this reserved territory should include.

I apprehend that it ought to include all that part which concerns only the life, whether inward or outward, of the individual, and does not affect the interests of others, or affects them only through the moral influence of example. With respect to the domain of the inward consciousness, the thoughts and feelings, and as much of external conduct as is personal only, involving no consequences, none at least of a painful or injurious kind, to other people: I hold that it is allowable in all, and in the more thoughtful and cultivated often a duty, to assert and promulgate, with all the force they are capable of, their opinion of what is good or bad, admirable or contemptible, but not to compel others to conform to that opinion; whether the force used is that of extra-legal coercion, or exerts itself by means of the law.

Even in those portions of conduct which do affect the interest of others, the onus of making out a case always lies on the defenders of legal prohibitions. It is not a merely constructive or presumptive injury to others, which will justify the interference of law with individual freedom. To be prevented from doing what one is inclined to, from acting according to one's own judgment of what is desirable, is not only always irksome, but always tends, *pro tanto*, to starve the development of some portion of the bodily or mental faculties, either sensitive or active; and unless the conscience of the individual goes freely with the legal restraint, it partakes, either in a great or in a small degree, of the degradation of slavery. Scarcely any degree of utility, short of absolute necessity, will justify a prohibitory regulation, unless it can also be made to recommend itself to the general conscience; unless persons of ordinary good intentions either believe already, or can be induced to believe, that the thing prohibited is a thing which they ought not to wish to do.

It is otherwise with governmental interferences which do not restrain individual free agency. When a government provides means of fulfilling a certain end, leaving individuals free to avail themselves of different means if in their opinion preferable, there is no infringement of liberty, no irksome or degrading restraint. One of the principal objections to government interference is then absent. There is, however, in almost all forms of government agency, one thing which is compulsory. the provision of the pecuniary means. These are derived from taxation; or, if existing in the form of an endowment derived from public property, they are still the cause of as much compulsory taxation as the sale or the annual proceeds of the property would enable to be dispensed with. And the objection necessarily attaching to compulsory contributions, is almost always greatly aggravated by the expensive precautions and onerous restrictions, which are indispensable to prevent evasion of a compulsory tax.

3. A second general objection to government agency, is that every increase of the functions devolving on the government is an increase of its power, both in the form of authority, and still more, in the indirect form of influence. The importance of this consideration, in respect of political freedom, has in general been quite sufficiently recognized, at least in England, but many, in latter times, have been prone to think that limitation of the powers of the government is only essential when the government itself is badly constituted; when it does not represent the people, but is the organ of a class, or coalition of classes: and that a government of sufficiently popular constitution might be trusted with any amount of power over the nation, since its power would be only that of the nation over itself. This might be true, if the nation, in such cases, did not practically mean a mere majority of the nation, and if minorities were only capable of oppressing, but not of being oppressed. Experience, however, proves that the depositaries of power who are mere delegates of the people, that is of a majority, are quite as ready (when they think they can count on popular support) as any organs of oligarchy to assume arbitrary power, and encroach unduly on the liberty of private life.

The public collectively is abundantly ready to impose, not only its generally narrow views of its interests, but its abstract opinions, and even its tastes, as laws binding upon individuals. And the present civilization tends so strongly to make the power of persons acting in masses the only substantial power in society, that there never was more necessity for surrounding individual independence of thought, speech, and conduct, with the most powerful defenses, in order to maintain that originality of mind and individuality of character, which are the only source of any real progress, and of most of the qualities which make the human race much superior to any herd of animals. Hence it is no less important in a democratic than in any other government, that all tendency on the part of public authorities to stretch their interference, and assume a power of any sort which can easily be dispensed with, should be regarded with unremitting jealousy. Perhaps this is even more important in a democracy than in any other form of political society; because where public opinion is sovereign, an individual who is oppressed by the sovereign does not, as in most other states of things, find a rival power to which he can appeal for relief, or, at all events, for sympathy.

4. A third general objection to government agency, rests on the principle of the division of labor. Every additional function undertaken by the government, is a fresh occupation imposed upon a body already overcharged with duties. A natural consequence is that most things are ill done; much not done at all, because the government is not able to do it without delays which are fatal to its purpose; that the more troublesome and less showy, of the functions undertaken, are postponed or neglected, and an excuse is always ready for the neglect; while the heads of the administration have their minds so fully taken up with official details, in however perfunctory a manner superintended, that they have no time or thought to spare for the great interests of the state, and the preparation of enlarged measures of social improvement....

5. But though a better organization of governments would greatly diminish the force of the objection to the mere multiplication of their duties, it would still remain true that in all the more advanced communities, the great majority of things are worse done by the intervention of government, than the individuals most interested in the matter would do them, or cause them to be done, if left to themselves. The grounds of this truth are expressed with tolerable exactness in the popular dictum, that people understand their own business and their own interests better, and care for them more, than the government does, or can be expected to do. This maxim holds true throughout the greatest part of the business of life, and wherever it is true we ought to condemn every kind of government intervention that conflicts with it. The inferiority of government agency, for example, in any of the common operations of industry or commerce, is proved by the fact, that it is hardly ever able to maintain itself in equal competition with individual agency, where the individuals possess the requisite degree of industrial enterprise, and can command the necessary assemblage of means. All the facilities which a government enjoys of access to information; all the means which it possesses of remunerating, and therefore of commanding, the best available talent in the market—are not an equivalent for the one great disadvantage of an inferior interest in the result.

It must be remembered, besides, that even if a government were superior in intelligence and knowledge to any single individual in the nation, it must be inferior to all the individuals of the nation taken together. It can neither possess in itself, nor enlist in its service, more than a portion of the acquirements and capacities which the country contains, applicable to any given purpose. There must be many persons equally qualified for the work with those whom the government employs, even if it selects its instruments with no reference to any consideration but their fitness. Now these are the very persons into whose hands, in the cases of most common occurrence, a system of individual agency naturally tends to throw the work, because they are capable of doing it better or on cheaper terms than any other persons. So far as this is the case, it is evident that government, by excluding or even by superseding individual agency, either substitutes a less qualified instrumentality for one better qualified, or at any rate substitutes its own mode of accomplishing the work, for all the variety of modes which would be tried by a number of equally qualified persons aiming at the same end; a competition by many degrees more propitious to the progress of improvement than any uniformity of system.

6. I have reserved for the last place one of the strongest of the reasons against the extension of government agency. Even if the government could comprehend within itself, in each department, all the most eminent intellectual capacity and active talent of the nation, it would not be the less desirable that the conduct of a large portion of the affairs of the society should be left in the hands of the persons immediately interested in them. The business of life is an essential part of the practical education of a people; without which, book and school instruction, though most necessary and salutary, does not suffice to qualify them for conduct, and for the adaptation of means to ends. Instruction is only one of the desiderata of mental improvement; another, almost as indispensable, is a vigorous exercise of the active energies; labor, contrivance, judgment, self-control: and the natural stimulus to these is the difficulties of life.... A people among whom there is no habit of spontaneous action for a collective interest—who look habitually to their government to command or prompt them in all matters of joint concern—who expect to have everything done for them, except what can be made an affair of mere habit and routine—have their faculties only half developed; their education is defective in one of its most important branches.

Not only is the cultivation of the active faculties by exercise, diffused through the whole community, in itself one of the most valuable of national possessions: it is rendered, not less, but more necessary, when a high degree of that indispensable culture is systematically kept up in the chiefs and functionaries of the state. There cannot be a combination of circumstances more dangerous to human welfare, than that in which intelligence and talent are maintained at a high standard within a governing corporation, but starved and discouraged outside the pale. Such a system, more completely than any other, embodies the idea of despotism, by arming with intellectual superiority as an additional weapon those who have already the legal power. It approaches as nearly as the organic difference between human beings and other animals admits, to the government of sheep by their shepherd, without anything like so strong an interest as the shepherd has in the thriving condition of the flock. The only security against political slavery is the check maintained over governors by the diffusion of intelligence, activity, and public spirit among the governed. Experience proves the extreme difficulty of permanently keeping up a sufficiently high standard of those qualities; a difficulty which increases, as the advance of civilization and security removes one after another of the hardships, embarrassments, and dangers against which individuals had formerly no resource but in their own strength, skill, and courage.

It is therefore of supreme importance that all classes of the community, down to the lowest, should have much to do for themselves; that as great a demand should be made upon their intelligence and virtue as it is in any respect equal to; that the government should not only leave as far as possible to their own faculties the conduct of whatever concerns themselves alone, but should suffer them, or rather encourage them, to manage as many as possible of their joint concerns by voluntary co-operation; since this discussion and management of collective interests is the great school of that public spirit, and the great source of that intelligence of public affairs, which are always regarded as the distinctive character of the public of free countries....

7. *Laisser-faire*, in short, should be the general practice: every departure from it, unless required by some great good, is a certain evil....

We have observed that, as a general rule, the business of life is better performed when those who have an immediate interest in it are left to take their own course, uncontrolled either by the mandate of the law or by the meddling of any public functionary. The persons, or some of the persons, who do the work, are likely to be better judges than the government, of the means of attaining the particular end at which they aim.... But if the workman is generally the best selector of means, can it be affirmed with the same universality, that the consumer, or person served, is the most competent judge of the end? Is the buyer always qualified to judge of the commodity? If not, the presumption in favor of the competition of the market does not apply to the case; and if the commodity be one, in the quality of which society has much at stake, the balance of advantages may be in favor of some mode and degree of intervention, by the authorized representatives of the collective interest of the state.

8. Now, the proposition that the consumer is a competent judge of the commodity, can be admitted only with numerous abatements and exceptions. He is generally the best judge (though even this is not true universally) of the material objects produced for his use. These are destined to supply some physical want, or gratify some taste or inclination, respecting which wants or inclinations there is no appeal from the person who feels them; or they are the means and appliances of some occupation, for the use of the persons engaged in it, who may be presumed to be judges of the things required in their own habitual employment. But there are other things, of the worth of which the demand of the market is by no means a test; things of which the utility does not consist in

ministering to inclinations, nor in serving the daily uses of life, and the want of which is least felt where the need is greatest. This is peculiarly true of those things which are chiefly useful as tending to raise the character of human beings. The uncultivated cannot be competent judges of cultivation. Those who most need to be made wiser and better, usually desire it least, and if they desired it, would be incapable of finding the way to it by their own lights.

It will continually happen, on the voluntary system, that, the end not being desired, the means will not be provided at all, or that, the persons requiring improvement having an imperfect or altogether erroneous conception of what they want, the supply called forth by the demand of the market will be anything but what is really required. Now any well-intentioned and tolerably civilized government may think, without presumption, that it does or ought to possess a degree of cultivation above the average of the community which it rules, and that it should therefore be capable of offering better education and better instruction to the people, than the greater number of them would spontaneously demand. Education, therefore, is one of those things which it is admissible in principle that a government should provide for the people. The case is one to which the reasons of the non-interference principle do not necessarily or universally extend.

With regard to elementary education, the exception to ordinary rules may, I conceive, justifiably be carried still further. There are certain primary elements and means of knowledge, which it is in the highest degree desirable that all human beings born into the community should acquire during childhood. If their parents, or those on whom they depend, have the power of obtaining for them this instruction, and fail to do it, they commit a double breach of duty, towards the children themselves, and towards the members of the community generally, who are all liable to suffer seriously from the consequences of ignorance and want of education in their fellow-citizens. It is therefore an allowable exercise of the powers of government to impose on parents the legal obligation of giving elementary instruction to children. This, however, cannot fairly be done, without taking measures to insure that such instruction shall be always accessible to them, either gratuitously or at a trifling expense.

It may indeed be objected that the education of children is one of those expenses which parents, even of the laboring class, ought to defray; that it is desirable that they should feel it incumbent on them to provide by their own means for the fulfillment of their duties, and that by giving education at the cost of others, just as much by giving subsistence, the standard of necessary wages is proportionally lowered, and the springs of exertion and self-restraint is so much relaxed. This argument could, at best, be only valid if the question were that of substituting a public provision for what individuals would otherwise do for themselves; if all parents in the laboring class recognized and practiced the duty of giving instruction to their children at their own expense. But inasmuch as parents do not practice this duty, and do not include education among those necessary expenses which their wages must provide for, therefore the general rate of wages is not high enough to bear those expenses, and they must be borne from some other source. And this is not one of the cases in which the tender of help perpetuates the state of things which renders help necessary. Instruction, when it is really such, does not enervate, but strengthens as well as enlarges the active faculties: in whatever manner acquired, its effect on the mind is favorable to the spirit of independence: and when, unless had gratuitously, it would not be had at all, help in this form has the opposite tendency to that which in so many other cases makes it objectionable; it is help towards doing without help....

One thing must be strenuously insisted on; that the government must claim no monopoly for its education, either in the lower or in the higher branches; must exert neither authority nor influence to induce the people to resort to its teachers in preference to others, and must confer no peculiar advantages on those who have been instructed by them.... It would be justified in requiring from all the people that they shall possess instruction in certain things, but not in prescribing to them how or from whom they shall obtain it.

9. In the matter of education, the intervention of government is justifiable, because the case is not one in which the interest and judgment of the consumer are a sufficient security for the goodness of the commodity. Let us now consider another class of cases, where there is no person in the situation of a consumer, and where the interest and judgment to be relied on are those of the agent himself; as in the conduct of any business in which he is exclusively interested, or in entering into any contract or engagement by which he himself is to be bound.

The ground of the practical principle of non-interference must here be, that most persons take a juster and more intelligent view of their own interest, and of the means of promoting it, than can either be prescribed to them by a general enactment of the legislature, or pointed out in the particular case by a public functionary. The maxim is unquestionably sound as a general rule; but there is no difficulty in perceiving some very large and conspicuous exceptions to it. These may be classed under several heads.

First: The individual who is presumed to be the best judge of his own interests may be incapable of judging or acting for himself; may be a lunatic, an idiot, an infant: or though not wholly incapable, may be of immature years and judgment. In this case the foundation of the *laisser-faire* principle breaks down entirely. The person most interested is not the best judge of the matter, nor a competent judge at all. Insane persons are everywhere regarded as proper objects of the care of the state. In the case of children and young persons, it is common to say, that though they cannot judge for themselves, they have their parents or other relatives to judge for them. But this removes the question into a different category; making it no longer a question whether the government should interfere with individuals in the direction of their own conduct and interests, but whether it should leave absolutely in their power the conduct and interests of somebody else.

Parental power is as susceptible of abuse as any other power, and is, as a matter of fact, constantly abused. If laws do not succeed in preventing parents from brutally ill-treating, and even from murdering their children, far less ought it to be presumed that the interests of children will never be sacrificed, in more commonplace and less revolting ways, to the selfishness or the ignorance of their parents. Whatever it can be clearly seen that parents ought to do or forbear for the interest of children, the law is warranted, if it is able, in compelling to be done or forborne, and is generally bound to do so. To take an example from the peculiar province of political economy; it is right that children, and young persons not yet arrived at maturity, should be protected so far as the eye and hand of the state can reach, from being over-worked. Laboring for too many hours in the day, or on work beyond their strength, should not be permitted to them, for if permitted it may always be compelled. Freedom of contract, in the case of children, is but another word for freedom of coercion. Education also, the best which circumstances admit of their receiving, is not a thing which parents or relatives, from indifference, jealousy, or avarice, should have it in their power to withhold.

The reasons for legal intervention in favor of children, apply not less strongly to the case of those unfortunate slaves and victims of the most brutal part of mankind, the lower animals. It is by the grossest misunderstanding of the principles of liberty, that the infliction of exemplary punishment on ruffianism practiced towards these defenseless creatures has been treated as a meddling by government with things beyond its province; an interference with domestic life. The domestic life of domestic tyrants is one of the things which it is the most imperative on the law to interfere with; and it is to be regretted that metaphysical scruples respecting the nature and source of the authority of government, should induce many warm supporters of laws against cruelty to animals, to seek for a justification of such laws in the incidental consequences of the indulgence of ferocious habits to the interests of human beings, rather than in the intrinsic merits of the case itself. What it would be the duty of a human being, possessed of the requisite physical strength, to prevent by force if attempted in his presence, it cannot be less incumbent on society generally to repress. The existing laws of England on the subject are chiefly defective in the trifling, often almost nominal, maximum, to which the penalty even in the worst cases is limited.

Among those members of the community whose freedom of contract ought to be controlled by the legislature for their own protection, on account (it is said) of their dependent position, it is frequently proposed to include women: and in the existing Factory Acts, their labor, in common with that of young persons, has been placed under peculiar restrictions. But the classing together, for this and other purposes, of women and children, appears to me both indefensible in principle and mischievous in practice.

Children below a certain age *cannot* judge or act for themselves; up to a considerably greater age they are inevitably more or less disqualified for doing so; but women are as capable as men of appreciating and managing their own concerns, and the only hindrance to their doing so arises from the injustice of their present social position. When the law makes everything which the wife acquires, the property of the husband, while by compelling her to live with him it forces her to submit to almost any amount of moral and even physical tyranny which he may choose to inflict, there is some ground for regarding every act done by her as done under coercion: but it is the great error of reformers and philanthropists in our time, to nibble at the consequences of unjust power, instead of redressing the injustice itself. If women had as absolute a control as men have, over their own persons and their own patrimony or acquisitions, there would be no plea for limiting their hours of laboring for themselves, in order that they might have time to labor for the husband, in what is called, by the advocates of restriction, *his* home. Women employed in factories are the only women in the laboring rank of life whose position is not that of slaves and drudges; precisely because they cannot easily be compelled to work and earn wages in factories against their will. For improving the condition of women, it should, in the contrary, be an object to give them the readiest access to independent industrial employment, instead of closing, either entirely or partially, that which is already open to them.

10. A second exception to the doctrine that individuals are the best judges of their own interest, is when an individual attempts to decide irrevocably now, what will be best for his interest at some future and distant time. The presumption in favor of individual judgment is only legitimate, where the judgment is grounded on actual, and especially on present, personal experience; not where it is formed antecedently to experience, and not suffered to be reversed even after experience has condemned it. When persons have bound themselves by a contract, not simply to do some one thing, but to continue doing something for ever or for a prolonged period, without any power of revoking the engagement, the presumption which their perseverance in that course of conduct would otherwise raise in favor of its being advantageous to them, does not exist; and any such presumption which can be grounded on their having voluntarily entered into the contract, perhaps at an early age, and without any real knowledge of what they undertook, is commonly next to null.

The practical maxim of leaving contracts free is not applicable without great limitations in case of engagement in perpetuity; and the law should be extremely jealous of such engagements; should refuse its sanction to them, when the obligations they impose are such as the contracting party cannot be a competent judge of; if it ever does sanction them, it should take every possible security for their being contracted with foresight and deliberation; and in compensation for not permitting the parties themselves to revoke their engagement, should grant them a release from it, on a sufficient case being made out before an impartial authority. These considerations are eminently applicable to marriage, the most important of all cases of engagement for life.

11. The third exception which I shall notice, to the doctrine that government cannot manage the affairs of individuals as well as the individuals themselves, has reference to the great class of cases in which the individuals can only manage the concern by delegated agency, and in which the so-called private management is, in point of fact, hardly better entitled to be called management by the persons interested, than administration by a public officer. Whatever, if left to spontaneous agency, can only be done by joint-stock associations, will often be as well, and sometimes better done, as far as the actual work is concerned, by the state....

For these reasons, most things which are likely to be even tolerably done by voluntary associations, should, generally speaking, be left to them; it does not follow that the manner in which those associations perform their work should be entirely uncontrolled by the government. There are many cases in which the agency, of whatever nature, by which a service is performed, is certain, from the nature of the case, to be virtually single; in which a practical monopoly, with all the power it confers of taxing the community, cannot be prevented from existing. I have already more than once adverted to the case of the gas and water companies, among which, though perfect freedom is allowed to competition, none really takes place, and practically they are found to be even more irresponsible, and unapproachable by individual complaints, than the government....

But in the many analogous cases which it is best to resign to voluntary agency, the community needs some other security for the fit performance of the service than the interest of the managers; and it is the part of the government, either to subject the business to reasonable conditions for the general advantage, or to retain such power over it, that the profits of the monopoly may at least be obtained for the public. This applies to the case of a road, a canal, or a railway. These are always, in a great degree, practical monopolies; and a government which concedes such monopoly unreservedly to a private company, does much the same thing as if it allowed an individual or an association to levy any tax they chose, for their own benefit, on all the malt produced in the country, or on all the cotton imported into it. To make the concession for a limited time is generally justifiable, on the principle which justifies patents for invention: but the state should either reserve to itself a reversionary property in such public works, or should retain, and freely exercise, the right of fixing a maximum of fares and charges, and, from time to time, varying that maximum. It is perhaps necessary to remark, that the state may be the proprietor of canals or railways without itself working them; and that they will almost always be better worked by means of a company renting the railway or canal for a limited period from the state.

12. To a fourth case of exception I must request particular attention, it being one to which as it appears to me, the attention of political economists has not yet been sufficiently drawn. There are matters in which the interference of law is required, not to overrule the judgment of individuals respecting their own

interest, but to give effect to that judgment: they being unable to give effect to it except by concert, which concert again cannot be effectual unless it receives validity and sanction from the law. For illustration, and without prejudging the particular point, I may advert to the question of diminishing the hours of labor. Let us suppose, what is at least supposable, whether it be the fact or not—that a general reduction of the hours of factory labor, say from ten to nine, would be for the advantage of the workpeople: that they would receive as high wages, or nearly as high, for nine hours' labor as they receive for ten. If this would be the result, and if the operatives generally are convinced that it would, the limitation, some may say, will be adopted spontaneously. I answer, that it will not be adopted unless the body of operatives bind themselves to one another to abide by it. A workman who refused to work more than nine hours while there were others who worked ten, would either not be employed at all, or if employed, must submit to lose one-tenth of his wages. However convinced, therefore, he may be that it is the interest of the class to work short time, it is contrary to his own interest to set the example, unless he is well assured that all or most others will follow it....

The principle that each is the best judge of his own interest, understood as these objectors understand it, would prove that governments ought not to fulfill any of their acknowledged duties—ought not, in fact, to exist at all. It is greatly the interest of the community, collectively and individually, not to rob or defraud one another. But there is not the less necessity for laws to punish robbery and fraud; because, though it is the interest of each that nobody should rob or cheat, it is not any one's interest to refrain from robbing and cheating others when all others are permitted to rob and cheat him. Penal laws exist at all, chiefly for this reason—because even an unanimous opinion that a certain line of conduct is for the general interest, does not always make it people's individual interest to adhere to that line of conduct.

13. Fifthly; the argument against government interference grounded on the maxim that individuals are the best judges of their own interest, cannot apply to the very large class of cases, in which those acts of individuals with which the government claims to interfere, are not done by those individuals for their own interest, but for the interest of other people. This includes, among other things, the important and much agitated subject of public charity. Though individuals should, in general, be left to do for themselves whatever it can reasonably be expected that they should be capable of doing, yet when they are at any rate not to be left to themselves, but to be helped by other people, the question arises whether it is better that they should receive this help exclusively from individuals, and therefore uncertainly and casually, or by systematic arrangements, in which society acts through its organ, the state....

In all cases of helping, there are two sets of consequences to be considered; the consequences of the assistance itself, and the consequences of relying on the assistance. The former are generally beneficial, but the latter, for the most part, injurious; so much so, in many cases, as greatly to outweigh the value of the benefit. And this is never more likely to happen than in the very cases where the need of help is the most intense. There are few things for which it is more mischievous that people should rely on the habitual aid of others, than for the means of subsistence, and unhappily there is no lesson which they more easily learn. The problem to be solved is therefore one of peculiar nicety as well as importance; how to give the greatest amount of needful help, with the smallest encouragement to undue reliance on it.

Energy and self-dependence are, however, liable to be impaired by the absence of help, as well as by its excess. It is even more fatal to exertion to have no hope of succeeding by it, than to be assured of succeeding without it. When the condition of any one is so disastrous that his energies are paralyzed by discouragement, assistance is a tonic, not a sedative: it braces instead of deadening the active faculties: always provided that the assistance is not such as to dispense with self-help, by substituting itself for the person's own labor, skill, and prudence, but is limited to affording him a better hope of attaining success by those legitimate means. This accordingly is a test to which all plans of philanthropy and benevolence should be brought, whether intended for the benefit of individuals or of classes, and whether conducted on the voluntary or on the government principle....

But if, consistently with guaranteeing all persons against absolute want, the condition of those who are supported by legal charity can be kept considerably less desirable than the condition of those who find support for themselves, none but beneficial consequences can arise from a law which renders it impossible for any person, except by his own choice, to die from insufficiency of food. That in England at least this supposition can be realized, is proved by the experience of a long period preceding the close of the last century, as well as by that of many highly pauperized districts in more recent times, which have been dispauperized by adopting strict rules of poor-law administration, to the great and permanent benefit of the whole laboring class. There is probably no country in which, by varying the means suitably to the character of the people, a legal provision for the destitute might not be made compatible with the observance of the conditions necessary to its being innocuous.

Subject to these conditions, I conceive it to be highly desirable, that the certainty of subsistence should be held out by law to the destitute able-bodied, rather than that their relief should depend on voluntary charity. In the first place, charity almost always does too much or too little: it lavishes its bounty in one place, and leaves people to starve in another. Secondly, since the state must necessarily provide subsistence for the criminal poor while undergoing punishment, not to do the same for the poor who have not offended is to give a premium on crime. And lastly, if the poor are left to individual charity, a vast amount of mendacity is inevitable. What the state may and should abandon to private charity, is the task of distinguishing between one case of real necessity and another. Private charity can give more to the more deserving. The state must act by general rules. It cannot undertake to discriminate between the deserving and the undeserving indigent. It owes no more than subsistence to the first, and can give no less to the last. What is said about the injustice of a law which has no better treatment for the merely unfortunate poor than for the ill-conducted, is founded on a misconception of the province of law and public authority. The dispensers of public relief have no business to be inquisitors....

15. It is a proper office of government to build and maintain lighthouses, establish buoys, &c. for the security of navigation: for since it is impossible that the ships at sea which are benefited by a lighthouse, should be made to pay a toll on the occasion of its use, no one would build lighthouses from motives of personal interest, unless indemnified and rewarded from a compulsory levy made by the state. There are many scientific researches, of great value to a nation and to mankind, requiring assiduous devotion of time and labor, and not infrequently great expense, by persons who can obtain a high price for their services in other ways. If the government had no power to grant indemnity for expense, and remuneration for time and labor thus employed, such researches could only be undertaken by the very few persons who, with an independent fortune, unite technical knowledge, laborious habits, and either great public spirit, or an ardent desire of scientific celebrity.

Connected with this subject is the question of providing by means of endowments or salaries, for the maintenance of what has been called a learned class. The cultivation of speculative knowledge, though one of the most useful of all employments, is a service rendered to a community collectively, not individually, and one consequently for which it is, *primâ facie*, reasonable that the community collectively should pay; since it gives no claim on any individual for a pecuniary remuneration; and unless a provision is made for such services from some public fund, there is not only no encouragement to them, but there is as much discouragement as is implied in the impossibility of gaining a living by such pursuits, and the necessity consequently imposed on most of those who would be capable of them, to employ the greatest part of their time in gaining a subsistence. The evil, however, is greater in appearance than in reality. The greatest things, it has been said, have generally been done by those who had the least time at their disposal; and the occupation of some hours every day in a routine employment, has often been found compatible with the most brilliant achievements in literature and philosophy. Yet there are investigations and experiments which require not only a long but a continuous devotion of time and attention: there are also occupations which so engross and fatigue the mental faculties, as to be inconsistent with any vigorous employment of them upon other subjects, even in any intervals of leisure. It is highly desirable, therefore, that there should be a mode of insuring to the public the services of scientific discoverers, and perhaps of some other classes of savants, by affording them the means of support consistently with devoting a sufficient portion of time to their peculiar pursuits....

16. The preceding heads comprise, to the best of my judgment, the whole of the exceptions to the practical maxim, that the business of society can be

best performed by private and voluntary agency. It is, however, necessary to add, that the intervention of government cannot always practically stop short at the limit which defines the cases intrinsically suitable for it. In the particular circumstances of a given age or nation, there is scarcely anything really important to the general interest, which it may not be desirable, or even necessary, that the government should take upon itself, not because private individuals cannot effectually perform it, but because they will not. At some times and places there will be no roads, docks, harbors, canals, works of irrigation, hospitals, schools, colleges, printing-presses, unless the government establishes them; the public being either too poor to command the necessary resources, or too little advanced in intelligence to appreciate the ends, or not sufficiently practiced in joint action to be capable of the means. This is true, more or less, of all countries inured to despotism, and particularly of those in which there is a very wide distance in civilization between the people and the government: as in those which have been conquered and are retained in subjection by a more energetic and more cultivated people.

In many parts of the world, the people can do nothing for themselves which requires large means and combined action: all such things are left undone, unless done by the state. In these cases, the mode in which the government can most surely demonstrate the sincerity with which it intends the greatest good of its subjects, is by doing the things which are made incumbent on it by the helplessness of the public, in such a manner as shall tend not to increase and perpetuate, but to correct that helplessness. A good government will give all its aid in such a shape as to encourage and nurture any rudiments it may find of a spirit of individual exertion. It will be assiduous in removing obstacles and discouragements to voluntary enterprise, and in giving whatever facilities and whatever direction and guidance may be necessary: its pecuniary means will be applied, when practicable, in aid of private efforts rather than in supersession of them, and it will call into play its machinery of rewards and honors to elicit such efforts. Government aid, when given merely in default of private enterprise, should be so given as to be as far as possible a course of education for the people in the art of accomplishing great objects by individual energy and voluntary co-operation.

John Stuart Mill

On Liberty

Chapter I: Introductory

The subject of this Essay is not the so-called Liberty of the Will, so unfortunately opposed to the misnamed doctrine of Philosophical Necessity; but
Civil, or Social Liberty: the nature and limits of the power which can be legitimately exercised by society over the individual. A question seldom stated, and
hardly ever discussed, in general terms, but which profoundly influences *the
practical controversies of the age* (italics added) by its latent presence, and is likely
soon to make itself recognized as the vital question of the future. It is so far
from being new, that, in a certain sense, it has divided mankind, almost from
the remotest ages; but in the stage of progress into which the more civilized
portions of the species have now entered, it presents itself under new conditions, and requires a different and more fundamental treatment.

The struggle between Liberty and Authority is the most conspicuous feature in the portions of history with which we are earliest familiar, particularly
in that of Greece, Rome, and England. But in old times this contest was
between subjects, or some classes of subjects, and the Government. By liberty,
was meant protection against the tyranny of the political rulers.... The aim,
therefore, of patriots was to set limits to the power which the ruler should be

suffered to exercise over the community; and this limitation was what they meant by liberty.

It was attempted in two ways. First, by obtaining a recognition of certain immunities, called political liberties or rights, which it was to be regarded as a breach of duty in the ruler to infringe, and which, if he did infringe, specific resistance, or general rebellion, was held to be justifiable. A second, and generally a later expedient, was the establishment of constitutional checks, by which the consent of the community, or of a body of some sort, supposed to represent its interests, was made a necessary condition to some of the more important acts of the governing power....

But, in political and philosophical theories, as well as in persons, success discloses faults and infirmities which failure might have concealed from observation. The notion, that the people have no need to limit their power over themselves, might seem axiomatic, when popular government was a thing only dreamed about, or read of as having existed at some distant period of the past. Neither was that notion necessarily disturbed by such temporary aberrations as those of the French Revolution, the worst of which were the work of an usurping few, and which, in any case, belonged, not to the permanent working of popular institutions, but to a sudden and convulsive outbreak against monarchical and aristocratic despotism.

In time, however, a democratic republic came to occupy a large portion of the earth's surface, and made itself felt as one of the most powerful members of the community of nations; and elective and responsible government became subject to the observations and criticisms which wait upon a great existing fact. It was now perceived that such phrases as "self-government," and "the power of the people over themselves," do not express the true state of the case. The "people" who exercise the power are not always the same people with those over whom it is exercised; and the "self-government" spoken of is not the government of each by himself, but of each by all the rest. The will of the people, moreover, practically means the will of the most numerous or the most active part of the people; the majority, or those who succeed in making themselves accepted as the majority; the people, consequently, may desire to oppress a part of their number; and precautions are as much needed against this as against any other abuse of power. The limitation, therefore, of the power of government over individuals loses none of its importance when the holders of power are regularly accountable to the community, that is, to the strongest party therein. This view of things, recommending itself equally to the intelligence of thinkers and to the inclination of those important classes in European society to whose real or supposed interests democracy is adverse, has had no difficulty in establishing itself; and in political speculations "the tyranny of the majority" is now generally included among the evils against which society requires to be on its guard.

Like other tyrannies, the tyranny of the majority was at first, and is still vulgarly, held in dread, chiefly as operating through the acts of the public authorities. But reflecting persons perceived that when society is itself the tyrant—society collectively, over the separate individuals who compose it—its means of tyrannizing are not restricted to the acts which it may do by the hands of its political functionaries. Society can and does execute its own mandates: and if it issues wrong mandates instead of right, or any mandates at all in things with which it ought not to meddle, it practices a social tyranny more formidable than many kinds of political oppression, since, though not usually upheld by such extreme penalties, it leaves fewer means of escape, penetrating much more deeply into the details of life, and enslaving the soul itself. Protection, therefore, against the tyranny of the magistrate is not enough: there needs protection also against the tyranny of the prevailing opinion and feeling; against the tendency of society to impose, by other means than civil penalties, its own ideas and practices as rules of conduct on those who dissent from them; to fetter the development, and, if possible, prevent the formation, of any individuality not in harmony with its ways, and compel all characters to fashion themselves upon the model of its own. There is a limit to the legitimate interference of collective opinion with individual independence: and to find that limit, and maintain it against encroachment, is as indispensable to a good condition of human affairs, as protection against political despotism.

But though this proposition is not likely to be contested in general terms, the practical question, where to place the limit—how to make the fitting adjustment between individual independence and social control—is a subject on which nearly everything remains to be done. All that makes existence valuable to any one, depends on the enforcement of restraints upon the actions of other people. Some rules of conduct, therefore, must be imposed, by law in the first place, and by opinion on many things which are not fit subjects for the operation of law. What these rules should be, is the principal question in human affairs; but if we except a few of the most obvious cases, it is one of those which least progress has been made in resolving. No two ages, and scarcely any two countries, have decided it alike; and the decision of one age or country is a wonder to another. Yet the people of any given age and country no more suspect any difficulty in it, than if it were a subject on which mankind had always been agreed. The rules which obtain among themselves appear to them self-evident and self-justifying. This all but universal illusion is one of the examples of the magical influence of custom, which is not only, as the proverb says, a second nature, but is continually mistaken for the first.

The effect of custom, in preventing any misgiving respecting the rules of conduct which mankind impose on one another, is all the more complete because the subject is one on which it is not generally considered necessary that reasons should be given, either by one person to others, or by each to himself. People are accustomed to believe, and have been encouraged in the belief by some who aspire to the character of philosophers, that their feelings, on subjects of this nature, are better than reasons, and render reasons unnecessary. The practical principle which guides them to their opinions on the regulation of human conduct, is the feeling in each person's mind that everybody should be required to act as he, and those with whom he sympathizes, would like them to act. No one, indeed, acknowledges to himself that his standard of judgment is his own liking; but an opinion on a point of conduct, not supported by reasons, can only count as one person's preference; and if the reasons, when given, are a mere appeal to a similar preference felt by other people, it is still only many people's liking instead of one....

The likings and dislikings of society, or of some powerful portion of it, are thus the main thing which has practically determined the rules laid down for general observance, under the penalties of law or opinion. And in general, those who have been in advance of society in thought and feeling, have left this condition of things unassailed in principle, however they may have come into conflict with it in some of its details. They have occupied themselves rather in inquiring what things society ought to like or dislike, than in questioning whether its likings or dislikings should be a law to individuals. They preferred endeavoring to alter the feelings of mankind on the particular points on which they were themselves heretical, rather than make common cause in defense of freedom, with heretics generally. The only case in which the higher ground has been taken on principle and maintained with consistency, by any but an individual here and there, is that of religious belief: a case instructive in many ways, and not least so as forming a most striking instance of the fallibility of what is called the moral sense: for the odium theological, in a sincere bigot, is one of the most unequivocal cases of moral feeling....

The great writers to whom the world owes what religious liberty it possesses, have mostly asserted freedom of conscience as an indefeasible right, and denied absolutely that a human being is accountable to others for his religious belief. Yet so natural to mankind is intolerance in whatever they really care about, that religious freedom has hardly anywhere been practically realized, except where religious indifference, which dislikes to have its peace disturbed by theological quarrels, has added its weight to the scale. In the minds of almost all religious persons, even in the most tolerant countries, the duty of toleration is admitted with tacit reserves. One person will bear with dissent in matters of church government, but not of dogma; another can tolerate everybody, short of a Papist or an Unitarian; another, every one who believes in revealed religion; a few extend their charity a little further, but stop at the belief in a God and in a future state. Wherever the sentiment of the majority is still genuine and intense, it is found to have abated little of its claim to be obeyed....

The object of this Essay is to assert one very simple principle, as entitled to govern absolutely the dealings of society with the individual in the way of compulsion and control, whether the means used be physical force in the form of legal penalties, or the moral coercion of public opinion. That principle is, that the sole end for which mankind are warranted, individually or collectively, in interfering with the liberty of action of any of their number, is self-protection. That the only purpose for which power can be rightfully exercised over any member of a civilized community, against his will, is to prevent harm to others. His own good, either physical or moral, is not a sufficient warrant. He cannot rightfully be compelled to do or forbear because it will be better for him to do so, because it will make him happier, because, in the opinions of others, to do so would be wise, or even right. These are good reasons for remonstrating with him, or reasoning with him, or persuading him, or entreating him, but not for compelling him, or visiting him with any evil in case he do otherwise. To justify that, the conduct from which it is desired to deter him, must be calculated to produce evil to some one else. The only part of the conduct of any one, for which he is amenable to society, is that which concerns others. In the part which merely concerns himself, his independence is, of right, absolute. Over himself, over his own body and mind, the individual is sovereign.

It is, perhaps, hardly necessary to say that this doctrine is meant to apply only to human beings in the maturity of their faculties. We are not speaking of children, or of young persons below the age which the law may fix as that of manhood or womanhood. Those who are still in a state to require being taken care of by others, must be protected against their own actions as well as against external injury. For the same reason, we may leave out of consideration those backward states of society in which the race itself may be considered as in its nonage. The early difficulties in the way of spontaneous progress are so great, that there is seldom any choice of means for overcoming them; and a ruler full of the spirit of improvement is warranted in the use of any expedients that will attain an end, perhaps otherwise unattainable. Despotism is a legitimate mode of government in dealing with barbarians, provided the end be their improvement, and the means justified by actually effecting that end. Liberty, as a principle, has no application to any state of things anterior to the time when mankind have become capable of being improved by free and equal discussion. Until then, there is nothing for them but implicit obedience to an Akbar or a Charlemagne, if they are so fortunate as to find one. But as soon as mankind have attained the capacity of being guided to their own improvement by conviction or persuasion (a period long since reached in all nations with whom we need here concern ourselves), compulsion, either in the direct form or in that of pains and penalties for non-compliance, is no longer admissible as a means to their own good, and justifiable only for the security of others.

It is proper to state that I forego any advantage which could be derived to my argument from the idea of abstract right, as a thing independent of utility. I regard utility as the ultimate appeal on all ethical questions; but it must be utility in the largest sense, grounded on the permanent interests of man as a progressive being. Those interests, I contend, authorize the subjection of individual spontaneity to external control, only in respect to those actions of each, which concern the interest of other people. If any one does an act hurtful to others, there is a *prima facie* case for punishing him, by law, or, where legal penalties are not safely applicable, by general disapprobation. There are also many positive acts for the benefit of others, which he may rightfully be compelled to perform; such as, to give evidence in a court of justice; to bear his fair share in the common defense, or in any other joint work necessary to the interest of the society of which he enjoys the protection; and to perform certain acts of individual beneficence, such as saving a fellow-creature's life, or interposing to protect the defenseless against ill-usage, things which whenever it is obviously a man's duty to do, he may rightfully be made responsible to society for not doing. A person may cause evil to others not only by his actions but by his inaction, and in either case he is justly accountable to them for the injury. The latter case, it is true, requires a much more cautious exercise of compulsion than the former. To make any one answerable for doing evil to others, is the rule; to make him answerable for not preventing evil, is, comparatively speaking, the exception....

But there is a sphere of action in which society, as distinguished from the individual, has, if any, only an indirect interest; comprehending all that portion of a person's life and conduct which affects only himself, or if it also affects others, only with their free, voluntary, and undeceived consent and participation. When I say only himself, I mean directly, and in the first instance: for whatever affects himself, may affect others through himself; and the objection which may be grounded on this contingency, will receive consideration in the sequel.

This, then, is the appropriate region of human liberty. It comprises, first, the inward domain of consciousness; demanding liberty of conscience, in the most comprehensive sense; liberty of thought and feeling; absolute freedom of opinion and sentiment on all subjects, practical or speculative, scientific, moral, or theological. The liberty of expressing and publishing opinions may seem to fall under a different principle, since it belongs to that part of the conduct of an individual which concerns other people; but, being almost of as much importance as the liberty of thought itself, and resting in great part on the same reasons, is practically inseparable from it. Secondly, the principle requires liberty of tastes and pursuits; of framing the plan of our life to suit our own character; of doing as we like, subject to such consequences as may follow: without impediment from our fellow-creatures, so long as what we do does not harm them, even though they should think our conduct foolish, perverse, or wrong. Thirdly, from this liberty of each individual, follows the liberty, within the same limits, of combination among individuals; freedom to unite, for any purpose not involving harm to others: the persons combining being supposed to be of full age, and not forced or deceived.

No society in which these liberties are not, on the whole, respected, is free, whatever may be its form of government; and none is completely free in which they do not exist absolute and unqualified. The only freedom which deserves the name, is that of pursuing our own good in our own way, so long as we do not attempt to deprive others of theirs, or impede their efforts to obtain it. Each is the proper guardian of his own health, whether bodily, or mental and spiritual.

Mankind are greater gainers by suffering each other to live as seems good to themselves, than by compelling each to live as seems good to the rest....

It will be convenient for the argument, if, instead of at once entering upon the general thesis, we confine ourselves in the first instance to a single branch of it, on which the principle here stated is, if not fully, yet to a certain point, recognized by the current opinions. This one branch is the Liberty of Thought: from which it is impossible to separate the cognate liberty of speaking and of writing....

Chapter II: Of The Liberty Of Thought And Discussion

The time, it is to be hoped, is gone by, when any defense would be necessary of the "liberty of the press" as one of the securities against corrupt or tyrannical government. No argument, we may suppose, can now be needed, against permitting a legislature or an executive, not identified in interest with the people, to prescribe opinions to them, and determine what doctrines or what arguments they shall be allowed to hear. This aspect of the question, besides, has been so often and so triumphantly enforced by preceding writers, that it needs not be specially insisted on in this place. Though the law of England, on the subject of the press, is as servile to this day as it was in the time of the Tudors, there is little danger of its being actually put in force against political discussion, except during some temporary panic, when fear of insurrection drives ministers and judges from their propriety;* and, speaking generally, it is not, in constitutional countries, to be apprehended, that the government, whether completely responsible to the people or not, will often attempt to control the expression of opinion, except when in doing so it makes itself the organ of the general intolerance of the public....

If all mankind minus one, were of one opinion, and only one person were of the contrary opinion, mankind would be no more justified in silencing that one person, than he, if he had the power, would be justified in silencing mankind. Were an opinion a personal possession of no value except to the owner; if to be obstructed in the enjoyment of it were simply a private injury, it would make some difference whether the injury was inflicted only on a few persons or on many. But the peculiar evil of silencing the expression of an opinion is, that it is robbing the human race; posterity as well as the existing generation; those who dissent from the opinion, still more than those who hold it. If the

---

*'These words [*Editors' Comment: J. S. Mill's First Footnote*] had scarcely been written, when, as if to give them an emphatic contradiction, occurred the Government Press Prosecutions of 1858....If the arguments of the present chapter are of any validity, there ought to exist the fullest liberty of professing and discussing, as a matter of ethical conviction, any doctrine, however immoral it may be considered."

opinion is right, they are deprived of the opportunity of exchanging error for truth: if wrong, they lose, what is almost as great a benefit, the clearer perception and livelier impression of truth, produced by its collision with error.

It is necessary to consider separately these two hypotheses, each of which has a distinct branch of the argument corresponding to it. We can never be sure that the opinion we are endeavoring to stifle is a false opinion; and if we were sure, stifling it would be an evil still.

First: the opinion which it is attempted to suppress by authority may possibly be true. Those who desire to suppress it, of course deny its truth; but they are not infallible. They have no authority to decide the question for all mankind, and exclude every other person from the means of judging. To refuse a hearing to an opinion, because they are sure that it is false, is to assume that their certainty is the same thing as absolute certainty. All silencing of discussion is an assumption of infallibility. Its condemnation may be allowed to rest on this common argument, not the worse for being common....

But I must be permitted to observe, that it is not the feeling sure of a doctrine (be it what it may) which I call an assumption of infallibility. It is the undertaking to decide that question for others, without allowing them to hear what can be said on the contrary side. And I denounce and reprobate this pretension not the less, if put forth on the side of my most solemn convictions. However positive any one's persuasion may be, not only of the falsity but of the pernicious consequences—not only of the pernicious consequences, but (to adopt expressions which I altogether condemn) the immorality and impiety of an opinion; yet if, in pursuance of that private judgment, though backed by the public judgment of his country or his cotemporaries, he prevents the opinion from being heard in its defense, he assumes infallibility. And so far from the assumption being less objectionable or less dangerous because the opinion is called immoral or impious, this is the case of all others in which it is most fatal. These are exactly the occasions on which the men of one generation commit those dreadful mistakes, which excite the astonishment and horror of posterity. It is among such that we find the instances memorable in history, when the arm of the law has been employed to root out the best men and the noblest doctrines; with deplorable success as to the men, though some of the doctrines have survived to be (as if in mockery) invoked, in defense of similar conduct towards those who dissent from them, or from their received interpretation....

Let us now pass to the second division of the argument, and dismissing the supposition that any of the received opinions may be false, let us assume them to be true, and examine into the worth of the manner in which they are likely to be held, when their truth is not freely and openly canvassed. However unwillingly a person who has a strong opinion may admit the possibility that his opinion may be false, he ought to be moved by the consideration that however true it may be, if it is not fully, frequently, and fearlessly discussed, it will be held as a dead dogma, not a living truth....

It still remains to speak of one of the principal causes which make diversity of opinion advantageous, and will continue to do so until mankind shall have entered a stage of intellectual advancement which at present seems at an incalculable distance. We have hitherto considered only two possibilities: that the received opinion may be false, and some other opinion, consequently, true; or that, the received opinion being true, a conflict with the opposite error is essential to a clear apprehension and deep feeling of its truth.

But there is a commoner case than either of these; when the conflicting doctrines, instead of being one true and the other false, share the truth between them; and the nonconforming opinion is needed to supply the remainder of the truth, of which the received doctrine embodies only a part. Popular opinions, on subjects not palpable to sense, are often true, but seldom or never the whole truth. They are a part of the truth; sometimes a greater, sometimes a smaller part, but exaggerated, distorted, and disjoined from the truths by which they ought to be accompanied and limited. Heretical opinions, on the other hand, are generally some of these suppressed and neglected truths, bursting the bonds which kept them down, and either seeking reconciliation with the truth contained in the common opinion, or fronting it as enemies, and setting themselves up, with similar exclusiveness, as the whole truth. The latter case is hitherto the most frequent, as, in the human mind, one-sidedness has always been the rule, and many-sidedness the exception.

Hence, even in revolutions of opinion, one part of the truth usually sets while another rises. Even progress, which ought to super add, for the most part only substitutes, one partial and incomplete truth for another; improvement consisting chiefly in this, that the new fragment of truth is more wanted, more adapted to the needs of the time, than that which it displaces. Such being the partial character of prevailing opinions, even when resting on a true foundation, every opinion which embodies somewhat of the portion of truth which the common opinion omits, ought to be considered precious, with whatever amount of error and confusion that truth may be blended. No sober judge of human affairs will feel bound to be indignant because those who force on our notice truths which we should otherwise have overlooked, overlook some of those which we see. Rather, he will think that so long as popular truth is one-sided, it is more desirable than otherwise that unpopular truth should have one-sided asserters too; such being usually the most energetic, and the most likely to compel reluctant attention to the fragment of wisdom which they proclaim as if it were the whole....

We have now recognized the necessity to the mental well-being of mankind (on which all their other well-being depends) of freedom of opinion, and freedom of the expression of opinion, on four distinct grounds; which we will now briefly recapitulate.

First, if any opinion is compelled to silence, that opinion may, for aught we can certainly know, be true. To deny this is to assume our own infallibility.

Secondly, though the silenced opinion be an error, it may, and very commonly does, contain a portion of truth; and since the general or prevailing opinion on any subject is rarely or never the whole truth, it is only by the collision of adverse opinions that the remainder of the truth has any chance of being supplied.

Thirdly, even if the received opinion be not only true, but the whole truth; unless it is suffered to be, and actually is, vigorously and earnestly contested, it will, by most of those who receive it, be held in the manner of a prejudice, with little comprehension or feeling of its rational grounds.

And not only this, but, fourthly, the meaning of the doctrine itself will be in danger of being lost, or enfeebled, and deprived of its vital effect on the character and conduct: the dogma becoming a mere formal profession, inefficacious for good, but cumbering the ground, and preventing the growth of any real and heartfelt conviction, from reason or personal experience.

Chapter III: On Individuality, as one of the Elements of Well Being

No one pretends that actions should be as free as opinions. On the contrary, even opinions lose their immunity, when the circumstances in which they are expressed are such as to constitute their expression a positive instigation to some mischievous act. An opinion that corn-dealers are starvers of the poor, or that private property is robbery, ought to be unmolested when simply circulated through the press, but may justly incur punishment when delivered orally to an excited mob assembled before the house of a corn-dealer, or when handed about among the same mob in the form of a placard. Acts of whatever kind, which, without justifiable cause, do harm to others, may be, and in the more important cases absolutely require to be, controlled by the unfavorable sentiments, and, when needful, by the active interference of mankind. The liberty of the individual must be thus far limited; he must not make himself a nuisance to other people....

Human nature is not a machine to be built after a model, and set to do exactly the work prescribed for it, but a tree, which requires to grow and develop itself on all sides, according to the tendency of the inward forces which make it a living thing....

In our times, from the highest class of society down to the lowest every one lives as under the eye of a hostile and dreaded censorship. Not only in what concerns others, but in what concerns only themselves, the individual, or the family, do not ask themselves—what do I prefer? Or, what would suit my character and disposition? Or, what would allow the best and highest in me to have fair play, and enable it to grow and thrive? They ask themselves, what is suitable to my position? What is usually done by persons of my station and pecuniary circumstances? Or (worse still) what is usually done by persons of a station and circumstances superior to mine? I do not mean that they choose what is customary, in preference to what suits their own inclination. It does not occur to them to have any inclination, except for what is customary. Thus the mind itself is bowed to the yoke: even in what people do for pleasure, conformity is the first thing thought of; they like in crowds; they exercise choice only among things commonly done: peculiarity of taste, eccentricity of conduct, are shunned equally with crimes: until by dint of not following their own nature, they have no nature to follow: their human capacities are withered and starved: they become incapable of any strong wishes or native pleasures, and are generally without either opinions or feelings of home growth, or properly their own. Now is this, or is it not, the desirable condition of human nature?...

Precisely because the tyranny of opinion is such as to make eccentricity a reproach, it is desirable, in order to break through that tyranny, that people should be eccentric. Eccentricity has always abounded when and where strength of character has abounded; and the amount of eccentricity in a society has generally been proportional to the amount of genius, mental vigor, and moral courage which it contained. That so few now dare to be eccentric, marks the chief danger of the time.

I have said that it is important to give the freest scope possible to uncustomary things, in order that it may in time appear which of these are fit to be converted into customs. But independence of action, and disregard of custom are not solely deserving of encouragement for the chance they afford that better modes of action, and customs more worthy of general adoption, may be struck out; nor is it only persons of decided mental superiority who have a just claim to carry on their lives in their own way. There is no reason that all human existences should be constructed on some one, or some small number of patterns. If a person possesses any tolerable amount of common sense and experience, his own mode of laying out his existence is the best, not because it is the best in itself, but because it is his own mode. Human beings are not like sheep; and even sheep are not indistinguishably alike....

The despotism of custom is everywhere the standing hindrance to human advancement, being in unceasing antagonism to that disposition to aim at something better than customary, which is called, according to circumstances, the spirit of liberty, or that of progress or improvement. The spirit of improvement is not always a spirit of liberty, for it may aim at forcing improvements on an unwilling people; and the spirit of liberty, in so far as it resists such attempts, may ally itself locally and temporarily with the opponents of improvement; but the only unfailing and permanent source of improvement is liberty, since by it there are as many possible independent centers of improvement as there are individuals. The progressive principle, however, in either shape, whether as the love of liberty or of improvement, is antagonistic to the sway of Custom, involving at least emancipation from that yoke; and the contest between the two constitutes the chief interest of the history of mankind....

Chapter IV: Of The Limits To The Authority Of Society Over The Individual

What, then, is the rightful limit to the sovereignty of the individual over himself? Where does the authority of society begin? How much of human life should be assigned to individuality, and how much to society?

Each will receive its proper share, if each has that which more particularly concerns it. To individuality should belong the part of life in which it is chiefly the individual that is interested; to society, the part which chiefly interests society.

Though society is not founded on a contract, and though no good purpose is answered by inventing a contract in order to deduce social obligations from it, every one who receives the protection of society owes a return for the benefit, and the fact of living in society renders it indispensable that each should be bound to observe a certain line of conduct towards the rest. This conduct consists first, in not injuring the interests of one another; or rather certain interests, which, either by express legal provision or by tacit understanding, ought to be considered as rights; and secondly, in each person's bearing his share (to be fixed on some equitable principle) of the labors and sacrifices incurred for defending the society or its members from injury and molestation. These conditions society is justified in enforcing at all costs to those who endeavor to withhold fulfillment. Nor is this all that society may do. The acts of an individual may be hurtful to others, or wanting in due consideration for their welfare, without going the length of violating any of their constituted rights. The offender may then be justly punished by opinion, though not by law. As soon as any part of a person's conduct affects prejudicially the interests of others, society has jurisdiction over it, and the question whether the general welfare will or will not be promoted by interfering with it, becomes open to discussion. But there is no room for entertaining any such question when a person's conduct affects the interests of no persons besides himself, or needs not affect them unless they like (all the persons concerned being of full age, and the ordinary amount of understanding). In all such cases there should be perfect freedom, legal and social, to do the action and stand the consequences.

It would be a great misunderstanding of this doctrine to suppose that it is one of selfish indifference, which pretends that human beings have no business with each other's conduct in life, and that they should not concern themselves about the well-doing or well-being of one another, unless their own interest is involved. Instead of any diminution, there is need of a great increase of disinterested exertion to promote the good of others. But disinterested benevolence can find other instruments to persuade people to their good, than whips and scourges, either of the literal or the metaphorical sort. I am the last person to undervalue the self-regarding virtues; they are only second in importance, if even second, to the social. It is equally the business of education to cultivate both. But even education works by conviction and persuasion as well as by compulsion, and it is by the former only that, when the period of education is past, the self-regarding virtues should be inculcated.

Human beings owe to each other help to distinguish the better from the worse, and encouragement to choose the former and avoid the latter. They should be forever stimulating each other to increased exercise of their higher faculties, and increased direction of their feelings and aims towards wise instead of foolish, elevating instead of degrading, objects and contemplations. But neither one person, nor any number of persons, is warranted in saying to another human creature of ripe years, that he shall not do with his life for his own benefit what he chooses to do with it. He is the person most interested in his own well-being: the interest which any other person, except in cases of strong personal attachment, can have in it, is trifling, compared with that which he himself has; the interest which society has in him individually (except as to his conduct to others) is fractional, and altogether indirect: while, with respect to his own feelings and circumstances, the most ordinary man or woman has means of knowledge immeasurably surpassing those that can be possessed by any one else. The interference of society to overrule his judgment and purposes in what only regards himself, must be grounded on general presumptions; which may be altogether wrong, and even if right, are as likely as not to be misapplied to individual cases, by persons no better acquainted with the circumstances of such cases than those are who look at them merely from without. In this department, therefore, of human affairs, Individuality has its proper field of action....

The distinction here pointed out between the part of a person's life which concerns only himself, and that which concerns others, many persons will refuse to admit. How (it may be asked) can any part of the conduct of a member of society be a matter of indifference to the other members? No person is an entirely isolated being; it is impossible for a person to do anything seriously or permanently hurtful to himself, without mischief reaching at least to his near connections, and often far beyond them. If he injures his property, he does harm to those who directly or indirectly derived support from it, and usually diminishes, by a greater or less amount, the general resources of the community. If he deteriorates his bodily or mental faculties, he not only brings evil upon all who depended on him for any portion of their happiness, but disqualifies himself for rendering the services which he owes to his fellow-creatures generally; perhaps becomes a burthen on their affection or benevolence; and if such conduct were very frequent, hardly any offence that is committed would detract more from the general sum of good. Finally, if by his vices or follies a person does no direct harm to others, he is nevertheless (it may be said) injurious by his example; and ought to be compelled to control himself, for the sake of those whom the sight or knowledge of his conduct might corrupt or mislead.

And even (it will be added) if the consequences of misconduct could be confined to the vicious or thoughtless individual, ought society to abandon to their own guidance those who are manifestly unfit for it? If protection against themselves is confessedly due to children and persons under age, is not society equally bound to afford it to persons of mature years who are equally incapable of self-government? If gambling, or drunkenness, or incontinence, or idleness, or uncleanliness, are as injurious to happiness, and as great a hindrance to improvement, as many or most of the acts prohibited by law, why (it may be asked) should not law, so far as is consistent with practicability and social convenience, endeavor to repress these also? And as a supplement to the unavoidable imperfections of law, ought not opinion at least to organize a powerful police against these vices, and visit rigidly with social penalties those who are known to practice them? There is no question here (it may be said) about restricting individuality, or impeding the trial of new and original experiments in living. The only things it is sought to prevent are things which have been tried and condemned from the beginning of the world until now; things which experience has shown not to be useful or suitable to any person's individuality. There must be some length of time and amount of experience, after which a moral or prudential truth may be regarded as established: and it is merely desired to prevent generation after generation from falling over the same precipice which has been fatal to their predecessors.

I fully admit that the mischief which a person does to himself may seriously affect, both through their sympathies and their interests, those nearly connected with him, and in a minor degree, society at large. When, by conduct of this sort, a person is led to violate a distinct and assignable obligation to any other person or persons, the case is taken out of the self-regarding class, and becomes amenable to moral disapprobation in the proper sense of the term.... Again, in the frequent case of a man who causes grief to his family by addiction to bad habits, he deserves reproach for his unkindness or ingratitude; but so he may for cultivating habits not in themselves vicious, if they are painful to those with whom he passes his life, or who from personal ties are dependent on him for their comfort.

Whoever fails in the consideration generally due to the interests and feelings of others, not being compelled by some more imperative duty, or justified by allowable self-preference, is a subject of moral disapprobation for that failure, but not for the cause of it, nor for the errors, merely personal to himself, which may have remotely led to it. In like manner, when a person disables himself, by conduct purely self-regarding, from the performance of some definite duty incumbent on him to the public, he is guilty of a social offence. No person ought to be punished simply for being drunk; but a soldier or a policeman should be punished for being drunk on duty. Whenever, in short, there is a definite damage, or a definite risk of damage, either to an individual or to the public, the case is taken out of the province of liberty, and placed in that of morality or law....

But the strongest of all the arguments against the interference of the public with purely personal conduct, is that when it does interfere, the odds are that it interferes wrongly, and in the wrong place. On questions of social morality, of duty to others, the opinion of the public, that is, of an overruling majority, though often wrong, is likely to be still oftener right; because on such questions they are only required to judge of their own interests; of the manner in which some mode of conduct, if allowed to be practiced, would affect themselves. But the opinion of a similar majority, imposed as a law on the minority, on questions of self-regarding conduct, is quite as likely to be wrong as right; for in these cases public opinion means, at the best, some people's opinion of what is good or bad for other people; while very often it does not even mean that; the public, with the most perfect indifference, passing over the pleasure or convenience of those whose conduct they censure, and considering only their own preference.

There are many who consider as an injury to themselves any conduct which they have a distaste for, and resent it as an outrage to their feelings; as a religious bigot, when charged with disregarding the religious feelings of others, has been known to retort that they disregard his feelings, by persisting in their abominable worship or creed. But there is no parity between the feeling of a person for his own opinion, and the feeling of another who is offended at his holding it; no more than between the desire of a thief to take a purse, and the desire of the right owner to keep it. And a persons taste is as much his own peculiar concern as his opinion or his purse. It is easy for any one to imagine an ideal public, which leaves the freedom and choice of individuals in all uncertain matters undisturbed, and only requires them to abstain from modes of conduct which universal experience has condemned. But where has there been seen a public which set any such limit to its censorship? or when does the public trouble itself about universal experience? In its interferences with personal conduct it is seldom thinking of anything but the enormity of acting or feeling differently from itself; and this standard of judgment, thinly disguised, is held up to mankind as the dictate of religion and philosophy, by nine-tenths of all moralists and speculative writers. These teach that things are right because they are right; because we feel them to be so. They tell us to search in our own minds and hearts for laws of conduct binding on ourselves and on all others. What can the poor public do but apply these instructions, and make their own personal feelings of good and evil, if they are tolerably unanimous in them, obligatory on all the world?...

As a first instance, consider the antipathies which men cherish on no better grounds than that persons whose religious opinions are different from theirs, do not practice their religious observances, especially their religious abstinences. To cite a rather trivial example, nothing in the creed or practice of Christians does more to envenom the hatred of Mahomedans against them, than the fact of their eating pork. There are few acts which Christians and Europeans regard with more unaffected disgust, than Mussulmans regard this particular mode of satisfying hunger. It is, in the first place, an offence against their religion; but this circumstance by no means explains either the degree or the kind of their repugnance; for wine also is forbidden by their religion, and to partake of it is by all Mussulmans accounted wrong, but not disgusting. Their aversion to the flesh of the "unclean beast" is, on the contrary, of that peculiar character, resembling an instinctive antipathy, which the idea of uncleanness, when once it thoroughly sinks into the feelings, seems always to excite even in those whose personal habits are anything but scrupulously cleanly, and of which the sentiment of religious impurity, so intense in the Hindus, is a remarkable example. Suppose now that in a people, of whom the majority were Mussulmans, that majority should insist upon not permitting pork to be eaten within the limits of the country. This would be nothing new in Mahomedan countries. Would it be a legitimate exercise of the moral authority of public opinion? and if not, why not? The practice is really revolting to such a public. They also sincerely think that it is forbidden and abhorred by the Deity. Neither could the prohibition be censured as religious persecution. It might be religious in its origin, but it would not be persecution for religion, since nobody's religion makes it a duty to eat pork. The only tenable ground of condemnation would be, that with the personal tastes and self-regarding concerns of individuals the public has no business to interfere.

To come somewhat nearer home: the majority of Spaniards consider it a gross impiety, offensive in the highest degree to the Supreme Being, to worship him in any other manner than the Roman Catholic; and no other public worship is lawful on Spanish soil. The people of all Southern Europe look upon a married clergy as not only irreligious, but unchaste, indecent, gross, disgusting. What do Protestants think of these perfectly sincere feelings, and of the attempt to enforce them against non-Catholics? Yet, if mankind are justified in interfering with each other's liberty in things which do not concern the interests of others, on what principle is it possible consistently to exclude these cases? or who can blame people for desiring to suppress what they regard as a scandal in the sight of God and man? No stronger case can be shown for prohibiting anything which is regarded as a personal immorality, than is made out for suppressing these practices in the eyes of those who regard them as impieties; and unless we are willing to adopt the logic of persecutors, and to say that we may persecute others because we are right, and that they must not persecute us because they are wrong, we must beware of admitting a principle of which we should resent as a gross injustice the application to ourselves....

We have only further to suppose a considerable diffusion of Socialist opinions, and it may become infamous in the eyes of the majority to possess more property than some very small amount, or any income not earned by manual labor. Opinions similar in principle to these, already prevail widely among the artisan class, and weigh oppressively on those who are amenable to the opinion chiefly of that class, namely, its own members. It is known that the bad workmen who form the majority of the operatives in many branches of industry, are decidedly of opinion that bad workmen ought to receive the same wages as good, and that no one ought to be allowed, through piecework or otherwise, to earn by superior skill or industry more than others can without it. And they employ a moral police, which occasionally becomes a physical one, to deter skilful workmen from receiving, and employers from giving, a larger remuneration for a more useful service. If the public have any jurisdiction over private concerns, I cannot see that these people are in fault, or that any individual's particular public can be blamed for asserting the same authority over his individual conduct, which the general public asserts over people in general.

But, without dwelling upon supposititious cases, there are, in our own day, gross usurpations upon the liberty of private life actually practiced, and still greater ones threatened with some expectation of success, and opinions propounded which assert an unlimited right in the public not only to prohibit by law everything which it thinks wrong, but in order to get at what it thinks wrong, to prohibit any number of things which it admits to be innocent.

Under the name of preventing intemperance, the people of one English colony, and of nearly half the United States, have been interdicted by law from making any use whatever of fermented drinks, except for medical purposes: for prohibition of their sale is in fact, as it is intended to be, prohibition of their use. And though the impracticability of executing the law has caused its repeal in several of the States which had adopted it, including the one from which it derives its name, an attempt has notwithstanding been commenced, and is prosecuted with considerable zeal by many of the professed philanthropists, to agitate for a similar law in this country…. A theory of "social rights," the like of which probably never before found its way into distinct language: being nothing short of this—that it is the absolute social right of every individual, that every other individual shall act in every respect exactly as he ought; that whosoever fails thereof in the smallest particular, violates my social right, and entitles me to demand from the legislature the removal of the grievance. So monstrous a principle is far more dangerous than any single interference with liberty; there is no violation of liberty which it would not justify; it acknowledges no right to any freedom whatever, except perhaps to that of holding opinions in secret, without ever disclosing them….

Another important example of illegitimate interference with the rightful liberty of the individual, not simply threatened, but long since carried into triumphant effect, is Sabbatarian legislation. Without doubt, abstinence on one day in the week, so far as the exigencies of life permit, from the usual daily occupation, though in no respect religiously binding on any except Jews, is a highly beneficial custom. And inasmuch as this custom cannot be observed without a general consent to that effect among the industrious classes, therefore, in so far as some persons by working may impose the same necessity on others, it may be allowable and right that the law should guarantee to each the observance by others of the custom, by suspending the greater operations of industry on a particular day. But this justification, grounded on the direct interest which others have in each individual's observance of the practice, does not apply to the self-chosen occupations in which a person may think fit to employ his leisure; nor does it hold good, in the smallest degree, for legal restrictions on amusements. It is true that the amusement of some is the day's work of others; but the pleasure, not to say the useful recreation, of many, is worth the labor of a few, provided the occupation is freely chosen, and can be freely resigned....

I cannot refrain from adding to these examples of the little account commonly made of human liberty, the language of downright persecution which breaks out from the press of this country, whenever it feels called on to notice the remarkable phenomenon of Mormonism. Much might be said on the unexpected and instructive fact, that an alleged new revelation, and a religion founded on it, the product of palpable imposture, not even supported by the prestige of extraordinary qualities in its founder, is believed by hundreds of thousands, and has been made the foundation of a society, in the age of newspapers, railways, and the electric telegraph. What here concerns us is, that this religion, like other and better religions, has its martyrs; that its prophet and founder was, for his teaching, put to death by a mob; that others of its adherents lost their lives by the same lawless violence; that they were forcibly expelled, in a body, from the country in which they first grew up; while, now that they have been chased into a solitary recess in the midst of a desert, many in this country openly declare that it would be right (only that it is not convenient) to send an expedition against them, and compel them by force to conform to the opinions of other people. The article of the Mormonite doctrine which is the chief provocative to the antipathy which thus breaks through the ordinary restraints of religious tolerance, is its sanction of polygamy; which, though permitted to Mahomedans, and Hindus, and Chinese, seems to excite unquenchable animosity when practiced by persons who speak English, and profess to be a kind of Christians.

No one has a deeper disapprobation than I have of this Mormon institution; both for other reasons, and because, far from being in any way countenanced by the principle of liberty, it is a direct infraction of that principle, being a mere riveting of the chains of one-half of the community, and an emancipation of the other from reciprocity of obligation towards them. Still, it must be remembered that this relation is as much voluntary on the part of the women concerned in it, and who may be deemed the sufferers by it, as is the case with any other form of the marriage institution; and however surprising this fact may appear, it has its explanation in the common ideas and customs of the world, which teaching women to think marriage the one thing needful, make it intelligible that many a woman should prefer being one of several wives, to not being a wife at all. Other countries are not asked to recognize such unions, or release any portion of their inhabitants from their own laws on the score of Mormonite opinions. But when the dissentients have conceded to the hostile sentiments of others, far more than could justly be demanded; when they have left the countries to which their doctrines were unacceptable, and established themselves in a remote corner of the earth, which they have been the first to render habitable to human beings; it is difficult to see on what principles but those of tyranny they can be prevented from living there under what laws they please, provided they commit no aggression on other nations, and allow perfect freedom of departure to those who are dissatisfied with their ways....

Chapter V: Applications

The principles asserted in these pages must be more generally admitted as the basis for discussion of details, before a consistent application of them to all the various departments of government and morals can be attempted with any prospect of advantage. The few observations I propose to make on questions of detail, are designed to illustrate the principles, rather than to follow them out to their consequences. I offer, not so much applications, as specimens of application; which may serve to bring into greater clearness the meaning and limits of the two maxims which together form the entire doctrine of this Essay, and to assist the judgment in holding the balance between them, in the cases where it appears doubtful which of them is applicable to the case.

The maxims are, first, that the individual is not accountable to society for his actions, in so far as these concern the interests of no person but himself. Advice, instruction, persuasion, and avoidance by other people if thought necessary by them for their own good, are the only measures by which society can justifiably express its dislike or disapprobation of his conduct. Secondly, that for such actions as are prejudicial to the interests of others, the individual is accountable, and may be subjected either to social or to legal punishment, if society is of opinion that the one or the other is requisite for its protection.

In the first place, it must by no means be supposed, because damage, or probability of damage, to the interests of others, can alone justify the interference of society, that therefore it always does justify such interference. In many cases, an individual, in pursuing a legitimate object, necessarily and therefore legitimately causes pain or loss to others, or intercepts a good which they had a reasonable hope of obtaining. Such oppositions of interest between individuals often arise from bad social institutions, but are unavoidable while those institutions last; and some would be unavoidable under any institutions. Whoever succeeds in an overcrowded profession, or in a competitive examination; whoever is preferred to another in any contest for an object which both desire, reaps benefit from the loss of others, from their wasted exertion and their disappointment. But it is, by common admission, better for the general interest of mankind, that persons should pursue their objects undeterred by this sort of consequences. In other words, society admits no right, either legal or moral, in the disappointed competitors, to immunity from this kind of suffering; and feels called on to interfere, only when means of success have been employed which it is contrary to the general interest to permit—namely, fraud or treachery, and force.

Again, trade is a social act. Whoever undertakes to sell any description of goods to the public, does what affects the interest of other persons, and of society in general; and thus his conduct, in principle, comes within the jurisdiction of society: accordingly, it was once held to be the duty of governments, in all cases which were considered of importance, to fix prices, and regulate the processes of manufacture. But it is now recognized, though not till after a long struggle, that both the cheapness and the good quality of commodities are most effectually provided for by leaving the producers and sellers perfectly free, under the sole check of equal freedom to the buyers for supplying themselves elsewhere. This is the so-called doctrine of Free Trade, which rests on grounds different from, though equally solid with, the principle of individual liberty asserted in this Essay. Restrictions on trade, or on production for purposes of trade, are indeed restraints; and all restraint, *qua restraint*, is an evil: but the restraints in question affect only that part of conduct which society is competent to restrain, and are wrong solely because they do not really produce the results which it is desired to produce by them....

One of these examples, that of the sale of poisons, opens a new question; the proper limits of what may be called the functions of police; how far liberty may legitimately be invaded for the prevention of crime, or of accident. It is one of the undisputed functions of government to take precautions against crime before it has been committed, as well as to detect and punish it afterwards. The preventive function of government, however, is far more liable to be abused, to the prejudice of liberty, than the punitory function; for there is hardly any part of the legitimate freedom of action of a human being which would not admit of being represented, and fairly too, as increasing the facilities for some form or other of delinquency. Nevertheless, if a public authority, or even a private person, sees any one evidently preparing to commit a crime, they are not bound to look on inactive until the crime is committed, but may interfere to prevent it. If poisons were never bought or used for any purpose except the commission of murder, it would be right to prohibit their manufacture and sale. They may, however, be wanted not only for innocent but for useful purposes, and restrictions cannot be imposed in the one case without operating in the other.

Again, it is a proper office of public authority to guard against accidents. If either a public officer or any one else saw a person attempting to cross a bridge which had been ascertained to be unsafe, and there were no time to warn him of his danger, they might seize him and turn him back, without any real infringement of his liberty; for liberty consists in doing what one desires, and he does not desire to fall into the river. Nevertheless, when there is not a certainty, but only a danger of mischief, no one but the person himself can judge of the sufficiency of the motive which may prompt him to incur the risk: in this case, therefore, (unless he is a child, or delirious, or in some state of excitement or absorption incompatible with the full use of the reflecting faculty) he ought, I conceive, to be only warned of the danger; not forcibly prevented from exposing himself to it.

Similar considerations, applied to such a question as the sale of poisons, may enable us to decide which among the possible modes of regulation are or are not contrary to principle. Such a precaution, for example, as that of labeling the drug with some word expressive of its dangerous character, may be enforced without violation of liberty: the buyer cannot wish not to know that the thing he possesses has poisonous qualities. But to require in all cases the certificate of a medical practitioner, would make it sometimes impossible, always expensive, to obtain the article for legitimate uses....

Again, there are many acts which, being directly injurious only to the agents themselves, ought not to be legally interdicted, but which, if done publicly, are a violation of good manners, and coming thus within the category of offences against others, may rightfully be prohibited. Of this kind are offences against decency; on which it is unnecessary to dwell, the rather as they are only connected indirectly with our subject, the objection to publicity being equally strong in the case of many actions not in themselves condemnable, nor supposed to be so.

There is another question to which an answer must be found, consistent with the principles which have been laid down. In cases of personal conduct supposed to be blamable, but which respect for liberty precludes society from preventing or punishing, because the evil directly resulting falls wholly on the agent; what the agent is free to do, ought other persons to be equally free to counsel or instigate? This question is not free from difficulty. The case of a person who solicits another to do an act, is not strictly a case of self-regarding conduct. To give advice or offer inducements to any one, is a social act, and may, therefore, like actions in general which affect others, be supposed amenable to social control. But a little reflection corrects the first impression, by showing that if the case is not strictly within the definition of individual liberty, yet the reasons on which the principle of individual liberty is grounded, are applicable to it. If people must be allowed, in whatever concerns only themselves, to act as seems best to themselves at their own peril, they must equally be free to consult with one another about what is fit to be so done; to exchange opinions, and give and receive suggestions. Whatever it is permitted to do, it must be permitted to advise to do. The question is doubtful, only when the instigator derives a personal benefit from his advice; when he makes it his occupation, for subsistence or pecuniary gain, to promote what society and the State consider to be an evil. Then, indeed, a new element of complication is introduced; namely, the existence of classes of persons with an interest opposed to what is considered as the public weal, and whose mode of living is grounded on the counteraction of it.

Ought this to be interfered with, or not? Fornication, for example, must be tolerated, and so must gambling; but should a person be free to be a pimp, or to keep a gambling-house? The case is one of those which lie on the exact boundary line between two principles, and it is not at once apparent to which of the two it properly belongs. There are arguments on both sides....

There can surely, it may be urged, be nothing lost, no sacrifice of good, by so ordering matters that persons shall make their election, either wisely or foolishly, on their own prompting, as free as possible from the arts of persons who stimulate their inclinations for interested purposes of their own. Thus (it may be said) though the statutes respecting unlawful games are utterly indefensible—though all persons should be free to gamble in their own or each other's houses, or in any place of meeting established by their own subscriptions, and open only to the members and their visitors—yet public gambling-houses should not be permitted. It is true that the prohibition is never effectual, and that, whatever amount of tyrannical power may be given to the police, gambling-houses can always be maintained under other pretences; but they may be compelled to conduct their operations with a certain degree of secrecy and mystery, so that nobody knows anything about them but those who seek them; and more than this, society ought not to aim at. There is considerable force in these arguments. I will not venture to decide whether they are sufficient to justify the moral anomaly of punishing the accessory, when the principal is (and must be) allowed to go free; of fining or imprisoning the procurer, but not the fornicator, the gambling-house keeper, but not the gambler. Still less ought the common operations of buying and selling to be interfered with on analogous grounds....

A further question is, whether the State, while it permits, should nevertheless indirectly discourage conduct which it deems contrary to the best interests of the agent; whether, for example, it should take measures to render the means of drunkenness more costly, or add to the difficulty of procuring them by limiting the number of the places of sale. On this as on most other practical questions, many distinctions require to be made. To tax stimulants for the sole purpose of making them more difficult to be obtained, is a measure differing only in degree from their entire prohibition; and would be justifiable only if that were justifiable. Every increase of cost is a prohibition, to those whose means do not come up to the augmented price; and to those who do, it is a penalty laid on them for gratifying a particular taste. Their choice of pleasures, and their mode of expending their income, after satisfying their legal and moral obligations to the State and to individuals, are their own concern, and must rest with their own judgment. These considerations may seem at first sight to condemn the selection of stimulants as special subjects of taxation for purposes of revenue. But it must be remembered that taxation for fiscal purposes is absolutely inevitable; that in most countries it is necessary that a considerable part of that taxation should be indirect; that the State, therefore, cannot help imposing penalties, which to some persons may be prohibitory, on the use of some articles of consumption. It is hence the duty of the State to consider, in the imposition of taxes, what commodities the consumers can best spare; and *à fortiori*, to select in preference those of which it deems the use, beyond a very moderate quantity, to be positively injurious. Taxation, therefore, of stimulants, up to the point which produces the largest amount of revenue is not only admissible, but to be approved of....

It was pointed out in an early part of this Essay, that the liberty of the individual, in things wherein the individual is alone concerned, implies a corresponding liberty in any number of individuals to regulate by mutual agreement such things as regard them jointly, and regard no persons but themselves. This question presents no difficulty, so long as the will of all the persons implicated remains unaltered; but since that will may change, it is often necessary, even in things in which they alone are concerned, that they should enter into engagements with one another; and when they do, it is fit, as a general rule, that those engagements should be kept. Yet, in the laws, probably, of every country, this general rule has some exceptions. Not only persons are not held to engagements which violate the rights of third parties, but it is sometimes considered a sufficient reason for releasing them from an engagement, that it is injurious to themselves. In this and most other civilized countries, for example, an engagement by which a person should sell himself, or allow himself to be sold, as a slave, would be null and void; neither enforced by law nor by opinion. The ground for thus limiting his power of voluntarily disposing of his own lot in life, is apparent, and is very clearly seen in this extreme case. The reason for not interfering, unless for the sake of others, with a person's voluntary acts, is consideration for his liberty. His voluntary choice is evidence that what he so chooses is desirable, or at the least endurable, to him, and his good is on the whole best provided for by allowing him to take his own means of pursuing it. But by selling himself for a slave, he abdicates his liberty; he foregoes any future use of it beyond that single act. He therefore defeats, in his own case, the very purpose which is the justification of allowing him to dispose of himself. He is no longer free; but is thenceforth in a position which has no longer the presumption in its favor, that would be afforded by his voluntarily remaining in it. The principle of freedom cannot require that he should be free not to be free. It is not freedom, to be allowed to alienate his freedom....

When a person, either by express promise or by conduct, has encouraged another to rely upon his continuing to act in a certain way—to build expectations and calculations, and stake any part of his plan of life upon that supposition—a new series of moral obligations arises on his part towards that person, which may possibly be overruled, but cannot be ignored. And again, if the relation between two contracting parties has been followed by consequences to others; if it has placed third parties in any peculiar position, or, as in the case of marriage, has even called third parties into existence, obligations arise on the part of both the contracting parties towards those third persons, the fulfillment of which, or at all events the mode of fulfillment, must be greatly affected by the continuance or disruption of the relation between the original parties to the contract. It does not follow, nor can I admit, that these obligations extend to requiring the fulfillment of the contract at all costs to the happiness of the reluctant party; but they are a necessary element in the question; and even if, as Von Humboldt maintains, they ought to make no difference in the legal freedom of the parties to release themselves from the engagement (and I also hold that they ought not to make much difference), they necessarily make a great difference in the moral freedom. A person is bound to take all these circumstances into account, before resolving on a step which may affect such important interests of others; and if he does not allow proper weight to those interests, he is morally responsible for the wrong. I have made these obvious remarks for the better illustration of the general principle of liberty, and not because they are at all needed on the particular question, which, on the contrary, is usually discussed as if the interest of children was everything, and that of grown persons nothing.

I have already observed that, owing to the absence of any recognized general principles, liberty is often granted where it should be withheld, as well as withheld where it should be granted; and one of the cases in which, in the modern European world, the sentiment of liberty is the strongest, is a case where, in my view, it is altogether misplaced. A person should be free to do as he likes in his own concerns; but he ought not to be free to do as he likes in acting for another, under the pretext that the affairs of the other are his own affairs. The State, while it respects the liberty of each in what specially regards himself, is bound to maintain a vigilant control over his exercise of any power which it allows him to possess over others. This obligation is almost entirely disregarded in the case of the family relations, a case, in its direct influence on human happiness, more important than all others taken together.

The almost despotic power of husbands over wives needs not be enlarged upon here, because nothing more is needed for the complete removal of the evil, than that wives should have the same rights, and should receive the protection of law in the same manner, as all other persons; and because, on this subject, the defenders of established injustice do not avail themselves of the plea of liberty, but stand forth openly as the champions of power. It is in the case of children, that misapplied notions of liberty are a real obstacle to the fulfillment by the State of its duties. One would almost think that a man's children were supposed to be literally, and not metaphorically, a part of himself, so jealous is opinion of the smallest interference of law with his absolute and exclusive control over them; more jealous than of almost any interference with his own freedom of action: so much less do the generality of mankind value liberty than power.

Consider, for example, the case of education. Is it not almost a self-evident axiom, that the State should require and compel the education, up to a certain standard, of every human being who is born its citizen? Yet who is there that is not afraid to recognize and assert this truth? Hardly any one indeed will deny that it is one of the most sacred duties of the parents (or, as law and usage now stand, the father), after summoning a human being into the world, to give to that being an education fitting him to perform his part well in life towards others and towards himself. But while this is unanimously declared to be the father's duty, scarcely anybody, in this country, will bear to hear of obliging him to perform it. Instead of his being required to make any exertion or sacrifice for securing education to the child, it is left to his choice to accept it or not when it is provided gratis! It still remains unrecognized, that to bring a child into existence without a fair prospect of being able, not only to provide food for its body, but instruction and training for its mind, is a moral crime, both against the unfortunate offspring and against society; and that if the parent does not fulfill this obligation, the State ought to see it fulfilled, at the charge, as far as possible, of the parent....

All that has been said of the importance of individuality of character, and diversity in opinions and modes of conduct, involves, as of the same unspeakable importance, diversity of education. A general State education is a mere contrivance for molding people to be exactly like one another: and as the mould in which it casts them is that which pleases the predominant power in the government, whether this be a monarch, a priesthood, an aristocracy, or the majority of the existing generation, in proportion as it is efficient and successful, it establishes a despotism over the mind, leading by natural tendency to one over the body. An education established and controlled by the State should only exist, if it exist at all, as one among many competing experiments, carried on for the purpose of example and stimulus, to keep the others up to a certain standard of excellence....

The instrument for enforcing the law could be no other than public examinations, extending to all children, and beginning at an early age. An age might be fixed at which every child must be examined, to ascertain if he (or she) is able to read. If a child proves unable, the father, unless he has some sufficient ground of excuse, might be subjected to a moderate fine, to be worked out, if necessary, by his labor, and the child might be put to school at his expense. Once in every year the examination should be renewed, with a gradually extending range of subjects, so as to make the universal acquisition, and what is more, retention, of a certain minimum of general knowledge, virtually compulsory. Beyond that minimum, there should be voluntary examinations on all subjects, at which all who come up to a certain standard of proficiency might claim a certificate. To prevent the State from exercising, through these arrangements, an improper influence over opinion, the knowledge required for passing an examination (beyond the merely instrumental parts of knowledge, such as languages and their use) should, even in the higher classes of examinations, be confined to facts and positive science exclusively. The examinations on religion, politics, or other disputed topics, should not turn on the truth or falsehood of opinions, but on the matter of fact that such and such an opinion is held, on such grounds, by such authors, or schools, or churches....

It is not in the matter of education only, that misplaced notions of liberty prevent moral obligations on the part of parents from being recognized, and legal obligations from being imposed, where there are the strongest grounds for the former always, and in many cases for the latter also. The fact itself, of causing the existence of a human being, is one of the most responsible actions in the range of human life. To undertake this responsibility—to bestow a life which may be either a curse or a blessing—unless the being on whom it is to be bestowed will have at least the ordinary chances of a desirable existence, is a crime against that being. And in a country either over-peopled or threatened with being so, to produce children, beyond a very small number, with the effect of reducing the reward of labor by their competition, is a serious offence against all who live by the remuneration of their labor....

I have reserved for the last place a large class of questions respecting the limits of government interference, which, though closely connected with the subject of this Essay, do not, in strictness, belong to it. These are cases in which the reasons against interference do not turn upon the principle of liberty: the question is not about restraining the actions of individuals, but about helping them: it is asked whether the government should do, or cause to be done, something for their benefit, instead of leaving it to be done by themselves, individually, or in voluntary combination.

The objections to government interference, when it is not such as to involve infringement of liberty, may be of three kinds.

The first is, when the thing to be done is likely to be better done by individuals than by the government. Speaking generally, there is no one so fit to conduct any business, or to determine how or by whom it shall be conducted, as those who are personally interested in it. This principle condemns the interferences, once so common, of the legislature, or the officers of government, with the ordinary processes of industry. But this part of the subject has been sufficiently enlarged upon by political economists, and is not particularly related to the principles of this Essay.

The second objection is more nearly allied to our subject. In many cases, though individuals may not do the particular thing so well, on the average, as the officers of government, it is nevertheless desirable that it should be done by them, rather than by the government, as a means to their own mental education—a mode of strengthening their active faculties, exercising their judgment, and giving them a familiar knowledge of the subjects with which they are thus left to deal. This is a principal, though not the sole, recommendation of jury trial (in cases not political); of free and popular local and municipal institutions; of the conduct of industrial and philanthropic enterprises by voluntary associations. These are not questions of liberty, and are connected with that subject only by remote tendencies; but they are questions of development....

The third, and most cogent reason for restricting the interference of government, is the great evil of adding unnecessarily to its power. Every function superadded to those already exercised by the government, causes its influence over hopes and fears to be more widely diffused, and converts, more and more, the active and ambitious part of the public into hangers-on of the government, or of some party which aims at becoming the government. If the roads, the railways, the banks, the insurance offices, the great joint-stock companies, the universities, and the public charities, were all of them branches of the government; if, in addition, the municipal corporations and local boards, with all that now devolves on them, became departments of the central administration; if the employees of all these different enterprises were appointed and paid by the government, and looked to the government for every rise in life; not all the freedom of the press and popular constitution of the legislature would make this or any other country free otherwise than in name.

And the evil would be greater, the more efficiently and scientifically the administrative machinery was constructed—the more skilful the arrangements for obtaining the best qualified hands and heads with which to work it. In England it has of late been proposed that all the members of the civil service of government should be selected by competitive examination, to obtain for those employments the most intelligent and instructed persons procurable; and much has been said and written for and against this proposal. One of the arguments most insisted on by its opponents, is that the occupation of a permanent official servant of the State does not hold out sufficient prospects of emolument and importance to attract the highest talents, which will always be able to find a more inviting career in the professions, or in the service of companies and other public bodies. One would not have been surprised if this argument had been used by the friends of the proposition, as an answer to its principal difficulty. Coming from the opponents it is strange enough. What is urged as an objection is the safety-valve of the proposed system.

If indeed all the high talent of the country could be drawn into the service of the government, a proposal tending to bring about that result might well inspire uneasiness. If every part of the business of society which required organized concert, or large and comprehensive views, were in the hands of the government, and if government offices were universally filled by the ablest men, all the enlarged culture and practiced intelligence in the country, except the purely speculative, would be concentrated in a numerous bureaucracy, to whom alone the rest of the community would look for all things: the multitude for direction and dictation in all they had to do; the able and aspiring for personal advancement. To be admitted into the ranks of this bureaucracy, and when admitted, to rise therein, would be the sole objects of ambition. Under this régime, not only is the outside public ill-qualified, for want of practical experience, to criticize or check the mode of operation of the bureaucracy, but even if the accidents of despotic or the natural working of popular institutions occasionally raise to the summit a ruler or rulers of reforming inclinations, no reform can be effected which is contrary to the interest of the bureaucracy....

To determine the point at which evils, so formidable to human freedom and advancement, begin, or rather at which they begin to predominate over the benefits attending the collective application of the force of society, under its recognized chiefs, for the removal of the obstacles which stand in the way of its well-being; to secure as much of the advantages of centralized power and intelligence, as can be had without turning into governmental channels too great a proportion of the general activity—is one of the most difficult and complicated questions in the art of government. It is, in a great measure, a question of detail, in which many and various considerations must be kept in view, and no absolute rule can be laid down. But I believe that the practical principle in which safety resides, the ideal to be kept in view, the standard by which to test all arrangements intended for overcoming the difficulty, may be conveyed in these words: the greatest dissemination of power consistent with efficiency; but the greatest possible centralization of information, and diffusion of it from the center....

John Stuart Mill

The Subjection of Women

Chapter I: The Principle Of Perfect Equality

The object of this Essay is to explain as clearly as I am able the grounds of an opinion which I have held from the very earliest period when I had formed any opinions at all on social or political matters, and which, instead of being weakened or modified, has been constantly growing stronger by the progress reflection and the experience of life. That the principle which regulates the existing social relations between the two sexes—the legal subordination of one sex to the other—is wrong itself, and now one of the chief hindrances to human improvement; and that it ought to be replaced by a principle of perfect equality, admitting no power or privilege on the one side, nor disability on the other.

The very words necessary to express the task I have undertaken, show how arduous it is. But it would be a mistake to suppose that the difficulty of the case must lie in the insufficiency or obscurity of the grounds of reason on which my convictions. The difficulty is that which exists in all cases in which there is a mass of feeling to be contended against. So long as opinion is strongly rooted in the feelings, it gains rather than loses instability by having a preponderating weight of argument against it. For if it were accepted as a result of argument, the refutation of the argument might shake the solidity of the conviction; but when it rests solely on feeling, the worse it fares in argumentative contest, the more persuaded adherents are that their feeling must have some deeper ground, which the arguments do not reach; and while the feeling remains, it is always throwing up fresh entrenchments of argument to repair any breach made in the old. And there are so many causes tending to make the feelings connected with this subject the most intense and most deeply-rooted of those which gather round and protect old institutions and custom, that we need not wonder to find them as yet less undermined and loosened than any of the rest by the progress of the great modern spiritual and social transition; nor suppose that the barbarisms to which men cling longest must be less barbarisms than those which they earlier shake off....

The *a priori* presumption is in favor of freedom and impartiality. It is held that there should be no restraint not required by the general good, and that the law should be no respecter of persons but should treat all alike, save where dissimilarity of treatment is required by positive reasons, either of justice or of policy. But of none of these rules of evidence will the benefit be allowed to those who maintain the opinion I profess. It is useless me to say that those who maintain the doctrine that men have a right to command and women are under an obligation obey, or that men are fit for government and women unfit, on the affirmative side of the question, and that they are bound to show positive evidence for the assertions, or submit to their rejection. It is equally unavailing for me to say that those who deny to women any freedom or privilege rightly allow to men, having the double presumption against them that they are opposing freedom and recommending partiality, must held to the strictest proof of their case, and unless their success be such as to exclude all doubt, the judgment ought to against them. These would be thought good pleas in any common case; but they will not be thought so in this instance. Before I could hope to make any impression, I should be expected not only to answer all that has ever been said by those who take the other side of the question, but to imagine that could be said by them—to find them in reasons, as I as answer all I find: and besides refuting all arguments for the affirmative, I shall be called upon for invincible positive arguments to prove a negative. And even if I could do all and leave the opposite party with a host of unanswered arguments against them, and not a single unrefuted one on side, I should be thought to have done little; for a cause supported on the one hand by universal usage, and on the other by so great a preponderance of popular sentiment, is supposed to have a presumption in its favor, superior to any conviction which an appeal to reason has power to produce in any intellects but those of a high class....

It is one of the characteristic prejudices of the reaction of the nineteenth century against the eighteenth, to accord to the unreasoning elements in human nature the infallibility which the eighteenth century is supposed to have ascribed to the reasoning elements. For the apotheosis of Reason we have substituted that of Instinct; and we call thing instinct which we find in ourselves and for which we cannot trace any rational foundation. This idolatry, infinitely more degrading than the other, and the most pernicious of the false worships of the present day, of all of which it is now the main support, will probably hold its ground until it gives way before a sound psychology laying bare the real root of much that is bowed down to as the intention of Nature and ordinance of God. As regards the present question, I am willing to accept the unfavorable conditions which the prejudice assigns to me. I consent that established custom, and the general feelings, should be deemed conclusive against me, unless that custom and feeling from age to age can be shown to have owed their existence to other causes than their soundness, and to have derived their power from the worse rather than the better parts of human nature. I am willing that judgment should go against me, unless I can show that my judge has been tampered with. The concession is not so great as it might appear; for to prove this, is by far the easiest portion of my task.

The generality of a practice is in some cases a strong presumption that it is, or at all events once was, conducive to laudable ends. This is the case, when the practice was first adopted, or afterwards kept up, as a means to such ends, and was grounded on experience of the mode in which they could be most effectually attained. If the authority of men over women, when first established, had been the result of a conscientious comparison between different modes of constituting the government of society; if, after trying various other modes of social organization—the government of women over men, equality between the two, and such mixed and divided modes of government as might be invented—it had been decided, on the testimony of experience, that the mode in which women are wholly under the rule of men, having no share at all in public concerns, and each in private being under the legal obligation of obedience to the man with whom she has associated her destiny, was the arrangement most conducive to the happiness and well-being of both; its general adoption might then be fairly thought to be some evidence that, at the time when it was adopted, it was the best: though even then the considerations which recommended it may, like so many other primeval social facts of the greatest importance, have subsequently, in the course of ages, ceased to exist. But the state of the case is in every respect the reverse of this.

In the first place, the opinion in favor of the present system, which entirely subordinates the weaker sex to the stronger, rests upon theory only; for there never has been trial made of any other: so that experience, in the sense in which it is vulgarly opposed to theory, cannot be pretended to have pronounced any verdict. And in the second place, the adoption of this system of inequality never was the result of deliberation, or forethought, or any social ideas, or any notion whatever of what conduced to the benefit of humanity or the good order of society. It arose simply from the fact that from the very earliest twilight of human society, every woman (owing to the value attached to her by men, combined with her inferiority in muscular strength) was found in a state of bondage to some man. Laws and systems of polity always begin by recognizing the relations they find already existing between individuals....

In early times, the great majority of the male sex were slaves, as well as the whole of the female. And many ages elapsed, some of them ages of high cultivation, before any thinker was bold enough to question the rightfulness, and the absolute social necessity, either of the one slavery or of the other. By degrees such thinkers did arise; and (the general progress of society assisting) the slavery of the male sex has, in all the countries of Christian Europe at least (though, in one of them, only within the last few years) been at length abolished, and that of the female sex has been gradually changed into a milder form of dependence. But this dependence, as it exists at present, is not an original institution, taking a fresh start from considerations of justice and social expediency—it is the primitive state of slavery lasting on, through successive mitigations and modifications occasioned by the same causes which have softened the general manners, and brought all human relations more under the control of justice and the influence of humanity. It has not lost the taint of its brutal origin. No presumption in its favor, therefore, can be drawn from the fact of its existence. The only such presumption which it could be supposed to have, must be grounded on its having lasted till now, when so many other things which came down from the same odious source have been done away with. And this, indeed, is what makes it strange to ordinary ears, to hear it asserted that the inequality of rights between men and women has no other source than the law of the strongest....

The truth is, that people of the present and the last two or three generations have lost all practical sense of the primitive condition of humanity; and only the few who have studied history accurately, or have much frequented the parts of the world occupied by the living representatives of ages long past, are able to form any mental picture of what society then was. People are not aware how entirely, in former ages, the law of superior strength was the rule of life; how publicly and openly it was avowed, I do not say cynically or shamelessly—for these words imply a feeling that there was something in it to be ashamed of, and no such notion could find a place in the faculties of any person in those ages, except a philosopher or a saint. History gives a cruel experience of human nature, in showing how exactly the regard due to the life, possessions, and entire earthly happiness of any class of persons, was measured by what they had the power of enforcing; how all who made any resistance to authorities that had arms in their hands, however dreadful might be the provocation, had not only the law of force but all other laws, and all the notions of social obligation against them; and in the eyes of those whom they resisted, were not only guilty of crime, but of the worst of all crimes, deserving the most cruel chastisement which human beings could inflict. The first small vestige of a feeling of obligation in a superior to acknowledge any right in inferiors, began when he had been induced, for convenience, to make some promise to them. Though these promises, even when sanctioned by the most solemn oaths, were for many ages revoked or violated on the most trifling provocation or temptation, it is probably that this, except by persons of still worse than the average morality, was seldom done without some twinges of conscience....

If people are mostly so little aware how completely, during the greater part of the duration of our species, the law of force was the avowed rule of general conduct, any other being only a special and exceptional consequence of peculiar ties—and from how very recent a date it is that the affairs of society in general have been even pretended to be regulated according to any moral law; as little do people remember or consider, how institutions and customs which never had any ground but the law of force, last on into ages and states of general opinion which never would have permitted their first establishment. Less than forty years ago, Englishmen might still by law hold human beings in bondage as saleable property: within the present century they might kidnap them and carry them off, and work them literally to death. This absolutely extreme case of the law of force, condemned by those who can tolerate almost every other form of arbitrary power, and which, of all others presents features the most revolting to the feelings of all who look at it from an impartial position, was the law of civilized and Christian England within the memory of persons now living: and in one half of Anglo-Saxon America three or four years ago, not only did slavery exist, but the slave-trade, and the breeding of slaves expressly for it, was a general practice between slave states. Yet not only was there a greater strength of sentiment against it, but, in England at least, a less amount either of feeling or of interest in favor of it, than of any other of the customary abuses of force: for its motive was the love of gain, unmixed and undisguised; and those who profited by it were a very small numerical fraction of the country, while the natural feeling of all who were not personally interested in it, was unmitigated abhorrence....

Some will object, that a comparison cannot fairly be made between the government of the male sex and the forms of unjust power which I have adduced in illustration of it, since these are arbitrary, and the effect of mere usurpation, while it on the contrary is natural. But was there ever any domination which did not appear natural to those who possessed it? There was a time when the division of mankind into two classes, a small one of masters and a numerous one of slaves, appeared, even to the most cultivated minds, to be natural, and the only natural, condition of the human race. No less an intellect, and one which contributed no less to the progress of human thought, than Aristotle, held this opinion without doubt or misgiving; and rested it on the same premises on which the same assertion in regard to the dominion of men over women is usually based, namely that there are different natures among mankind, free natures, and slave natures; that the Greeks were of a free nature, the barbarian races of Thracians and Asiatics of a slave nature. But why need I go back to Aristotle? Did not the slave-owners of the Southern United States maintain the same doctrine, with all the fanaticism with which men cling to the theories that justify their passions and legitimate their personal interests? Did they not call heaven and earth to witness that the dominion of the white man over the black is natural, that the black race is by nature incapable of freedom, and marked out for slavery? some even going so far as to say that the freedom of manual laborers is an unnatural order of things anywhere. Again, the theorists of absolute monarchy have always affirmed it to be the only natural form of government; issuing from the patriarchal, which was the primitive and spontaneous form of society, framed on the model of the paternal, which is anterior to society itself, and, as they contend, the most natural authority of all....

But, it will be said, the rule of men over women differs from all these others in not being a rule a rule of force: it is accepted voluntarily; women make no complaint, and are consenting parties to it. In the first place, a great number of women do not accept it. Ever since there have been women able to make their sentiments known by their writings (the only mode of publicity which society permits to them), an increasing number of them have recorded protests against their present social condition: and recently many thousands of them, headed by the most eminent women known to the public, have petitioned Parliament for their admission to the Parliamentary Suffrage The claim of women to be educated as solidly, and in the same branches of knowledge, as men, is urged with growing intensity, and with a great prospect of success; while the demand for their admission into professions and occupations hitherto closed against them, becomes every year more urgent. Though there are not in this country, as there are in the United States, periodical conventions and an organized party to agitate for the Rights of Women, there is a numerous and active society organized and managed by women, for the more limited object of obtaining the political franchise. Nor is it only in our own country and in America that women are beginning to protest, more or less collectively, against the disabilities under which they labor. France, and Italy, and Switzerland, and Russia now afford examples of the same thing. How many more women there are who silently cherish similar aspirations, no one can possibly know; but there are abundant tokens how many would cherish them, were they not so strenuously taught to repress them as contrary to the proprieties of their sex. It must be remembered, also, that no enslaved class ever asked for complete liberty at once....

When we put together three things—first, the natural attraction between opposite sexes; secondly, the wife's entire dependence on the husband, every privilege or pleasure she has being either his gift, or depending entirely on his will; and lastly, that the principal object of human pursuit, consideration, and all objects of social ambition, can in general be sought or obtained by her only through him, it would be a miracle if the object of being attractive to men had not become the polar star of feminine education and formation of character. And, this great means of influence over the minds of women having been acquired, an instinct of selfishness made men avail themselves of it to the utmost as a means of holding women in subjection, by representing to them meekness, submissiveness, and resignation of all individual will into the hands of a man, as an essential part of sexual attractiveness. Can it be doubted that any of the other yokes which mankind have succeeded in breaking, would have subsisted till now if the same means had existed, and had been so sedulously used, to bow down their minds to it? If it had been made the object of the life of every young plebeian to find personal favor in the eyes of some patrician, of every young serf with some seigneur; if domestication with him, and a share of his personal affections, had been held out as the prize which they all should look out for, the most gifted and aspiring being able to reckon on the most desirable prizes; and if, when this prize had been obtained, they had been shut out by a wall of brass from all interests not centering in him, all feelings and desires but those which he shared or inculcated; would not serfs and seigneurs, plebeians and patricians, have been as broadly distinguished at this day as men and women are? And would not all but a thinker here and there, have believed the distinction to be a fundamental and unalterable fact in human nature?

The preceding considerations are amply sufficient to show that custom, however universal it may be, affords in this case no presumption, and ought not to create any prejudice, in favor of the arrangements which place women in social and political subjection to men. But I may go farther, and maintain that the course of history, and the tendencies of progressive human society, afford not only no presumption in favor of this system of inequality of rights, but a strong one against it; and that, so far as the whole course of human improvement up to the time, the whole stream of modern tendencies, warrants any inference on the subject, it is, that this relic of the past is discordant with the future, and must necessarily disappear.

For, what is the peculiar character of the modern world—the difference which chiefly distinguishes modern institutions, modern social ideas, modern life itself, from those of times long past? It is, that human beings are no longer born to their place in life, and chained down by an inexorable bond to the place they are born to, but are free to employ their faculties, and such favorable chances as offer, to achieve the lot which may appear to them most desirable. Human society of old was constituted on a very different principle. All were born to a fixed social position, and were mostly kept in it by law, or interdicted from any means by which they could emerge from it. As some men are born white and others black, so some were born slaves and others freemen and citizens; some were born patricians, others plebeians; some were born feudal nobles, others commoners and *roturiers*. A slave or serf could never make himself free, nor, except by the will of his master, become so. In most European countries it was not till towards the close of the middle ages, and as a consequence of the growth of regal power, that commoners could be ennobled. Even among nobles, the eldest son was born the exclusive heir to the paternal possessions, and a long time elapsed before it was fully established that the father could disinherit him. Among the industrious classes, only those who were born members of a guild, or were admitted into it by its members, could lawfully practice their calling within its local limits; and nobody could practice any calling deemed important, in any but the legal manner by processes authoritatively prescribed. Manufacturers have stood in the pillory for presuming to carry on their business by new and improved methods....

The modern conviction, the fruit of a thousand years of experience, is, that things in which the individual is the person directly interested, never go right but as they are left to his own discretion; and that any regulation of them by authority, except to protect the rights of others, is sure to be mischievous. This conclusion slowly arrived at, and not adopted until almost every possible application of the contrary theory had been made with disastrous result, now (in the industrial department) prevails universally in the most advanced countries, almost universally in all that have pretensions to any sort of advancement. It is not that all processes are supposed to be equally good, or all persons to be equally qualified for everything; but that freedom of individual choice is now known to be the only thing which procures the adoption of the best processes, and throws each operation into the hands of those who are best qualified for it. Nobody thinks it necessary to make a law that only a strong-armed man shall be a blacksmith. Freedom and competition suffice to make blacksmiths strong-armed men, because the weak armed can earn more by engaging in occupations for which they are more fit. In consonance with this doctrine, it is felt to be an overstepping of the proper bounds of authority to fix beforehand, on some general presumption, that certain persons are not fit to do certain things. It is now thoroughly known and admitted that if some such presumptions exist, no such presumption is infallible. Even if it be well grounded in a majority of cases, which it is very likely not to be, there will be a minority of exceptional cases in which it does not hold: and in those it is both an injustice to the individuals, and a detriment to society, to place barriers in the way of their using their faculties for their own benefit and for that of others. In the cases, on the other hand, in which the unfitness is real, the ordinary motives of human conduct will on the whole suffice to prevent the incompetent person from making, or from persisting in, the attempt.

If this general principle of social and economical science is not true; if individuals, with such help as they can derive from the opinion of those who know them, are not better judges than the law and the government, of their own capacities and vocation; the world cannot too soon abandon this principle, and return to the old system of regulations and disabilities. But if the principle is true, we ought to act as if we believed it, and not to ordain that to be born a girl instead of a boy, any more than to be born black instead of white, or a commoner instead of a nobleman, shall decide the person's position through all life—shall interdict people from all the more elevated social positions, and from all, except a few, respectable occupations. Even were we to admit the utmost that is ever pretended a to the superior fitness of men for all the functions now reserve to them, the same argument applies which forbids a legal qualification for Members of Parliament. If only once in a dozen years the conditions of eligibility exclude a fit person, there is a real loss, while the exclusion of thousands of unfit persons is no gain; for if the constitution of the electoral body disposes them to choose unfit persons, there are always plenty of such persons to choose from. In all things of any difficulty and importance, those who can do them well are fewer than the need, even with the most unrestricted latitude of choice: and any limitation of the field of selection deprives society of some chances of being served by the competent, without ever saving it from the incompetent....

The least that can be demanded is, that the question should not be considered as prejudged by existing fact and existing opinion, but open to discussion on its merits, as a question of justice and expediency: the decision on this, as on any of the other social arrangements of mankind, depending on what an enlightened estimate of tendencies and consequences may show to be most advantageous to humanity in general, without distinction of sex. And the discussion must be a real discussion, descending to foundations, and not resting satisfied with vague and general assertions. It will not do, for instance to assert in general terms, that the experience of mankind has pronounced in favor of the existing system. Experience cannot possibly have decided between two courses, so long as there has only been experience of one. If it be said that the doctrine of the equality of the sexes rests only on theory, it must be remembered that the contrary doctrine also has only theory to rest upon. All that is proved in its favor by direct experience, is that mankind have been able to exist under it, and to attain the degree of improvement and prosperity which we now see; but whether that prosperity has been attained sooner, or is now greater, than it would have been under the other system, experience does not say. On the other hand, experience does say, that every step in improvement has been so invariably accompanied by a step made in raising the social position of women, that historians and philosophers have been led to adopt their elevation or debasement as on the whole the surest test and most correct measure of the civilization of a people or an age. Through all the progressive period of human history, the condition of women has been approaching nearer to equality with men. This does not of itself prove that the assimilation must goon to complete equality; but it assuredly affords some presumption that such is the case....

I have dwelt so much on the difficulties which at present obstruct any real knowledge by men of the true nature of women, because in this as in so many other things *opinio copiae inter maximas causas inopiae est*; and there is little chance of reasonable thinking on the matter while people flatter themselves that they perfectly understand a subject of which most men know absolutely nothing, and of which it is at present impossible that any man, or all men taken together, should have knowledge which can qualify them to lay down the law to women as to what is, or is not, their vocation. Happily, no such knowledge is necessary for any practical purpose connected with the position of women is relation to society and life. For, according to all the principles involved in modern society, the question rests with women themselves—to be decided by their own experience, and by the use of their own faculties. There are no means of finding what either one person or many can do, but by trying—and no means by which anyone else can discover for them what it is for their happiness to do or leave undone.

One thing we may be certain of—that what is contrary to women's nature to do, they never will be made to do by simply giving their nature free play. The anxiety of mankind to interfere in behalf of nature, for fear lest nature should not succeed in effecting its purpose, is an altogether unnecessary solicitude. What women by nature cannot do, it is quite superfluous to forbid them from doing. What they can do, but not so well as the men who are their competitors, competition suffices to exclude them from; since nobody asks for protective duties and bounties in favor of women; it is only asked that the present bounties and protective duties in favor of men should be recalled. If women have a greater natural inclination for some things than for others, there is no need of laws or social inculcation to make the majority of them do the former in preference to the latter. Whatever women's services are most wanted for, the free play of competition will hold out the strongest inducements to them to undertake. And, as the words imply, they are most wanted for the things for which they are most fit; by the apportionment of which to them, the collective faculties of the two sexes can be applied on the whole with the greatest sum of valuable result.

Chapter IV: The Benefits Of Equality

What good are we to expect from the changes proposed in our customs and institutions? Would mankind be at all better off if women were free?...

The principle of the modern movement in morals and politics, is that conduct, and conduct alone, entitles to respect: that not what men are, but what they do, constitutes their claim to deference; that, above all, merit, and not birth, is the only rightful claim to power and authority. If no authority, not in its nature temporary, were allowed to one human being over another, society would not be employed in building up propensities with one hand which it has to curb with the other. The child would really, for the first time in man's existence on earth, be trained in the way he should go, and when he was old there would be a chance that he would not depart from it. But so long as the right of the strong to power over the weak rules in the very heart of society, the attempt to make the equal right of the weak the principle of its outward actions will always be an uphill struggle; for the law of justice, which is also that of Christianity, will never get possession of men's inmost sentiments; they will be working against it, even when bending to it.

The second benefit to be expected from giving to women the free use of their faculties, by leaving them the free choice of their employments, and opening to them the same field of occupation and the same prizes and encouragements as to other human beings, would be that of doubling the mass of mental faculties available for the higher service of humanity. Where there is now one person qualified to benefit mankind and promote the general improvement, as a public teacher, or an administrator of some branch of public or social affairs, there would then be a chance of two. Mental superiority of any kind is at present everywhere so much below the demand; there is such a deficiency of persons competent to do excellently anything which it requires any considerable amount of ability to do; that the loss to the world, by refusing to make use of one half of the whole quantity of talent it possesses, is extremely serious. It is true that this amount of mental power is not totally lost. Much of it is employed, and would in any case be employed, in domestic management, and in the few other occupations open to women; and from the remainder indirect benefit is in many individual cases obtained, through the personal influence of individual women over individual men. But these benefits are partial; their range is extremely circumscribed; and if they must be admitted, on the one hand, as a deduction from the amount of fresh social power that would be acquired by giving freedom to one-half of the whole sum of human intellect, there must be added, on the other, the benefit of the stimulus that would be given to the intellect of men by the competition; or (to use a more true expression) by the necessity that would be imposed on them of deserving presidency before they could expect to obtain it.

This great accession to the intellectual power of the species, and to the amount of intellect available for the good management of its affairs, would be obtained, partly, through the better and more complete intellectual education of women, which would then improve *pari passu* with that of men. Women in general would be brought up equally capable of understanding business, public affairs, and the higher matters of speculation, with men In the same class of society; and the select few of the one as well as of the other sex, who were qualified not only to comprehend what is done or thought by others, but to think or do something considerable themselves, would meet with the same facilities for improving and training their capacities in the one sex as in the other. In this way, the widening of the sphere of action for women would operate for good, by raising their education to the level of that of men, and making the one participate in all improvements made in the other. But independently of this, the mere breaking down of the barrier would of itself have an educational virtue of the highest worth. The mere getting rid of the idea that all the wider subjects of thought and action, all the things which are of general and not solely of private interest, are men's business, from which women are to be warned off—positively interdicted from most of it, coldly tolerated in the little which is allowed them—the mere consciousness a woman would then have of being a human being like any other, entitled to choose her pursuits, urged or invited by the same inducements as anyone else to interest herself in whatever is interesting to human beings, entitled to exert the share of influence on all human concerns which belongs to an individual opinion, whether she attempted actual participation in them or not—this alone would effect an immense expansion of the faculties of women, as well as enlargement of the range of their moral sentiments.

Besides the addition to the amount of individual talent available for the conduct of human affairs, which certainly are not at present so abundantly provided in that respect that they can afford to dispense with one-half of what nature proffers; the opinion of women would then possess a more beneficial, rather than a greater, influence upon the general mass of human belief and sentiment. I say a more beneficial, rather than a greater influence; for the influence of women over the general tone of opinion has always, or at least from the earliest known period, been very considerable. The influence of mothers on the early character of their sons, and the desire of young men to recommend themselves to young women, have in all recorded times been important agencies in the formation of character, and have determined some of the chief steps in the progress of civilization....

The great and continually increasing mass of unenlightened and short-sighted benevolence, which, taking the care of people's lives out of their own hands, and relieving them from the disagreeable consequences of their own acts, saps the very foundations of the self-respect, self-help, and self-control which are the essential conditions both of individual prosperity and of social virtue—this waste of resources and of benevolent feelings in doing harm instead of good, is immensely swelled by women's contributions, and stimulated by their influence. Not that this is a mistake likely to be made by women, where they have actually the practical management of schemes of beneficence.... These considerations show how usefully the part which women take in the formation of general opinion, would be modified for the better by that more enlarged instruction, and practical conversancy with the things which their opinions influence, that would necessarily arise from their social and political emancipation. But the improvement it would work through the influence they exercise, each in her own family, would be still more remarkable....

There is another very injurious aspect in which the effect, not of women's disabilities directly, but of the broad line of difference which those disabilities create between the education and character of a woman and that of a man, requires to be considered. Nothing can be more unfavorable to that union of thoughts and inclinations which is the ideal of married life. Intimate society between people radically dissimilar to one another, is an idle dream. Unlikeness may attract, but it is likeness which retains; and in proportion to the likeness is the suitability of the individuals to give each other a happy life. While women are so unlike men, it is not wonderful that selfish men should feel the need of arbitrary power in their own hands, to arrest *in limine* the life-long conflict of inclinations, by deciding every question on the side of their own preference. When people are extremely unlike, there can be no real identity of interest. Very often there is conscientious difference of opinion between married people, on the highest points of duty. Is there any reality in the marriage union where this takes place? Yet it is not uncommon anywhere, when the woman has any earnestness of character; and it is a very general case indeed in Catholic countries, when she is supported in her dissent by the only other authority to which she is taught to bow, the priest. With the usual barefacedness of power not accustomed to find itself disputed, the influence of priests over women is attacked by Protestant and Liberal writers, less for being bad in itself, than because it is a rival authority to the husband, and raises up a revolt against his infallibility....

At the present time, the progress of civilization, and the turn of opinion against the rough amusements and convivial excesses which formerly occupied most men in their hours of relaxation—together with (it must be said) the improved tone of modern feeling as to the reciprocity of duty which binds the husband towards the wife—have thrown the man very much more upon home and its inmates, for his personal and social pleasures: while the kind and degree of improvement which has been made in women's education, has made them in some degree capable of being his companions in ideas and mental taste, while leaving them, in most cases, still hopelessly inferior to him. His desire of mental communion is thus in general satisfied by a communion from which he learns nothing. An unimproving and unstimulating companionship is substituted for (what he might otherwise have been obliged to seek) the society of his equals in powers and his fellows in the higher pursuits. We see, accordingly, that young men of the greatest promise generally cease to improve as soon as they marry, and, not improving, inevitably degenerate. If the wife does not push the husband forward, she always holds him back. He ceases to care for what she does not care for; he no longer desires, and ends by disliking and shunning, society congenial to his former aspirations, and which would now shame his falling-off from them; his higher faculties both of mind and heart cease to be called into activity. And this change coinciding with the new and selfish interests which are created by the family, after a few years he differs in no material respect from those who have never had wishes for anything but the common vanities and the common pecuniary objects.

What marriage may be in the case of two persons of cultivated faculties, identical in opinions and purposes, between whom there exists that best kind of equality, similarity of powers and capacities with reciprocal superiority in them—so that each can enjoy the luxury of looking up to the other, and can have alternately the pleasure of leading and of being led in the path of development—I will not attempt to describe. To those who can conceive it, there is no need; to those who cannot, it would appear the dream of an enthusiast. But I maintain, with the profoundest conviction, that this, and this only, is the ideal of marriage; and that all opinions, customs, and institutions which favor any other notion of it, or turn the conceptions and aspirations connected with it into any other direction, by whatever pretences they may be colored, are relics of primitive barbarism. The moral regeneration of mankind will only really commence, when the most fundamental of the social relations is placed under the rule of equal justice, and when human beings learn to cultivate their strongest sympathy with an equal in rights and in cultivation.

Thus far, the benefits which it has appeared that the world would gain by ceasing to make sex a disqualification for privileges and a badge of subjection, are social rather than individual; consisting in an increase of the general fund of thinking and acting power, and an improvement in the general conditions of the association of men with women. But it would be a grievous understatement of the case to omit the most direct benefit of all, the unspeakable gain in private happiness to the liberated half of the species; the difference to them between a life of subjection to the will of others, and a life of rational freedom. After the primary necessities of food and raiment, freedom is the first and strongest want of human nature. While mankind are lawless, their desire is for lawless freedom. When they have learnt to understand the meaning of duty and the value of reason, they incline more and more to be guided and restrained by these in the exercise of their freedom; but they do not therefore desire freedom less; they do not become disposed to accept the will of other people as the representative and interpreter of those guiding principles. on the contrary, the communities in which the reason has been most cultivated, and in which the idea of social duty has been most powerful, are those which have most strongly asserted the freedom of action of the individual—the liberty of each to govern his conduct by his own feelings of duty, and by such laws and social restraints as his own conscience can subscribe to.

He who would rightly appreciate the worth of personal independence as an element of happiness, should consider the value he himself puts upon it as an ingredient of his own. There is no subject on which there is a greater habitual difference of judgment between a man judging for himself, and the same man judging for other people. When he hears others complaining that they are not allowed freedom of action—that their own will has not sufficient influence in the regulation of their affairs—his inclination is, to ask, what are their grievances? What positive damage they sustain? And in what respect they consider their affairs to be mismanaged? And if they fail to make out, in answer to these questions, what appears to him a sufficient case, he turns a deaf ear, and regards their complaint as the fanciful querulousness of people whom nothing reasonable will satisfy. But he has a quite different standard of judgment when he is deciding for himself. Then, the most unexceptionable administration of his interests by a tutor set over him, does not satisfy his feelings: his personal exclusion from the deciding authority appears itself the greatest grievance of all, rendering it superfluous even to enter into the question of mismanagement. It is the same with nations. What citizen of a free country would listen to any offers of good and skilful administration, in return for the abdication of freedom? Even if he could believe that good and skilful administration can exist among a people ruled by a will not their own, would not the consciousness of working out their own destiny under their own moral responsibility be a compensation to his feelings for great rudeness and imperfection in the details of public affairs? Let him rest assured that whatever he feels on this point, women feel in a fully equal degree....

But it is not only through the sentiment of personal dignity, that the free direction and disposal of their own faculties is a source of individual happiness, and to be fettered and restricted in it, a source of unhappiness, to human beings, and not least to women. There is nothing, after disease, indigence, and guilt, so fatal to the pleasurable enjoyment of life as the want of a worthy outlet for the active faculties....Of such women, and of those others to whom this duty has not been committed at all—many of whom pine through life with the consciousness of thwarted vocations, and activities which are not suffered to expand—the only resources, speaking generally, are religion and charity. But their religion, though it may be one of feeling, and of ceremonial observance, cannot be a religion of action, unless in the form of charity. For charity many of them are by nature admirably fitted; but to practice it usefully, or even without doing mischief, requires the education, the manifold preparation, the knowledge and the thinking powers, of a skilful administrator.

There are few of the administrative functions of government for which a person would not be fit, who is fit to bestow charity usefully. In this as in other cases (pre-eminently in that of the education of children), the duties permitted to women cannot be performed properly, without their being trained for duties which, to the great loss of society, are not permitted to them. And here let me notice the singular way in which the question of women's disabilities is frequently presented to view, by those who find it easier to draw a ludicrous picture of what they do not like, than to answer the arguments for it. When it is suggested that women's executive capacities and prudent counsels might sometimes be found valuable in affairs of State, these lovers of fun hold up to the ridicule of the world, as sitting in Parliament or in the Cabinet, girls in their teens, or young wives of two or three and twenty, transported bodily, exactly as they are, from the drawing-room to the House of Commons. They forget that males are not usually selected at this early age for a seat in Parliament, or for responsible political functions. Common sense would tell them that if such trusts were confided to women, it would be to such as having no special vocation for married life, or preferring another employment of their faculties (as many women even now prefer to marriage some of the few honorable occupations within their reach), have spent the best years of their youth in attempting to qualify themselves for the pursuits in which they desire to engage; or still more frequently perhaps, widows or wives of forty or fifty, by whom the knowledge of life and faculty of government which they have acquired in their families, could by the aid of appropriate studies be made available on a less contracted scale. There is no country of Europe in which the ablest men have not frequently experienced, and keenly appreciated, the value of the advice and help of clever and experienced women of the world, in the attainment both of private and of public objects; and there are important

matters of public administration to which few men are equally competent
with such women; among others, the detailed control of expenditure....

When we consider the positive evil caused to the disqualified half of the
human race by their disqualification—first in the loss of the most inspiriting
and elevating kind of personal enjoyment, and next in the weariness, disappointment, and profound dissatisfaction with life, which are so often the substitute for it; one feels that among all the lessons which men require for carrying
on the struggle against the inevitable imperfections of their lot on earth, there
is no lesson which they more need, than not to add to the evils which nature
inflicts, by their jealous and prejudiced restrictions on one another. Their vain
fears only substitute other and worse evils for those which they are idly appre-
hensive of: while every restraint on the freedom of conduct of any of their
human fellow-creatures (otherwise than by making them responsible for any
evil actually caused by it), dries up *pro tanto* the principal fountain of human
happiness, and leaves the species less rich, to an inappreciable degree, in all
that makes life valuable to the individual human being.

K. Marx and F. Engels

The Communist Manifesto

Introduction: The Spectre Haunting Europe

A spectre is haunting Europe—the spectre of communism. All the powers of old Europe have entered into a holy alliance to exorcise this spectre: Pope and Tsar, Metternich and Guizot, French Radicals and German police-spies.

Where is the party in opposition that has not been decried as communistic by its opponents in power? Where is the opposition that has not hurled back the branding reproach of communism, against the more advanced opposition parties, as well as against its reactionary adversaries?...

Bourgeois and Proletarians

The history of all hitherto existing society is the history of class struggles.

Freeman and slave, patrician and plebian, lord and serf, guild-master and journeyman, in a word, oppressor and oppressed, stood in constant opposition to one another, carried on an uninterrupted, now hidden, now open fight, a fight that each time ended, either in a revolutionary reconstitution of society at large, or in the common ruin of the contending classes.

In the earlier epochs of history, we find almost everywhere a complicated arrangement of society into various orders, a manifold gradation of social rank. In ancient Rome we have patricians, knights, plebians, slaves; in the Middle Ages, feudal lords, vassals, guild-masters, journeymen, apprentices, serfs; in almost all of these classes, again, subordinate gradations....

Our epoch, the epoch of the bourgeoisie, possesses, however, this distinct feature: it has simplified class antagonisms. Society as a whole is more and more splitting up into two great hostile camps, into two great classes directly facing each other—bourgeoisie and proletariat....

The discovery of America, the rounding of the Cape, opened up fresh ground for the rising bourgeoisie. The East-Indian and Chinese markets, the colonization of America, trade with the colonies, the increase in the means of exchange and in commodities generally, gave to commerce, to navigation, to industry, an impulse never before known, and thereby, to the revolutionary element in the tottering feudal society, a rapid development....

Modern industry has established the world market, for which the discovery of America paved the way. This market has given an immense development to commerce, to navigation, to communication by land. This development has, in turn, reacted on the extension of industry; and in proportion as industry, commerce, navigation, railways extended, in the same proportion the bourgeoisie developed, increased its capital, and pushed into the background every class handed down from the Middle Ages.

We see, therefore, how the modern bourgeoisie is itself the product of a long course of development, of a series of revolutions in the modes of production and of exchange....

The bourgeoisie has at last, since the establishment of Modern Industry and of the world market, conquered for itself, in the modern representative state, exclusive political sway. The executive of the modern state is but a committee for managing the common affairs of the whole bourgeoisie.

The Bourgeoisie as a Revolutionary Force

The bourgeoisie, historically, has played a most revolutionary part.

The bourgeoisie, wherever it has got the upper hand, has put an end to all feudal, patriarchal, idyllic relations. It has pitilessly torn asunder the motley feudal ties that bound man to his "natural superiors," and has left no other nexus between people than naked self-interest, than callous "cash payment." It has drowned out the most heavenly ecstasies of religious fervor, of chivalrous enthusiasm, of philistine sentimentalism, in the icy water of egotistical calculation. It has resolved personal worth into exchange value, and in place of the numberless indefeasible chartered freedoms, has set up that single, unconscionable freedom—Free Trade. In one word, for exploitation, veiled by religious and political illusions, it has substituted naked, shameless, direct, brutal exploitation.

The bourgeoisie has stripped of its halo every occupation hitherto honored and looked up to with reverent awe. It has converted the physician, the lawyer, the priest, the poet, the man of science, into its paid wage laborers.

The bourgeoisie has torn away from the family its sentimental veil, and has reduced the family relation into a mere money relation.

The bourgeoisie has disclosed how it came to pass that the brutal display of vigor in the Middle Ages, which reactionaries so much admire, found its fitting complement in the most slothful indolence. It has been the first to show what man's activity can bring about. It has accomplished wonders far surpassing Egyptian pyramids, Roman aqueducts, and Gothic cathedrals; it has conducted expeditions that put in the shade all former exoduses of nations and crusades.

The bourgeoisie cannot exist without constantly revolutionizing the instruments of production, and thereby the relations of production, and with them the whole relations of society. Conservation of the old modes of production in unaltered form, was, on the contrary, the first condition of existence for all earlier industrial classes. Constant revolutionizing of production, uninterrupted disturbance of all social conditions, everlasting uncertainty and agitation distinguish the bourgeois epoch from all earlier ones. All fixed, fast frozen relations, with their train of ancient and venerable prejudices and opinions, are swept away, all new-formed ones become antiquated before they can ossify. All that is solid melts into air, all that is holy is profaned, and man is at last compelled to face with sober senses his real condition of life and his relations with his kind.

The need of a constantly expanding market for its products chases the bourgeoisie over the entire surface of the globe. It must nestle everywhere, settle everywhere, establish connections everywhere.

The bourgeoisie has, through its exploitation of the world market, given a cosmopolitan character to production and consumption in every country. To the great chagrin of reactionaries, it has drawn from under the feet of industry the national ground on which it stood. All old-established national industries have been destroyed or are daily being destroyed. They are dislodged by new industries, whose introduction becomes a life and death question for all civilized nations, by industries that no longer work up indigenous raw material, but raw material drawn from the remotest zones; industries whose products are consumed, not only at home, but in every quarter of the globe. In place of the old wants, satisfied by the production of the country, we find new wants, requiring for their satisfaction the products of distant lands and climes. In place of the old local and national seclusion and self-sufficiency, we have intercourse in every direction, universal inter-dependence of nations. And as in material, so also in intellectual production. The intellectual creations of individual nations become common property. National one-sidedness and narrow-mindedness become more and more impossible, and from the numerous national and local literatures, there arises a world literature.

The bourgeoisie, by the rapid improvement of all instruments of production, by the immensely facilitated means of communication, draws all, even the most barbarian, nations into civilization. The cheap prices of commodities are the heavy artillery with which it forces the barbarians' intensely obstinate hatred of foreigners to capitulate. It compels all nations, on pain of extinction, to adopt the bourgeois mode of production; it compels them to introduce what it calls civilization into their midst, i.e., to become bourgeois themselves. In one word, it creates a world after its own image.

The bourgeoisie has subjected the country to the rule of the towns. It has created enormous cities, has greatly increased the urban population as compared with the rural, and has thus rescued a considerable part of the population from the idiocy of rural life. Just as it has made the country dependent on the towns, so it has made barbarian and semi-barbarian countries dependent on the civilized ones, nations of peasants on nations of bourgeois, the East on the West.

The bourgeoisie keeps more and more doing away with the scattered state of the population, of the means of production, and of property. It has agglomerated population, centralized the means of production, and has concentrated property in a few hands. The necessary consequence of this was political centralization. Independent, or but loosely connected provinces, with separate interests, laws, governments, and systems of taxation, became lumped together into one nation, with one government, one code of laws, one national class interest, one frontier, and one customs tariff.

The bourgeoisie, during its rule of scarce one hundred years, has created more massive and more colossal productive forces than have all preceding generations together. Subjection of nature's forces to man, machinery, application of chemistry to industry and agriculture, steam navigation, railways, electric telegraphs, clearing of whole continents for cultivation, canalization or rivers, whole populations conjured out of the ground—what earlier century had even a presentiment that such productive forces slumbered in the lap of social labor?

We see then: the means of production and of exchange, on whose foundation the bourgeoisie built itself up, were generated in feudal society. At a certain stage in the development of these means of production and of exchange, the conditions under which feudal society produced and exchanged, the feudal organization of agriculture and manufacturing industry, in one word, the feudal relations of property became no longer compatible with the already developed productive forces; they became so many fetters. They had to be burst asunder; they were burst asunder.

Into their place stepped free competition, accompanied by a social and political constitution adapted in it, and the economic and political sway of the bourgeois class.

"Modern Bourgeois Society"

A similar movement is going on before our own eyes. Modern bourgeois society, with its relations of production, of exchange and of property, a society that has conjured up such gigantic means of production and of exchange, is like the sorcerer who is no longer able to control the powers of the nether world whom he has called up by his spells. For many a decade past, the history of industry and commerce is but the history of the revolt of modern productive forces against modern conditions of production, against the property relations that are the conditions for the existence of the bourgeois and of its rule.

It is enough to mention the commercial crises that, by their periodical return, put the existence of the entire bourgeois society on its trial, each time more threateningly. In these crises, a great part not only of the existing products, but also of the previously created productive forces, are periodically destroyed. In these crises, there breaks out an epidemic that, in all earlier epochs, would have seemed an absurdity—the epidemic of over-production. Society suddenly finds itself put back into a state of momentary barbarism; it appears as if a famine, a universal war of devastation, had cut off the supply of every means of subsistence; industry and commerce seem to be destroyed. And why?

Because there is too much civilization, too much means of subsistence, too much industry, too much commerce. The productive forces at the disposal of society no longer tend to further the development of the conditions of bourgeois property; on the contrary, they have become too powerful for these conditions, by which they are fettered, and so soon as they overcome these fetters, they bring disorder into the whole of bourgeois society, endanger the existence of bourgeois property. The conditions of bourgeois society are too narrow to comprise the wealth created by them. And how does the bourgeoisie get over these crises? On the one hand, by enforced destruction of a mass of productive forces; on the other, by the conquest of new markets, and by the more thorough exploitation of the old ones. That is to say, by paving the way for more extensive and more destructive crises, and by diminishing the means whereby crises are prevented.

The weapons with which the bourgeoisie felled feudalism to the ground are now turned against the bourgeoisie itself.

The Development of the Proletarians into a Class

But not only has the bourgeoisie forged the weapons that bring death to itself; it has also called into existence the men who are to wield those weapons—the modern working class—the proletarians.

In proportion as the bourgeoisie, i.e., capital, is developed, in the same proportion is the proletariat, the modern working class, developed—a class of laborers, who live only so long as they find work, and who find work only so long as their labor increases capital. These laborers, who must sell themselves piecemeal, are a commodity, like every other article of commerce, and are consequently exposed to all the vicissitudes of competition, to all the fluctuations of the market.

Owing to the extensive use of machinery, and to the division of labor, the work of the proletarians has lost all individual character, and, consequently, all charm for the workman. He becomes an appendage of the machine, and it is only the most simple, most monotonous, and most easily acquired knack, that is required of him. Hence, the cost of production of a workman is restricted, almost entirely, to the means of subsistence that he requires for maintenance, and for the propagation of his race. But the price of a commodity, and therefore also of labor, is equal to its cost of production. In proportion, therefore, as the repulsiveness of the work increases, the wage decreases. What is more, in proportion as the use of machinery and division of labor increases, in the same proportion the burden of toil also increases, whether by prolongation of the working hours, by the increase of the work exacted in a given time, or by increased speed of machinery, etc.

Modern Industry has converted the little workshop of the patriarchal master into the great factory of the industrial capitalist. Masses of laborers, crowded into the factory, are organized like soldiers. As privates of the industrial army, they are placed under the command of a perfect hierarchy of officers and sergeants. Not only are they slaves of the bourgeois class, and of the bourgeois state; they are daily and hourly enslaved by the machine, by the over looker, and, above all, in the individual bourgeois manufacturer himself. The more openly this despotism proclaims gain to be its end and aim, the more petty, the more hateful and the more embittering it is....

No sooner is the exploitation of the laborer by the manufacturer, so far at an end, that he receives his wages in cash, than he is set upon by the other portion of the bourgeoisie, the landlord, the shopkeeper, the pawnbroker, etc.

The lower strata of the middle class—the small trades people, shopkeepers, and retired tradesmen generally, the handicraftsmen and peasants—all these sink gradually into the proletariat, partly because their diminutive capital does not suffice for the scale on which Modern Industry is carried on, and is swamped in the competition with the large capitalists, partly because their specialized skill is rendered worthless by new methods of production. Thus, the proletariat is recruited from all classes of the population....

But with the development of industry, the proletariat not only increases in number; it becomes concentrated in greater masses, its strength grows, and it feels that strength more. The various interests and conditions of life within the ranks of the proletariat are more and more equalized, in proportion as machinery obliterates all distinctions of labor, and nearly everywhere reduces wages to the same low level. The growing competition among the bourgeois, and the resulting commercial crises, make the wages of the workers ever more fluctuating. The increasing improvement of machinery, ever more rapidly developing, makes their livelihood more and more precarious; the collisions between individual workmen and individual bourgeois take more and more the character of collisions between two classes. Thereupon, the workers begin to form combinations (trade unions) against the bourgeois; they club together in order to keep up the rate of wages; they found permanent associations in order to make provision beforehand for these occasional revolts. Here and there, the contest breaks out into riots....This organization of the proletarians into a class, and, consequently, into a political party, is continually being upset again by the competition between the workers themselves. But it ever rises up again, stronger, firmer, mightier. It compels legislative recognition of particular interests of the workers, by taking advantage of the divisions among the bourgeoisie itself. Thus, the Ten-Hours Bill in England was carried....

Further, as we have already seen, entire sections of the ruling class are, by the advance of industry, precipitated into the proletariat, or are at least threatened in their conditions of existence. These also supply the proletariat with fresh elements of enlightenment and progress.

Finally, in times when the class struggle nears the decisive hour, the progress of dissolution going on within the ruling class, in fact within the whole range of old society, assumes such a violent, glaring character, that a small section of the ruling class cuts itself adrift, and joins the revolutionary class, the class that holds the future in its hands. Just as, therefore, at an earlier period, a section of the nobility went over to the bourgeoisie, so now a portion of the bourgeoisie goes over to the proletariat, and in particular, a portion of the bourgeois ideologists, who have raised themselves to the level of comprehending theoretically the historical movement as a whole.

Of all the classes that stand face to face with the bourgeoisie today, the proletariat alone is a genuinely revolutionary class. The other classes decay and finally disappear in the face of Modern Industry; the proletariat is its special and essential product.

The lower middle class, the small manufacturer, the shopkeeper, the artisan, the peasant, all these fight against the bourgeoisie, to save from extinction their existence as fractions of the middle class. They are therefore not revolutionary, but conservative. Nay, more, they are reactionary, for they try to roll back the wheel of history. If, by chance, they are revolutionary, they are only so in view of their impending transfer into the proletariat; they thus defend not their present, but their future interests; they desert their own standpoint to place themselves at that of the proletariat.

The "dangerous class," the social scum, that passively rotting mass thrown off by the lowest layers of the old society, may, here and there, be swept into the movement by a proletarian revolution; its conditions of life, however, prepare it far more for the part of a bribed tool of reactionary intrigue.

In the condition of the proletariat, those of old society at large are already virtually swamped. The proletarian is without property; his relation to his wife and children has no longer anything in common with the bourgeois family relations; modern industry labor, modern subjection to capital, the same in England as in France, in America as in Germany, has stripped him of every trace of national character. Law, morality, religion, are to him so many bourgeois prejudices, behind which lurk in ambush just as many bourgeois interests....

The Bourgeoisie Produces its Own Grave-Diggers

Hitherto, every form of society has been based, as we have already seen, on the antagonism of oppressing and oppressed classes. But in order to oppress a class, certain conditions must be assured to it under which it can, at least, continue its slavish existence. The serf, in the period of serfdom, raised himself to membership in the commune, just as the petty bourgeois, under the yoke of the feudal absolutism, managed to develop into a bourgeois. The modern laborer, on the contrary, instead of rising with the process of industry, sinks deeper and deeper below the conditions of existence of his own class. He becomes a pauper, and pauperism develops more rapidly than population and wealth. And here it becomes evident that the bourgeoisie is unfit any longer to be the ruling class in society, and to impose its conditions of existence upon society as an overriding law. It is unfit to rule because it is incompetent to assure an existence to its slave within his slavery, because it cannot help letting him sink into such a state, that it has to feed him, instead of being fed by him. Society can no longer live under this bourgeoisie, in other words, its existence is no longer compatible with society.

The essential conditions for the existence and for the sway of the bourgeois class is the formation and augmentation of capital; the condition for capital is wage labor. Wage labor rests exclusively on competition between the laborers. The advance of industry, whose involuntary promoter is the bourgeoisie, replaces the isolation of the laborers, due to competition, by the revolutionary combination, due to association. The development of Modern Industry, therefore, cuts from under its feet the very foundation on which the bourgeoisie produces and appropriates products. What the bourgeoisie therefore produces, above all, are its own grave-diggers. Its fall and the victory of the proletariat are equally inevitable.

The Relationship Between the Proletarians and the Communists

In what relation do the Communists stand to the proletarians as a whole? The Communists do not form a separate party opposed to the other working-class parties.

They have no interests separate and apart from those of the proletariat as a whole.

They do not set up any sectarian principles of their own, by which to shape and mold the proletarian movement.

The Communists are distinguished from the other working-class parties by this only:

(1) In the national struggles of the proletarians of the different countries, they point out and bring to the front the common interests of the entire proletariat, independently of all nationality.

(2) In the various stages of development which the struggle of the working class against the bourgeoisie has to pass through, they always and everywhere represent the interests of the movement as a whole.

The Communists, therefore, are on the one hand practically, the most advanced and resolute section of the working-class parties of every country, that section which pushes forward all others; on the other hand, theoretically, they have over the great mass of the proletariat the advantage of clearly understanding the lines of march, the conditions, and the ultimate general results of the proletarian movement.

The immediate aim of the Communists is the same as that of all other proletarian parties: Formation of the proletariat into a class, overthrow of the bourgeois supremacy, conquest of political power by the proletariat.

"The Distinguishing Feature of Communism: Abolition of Private Property"

The theoretical conclusions of the Communists are in no way based on ideas or principles that have been invented, or discovered, by this or that would-be universal reformer.

They merely express, in general terms, actual relations springing from an existing class struggle, from a historical movement going on under our very eyes. The abolition of existing property relations is not at all a distinctive feature of communism.

All property relations in the past have continually been subject to historical change consequent upon the change in historical conditions.

The French Revolution, for example, abolished feudal property in favor of bourgeois property.

The distinguishing feature of communism is not the abolition of property generally, but the abolition of bourgeois property. But modern bourgeois private property is the final and most complete expression of the system of producing and appropriating products that is based on class antagonisms, on the exploitation of the many by the few.

In this sense, the theory of the Communists may be summed up in the single sentence: Abolition of private property....

Bourgeois Society and Communist Society

In bourgeois society, living labor is but a means to increase accumulated labor. In communist society, accumulated labor is but a means to widen, to enrich, to promote the existence of the laborer.

In bourgeois society, therefore, the past dominates the present; in communist society, the present dominates the past. In bourgeois society, capital is independent and has individuality, while the living person is dependent and has no individuality.

And the abolition of this state of things is called by the bourgeois, abolition of individuality and freedom! And rightly so. The abolition of bourgeois individuality, bourgeois independence, and bourgeois freedom is undoubtedly aimed at.

By freedom is meant, under the present bourgeois conditions of production, free trade, free selling and buying.

But if selling and buying disappears, free selling and buying disappears also. This talk about free selling and buying, and all the other "brave words" of our bourgeois about freedom in general, have a meaning, if any, only in contrast with restricted selling and buying, with the fettered traders of the Middle Ages, but have no meaning when opposed to the communist abolition of buying and selling, or the bourgeois conditions of production, and of the bourgeoisie itself.

You are horrified at our intending to do away with private property. But in your existing society, private property is already done away with for nine-tenths of the population; its existence for the few is solely due to its non-existence in the hands of those nine-tenths.

You reproach us, therefore, with intending to do away with a form of property, the necessary condition for whose existence is the non-existence of any property for the immense majority of society.

In one word, you reproach us with intending to do away with your property. Precisely so; that is just what we intend.

From the moment when labor can no longer be converted into capital, money, or rent, into a social power capable of being monopolized, i.e., from the moment when individual property can no longer be transformed into bourgeois property, into capital, from that moment, you say, individuality vanishes.

You must, therefore, confess that by "individual" you mean no other person than the bourgeois, than the middle-class owner of property. This person must, indeed, be swept out of the way, and made impossible.

Communism deprives no man of the power to appropriate the products of society; all that it does is to deprive him of the power to subjugate the labor of others by means of such appropriations.

It has been objected that upon the abolition of private property, all work will cease, and universal laziness will overtake us.

According to this, bourgeois society ought long ago to have gone to the dogs through sheer idleness; for those who acquire anything, do not work. The whole of this objection is but another expression of the tautology: There can no longer be any wage labor when there is no longer any capital.

All objections urged against the communistic mode of producing and appropriating material products, have, in the same way, been urged against the communistic mode of producing and appropriating intellectual products. Just as to the bourgeois, the disappearance of class property is the disappearance of production itself, so the disappearance of class culture is to him identical with the disappearance of all culture.

That culture, the loss of which he laments, is, for the enormous majority, a mere training to act as a machine.

"Bourgeois Notions of Freedom"

But don't wrangle with us so long as you apply, to our intended abolition of bourgeois property, the standard of your bourgeois notions of freedom, culture, law, etc. Your very ideas are but the outgrowth of the conditions of your bourgeois production and bourgeois property, just as your jurisprudence is but the will of your class made into a law for all, a will whose essential character and direction are determined by the economical conditions of existence of your class.

The selfish misconception that induces you to transform into eternal laws of nature and of reason the social forms stringing from your present mode of production and form of property—historical relations that rise and disappear in the progress of production—this misconception you share with every ruling class that has preceded you. What you see clearly in the case of ancient property, what you admit in the case of feudal property, you are of course forbidden to admit in the case of your own bourgeois form of property.

Abolition of the family! Even the most radical flare up at this infamous proposal of the Communists.

On what foundation is the present family, the bourgeois family, based? On capital, on private gain. In its completely developed form, this family exists only among the bourgeoisie. But this state of things finds its complement in the practical absence of the family among proletarians, and in public prostitution.

The bourgeois family will vanish as a matter of course when its complement vanishes, and both will vanish with the vanishing of capital.

Do you charge us with wanting to stop the exploitation of children by their parents? To this crime we plead guilty.

But, you say, we destroy the most hallowed of relations, when we replace home education by social.

And your education! Is not that also social, and determined by the social conditions under which you educate, by the intervention direct or indirect, of society, by means of schools, etc.? The Communists have not intended the intervention of society in education; they do but seek to alter the character of that intervention, and to rescue education from the influence of the ruling class.

The bourgeois claptrap about the family and education, about the hallowed correlation of parents and child, becomes all the more disgusting, the more, by the action of Modern Industry, all the family ties among the proletarians are torn asunder, and their children transformed into simple articles of commerce and instruments of labor.

But you Communists would introduce community of women, screams the bourgeoisie in chorus.

The bourgeois sees his wife a mere instrument of production. He hears that the instruments of production are to be exploited in common, and, naturally, can come to no other conclusion that the lot of being common to all will likewise fall to the women.

He has not even a suspicion that the real point aimed at is to do away with the status of women as mere instruments of production.

For the rest, nothing is more ridiculous than the virtuous indignation of our bourgeois at the community of women which, they pretend, is to be openly and officially established by the Communists. The Communists have no need to introduce free love; it has existed almost from time immemorial.

Our bourgeois, not content with having wives and daughters of their proletarians at their disposal, not to speak of common prostitutes, take the greatest pleasure in seducing each others wives. (Ah, those were the days!)

Bourgeois marriage is, in reality, a system of wives in common and thus, at the most, what the Communists might possibly be reproached with is that they desire to introduce, in substitution for a hypocritically concealed, an openly legalized system of free love. For the rest, it is self-evident that the abolition of the present system of production must bring with it the abolition of free love springing from that system, i.e., of prostitution both public and private.

The Communists are further reproached with desiring to abolish countries and nationality.

"The Workers Have No Country"

The workers have no country. We cannot take from them what they have not got. Since the proletariat must first of all acquire political supremacy, must rise to be the leading class of the nation, must constitute itself the nation, it is, so far, itself national, though not in the bourgeois sense of the word.

National differences and antagonism between peoples are daily more and more vanishing, owing to the development of the bourgeoisie, to freedom of commerce, to the world market, to uniformity in the mode of production and in the conditions of life corresponding thereto.

The supremacy of the proletariat will cause them to vanish still faster. United action of the leading civilized countries at least is one of the first conditions for the emancipation of the proletariat.

In proportion as the exploitation of one individual by another will also be put an end to, the exploitation of one nation by another will also be put an end to. In proportion as the antagonism between classes within the nation vanishes, the hostility of one nation to another will come to an end.

Further Charges Against Communism

The charges against communism made from a religious, a philosophical and, generally, from an ideological standpoint, are not deserving of serious examination.

Does it require deep intuition to comprehend that man's ideas, views, and conception, in one word, man's consciousness, changes with every change in the conditions of his material existence, in his social relations and in his social life?

What else does the history of ideas prove, than that intellectual production changes its character in proportion as material production is changed? The ruling ideas of each age have ever been the ideas of its ruling class....

"Undoubtedly," it will be said, "religious, moral, philosophical, and juridical ideas have been modified in the course of historical development. But religion, morality, philosophy, political science, and law, constantly survived this change."

"There are, besides, eternal truths, such as Freedom, Justice, etc., that are common to all states of society. But communism abolishes eternal truths, it abolishes all religion, and all morality, instead of constituting them on a new basis; it therefore acts in contradiction to all past historical experience."

What does this accusation reduce itself to? The history of all past society has consisted in the development of class antagonisms, antagonisms that assumed different forms at different epochs.

But whatever form they may have taken, one fact is common to all past ages, viz., the exploitation of one part of society by the other. No wonder, then, that the social consciousness of past ages, despite all the multiplicity and variety it displays, moves within certain common forms, or general ideas, which cannot completely vanish except with the total disappearance of class antagonisms.

The communist revolution is the most radical rupture with traditional relations; no wonder that its development involved the most radical rupture with traditional ideas.

But let us have done with the bourgeois objections to communism.

Ten Point Program to "Win the Battle of Democracy"

We have seen above that the first step in the revolution by the working class is to raise the proletariat to the position of ruling class to win the battle of democracy.

The proletariat will use its political supremacy to wrest, by degree, all capital from the bourgeoisie, to centralize all instruments of production in the hands of the state, i.e., of the proletariat organized as the ruling class; and to increase the total productive forces as rapidly as possible.

Of course, in the beginning, this cannot be effected except by means of despotic inroads on the rights of property, and on the conditions of bourgeois production; by means of measures, therefore, which appear economically insufficient and untenable, but which, in the course of the movement, outstrip themselves, necessitate further inroads upon the old social order, and are unavoidable as a means of entirely revolutionizing the mode of production.

These measures will, of course, be different in different countries.

Nevertheless, in most advanced countries, the following will be pretty generally applicable.

1. Abolition of property in land and application of all rents of land to public purposes.
2. A heavy progressive or graduated income tax.
3. Abolition of all rights of inheritance.
4. Confiscation of the property of all emigrants and rebels.
5. Centralization of credit in the banks of the state, by means of a national bank with state capital and an exclusive monopoly.
6. Centralization of the means of communication and transport in the hands of the state.
7. Extension of factories and instruments of production owned by the state; the bringing into cultivation of waste lands, and the improvement of the soil generally in accordance with a common plan.
8. Equal obligation of all to work. Establishment of industrial armies, especially for agriculture.
9. Combination of agriculture with manufacturing industries; gradual abolition of all the distinction between town and country by a more equable distribution of the populace over the country.

10. Free education for all children in public schools. Abolition of children's factory labor in its present form. Combination of education with industrial production, etc.

"The Free Development of All"

When, in the course of development, class distinctions have disappeared, and all production has been concentrated in the hands of a vast association of the whole nation, the public power will lose its political character. Political power, properly so called, is merely the organized power of one class for oppressing another. If the proletariat during its contest with the bourgeoisie is compelled, by the force of circumstances, to organize itself as a class; if, by means of a revolution, it makes itself the ruling class, and, as such, sweeps away by force the old conditions of production, then it will, along with these conditions, have swept away the conditions for the existence of class antagonisms and of classes generally, and will thereby have abolished its own supremacy as a class.

In place of the old bourgeois society, with its classes and class antagonisms, we shall have an association in which the free development of each is the condition for the free development of all.

Reactionary Socialism

A. Feudal Socialism

Owing to their historical position, it became the vocation of the aristocracies of France and England to write pamphlets against modern bourgeois society. In the French Revolution of July 1830, and in the English reform agitation, these aristocracies again succumbed to the hateful upstart. Thenceforth, a serious political struggle was altogether out of the question. A literary battle alone remained possible. But even in the domain of literature, the old cries of the restoration period had become impossible.

In order to arouse sympathy, the aristocracy was obliged to lose sight, apparently, of its own interests, and to formulate its indictment against the bourgeoisie in the interest of the exploited working class alone. Thus, the aristocracy took their revenge by singing lampoons on their new masters and whispering in his ears sinister prophesies of coming catastrophe.

In this way arose feudal socialism: half lamentation, half lampoon; half an echo of the past, half menace of the future; at times, by its bitter, witty and incisive criticism, striking the bourgeoisie to the very heart's core, but always ludicrous in its effect, through total incapacity to comprehend the march of modern history.

The aristocracy, in order to rally the people to them, waved the proletarian alms-bag in front for a banner. But the people, so often as it joined them, saw on their hindquarters the old feudal coats of arms, and deserted with loud and irreverent laughter….

For the rest, so little do they conceal the reactionary character of their criticism that their chief accusation against the bourgeois amounts to this: that under the bourgeois regime a class is being developed which is destined to cut up, root and branch, the old order of society.

What they upbraid the bourgeoisie with is not so much that it creates a proletariat as that it creates a revolutionary proletariat….

Nothing is easier than to give Christian asceticism a socialist tinge. Has not Christianity declaimed against private property, against marriage, against the state? Has it not preached in the place of these, charity and poverty, celibacy and mortification of the flesh, monastic life and Mother Church? Christian socialism is but the holy water with which the priest consecrates the heartburnings of the aristocrat.

B. Petty-Bourgeois Socialism

In countries where modern civilization has become fully developed, a new class of petty bourgeois has been formed, fluctuating between proletariat and bourgeoisie, and ever renewing itself a supplementary part of bourgeois society. The individual members of this class, however, as being constantly hurled down into the proletariat by the action of competition, and, as Modern Industry develops, they even see the moment approaching when they will completely disappear as an independent section of modern society, to be replaced in manufactures, agriculture and commerce, by over lookers, bailiffs and shop men.

In countries like France, where the peasants constitute far more than half of the population, it was natural that writers who sided with the proletariat against the bourgeoisie should use, in their criticism of the bourgeois regime, the standard of the peasant and petty bourgeois, and from the standpoint of these intermediate classes, should take up the cudgels for the working class. Thus arose petty-bourgeois socialism. Sismondi was the head of this school, not only in France but also in England.

This school of socialism dissected with great acuteness the contradictions in the conditions of modern production. It laid bare the hypocritical apologies of economists. It proved, incontrovertibly, the disastrous effects of machinery and division of labor; the concentration of capital and land in a few hands; overproduction and crises; it pointed out the inevitable ruin of the petty bourgeois and peasant, the misery of the proletariat, the anarchy in production, the crying inequalities in the distribution of wealth, the industrial war of extermination between nations, the dissolution of old moral bonds, of the old family relations, of the old nationalities.

In it positive aims, however, this form of socialism aspires either to restoring the old means of production and of exchange, and with them the old property relations, and the old society, or to cramping the modern means of production and of exchange within the framework of the old property relations that have been, and were bound to be, exploded by those means. In either case, it is both reactionary and Utopian.

Its last words are: corporate guilds for manufacture; patriarchal relations in agriculture.

Ultimately, when stubborn historical facts had dispersed all intoxicating effects of self-deception, this form of socialism ended in a miserable hangover.

C. German or "True" Socialism

The socialist and communist literature of France, a literature that originated under the pressure of a bourgeoisie in power, and that was the expressions of the struggle against this power, was introduced into Germany at a time when the bourgeoisie in that country had just begun its contest with feudal absolutism....

German philosophers, would-be philosophers, and beaux esprits (men of letters), eagerly

The work of the German literati consisted solely in bringing the new French ideas into harmony with their ancient philosophical conscience, or rather, in annexing the French ideas without deserting their own philosophic point of view.

This annexation took place in the same way in which a foreign language is appropriated, namely, by translation.

It is well known how the monks wrote silly lives of Catholic saints over the manuscripts on which the classical works of ancient heathendom had been written. The German literati reversed this process with the profane French literature. They wrote their philosophical nonsense beneath the French original. For instance, beneath the French criticism of the economic functions of money, they wrote "alienation of humanity," and beneath the French criticism of the bourgeois state they wrote "dethronement of the category of the general," and so forth....

The French socialist and communist literature was thus completely emasculated. And, since it ceased, in the hands of the German, to express the struggle of one class with the other, he felt conscious of having overcome "French one-sidedness" and of representing, not true requirements, but the requirements of truth; not the interests of the proletariat, but the interests of human nature, of man in general, who belongs to no class, has no reality, who exists only in the misty realm of philosophical fantasy....

German socialism forgot, in the nick of time, that the French criticism, whose silly echo it was, presupposed the existence of modern bourgeois society, with its corresponding economic conditions of existence, and the political constitution adapted thereto, the very things whose attainment was the object of the pending struggle in Germany.

To the absolute governments, with their following of parsons, professors, country squires, and officials, it served as a welcome scarecrow against the threatening bourgeoisie.

It was a sweet finish, after the bitter pills of flogging and bullets, with which these same governments, just at that time, dosed the German working-class risings.

While this "True" Socialism thus served the government as a weapon for fighting the German bourgeoisie, it, at the same time, directly represented a reactionary interest, the interest of German philistines. In Germany, the petty-bourgeois class, a relic of the sixteenth century, and since then constantly cropping up again under the various forms, is the real social basis of the existing state of things....

Conservative or Bourgeois Socialism

A part of the bourgeoisie is desirous of redressing social grievances in order to secure the continued existence of bourgeois society.

To this section belong economists, philanthropists, humanitarians, improvers of the condition of the working class, organizers of charity, members of societies for the prevention of cruelty to animals, temperance fanatics, hole-and-corner reformers of every imaginable kind. This form of socialism has, moreover, been worked out into complete systems.

We may cite Proudhon's *Philosophy of Poverty* as an example of this form.

The socialistic bourgeois want all the advantages of modern social conditions without the struggles and dangers necessarily resulting there from. They desire the existing state of society, minus its revolutionary and disintegrating elements. They wish for a bourgeoisie without a proletariat. The bourgeoisie naturally conceives the world in which it is supreme to be the best; and bourgeois socialism develops this comfortable conception into various more or less complete systems. In requiring the proletariat to carry out such a system, and thereby to march straightaway into the social New Jerusalem, it but requires in reality that the proletariat should remain within the bounds of existing society, but should cast away all its hateful ideas concerning the bourgeoisie.

A second, and more practical, but less systematic, form of this socialism sought to depreciate every revolutionary movement in the eyes of the working class by showing that no mere political reform, but only a change in the material conditions of existence, in economical relations, could be of any advantage to them. By changes in the material conditions of existence, this form of socialism, however, by no means understands abolition of the bourgeois relations of production, an abolition that can be affected only by a revolution, but administrative reforms, based on the continued existence of these relations; reforms, therefore, that in no respect affect the relations between capital and labor, but, at the best, lessen the cost, and simplify the administrative work of bourgeois government.

Bourgeois socialism attains adequate expression when, and only when, it becomes a mere figure of speech.

Free trade: for the benefit of the working class. Protective duties: for the benefit of the working class. Prison reform: for the benefit of the working class. This is the last word and the only seriously meant word of bourgeois socialism. It is summed up in the phrase: the bourgeois is a bourgeois—for the benefit of the working class.

Critical — Utopian Socialism and Communism

The socialist and communist systems, properly so called, those of Saint-Simon, Fourier, Owen, and others, spring into existence in the early undeveloped period, described above, of the struggle between proletariat and bourgeoisie.

The founders of these systems see, indeed, the class antagonisms, as well as the action of the decomposing elements in the prevailing form of society. But the proletariat, as yet in its infancy, offers to them the spectacle of a class without any historical initiative or any independent political movement.

Since the development of class antagonism keeps even pace with the development of industry, the economic situation, as they find it, does not as yet offer to them the material conditions for the emancipation of the proletariat. They therefore search after a new social science, after new social laws, that are to create these conditions.

Historical action is to yield to their personal inventive action; historically created conditions of emancipation to fantastic ones; and the gradual, spontaneous class organization of the proletariat to an organization of society especially contrived by these inventors. Future history resolves itself, in their eyes, into the propaganda and the practical carrying out of their social plans.

In the formation of their plans, they are conscious of caring chiefly for the interests of the working class, as being the most suffering class. Only from the point of view of being the most suffering class does the proletariat exist for them.

The undeveloped state of the class struggle, as well as their own surroundings, causes Socialists of this kind to consider themselves far superior to all class antagonisms. They want to improve the condition of every member of society, even that of the most favored. Hence, they habitually appeal to society at large, without the distinction of class; nay, by preference, to the ruling class. For how can people when once they understand their system, fail to see in it the best possible plan of the best possible state of society?

Hence, they reject all political, and especially all revolutionary action; they wish to attain their ends by peaceful means, necessarily doomed to failure, and by the force of example, to pave the way for the new social gospel.

Such fantastic pictures of future society, painted at a time when the proletariat is still in a very undeveloped state and has but a fantastic conception of its own position, correspond with the first instinctive yearnings of that class for a general reconstruction of society....

The significance of critical-utopian socialism and communism bears an inverse relation to historical development. In proportion as the modern class struggle develops and takes definite shape, this fantastic standing apart from the contest, these fantastic attacks on it, lose all practical value and all theoretical justifications. Therefore, although the originators of these systems were, in many respects, revolutionary, their disciples have, in every case, formed mere reactionary sects. They hold fast by the original views of their masters, in opposition to the progressive historical development of the proletariat. They, therefore, endeavor, and that consistently, to deaden the class struggle and to reconcile the class antagonisms. They still dream of experimental realization of their social utopias, of founding isolated phalansteres, of establishing "Home Colonies," or setting up a "Little Icaria," pocket editions of the New Jerusalem, and to realize all these castles in the air, they are compelled to appeal to the feelings and purses of the bourgeois. By degrees, they sink into the category of the reactionary conservative socialists depicted above, differing from these only by more systematic pedantry, and by their fanatical and superstitious belief in the miraculous effects of their social science.

They, therefore, violently oppose all political action on the part of the working class; such action, according to them, can only result from blind unbelief in the new gospel.

The Owenites in England, and the Fourierists in France, respectively, oppose the Chartists and the Reformistes.

The Communists in Relation to the Various Existing Opposition Parties

The Communists turn their attention chiefly to Germany, because that country is on the eve of a bourgeois revolution that is bound to be carried out under more advanced conditions of European civilization and with a much more developed proletariat than that of England was in the seventeenth, and France in the eighteenth century, and because the bourgeois revolution in Germany will be but the prelude to an immediately following proletarian revolution.

In short, the Communists everywhere support every revolutionary movement against the existing social and political order of things.

In all these movements, they bring to the front, as the leading question in each, the property question, no matter what its degree of development at the time.

Finally, they labor everywhere for the union and agreement of the democratic parties of all countries.

The Communists disdain to conceal their views and aims. They openly declare that their ends can be attained only by the forcible overthrow of all existing social conditions. Let the ruling classes tremble at a communist revolution. The proletarians have nothing to lose but their chains. They have a world to win.

Workingmen of all countries, unite!

Karl Marx

Das Kapital

Volume One, Part I: Commodities and Money

Chapter One: Commodities

Section 1 The Two Factors of a Commodity: Use Value and (Exchange) Value
The wealth of those societies in which the capitalist mode of production prevails, presents itself as "an immense accumulation of commodities," its unit being a single commodity. Our investigation must therefore begin with the analysis of a commodity.

A commodity is, in the first place, an object outside us, a thing that by its properties satisfies human wants of some sort or another. The nature of such wants, whether, for instance, they spring from the stomach or from fancy, makes no difference. Neither are we here concerned to know how the object satisfies these wants, whether directly as means of subsistence, or indirectly as means of production.

Every useful thing, as iron, paper, &c., may be looked at from the two points of view of quality and quantity. It is an assemblage of many properties, and may therefore be of use in various ways. To discover the various uses of things is the work of history. So also is the establishment of socially-recognized standards of measure for the quantities of these useful objects. The diversity of these measures has its origin partly in the diverse nature of the objects to be measured, partly in convention.

The utility of a thing makes it a use value. But this utility is not a thing of air. Being limited by the physical properties of the commodity, it has no existence apart from that commodity. A commodity, such as iron, corn, or a diamond, is therefore, so far as it is a material thing, a use value, something useful. This property of a commodity is independent of the amount of labor required to appropriate its useful qualities. When treating of use value, we always assume to be dealing with definite quantities, such as dozens of watches, yards of linen, or tons of iron. The use values of commodities furnish the material for a special study, that of the commercial knowledge of commodities. Use values become a reality only by use or consumption: they also constitute the substance of all wealth, whatever may be the social form of that wealth. In the form of society we are about to consider, they are, in addition, the material depositories of exchange value.

Exchange value, at first sight, presents itself as a quantitative relation, as the proportion in which values in use of one sort are exchanged for those of another sort, a relation constantly changing with time and place. Hence exchange value appears to be something accidental and purely relative, and consequently an intrinsic value, i.e., an exchange value that is inseparably connected with, inherent in commodities, seems a contradiction in terms. Let us consider the matter a little more closely….

Let us take two commodities, e.g., corn and iron. The proportions in which they are exchangeable, whatever those proportions may be, can always be represented by an equation in which a given quantity of corn is equated to some quantity of iron: e.g., 1 quarter corn = x cwt. iron. What does this equation tell us? It tells us that in two different things—in 1 quarter of corn and x cwt. of iron, there exists in equal quantities something common to both. The two things must therefore be equal to a third, which in itself is neither the one nor the other. Each of them, so far as it is exchange value, must therefore be reducible to this third….

If then we leave out of consideration the use value of commodities, they have only one common property left, that of being products of labor. But even the product of labor itself has undergone a change in our hands. If we make abstraction from its use value, we make abstraction at the same time from the material elements and shapes that make the product a use value; we see in it no longer a table, a house, yarn, or any other useful thing. Its existence as a material thing is put out of sight. Neither can it any longer be regarded as the product of the labor of the joiner, the mason, the spinner, or of any other definite kind of productive labor. Along with the useful qualities of the products themselves, we put out of sight both the useful character of the various kinds of labor embodied in them, and the concrete forms of that labor; there is nothing left but what is common to them all; all are reduced to one and the same sort of labor, human labor in the abstract….

We have seen that when commodities are exchanged, their exchange value manifests itself as something totally independent of their use value. But if we abstract from their use value, there remains their Value as defined above. Therefore, the common substance that manifests itself in the exchange value of commodities, whenever they are exchanged, is their value. The progress of our investigation will show that exchange value is the only form in which the value of commodities can manifest itself or be expressed. For the present, however, we have to consider the nature of value independently of this, its form.

A use value, or useful article, therefore, has value only because human labor in the abstract has been embodied or materialized in it. How, then, is the magnitude of this value to be measured? Plainly, by the quantity of the value-creating substance, the labor, contained in the article. The quantity of labor, however, is measured by its duration, and labor time in its turn finds its standard in weeks, days, and hours.

Some people might think that if the value of a commodity is determined by the quantity of labor spent on it, the more idle and unskillful the laborer, the more valuable would his commodity be, because more time would be required in its production. The labor, however, that forms the substance of value, is homogeneous human labor, expenditure of one uniform labor power. The total labor power of society, which is embodied in the sum total of the values of all commodities produced by that society, counts here as one homogeneous mass of human labor power, composed though it be of innumerable individual units. Each of these units is the same as any other, so far as it has the character of the average labor power of society, and takes effect as such; that is, so far as it requires for producing a commodity, no more time than is needed on an average, no more than is socially necessary. The labor time socially necessary is that required to produce an article under the normal conditions of production, and with the average degree of skill and intensity prevalent at the time. The introduction of power-looms into England probably reduced by one-half the labor required to weave a given quantity of yarn into cloth. The hand-loom weavers, as a matter of fact, continued to require the same time as before; but for all that, the product of one hour of their labor represented after the change only half an hour's social labor, and consequently fell to one-half its former value.

We see then that that which determines the magnitude of the value of any article is the amount of labor socially necessary, or the labor time socially necessary for its production. Each individual commodity, in this connection, is to be considered as an average sample of its class. Commodities, therefore, in which equal quantities of labor are embodied, or which can be produced in the same time, have the same value. The value of one commodity is to the value of any other, as the labor time necessary for the production of the one is to that necessary for the production of the other. "As values, all commodities are only definite masses of congealed labor time...."

Section 4 The Fetishism of Commodities and the Secret Thereof

A commodity appears, at first sight, a very trivial thing, and easily understood. Its analysis shows that it is, in reality, a very queer thing, abounding in metaphysical subtleties and theological niceties. So far as it is a value in use, there is nothing mysterious about it, whether we consider it from the point of view that by its properties it is capable of satisfying human wants, or from the point that those properties are the product of human labor. It is as clear as noon-day, that man, by his industry, changes the forms of the materials furnished by Nature, in such a way as to make them useful to him. The form of wood, for instance, is altered, by making a table out of it. Yet, for all that, the table continues to be that common, every-day thing, wood. But, so soon as it steps forth as a commodity, it is changed into something transcendent. It not only stands with its feet on the ground, but, in relation to all other commodities, it stands on its head, and evolves out of its wooden brain grotesque ideas, far more wonderful than "table-turning" ever was.

The mystical character of commodities does not originate, therefore, in their use value. Just as little does it proceed from the nature of the determining factors of value. For, in the first place, however varied the useful kinds of labor, or productive activities, may be, it is a physiological fact, that they are functions of the human organism, and that each such function, whatever may be its nature or form, is essentially the expenditure of human brain, nerves, muscles, &c. Secondly, with regard to that which forms the ground-work for the quantitative determination of value, namely, the duration of that expenditure, or the quantity of labor, it is quite clear that there is a palpable difference between its quantity and quality. In all states of society, the labor time that it costs to produce the means of subsistence, must necessarily be an object of interest to mankind, though not of equal interest in different stages of development. And lastly, from the moment that men in any way work for one another, their labor assumes a social form.

Whence, then, arises the enigmatical character of the product of labor, so soon as it assumes the form of commodities? Clearly from this form itself. The equality of all sorts of human labor is expressed objectively by their products all being equally values; the measure of the expenditure of labor power by the duration of that expenditure, takes the form of the quantity of value of the products of labor; and finally the mutual relations of the producers, within which the social character of their labor affirms itself, take the form of a social relation between the products.

A commodity is therefore a mysterious thing, simply because in it the social character of men's labor appears to them as an objective character stamped upon the product of that labor; because the relation of the producers to the sum total of their own labor is presented to them as a social relation, existing not between themselves, but between the products of their labor. This is the reason why the products of labor become commodities, social things whose qualities are at the same time perceptible and imperceptible by the senses....There it is a definite social relation between men, that assumes, in their eyes, the fantastic form of a relation between things. In order, therefore, to find an analogy, we must have recourse to the mist-enveloped regions of the religious world. In that world the productions of the human brain appear as independent beings endowed with life, and entering into relation both with one another and the human race. So it is in the world of commodities with the products of men's hands. This I call the Fetishism which attaches itself to the products of labor, so soon as they are produced as commodities, and which is therefore inseparable from the production of commodities.

This Fetishism of commodities has its origin, as the foregoing analysis has already shown, in the peculiar social character of the labor that produces them....

Since Robinson Crusoe's experiences are a favorite theme with political economists, let us take a look at him on his island. Moderate though he be, yet some few wants he has to satisfy, and must therefore do a little useful work of various sorts, such as making tools and furniture, taming goats, fishing and hunting. Of his prayers and the like we take no account, since they are a source of pleasure to him, and he looks upon them as so much recreation. In spite of the variety of his work, he knows that his labor, whatever its form, is but the activity of one and the same Robinson, and consequently, that it consists of nothing but different modes of human labor. Necessity itself compels him to apportion his time accurately between his different kinds of work. Whether one kind occupies a greater space in his general activity than another, depends on the difficulties, greater or less as the case may be, to be overcome in attaining the useful effect aimed at. This our friend Robinson soon learns by experience, and having rescued a watch, ledger, and pen and ink from the wreck, commences, like a true-born Briton, to keep a set of books. His stock-book contains a list of the objects of utility that belong to him, of the operations necessary for their production; and lastly, of the labor time that definite quantities of those objects have, on an average, cost him. All the relations between Robinson and the objects that form this wealth of his own creation, are here so simple and clear as to be intelligible without exertion, even to Mr. Sedley Taylor. And yet those relations contain all that is essential to the determination of value.

Let us now transport ourselves from Robinson's island bathed in light to the European middle ages shrouded in darkness. Here, instead of the independent man, we find everyone dependent, serfs and lords, vassals and suzerains, laymen and clergy. Personal dependence here characterizes the social relations of production just as much as it does the other spheres of life organized on the basis of that production. But for the very reason that personal dependence forms the ground-work of society, there is no necessity for labor and its products to assume a fantastic form different from their reality. They take the shape, in the transactions of society, of services in kind and payments in kind. Here the particular and natural form of labor, and not, as in a society based on production of commodities, its general abstract form is the immediate social form of labor. Compulsory labor is just as properly measured by time, as commodity-producing labor; but every serf knows that what he expends in the service of his lord, is a definite quantity of his own personal labor power. The tithe to be rendered to the priest is more matter of fact than his blessing. No matter, then, what we may think of the parts played by the different classes of people themselves in this society, the social relations between individuals in the performance of their labor, appear at all events as their own mutual personal relations, and are not disguised under the shape of social relations between the products of labor.

For an example of labor in common or directly associated labor, we have no occasion to go back to that spontaneously developed form which we find on the threshold of the history of all civilized races. We have one close at hand in the patriarchal industries of a peasant family, that produces corn, cattle, yarn, linen, and clothing for home use. These different articles are, as regards the family, so many products of its labor, but as between themselves, they are not commodities. The different kinds of labor, such as tillage, cattle tending, spinning, weaving and making clothes, which result in the various products, are in themselves, and such as they are, direct social functions, because functions of the family, which, just as much as a society based on the production of commodities, possesses a spontaneously developed system of division of labor. The distribution of the work within the family, and the regulation of the labor time of the several members, depend as well upon differences of age and sex as upon natural conditions varying with the seasons. The labor power of each individual, by its very nature, operates in this case merely as a definite portion of the whole labor power of the family, and therefore, the measure of the expenditure of individual labor power by its duration, appears here by its very nature as a social character of their labor.

Let us now picture to ourselves, by way of change, a community of free individuals, carrying on their work with the means of production in common, in which the labor power of all the different individuals is consciously applied as the combined labor power of the community. All the characteristics of Robinson's labor are here repeated, but with this difference, that they are social, instead of individual. Everything produced by him was exclusively the result of his own personal labor, and therefore simply an object of use for himself. The total product of our community is a social product. One portion serves as fresh means of production and remains social. But another portion is consumed by the members as means of subsistence. A distribution of this portion amongst them is consequently necessary. The mode of this distribution will vary with the productive organization of the community, and the degree of historical development attained by the producers. We will assume, but merely for the sake of a parallel with the production of commodities, that the share of each individual producer in the means of subsistence is determined by his labor time. Labor time would, in that case, play a double part. Its apportionment in accordance with a definite social plan maintains the proper proportion between the different kinds of work to be done and the various wants of the community. On the other hand, it also serves as a measure of the portion of the common labor borne by each individual, and of his share in the part of the total product destined for individual consumption. The social relations of the individual producers, with regard both to their labor and to its products, are in this case perfectly simple and intelligible, and that with regard not only to production but also to distribution.

The religious world is but the reflex of the real world. And for a society based upon the production of commodities, in which the producers in general enter into social relations with one another by treating their products as commodities and values, whereby they reduce their individual private labor to the standard of homogeneous human labor — for such a society, Christianity with its cultus of abstract man, more especially in its bourgeois developments, Protestantism, Deism, &c., is the most fitting form of religion.... This narrowness is reflected in the ancient worship of Nature, and in the other elements of the popular religions. The religious reflex of the real world can, in any case, only then finally vanish, when the practical relations of every-day life offer to man none but perfectly intelligible and reasonable relations with regard to his fellowmen and to Nature.

The life-process of society, which is based on the process of material production, does not strip off its mystical veil until it is treated as production by freely associated men, and is consciously regulated by them in accordance with a settled plan. This, however, demands for society a certain material ground-work or set of conditions of existence which in their turn are the spontaneous product of a long and painful process of development.

Political Economy has indeed analyzed, however incompletely, value and its magnitude, and has discovered what lies beneath these forms. But it has never once asked the question why labor is represented by the value of its product and labor time by the magnitude of that value. These formulæ, which bear it stamped upon them in unmistakable letters that they belong to a state of society, in which the process of production has the mastery over man, instead of being controlled by him, such formulæ appear to the bourgeois intellect to be as much a self-evident necessity imposed by Nature as productive labor itself. Hence forms of social production that preceded the bourgeois form, are treated by the bourgeoisie in much the same way as the Fathers of the Church treated pre-Christian religions.

To what extent some economists are misled by the Fetishism inherent in commodities, or by the objective appearance of the social characteristics of labor, is shown, amongst other ways, by the dull and tedious quarrel over the part played by Nature in the formation of exchange value. Since exchange value is a definite social manner of expressing the amount of labor bestowed upon an object, Nature has no more to do with it, than it has in fixing the course of exchange....

Part II: The Transformation of Money into Capital

Chapter Four: The General Formula for Capital

The first distinction we notice between money that is money only, and money that is capital, is nothing more than a difference in their form of circulation.

The simplest form of the circulation of commodities is C-M-C, the transformation of commodities into money, and the change of the money back again into commodities; or selling in order to buy. But alongside of this form we find another specifically different form: M-C-M, the transformation of money into commodities, and the change of commodities back again into money; or buying in order to sell. Money that circulates in the latter manner is thereby transformed into, becomes capital, and is already potentially capital.

Now let us examine the circuit M-C-M a little closer. It consists, like the other, of two antithetical phases. In the first phase, M-C, or the purchase, the money is changed into a commodity. In the second phase, C-M, or the sale, the commodity is changed back again into money. The combination of these two phases constitutes the single movement whereby money is exchanged for a commodity, and the same commodity is again exchanged for money; whereby a commodity is bought in order to be sold, or, neglecting the distinction in form between buying and selling, whereby a commodity is bought with money, and then money is bought with a commodity. The result, in which the phases of the process vanish, is the exchange of money for money, M-M. If I purchase 2,000 lbs. of cotton for £100, and resell the 2,000 lbs. of cotton for £110, I have, in fact, exchanged £100 for £110, money for money.

Now it is evident that the circuit M-C-M would be absurd and without meaning if the intention were to exchange by this means two equal sums of money, £100 for £100. The miser's plan would be far simpler and surer; he sticks to his £100 instead of exposing it to the dangers of circulation. And yet, whether the merchant who has paid £100 for his cotton sells it for £110, or lets it go for £100, or even £50, his money has, at all events, gone through a characteristic and original movement, quite different in kind from that which it goes through in the hands of the peasant who sells corn, and with the money thus set free buys clothes. We have therefore to examine first the distinguishing characteristics of the forms of the circuits M-C-M and C-M-C, and in doing this the real difference that underlies the mere difference of form will reveal itself....

What, however, first and foremost distinguishes the circuit C-M-C from the circuit M-C-M, is the inverted order of succession of the two phases. The simple circulation of commodities begins with a sale and ends with a purchase, while the circulation of money as capital begins with a purchase and ends with a sale. In the one case both the starting-point and the goal are commodities, in the other they are money. In the first form the movement is brought about by the intervention of money, in the second by that of a commodity.

In the circulation C-M-C, the money is in the end converted into a commodity, that serves as a use-value; it is spent once for all. In the inverted form, M-C-M, on the contrary, the buyer lays out money in order that, as a seller, he may recover money. By the purchase of his commodity he throws money into circulation, in order to withdraw it again by the sale of the same commodity. He lets the money go, but only with the sly intention of getting it back again. The money, therefore, is not spent, it is merely advanced.

In the circuit C-M-C, the same piece of money changes its place twice. The seller gets it from the buyer and pays it away to another seller. The complete circulation, which begins with the receipt, concludes with the payment, of money for commodities. It is the very contrary in the circuit M-C-M. Here it is not the piece of money that changes its place twice, but the commodity. The buyer takes it from the hands of the seller and passes it into the hands of another buyer. Just as in the simple circulation of commodities the double change of place of the same piece of money effects its passage from one hand into another, so here the double change of place of the same commodity brings about the reflux of the money to its point of departure.

Such reflux is not dependent on the commodity being sold for more than was paid for it. This circumstance influences only the amount of the money that comes back. The reflux itself takes place, so soon as the purchased commodity is resold, in other words, so soon as the circuit M-C-M is completed. We have here, therefore, a palpable difference between the circulation of money as capital, and its circulation as mere money.

The circuit C-M-C comes completely to an end, so soon as the money brought in by the sale of one commodity is abstracted again by the purchase of another.

If, nevertheless, there follows a reflux of money to its starting-point, this can only happen through a renewal or repetition of the operation. If I sell a quarter of corn for £3, and with this £3 buy clothes, the money, so far as I am concerned, is spent and done with. It belongs to the clothes merchant. If I now sell a second quarter of corn, money indeed flows back to me, not however as a sequel to the first transaction, but in consequence of its repetition. The money again leaves me, so soon as I complete this second transaction by a fresh purchase. Therefore, in the circuit C-M-C, the expenditure of money has nothing to do with its reflux. On the other hand, in M-C-M, the reflux of the money is conditioned by the very mode of its expenditure. Without this reflux, the operation fails, or the process is interrupted and incomplete, owing to the absence of its complementary and final phase, the sale.

The circuit C-M-C starts with one commodity, and finishes with another, which falls out of circulation and into consumption. Consumption, the satisfaction of wants, in one word, use-value, is its end and aim. The circuit M-C-M, on the contrary, commences with money and ends with money. Its leading motive, and the goal that attracts it, is therefore mere exchange-value....

As the conscious representative of this movement, the possessor of money becomes a capitalist. His person, or rather his pocket, is the point from which the money starts and to which it returns. The expansion of value, which is the objective basis or main-spring of the circulation M-C-M, becomes his subjective aim, and it is only in so far as the appropriation of ever more and more wealth in the abstract becomes the sole motive of his operations, that he functions as a capitalist, that is, as capital personified and endowed with consciousness and a will. Use-values must therefore never be looked upon as the real aim of the capitalist; neither must the profit on any single transaction. The restless never-ending process of profit-making alone is what he aims at. This boundless greed after riches, this passionate chase after exchange-value, is common to the capitalist and the miser; but while the miser is merely a capitalist gone mad, the capitalist is a rational miser. The never-ending augmentation of exchange-value, which the miser strives after, by seeking to save his money from circulation, is attained by the more acute capitalist, by constantly throwing it afresh into circulation.

The independent form, i.e., the money-form, which the value of commodities assumes in the case of simple circulation, serves only one purpose, namely, their exchange, and vanishes in the final result of the movement. On the other hand, in the circulation M-C-M, both the money and the commodity represent only different modes of existence of value itself, the money its general mode, and the commodity its particular, or, so to say, disguised mode. It is constantly changing from one form to the other without thereby becoming lost, and thus assumes an automatically active character. If now we take in turn each of the two different forms which self-expanding value successively assumes in the course of its life, we then arrive at these two propositions: Capital is money: Capital is commodities. In truth, however, value is here the active factor in a process, in which, while constantly assuming the form in turn of money and commodities, it at the same time changes in magnitude, differentiates itself by throwing off surplus-value from itself; the original value, in other words, expands spontaneously. For the movement, in the course of which it adds surplus-value, is its own movement, its expansion, therefore, is automatic expansion. Because it is value, it has acquired the occult quality of being able to add value to itself. It brings forth living offspring, or, at the least, lays golden eggs....

Buying in order to sell, or, more accurately, buying in order to sell dearer, M-C-M', appears certainly to be a form peculiar to one kind of capital alone, namely, merchants' capital. But industrial capital too is money, that is changed into commodities, and by the sale of these commodities, is re-converted into more money. The events that take place outside the sphere of circulation, in the interval between the buying and selling, do not affect the form of this movement. Lastly, in the case of interest-bearing capital, the circulation M-C-M' appears abridged. We have its result without the intermediate stage, in the form M-M', "en style lapidaire" so to say, money that is worth more money, value that is greater than itself.

M-C-M' is therefore in reality the general formula of capital as it appears *prima facie* within the sphere of circulation.

Chapter Six: The Buying and Selling of Labor-Power

The change of value that occurs in the case of money intended to be converted into capital, cannot take place in the money itself, since in its function of means of purchase and of payment, it does no more than realize the price of the commodity it buys or pays for; and, as hard cash, it is value petrified, never varying. Just as little can it originate in the second act of circulation, the re-sale of the commodity, which does no more than transform the article from its bodily form back again into its money-form. The change must, therefore, take place in the commodity bought by the first act, M-C, but not in its value, for equivalents are exchanged, and the commodity is paid for at its full value. We are, therefore, forced to the conclusion that the change originates in the use-value, as such, of the commodity, i.e., in its consumption. In order to be able to extract value from the consumption of a commodity, our friend, Moneybags, must be so lucky as to find, within the sphere of circulation, in the market, a commodity, whose use-value possesses the peculiar property of being a source of value, whose actual consumption, therefore, is itself an embodiment of labor, and, consequently, a creation of value. The possessor of money does find on the market such a special commodity in capacity for labor or labor-power.

By labor-power or capacity for labor is to be understood the aggregate of those mental and physical capabilities existing in a human being, which he exercises whenever he produces a use-value of any description.

But in order that our owner of money may be able to find labor-power offered for sale as a commodity, various conditions must first be fulfilled. The exchange of commodities of itself implies no other relations of dependence than those which, result from its own nature. On this assumption, labor-power can appear upon the market as a commodity, only if, and so far as, its possessor, the individual whose labor-power it is, offers it for sale, or sells it, as a commodity. In order that he may be able to do this, he must have it at his disposal, must be the untrammeled owner of his capacity for labor, i.e., of his person. He and the owner of money meet in the market, and deal with each other as on the basis of equal rights, with this difference alone, that one is buyer, the other seller; both, therefore, equal in the eyes of the law. The continuance of this relation demands that the owner of the labor-power should sell it only for a definite period, for if he were to sell it rump and stump, once for all, he would be selling himself, converting himself from a free man into a slave, from an owner of a commodity into a commodity. He must constantly look upon his labor-power as his own property, his own commodity, and this he can only do by placing it at the disposal of the buyer temporarily, for a definite period of time. By this means alone can he avoid renouncing his rights of ownership over it.

The second essential condition to the owner of money finding labor-power in the market as a commodity is this: that the laborer instead of being in the position to sell commodities in which his labor is incorporated, must be obliged to offer for sale as a commodity that very labor-power, which exists only in his living self.

In order that a man may be able to sell commodities other than labor-power, he must of course have the means of production, as raw material, implements, &c. No boots can be made without leather. He requires also the means of subsistence. Nobody—not even "a musician of the future"—can live upon future products, or upon use-values in an unfinished state; and ever since the first moment of his appearance on the world's stage, man always has been, and must still be a consumer, both before and while he is producing. In a society where all products assume the form of commodities, these commodities must be sold after they have been produced, it is only after their sale that they can serve in satisfying the requirements of their producer. The time necessary for their sale is superadded to that necessary for their production.

For the conversion of his money into capital, therefore, the owner of money must meet in the market with the free laborer, free in the double sense, that as a free man he can dispose of his labor-power as his own commodity, and that on the other hand he has no other commodity for sale, is short of everything necessary for the realization of his labor-power.

The question why this free laborer confronts him in the market, has no interest for the owner of money, who regards the labor-market as a branch of the general market for commodities. And for the present it interests us just as little. We cling to the fact theoretically, as he does practically. One thing, however, is clear—Nature does not produce on the one side owners of money or commodities, and on the other men possessing nothing but their own labor-power. This relation has no natural basis, neither is its social basis one that is common to all historical periods. It is clearly the result of a past historical development, the product of many economic revolutions, of the extinction of a whole series of older forms of social production.

So, too, the economic categories, already discussed by us, bear the stamp of history. Definite historical conditions are necessary that a product may become a commodity. It must not be produced as the immediate means of subsistence of the producer himself. Had we gone further, and inquired under what circumstances all, or even the majority of products take the form of commodities, we should have found that this can only happen with production of a very specific kind, capitalist production. Such an inquiry, however, would have been foreign to the analysis of commodities. Production and circulation of commodities can take place, although the great mass of the objects produced are intended for the immediate requirements of their producers, are not turned into commodities, and consequently social production is not yet by a long way dominated in its length and breadth by exchange-value. The appearance of products as commodities pre-supposes such a development of the social division of labor, that the separation of use-value from exchange-value, a separation which first begins with barter, must already have been completed....

We must now examine more closely this peculiar commodity, labor-power. Like all others it has a value. How is that value determined?

The value of labor-power is determined, as in the case of every other commodity, by the labor-time necessary for the production, and consequently also the reproduction, of this special article. So far as it has value, it represents no more than a definite quantity of the average labor of society incorporated in it. Labor-power exists only as a capacity, or power of the living individual. Its production consequently pre-supposes his existence. Given the individual, the production of labor-power consists in his reproduction of himself or his maintenance. For his maintenance he requires a given quantity of the means of subsistence. Therefore the labor-time requisite for the production of labor-power reduces itself to that necessary for the production of those means of subsistence; in other words, the value of labor-power is the value of the means of subsistence necessary for the maintenance of the laborer....

Some of the means of subsistence, such as food and fuel, are consumed daily, and a fresh supply must be provided daily. Others such as clothes and furniture last for longer periods and require to be replaced only at longer intervals. One article must be bought or paid for daily, another weekly, another quarterly, and so on. But in whatever way the sum total of these outlays may be spread over the year, they must be covered by the average income, taking one day with another....

The minimum limit of the value of labor-power is determined by the value of the commodities, without the daily supply of which the laborer cannot renew his vital energy, consequently by the value of those means of subsistence that are physically indispensable. If the price of labor-power fall to this minimum, it falls below its value, since under such circumstances it can be maintained and developed only in a crippled state. But the value of every commodity is determined by the labor-time requisite to turn it out so as to be of normal quality....

In every country in which the capitalist mode of production reigns, it is the custom not to pay for labor-power before it has been exercised for the period fixed by the contract, as for example, the end of each week. In all cases, therefore, the use-value of the labor-power is advanced to the capitalist: the laborer allows the buyer to consume it before he receives payment of the price; he everywhere gives credit to the capitalist. That this credit is no mere fiction, is shown not only by the occasional loss of wages on the bankruptcy of the capitalist, but also by a series of more enduring consequences. Nevertheless, whether money serves as a means of purchase or as a means of payment, this makes no alteration in the nature of the exchange of commodities. The price of the labor-power is fixed by the contract, although it is not realized till later, like the rent of a house. The labor-power is sold, although it is only paid for at a later period. It will, therefore, be useful, for a clear comprehension of the relation of the parties, to assume provisionally, that the possessor of labor-power, on the occasion of each sale, immediately receives the price stipulated to be paid for it....

Part III: The Production of Absolute Surplus-Value

Chapter Seven: The Labor-Process and the Process of Producing Surplus-Value

Section 1. The Labor-Process or the Production of Use Values

The capitalist buys labor-power in order to use it; and labor-power in use is labor itself. The purchaser of labor-power consumes it by setting the seller of it to work. By working, the latter becomes actually, what before he only was potentially, labor-power in action, a laborer. In order that his labor may re-appear in a commodity, he must, before all things, expend it on something useful, on something capable of satisfying a want of some sort. Hence, what the capitalist sets the laborer to produce, is a particular use-value, a specified article. The fact that the production of use-values, or goods, is carried on under the control of a capitalist and on his behalf, does not alter the general character of that production. We shall, therefore, in the first place, have to consider the labor-process independently of the particular form it assumes under given social conditions.

Labor is, in the first place, a process in which both man and Nature participate, and in which man of his own accord starts, regulates, and controls the material re-actions between himself and Nature. He opposes himself to Nature as one of her own forces, setting in motion arms and legs, head and hands, the natural forces of his body, in order to appropriate Nature's productions in a form adapted to his own wants. By thus acting on the external world and changing it, he at the same time changes his own nature. He develops his slumbering powers and compels them to act in obedience to his sway. We are not now dealing with those primitive instinctive forms of labor that remind us of the mere animal. An immeasurable interval of time separates the state of things in which a man brings his labor-power to market for sale as a commodity, from that state in which human labor was still in its first instinctive stage. We pre-suppose labor in a form that stamps it as exclusively human. A spider conducts operations that resemble those of a weaver, and a bee puts to shame many an architect in the construction of her cells. But what distinguishes the worst architect from the best of bees is this, that the architect raises his structure in imagination before he erects it in reality.

At the end of every labor-process, we get a result that already existed in the imagination of the laborer at its commencement. He not only effects a change of form in the material on which he works, but he also realizes a purpose of his own that gives the law to his modus operandi, and to which he must subordinate his will. And this subordination is no mere momentary act. Besides the exertion of the bodily organs, the process demands that, during the whole operation, the workman's will be steadily in consonance with his purpose. This means close attention. The less he is attracted by the nature of the work, and the mode in which it is carried on, and the less, therefore, he enjoys it as something which gives play to his bodily and mental powers, the more close his attention is forced to be.

The elementary factors of the labor-process are 1, the personal activity of man, i.e., work itself, 2, the subject of that work, and 3, its instruments....

If then, on the one hand, finished products are not only results, but also necessary conditions, of the labor-process, on the other hand, their assumption into that process, their contact with living labor, is the sole means by which they can be made to retain their character of use-values, and be utilized....

The labor-process, resolved as above into its simple elementary factors, is human action with a view to the production of use-values, appropriation of natural substances to human requirements; it is the necessary condition for effecting exchange of matter between man and Nature; it is the everlasting Nature-imposed condition of human existence, and therefore is independent of every social phase of that existence, or rather, is common to every such phase. It was, therefore, not necessary to represent our laborer in connection with other laborers; man and his labor on one side, Nature and its materials on the other, sufficed. As the taste of the porridge does not tell you who grew the oats, no more does this simple process tell you of itself what are the social conditions under which it is taking place, whether under the slave-owner's brutal lash, or the anxious eye of the capitalist, whether Cincinnatus carries it on in tilling his modest farm or a savage in killing wild animals with stones.

Let us now return to our would-be capitalist. We left him just after he had purchased, in the open market, all the necessary factors of the labor-process-its objective factors, the means of production, as well as its subjective factor, labor-power. With the keen eye of an expert, he has selected the means of production and the kind of labor-power best adapted to his particular trade, be it spinning, boot making, or any other kind. He then proceeds to consume the commodity, the labor-power that he has just bought, by causing the laborer, the impersonation of that labor-power, to consume the means of production by his labor. The general character of the labor-process is evidently not changed by the fact, that the laborer works for the capitalist instead of for himself; moreover, the particular methods and operations employed in boot making or spinning are not immediately changed by the intervention of the capitalist. He must begin by taking the labor-power as he finds it in the market, and consequently be satisfied with labor of such a kind as would be found in the period immediately preceding the rise of capitalists. Changes in the methods of production by the subordination of labor to capital, can take place only at a later period, and therefore will have to be treated of in a later chapter.

The labor-process, turned into the process by which the capitalist consumes labor-power, exhibits two characteristic phenomena. First, the laborer works under the control of the capitalist to whom his labor belongs; the capitalist taking good care that the work is done in a proper manner, and that the means of production are used with intelligence, so that there is no unnecessary waste of raw material, and no wear and tear of the implements beyond what is necessarily caused by the work.

Secondly, the product is the property of the capitalist and not that of the laborer, its immediate producer. Suppose that a capitalist pays for a day's labor-power at its value; then the right to use that power for a day belongs to him, just as much as the right to use any other commodity, such as a horse that he has hired for the day. To the purchaser of a commodity belongs its use, and the seller of labor-power, by giving his labor, does no more, in reality, than part with the use-value that he has sold. From the instant he steps into the workshop, the use-value of his labor-power, and therefore also its use, which is labor, belongs to the capitalist. By the purchase of labor-power, the capitalist incorporates labor, as a living ferment, with the lifeless constituents of the product. From his point of view, the labor-process is nothing more than the consumption of the commodity purchased, i.e., of labor-power; but this consumption cannot be effected except by supplying the labor-power with the means of production. The labor-process is a process between things that the capitalist has purchased, things that have become his property. The product of this process belongs, therefore, to him, just as much as does the wine which is the product of a process of fermentation completed in his cellar.

Section 2. The Production of Surplus Value

We know that the value of each commodity is determined by the quantity of labor expended on and materialized in it, by the working-time necessary, under given social conditions, for its production. This rule also holds good in the case of the product that accrued to our capitalist, as the result of the labor-process carried on for him. Assuming this product to be 10 lbs. of yarn, our first step is to calculate the quantity of labor realized in it.

For spinning the yarn, raw material is required; suppose in this case 10 lbs. of cotton. We have no need at present to investigate the value of this cotton, for our capitalist has, we will assume, bought it at its full value, say of ten shillings. In this price the labor required for the production of the cotton is already expressed in terms of the average labor of society. We will further assume that the wear and tear of the spindle, which, for our present purpose, may represent all other instruments of labor employed, amounts to the value of 2s. If, then, twenty-four hours' labor, or two working-days, are required to produce the quantity of gold represented by twelve shillings, we have here, to begin with, two days' labor already incorporated in the yarn.

We must not let ourselves be misled by the circumstance that the cotton has taken a new shape while the substance of the spindle has to a certain extent been used up. By the general law of value, if the value of 40 lbs. of yarn = the value of 40 lbs. of cotton + the value of a whole spindle, i.e., if the same working-time is required to produce the commodities on either side of this equation, then 10 lbs. of yarn are an equivalent for 10 lbs. of cotton, together with one-fourth of a spindle. In the case we are considering the same working-time is materialized in the 10 lbs. of yarn on the one hand, and in the 10 lbs. of cotton and the fraction of a spindle on the other. Therefore, whether value appears in cotton, in a spindle, or in yarn, makes no difference in the amount of that value. The spindle and cotton, instead of resting quietly side by side, join together in the process, their forms are altered, and they are turned into yarn; but their value is no more affected by this fact than it would be if they had been simply exchanged for their equivalent in yarn.

The labor required for the production of the cotton, the raw material of the yarn, is part of the labor necessary to produce the yarn, and is therefore contained in the yarn. The same applies to the labor embodied in the spindle, without whose wear and tear the cotton could not be spun.

Hence, in determining the value of the yarn, or the labor-time required for its production, all the special processes carried on at various times and in different places, which were necessary, first to produce the cotton and the wasted portion of the spindle, and then with the cotton and spindle to spin the yarn, may together be looked on as different and successive phases of one and the same process. The whole of the labor in the yarn is past labor; and it is a matter of no importance that the operations necessary for the production of its constituent elements were carried on at times which, referred to the present, are more remote than the final operation of spinning. If a definite quantity of labor, say thirty days, is requisite to build a house, the total amount of labor incorporated in it is not altered by the fact that the work of the last day is done twenty-nine days later than that of the first. Therefore the labor contained in the raw material and the instruments of labor can be treated just as if it were labor expended in an earlier stage of the spinning process, before the labor of actual spinning commenced.

The values of the means of production, i.e., the cotton and the spindle, which values are expressed in the price of twelve shillings, are therefore constituent parts of the value of the yarn, or, in other words, of the value of the product.

Two conditions must nevertheless be fulfilled. First, the cotton and spindle must concur in the production of a use-value; they must in the present case become yarn. Value is independent of the particular use-value by which it is borne, but it must be embodied in a use-value of some kind. Secondly, the time occupied in the labor of production must not exceed the time really necessary under the given social conditions of the case. Therefore, if no more than I lb. of cotton be requisite to spin 11 lbs. of yarn, care must be taken that no more than this weight of cotton is consumed in the production of 11 lbs. of yarn; and similarly with regard to the spindle. Though the capitalist have a hobby, and use a gold instead of a steel spindle, yet the only labor that counts for anything in the value of the yarn is that which would be required to produce a steel spindle, because no more is necessary under the given social conditions.

We now know what portion of the value of the yarn is owing to the cotton and the spindle. It amounts to twelve shillings or the value of two days' work. The next point for our consideration is, what portion of the value of the yarn is added to the cotton by the labor of the spinner....

While the laborer is at work, his labor constantly undergoes a transformation: from being motion, it becomes an object without motion; from being the laborer working, it becomes the thing produced. At the end of one hour's spinning, that act is represented by a definite quantity of yarn; in other words, a definite quantity of labor, namely that of one hour, has become embodied in the cotton. We say labor, i.e., the expenditure of his vital force by the spinner, and not spinning labor, because the special work of spinning counts here, only so far as it is the expenditure of labor-power in general, and not in so far as it is the specific work of the spinner.

In the process we are now considering it is of extreme importance, that no more time be consumed in the work of transforming the cotton into yarn than is necessary under the given social conditions. If under normal, i.e., average social conditions of production, a pounds of cotton ought to be made into b pounds of yarn by one hour's labor, then a day's labor does not count as 12 hours' labor unless 12 a pounds of cotton have been made into 12 b pounds of yarn; for in the creation of value, the time that is socially necessary alone counts.

Not only the labor, but also the raw material and the product now appear in quite a new light, very different from that in which we viewed them in the labor-process pure and simple. The raw material serves now merely as an absorbent of a definite quantity of labor. By this absorption it is in fact changed into yarn, because it is spun, because labor-power in the form of spinning is added to it; but the product, the yarn, is now nothing more than a measure of the labor absorbed by the cotton. If in one hour 1 2/3 lbs. of cotton can be spun into 1 2/3 lbs. of yarn, then 10 lbs. of yarn indicate the absorption of 6 hours' labor. Definite quantities of product, these quantities being determined by experience, now represent nothing but definite quantities of labor, definite masses of crystallized labor-time. They are nothing more than the materialization of so many hours or so many days of social labor....

We assumed, on the occasion of its sale, that the value of a day's labor-power is three shillings, and that six hours' labor is incorporated in that sum; and consequently that this amount of labor is requisite to produce the necessaries of life daily required on an average by the laborer. If now our spinner by working for one hour, can convert 1 2/3 lbs. of cotton into 1 2/3 lbs. of yarn, it follows that in six hours he will convert 10 lbs. of cotton into 10 lbs. of yarn. Hence, during the spinning process, the cotton absorbs six hours' labor. The same quantity of labor is also embodied in a piece of gold of the value of three shillings. Consequently by the mere labor of spinning, a value of three shillings is added to the cotton.

Let us now consider the total value of the product, the 10 lbs. of yarn. Two and a half days' labor has been embodied in it, of which two days were contained in the cotton and in the substance of the spindle worn away, and half a day was absorbed during the process of spinning. This two and a half days' labor is also represented by a piece of gold of the value of fifteen shillings. Hence, fifteen shillings is an adequate price for the 10 lbs. of yarn, or the price of one pound is eighteen pence.

Our capitalist stares in astonishment. The value of the product is exactly equal to the value of the capital advanced. The value so advanced has not expanded, no surplus-value has been created, and consequently money has not been converted into capital. The price of the yarn is fifteen shillings, and fifteen shillings were spent in the open market upon the constituent elements of the product, or, what amounts to the same thing, upon the factors of the labor-process; ten shillings were paid for the cotton, two shillings for the substance of the spindle worn away, and three shillings for the labor-power. The swollen value of the yarn is of no avail, for it is merely the sum of the values formerly existing in the cotton, the spindle, and the labor-power: out of such a simple addition of existing values, no surplus-value can possibly arise. These separate values are now all concentrated in one thing; but so they were also in the sum of fifteen shillings, before it was split up into three parts, by the purchase of the commodities.

There is in reality nothing very strange in this result. The value of one pound of yarn being eighteen pence, if our capitalist buys 10 lbs. of yarn in the market, he must pay fifteen shillings for them. It is clear that, whether a man buys his house ready built, or gets it built for him, in neither case will the mode of acquisition increase the amount of money laid out on the house.

Our capitalist, who is at home in his vulgar economy, exclaims: "Oh! but I advanced my money for the express purpose of making more money." The way to Hell is paved with good intentions, and he might just as easily have intended to make money, without producing at all. He threatens all sorts of things. He won't be caught napping again. In future he will buy the commodities in the market, instead of manufacturing them himself. But if all his brother capitalists were to do the same, where would he find his commodities in the market? And his money he cannot eat. He tries persuasion. "Consider my abstinence; I might have played ducks and drakes with the 15 shillings; but instead of that I consumed it productively, and made yarn with it." Very well, and by way of reward he is now in possession of good yarn instead of a bad conscience; and as for playing the part of a miser, it would never do for him to relapse into such bad ways as that; we have seen before to what results such asceticism leads. Besides, where nothing is, the king has lost his rights; whatever may be the merit of his abstinence, there is nothing wherewith specially to remunerate it, because the value of the product is merely the sum of the values of the commodities that were thrown into the process of production…

A service is nothing more than the useful effect of a use-value, be it of a commodity, or be it of labor. But here we are dealing with exchange-value. The capitalist paid to the laborer a value of 3 shillings, and the laborer gave him back an exact equivalent in the value of 3 shillings, added by him to the cotton: he gave him value for value. Our friend, up to this time so purse-proud, suddenly assumes the modest demeanor of his own workman, and exclaims: "Have I myself not worked? Have I not performed the labor of superintendence and of overlooking the spinner? And does not this labor, too, create value?" His over looker and his manager try to hide their smiles. Meanwhile, after a hearty laugh, he re-assumes his usual mien. Though he chanted to us the whole creed of the economists, in reality, he says, he would not give a brass farthing for it. He leaves this and all such like subterfuges and juggling tricks to the professors of Political Economy, who are paid for it. He himself is a practical man; and though he does not always consider what he says outside his business, yet in his business he knows what he is about.

Let us examine the matter more closely. The value of a day's labor-power amounts to 3 shillings, because on our assumption half a day's labor is embodied in that quantity of labor-power, i.e., because the means of subsistence that are daily required for the production of labor-power, cost half a day's labor. But the past labor that is embodied in the labor-power, and the living labor that it can call into action; the daily cost of maintaining it, and its daily expenditure in work, are two totally different things. The former determines the exchange-value of the labor-power, the latter is its use-value. The fact that half a day's labor is necessary to keep the laborer alive during 24 hours, does not in any way prevent him from working a whole day. Therefore, the value of labor-power, and the value which that labor-power creates in the labor-process, are two entirely different magnitudes; and this difference of the two values was what the capitalist had in view, when he was purchasing the labor-power.

The useful qualities that labor-power possesses, and by virtue of which it makes yarn or boots, were to him nothing more than a *conditio sine qua non*; for in order to create value, labor must be expended in a useful manner. What really influenced him was the specific use-value which this commodity possesses of being a source not only of value, but of more value than it has itself. This is the special service that the capitalist expects from labor-power, and in this transaction he acts in accordance with the "eternal laws" of the exchange of commodities. The seller of labor-power, like the seller of any other commodity, realizes its exchange-value, and parts with its use-value. He cannot take the one without giving the other. The use-value of labor-power, or in other words, labor, belongs just as little to its seller, as the use-value of oil after it has been sold belongs to the dealer who has sold it. The owner of the money has paid the value of a day's labor-power; his, therefore, is the use of it for a day; a day's labor belongs to him. The circumstance, that on the one hand the daily sustenance of labor-power costs only half a day's labor, while on the other hand the very same labor-power can work during a whole day, that consequently the value which its use during one day creates, is double what he pays for that use, this circumstance is, without doubt, a piece of good luck for the buyer, but by no means an injury to the seller.

Our capitalist foresaw this state of things, and that was the cause of his laughter. The laborer therefore finds, in the workshop, the means of production necessary for working, not only during six, but during twelve hours. Just as during the six hours' process our 10 lbs. of cotton absorbed six hours' labor, and became 10 lbs. of yarn, so now, 20 lbs. of cotton will absorb 12 hours' labor and be changed into 20 lbs. of yarn....The value of the yarn is 30 shillings. Therefore the value of the product is 1/9 greater than the value advanced for its production; 27 shillings have been transformed into 30 shillings; a surplus-value of 3 shillings has been created. The trick has at last succeeded; money has been converted into capital.

Section 1. Limits of the Working Day

We started with the supposition that labor-power is bought and sold at its value. Its value, like that of all other commodities, is determined by the working-time necessary to its production. If the production of the average daily means of subsistence of the laborer takes up 6 hours, he must work, on the average, 6 hours every day, to produce his daily labor-power, or to reproduce the value received as the result of its sale. The necessary part of his working-day amounts to 6 hours, and is, therefore, *caeteris paribus*, a given quantity. But with this, the extent of the working-day itself is not yet given.

Let us assume that the line A——B represents the length of the necessary working-time, say 6 hours. If the labor be prolonged 1, 3, or 6 hours beyond A——B, we have 3 other lines

```
Working day 1        Working day II       Working day III
A-------B--C         A-------B----C       A-------B-------C
```

representing 3 different working-days of 7, 9, and 12 hours. The extension B——C of the line A——B represents the length of the surplus-labor. As the working-day is A——B + B——C or A——C, it varies with the variable quantity B——C. Since A——B is constant, the ratio of B——C to A——B can always be calculated. In working-day I, it is 1/6, in working-day II, 3/6, in working day III 6/6 of A——B. Since further the ratio (surplus working-time)/(necessary working-time), determines the rate of the surplus-value, the latter is given by the ratio of B——C to A——B. It amounts in the 3 different working-days respectively to 16 2/3, 50 and 100 per cent. On the other hand, the rate of surplus-value alone would not give us the extent of the working-day. If this rate, e.g., were 100 per cent., the working-day might be of 8, 10, 12, or more hours. It would indicate that the 2 constituent parts of the working-day, necessary-labor and surplus-labor time, were equal in extent, but not how long each of these two constituent parts was....

The working-day is thus not a constant, but a variable quantity. One of its parts, certainly, is determined by the working-time required for the reproduction of the labor-power of the laborer himself. But its total amount varies with the duration of the surplus-labor. The working-day is, therefore, determinable, but is, per se, indeterminate....

Capital is dead labor, that, vampire-like, only lives by sucking living labor, and lives the more, the more labor it sucks. The time during which the laborer works, is the time during which the capitalist consumes the labor-power he has purchased of him....

Hence is it that in the history of capitalist production, the determination of what is a working-day, presents itself as the result of a struggle, a struggle between collective capital, i.e., the class of capitalists, and collective labor, i.e., the working-class.

Part IV: Production of Relative Surplus-Value

Chapter Twelve: The Concept of Relative Surplus-Value

That portion of the working-day which merely produces an equivalent for the value paid by the capitalist for his labor-power, has, up to this point, been treated by us as a constant magnitude, and such in fact it is, under given conditions of production and at a given stage in the economic development of society. Beyond this, his necessary labor-time, the laborer, we saw, could continue to work for 2, 3, 4, 6, &c., hours. The rate of surplus-value and the length of the working-day depended on the magnitude of this prolongation. Though the necessary labor-time was constant, we saw, on the other hand, that the total working-day was variable.... Now suppose we have a working-day whose length, and whose apportionment between necessary labor and surplus-labor, are given....

Given the length of the working-day, the prolongation of the surplus-labor must of necessity originate in the curtailment of the necessary labor-time; the latter cannot arise from the former. In the example we have taken, it is necessary that the value of labor-power should actually fall by one-tenth, in order that the necessary labor-time may be diminished by one-tenth, i.e., from ten hours to nine, and in order that the surplus labor may consequently be prolonged from two hours to three.

Such a fall in the value of labor-power implies, however, that the same necessaries of life which were formerly produced in ten hours, can now be produced in nine hours. But this is impossible without an increase in the productiveness of labor. For example, suppose a shoemaker, with given tools, makes in one working-day of twelve hours, one pair of boots. If he must make two pairs in the same time, the productiveness of his labor must be doubled;

and this cannot be done, except by an alteration in his tools or in his mode of working, or in both. Hence, the conditions of production, i.e., his mode of production, and the labor-process itself, must be revolutionized. By increase in the productiveness of labor, we mean, generally, an alteration in the labor-process, of such a kind as to shorten the labor-time socially necessary for the production of a commodity, and to endow a given quantity of labor with the power of producing a greater quantity of use-value. Hitherto in treating of surplus-value, arising from a simple prolongation of the working-day, we have assumed the mode of production to be given and invariable. But when surplus-value has to be produced by the conversion of necessary labor into surplus-labor, it by no means suffices for capital to take over the labor-process in the form under which it has been historically handed down, and then simply to prolong the duration of that process. The technical and social conditions of the process, and consequently the very mode of production must be revolutionized, before the productiveness of labor can be increased. By that means alone can the value of labor-power be made to sink, and the portion of the working-day necessary for the reproduction of that value, be shortened.

The surplus-value produced by prolongation of the working-day, I call absolute surplus-value. On the other hand, the surplus-value arising from the curtailment of the necessary labor-time, and from the corresponding alteration in the respective lengths of the two components of the working-day, I call relative surplus-value.

In order to effect a fall in the value of labor-power, the increase in the productiveness of labor must seize upon those branches of industry whose products determine the value of labor-power, and consequently either belong to the class of customary means of subsistence, or are capable of supplying the place of those means. But the value of a commodity is determined, not only by the quantity of labor which the laborer directly bestows upon that commodity, but also by the labor contained in the means of production. For instance, the value of a pair of boots depends not only on the cobbler's labor, but also on the value of the leather, wax, thread, &c. Hence, a fall in the value of labor-power is also brought about by an increase in the productiveness of labor, and by a corresponding cheapening of commodities in those industries which supply the instruments of labor and the raw material, that form the material elements of the constant capital required for producing the necessaries of life. But an increase in the productiveness of labor in those branches of industry which supply neither the necessaries of life, nor the means of production for such necessaries, leaves the value of labor-power undisturbed....

Chapter Fourteen: Division of Labor and Manufacture

Section 4 Division of Labor in Manufacture, Division of Labor in Society
Division of labor in a society, and the corresponding tying down of individuals to a particular calling, develops itself, just as does the division of labor in manufacture, from opposite starting-points. Within a family, and after further

development within a tribe, there springs up naturally a division of labor, caused by differences of sex and age, a division that is consequently based on a purely physiological foundation, which division enlarges its materials by the expansion of the community, by the increase of population, and more especially, by the conflicts between different tribes, and the subjugation of one tribe by another. On the other hand, as I have before remarked, the exchange of products springs up at the points where different families, tribes, communities, come in contact; for, in the beginning of civilization, it is not private individuals but families, tribes, &c., that meet on an independent footing. Different communities find different means of production, and different means of subsistence in their natural environment. Hence, their modes of production, and of living, and their products are different. It is this spontaneously developed difference which, when different communities come in contact, calls forth the mutual exchange of products, and the consequent gradual conversion of those products into commodities...

Since the production and the circulation of commodities are the general pre-requisites of the capitalist mode of production, division of labor in manufacture demands, that division of labor in society at large should previously have attained a certain degree of development. Inversely, the former division reacts upon and develops and multiplies the latter. Simultaneously, with the differentiation of the instruments of labor, the industries that produce these instruments, become more and more differentiated. If the manufacturing system seize upon an industry, which, previously, was carried on in connection with others, either as a chief or as a subordinate industry, and by one producer, these industries immediately separate their connection, and become independent. If it seize upon a particular stage in the production of a commodity, the other stages of its production become converted into so many independent industries. It has already been stated, that where the finished article consists merely of a number of parts fitted together, the detail operations may re-establish themselves as genuine and separate handicrafts. In order to carry out more perfectly the division of labor in manufacture, a single branch of production is, according to the varieties of its raw material, or the various forms that one and the same raw material may assume, split up into numerous, and to some extent, entirely new manufactures....

But, in spite of the numerous analogies and links connecting them, division of labor in the interior of a society, and that in the interior of a workshop, differ not only in degree, but also in kind. The analogy appears most indisputable where there is an invisible bond uniting the various branches of trade. For instance the cattle-breeder produces hides, the tanner makes the hides into leather, and the shoemaker, the leather into boots. Here the thing produced by each of them is but a step towards the final form, which is the product of all their labors combined. There are, besides, all the various industries that supply the cattle-breeder, the tanner, and the shoemaker with the means of production. Now it is quite possible to imagine, with Adam Smith, that the difference between the above social division of labor, and the division in man-ufacture, is merely subjective, exists merely for the observer, who, in a manu-facture, can see with one glance, all the numerous operations being performed on one spot, while in the instance given above, the spreading out of the work over great areas, and the great number of people employed in each branch of labor, obscure the connection....

Division of labor within the workshop implies the undisputed authority of the capitalist over men, that are but parts of a mechanism that belongs to him. The division of labor within the society brings into contact independent com-modity-producers, who acknowledge no other authority but that of competi-tion, of the coercion exerted by the pressure of their mutual interests; just as in the animal kingdom, the *bellum omnium contra omnes* more or less preserves the conditions of existence of every species. The same bourgeois mind which praises division of labor in the workshop, life-long annexation of the laborer to a partial operation, and his complete subjection to capital, as being an organi-zation of labor that increases its productiveness that same bourgeois mind denounces with equal vigor every conscious attempt to socially control and regulate the process of production, as an inroad upon such sacred things as the rights of property, freedom and unrestricted play for the bent of the individual capitalist. It is very characteristic that the enthusiastic apologists of the factory system have nothing more damning to urge against a general organization of the labor of society, than that it would turn all society into one immense factory....

While division of labor in society at large, whether such division be brought about or not by exchange of commodities, is common to economic formations of society the most diverse, division of labor in the workshop, as practiced by manufacture, is a special creation of the capitalist mode of production alone.

Section 5. The Capitalistic Character of Manufacture

An increased number of laborers under the control of one capitalist is the natu-ral starting-point, as well of co-operation generally, as of manufacture in par-ticular. But the division of labor in manufacture makes this increase in the number of workmen a technical necessity. The minimum number that any given capitalist is bound to employ is here prescribed by the previously estab-lished division of labor. On the other hand, the advantages of further division are obtainable only by adding to the number of workmen, and this can be done only by adding multiples of the various detail groups. But an increase in the variable component of the capital employed necessitates an increase in its constant component, too, in the workshops, implements, &c., and, in particu-lar, in the raw material, the call for which grows quicker than the number of workmen. The quantity of it consumed in a given time, by a given amount of labor, increases in the same ratio as does the productive power of that labour in consequence of its division. Hence, it is a law, based on the very nature of manufacture, that the minimum amount of capital, which is bound to be in the

hands of each capitalist, must keep increasing; in other words, that the transformation into capital of the social means of production and subsistence must
keep extending....

"The understandings of the greater part of men," says Adam Smith, "are
necessarily formed by their ordinary employments. The man whose whole life
is spent in performing a few simple operations ... has no occasion to exert his
understanding... He generally becomes as stupid and ignorant as it is possible
for a human creature to become."

After describing the stupidity of the detail labourer he goes on:

> "The uniformity of his stationary life naturally corrupts the courage of his mind...
> It corrupts even the activity of his body and renders him incapable of exerting his
> strength with vigour and perseverance in any other employments than that to
> which he has been bred. His dexterity at his own particular trade seems in this
> manner to be acquired at the expense of his intellectual, social, and martial vir-
> tues. But in every improved and civilized society, this is the state into which the
> laboring poor, that is, the great body of the people, must necessarily fall."

For preventing the complete deterioration of the great mass of the people
by division of labor, A. Smith recommends education of the people by the
State, but prudently, and in homeopathic doses... Some crippling of body and
mind is inseparable even from division of labour in society as a whole. Since,
however, manufacture carries this social separation of branches of labour
much further, and also, by its peculiar division, attacks the individual at the
very roots of his life, it is the first to afford the materials for, and to give a start
to, industrial pathology.

Chapter Fifteen: Machinery and Modern Industry

Section 1. The Development of Machinery
John Stuart Mill says in his "Principles of Political Economy": "It is question-
able if all the mechanical inventions yet made have lightened the day's toil of
any human being." That is, however, by no means the aim of the capitalistic
application of machinery. Like every other increase in the productiveness of
labor, machinery is intended to cheapen commodities, and, by shortening that
portion of the working-day, in which the laborer works for himself, to lengthen
the other portion that he gives, without an equivalent, to the capitalist. In
short, it is a means for producing surplus-value.

In manufacture, the revolution in the mode of production begins with the
labor-power, in modern industry it begins with the instruments of labor. Our
first inquiry then is, how the instruments of labor are converted from tools into
machines, or what is the difference between a machine and the implements of
a handicraft? We are only concerned here with striking and general characteristics; for epochs in the history of society are no more separated from each
other by hard and fast lines of demarcation, than are geological epochs....

Section 3. The Proximate Effects of machinery on the Workman
A. Appropriation of Supplementary Labor-Power by Capital. The Employment of Women and Children

The value of labor-power was determined, not only by the labor-time necessary to maintain the individual adult laborer, but also by that necessary to maintain his family. Machinery, by throwing every member of that family on to the labor-market, spreads the value of the man's labor-power over his whole family. It thus depreciates his labor-power. To purchase the labor-power of a family of four workers may, perhaps, cost more than it formerly did to purchase the labor-power of the head of the family, but, in return, four days' labor takes the place of one, and their price falls in proportion to the excess of the surplus-labor of four over the surplus-labor of one. In order that the family may live, four people must now, not only labor, but expend surplus-labor for the capitalist. Thus we see, that machinery, while augmenting the human material that forms the principal object of capital's exploiting power, at the same time raises the degree of exploitation....

The moral degradation caused by the capitalistic exploitation of women and children has been so exhaustively depicted by F. Engels in his "Lage der Arbeitenden Klasse Englands," and other writers, that I need only mention the subject in this place. But the intellectual desolation artificially produced by converting immature human beings into mere machines for the fabrication of surplus-value, a state of mind clearly distinguishable from that natural ignorance which keeps the mind fallow without destroying its capacity for development, its natural fertility, this desolation finally compelled even the English Parliament to make elementary education a compulsory condition to the "productive" employment of children under 14 years, in every industry subject to the Factory Acts. The spirit of capitalist production stands out clearly in the ludicrous wording of the so-called education clauses in the Factory Acts, in the absence of an administrative machinery, an absence that again makes the compulsion illusory, in the opposition of the manufacturers themselves to these education clauses, and in the tricks and dodges they put in practice for evading them....

B. Prolongation of the Working-Day

If machinery be the most powerful means for increasing the productiveness of labor—i.e., for shortening the working-time required in the production of a commodity, it becomes in the hands of capital the most powerful means, in those industries first invaded by it, for lengthening the working-day beyond all bounds set by human nature. It creates, on the one hand, new conditions by which capital is enabled to give free scope to this its constant tendency, and on the other hand, new motives with which to whet capital's appetite for the labor of others....

If, then, the capitalistic employment of machinery, on the one hand, supplies new and powerful motives to an excessive lengthening of the working-day, and radically changes, as well the methods of labor, as also the character of the social working organism, in such a manner as to break down all opposition to this tendency, on the other hand it produces, partly by opening out to the capitalist new strata of the working-class, previously inaccessible to him, partly by setting free the laborers it supplants, a surplus working population, which is compelled to submit to the dictation of capital.

Hence that remarkable phenomenon in the history of Modern Industry, that machinery sweeps away every moral and natural restriction on the length of the working-day. Hence, too, the economic paradox, that the most powerful instrument for shortening labor-time, becomes the most unfailing means for placing every moment of the laborer's time and that of his family, at the disposal of the capitalist for the purpose of expanding the value of his capital....

Section 4. The Factory
Although then, technically speaking, the old system of division of labor is thrown overboard by machinery, it hangs on in the factory, as a traditional habit handed down from Manufacture, and is afterwards systematically remolded and established in a more hideous form by capital, as a means of exploiting labor-power. The life-long specialty of handling one and the same tool, now becomes the life-long specialty of serving one and the same machine. Machinery is put to a wrong use, with the object of transforming the workman, from his very childhood, into a part of a detail-machine. In this way, not only are the expenses of his reproduction considerably lessened, but at the same time his helpless dependence upon the factory as a whole, and therefore upon the capitalist, is rendered complete. Here as everywhere else, we must distinguish between the increased productiveness due to the development of the social process of production, and that due to the capitalist exploitation of that process. In handicrafts and manufacture, the workman makes use of a tool, in the factory, the machine makes use of him. There the movements of the instrument of labor proceed from him, here it is the movements of the machine that he must follow. In manufacture the workmen are parts of a living mechanism. In the factory we have a lifeless mechanism independent of the workman, who becomes its mere living appendage.

> "The miserable routine of endless drudgery and toil in which the same mechanical process is gone through over and over again, is like the labor of Sisyphus. The burden of labor, like the rock, keeps ever falling back on the worn-out laborer."   [Engels, *The Condition of the Working Class*]

At the same time that factory work exhausts the nervous system to the uttermost, it does away with the many-sided play of the muscles, and confiscates every atom of freedom, both in bodily and intellectual activity. The lightening of the labor, even, becomes a sort of torture, since the machine does not free the laborer from work, but deprives the work of all interest. Every kind of capitalist production, in so far as it is not only a labor-process, but also a process of creating surplus-value, has this in common, that it is not the work-man that employs the instruments of labor, but the instruments of labor that employ the workman. But it is only in the factory system that this inversion for the first time acquires technical and palpable reality. By means of its conversion into an automaton, the instrument of labor confronts the laborer, during the labor-process, in the shape of capital, of dead labor, that dominates, and pumps dry, living labor-power. The separation of the intellectual powers of production from the manual labor, and the conversion of those powers into the might of capital over labor, is, as we have already shown, finally completed by modern industry erected on the foundation of machinery.

The special skill of each individual insignificant factory operative vanishes as an infinitesimal quantity before the science, the gigantic physical forces, and the mass of labor that are embodied in the factory mechanism and, together with that mechanism, constitute the power of the "master." This "master," therefore, in whose brain the machinery and his monopoly of it are inseparably united, whenever he falls out with his "hands," contemptuously tells them: "The factory operatives should keep in wholesome remembrance the fact that theirs is really a low species of skilled labor; and that there is none which is more easily acquired, or of its quality more amply remunerated, or which by a short training of the least expert can be more quickly, as well as abundantly, acquired.... The master's machinery really plays a far more important part in the business of production than the labor and the skill of the operative, which six months' education can teach, and a common laborer can learn."

The technical subordination of the workman to the uniform motion of the instruments of labor, and the peculiar composition of the body of workpeople, consisting as it does of individuals of both sexes and of all ages, give rise to a barrack discipline, which is elaborated into a complete system in the factory, and which fully develops the before mentioned labor of overlooking, thereby dividing the workpeople into operatives and over lookers, into private soldiers and sergeants of an industrial army....

Section 6. Workpeople Displaced by Machinery
The laborers that are thrown out of work in any branch of industry, can no doubt seek for employment in some other branch. If they find it, and thus renew the bond between them and the means of subsistence, this takes place only by the intermediary of a new and additional capital that is seeking investment; not at all by the intermediary of the capital that formerly employed them and was afterwards converted into machinery. And even should they find employment, what a poor look-out is theirs! Crippled as they are by division of labor, these poor devils are worth so little outside their old trade, that they cannot find admission into any industries, except a few of inferior kind, that are over-supplied with underpaid workmen. Further, every branch of industry attracts each year a new stream of men, who furnish a contingent from which to fill up vacancies, and to draw a supply for expansion. So soon

as machinery sets free a part of the workmen employed in a given branch of industry, the reserve men are also diverted into new channels of employment, and become absorbed in other branches; meanwhile the original victims, during the period of transition, for the most part starve and perish....

Section 7. Repulsion and Attraction of Workpeople by the Factory System

All political economists of any standing admit that the introduction of new machinery has a baneful effect on the workmen in the old handicrafts and manufactures with which this machinery at first competes. Almost all of them bemoan the slavery of the factory operative. And what is the great trump-card that they play? That machinery, after the horrors of the period of introduction and development have subsided, instead of diminishing, in the long run increases the number of the slaves of labor! Yes, Political Economy revels in the hideous theory, hideous to every "philanthropist" who believes in the eternal Nature-ordained necessity for capitalist production, that after a period of growth and transition, even its crowning success, the factory system based on machinery, grinds down more workpeople than on its first introduction it throws on the streets....

The enormous power, inherent in the factory system, of expanding by jumps, and the dependence of that system on the markets of the world, necessarily beget feverish production, followed by over-filling of the markets, whereupon contraction of the markets brings on crippling of production. The life of modern industry becomes a series of periods of moderate activity, prosperity, over-production, crisis and stagnation. The uncertainty and instability to which machinery subjects the employment, and consequently the conditions of existence, of the operatives become normal, owing to these periodic changes of the industrial cycle. Except in the periods of prosperity, there rages between the capitalists the most furious combat for the share of each in the markets. This share is directly proportional to the cheapness of the product. Besides the rivalry that this struggle begets in the application of improved machinery for replacing labor-power, and of new methods of production, there also comes a time in every industrial cycle, when a forcible reduction of wages beneath the value of labor-power, is attempted for the purpose of cheapening commodities.

Section 9. The Factory Acts. Sanitary and Education Clauses

Modern Industry, as we have seen, sweeps away by technical means the manufacturing division of labor, under which each man is bound hand and foot for life to a single detail-operation. At the same time, the capitalistic form of that industry reproduces this same division of labor in a still more monstrous shape; in the factory proper, by converting the workman into a living appendage of the machine; and everywhere outside the Factory, partly by the sporadic use of machinery and machine workers, partly by re-establishing the division of labor on a fresh basis by the general introduction of the labor of women and children, and of cheap unskilled labor....

Part V: The Production of Absolute and of Relative Surplus-Value

Chapter Sixteen: Absolute and Relative Surplus-Value

The prolongation of the working-day beyond the point at which the laborer would have produced just an equivalent for the value of his labor-power, and the appropriation of that surplus-labor by capital, this is production of absolute surplus-value. It forms the general groundwork of the capitalist system, and the starting-point for the production of relative surplus-value. The latter pre-supposes that the working-day is already divided into two parts, necessary labor, and surplus-labor. In order to prolong the surplus-labor, the necessary labor is shortened by methods whereby the equivalent for the wages is produced in less time. The production of absolute surplus-value turns exclusively upon the length of the working-day; the production of relative surplus-value, revolutionizes out and out the technical processes of labor, and the composition of society. It therefore pre-supposes a specific mode, the capitalist mode of production, a mode which, along with its methods, means, and conditions, arises and develops itself spontaneously on the foundation afforded by the formal subjection of labor to capital. In the course of this development, the formal subjection is replaced by the real subjection of labor to capital....

Chapter Twenty-Five: The General Law of Capitalist Accumulation

Section 1. The Increased Demand for Labor-Power that Accompanies Accumulation, the Composition of Capital Remaining the Same

In this chapter we consider the influence of the growth of capital on the lot of the laboring class. The most important factor in this inquiry is the composition of capital and the changes it undergoes in the course of the process of accumulation.

The composition of capital is to be understood in a two-fold sense. On the side of value, it is determined by the proportion in which it is divided into constant capital or value of the means of production, and variable capital or value of labor-power, the sum total of wages. On the side of material, as it functions in the process of production, all capital is divided into means of production and living labor-power. This latter composition is determined by the relation between the mass of the means of production employed, on the one hand, and the mass of labor necessary for their employment on the other. I call the former the value-composition, the latter the technical composition of capital. Between the two there is a strict correlation. To express this, I call the value-composition of capital, in so far as it is determined by its technical composition and mirrors the changes of the latter, the organic composition of capital. Wherever I refer to the composition of capital, without further qualification, its organic composition is always understood.

The many individual capitals invested in a particular branch of production have, one with another, more or less different compositions. The average of their individual compositions gives us the composition of the total capital in this branch of production. Lastly, the average of these averages, in all branches of production, gives us the composition of the total social capital of a country, and with this alone are we, in the last resort, concerned in the following investigation.

Growth of capital involves growth of its variable constituent or of the part invested in labor-power. A part of the surplus-value turned into additional capital must always be re-transformed into variable capital, or additional labor-fund. If we suppose that, all other circumstances remaining the same, the composition of capital also remains constant (i.e., that a definite mass of means of production constantly needs the same mass of labor-power to set it in motion), then the demand for labor and the subsistence-fund of the laborers clearly increase in the same proportion as the capital, and the more rapidly, the more rapidly the capital increases. Since the capital produces yearly a surplus-value, of which one part is yearly added to the original capital; since this increment itself grows yearly along with the augmentation of the capital already functioning; since lastly, under special stimulus to enrichment, such as the opening of new markets, or of new spheres for the outlay of capital in consequence of newly developed social wants, &c., the scale of accumulation may be suddenly extended, merely by a change in the division of the surplus-value or surplus-product into capital and revenue, the requirements of accumulating capital may exceed the increase of labor-power or of the number of laborers; the demand for laborers may exceed the supply, and, therefore, wages may rise. This must, indeed, ultimately be the case if the conditions supposed above continue.... Accumulation of capital is, therefore, increase of the proletariat.

Classical economy grasped this fact so thoroughly that Adam Smith, Ricardo, &c., as mentioned earlier, inaccurately identified accumulation with the consumption, by the productive laborers, of all the capitalized, part of the surplus-product, or with its transformation into additional wage-laborers....

The law of capitalistic accumulation, metamorphosed by economists into a pretended Law of Nature, in reality merely states that the very nature of accumulation excludes every diminution in the degree of exploitation of labor, and every rise in the price of labor, which could seriously imperil the continual reproduction, on an ever-enlarging scale, of the capitalistic relation. It cannot be otherwise in a mode of production in which the laborer exists to satisfy the needs of self-expansion of existing values, instead of, on the contrary, material wealth existing to satisfy the needs of development on the part of the laborer. As, in religion, man is governed by the products of his own brain, so in capitalistic production, he is governed by the products of his own hand.

Section 3. Progressive Production of a Relative Surplus-Population or Industrial Reserve Army

The accumulation of capital, though originally appearing as its quantitative extension only, is effected, as we have seen, under a progressive qualitative change in its composition, under a constant increase of its constant, at the expense of its variable constituent.

The specifically capitalist mode of production, the development of the productive power of labor corresponding to it, and the change thence resulting in the organic composition of capital, do not merely keep pace with the advance of accumulation, or with the growth of social wealth. They develop at a much quicker rate, because mere accumulation, the absolute increase of the total social capital, is accompanied by the centralization of the individual capitals of which that total is made up; and because the change in the technological composition of the additional capital goes hand in hand with a similar change in the technological composition of the original capital....

But if a surplus laboring population is a necessary product of accumulation or of the development of wealth on a capitalist basis, this surplus-population becomes, conversely, the lever of capitalistic accumulation, nay, a condition of existence of the capitalist mode of production. It forms a disposable industrial reserve army, that belongs to capital quite as absolutely as if the latter had bred it at its own cost. Independently of the limits of the actual increase of population, it creates, for the changing needs of the self-expansion of capital, a mass of human material always ready for exploitation. With accumulation, and the development of the productiveness of labor that accompanies it, the power of sudden expansion of capital grows also; it grows, not merely because the elasticity of the capital already functioning increases, not merely because the absolute wealth of society expands, of which capital only forms an elastic part, not merely because credit, under every special stimulus, at once places an unusual part of this wealth at the disposal of production in the form of additional capital; it grows, also, because the technical conditions of the process of production themselves—machinery, means of transport, &c—now admit of the rapidest transformation of masses of surplus-product into additional means of production....

The expansion by fits and starts of the scale of production is the preliminary to its equally sudden contraction; the latter again evokes the former, but the former is impossible without disposable human material, without an increase, in the number of laborers independently of the absolute growth of the population. This increase is effected by the simple process that constantly "sets free" a part of the laborers; by methods which lessen the number of laborers employed in proportion to the increased production. The whole form of the movement of modem industry depends, therefore, upon the constant transformation of a part of the laboring population into unemployed or half-employed hands.

The superficiality of Political Economy shows itself in the fact that it looks upon the expansion and contraction of credit, which is a mere symptom of the periodic changes of the industrial cycle, as their cause. As the heavenly bodies, once thrown into a certain definite motion, always repeat this, so is it with social production as soon as it is once thrown into this movement of alternate expansion and contraction. Effects, in their turn, become causes, and the varying accidents of the whole process, which always reproduces its own conditions, take on the form of periodicity. When this periodicity is once consolidated, even Political Economy then sees that the production of a relative surplus-population—i.e., surplus with regard to the average needs of the self-expansion of capital—is a necessary condition of modern industry....

Even Malthus recognizes overpopulation as a necessity of modern industry, though, after his narrow fashion, he explains it by the absolute over-growth of the laboring population, not by their becoming relatively supernumerary. He says: "Prudential habits with regard to marriage, carried to a considerable extent among the laboring class of a country mainly depending upon manufactures and commerce, might injure it.... From the nature of a population, an increase of laborers cannot be brought into market in consequence of a particular demand till after the lapse of 16 or 18 years, and the conversion of revenue into capital, by saving, may take place much more rapidly: a country is always liable to an increase in the quantity of the funds for the maintenance of labor faster than the increase of population." [*Editors' Comment: Marx has a footnote reference here saying that "Malthus finally discovers, with the help of Sismondi, the beautiful Trinity of capitalistic production: over-production, over-population, over-consumption—three very delicate monsters indeed.*]

After Political Economy has thus demonstrated the constant production of a relative surplus-population of laborers to be a necessity of capitalistic accumulation, she very aptly, in the guise of an old maid, puts in the mouth of her "beau ideal" of a capitalist the following words addressed to those supernumeraries thrown on the streets by their own creation of additional capital: "We manufacturers do what we can for you, whilst we are increasing that capital on which you must subsist, and you must do the rest by accommodating your numbers to the means of subsistence."

Section 4. Different Forms of the Relative Surplus-Population. The General Law of Capitalistic Accumulation

The relative surplus-population exists in every possible form. Every laborer belongs to it during the time when he is only partially employed or wholly unemployed. Not taking into account the great periodically recurring forms that the changing phases of the industrial cycle impress on it, now an acute form during the crisis, then again a chronic form during dull times—it has always three forms, the floating, the latent, the stagnant....

The third category of the relative surplus-population, the stagnant, forms a part of the active labor army, but with extremely irregular employment. Hence it furnishes to capital an inexhaustible reservoir of disposable labor-power. Its conditions of life sink below the average normal level of the working-class; this makes it at once the broad basis of special branches of capitalist exploitation. It is characterized by maximum of working-time, and minimum of wages. We have learnt to know its chief form under the rubric of "domestic industry...."

The lowest sediment of the relative surplus-population finally dwells in the sphere of pauperism. Exclusive of vagabonds, criminals, prostitutes, in a word, the "dangerous" classes, this layer of society consists of three categories. First, those able to work. One need only glance superficially at the statistics of English pauperism to find that the quantity of paupers increases with every crisis, and diminishes with every revival of trade. Second, orphans and pauper children. These are candidates for the industrial reserve army, and are, in times of great prosperity, as 1860, e.g., speedily and in large numbers enrolled in the active army of laborers. Third, the demoralized and ragged, and those unable to work, chiefly people who succumb to their incapacity for adaptation, due to the division of labor; people who have passed the normal age of the laborer; the victims of industry, whose number increases with the increase of dangerous machinery, of mines, chemical works, &c., the mutilated, the sickly, the widows, &c. Pauperism is the hospital of the active labor-army and the dead weight of the industrial reserve army. Its production is included in that of the relative surplus-population, its necessity in theirs; along with the surplus-population, pauperism forms a condition of capitalist production, and of the capitalist development of wealth. It enters into the *faux frais* of capitalist production; but capital knows how to throw these, for the most part, from its own shoulders on to those of the working-class and the lower middle class.

The greater the social wealth, the functioning capital, the extent and energy of its growth, and, therefore, also the absolute mass of the proletariat and the productiveness of its labor, the greater is the industrial reserve army. The same causes which develop the expansive power of capital, develop also the labor-power at its disposal. The relative mass of the industrial reserve army increases therefore with the potential energy of wealth. But the greater this reserve army in proportion to the active labor-army, the greater is the mass of a consolidated surplus-population, whose misery is in inverse ratio to its torment of labor. The more extensive, finally, the lazarus-layers of the working-class, and the industrial reserve army, the greater is official pauperism. *This is the absolute general law of capitalist accumulation* [italics in original]. ...

We saw in Part IV., when analyzing the production of relative surplus-value: within the capitalist system all methods for raising the social productiveness of labor are brought about at the cost of the individual laborer; all means for the development of production transform themselves into means of domination over, and exploitation of, the producers; they mutilate the laborer into a fragment of a man, degrade him to the level of an appendage of a machine, destroy every remnant of charm in his work and turn it into a hated toil; they estrange from him the intellectual potentialities of the labor-process in the same proportion as science is incorporated in it as an independent power; they distort the conditions under which he works, subject him during the labor-process to a despotism the more hateful for its meanness; they transform his life-time into working-time, and drag his wife and child beneath the wheels of the Juggernaut of capital.

But all methods for the production of surplus-value are at the same time methods of accumulation; and every extension of accumulation becomes again a means for the development of those methods. It follows therefore that in proportion as capital accumulates, the lot of the laborer, be his payment high or low, must grow worse. The law, finally, that always equilibrates the relative surplus-population, or industrial reserve army, to the extent and energy of accumulation, this law rivets the laborer to capital more firmly than the wedges of Vulcan did Prometheus to the rock. It establishes an accumulation of misery, corresponding with accumulation of capital. Accumulation of wealth at one pole is, therefore, at the same time accumulation of misery, agony of toil slavery, ignorance, brutality, mental degradation, at the opposite pole, i.e., on the side of the class that produces its own product in the form of capital. This antagonistic character of capitalistic accumulation is enunciated in various forms by political economists, although by them it is confounded with phenomena, certainly to some extent analogous, but nevertheless essentially distinct, and belonging to pre-capitalistic modes of production.

Part VIII: The So-Called Primitive Accumulation

Chapter Thirty-Two: Historical Tendency of Capitalist Accumulation

As soon as this process of transformation has sufficiently decomposed the old society from top to bottom, as soon as the laborers are turned into proletarians, their means of labor into capital, as soon as the capitalist mode of production stands on its own feet, then the further socialization of labor and further transformation of the land and other means of production into socially exploited and, therefore, common means of production, as well as the further expropriation of private proprietors, takes a new form. That which is now to be expropriated is no longer the laborer working for himself, but the capitalist exploiting many laborers. This expropriation is accomplished by the action of the immanent laws of capitalistic production itself, by the centralization of capital.

One capitalist always kills many. Hand in hand with this centralization, or this expropriation of many capitalists by few, develop, on an ever-extending scale, the co-operative form of the labor-process, the conscious technical application of science, the methodical cultivation of the soil, the transformation of the instruments of labor into instruments of labor only usable in common, the economizing of all means of production by their use as means of production of combined, socialized labor, the entanglement of all peoples in the net of the world-market, and with this, the international character of the capitalistic regime. Along with the constantly diminishing number of the magnates of capital, who usurp and monopolize all advantages of this process of transformation, grows the mass of misery, oppression, slavery, degradation, exploitation; but with this too grows the revolt of the working-class, a class always increasing in numbers, and disciplined, united, organized by the very mechanism of the process of capitalist production itself. The monopoly of capital becomes a fetter upon the mode of production, which has sprung up and flourished along with, and under it. Centralization of the means of production and socialization of labor at last reach a point where they become incompatible with their capitalist integument. Thus integument is burst asunder. The knell of capitalist private property sounds. The expropriators are expropriated.

The capitalist mode of appropriation, the result of the capitalist mode of production, produces capitalist private property. This is the first negation of individual private property, as founded on the labor of the proprietor. But capitalist production begets, with the inexorability of a law of Nature, its own negation. It is the negation of negation. This does not re-establish private property for the producer, but gives him individual property based on the acquisition of the capitalist era: i.e., on co-operation and the possession in common of the land and of the means of production.

The transformation of scattered private property, arising from individual labor, into capitalist private property is, naturally, a process, incomparably more protracted, violent, and difficult, than the transformation of capitalistic private property, already practically resting on socialized production, into socialized property. In the former case, we had the expropriation of the mass of the people by a few usurpers; in the latter, we have the expropriation of a few usurpers by the mass of the people.

Das Kapital: Volume Three, Part VII

Chapter Forty-Eight: The Trinity Formula

Like all its predecessors, the capitalist process of production proceeds under definite material conditions, which are, however, simultaneously the bearers of definite social relations entered into by individuals in the process of reproducing their life. Those conditions, like these relations, are on the one hand prerequisites, on the other hand results and creations of the capitalist process of production; they are produced and reproduced by it. We saw also that capital—and the capitalist is merely capital personified and functions in the process of production solely as the agent of capital—in its corresponding social process of production, pumps a definite quantity of surplus-labor out of the direct producers, or laborers; capital obtains this surplus-labor without an equivalent, and in essence it always remains forced labor—no matter how much it may seem to result from free contractual agreement. This surplus-labor appears as surplus-value, and this surplus-value exists as a surplus-product. Surplus-labor in general, as labor performed over and above the given requirements, must always remain. In the capitalist as well as in the slave system, etc., it merely assumes an antagonistic form and is supplemented by complete idleness of a stratum of society....

The actual wealth of society, and the possibility of constantly expanding its reproduction process, therefore, do not depend upon the duration of surplus-labor, but upon its productivity and the more or less copious conditions of production under which it is performed. In fact, the realm of freedom actually begins only where labor which is determined by necessity and mundane considerations ceases; thus in the very nature of things it lies beyond the sphere of actual material production. Just as the savage must wrestle with Nature to satisfy his wants, to maintain and reproduce life, so must civilized man, and he must do so in all social formations and under all possible modes of production. With his development this realm of physical necessity expands as a result of his wants; but, at the same time, the forces of production which satisfy these wants also increase. Freedom in this field can only consist in socialized man, the associated producers, rationally regulating their interchange with Nature, bringing it under their common control, instead of being ruled by it as by the blind forces of Nature; and achieving this with the least expenditure of energy and under conditions most favorable to, and worthy of, their human nature. But it nonetheless still remains a realm of necessity. Beyond it begins that development of human energy which is an end in itself, the true realm of freedom, which, however, can blossom forth only with this realm of necessity as its basis. The shortening of the working day is its basic prerequisite.

Fredrick Engels

Socialism: Utopian and Scientific

The Origin of Utopian Socialism

Modern Socialism is, in its essence, the direct product of the recognition, on the one hand, of the class antagonisms existing in the society of today between proprietors and non-proprietors, between capitalists and wage-workers; on the other hand, of the anarchy existing in production. But, in its theoretical form, modern Socialism originally appears ostensibly as a more logical extension of the principles laid down by the great French philosophers of the 18th century. Like every new theory, modern Socialism had, at first, to connect itself with the intellectual stock-in-trade ready to its hand, however deeply its roots lay in material economic facts.

The great men, who in France prepared men's minds for the coming revolution, were themselves extreme revolutionists. They recognized no external authority of any kind whatever. Religion, natural science, society, political institutions—everything was subjected to the most unsparing criticism: everything must justify its existence before the judgment-seat of reason or give up existence. Reason became the sole measure of everything. It was the time when, as Hegel says, the world stood upon its head first in the sense that the human head, and the principles arrived at by its thought, claimed to be the basis of all human action and association; but by and by, also, in the

447

wider sense that the reality which was in contradiction to these principles had, in fact, to be turned upside down. Every form of society and government then existing, every old traditional notion, was flung into the lumber-room as irrational; the world had hitherto allowed itself to be led solely by prejudices; everything in the past deserved only pity and contempt. Now, for the first time, appeared the light of day, the kingdom of reason; henceforth superstition, injustice, privilege, oppression, were to be superseded by eternal truth, eternal Right, equality based on Nature and the inalienable rights of man.

We know today that this kingdom of reason was nothing more than the idealized kingdom of the bourgeoisie; that this eternal Right found its realization in bourgeois justice; that this equality reduced itself to bourgeois equality before the law; that bourgeois property was proclaimed as one of the essential rights of man; and that the government of reason, the *Contrat Social* of Rousseau, came into being, and only could come into being, as a democratic bourgeois republic. The great thinkers of the 18th century could, no more than their predecessors, go beyond the limits imposed upon them by their epoch....

The demand for equality...was extended also to the social conditions of individuals. It was not simply class privileges that were to be abolished, but class distinctions themselves. A Communism, ascetic, denouncing all the pleasures of life, Spartan, was the first form of the new teaching. Then came the three great Utopians: Saint-Simon, to whom the middle-class movement, side by side with the proletarian, still had a certain significance; Fourier; and Owen, who in the country where capitalist production was most developed, and under the influence of the antagonisms begotten of this, worked out his proposals for the removal of class distinction systematically and in direct relation to French materialism.

One thing is common to all three. Not one of them appears as a representative of the interests of that proletariat which historical development had, in the meantime, produced. Like the French philosophers, they do not claim to emancipate a particular class to begin with, but all humanity at once. Like them, they wish to bring in the kingdom of reason and eternal justice, but this kingdom, as they see it, is as far as Heaven from Earth, from that of the French philosophers.

For, to our three social reformers, the bourgeois world, based upon the principles of these philosophers, is quite as irrational and unjust, and, therefore, finds its way to the dust-hole quite as readily as feudalism and all the earlier stages of society. If pure reason and justice have not, hitherto, ruled the world, this has been the case only because men have not rightly understood them. What was wanted was the individual man of genius, who has now arisen and who understands the truth. That he has now arisen, that the truth has now been clearly understood, is not an inevitable event, following of necessity in the chains of historical development, but a mere happy accident.

He might just as well have been born 500 years earlier, and might then have spared humanity 500 years of error, strife, and suffering.

We saw how the French philosophers of the 18th century, the forerunners of the Revolution, appealed to reason as the sole judge of all that is. A rational government, rational society, were to be founded; everything that ran counter to eternal reason was to be remorselessly done away with. We saw also that this eternal reason was in reality nothing but the idealized understanding of the 18th century citizen, just then evolving into the bourgeois. The French Revolution had realized this rational society and government.

But the new order of things, rational enough as compared with earlier conditions, turned out to be by no means absolutely rational. The state based upon reason completely collapsed. Rousseau's *Contrat Social* had found its realization in the Reign of Terror, from which the bourgeoisie, who had lost confidence in their own political capacity, had taken refuge first in the corruption of the Directorate, and, finally, under the wing of the Napoleonic despotism. The promised eternal peace was turned into an endless war of conquest. The society based upon reason had fared no better. The antagonism between rich and poor, instead of dissolving into general prosperity, had become intensified by the removal of the guild and other privileges, which had to some extent bridged it over, and by the removal of the charitable institutions of the Church. The "freedom of property" from feudal fetters, now veritably accomplished, turned out to be, for the small capitalists and small proprietors, the freedom to sell their small property, crushed under the overmastering competition of the large capitalists and landlords, to these great lords, and thus, as far as the small capitalists and peasant proprietors were concerned, became "freedom from property."

The development of industry upon a capitalistic basis made poverty and misery of the working masses conditions of existence of society. Cash payment became more and more, in Carlyle's phrase, the sole nexus between man and man. The number of crimes increased from year to year. Formerly, the feudal vices had openly stalked about in broad daylight; though not eradicated, they were now at any rate thrust into the background. In their stead, the bourgeois vices, hitherto practiced in secret, began to blossom all the more luxuriantly. Trade became to a greater and greater extent cheating. The "fraternity" of the revolutionary motto was realized in the chicanery and rivalries of the battle of competition. Oppression by force was replaced by corruption; the sword, as the first social lever, by gold. The right of the first night was transferred from the feudal lords to the bourgeois manufacturers. Prostitution increased to an extent never heard of. Marriage itself remained, as before, the legally recognized form, the official cloak of prostitution, and, moreover, was supplemented by rich crops of adultery.

In a word, compared with the splendid promises of the philosophers, the social and political institutions born of the "triumph of reason" were bitterly disappointing caricatures. All that was wanting was the men to formulate this disappointment, and they came with the turn of the century. In 1802, Saint-Simon's Geneva letters appeared; in 1808 appeared Fourier's first work, although the groundwork of his theory dated from 1799; on January 1, 1800, Robert Owen undertook the direction of New Lanark....

The Contribution of Saint-Simon

Saint-Simon was a son of the great French Revolution, at the outbreak of which he was not yet 30. The Revolution was the victory of the 3rd estate—i.e., of the great masses of the nation, working in production and in trade, over the privileged idle classes, the nobles and the priests. But the victory of the 3rd estate soon revealed itself as exclusively the victory of a smaller part of this "estate," as the conquest of political power by the socially privileged section of it—i.e., the propertied bourgeoisie. And the bourgeoisie had certainly developed rapidly during the Revolution, partly by speculation in the lands of the nobility and of the Church, confiscated and afterwards put up for sale, and partly by frauds upon the nation by means of army contracts. It was the domination of these swindlers that, under the Directorate, brought France to the verge of ruin, and thus gave Napoleon the pretext for his coup d'état.

Hence, to Saint-Simon the antagonism between the 3rd Estate and the privileged classes took the form of an antagonism between "workers" and "idlers." The idlers were not merely the old privileged classes, but also all who, without taking any part in production or distribution, lived on their incomes. And the workers were not only the wageworkers, but also the manufacturers, the merchants, the bankers. That the idlers had lost the capacity for intellectual leadership and political supremacy had been proved, and was by the Revolution finally settled. That the non-possessing classes had not this capacity seemed to Saint-Simon proved by the experiences of the Reign of Terror. Then, who was to lead and command?

According to Saint-Simon, science and industry, both united by a new religious bond, destined to restore that unity of religious ideas which had been lost since the time of the Reformation—a necessarily mystic and rigidly hierarchic "new Christianity." But science, that was the scholars; and industry, that was, in the first place, the working bourgeois, manufacturers, merchants, bankers. These bourgeois were, certainly, intended by Saint-Simon to transform themselves into a kind of public officials, of social trustees; but they were still to hold, vis-à-vis of the workers, a commanding and economically privileged position. The bankers especially were to be called upon to direct the whole of social production by the regulation of credit. This conception was in exact keeping with a time in which Modern Industry in France and, with it, the chasm between bourgeoisie and proletariat was only just coming into existence. But what Saint-Simon especially lays stress upon is this: what interests him first, and above all other things, is the lot of the class that is the most numerous and the most poor ("la classe la plus nombreuse et la plus pauvre").

Already in his [1803] Geneva letters, Saint-Simon lays down the proposition that "all men ought to work." In the same work he recognizes also that the Reign of Terror was the reign of the non-possessing masses. "See," says he to them, "what happened in France at the time when your comrades held sway there; they brought about a famine."

But to recognize the French Revolution as a class war, and not simply one between nobility and bourgeoisie, but between nobility, bourgeoisie, and the non-possessors, was, in the year 1802, a most pregnant discovery. In 1816, he declares that politics is the science of production, and foretells the complete absorption of politics by economics. The knowledge that economic conditions are the basis of political institutions appears here only in embryo. Yet what is here already very plainly expressed is the idea of the future conversion of political rule over men into an administration of things and a direction of processes of production — that is to say, the "abolition of the state," about which recently there has been so much noise....

The Contribution of Fourier

Fourier takes the bourgeoisie, their inspired prophets before the Revolution, and their interested eulogists after it, at their own word. He lays bare remorselessly the material and moral misery of the bourgeois world. He confronts it with the earlier philosophers' dazzling promises of a society in which reason alone should reign, of a civilization in which happiness should be universal, of an illimitable human perfectibility, and with the rose-colored phraseology of the bourgeois ideologists of his time. He points out how everywhere the most pitiful reality corresponds with the most high-sounding phrases, and he overwhelms this hopeless fiasco of phrases with his mordant sarcasm.

Fourier is not only a critic, his imperturbably serene nature makes him a satirist, and assuredly one of the greatest satirists of all time. He depicts, with equal power and charm, the swindling speculations that blossomed out upon the downfall of the Revolution, and the shop keeping spirit prevalent in, and characteristic of, French commerce at that time. Still more masterly is his criticism of the bourgeois form of the relations between sexes, and the position of woman in bourgeois society. He was the first to declare that in any given society the degree of woman's emancipation is the natural measure of the general emancipation.

But Fourier is at his greatest in his conception of the history of society. He divides its whole course, thus far, into four stages of evolution—savagery, barbarism, the patriarchate, civilization. This last is identical with the so-called civil, or bourgeois, society of today—i.e., with the social order that came in with the 16th century. He proves "that the civilized stage raises every vice practiced by barbarism in a simple fashion into a form of existence, complex, ambiguous, equivocal, hypocritical"—that civilization moves "in a vicious circle", in contradictions which it constantly reproduces without being able to solve them; hence it constantly arrives at the very opposite to that which it wants to attain, or pretends to want to attain, so that, e.g., "under civilization poverty is born of superabundance itself."

Fourier, as we see, uses the dialectic method in the same masterly way as his contemporary, Hegel. Using these same dialectics, he argues against talk about illimitable human perfectibility, that every historical phase has its period of ascent and also its period of descent, and he applies this observation to the future of the whole human race. As Kant introduced into natural science the idea of the ultimate destruction of the Earth, Fourier introduced into historical science that of the ultimate destruction of the human race....

The Contribution of Robert Owen

At this juncture, there came forward as a reformer a manufacturer 29-years-old—a man of almost sublime, childlike simplicity of character, and at the same time one of the few born leaders of men. Robert Owen had adopted the teaching of the materialistic philosophers: that man's character is the product, on the one hand, of heredity; on the other, of the environment of the individual during his lifetime, and especially during his period of development. In the industrial revolution most of his class saw only chaos and confusion, and the opportunity of fishing in these troubled waters and making large fortunes quickly. He saw in it the opportunity of putting into practice his favorite theory, and so of bringing order out of chaos. He had already tried it with success, as superintendent of more than 500 men in a Manchester factory. From 1800 to 1829, he directed the great cotton mill at New Lanark, in Scotland, as managing partner, along the same lines, but with greater freedom of action and with a success that made him a European reputation. A population, originally consisting of the most diverse and, for the most part, very demoralized elements, a population that gradually grew to 2,500, he turned into a model colony, in which drunkenness, police, magistrates, lawsuits, poor laws, charity, were unknown. And all this simply by placing the people in conditions worthy of human beings, and especially by carefully bringing up the rising generation. He was the founder of infant schools, and introduced them first at New Lanark. At the age of two, the children came to school, where they enjoyed themselves so much that they could scarcely be got home again. Whilst his competitors worked their people 13 or 14 hours a day, in New Lanark the working day was only 10 and a half hours. When a crisis in cotton stopped work for four months, his workers received their full wages all the time. And with all this the business more than doubled in value, and to the last yielded large profits to its proprietors....

The Limitations of the Utopian Socialists

The Utopians' mode of thought has for a long time governed the Socialist ideas of the 19th century, and still governs some of them. Until very recently, all French and English Socialists did homage to it. The earlier German Communism, including that of Weitling, was of the same school. To all these, Socialism is the expression of absolute truth, reason and justice, and has only to be discovered to conquer all the world by virtue of its own power. And as an absolute truth is independent of time, space, and of the historical development of man, it is a mere accident when and where it is discovered. With all this, absolute truth, reason, and justice are different with the founder of each different school. And as each one's special kind of absolute truth, reason, and justice is again conditioned by his subjective understanding, his conditions of existence, the measure of his knowledge and his intellectual training, there is no other ending possible in this conflict of absolute truths than that they shall be mutually exclusive of one another. Hence, from this nothing could come but a kind of eclectic, average Socialism, which, as a matter of fact, has up to the present time dominated the minds of most of the socialist workers in France and England. Hence, a mish-mash allowing of the most manifold shades of opinion: a mish-mash of such critical statements, economic theories, pictures of future society by the founders of different sects, as excite a minimum of opposition; a mish-mash which is the more easily brewed the more definite sharp edges of the individual constituents are rubbed down in the stream of debate, like rounded pebbles in a brook.

To make a science of Socialism, it had first to be placed upon a real basis.

The Decline of Metaphysics and the Emergence of Dialectics

In the meantime, along with and after the French philosophy of the 18th century, had arisen the new German philosophy, culminating in Hegel.

Its greatest merit was the taking up again of dialectics as the highest form of reasoning. The old Greek philosophers were all born natural dialecticians, and Aristotle, the most encyclopedic of them, had already analyzed the most essential forms of dialectic thought. The newer philosophy, on the other hand, although in it also dialectics had brilliant exponents (e.g. Descartes and Spinoza), had, especially through English influence, become more and more rigidly fixed in the so-called metaphysical mode of reasoning, by which also the French of the 18th century were almost wholly dominated, at all events in their special philosophical work. Outside philosophy in the restricted sense, the French nevertheless produced masterpieces of dialectic. We need only call to mind Diderot's *Le Neveu de Rameau*, and Rousseau's *Discours sur l'origine et les fondements de l'inegalite parmi less hommes....*

To the metaphysician, things and their mental reflexes, ideas, are isolated, are to be considered one after the other and apart from each other, are objects of investigation fixed, rigid, given once for all. He thinks in absolutely irreconcilable antitheses. His communication is 'yea, yea; nay, nay'; for whatsoever is more than these cometh of evil." For him, a thing either exists or does not exist; a thing cannot at the same time be itself and something else. Positive and negative absolutely exclude one another; cause and effect stand in a rigid antithesis, one to the other.

At first sight, this mode of thinking seems to us very luminous, because it is that of so-called sound common sense. Only sound commonsense, respectable fellow that he is, in the homely realm of his own four walls, has very wonderful adventures directly he ventures out into the wide world of research. And the metaphysical mode of thought, justifiable and necessary as it is in a number of domains whose extent varies according to the nature of the particular object of investigation, sooner or later reaches a limit, beyond which it becomes one-sided, restricted, abstract, lost in insoluble contradictions. In the contemplation of individual things, it forgets the connection between them; in the contemplation of their existence, it forgets the beginning and end of that existence; of their repose, it forgets their motion. It cannot see the woods for the trees.

For everyday purposes, we know and can say, e.g., whether an animal is alive or not. But, upon closer inquiry, we find that his is, in many cases, a very complex question, as the jurists know very well. They have cudgeled their brains in vain to discover a rational limit beyond which the killing of the child in its mother's womb is murder. It is just as impossible to determine absolutely the moment of death, for physiology proves that death is not an instantaneous, momentary phenomenon, but a very protracted process.

In like manner, every organized being is every moment the same and not the same; every moment, it assimilates matter supplied from without, and gets rid of other matter; every moment, some cells of its body die and others build themselves anew; in a longer or shorter time, the matter of its body is completely renewed, and is replaced by other molecules of matter, so that every organized being is always itself, and yet something other than itself.

Further, we find upon closer investigation that the two poles of an antithesis, positive and negative, e.g., are as inseparable as they are opposed, and that despite all their opposition, they mutually interpenetrate. And we find, in like manner, that cause and effect are conceptions which only hold good in their application to individual cases; but as soon as we consider the individual cases in their general connection with the universe as a whole, they run into each other, and they become confounded when we contemplate that universal action and reaction in which causes and effects are eternally changing places, so that what is effect here and now will be cause there and then, and vice versa.

None of these processes and modes of thought enters into the framework of metaphysical reasoning. Dialectics, on the other hand, comprehends things and their representations, ideas, in their essential connection, concatenation, motion, origin and ending. Such processes as those mentioned above are, therefore, so many corroborations of its own method of procedure.

"Nature is the Proof of Dialectics"

Nature is the proof of dialectics, and it must be said for modern science that it has furnished this proof with very rich materials increasingly daily, and thus has shown that, in the last resort, Nature works dialectically and not metaphysically; that she does not move in the eternal oneness of a perpetually recurring circle, but goes through a real historical evolution. In this connection, Darwin must be named before all others. He dealt the metaphysical conception of Nature the heaviest blow by his proof that all organic beings, plants, animals, and man himself, are the products of a process of evolution going on through millions of years. But, the naturalists, who have learned to think dialectically, are few and far between, and this conflict of the results of discovery with preconceived modes of thinking, explains the endless confusion now reigning in theoretical natural science, the despair of teachers as well as learners, of authors and readers alike.

An exact representation of the universe, of its evolution, of the development of mankind, and of the reflection of this evolution in the minds of men, can therefore only be obtained by the methods of dialectics with its constant regard to the innumerable actions and reactions of life and death, of progressive or retrogressive changes. And in this spirit, the new German philosophy has worked. Kant began his career by resolving the stable Solar system of Newton and its eternal duration, after the famous initial impulse had once been given, into the result of a historical process, the formation of the Sun and all the planets out of a rotating, nebulous mass. From this, he at the same time drew the conclusion that, given this origin of the Solar system, its future death followed of necessity. His theory, half a century later, was established mathematically by Laplace, and half a century after that, the spectroscope proved the existence in space of such incandescent masses of gas in various stages of condensation.

"The Hegelian System" and "German Idealism"

This new German philosophy culminated in the Hegelian system. In this system—and herein is its great merit—for the first time the whole world, natural, historical, intellectual, is represented as a process—i.e., as in constant motion, change, transformation, development; and the attempt is made to trace out the internal connection that makes a continuous whole of all this movement and development. From this point of view, the history of mankind no longer

appeared as a wild whirl of senseless deeds of violence, all equally condemnable at the judgment seat of mature philosophic reason and which are best
forgotten as quickly as possible, but as the process of evolution of man himself. It was now the task of the intellect to follow the gradual march of this
process through all its devious ways, and to trace out the inner law running
through all its apparently accidental phenomena.

That the Hegelian system did not solve the problem it propounded is here
immaterial. Its epoch-making merit was that it propounded the problem. This
problem is one that no single individual will ever be able to solve. Although
Hegel was—with Saint-Simon—the most encyclopedic mind of his time, yet
he was limited, first, by the necessary limited extent of his own knowledge
and, second, by the limited extent and depth of the knowledge and conceptions of his age. To these limits, a third must be added; Hegel was an idealist.
To him, the thoughts within his brain were not the more or less abstract pictures of actual things and processes, but, conversely, things and their evolution were only the realized pictures of the "Idea", existing somewhere from
eternity before the world was. This way of thinking turned everything upside
down, and completely reversed the actual connection of things in the world.
Correctly and ingeniously as many groups of facts were grasped by Hegel,
yet, for the reasons just given, there is much that is botched, artificial, labored,
in a word, wrong in point of detail. The Hegelian system, in itself, was a colossal miscarriage—but it was also the last of its kind.

It was suffering, in fact, from an internal and incurable contradiction. Upon
the one hand, its essential proposition was the conception that human history
is a process of evolution, which, by its very nature, cannot find its intellectual
final term in the discovery of any so-called absolute truth. But, on the other
hand, it laid claim to being the very essence of this absolute truth. A system of
natural and historical knowledge, embracing everything, and final for all time,
is a contradiction to the fundamental law of dialectic reasoning.

This law, indeed, by no means excludes, but, on the contrary, includes the
idea that the systematic knowledge of the external universe can make giant
strides from age to age.

The Emergence of "Modern Materialism"

The perception of the fundamental contradiction in German idealism led necessarily back to materialism, but—*nota bene*—not to the simply metaphysical,
exclusively mechanical materialism of the 18th century. Old materialism
looked upon all previous history as a crude heap of irrationality and violence;
modern materialism sees in it the process of evolution of humanity, and aims
at discovering the laws thereof. With the French of the 18th century, and even
with Hegel, the conception obtained of Nature as a whole—moving in narrow
circles, and forever immutable, with its eternal celestial bodies, as Newton,

and unalterable organic species, as Linnaeus, taught. Modern materialism embraces the more recent discoveries of natural science, according to which Nature also has its history in time, the celestial bodies, like the organic species that, under favorable conditions, people them, being born and perishing. And even if Nature, as a whole, must still be said to move in recurrent cycles, these cycles assume infinitely larger dimensions. In both aspects, modern materialism is essentially dialectic, and no longer requires the assistance of that sort of philosophy which, queen-like, pretended to rule the remaining mob of sciences. As soon as each special science is bound to make clear its position in the great totality of things and of our knowledge of things, a special science dealing with this totality is superfluous or unnecessary. That which still survives of all earlier philosophy is the science of thought and its law—formal logic and dialectics. Everything else is subsumed in the positive science of Nature and history.

"A Decisive Change in the Conception of History"

Whilst, however, the revolution in the conception of Nature could only be made in proportion to the corresponding positive materials furnished by research, already much earlier certain historical facts had occurred which led to a decisive change in the conception of history. In 1831, the first working-class rising took place in Lyons; between 1838 and 1842, the first national working-class movement, that of the English Chartists, reached its height. The class struggle between proletariat and bourgeoisie came to the front in the history of the most advanced countries in Europe, in proportion to the development, upon the one hand, of modern industry, upon the other, of the newly-acquired political supremacy of the bourgeoisie. Facts more and more strenuously gave the lie to the teachings of bourgeois economy as to the identity of the interests of capital and labor, as to the universal harmony and universal prosperity that would be the consequence of unbridled competition. All these things could no longer be ignored, any more than the French and English Socialism, which was their theoretical, though very imperfect, expression. But the old idealist conception of history, which was not yet dislodged, knew nothing of class struggles based upon economic interests, knew nothing of economic interests; production and all economic relations appeared in it only as incidental, subordinate elements in the "history of civilization."

The new facts made imperative a new examination of all past history. Then it was seen that all past history, with the exception of its primitive stages, was the history of class struggles; that these warring classes of society are always the products of the modes of production and of exchange—In a word, of the economic conditions of their time; that the economic structure of society always furnishes the real basis, starting from which we can alone work out the ultimate explanation of the whole superstructure of juridical and political institutions as well as of the religious, philosophical, and other ideas of a given historical period. Hegel has freed history from metaphysics—he made it dialectic; but his conception of history was essentially idealistic. But now idealism was driven from its last refuge, the philosophy of history; now a materialistic treatment of history was propounded, and a method found of explaining man's "knowing" by his "being," instead of, as heretofore, his "being" by his "knowing."

From that time forward, Socialism was no longer an accidental discovery of this or that ingenious brain, but the necessary outcome of the struggle between two historically developed classes—the proletariat and the bourgeoisie. Its task was no longer to manufacture a system of society as perfect as possible, but to examine the historical economic succession of events from which these classes and their antagonism had of necessity sprung, and to discover in the economic conditions thus created the means of ending the conflict. But the Socialism of earlier days was as incompatible with this materialist conception as the conception of Nature of the French materialists was with dialectics and modern natural science. The Socialism of earlier days certainly criticized the existing capitalistic mode of production and its consequences. But it could not explain them, and, therefore, could not get the mastery of them. It could only simply reject them as bad. The more strongly this earlier Socialism denounced the exploitations of the working-class, inevitable under Capitalism, the less able was it clearly to show in what this exploitation consisted and how it arose. But for this it was necessary to present the capitalistic mode of production in its historical connection and its inevitableness during a particular historical period, and therefore, also, to present its inevitable downfall; and to lay bare its essential character, which was still a secret. This was done by the discovery of surplus-value.

"Socialism Became a Science"

It was shown that the appropriation of unpaid labor is the basis of the capitalist mode of production and of the exploitation of the worker that occurs under it; that even if the capitalist buys the labor power of his laborer at its full value as a commodity on the market, he yet extracts more value from it than he paid for; and that in the ultimate analysis, this surplus-value forms those sums of value from which are heaped up constantly increasing masses of capital in the hands of the possessing classes. The genesis of capitalist production and the production of capital were both explained.

These two great discoveries, the materialistic conception of history and the revelation of the secret of capitalistic production through surplus value, we owe to Marx. With these discoveries, Socialism became a science. The next thing was to work out all its details and relations.

"The Materialist Conception of History"

The materialist conception of history starts from the proposition that the production of the means to support human life and, next to production, the exchange of things produced, is the basis of all social structure; that in every society that has appeared in history, the manner in which wealth is distributed and society divided into classes or orders is dependent upon what is produced, how it is produced, and how the products are exchanged. From this point of view, the final causes of all social changes and political revolutions are to be sought, not in men's brains, not in men's better insights into eternal truth and justice, but in changes in the modes of production and exchange. They are to be sought, not in the philosophy, but in the economics of each particular epoch. The growing perception that existing social institutions are unreasonable and unjust, that reason has become unreason, and right wrong, is only proof that in the modes of production and exchange changes have silently taken place with which the social order, adapted to earlier economic conditions, is no longer in keeping. From this it also follows that the means of getting rid of the incongruities that have been brought to light must also be present, in a more or less developed condition, within the changed modes of production themselves. These means are not to be invented by deduction from fundamental principles, but are to be discovered in the stubborn facts of the existing system of production.

"What is, then, the position of Modern Socialism?"

The present situation of society—this is now pretty generally conceded—is the creation of the ruling class of today, of the bourgeoisie. The mode of production peculiar to the bourgeoisie, known, since Marx, as the capitalist mode of production, was incompatible with the feudal system, with the privileges it conferred upon individuals, entire social ranks and local corporations, as well as with the hereditary ties of subordination which constituted the framework of its social organization. The bourgeoisie broke up the feudal system and built upon its ruins the capitalist order of society, the kingdom of free competition, of personal liberty, of the equality, before the law, of all commodity owners, of all the rest of the capitalist blessings. Thenceforward, the capitalist mode of production could develop in freedom. Since steam, machinery, and the making of machines by machinery transformed the older manufacture into modern industry, the productive forces, evolved under the guidance of the bourgeoisie, developed with a rapidity and in a degree unheard of before. But just as the older manufacture, in its time, and handicraft, becoming more developed under its influence, had come into collision with the feudal trammels of the guilds, so now modern industry, in its complete development, comes into collision with the bounds within which the capitalist mode of production holds it confined. The new productive forces have already outgrown the capitalistic mode of using them. And this conflict between productive forces and modes of production is not a conflict engendered in the mind of man, like that between original sin and divine justice. It exists, in fact, objectively, outside us, independently of the will and actions even of the men that have brought it on. Modern Socialism is nothing but the reflex, in thought, of this conflict in fact; its ideal reflection in the minds, first, of the class directly suffering under it, the working class.

"Anarchy Reigns in Socialized Production"

The spinning wheel, the handloom, the blacksmith's hammer, were replaced by the spinning-machine, the power-loom, the steam-hammer; the individual workshop, by the factory implying the co-operation of hundreds and thousands of workmen. In like manner, production itself changed from a series of individual into a series of social acts, and the production from individual to social products. The yarn, the cloth, the metal articles that now come out of the factory were the joint product of many workers, through whose hands they had successively to pass before they were ready. No one person could say of them: "I made that; this is my product...."

Then came the concentration of the means of production and of the producers in large workshops and manufactories, their transformation into actual socialized means of production and socialized producers. But the socialized producers and means of production and their products were still treated, after this change, just as they had been before—i.e., as the means of production and the products of individuals. Hitherto, the owner of the instruments of labor had himself appropriated the product, because, as a rule, it was his own product and the assistance of others was the exception. Now, the owner of the instruments of labor always appropriated to himself the product, although it was no longer his product but exclusively the product of the labor of others. Thus, the products now produced socially were not appropriated by those who had actually set in motion the means of production and actually produced the commodities, but by the capitalists. The means of production, and production itself, had become in essence socialized. But they were subjected to a form of appropriation which presupposes the private production of individuals, under which, therefore, every one owns his own product and brings it to market. The mode of production is subjected to this form of appropriation, although it abolishes the conditions upon which the latter rests.

This contradiction, which gives to the new mode of production its capitalistic character, contains the germ of the whole of the social antagonisms of today. The greater the mastery obtained by the new mode of production over all important fields of production and in all manufacturing countries, the more it reduced individual production to an insignificant residuum, the more clearly was brought out the incompatibility of socialized production with capitalistic appropriation....

The Immanent laws of the "Capitalistic Mode of Production"

But the production of commodities, like every other form of production, has it peculiar, inherent laws inseparable from it; and these laws work, despite anarchy, in and through anarchy. They reveal themselves in the only persistent form of social inter-relations—i.e., in exchange—and here they affect the individual producers as compulsory laws of competition. They are, at first, unknown to these producers themselves, and have to be discovered by them gradually and as the result of experience. They work themselves out, therefore, independently of the producers, and in antagonism to them, as inexorable natural laws of their particular form of production. The product governs the producers....

Finally, modern industry and the opening of the world-market made the struggle universal, and at the same time gave it an unheard-of virulence. Advantages in natural or artificial conditions of production now decide the existence or non-existence of individual capitalists, as well as of whole industries and countries. He that falls is remorselessly cast aside. It is the Darwinian struggle of the individual for existence transferred from Nature to society with intensified violence. The conditions of existence natural to the animal appear as the final term of human development. The contradiction between socialized production and capitalistic appropriation now presents itself as an antagonism between the organization of production in the individual workshop and the anarchy of production in society generally.

The capitalistic mode of production moves in these two forms of the antagonism immanent to it from its very origin. It is never able to get out of that "vicious circle" which Fourier had already discovered. What Fourier could not, indeed, see in his time is that this circle is gradually narrowing; that the movement becomes more and more a spiral, and must come to an end, like the movement of planets, by collision with the centre. It is the compelling force of anarchy in the production of society at large that more and more completely turns the great majority of men into proletarians; and it is the masses of the proletariat again who will finally put an end to anarchy in production. It is the compelling force of anarchy in social production that turns the limitless perfectibility of machinery under modern industry into a compulsory law by which every individual industrial capitalist must perfect his machinery more and more, under penalty of ruin.

"The Perfecting of Machinery"

But the perfecting of machinery is making human labor superfluous. If the introduction and increase of machinery means the displacement of millions of manual by a few machine-workers, improvement in machinery means the displacement of more and more of the machine-workers themselves. It means, in the last instance, the production of a number of available wage workers in excess of the average needs of capital, the formation of a complete industrial reserve army, as I called it in 1845, available at the times when industry is working at high pressure, to be cast out upon the street when the inevitable crash comes, a constant dead weight upon the limbs of the working-class in its struggle for existence with capital, a regulator for keeping of wages down to the low level that suits the interests of capital.

Thus it comes about, to quote Marx, that machinery becomes the most powerful weapon in the war of capital against the working-class; that the instruments of labor constantly tear the means of subsistence out of the hands of the laborer; that they very product of the worker is turned into an instrument for his subjugation....

We have seen that the ever-increasing perfectibility of modern machinery is, by the anarchy of social production, turned into a compulsory law that forces the individual industrial capitalist always to improve his machinery, always to increase its productive force. The bare possibility of extending the field of production is transformed for him into a similarly compulsory law. The enormous expansive force of modern industry, compared with which that of gases is mere child's play, appears to us now as a necessity for expansion, both qualitative and quantitative, that laughs at all resistance. Such resistance is offered by consumption, by sales, by the markets for the products of modern industry. But the capacity for extension, extensive and intensive, of the markets is primarily governed by quite different laws that work much less energetically. The extension of the markets cannot keep pace with the extension of production. The collision becomes inevitable, and as this cannot produce any real solution so long as it does not break in pieces the capitalist mode of production, the collisions become periodic. Capitalist production has begotten another "vicious circle...."

"The Socialized Organization of Production"

The fact that the socialized organization of production within the factory has developed so far that it has become incompatible with the anarchy of production in society, which exists side by side with and dominates it, is brought home to the capitalist themselves by the violent concentration of capital that occurs during crises, through the ruin of many large, and a still greater number of small, capitalists. The whole mechanism of the capitalist mode of production breaks down under the pressure of the productive forces, its own creations. It is no longer able to turn all this mass of means of production into capital. They lie fallow, and for that very reason the industrial reserve army must also lie fallow. Means of production, means of subsistence, available laborers, all the elements of production and of general wealth, are present in abundance. But "abundance becomes the source of distress and want" (Fourier), because it is the very thing that prevents the transformation of the means of production and subsistence into capital....

If the crises demonstrate the incapacity of the bourgeoisie for managing any longer modern productive forces, the transformation of the great establishments for production and distribution into joint-stock companies, trusts, and State property, show how unnecessary the bourgeoisie are for that purpose. All the social functions of the capitalist has no further social function than that of pocketing dividends, tearing off coupons, and gambling on the Stock Exchange, where the different capitalists despoil one another of their capital. At first, the capitalistic mode of production forces out the workers. Now, it forces out the capitalists, and reduces them, just as it reduced the workers, to the ranks of the surplus-population, although not immediately into those of the industrial reserve army.

But, the transformation—either into joint-stock companies and trusts, or into State-ownership—does not do away with the capitalistic nature of the productive forces. In the joint-stock companies and trusts, this is obvious. And the modern State, again, is only the organization that bourgeois society takes on in order to support the external conditions of the capitalist mode of production against the encroachments as well of the workers as of individual capitalists. The modern state, no matter what its form, is essentially a capitalist machine—the state of the capitalists, the ideal personification of the total national capital. The more it proceeds to the taking over of productive forces, the more does it actually become the national capitalist, the more citizens does it exploit. The workers remain wage-workers—proletarians. The capitalist relation is not done away with. It is, rather, brought to a head. But, brought to a head, it topples over. State-ownership of the productive forces is not the solution of the conflict, but concealed within it are the technical conditions that form the elements of that solution.

This solution can only consist in the practical recognition of the social nature of the modern forces of production, and therefore in the harmonizing with the socialized character of the means of production. And this can only come about by society openly and directly taking possession of the productive forces which have outgrown all control, except that of society as a whole. The social character of the means of production and of the products today reacts against the producers, periodically disrupts all production and exchange, acts only like a law of Nature working blindly, forcibly, destructively. But, with the taking over by society of the productive forces, the social character of the means of production and of the products will be utilized by the producers with a perfect understanding of its nature, and instead of being a source of disturbance and periodical collapse, will become the most powerful lever of production itself.

Active social forces work exactly like natural forces: blindly, forcibly, destructively, so long as we do not understand, and reckon with, them. But, when once we understand them, when once we grasp their action, their direction, their effects, it depends only upon ourselves to subject them more and more to our own will, and, by means of them, to reach our own ends. And this holds quite especially of the mighty productive forces of today. As long as we obstinately refuse to understand the nature and the character of these social means of action—and this understanding goes against the grain of the capitalist mode of production, and its defenders—so long these forces are at work in spite of us, in opposition to us, so long they master us, as we have shown above in detail.

But when once their nature is understood, they can, in the hand working together, be transformed from master demons into willing servants. The difference is as that between the destructive force of electricity in the lightning in the storm, and electricity under command in the telegraph and the voltaic arc; the difference between a conflagration, and fire working in the service of man. With this recognition, at last, of the real nature of the productive forces of today, the social anarchy of production gives place to a social regulation of production upon a definite plan, according to the needs of the community and of each individual. Then the capitalist mode of appropriation, in which the product enslaves first the producer, and then the appropriator, is replaced by the mode of appropriation of the products that is based upon the nature of the modern means of production; upon the one hand, direct social appropriation, as means to the maintenance and extension of production—on the other, direct individual appropriation, as means of subsistence and of enjoyment.

Whilst the capitalist mode of production more and more completely transforms the great majority of the population into proletarians, it creates the power which, under penalty of its own destruction, is forced to accomplish this revolution. Whilst it forces on more and more of the transformation of the vast means of production, already socialized, into State property, it shows itself the way to accomplishing this revolution. The proletariat seizes political power and turns the means of production into State property.

The Withering Away of the State

But, in doing this, it abolishes itself as proletariat, abolishes all class distinction and class antagonisms, abolishes also the State as State. Society, thus far, based upon class antagonisms, had need of the State. That is, of an organization of the particular class which was, pro tempore, the exploiting class, an organization for the purpose of preventing any interference from without with the existing conditions of production, and, therefore, especially, for the purpose of forcibly keeping the exploited classes in the condition of oppression corresponding with the given mode of production (slavery, serfdom, wage-labor). The State was the official representative of society as a whole; the gathering of it together into a visible embodiment. But, it was this only in so far as it was the State of that class which itself represented, for the time being, society as a whole....

When, at last, it becomes the real representative of the whole of society, it renders itself unnecessary. As soon as there is no longer any social class to be held in subjection; as soon as class rule, and the individual struggle for existence based upon our present anarchy in production, with the collisions and excesses arising from these, are removed, nothing more remains to be repressed, and a special repressive force, a State, is no longer necessary. The first act by virtue of which the State really constitutes itself the representative of the whole of society—the taking possession of the means of production in the name of society—this is, at the same time, its last independent act as a State. State interference in social relations becomes, in one domain after another, superfluous, and then dies out of itself; *the government of persons is replaced by the administration of things,* and by the conduct of processes of production. [Italics added.] The State is not "abolished." It dies out. This gives the measure of the value of the phrase: "a free State," both as to its justifiable use at times by agitators, and as to its ultimate scientific inefficiency; and also of the demands of the so-called anarchists for the abolition of the State out of hand.

Since the historical appearance of the capitalist mode of production, the appropriation by society of all the means of production has often been dreamed of, more or less vaguely, by individuals, as well as by sects, as the ideal of the future. But it could become possible, could become a historical necessity, only when the actual conditions for its realization were there. Like every other social advance, it becomes practicable, not by men understanding that the existence of classes is in contradiction to justice, equality, etc., not by the mere willingness to abolish these classes, but by virtue of certain new economic conditions. The separation of society into an exploiting and an exploited class, a ruling and an oppressed class, was the necessary consequences of the deficient and restricted development of production in former times....

With the seizing of the means of production by society, production of commodities is done away with, and, simultaneously, the mastery of the product over the producer. Anarchy in social production is replaced by systematic, definite organization.

The struggle for individual existence disappears. Then, for the first time, man, in a certain sense, is finally marked off from the rest of the animal kingdom, and emerges from mere animal conditions of existence into really human ones. The whole sphere of the conditions of life which environ man, and which have hitherto ruled man, now comes under the dominion and control of man, who for the first time becomes the real, conscious lord of nature, because he has now become master of his own social organization. The laws of his own social action, hitherto standing face-to-face with man as laws of Nature foreign to, and dominating him, will then be used with full understanding, and so mastered by him. Man's own social organization, hitherto confronting him as a necessity imposed by Nature and History, now becomes the result of his own free action. The extraneous objective forces that have, hitherto, governed history, pass under the control of man himself. Only from that time will man himself, more and more consciously, make his own history—only from that time will the social causes set in movement by him have, in the main and in a constantly growing measure, the results intended by him. It is the ascent of man from the kingdom of necessity to the kingdom of freedom.

Index

Also of Interest

The Two Faces of Liberalism

How the Hoover-Roosevelt Debate Shapes the 21st Century Original Material Selected and edited by Gordon Lloyd 2007, 430pp, ISBN 978-0-97640412-5

The original readings selected and edited here will encourage us to take a fresh look at the material surrounding the New Deal controversy. The speeches and addresses of Franklin D. Roosevelt and Herbert Hoover, along with sample Acts of Congress, the presidential platforms of the two major political parties, as well as critical Supreme Court decisions that first declared the core legislation to be unconstitutional and then constitutionalzed the New Deal, have been collected under one roof and assembled in an accessible and yet comprehensive fashion.

The aim of this collection is not to substantiate or disprove any of the prevailing theories regarding the Great Depression and the New Deal. The aim is to present the original arguments which will allow the actors and documents to speak for themselves, thus promoting a conversation between the present generation and the most prominent actors of the New Deal era.

Reviews
"Lloyd has skillfully juxtaposed important documents in a way that highlights the stark differences between Hoover and Roosevelt. Even historians who are wholly familiar with the public materials and private letters included in this volume will appreciate viewing them in one collection arranged in such a logical manner." **The Annals of Iowa**

"This essentially backward-looking project takes the form of an archeological dig, the first stage of which is to bulldoze from the site sprawling acres of tendentious scholarship. We are thus indebted to political scientist Gordon Lloyd, who in this splendid edited collection, has applied his bulldozer the New Deal era." **Claremont Review of Books**

"This well-conceived and thought-provoking documentary volume casts fresh light on a clash of political philosophies that roiled American life for a generation and continues to affect it to this day." **George H. Nash, Historian**

"It is a fine collection and I learned much by reading Hoover and Roosevelt together." **Burt Folsom, Professor of History, Hillsdale College, Michigan**

Available from www.scrivenerpublishing.com